The Brainerd Journal

Indians of the Southeast

Series Editors

Theda Perdue
University of Kentucky
Michael D. Green
University of Kentucky

Advisory Editors

Leland Ferguson
University of South Carolina
Mary Young
University of Rochester

The Brainerd Journal
A Mission to the Cherokees, 1817-1823

Edited and introduced by
Joyce B. Phillips and Paul Gary Phillips

University of Nebraska Press
Lincoln and London

© 1998 by the University of Nebraska Press
Manufactured in the United States of America

⊗ The paper in this book meets the minimum requirements of
American National Standard for Information Sciences—Permanence
of Paper for Printed Library Materials, ANSI-Z39.48-1984.

Library of Congress Cataloging-in-Publication Data

The Brainerd journal : a mission to the Cherokees, 1817-1823 / edited and
introduced by Joyce B. Phillips and Paul Gary Phillips.
   p. cm. — (Indians of the Southeast)
Includes bibliographical references and index.
ISBN 0-8032-3718-9 (cl : alk. paper)
1. Brainerd Mission—History. 2. Cherokee Indians—Missions.
3. Cherokee Indians—History—19th century—Sources.
4. Missionaries—Tennessee—Diaries. 5. Missionaries—Tennessee—
Correspondence. I. Phillips, Joyce B., 1948- . II. Phillips,
Paul Gary, 1945- . III. Series.
E99.C5B748 1998
976.8′8204—dc21   98-4021
                                                 CIP

This book is dedicated to

The memory of
Redwing:
Maude Hoyt McSpadden Phillips (1885-1965)

and to

our son Andrew and our daughter Tiffany,
who share the same heritage

Table of Contents

Illustrations and Maps

Series Editors' Introduction

The ethnohistory of the Native peoples of the Southeast depends
heavily on non-Native records. Travel accounts, trade records,
minutes of treaty conferences, and reports of government agents form
much of the documentation on which scholars depend. Perhaps the
richest source for Cherokee history is the record left by various
missionaries who lived among them, particularly those sent by the
American Board of Commissioners for Foreign Missions, an
interdenominational—largely Presbyterian and Congregationalist—
missionary society headquartered in Boston. In this volume, Joyce
and Gary Phillips present the meticulously transcribed and
carefully annotated journal of the first five years of the Brainerd
Mission, the center of the American Board's efforts among the
Cherokees. The role of the missionaries in this period of Cherokee
history was central since they provided much of the education and
technical assistance that transformed the Cherokees. Their own
account of how they struggled to Christianize and "civilize" the
Cherokees is compelling. Equally important, however, is the
Cherokee voice that emerges indirectly from the entries in this
journal. Two domestic worlds intersected as Cherokee families
entrusted their children to missionaries, economies converged as
missionaries bought corn from Cherokees and in turn provided them
with the services of millers and blacksmiths, and ideas mingled as
Cherokees and missionaries tried to make sense of each other's
values and beliefs. In recording these encounters, the missionaries
articulated fascinating details about the daily lives of Cherokees as
well as their private reactions to public events. By making the
journal widely available, the editors of this series seek to enable
others to hear that Cherokee voice as well as experience the
hardships and triumphs of the missionaries. Scholars will find this
a useful introduction to the much larger collection of American Board
Papers; students will have an accessible source for their own

research in Cherokee history; genealogists will welcome the editors' attempt to identify individuals and their relations; and more casual readers will find a satisfying first-hand account of life in the early nineteenth-century Cherokee Nation.

Theda Perdue   Michael D. Green

The Cherokee Nation 1817-1823. Map adapted from Henry Thompson Malone *Cherokees of the Old South*. Copyright 1956 by University of Georgia Press. Used by permission of the publisher.

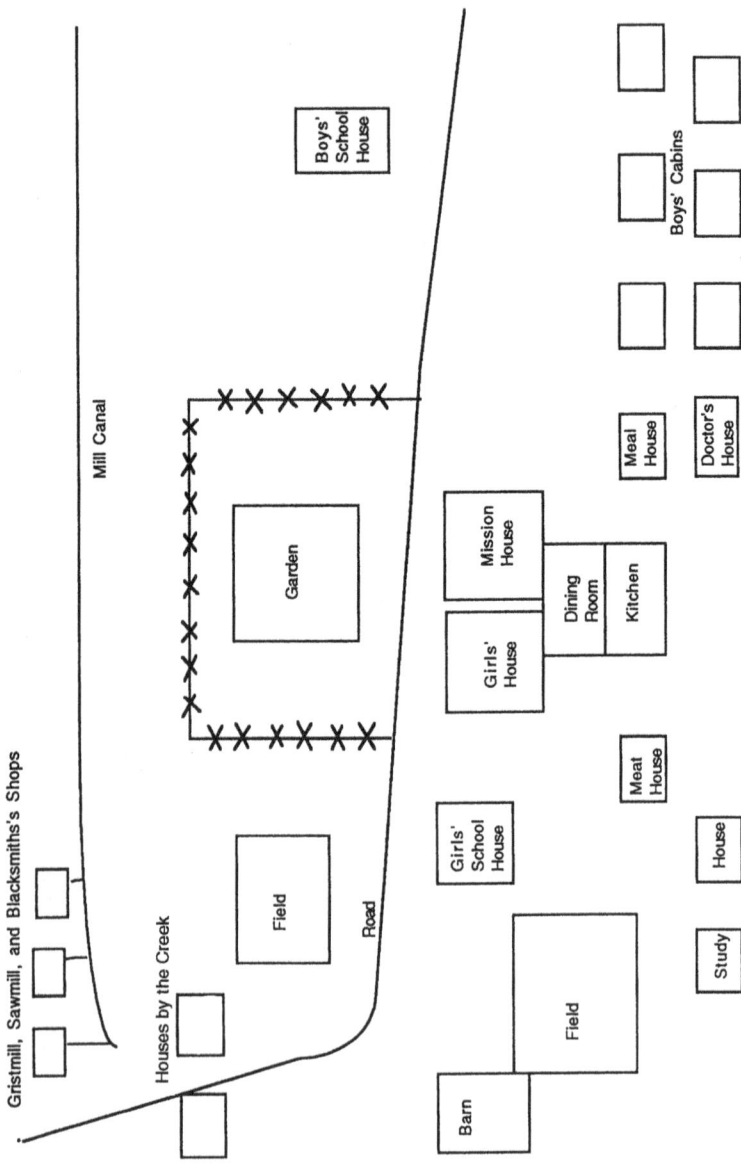

Layout of Brainerd Mission Station. Adapted from hand-drawn maps in the American Board Papers, Houghton Library, Harvard University, ABC 18.3.1 v. 2, Item 161, 169. Used by permission of the Houghton Library.

Map of Brainerd Mission's farmland and acreage. Hand-drawn in 1822 at the time of Jeremiah Evart's visit to Brainerd. American Board Papers, ABC 18.3.1 v.2, Item 169. Reproduced from microfilm by permission from Houghton Library and Primary Source Media.

Brainerd mission journal continued.

Dec. 1. Received information by the Agent that a cherokee in the lower part of the nation has an Osage boy, 9 or 10 years old, who was brought over captive by them on the return of the cherokees from their expedition against that tribe, a little more than a year ago — that the man now about to return to the Arkansas, & would leave their boy with us, if any one would go after him. We were also told that also, in the same family, there was a captive girl somewhat older than this boy, & that she was a sister of the Osage girl now with us. It was thought probable they might be persuaded to leave both the girl & the boy.

2. Further enquiry was made respecting those Osage children, & it was thought best to go after them immediately.

3rd Bro. Hoyt & his son Milo, set out in quest of the little captives.

12th Br. H. & his son returned. They had traveled between 2 & 3 hundred miles — lay in the woods three nights — encountered several storms, swam one creek &c but could not obtain the objects of their pursuit. They found both the children — The girl is indeed Lydia Carters sister, & appears to be about 15. The boy is younger than we expected, perhaps 4 or 5. It was very painful to leave these children — to be taken back again to the deep shades of the forest, after being brought so near to the light — but nothing could be done to prevent it. The owner of the boy said the Agent had misunderstood him.

In this tour Br. H. spent 2 nights & a day at Catharine Br owns fathers. He was received with great cordiality by the whole family, & Catharines joy was so great that she says & I felt myself more than paid for the fatigues of the whole journey, by the first evening opportunity. Catharine said it had been very dark times with her since she left Brainerd. All around her were engaged for the riches & pleasures of

Foreword

There can be no doubt that the activities of the American Board of Commissioners for Foreign Missions were important to the Chero-kee Nation. The missionaries were invited to educate Cherokee children. What greater trust could the Cherokee repose in the white man? The missionaries were invited to preach the Gospel, which was embraced by many tribal members through baptism. Again, what greater trust could the Cherokee repose in the white man?

In return, the white missionaries walked the delicate line between imposing (religion, language, and "civilized ways") and plodding—regular classes, both for education and religion. Eventally many missionaries learned the Cherokee language. This was appreciated by tribal members, some of whom already spoke English. All classes were conducted in English, even after the introduction of Sequoyah's alphabet.

The Cherokees' strong, continuing interest in both education and religion, demonstrated in this Journal as of 1817, can be seen as part of Cherokee culture. In the 1839 Constitution, signed to continue the government after the Trail of Tears, we find in Article VI: Sec. 9. "Religion, morality and knowledge, being necessary to good government, the preservation of liberty and the happiness of mankind, schools, and the means of education, shall forever be encouraged in this Nation."

The National Council enacted legislation to carry out this Constitutional provision and the first "Superintendent of Education of the Cherokee Nation" was appointed in 1841. As finances permitted, the Nation opened schools for each sex. The Cherokee Female Seminary opened in 1851, one day after the Cherokee Male Seminary. Each provided a four year high school education and was established and operated by the Nation. The Seminaries, although closed for a time during and after the Civil War, operated until after Oklahoma statehood in 1907. The Female Seminary was the first school for girls west of the Mississippi River and was set up by staff and graduates of Mount Holyoke College, South Hadley, Massachusetts.

I had a special interest in reading this transcription of the *Brainerd Journal* for two reasons—first, my work with the Cherokee Nation and second, my family. I have been a Justice of the Cherokee Nation's highest court since 1976. For just under fourteen years, I was Chief Justice of the Cherokee Nation—longer than anyone I can discover since we Cherokees started recording our judicial proceedings (1823). I was also a long-time trustee and Executive Committee member of the Cherokee National Historical Society.

My study of Cherokee history dovetails with my familial interest in the Brainerd Mission. Gary Phillips, the co-transcriber, and I are direct descendants of both the mission's first superintendent Rev. Ard Hoyt and Assistant Principal Chief George Lowrey. Gary's grandmother, Maude Hoyt McSpadden Phillips (1885-1965), and my grandmother, Elizabeth Peach McSpadden Milam (1883-1954) were sisters. Both graduated from the Cherokee Female Seminary, in Tahlequah, Indian Territory (now Oklahoma) in the Class of 1903.

Our grandmothers were themselves grandchildren of Hinman Booth Hoyt (1828-1863). Hinman's parents were Milo Hoyt and Lydia Lowrey, who were married at Brainerd Mission in 1820. You'll read of their marriage on February 24, 1820. Their marriage represented the union of the recently-arrived missionaries (Milo) and the Cherokees who welcomed them (Lydia).

In 1904, my grandmother Elizabeth Peach McSpadden married J. Bartley Milam (1884-1949); he served as Principal Chief of the Cherokees from 1941 until his death eight years later. The Cherokee Nation had been effectively disbanded in 1907 when Oklahoma became a state. Until 1941, the Principal Chief would be appointed by the U.S. President for only one day at a time, in order to sign official documents. So, when J.B. Milam was appointed to two one-year terms, and then two four-year terms, he had an opportunity to re-vitalize the tribe.

He did so by calling a meeting of enrolled Cherokees and securing authority to hire attorneys to press the tribe's claims before the recently created Indian Claims Commission. His efforts started what has become a tribal government representing over 193,000 members, located in all fifty states and many foreign countries.

Each of these enrolled tribal members of today owes a debt to the Brainerd Mission, to Rev. Ard Hoyt and to many other missionaries. This debt is recognized in part by reading the *Brainerd Journal* and reflecting on the hardships which these men and women of God faced—and overcame.

Philip H. Viles Jr.
Associate Justice of the Cherokee Nation
Tulsa, Oklahoma

Introduction

Whether it be in 2017, 1917, or 1817, January is not a good month to travel from New England to Tennessee. Yet, in January 1817, Reverend Cyrus Kingsbury trudged through the terrain surrounding Lookout Mountain to establish the Brainerd Mission on the Chickamauga Creek—the area which later became Chattanooga, Tennessee. Sent by the New England based American Board of Commissioners for Foreign Missions (ABCFM), Kingsbury sought, with the encouragement and approval of the Cherokee Council, to bring to the Cherokees education and Christianity, tools for acculturation which in turn provided the "civilizing" effect sought by both the United States government and the Cherokees themselves. Having set up a school and mission for the them, Kingsbury served only one year at the Chickamauga location and then left for the Choctaw Nation to open another American Board mission. In his place, Ard Hoyt, Daniel Butrick, Moody Hall, William Chamberlin, Elizur Butler, John Vail, John Elsworth, Ainsworth Blunt, and others carried forward the work of the Brainerd Mission. In the *Brainerd Journal*, these missionaries recorded their efforts to build a mission, to reach the Cherokees with education and the gospel, and to communicate the details of their daily lives.

The *Brainerd Journal* presents the missionaries in action. While other white men had entered the Cherokee Nation in search of personal gain through trading or land speculation, these missionaries from the American Board sought neither profit nor land, but rather sought the treasure of the soul. In short, they bent their backs to cultivate the mind as well as the soil. They were to be "able & willing to labour with their own hands that they literally endure hardness as good soldiers."[1]

The missionaries provided secular books as well as the message of the "good book," and skills in farming and "social" living. Their outpost stood well-stocked, not as an armory, but with tools for "civilization," for these men and women brought with them their own New England culture, values, and way of life. Many Cherokee leaders welcomed the missionary and his cache of learning because these Cherokee leaders, as a result of years of turmoil and strife on the white frontier, desired to preserve their people even if it meant modifying their culture.

The *Brainerd Journal* provides insight into the meeting of two peoples of different cultures. The New England missionaries were from a culture influenced by a religious revival known as the Second Awakening which motivated the missionaries, such as those who established Brainerd, to engage in preaching the gospel to Indians in North America and to other "aborigines" around the world. Not only did this religious revival spiritually awaken the New Englanders themselves, but the revival implanted a firm belief within the New England Congregationalists that their benevolence must extend beyond themselves, their cities, and their villages. Equipped with this belief, each missionary sought to follow the Bible's great command to "Go ye into all the world and preach the gospel."[2] Following such a command required financial support so that the missionaries could focus on their "mission." Organizers of the missionary movement set up philanthropic societies funded mainly by the rich in New England. Soon the general public felt the religious zeal of revivalism; as the religious movement swelled, these funding societies evolved into "cent" societies where even the non-affluent could participate by donating a small amount—as little as one cent—to benefit the missionary cause.[3]

The missionary outreach to the Indians fit the government's Indian policy which promoted "civilizing" the Indians. Federal policy makers and missionaries agreed that "civilization" was inseparable from Christianization. Therefore, during the period 1800 to 1830 many religious groups met the call of government as well as God and dispatched missionaries to reside among the Indian tribes for the joint purpose of "civilizing" and Christianizing the "heathen." One such missionary, Presbyterian minister Gideon Blackburn, educated a generation of Cherokees before the American Board missionaries appeared on the scene.[4] At the same time, the Moravians conducted missionary work among the Indians and established in Cherokee Georgia the Springplace Mission which John and Anna Gambold operated near the site of Cherokee leader James Vann's home. The Gambolds arrived prior to the Brainerd missionaries and continued in their missionary endeavor during the same time as these missionaries from the American Board.[5] Numerous references to the Gambolds and their ministry appear in the *Brainerd Journal* as American Board missionaries and their students travel to and from Springplace.

Other groups, in addition to the Moravians, worked in the Cherokee Nation. Baptists Humphrey Posey and Evan Jones preached in the Valley Towns populated by the traditionalist Cherokees.[6] The Methodists, who comprised the last group to arrive on the mission field, also ministered to the Cherokee people. Yet, the American Board missionaries, because of the Brainerd mission's size and the establishment of satellite mission stas as well as the support of government, philanthropists, and generous "cent" societies, became a major influence in educating and "civilizing" the Cherokees.

The American Board originated in 1810 when a group of men gathered in Farmington, Massachusetts, to establish a world-wide missionary society. Organized and promoted mainly by the Congregationalist churches of New England and also the Presbyterians, American Board founders included Rev. Dr. Samuel Worcester, pastor of the Tabernacle Church in Salem, Massachusetts,[7] and seventeen year-old Andover student Samuel J. Mills whose enthusiasm for missions ameliorated their disparate status.[8] In total, nine men comprised the first mission board with Worcester assuming the position of Corresponding Secretary. By the second year of the American Board's existence, *Panoplist* editor Jeremiah Evarts had joined the group and become the treasurer.[9] In order to function effectively, the American Board established a managing committee staffed by elected officers known as the Prudential Committee. After two years of promoting their intentions, the American Board sent out the first missionaries to India and Ceylon. In addition to establishing a world-wide outreach, the Board also suggested establishing missions among the "aborigines" on the American continent, more specifically among the "southern tribes of Indians [who] offered the most promising material upon which to begin to work."[10] Relative to the American Indian, the American Board's "7th Annual Report" of September 1816 proposed a mission statement and goal:

> To establish schools in the different parts of the tribe under the missionary direction and superintendence, for the instruction of the rising generation in common school learning, in the useful arts of life, and in Christianity, so as gradually, with the divine blessing to make the whole tribe English in the language, civilized in their habits, and Christian in their religion.[11]

When Kingsbury arrived in the Cherokee Nation in 1817, he fully embraced the mission statement, setting a course to accomplish this objective. Kingsbury submitted a proposal to the Cherokee Council that the American Board establish a school and mission in the Cherokee Nation; his proposal won the approval and support of the Council as well as leaders such as Pathkiller, Major Ridge, Charles Hicks, John Ross, and George Lowrey. These influential leaders encouraged the Cherokees to become a "civilized" society and embraced the educational assistance promised by the missionaries.[12]

The site chosen for the mission lay on the Chickamauga Creek occupying the plot of land previously owned by trader and former British agent, John McDonald. Kingsbury selected this site primarily because Cherokees of mixed-ancestry and social influence populated the surrounding area. Kingsbury felt that "those who will be first educated will be the children of half breeds & of the leading men in the nation. On their education & influence the character of the nation will very much depend."[13] However, American Board missionary Daniel S. Butrick, arriving in 1818, disagreed with this ethnocentric and elitist attitude. Rejecting the notion that the upper class Cherokee must be the first to be educated, Butrick sought out the traditional Cherokees and endeavored to learn the traditional customs and language.[14] Just as Kingsbury thought, the missionaries' first success did come from bi-cultural Cherokees of mixed-ancestry rather than the people more wedded to traditional culture. Many people of mixed-ancestry enjoyed a "peculiar status in the tribe" as cultural brokers, and they more cordially embraced the idea of missionaries in their nation.[15] Therefore, the American Board, by their own design as well as the inclination of their selected students, ended up ministering to many of those individuals who, by 1838, emerged as the shapers of Cherokee society.

From the time of his arrival in the Cherokee Nation, Kingsbury maintained daily notes of his experiences at the "Chickamauga Mission," later renamed Brainerd. However, Ard Hoyt, upon his arrival in early 1818, assumed the duty of converting Kingsbury's notes into a formal journal and then forwarding the journal to the Prudential Committee. For seven years Hoyt and other missionaries continued to correspond with headquarters through this formal journal. From this correspondence of January 1817 to December 1823 emerged the *Brainerd Journal*.

Though this daily reporting ceased in December 1823, the Brainerd Mission actively ministered to the Cherokees until the mission closed August 19, 1838, just before the Cherokee Removal.[16] During this later period, 1824-1838, the missionaries continually communicated with the American Board, but instead of an official journal, the missionaries wrote letters, short reports, and personal journals such as those Daniel Butrick and William Chamberlin kept of their itinerant evangelizing.[17]

This transcription presents the interaction of Cherokees and missionaries as seen through the eyes of those who lived the history they recorded. *The Brainerd Journal: A Mission to the Cherokees, 1817-1823* does not offer the perspective of the historian looking back and re-telling the story, but rather offers the complete, annotated transcription of the handwritten journal which reflects the meeting, the merging, and even the "colliding of cultures" in the voice of the missionary men and women who lived among the Cherokee.

A plethora of scholarly works document the acculturation of the Cherokee people and their subsequent removal. The reader is encouraged to turn to these histories for a more complete presentation of this struggle.[18] However, the *Brainerd Journal*, as a primary source document, provides the actual daily account of the meeting of two vibrant cultures without retrospective commentary or analysis. The biases, the comments, and the opinions found within the pages of this journal are those of the nineteenth century missionaries who wrote them. The journal writers, as evangelists for the cause of salvation and spiritual awakening, did not concern themselves with an analysis of Cherokee acculturation or their role within that cultural process, yet today the words recorded in this journal trace "civilization's" broader context with all its values, both positive and negative. The *Brainerd Journal* reveals a microcosm of the broader civilization and provides a contact point for observing Cherokee acculturation.

While the *Brainerd Journal* illuminates the lives of articulate and interesting people as they lived in another cultural setting, it also describes history in the making as events, situations, and people of historical significance drift in and out of the pages as if the reader of the journal, through some previous knowledge, should know what and who these events, situations, and people were. The journal can be read entirely without annotation and still be enjoyed, but the annotations included with the transcription reveal the background of events, the identity of individuals, and the locations of places written about within these pages.

How does the journal reflect the history of the Cherokees, of the missionaries, of the policies of the state and federal governments, and of the lives of the people? The answer is day by day. A brief discussion of Cherokee history and acculturation coupled with a few excerpts from the journal will serve to illustrate the point.

In *Salvation and the Savage*, Robert F. Berkhofer Jr. states that the study of acculturation—the study of the changes in culture as one cultural group comes into contact with another cultural group—is best accomplished at the point of contact of two cultures, and the Brainerd Mission provided one such point.[19] The missionaries brought New England values and lifestyle to the Cherokee Nation, and they looked for manifestations of these values and lifestyles in the Christianized Cherokees because the missionary defined a "Christian" as one possessing Euro-American manners, style of dress, language, law, and social life. Thus, motivated by religious revival, by the Second Awakening, and by the federal government, the missionaries "civilized," Christianized, and educated Cherokees, fully expecting the individual Cherokee to conform to the culture of New England, thus sowing the seeds for cultural change, that is, acculturation.[20]

As the missionaries had objectives in going to the Cherokee Nation, so the Cherokees had motives for receiving the missionaries and for opening their minds to education. Years of strife between the American colonists and the Cherokees motivated them to accept the U.S. government's Indian policy which promoted education and Christianity as the basis for relations with the new United States. As a result of the Cherokees' desire to retain their homeland, Cherokees began to embrace President George Washington's policy of "civilizing" Indians and their eventual integration into white society.

Changes in presidents and parties in power brought modifications of policy, and the impetus shifted from the idea that Indians could integrate into mainstream America, as promoted by Washington, to the idea that Indians were somehow different from whites.[21] With the policies of Jefferson, Monroe, and finally Jackson, the Cherokee people also found themselves faced with the possible threat of removal from their homeland. For years the United States demnded from the Cherokees one land cession after another, and at the same time urged a policy of integration and acculturation which, required Indians to abandon their traditional way of life and become more "white-like." This U.S. policy took their land away little by little and ultimately urged complete removal. Principal Chief Pathkiller, in a conversation with the missionaries through interpreter, John Arch, gave "what he called a history of this business since his own time." In this May 7, 1823 entry recorded in the *Brainerd Journal*, Pathkiller said:

> President Washington agreed where the line should be—had it run and marked—and told them this should always be the line between the Cherokees and white people—soon after there must be another treaty and another line—again another treaty and another line—and so on—always telling them this shall be the last line and always using the same reasons when they wished for more land viz. you have more land than you want,—you can live much better if you leave hunting, raise cattle, hogs, corn, and cotton—make your own clothes, and have your bread and meat always at hand .... But now (said he) the Georgians seemed determined to take this last little ....

Pathkiller and all the Cherokees fully recognized the shifting political sand on which they stood. He was very articulate in expressing their concerns and fears. Even though he died in 1827, by 1838 their fears were realized when the United States removed the Cherokees to Indian Territory.

The Cherokees could not forestall removal by becoming more like their non-Indian neighbors. Furthermore, not all Cherokees were enthusiastic about changing traditional ways. Some Cherokees saw no reason to abandon tradition and be assimilated by a "white" society that regarded them as inferior. Racism infected many whites who argued that the Indians could never join the mainstream of society because native people lacked the innate ability to become full citizens.[22] On June 24, 1818, Brainerd missionaries wrote to the Prudential Committee that the "prevailing opinion" of the Anglo-Americans who lived along the border of the Cherokee Nation was that "the Indian is by nature radically different from all other men, and that this difference presents an insurmountable barrier to his civilization." The Brainerd missionaries did not concur. Along with many Cherokees and other open-minded whites, they felt that the Cherokee people could acquire education, become Christian, and blend into Anglo-American society.

Even before Brainerd missionaries entered the Chickamauga area, Cherokee culture was in flux. The deerskin trade and war had dominated Cherokee lives in the eighteenth century,[23] but the 1791 Treaty of Holston promised to bring them peace and a new way of life—"civilization." By this treaty the United States would furnish the Cherokee people "with useful implements of husbandry."[24] This provision reflected the United States' view of Indians as "savages" who hunted and signaled the government's determination to turn these "savages" into "civilized" people who farmed. Unlike hunters, farmers would both add to the national wealth and prosperity and require less land. Under President Washington and Secretary of War Henry Knox, the federal government considered the Indians as "owners" of their land and as independent or foreign nations with whom the United States government must deal through treaties. Federal policy emphasized "civilizing" the Cherokees by making farmers of former Cherokee hunters, by making housewives who sewed and spun of Cherokee women who formerly farmed, and finally by absorbing into the United States the surplus Indian land, presumably no longer needed as hunting grounds.[25]

The need for more land by the United States stemmed partly from its increasing population and partly from a imperative soon to be described as manifest destinhe traditional roles of Cherokee men were hunters and warriors while white men were farmers fenced in and lashed to the plow. When white men began to move west, they asked: why do the Cherokees need all this land? Meanwhile, the Cherokees posed the converse: how much land does it take for "civilized men," farmers, to live? In answer to the white's question, traditional Cherokees could reply: since the Cherokee people were hunters, and since the game was not fenced and had a tendency to roam, much land was needed. Obviously, the good hunter, the Cherokee man, must follow the game within his territory, for the Cherokees were not territorial in the sense that the whites were. The answer to the Cherokees' question concerning land lay in the Anglo-American concept of individually owned realty. Sanctity of land title gave an individual and his heirs "rights." Native people had only the right to occupy the land, and use of vast acreage for hunting hardly seemed like occupancy to many whites. They demanded that Cherokees, as well as other Indian peoples, give up their limited claim.

Even before the Revolutionary War, the colonists pressured the Cherokees to give up more land. Colonists looked to the West and saw the American frontier stretching before them as an "unclaimed" land of opportunity. However, this frontier was not unoccupied, but rather already inhabited and "claimed" by Cherokees and other tribes. The whites' push for new land in the Cherokee Nation grew over time, escalating in intensity from 1721, when the Cherokee people made the first land cession to the colony of South Carolina, to the Removal in 1838, when the Cherokee people were driven from their homeland in the East.

The government's Indian policy also provided for agents who lived among each tribe and worked towards "civilizing" the Indians. At the same time, agents worked on behalf of the government to negotiate cessions of Indian land. In many entries, the *Brainerd Journal* speaks of Return Jonathan Meigs, the Cherokee agent for over twenty years. While the government used Meigs to oversee the "civilization" process and the land acquisition policy, the government used missionaries to implement the "civilization" program. The missionaries supplied the expertise to train the Indians while the federal government supplied plows, spinning wheels, and domestic farm animals.[26]

Jefferson continued the "civilization" program and elaborated on many of Washington's themes. The Cherokees must abandon tribal ownership of land and move toward owning their own farms. They must change from their matrilineal clan system to the white man's patrilineal model where land and possessions passed to a father's children, not to his sister's children.[27] Jefferson, however, encouraged those Cherokees who wanted to move away from white settlements to emigrate west. His policies also undermined Cherokee sovereignty in that construction of a federal road through the Cherokee Nation brought an influx of whites while negotiation of the Compact of 1802 with Georgia committed the United States to extinguish Indian land titles within that state's boundaries.

Throughout the time of the *Brainerd Journal*, the effects of the Compact of 1802 rippled through the missionaries' entries as Georgia pressured the U.S. to impose the compact. Georgia used various tactics to pressure, bribe, or force the Cherokees to give up land within the limits Georgia claimed. On November 7, 1823, the journal recorded the meeting of Georgia commissioners sent to negotiate a deal with the Cherokees: "We learn that the chiefs would not consent to cede any land, although great efforts were made on the part of the commissioners .... They [the Cherokee chiefs] appear determined not to part with their land on any conditions."

At this meeting the commissioners used bribery to pressure the Cherokee people into ceding more land; the Brainerd missionaries revealed the scheme in the November 11, 1823 entry: "a head man of the Creek nation, a half-blood, attended with the Commissioners [and] insinuated that the whites would have their country at all events, & this would be a good time to put money in their [the Cherokees'] own pockets." Constant pressure to negotiate land cessions continued until the Treaty of 1835, which agreed to complete removal of the Cherokees to Indian Territory.

Concurrent with the Compact of 1802 came pressure to construct a road through the center of the Cherokee Nation.[28] The road issue surfaced as early as 1798 under President John Adams. However, Adams left office before he could press for the right of way through the nation. For the incoming President Jefferson, military security and an easy flow of traffic between white settlements depended upon roads. When the U.S. first suggested road construction, the Cherokees rejected the idea. In fact, the council censured James Vann for merely building a wagon, much less constructing a road on which to use it, and with their censure, came the council's proclamation which forbade him to use the wagon at all. The *Brainerd Journal* recorded the Cherokee Council's primary objection: "If you have a waggon there must be waggon roads—& if waggon roads, the whites will be in amongst us." Although most Cherokees opposed the roads, the U.S. government and the new white settlers wanting to move west insisted. Through a treaty negotiated in October 1803, the United States received the desired permission from fourteen "progressive" Cherokee leaders who agreed to allow roads between Georgia and Tennessee.[29] Vann and other Cherokee entrepreneurs took advantage of the roads and charged tolls, set up ferries and taverns, and turned a profit.[30] The *Brainerd Journal* often mentioned these roads because the mission itself stood adjacent to the controversial Federal Road and became a stopping place for many overnight guests.

In 1807 with Jefferson's blessings, Meigs persuaded a group of Lower Town Cherokees to voluntarily remove, setting a dangerous precedent. Claiming to speak for the entire nation, the Lower Town Chiefs agreed to sell to the United States the Cherokees' remaining hunting grounds.[31] Lower Town Chief Doublehead was killed for his part in the sale of the hunting grounds as strong resistance swelled among rising young Upper Town leaders such as Charles Hicks and The Ridge. Hicks, Ridge, and other leaders saw no reason to give up more land and so attempted to restrain the Lower Town Cherokees who favored sale of land and removal.[32] This division between the

Upper and Lower Town leaders led to the 1810 voluntary removal of Lower Town Cherokees who went to Arkansas under Tahlonteskee's leadership.[33] Through Jefferson's Indian policy, white settlers gained 15,000 square miles of Cherokee land on which to settle and moved a portion of the Cherokees from their homeland to an area the United States recently had acquired in the Louisiana Purchase.[34]

Presidents Madison and Monroe carried on Jefferson's Indian policy. Since Monroe was President during the entire time the *Brainerd Journal* was written, the missionaries discussed many of his policies and the effect of these policies on the Cherokees and missionaries alike. The journal, therefore, captured the Cherokees' responses to the government's pressure for land cessions and removal.

Even after the Cherokees abandoned hunting and their hunting grounds, neighboring whites regarded their title as spurious. For years the Cherokees tried to restrain the flow of white settlers, who squatted illegally on their land, but to no avail. *The Brainerd Journal* recorded many instances where the Cherokees endured pressure either by threats of removal or white squatters. One such entry concerned John Brown, Cherokee headman and father of Brainerd student Catharine Brown. The journal stated that "white people would not suffer him to live" on the border land of the Cherokee Nation. He stated that "white people" stole his cattle, hogs, and horses until he "had little left." John Brown did not withstand this pressure; in fact, he later moved to Arkansas. When a white man who had married a Cherokee woman and had a Cherokee family told the missionaries that "White men are determined to have this country and it was likely he should be obliged to remove over the Mississippi," they reassured the man that if the Cherokee people moved, so would the missionaries and their schools.[35] This assurance probably did little to allay his fears. The December 11, 1822 *Brainerd Journal* entry pointed out "that many from Alabama and Georgia are so sanguine in their expectations that the Cherokee will give up that part of the country that they are exploring it to look the best places for settlement, and some have actually come on with their families supposing the land had been ceded." As the pressure increased, the Cherokee Nation submitted time after time to land cessions that totaled thousands of square miles of land. After the 1817 and 1819 treaties and land cessions, the Cherokee Nation controlled only 17,000 square miles of their original 124,000 square miles of native homeland.[36]

Both the Treaty of 1817 and 1819 encouraged emigration of the Indians to the West or the taking of reserves, a new tactic on the part of the government, and both treaties resulted in large losses of land for the Cherokee people. The removal to Arkansas was considered "voluntary," and as an incentive, the government offered rifles to those who wished to live in Arkansas and "hunt" in the traditional ways. Yet, an inconsistency existed between the government incentive of hunting rifles offered as reward for removing and the government policy of "civilizing" the Indians. This inconsistency did not go unnoticed by the missionaries. In an aside—the portion of the journal where they expressed their own opinions for only the Prudential Committee to read, but not for public release—the missionaries wrote on May 25, 1818:

{The Indians say they don't know how to understand their good Father the President. A few years ago he sent them a plough & a hoe—said it was not good for his red children to hunt, they must cultivate the earth. Now he tells them there is good hunting at the Arkansas; if they will go there he will give them rifles.} Perhaps it will be best not to publish the above which is in brackets.

In this quote there is no transcriber intrusion. The brackets and the underlining appear as originally written to the Prudential Committee expressing how the government Indian policy was indeed confusing.

The journal also records reaction to the new Civilization Fund Act enacted during Monroe's administration.[37] The fund's purpose was to further aid the civilization efforts largely undertaken by missionary societies such as the American Board. Many entries in the journal concern the missionaries erecting new school buildings or setting up their blacksmith shop and triphammer shop—all activities encouraged by government "civilization" policy.

Besides Cherokee reaction to government policy, the *Brainerd Journal* is replete with encouragement for Cherokees to abandon traditional ways and to take on the white manners and customs. The June 11, 1823 entry revealed the missionaries' civilizing efforts when the girls at the Brainerd School received certificates of merit for work well-done. Though not mentioned by name, the Cherokee girls' laudable accomplishments in the "civilized" labors of white women were enumerated:

since monday of last week, viz. they have made fifty hunting frocks, besides hemming a number of handkerchiefs & some other sewing, in addition to their usual work in other branches of labor which is assisting in the dining room, in the milking & in all the washings, doing the whole of their own washings & ironing, most of the ironing for the mission family & boys, & mending the boys clothes.[38]

The skills listed consist of typical domestic labors performed by Anglo-white women of the nineteenth century. Had these girls remained at home with their mothers, they would have learned the age-old Cherokee stories of Selu, the first woman, teaching the tribe to plant crops, as the women labored in the field planting corn.[39]

The acculturation of the Cherokees also involved a transformation from a matrilineal, community-oriented society to a society of patriarchal, nuclear families. In their traditional matrilineal society, kinship passed through the mother (as opposed to bilateral descent in white society) and the Cherokee mother's brother exerted a greater influence on a mother's children than did their own father. Furthermore, the social fabric of the matrilineal clan system dictated marriage laws, revenge laws, and inheritance laws.[40] In several instances the Brainerd journalist spoke of the importance of clan. The September 5, 1818 entry stated: "An uncle of one of the school girls called to day & frankly told us that the mother of the girl, having been informed that the children were not well fed, requested him to come & take the girl away." Here the uncle, not the father, came to collect the children. To Anglo-Americans, the father was the natural person to fetch the children, but for the Cherokees, maternal uncles assumed supervisory roles since they were the closest male relative. In addition, mothers expected their brothers to protect and train their children. Therefore, the uncle in this passage performed his duty when he came to collect the children, then assessed the situation, and concluded that the school was, in fact, a good place for the children.

As the "civilizing" policies of the United States and the transformation of Cherokee society proceeded, such traditional customs and practices changed. For instance, the individual Cherokee family unit separated from the community and began living on isolated farms. In essence, the Cherokee family became cutoff from the traditional community-oriented activities of a tribe. Because she was now isolated on a farm with only her husband and family, a Cherokee woman had little link to other women in her tribe.[41] What was once a tight cluster of homes in a village, now resembled a string of farms loosely scattered over an area which could easily stretch thirty miles or more.[42] This wide dispersion of Cherokee families detrimentally affected the missionaries' efforts to evangelize and draw a crowd together for worship services at the mission. The *Brainerd Journal* entry for December 29, 1818 expressed this disappointment: "As the people do not live in vilages, but scattered over the country from 2 to 10 miles apart; to collect in any place 20 or 30 who can understand our language, is as much as can be expected."

Changes in clan relationships and inheritance also challenged Cherokee traditional ways. With the shift from matrilineal clans to patriarchal nuclear families, the importance of the clan broke down. Traditionally, the clan held the right of revenge, so when the Cherokee Nation passed laws outlawing clan revenge and instituted the Lighthorse as the police force in the clan's stead, the clan's power diminished greatly. With the passage of one law after another, the Cherokee Nation slowly centralized tribal government which regulated tribal affairs and controlled relations with the United States government, rather than relying on the traditional clan system and town councils to maintain order and harmony.[43] Various *Brainerd Journal* entries point out the work of the Lighthorse and review the efforts of the centralized Cherokee Council to deal with the United States government's push for land cessions and treaties.

For Cherokees, the concept of inheritance—that is the passing on of personal possessions—held little importance because traditionally they de-emphasized accumulation of individual property.[44] As "civilization" progressed, though, the Cherokees began to accumulate private property as encouraged by the white society around them. Soon, a Cherokee family owned its domestic animals, house, and perhaps even slaves; in fact, some lived like Southern white planters.[45] Although the Cherokees still owned the land in common, these new customs of property accumulation contrasted directly with the community-oriented, clan-based Cherokee society.[46] The *Brainerd Journal* often mentioned the many black attendees at worship services and the Sunday school offered by the missionaries. These black attendees were mostly slaves held by Cherokee planters.

As changes in the basic fabric of Cherokee society took place, it was harder for them, especially traditional-minded Cherokees who lived away from the influence of the whites, to give up their ceremonies and rituals, which the missionaries condemned. Yet at the same time, the missionaries possessed an interest in the old customs, and they sometimes described Cherokee rituals and ceremonies in the *Brainerd Journal*.[47] The lengthy April 16, 1818 entry recorded Charles Hicks' recounting of Cherokee customs including matrilineage, clans, the Eagle Tail Dance, and the Green Corn Dance to help the Brainerd missionaries better understand the Cherokee people. The American Board's publication, the *Missionary Herald*, later published this long relation of Cherokee customs, presumably as evidence of the Cherokees' need for missions.[48]

The missionaries attempted to cope with cultural differences, and their successes and failures can be observed throughout the journal. The journal recorded that three boys left the mission grounds to attend a Cherokee ball play, a competition similar to lacrosse. The missionaries reprimanded the boys for their action, and, of the three, expelled the boy who had the longest attendance at Brainerd (see *Brainerd Journal*, July 6, 1822). This situation is a vivid example of the "clash of cultures" as the missionaries tried to take away from their Cherokee students the very customs that made the boys Cherokee. The boys, in turn, probably did not intend to disobey but merely continued to participate in what was to them a perfectly normal and acceptable activity. Yet to live at the Brainerd Mission, a New England-style boarding school, required Cherokee students to adopt the white style of clothing, speech, and family situation, and to leave tradition at home with the parents.

Thus, the Brainerd Mission opened its doors during a time of much change and tension in the Cherokee Nation. When the mission first opened, the mission grounds contained a simple mission house and school house. However, as more students and workers arrived, the missionaries constructed additional buildings to house the increasing numbers, including a school for girls and one for boys; separate living quarters for the missionaries, boys, and girls; a farm with several fields and pastures; a mill; and various kinds of out buildings. The mission grew into a complex that by the close of 1823 looked like a village. Such growth was clearly what the American Board had intended:

At Brainerd we must gradually, but as fast as circumstances permit, form a settlement, a village composed of white people, devoted to missionary in its various departments, and of Cherokees, willing to submit to the order and conform to the rules of Christianized society: a settlement, a village, in which all the employments, and advantages, and excellencies of Christian civilization shall be exhibited for the benefit of the surrounding children of the forest, and as a model for other establishments successively to be formed in other parts of the Indian countries.[49]

Over one hundred people lived at Brainerd in 1823. All the elements of a village existed: a preacher, a doctor, a school and two school teachers, a gristmill, a sawmill, a blacksmith shop, a grain warehouse, barns, stables, farm and vegetable fields, livestock, a smoke house, a wash house, and even a store room for all the supplies needed to feed, clothe, and educate approximately eighty to one hundred children. The storeroom held a variety of items shipped from benevolent societies in northern states. The storeroom must have looked like a nineteenth century dry goods store full of clothing, shoes, hats, various types of cloth, sewing notions, and school supplies. The village even had a library as part of the mission and school. The mission's gristmill, sawmill, and blacksmith shop not only met the needs of the mission but also aided the "civilizing" process for the Cherokee people. Additionally, the shops brought the mission cash payments and bartered food from Cherokees who availed themselves of these services.

Besides the Brainerd complex, between 1817 and 1823 the missionaries set up mission stations and schools at Taloney, Creek Path, Willstown, Hightower, and Turnip Mountain. The American Board provided the staff for the new missions as well as funds to supply the station. The United States government through the Civilization Fund provided additional support for these new schools. In several instances, however, eager Cherokees erected a building so that a local school could be ready for their children as soon as possible.

Brainerd and the smaller stations used the Lancastrian method of teaching, which achieved maximum teaching at least expense. In the classroom, one teacher taught subjects such as spelling, writing, and arithmetic by subdividing the one classroom into grades according to the students' ability. More advanced students became "monitors" who received special training from the teacher in order to help them teach the younger children. Instead of expensive books, the teacher used large cards with the lesson on each card.[50] Through this method the mission taught children to read and write English.

The first missionaries arrived in the Cherokee Nation expecting to teach in only English; as a result, they taught mainly those children with previous exposure to the English language, usually children of mixed-ancestry. The missionaries hesitated to speak in Cherokee, so interpreters became the medium for those students or church attendees who did not know English. In school, the older bi-lingual students often interpreted. In church, Cherokees such as Charles Reece and Brainerd student John Arch interpreted.

The missionaries also assumed the responsibility of teaching the children "civilized" industries such as weaving and spinning to girls, and farming and mechanical skills to boys. The Brainerd schoolteachers were expected to teach and supervise the students in and out of the classroom. After class session, the male schoolteacher supervised the boys in the field, while the female teacher supervised the girls' work. The journal routinely referred to the teaching of the "civilized" industries as the labors "out of school." However, the missionaries often found this continual daytime and evening time routine detrimental to their own well-being:

> We find it quite too much for any one man to teach the school, and labor with, and instruct, such a number of boys out of school. Br. Chamberlin has taken most of this labor upon himself untill his health has so entirely failed that he is scarcely able to teach the school, and the other brethren are necessarily as much engaged in their several departments that it is impossible for them so to attend to the labor of the boys, as to do them justice or to render their labor as productive as it otherwise might be.[51]

The missionaries brought with them their values and customs which gave rise to ethnocentrism. The missionaries' judgmental attitude often shaped their evaluations of people and events. The missionaries' bias was evident in their initial assessment of new Cherokee student John Arch in this January 26, 1819 journal entry:

> He spoke english, & his countenance indicated a mind, that might admit of improvement; but having the dress & dirty appearance of the most uncultivated part of the tribe, & withal a mind & body for so many years under the influence of these habits, we were sorry to hear him say any thing about entering the school .... We had often heard that the people in that part of

the nation from which he said he had come, were the most
ignorant & uncultivated of any in the whole tribe . . . .

After his education at Brainerd, John Arch became one of the
mission's most faithful and trusted interpreters, and the missionaries
acknowledged him as one of the finest examples of success in their
missionary cause. He had become like them: he was an Indian who
took on the culture of the white man.

The *Brainerd Journal* shows other results of the "civilizing" process.
At the Brainerd Mission school alone, over two hundred students
received some amount of education during the period 1817-1823.[52]
Even more students studied at the outlying mission stations. Granted,
some students stayed in school for just a short length of time, but such
notable Cherokee leaders as John Ridge, Elias Boudinot, David
Brown, and David Carter received an education at the Brainerd school
and later at the American Board's Foreign Mission School at
Cornwall, Connecticut.

The American Board, through the Brainerd Mission and its outlying local schools, advanced the government's civilization program
not only through the education of children, but through the teaching
of Anglo-American agricultural techniques. The missionaries
observed that the Cherokee people had never used oxen for farming.
New Englanders felt oxen were of great use, so the Brainerd
missionaries introduced them to the region. (See *Brainerd Journal* for
April 22, 1820.) The missionaries believed in pastures for their
domestic animals, especially milk cows, instead of the Southern
tradition of letting cows or hogs range freely in the woods. Several
times the *Brainerd Journal* recorded the missionaries' preference of
pasturage over range. Furthermore, the missionaries set up various
mills and shops to grind the Cherokees' corn, saw their lumber, and
make and repair their metal tools. The mission also provided
Cherokee families with European-style clothing and trained the men
in technical and mechanical skills—skills which the United States
government promoted through their Indian civilization policy.

Over the seven years of the journal, the Brainerd Mission evolved
as the "mother" mission. Other mission sites sprung up as groups of
Cherokee people, living in outlying areas of sixty to ninety miles
away, requested smaller schools to be established in their particular
district. The Prudential Committee approved the establishment of
these outlying schools.

As more local schools were built, the Cherokees wanted the Brainerd Mission to reduce its role as the "mother mission" because the large Brainerd complex became too obtrusive in the eyes of some Cherokee. The American Board's views on Brainerd changed, particularly after Jeremiah Evarts' 1822 tour of the Board's Indian missions. Chief Charles Hicks revealed Cherokee attitudes to Evarts:

> After the family had retired, he [Hicks] conversed very freely with Mr. Kingsbury & myself, relative to the concerns of the Cherokee mission. He said the people were displeased that so many persons had arrived at Brainerd; that they said the intention was to build a town, rather than teach a school. He added, that his own opinion of Brainerd had altered; that he thought that too much was expected there & that more good would be done by local schools. He said that there were various unfavorable reports in the nation, which arose from little things, but which had an unpleasant effect. He supposed if the expense at Brainerd were reduced one half, & the other half were laid out at local schools, at $600 each annually, much good would be produced.[53]

In the fall of 1823 several new missionaries from New England arrived at the Brainerd Mission, resulting in a total reorganization of the mission system, and on December 31, 1823, the *Brainerd Journal* ceased to be written as one continuous journal.

This missionary journal not only tells of the history of the missionary movement, supplies insight into the "civilizing" of the Cherokee people, and provides glimpses of Cherokee culture at that time, but it also tells of the intimate lives of the missionaries and their families. These people had a strong Christian faith; they trusted God for all their daily needs and in numerous entries wrote about feeling God's grace. However, they were also mortal beings subject to the same personality flaws and temptations as all people—Christian and non-Christian alike. Thus, in the journal the missionaries' character qualities peek through, especially concerning the running of the missionary stations and the opposing views of Ard Hoyt, as superintendent, and Moody Hall, as steward, at the Brainerd Mission. Their conflict continued when Hall moved from Brainerd to establish the Taloney station. Corresponding Secretary Samuel Worcester, when exhorting these missionaries to harmony among themselves, touched on this very point by saying that "missionaries are men: and like other christians, even the best, have their infirmities and imperfections." After pointing out that the missionaries' adversary can produce discord among missionaries, he added that "It is a humiliating fact that at almost every missionary station now existing he [the adversary] has succeeded, and in too many instances to a deplorable extent, in producing and fomenting discord among the Brethren."[54] Even though most entries show the missionaries' overwhelming trust and faith in God in their every day life, some entries provide glimpses of their "infirmities and imperfections" as well as their intimate lives. The journal tells of Daniel Butrick's frustration as he finds himself stranded on the wrong side of the creek at night in a pouring down rain storm (see *Brainerd Journal*, March 24, 1819), the sadness felt when a missionary's new born baby died, or the serious illnesses which afflicted each of the missionaries more than once.

Beyond these human qualities, the missionaries had different feelings and motivations for going into the Cherokee Nation. Most missionaries dedicated the rest of their lives to working at whatever mission they were called to serve. But, the journal reveals that a missionary was not always devoted to the cause. Missionary John Talmage had expectations of living in much the same manner as he had lived in the North, with his wife having to care for only her own family and her husband.[55] When he arrived at the mission, his family had to become part of a communal family; his wife was expected to care for others beyond her own family, and they had to learn how to live by a set of rules. The Talmages left Brainerd after only a few months, but they were the exception to the truly devoted missionary family. Daniel Butrick, the Hoyts, the Chamberlins, the Butlers, the Vails, the Deans, Elsworths, Parkers, Blunts, and Halls—all these families toiled with their hands and hearts to further their objectives which in turn hastened the acculturation of the Cherokee people.

Turning once again to the *Brainerd Journal* as a historical document, the missionaries recorded this "official" journal, now housed in the archives at the Houghton Library, Harvard University, on whatever paper was at hand, probably from items donated to them by the missionary societies. They wrote on short stationary-size paper or on longer-size stationary, while many submissions were on large "newsprint" size paper of 22" by 17" folded down the middle. The missionaries wrote on four sides, each side measuring 11" wide by 17" long. It was this last type of thin 22" x 17" paper which proved most susceptible to the tyranny of time, for today holes in the manuscript now appear where important words once stood. Yet overall, the journal is in readable form.

To record the journal, the missionaries most likely used quill pens since workable metal pens were not widely available until 1819 and were not mass produced until the 1830's. Also, the list of items donated to the mission shows quills being shipped to them, so in 1817-1823 the missionaries probably were using quill pens made from goose feathers (see *Brainerd Journal* for February 16, 1821 #9). The use of quill pens produced an interesting quality in the journal. Since each quill was individually cut, no two quills wrote exactly alike.[56] The differences in the quills could account for why the handwriting of the same person was so bold and clear in some entries, while other entries the writing was so faint.

For the transcriber, penmanship provided information well beyond the mere meaning of the sentences. Penmanship was the element which identified the writer of various sections of the journal. Ard Hoyt, William Chamberlin, Daniel Butrick, Darius Hoyt, an unidentified woman, and others penned various sections of the journal. Approximately nine different handwritings appeared during the seven years of the journal. The specific journalists were identified through a comparison of distinctly different penmanship found in the *Brainerd Journal*, letters, and private journals of Chamberlin, Butrick, Ard Hoyt, and Hoyt's son Darius. Though most of the journal was penned by identifiable missionaries, the recorders of several sections of the journal were unidentifiable and may simply have written as someone else dictated.

Penmanship and writing implements provide only a portion of the fascination in the journal. This journal also embodies a unique and sincere voice and a writing style indicative of the nineteenth century, not to mention a distinctive manner of spelling, abbreviation, and paragraphing. Therefore, as the transcribers endeavored to accurately convert the original manuscript to printed format, several issues required addressing, in particular, transcriber intrusion, use of brackets, indecipherable portions, and annotations.

Within every writing lies the voice of the author. Echoed through tone, syntax, and diction, the writer's voice strikes the ear, even in transcribing. As one reads, the journal lives, creating an intimacy between missionary writer and modern reader. In transcribing, the primary concern was to reflect each word as written without interjection of twentieth century vocabulary or values. Therefore, the journal will reflect the original writers—their feelings, their frustrations, their loves, and their fears which appear in their own words and in their own syntax—correct, politically or otherwise, by their own standards and not this century's.

The transcribers have endeavored to maintain the overall tone and voice of the missionaries who wrote. The vocabulary, sentence structure, and often illustrations not only reflected the nineteenth century, but were infused with religious language and metaphor. For example, in the January 26, 1817 entry, Cyrus Kingsbury said, "But alas! how little do I feel of that divine ardour which animated the heart of the pious David when he said, 'A day in thy house is better than a thousand.'" Such allusions to Bible verses and religious writing are common in the journal.

Another element of style, which added to the adventure of entering into the world of the nineteenth century Brainerd Mission was spelling, dictated by convention of the times or poor spelling habits. For example, such words as *until* spelled as *untill* or *scholar* spelled as *schollar* appear often in the journal. It would be convenient if the spelling were predictable as if a single author penned the *Brainerd Journal*. Such is not the case. Suffice it to say that all spellings, correct or incorrect by today's standard, appear as originally written.

The writer of the *Brainerd Journal* also irregularly used capitalization and constantly relied on abbreviations. However, the application of capitalization or abbreviation seemed to be more by whim than by rule. The word *Cherokee*, for instance, could be *Cherokee* or *cherokee*. As to abbreviations, *brot.* for *brought*, *bu* for *bushel*, *chh* for *church*, and *&c* for *etc.* appear among many others.

The formatting of paragraphs was, at best, scant. Generally, no indention was used to indicate paragraph beginning, and no line separation was provided as today, when "block" paragraphing is chosen. As a paragraph ended, the next paragraph began on the next line at the left margin. If the line ending the previous paragraph happened to be short, the transcribers were lucky. Otherwise, context dictated the paragraphing. In transcribing, paragraphing has been left as originally set down by the missionaries.

The mere fact that the journal is old and handwritten created problems in transcribing. Years alone can turn page to powder, and the *Brainerd Journal* is no exception. Even though the archivists have exerted great care to maintain the original journal, time is claiming bits and pieces to the extent that holes now appear where words used to be, and numerous foldings and unfoldings have creased away the words that were once there. The physical condition in many places have made reading the handwriting and overcoming the spelling and word choice even more of a challenge. In some instances, these conditions required a "best guess." Where a word was entirely unreadable, the transcribers used brackets [?] to indicate a missing word. When a word was present in the manuscript but partially unreadable, the transcribers indicated the possible letters or possible word such as [r?ed] or [received?]. In other instances the transcriber indicated why a word or words were missing by use of an explanatory intrusion such as [*hole in manuscript*]. The transcribers also used brackets to indicate added words such as: President [James] Monroe.

Occasionally the missionaries indicated portions of the journal which they did not want published in the *Missionary Herald.* The transcribers have elected to use braces { } to indicate those portions of the journal which the missionaries designated "not for publication."

The missionaries often crossed out words or lines of writing in the journal. In most instances the transcribers were able to transcribe these words or sentences and have indicated the original journalist's crossed-out lines with a strike over in the type.

Various titles appear within the text of the journal. As a portion of the journal was completed, the section was signed by those missionaries present and then mailed to the headquarters in New England. When the journalist started the next section of the journal, he titled the new section but did not endeavor to maintain consistent titles from one mailing of the journal to the next. Therefore, such titles as "Brainerd Journal," "Journal of the Mission at Brainerd," or "Brainerd Mission Journal" appear as each new section of the journal commences.

Since the journalist often generated the official journal from notes maintained by the missionaries and then later compiled the notes into a formal journal, he sometimes inadvertently omitted entries for a particular date or dates. Consequently, at the end of a section, the missionary added a list of "omissions" in non-chronological order. The transcribers took the liberty of integrating these "omissions" so that the entire manuscript now reads in proper chronological order.

When missionaries referred, directly or indirectly, to people, places, things, situations, or scripture, the transcribers provided explanatory information in notes or, rarely, in brackets within the text.

Since the missionaries knew that portions of the *Brainerd Journal* would be published in the *Missionary Herald*, they often kept the journal entry succinct. However, in personal letters to the Prudential Committee and others, the missionaries expounded on the details of a situation mentioned in the journal. In the notes, to more fully explain a situation, the transcribers have used direct quotes or paraphrases from missionaries' correspondence and journals. In addition, efforts have been made to identify in notes as many people as possible where their names first appear within the journal. A positive identification was not possible in all cases. Therefore, the transcribers have indicated possible and maybe the most probable identification based on other sources.

In addition to the notes, to enhance the contents of the journal, this book includes a transcription of other shorter documents found in the American Board Papers. These valuable documents, many compiled during Jeremiah Evarts' 1822 visit to Brainerd, include a descriptive list of the Cherokee towns in the Brainerd vicinity, a list of the missionaries' names and their families, a list of the people who had joined the church at Brainerd and Creek Path, and two lists of students who attended the school. These documents, included as Tables #1–#5 at the end of the transcribed journal, are valuable for research information in that they contain more than just names. For instance, the "Catalogue" of students found in Table #4 includes the approximate age of students, their Cherokee name with an explanation, and their place of residence in 1822. The compiled list of students in Table #5 often includes sibling relationships between students. In these records though, the missionaries many times included a student's "white person's" name, but not the student's Cherokee name.

The American Board of Commissioners for Foreign Missions had a vision, and the missionaries became the ones who carried out this vision and who diligently put down in writing all that occurred at that pivotal time in the Cherokee Nation's history. The transcribers are grateful that the missionaries, the American Board, and the Houghton Library had the foresight to organize and preserve these valuable documents in archival form for some 175 years. Publication of this document is by permission of the Houghton Library, Harvard University and the American Board of Commissioners for Foreign Missions' successor, the United Church Board for World Ministries. A research trip to the Houghton Library was provided through a grant by the American Philosophical Society, Phillips Fund for Native American Studies. We appreciate all the courteous and helpful librarians who made our research at the Houghton so successful.

A special thank you goes to those who guided us and encouraged us on this project, especially Theda Perdue, Professor of History at the University of Kentucky and editor of the "Indians of the Southeast" series, for her detailed and most diligent review of several drafts of the manuscript. Her knowledge of Native American History inspired us to further research. We express our sincere appreciation to William L. Anderson, Professor of History at Western Carolina University, for his invaluable comments on our initial manuscript, and to Duane H. King, Executive Director of the Southwest Museum in Los Angeles, for his encouragement that a transcription of the *Brainerd Journal* was needed, his readiness to always provide answers to our questions, and his proofreading of the Cherokee names in the "Catalogue of Students."

We are grateful to Rowena McClinton of Middle Tennessee University, for her valuable help in identifying individuals mentioned in both the *Brainerd Journal* and in the "Moravian Mission Diary." Thank you to Marilou Awiakta; Gary Moulton of the University of Nebraska; Tom Mooney and Virginia Vann Perry of the Cherokee Heritage Center; descendants of Collins McDonald, Jerry L. Clark and Rose Guthrie; and David Hirano and Fujiko Kitagawa of the United Church Board for World Ministries for responding to our queries. We acknowledge the librarians at Grossmont College for their assistance and are grateful for Marty Lewis' help in obtaining material through inter-library loan. The helpful assistance received from reference librarians at the National Archives in Atlanta, Georgia; San Diego State University; San Diego Family History Center; Escondido Pioneer Room; and Carlsbad Library was much appreciated.

We are indebted to Jeanne Martinez, who unselfishly devoted an entire summer helping proofread the entire manuscript as well as assisting with the index. We appreciate Stephanie Mood, Don Shannon, and Richard Best for reading versions of the Introduction as we proceeded. A special thank you to Judith and Paul Becker for their proofreading of portions of the final draft. Thank you to Bert Youde, Edward Hillary, Andrew Phillips, Mark Phillips, and Linda Nelson for their help as the project progressed. We are grateful to Tiffany Phillips, as well as our parents, who have always encouraged us in everything we have done.

Current Cherokee Associate Justice, former Cherokee Chief Justice, and faithful servant to the Cherokee Nation for fourteen years, Philip H. Viles, Jr. has not only written the Foreword to this book, but has provided these researchers with a wealth of information concerning the history of Gary Phillips' ancestors—the Lowrey family and the Hoyt family—two family names mentioned often in the journal.

It has truly been an inspiration to share in the lives of these Cherokees and missionaries as the transcription progressed and evolved. For us it was easy to be caught up in the words—to feel their success and suffering and to feel the anguish of the Cherokee people as they experienced the pressure of removal from their beloved country. The *Brainerd Journal* is no tedious daily diary, but a book stuffed full of the Cherokees' and missionaries' intimate lives and their view of the history of their times.

1817

Journal of the Mission to the Cherokees,
beginning with a few minutes from
the Journal of Brother Kingsbury
before the arrival of the brothers Hall & Williams

1817 Saturday Jan. 18. Arrive at Chickamaugah [Chickamauga], for the purpose of making preparations to commence & establish a Lancastrian school at that place.[1] The work is of the highest importance & I feel the need of imploring the divine aid & direction. The day is extremely cold. The houses both in this country & in Tennessee have generally wooden chimneys, are without glass, & the doors are obliged to be left open in the day time to admit light, so that one can hardly eat breakfast without a fit of the ague.

Sab. [Jan.] 19. Weather continues very cold for this country. Spend the day at the house on the plantation which we have purchased for the use of the school. Mr. McDonald, an old Scotch Gentleman, who has married a native, occupies it at present, but is soon to move out.[2] Had no opportunity this day to collect a congregation for preaching. Read some tracts, & converse & pray with the old people. The old gentleman thinks he never did any thing wrong.[3]

[Jan.] 20. Hear that some articles which I had ordered to be sent down the river had arrived at a Ware house about 6 miles distant. Go with small waggon to bring them.

[Jan.] 21. Go again for my goods to the Warehouse. Return again in safety, though late & the night dark & rainy.

[Jan.] 22. Rainy—Mr. McDonald is removing his effects to his grandsons about 4 miles distant, & I am busily employed in assisting him.

[Jan.] 23. House still in confusion by the moving posture of the old occupants.

[Jan.] 24. Labor to day in preparing a window for my house. The day is pleasant, and the old people bid farewell to their old habitation no more to return to live in it. They will leave a negro boy & girl to keep house & do my little affairs untill I can get assistance.[4] Two Indians call & tarry over night.

[Jan.] 25. My time is principally occupied in making those little arrangements which are always necessary at the commencement of a family establishment.
Charles Reece, a half breed, has been at work for me five days.[5] He is very industrious. Has had three sisters for his wives at the same time, one of whom is dead; & he has left the other two on account of the insolence of their mother—has left a good plantation, & a valuable stock of cattle, for them & his children, & taken another woman with whom he has begun anew in the world. This illustrates a striking trait in the Indian character. If they have differences with each other they will not contend but agree to separate.[6]

Sab. [Jan.] 26. Nobody to interrupt me to day—But alas! how little do I feel of that divine ardour which animated the heart of pious David when he said "a day in thy house is better than a thousand."[7] At 12 o'clock I preached at Mr. Nave's for the first time in the nation, about 2 miles distant, agreeable to appointment—15 to hear, 4 whites, 4 blacks, & 7 mixed blood Indians all attentive.[8]

[Jan.] 27. Write letter on business—go about 6 miles & engaged a half breed man & woman to live with me awhile. Also engaged two Indians to hunt me cows in the range which I can have the loan of a while for milk, & to bring up a steer which I have bought for beef.[9]

[Jan.] 28. The Cherokee woman I engaged yesterday arrived & I dismiss the black boy & girl.

[Jan.] 30. The Cherokee woman I have hired is industrious, & a tollerable cook. Very busy to day in killing the steer I had brought up. Two Indians were my butchers. They did it tolerably well, but made a bungling business of cutting it up. In the evening set my glass & put a window in my house.

Feb. 1. Two Indians bring in two turkeys & a Deer this morning.[10]

Sab. [Feb.] 2. Preached at Mr. Coodey's.[11] About 30 present, 1/3 mixed blood Cherokees, 1/3 whites & 1/3 blacks, slaves. Enjoyed some little freedom in the exercises, for which I desire to be thankful.—This evening the ground is covered with snow for the first time this winter, but since January came in it has been remarkably cold for this climate.

Mon. [Feb.] 3. Find it very difficult to procure help to do any kind of mechanical work.[12] Spent the day in rounding & preparing a grindstone. A hard snow.

[Feb.] 5. Very cold—have business from home. Evening—the ink freezes in my pen as I write by the fireside.

[Feb.] 6. Spent the day in hunting hogs in the woods which I wish to purchase.

[Feb.] 7. I am comfortably situated in many respects. But from the multitude of cares & business have no time to study either for my own improvement or for the instruction of the Indians.

Feb. 8. The Cherokee man & woman wish to go home. I know not what to do—am in great difficulty about help. But I have no reason to complain—my situation is comfortable when compared with that of theirs and whose shoe latchets I am not worthy to loose.

Sab. [Feb.] 9. A prospect of fair weather after an uncomfortable stormy week. There was an appointment for preaching at the mission house, but no one came. Some were from home & others made the weather an excuse.

[Feb.] 10. Go in quest of help; get an old black man & his wife from Mr. McDonald.

[Feb.] 13. Go out to day on business—Meet with Charles Hicks, one of the principal Chiefs.[13] He informs me an Indian on Highwasse [Hiwassee] river murdered his wife & children about a week since;[14] supposed to be occasioned by a disagreement respecting removing over the Mississippi, he wishing to go, she not.[15] The women in these parts are about to draw up a memorial to the National Council against an exchange of country.[16] This is done in cognizance of the hardships & suffering to which it is apprehended the woman & children will be exposed by a removal.

[Feb.] 15. Mr. Ross, a Cherokee by birth, [17] & who is a very respectable merchant in the neighborhood arrives from the Agency & brings a packet of letters for me from various friends.[18] A feast indeed.

Sab. [Feb.] 16. Mr. Coodey who is a respectable white man in the neighborhood, & married to a Cherokee sent his servant this morning to inform me that George McDonald died last night and that probably there would be few or no people at preaching today. Mr. McDonald was a son of the former occupant of the mission house & most of my hearers are relatives.[19]

[Feb.] 17. Attended funeral of McDonald. A decent coffin & grave was prepared. Prayer was attended at the house. There was not that order which we see in the Northern States but everything was decent & solemn.

[Feb.] 18. Leave my house in the care of a white man, who providentially called on me as he was passing, & set off for the settlement on business.[20] When I arrived at the ferry on Tennessee there was no one to take me over, & I was obliged to row myself & horse across. The river is here about three quarters of a mile wide, & it was dark before I got over, so that I had much difficulty to find the landing.

[Feb.] 25. Return home & find all things well. The time I spent in the settlement was employed in procuring various implements of husbandry, provisions &c [etc.].

[Feb.] 26. Rainy. Hear that Mr. McClelland & family whom I have engaged to live with me, are on their way from the settlements.[21] Set off to meet them. Got them safe over the creek by sundown.

[Feb.] 27. Very rainy. Waters rise fast & am obliged to ride several miles in the rains. In the evening I was seized with a violent cold & sore throat.

[Feb.] 28. Quite unwell. Was under the necessity of going to the Warehouse 6 miles; Indisposition increased. Heard that my dear Brethren & Sisters from N. York are within 70 miles.[22] At night annointed my neck, breast & feet with pounded onions & butter which soon relieved my pain, & I had a good nights sleep

March 1. I have daily occasion to notice the care of a kind providence, & the gracious interposition in favor of the mission. The night after Mr. McClellan[d] & family arrived the waters rose so as to stop all traveling for several days. My Boat with provisions can now come down, & my associates I expect in a few days, all in good time. Health much better.

Sab. [March] 2. A small number meet at my house for public worship, to whom I endeavored to explain & enforce the doctrine of total depravity.

[March] 4. Felt much anxiety about my brethren who are on the way. They have been by high water, & provisions both for man & beast are extremely scarse. Send Mr. McClellan[d] with supplies to meet them. About one hour after Brethren Hall & Williams arrived having passed the messenger by a different road.[23] They had left their wives at Mr. Gambolds, who is the Moravian missionary in this nation, & lives about 30 miles from Chickamaugah.[24] Our meeting produced peculiar sensations, & was such as might be expected at the first interview of those who are devoted family to the same great & good work of building up the cause of the Redeemer in this Heathen land. Our prayers & praises were mingled at the throne of grace.

[March] 5. Brethren Hall & Williams return to Mr. Gambolds to bring on their wives.

[March] 6. At about 12 Ock [o'clock] a hard rain commenced. I was apprehen-sive it might raise the creek so as to oblige my friends once more to stop before they reach Chickamaugah. After securing a load of provisions which two Indians had brought for me up the creek, I set off about 4 ock P.M. to meet them, & about an hour after dark I arrived at the house where they had taken lodgings for the night. Here for the first time I beheld the dear sisters who are to be our associates in the arduous work of civilizing & converting the savages of our wilderness. O! what thanks are due to our gracious Lord for raising up from among the daughters of our land those who are willing to make such sacrifices for his cause.

[March] 7. No rain to day. Started very early on our way to Chick-amaugah. Were highly favored in geting over the bad roads & creeks. Br. W. was flung from his horse but providentialy received no injury, & about 9 ock P.M. we all arrived in safety at the mission house.[25] Here we all united in devout praise & thanksgiving to God for his preserving many in many difficulties & dangers. Truly the Lord has been with the Brethren & Sisters on the way & brought them to their destined place in safety. But the severe indispositions of Br. Williams & Sister Hall, cast a shade over our minds on this other wise joyful occasion.

Journal of the Brethren United

Sab. March 9. Br. Kingsbury preached to about 40 persons, from Matt. 19:29. "Every one that hath forsaken houses &c". We are now a little band of Missionaries, who profess to have renounced the world for the sake of Christ. O! that we may be faithful to our covenant vows.

[March] 12. Our boat which we had expected for some time arrived with corn, potatoes, pork &c. The creek on which we live is navigable for large boats about 2 miles from its mouth. From this place to the Mission house is about 6 miles by land & 10 or 12 by water. We shall be obliged to take out our load & bring it up the creek in large canoes.

[March] 15. Since the arrival of our boat we have all been laboriously & constantly engaged in unloading it, & have had to work much in the night.
We feel thankful that we are situated where we can receive assistance from kind neighbors. We were in want of money, & to day Mr. Ross loaned us $100 for as long a time as we should want it.

Sab. [March] 16. Br. K. preached at the Ware house.

Sab. [March] 23. Br. K. preached at our own house, a respectable number attended. Two Indians came this day to trade with us. We told them it was our beloved day, & the great & good being above would be offended if we traded on this day. They seemed to understand us & we think were satisfied.

Sat. [March] 29. This week has been spent in labor so hard that our bodies are almost worn down, & even our spirits somewhat depressed. But why should we be cast down? Surely the object we are pursuing may well engage our hearts so entirely that we shall be willing to spend & be spent in this work; having always the fear of God before us.
We have frequent visits from our neighbors, both red & white. The Indians appear truly friendly. Our schollars are bright & active, & make good progress in their learning.

Mar. 31. We were much gratified receiving a letter & more provisions from Moravian friends, Mr. & Mrs. Gambold. We have the utmost assurance of their affection for us & their deep interest in our establishment.

Sab. April 6. This morning four Indians of the Creek Nation called to inquire the way to some place. We could understand only by signing. Concluded they wished to cross the creek & go to see a child about five miles from this place—we assisted them in crossing the creek & pointed out their path, they appeared well pleased. Their complexion is much darker than that of the Cherokees & they appear more barbarous.[26]

April 7. Br. K. set out for the settlements with some Indians to assist him, taking two perogues, to fetch shingles & supplies of provisions. An Indian from Fort Armstrong about 70 miles south of Chickamaugah on the Coosa river staid [stayed] with us for a night.[27] He had been one of Mr. Blackburn's pupils, & in him we saw a very good & encouraging specimen of what even a little learning will do for an Indian.[28] He is an agreeable, intelligent young man of easy manners, & by his industry has acquired some property. He expressed a strong desire for the success of this establishment as connected with the best good of his country men.

Sab. [April] 13. We have quite a respectable sabbath school; it is increasing. The blacks are much engaged.

[April] 14. This day we engaged a young man to labor on the farm for this season who appears steady & hopefully pious. O that we were never obliged to employ men of an opposite character. But all here are strangers, we know not even what this man be.

[April] 16. Br. K. returned & brought with him some men to work on our buildings.[29] He brought also a considerable supply of meal which was very welcome as we had been obliged to pound corn for our bread.

[April] 17. Br. W. is quite unwell, br. & sister H. are also indisposed.

Sab. [April] 20. About 60 persons attended ~~Br. K's~~ preaching. Nine blacks & three others attended our sunday school. We hope these poor ignorant souls may be benefited by our instruction.

[April] 27. Religious exercise again in our own house—a good number attended. Sunday school increased.

[April] 28. Br. K. again set out for the settlements.

May 1. Thirty-four families came to us at one time to buy corn. It was a time of great rain & every shed, stable & out house was occupied by them for shelter. They behaved very decently. While it was painful to see this people thus distressed for bread in this fertile land, where, if they knew how, they might raise an abundance with half the labor they now take to get this scanty pittance from us, it was highly pleasing to have it in our power to deal out to their present supplies, & at the same time to hope that we may be instrumental of putting them in a way to obtain an abundance of bread, & all other necessaries of life, by teaching them & their children to cultivate the earth.[30] But O! how did we long & hope to be the humble instruments of leading them to the "Bread of life", that their famishing souls might live![31]

[May] 3. Br. K. returned laden with fresh experience of the loving kindness & tender mercies of our covenant God.

[May] 4. Preaching at the mission house. Congregation & school as usual.

[May] 5th Br. K. went down the river to receive a bed & bedding which unknown friends had graciously given for the use of the establishment.

Sab. [May] 11. Preaching again at the mission house. It is our ardent prayer that the Spirit may bless the word.

[May] 12. Br. W. went out with one of our neighbors to buy cows for the use of the Mission.

[May] 14. A son & daughter of a chief came about 60 miles from their fathers to live with us. They are about 16 & 17 years old. Have rich clothing, many ornaments, & some knowledge of letters.[32]

[May] 15. Br. W. returned, having visited our dear friends Father & Mother Gambold & received from them many tokens of their affection & kindness to us. A member of their church very affectionately gave us a Cow & calf.[33] Four cows & calves were purchased.

Sab. [May] 18. Our congregation rather larger than usual.

[May] 21. Within three days we have had 5 schollars added to our family.[34]

Sab. [May] 25. Another boy came, & was received as a member of our school & family.[35]

[May] 26. Br. K. again set off for the settlement on business.

[May] 30. Br. K. returned.

Sab. June 1. Br. K. preached a funeral sermon on account of the death of sister Halls mother, the news of which reached us the week past. Our sunday school is increasing, & there are some hopeful appearances that it may be very useful to the blacks.

Feb. 27. [1818][36]

Rev. & Dear Sir,

The above extracts I have made at the special request of Brothers Kingsbury, Hall & Williams. All has been examined by them, & they request me to forward it in their name. We expect you have received a joint letter from us since my arrival here—yours to Brs. K. H. & W. of the 30th ult. they received last evening. It was immediately announced & a special meeting of all the brethren called to hear it read. It is always refreshing to hear from you, & peculiarly so to have the repeated assurance that our dear brethren at the North are disposed to do every thing in their power for the poor heathen in this region.— In regard to the manner in which we shall be distributed I trust each individual will be willing to be disposed of just as a majority of the brethren & of the Prud. Com. shall think best. Sister Hall is yet feeble—yesterday she left her room for a short time where she had been confined near 7 weeks. The rest of our numerous family are all about, & generally quite well. We rejoice in the prospect of seeing Esqr Evarts here. All the brethren salute you. You will pray for us; & give thanks to God for his abundant mercy & grace to us all.

> Accept the most affectionate regards
> of your unworthy brother
>
> Ard Hoyt

Rev. S. Worcester, Cor. Sec. A.B.C.F.M.

Continuation of Mission Journal, Chickamaugah, Cherokee Nation

June 8th No preaching at the Mission house to-day, Br. K. being absent on a journey to the settlements. A considerable number met for public worship—Brs. H. & W. lead in the exercises—One of Burders sermons was read.[37] First "one thing is needful."

Sab. [June] 15. Preaching from Prov. 22:6. About 100 were present who were very attentive & solemn.

[June] 16. ~~A letter was received from Col⁰ Meigs informing us that a present of 100 bushels of corn from the public Annuity would be made to this establishment.~~

[June] 19. We have for some time been much occupied in labor; particularly in geting supplies of corn & other articles up the creek, in which we have experienced much difficulty. We greatly lament that so much of our time is occupied in business not directly pertaining to the instruction of the people, but we are convinced that this labor is all necessary, and if we cannot get others to do it, we must perform it ourselves.[38]

Sab. [June] 22. Preaching at the Mission house. After service in English Br. K. addressed the Indians by an interpreter. Sunday school appears promising.

July 4th. Br. K. was called in this evening, for the first time, to attend to a difficulty in the school. The oldest class had been spelling, & having missed several words, the teacher told them to take a shorter lesson. John Ridge, a lad of about 15, said, in a hasty & petulant manner, that he would not have such short lessons, but would get his usual number of columns.[39] This was spoken in such a way that it could not be passed over. Some remarks were made to shew [show] the ingratitude of schollars treating their teachers with disrespect; especially when teachers had labored & done so much for them as we had done. "Little did we expect," it was said, ["] such a return from any of our schollars, & least of all did we expect it from John, a boy of whom we had great hopes". He burst into a flood of tears—said he meant no harm & was sorry he had given us so much trouble & pain.—We could freely forgive him.

[July] 6th. Had a very interesting visit today from the Ridge, one of the Chiefs & father of the lad just mentioned. He is a sensible man & has

had a daughter also at our school for some time. The children perceived on his arrival that something agitated his mind. We were dining. After dinner he said he had something to tell us, & he would tell it just as he heard it. "I heard" said he "that my children were so bad that you could not manage them, & had just to let them go wild. I came to see if it was true. If they conduct so it will not be good to keep them at school. I have brought a little Coosa (Creek) girl which I took in the war a prisoner, & design to leave her, if my own children are so bad, & see if she will do better." We told him the story was new to us; & that we were generally pleased with the conduct of his children. He clasped his hands, & raising his eyes to heaven in a kind of involuting adoration, expressed with strong emotions the gratitude of his heart. He appeared overjoyed at the happy disappointment. Exclaiming "Never was I so glad! As I was coming I often said to myself, can it be that my children, after all the advice I have given them, conduct in such a manner." Before he left us, he talked very affectionately with them. The conclusion was in the following words, "You know I have often talked with you, & gave you such advice as a father ought to give his children. I hope you will listen to it. I now leave you with these people (meaning the Missionaries) they will take care of you, & you must obey them as you would me." We suppose the report he heard was an idle one; & that it did not originate from the partial misconduct of his son.

July 11. We have no reason to complain of any of our pupils except one. His conduct has grieved us much. When endeavoring to shew [show] him his fault & persuade him to reform, our patience was greatly tried. We could see nothing like penitence, yet, after much suasions, he promised to submit to the authority of the Institution. Our schollars all make tolerable progress, some of them very great.

[July] 24. We were much straitened in our circumstances, & found ourselves considerably in debt, but we trusted in our good Lord, that he would in some way provide.

August 3. Our family has increased to about 50—nearly out of meat, & little prospect of geting more.

[Aug.] 19. Two schollars were expelled [from] the school for obstinate & persevering disobedience.[40]

[Aug.] 20. Sister Williams was safely delivered of a Daughter.

Sept. 19. Late at night the Rev. Elias Cornelius arrived at this station for the first time.[41]

Sab. Sept. 21. Our dear friend & brother Cornelius preached to a respectable & attentive audience upon these words "What shall it profit a man if he gains the whole world & looses [loses] his own soul."[42] His object was to shew to every one the immense worth of the soul, & the danger of its being lost, & that forever. He exhorted his hearers in the most solemn manner to attend immediately to the vast concerns of their souls.

Sept. 26. Br. Cornelius preached a lecture preparatory to the Lords supper. Text "Let a man examine himself &c".[43]

Sab. [Sept.] 28. After the formation of our little church, our dear brother Cornelius, whom the Lord sent here to refresh our souls, preached from the word of our divine Master "Do this in remembrance of me".[44] Truly he exhibited motives sufficient to cause us to lift up our heads & rejoice at the solemn yet pleasing prospect before us.

[Sept.] 28. This day we formed ourselves into a church, by assenting to & subscribing articles of faith & a covenant, which had been previously prepared.[45]

Oct. 2. Last satturday some Cherokees who had been employed by us in bringing boards up the Creek in a boat wished to go down for another load. We requested them to wait untill Monday, telling them "tomorrow is our beloved day, & the Good Spirit will be angry with us if we work, or employ men to work, on that day". They said this was good, & promised if we would let them take the boats down to day they would stay at some house tomorrow & be still untill monday. We gave them permission to go & they did as they had promised.

When they returned we asked them when they would come & get up more, They said "on Monday" adding "we will come no more to work on the good day; nor would we before if we had known it was wrong".

[Oct.] 4th This evening, met according to vote of our little church, for mutual conversation on the state of our souls.

[Oct.] 5*th* Some of our workmen give us great pain by their immoral conduct. And this aggravated by the consideration that it is commited on this ground which is consecrated to God by the prayers, tears & charities of his people.

[Oct.] 12. A young man who had been hired to work for us was this morning convicted of stealing mon[e]y from one of the workmen. This theft was commited on the Sabbath, while the rest of the family were engaged in religious worship. We are more & more deeply impressed with the importance of employing none but the true servants of Christ. O Lord send us such to do all the labor that must be performed here.

Oct. 13. Br. Cornelius left us with one of our schollars as interpreter, to attend a Council.

[Oct.] 14. Our well which had been dug 20 ft, & had the appearance of water within a short distance, caved in. This is the third attempt we have made & at considerable expense—now we do not expect to get a well this Season.

[Oct.] 21. Purchased & brought home for the use of the establishment 12 head of Cattle.

[Oct.] 22. This evening Br. C. & his interpreter returned. He had a most interesting meeting with the Indians at their Council. The Cherokees threw open their arms wide, are deeply interested in the cause of schools, & civilization. The Creeks, not having digested the subject, do not give a positive answer either way.

Nov. 2. Sab. Br. Cornelius preached from these words "Now is the acceptable time, now is the day of salvation."[46] The hearers were solemn & attentive; one Cherokee in particular appeared "pricked to the heart."[47] After meeting he went a few rods from the house & stood against a tree apparently in great agony. This being discovered Br. C. & Br. K. went to him & gave him some further instructions. His wounds were deepened untill (like Saul) he was unable to stand.[48] He fell on the ground, & burst into a flood of tears; after which he became a little more composed. Several others were much affected & deeply impressed under the preaching of the word.

Sab. Nov. 3. Some of our hearers appeared deeply impressed with divine truth.

[Nov.] 4. Two Cherokees & one white came to inquire "What they must do to be saved?" They appear to be anxious, inquirers, & much time was spent to instruct them.

[Nov.] 6. Br. C. took an affectionate leave of us to pros[e]cute his journey to N. Orleans. It was hard to part with this dear brother, who had been as a messenger of peace to us & instrumental in consoling & comforting our hearts.
Br. K. accompanied him one days journey.

Nov. 27. Rev. Mr. Donald from Rhea County Ten. came down to visit us & assist in the labors of the coming Sabbath.[49]

[Nov.] 28. Mr. Donald preached a lecture preparatory to Lords supper.

Sab. [Nov.] 29. A large number assembled for worship. Mr. Donald preached and the sacrament of the Lords supper was once more administered to the refreshing of our souls. The blessed Savior spread a table for us in this wilderness, & granted his presence. We have increasing hopes that the Lord has begun a good work in the heart of one of the schollars, & one or two of our neighbors. O may he carry on his work for the Redeemers sake!

Sab. Dec. 14. Br. K. was absent on business to the settlements. Burders sermon on the value of the soul was read. Some of the audience much affected; one raged woman wept most of the time. After the sunday school exercises Br. H. had an interesting conversation with the blacks, for substance as follows. Do you ever pray? Yes, we black people pray together every night. What do you pray for? We pray that God would bless us & make us good. Do you know that you are sinners? Yes, we very great sinners. When did you know you were wicked? When we came here last summer these good people told us so, & that make our heart sorry. Do you now think you are about good enough? O no! If we are not true in our heart to him (meaning God) he won't bless us. Do you think your prayers will save you? If we keep trying, God will come & bless us black people. How do you feel when you try to pray? Sometime all dark & heart heavy, & then our heart light & glad. What do you think about the dear Savior, who came into the world & died for poor lost sinners? We think he mighty good & love mankind mightily. Did you ever do any thing very bad? One immediately replied, he had been a great sinner, & worked on the Sabbath, but was very sorry & would not do so any more.

[Dec.] 15. Recvd a letter from Mr. Hoyt giving the pleasing inteligence that he with his family is on his way to join us[50] —a Mr. Butrick is to meet him at Savannah and come on with him,[51] & a Mr. Swift & a Mr. Chamberlin are expected soon to come on by another rout [route].[52] How cheering the thought that the Lord is sending fellow laborers into this great field. Will the Lord protect them on their way & in due time bring them to us, laden with rich experience of his goodness.

In behalf of the brethren, Yours affectionately,
Ard Hoyt

1818

Jan. 3, 1818. Towards evening heard that Br. Hoyt & family & Br. Butrick are on the road near our station.[1] Br. K. returned from the settlements about sun down, & immediately set off to meet them. He found them about four miles from our station at the house of one of the natives being unable to reach the mission house that night.

Sab. Jan. 4. Br. K. returned in the morning with Br. H. & family & Br. B. We have again occasion to record the signal mercies of the Lord. Our dear friends have enjoyed good health during their whole journey, & have been conducted in perfect safety both by land & by sea. This accession to our mission family will be of great service to us under our present circumstances. Br. Hoyt preached from Mark 16:15 "Go ye into all the world &c". We trust it was a good day to some.

Jan. 10. This was a day of anxiety, of joy, & of sorrow. In the morning, Sister Hall was safely delivered of a son. The dear little babe survived its birth but a few minutes. We had felt great anxiety, as to the result of sister Hall's confinement, on account of her very feeble state; &, in the event, have much cause to rejoice as well as to mourn. O that in all our afflictions we may ever say: "It is the Lord; let him do what seemeth him good".[2]

Sab. [Jan.] 11. The remains of the little babe were brought into our public assembly, & after prayers & a discourse adapted to the occasion, the mission family (including our schollars) & our little congregation, in solemn procession, followed them to "the house appointed for all living".[3] It was, to us, a solemn day. This was the first time we had been called to bury our dead in this heathen land; how soon some of us should be again called to perform this office for others in our family was known only to Him, "in whose hand are the life & breath of all living";[4] & we could not but feel that if we had any thing to do here we must do it quickly. O how soon shall we, with all this cherokee people now living, be in eternity! And, if they are not enlightened by the Gospel, where will be their immortal souls? "Where no vision is, the people perish".[5] Thy word O God, is truth;

thy ways are just. O, give us grace, that we may do with our might, what our hand findeth to do, for these our poor brethren, who sit in darkness, & in the shadow of death.

[Jan.] 16. Brothers Hoyt & Kingsbury visited at one of our neighbors ~~Coodey's~~. His wife was absent. ~~Mr. C.~~ The man conversed freely & feelingly on the subject of religion; is evidently very thoughtful, & has acquired tolerably correct ideas of the doctrines of the gospel, & of the nature & effects of practical piety.

[Jan.] 17. Four of our children returned, who had been absent for some time. Two of them we did not expect again; but they all manifested great cheerfulness.

Sab. [Jan.] 18. Br. B. preached from John 7:37.[6] There were a goodly number present; & they were all solemn. Those, of whose piety we have entertained hopes, give us comfortable evidence that they are in some measure grounded in the truth. Mr. Reese is one of a company of regulators, whose duty it is to settle difficulties, collect debts, &c.[7] Some of his companions are very profane; & when he reproves them they sometimes laugh at him, & call him "the missionaries' man". But he says, "I care nothing about that. I just let them say of me what they please. I must take care & do my duty to them. Sometimes I tell them I wish I was fit to be the missionaries' man: I would be mighty glad to go with these good people, if I was fit for it."

[Jan.] 21. This was an interesting day to us, & we trust it will be a day of joyful remembrance to all who are looking for the salvation of the heathen. Agreeable to previous notice given the chh [church] met for the purpose of examining candidates for admission to our ~~little chh~~ communion. Five of our neighbors attended the meeting. Three of them, (native Cherokees,) expressed a desire to be admitted to the chh, if we should think they possessed the requisite qualifications. Their examination was prayerfully attended to, & they gave us satisfactory evidence of their union to Christ, & were received to be propounded next Sabbath. The other two, (white men,) wished to open their hearts to us, & have us question them that we might be able to advise what to do; but were afraid to offer themselves as candidates lest they should come unworthily. These were examined.—We had some hope for at least one of them; but thought best to defer their baptism & admission to the chh, untill their evidences of a saving change should be more satisfactory to themselves & others.

These men did not appear dissatisfied with our decision, but left us apparently with great searchings of heart.

Jan. 24. The Father of Catharine Brown came for the purpose of taking her & his son Edward home.[8] He expressed great satisfaction with the treatment his children had received here; & says he shall be very glad to have them return again, if circumstances will permit, {but (living near the United States line) he has great trouble from some of his white neighbors, who steal his horses, hogs &c, & on this account he does not know but he shall be compelled to move over the Mississippi. He can tell better when his son returns from the Federal City.}[9] If he removes over the Mississippi he shall wish to have his children with him; but even in that case, he may possibly leave Catharine with us for a while. We had much conversation with this man, on the subject of our most holy religion; his daughter being our interpreter. He manifested a very discerning mind; heard with solemn attention; said he had never been told such things before; and appeared sensible, that we were seeking his welfare, in all that we said to him.

Sab. [Jan.] 25. As our beloved sister Catharine was expected to leave us before the time for administering the sacrament of the Lord's supper, she was this day admited to the holy ordinance of Baptism. The scene was solemn & impressive to us all; & we believe to our whole congregation, which was larger than it had been before this winter. We consider this girl as the first fruits of our labor in this heathen land. The thought of parting with her so soon is painful; but perhaps the Lord is taking her from us, that she may be more useful in promoting his cause in some other place. His will be done. The step father of one of our other female children whom we call Little Peggy came this day for the purpose of taking the girl away, as he & her mother were soon to move over the Mississippi, & the fond mother did not like to leave her daughter behind; but seeing how the girl was treated here, & believing it would be for her good to stay, he concluded to leave her for the present; & try to persuade her mother to go on without her.[10]

[Jan.] 26. Had much more conversation with Catharine's Father; ~~she interpreting, for he can speak no english~~. Perhaps there are few among the natives better informed or more inteligent than this man; yet, on the subject of religion, he had but few ideas of any kind. He believed in a Supreme Being, Creator of all things & that there would be a state of rewards & punishments for man beyond this life: &

appeared sensible that this short creed included many things above his comprehension & beyond his knowledge—as the character of this Supreme Being—the nature of these rewards, who would escape punishment &c. He appeared to have no idea of forgiveness on any terms. He expressed many thanks for the information we gave him; said all we told him appeared reasonable—that he should think much of it, & endeavor to learn more; expressed the greatest friendship at parting, & said, when his children had visited their friends, he should want to have them come back more than he now wanted them to go.

[*Jan.*] 27. Brs. Hoyt & Hall went out for the purpose of visiting several families of the natives.

[*Jan.*] 28. These brethren returned having visited 5 or 6 families. They were kindly received by all & had much interesting conversation. It is truly painful to see the ignorance of these people.[11] In no instance did a conversation with any one of the natives close without a visible seriousness; yet in several instances when first speaking to them on the most solemn & momentous subjects, they would laugh ~~like~~ ~~[mere?] idiots~~. At Brother Reece's, where the brethren spent the night, were three Cherokee women, who live about 25 miles from us.[12] With them the brethren talked much. Br. Reese, being interpreter, who also told them many things without assistance. One of the women appeared much affected, & often wept very freely as we told her of the sinfulness of man;—the suffering of the Savior—& forgiveness through him. She said she had before thought the wicked would be punished, & the good happy after death; but did not think there was any way for those, who had been once wicked, to be made good & happy. Her ideas of the happiness above appeared much confused: but she thought there was somewhere above a good man & woman who would make good people happy. She wished us to tell her what was wicked;—&, although evidently backward & ashamed to confess what she felt of her own guilt, said she knew that she had done wrong, & that she was sometimes so much afraid that she could not stay in her own house;—that she had often run away into the woods; but that did not help her, for she was afraid everywhere. When the duty & privilege of prayer were inculcated & recommended she asked if the Great Spirit could hear in her language. Being inquired of, whether she thought what we told her was good news, she answered "very good."—whether she thought her people about the place where she lived would be glad to hear these things, she said she had heard many of them say their old way was bad, & they must learn the Missionaries' way, for they believed the missionaries' way was right; & if it was right they ought to hear; & go with them. These women took a most affectionate leave of the brethren in the morning, & said, if they could, they would come to the mission house, & learn more of these good things.

Sab. Feb. 1st Our little house was crowded with a very solemn audience. {of all colours.} Charles Reese & Jane Coodey made a public profession of their faith, were baptized with their households, & received as members of this church.[13] It was to us indeed a joyful time, when we surrounded the table of our common Lord with these Cherokee converts; while we hoped & prayed, that these might be the first fruits of an abundant harvest, which the Lord would soon gather here.

After public service a Cherokee man & his wife readily accepted an invitation to tarry with us all night. Speaking to them by an interpreter we learnt that they had understood nothing of the preaching, & did not know the meaning of anything they had seen. The man said he had heard that we could tell him some way whereby bad people could be made good, & be happy when they died. He said he was bad himself & wanted to be good; & that he had come to learn what our way was. He & his wife had come 20 miles for this purpose. We indeavored to teach the first principles of the oracles of God, as well as we could by our interpreter. He asked many questions; said he had never heard these things before; thanked us for the information we had given him, & said all we had told him was good.

[Feb.] 2nd Brothers Hoyt & Kingsbury left home for the purpose of visiting some families of natives near the settlements, attend a wedding to which Br. K. had been invited, & transact some business in Tennessee. It is pleasing to see the natives beginning to leave their old customs of taking & leaving their wives without ceremony, & in place of this adopting the christian form of marriage.

[Feb.] 7th Br. Hoyt returned with a Cherokee girl for our school; having brought her on the horse behind him near fifty miles.[14] He left Br. Kingsbury to spend the Sabbath among the whites in the settlement; had preached once in his tour, & rode about 140 miles, chiefly in company with Br. K. They were kindly received in every family they visited.

[Feb.] 10th A white man came from Nick-o-jack [Nickajack] a place in the nation distant about 30 miles, to invite one of the missionaries to go & preach to the people there, and also to attend a wedding. ~~We hope the day is not far distant when all our Cherokee brothers will feel that "marriage is honorable in all" & know that "whore mongers & adulters God will judge".~~

Feb. 11. Br. Butrick set out with the above named man for Nickajack. Br. Kingsbury returned, having accomplished most of the business on which he went & preached twice on the Sabbath. He brot with him a Cherokee girl for the school.[15] By fatigue & riding in bad weather he had been in poor health, but soon recovered and came home well.

[Feb.] 13. Little Peggy (~~the girl~~ mentioned on the 25th ult) ~~a very fine girl~~ left us to go with her mother to the Arkansas. Parental affection induced the ~~parent~~ mother (perhaps against her better judgment,) to take her daughter with her, though we offered to provide for the ~~girl~~ child untill her education should be completed, & then to send her on.[16] May the Lord preserve the child, & make the instructions she has received a blessing to her & to her connections. She is affectionate & promising, & many prayers were offered for her at her departure.

Sab. [Feb.] 15. The weather was cold & uncomfortable; yet our house of worship was tolerably filled. Some hopeful appearances among the blacks in our Sabbath ~~Sunday~~ School. Several this day gave evidence of very serious impressions; one in particular, a free man whose name is Robin.[17] He conversed freely & sensibly—said he felt very differently from what he had done, but could not think he was a Christian: "This was too great a blessing for such an audacious wretch to enjoy."

[Feb.] 17th Br. Butrick returned—has preached three times in his tour, married one couple, visited a number of families, had some interesting conversation with some of the natives who could speak English, & was kindly received by all. He was deeply impressed with the importance of being able to speak in the language of the natives, or at least having a good interpreter. He also brought a small girl for the school.[18] Br. B. brought information that the Chiefs were met in Council at Etow-ee [Etowah], or Hightower as it is sometimes called, about 80 miles from us. Thinking it would be of service to the mission if one or two of us could be there before the council broke up, brothers Hoyt & Kingsbury set out immediately—taking with them ~~Edmond~~ward Brown, one of our scholars for interpreter.

[Feb.] 18. A storm of rain induced Brs. H. & K. to think the chiefs would disperse before they could get to the council house if they proceeded, therefore Br. H. returned & Br. K. concluded to go on to Father Gambold's, & return by Mr. Hicks's.

[Feb.] 21. Br. K. returned in health, had a prosperous journey, found our friends well at Spring-place, & brought some presents with much love. He also visited Mr. Hicks, & had much interesting conversation with him about the school, {& obtained his permission to employ two men who have small families, to work on the plantation for one year.}

[Feb.] 28. Rec'd 3 letters from Br. Cornelius, full of animating and refreshing intelligence.

March 1 Sab. The rain was so violent that we did not expect any one of our neighbors would come to meeting, but we were agreeably disappointed in the attendance of 9 or 10 blacks, & about as many Cherokees. These came in the storm from 3 to 6 miles, & were very attentive. The Cherokees were addressed thro. Br. Reece as interpreter.

Continuation of Journal

March 9. Our dear Sister Catharine returned to spend a few months more with us before she goes to the Arkansas Country. She was accompanied by John Brown & her brother Alexander. John would be glad to return to school, but the late death of his father had brought great care upon him {in business to which he must attend.}[19]
Catharine was closely examined in the course of her visit with respect to her faith in Christ by some white people, who were no friends to religion. They indeavored to embarrass her mind by bringing objections against the Bible. She replied that for her part she believed the Bible was true and hoped she always should. Her father & mother say they are very glad she had learned these good things & express a desire to be instructed in the good way themselves.

[March] 10. Br. Chamberlin arrived in good health. He had been detained about 10 days by sickness; in other respects his long & fatiguing journey had been prosperous.[20]

[March] 19. Church met according to previous appointment, for the purpose of examining such as might present themselves for admission to the church. Daniel McPherson (a white man) & Sally McDonald (a Cherokee)[21] One white man & one Cherokee woman

offered themselves. After prayerful examination we were unanimously of opinion that ~~Mr. McPherson~~ the man be directed to wait a while & endeavor to obtain more clear evidence of his right to Gospel ordinances & that ~~Sally McDonald~~ the Cherokee woman be accepted to be propounded for admission to the chh. In this examination Br. Reece took an active part & gave very clear evidence of his own knowledge of the Christian character. {We soon discovered that he was afraid ~~Mr. McPherson~~ the white man was building on his own works, & put some pertinent questions to that point. While examining the other candidate after posing a number of questions relative to her experience, it appeared he wished to know whether she had a forgiving spirit, & said "How should you feel if someone should come into your house & break your things to pieces? Would you not be angry & wish to hurt him?}

[*March*] 20th One white man & one Cherokee woman were examined & admitted to be propounded.

[*March*] 22. Brother Chamberlain & sister Flora Hoyt were married, in the presence of the congregation.[22]

Sab. [*March*] 29. How great & precious are the privileges, which we, as missionaries, & as a church, have this day enjoyed in the house of God, & around the table of our Lord? One white man & two natives (having previously given satisfactory evidence of their saving acquaintance with the gospel) made a public profession of their faith, & were baptized with their household consisting of seven young children.[23] The new converts, having entered into covenant & been received to the church, twenty two of the professed followers of Christ sat down together at the table of the Lord. ~~in this heathen land.~~ Four of the communicants (two white men and two Cherokees,) belong to the Moravian church at Springplace.[24] It was to us all truly "a feast of fat things; of fat things full of marrow; of wines on the lees well refined."[25] Seven of the communicants were Cherokees. Our red brethren & sisters ~~appeared to enjoy the feast as much as any of us &~~ ~~they~~ afterward declared that their joys exceeded every thing they had before conceived. The assembly was large, solemn & attentive, & we have reason to believe that some of the by-standers had a great desire to be with us: particularly one black woman, who afterwards asked how she felt on that occasion, answered, "I felt as if that was my company {meaning the communicants}" & "that they had left me alone in the wicked world." When asked if she was not displeased with them for leaving her behind, "O no!" said she, "I loved them with all my heart."

Mar. 31. Br. K. left us this morning for the settlements in order to make some preparations for the Choctaw missions. He expects to go as far as Knoxville, & to be absent about two weeks.

Sab. April 5. A number of Cherokees, who have not met with us, & some, who have never attended before, were present to hear the Gospel. Gen. 1:14 was expounded in the morning.[26] During the intermission the Cherokees were addressed thro Br. Reece as interpreter; &, after sermon in the afternoon they were again spoken to in the same manner, before the congregation was dismissed. A number of them afterwards went to our dwelling house, where Br. Reece (by our request) conversed with them some time in his own way, & then again interpreted for us. They were all attentive, & solemn. One man, who lives about 30 miles from us & had never attended before, appeared very desirous to learn—said all he heard appeared right & good so far as he could understand it, & he would come again & learn more. He also said he would go & tell his neighbors what he had heard, & ask them to come & hear for themselves. About twenty took dinner with us, at 5 oclock, & then departed, many of them apparently under serious impressions.

[April] 8th Agreeable to a resolution passed at our last meeting for business, we this day called the family together to attend public lecture.[27] These lectures are intended to be continued every Wednesday afternoon for the benefit of our family & neighbors. We also thought it would tend to our edification, & the edification of the new converts who might meet with us, to have a religious conference either in the school house or one of our private rooms, immediately after the close of lecture. A meeting of this kind was attended this day. ~~Br. W.'s room to our mutual comfort & edification.~~ We have usually had conferences & prayer meetings one or two evenings in the week for professers in the mission family. It was thought that if one of these weekly meetings were attended in the afternoon, as above, we should more frequently have our Christian neighbors with us.

[April] 9. A Cherokee woman, mother of one of our boys & very decent in her appearance, called on us for the first time. Being dressed neatly in the fashion of our country women ~~called Christian~~ we hoped

she had obtained from white people some knowledge of our God & Savior as well as of our manners & dress.

By sister Catharine, as interpreter, we soon found this woman willing to open her mind to us: &, after some introductory remarks, asked her if she had many thoughts about God, the Great Spirit. She replied "I do not think much about him." We inquired if she thought herself a sinner? She answered, No. Where she thought her spirit would be when her body died? She did not know that it would be anywhere. In short, she appeared to have thought very little on these most important subjects, & to have little or no expectations of living beyond the grave. She was told some of the first principles of our most holy religion, & said she had never heard these things before. She appeared solemn & somewhat affected, & before the close of the conversation said she believed she was a sinner—said also that she was willing to leave her son here a great while, that he might learn all these good things.

O how shall we white people answer when God inquires after our red brethren! Shall we use the language of some, & say, "It is of no use to preach the gospel to them;—they cannot be Christianized or civilized?" They have been for generations within the light of the gospel & will not regard it? Or shall we, in the language of humble confession say, "We have taught them some of our innocent customs, & many, very many, of our bad ones; but as it respects the gospel, most of them are as ignorant as if no white man had ever set his foot on this continent." From what we have observed, we verily believe this to be the truth, as to the great body of the full blooded Cherokees, & with few exceptions, it is little better with the half-breeds. From our observation we are led to believe that some of the Cherokees have a few correct ideas concerning the Supreme Being & a future state, whether they have obtained these mostly by tradition from their fathers, or from intercourse with the whites, we cannot determine, but even these few correct ideas appear to have little or no place among what may be called the lower class of this people.

Cases similar to the one which has occasioned these remarks very frequently occur here; & we think if Christians generally could see the state of this people as it really is, exertions for their relief would be increased an hundred fold.

There is nothing among this people to oppose the gospel, except their ignorance & the depravity of the human heart. They have not, as in the case with most heathen nations, a system of false religion, handed down from their fathers, which must be overturned in order to make way for the Gospel.[28] They are rather, as the prophet foretold the children of Israel would be, "Without a sacrifice, & without an image, & without an ephod, & without a teraphim".[29]

Sabbath, April 12. In addition to our usual congregation were the Cherokees who attended last Sabbath, and some more.[30] The afternoon sermon was shortened to give time to speak to them. Brother Reece interpreted. They were attentive and solemn while we were speaking to them, but after we had ceased and Br. R. had addressed them without our assistance, and according to the feelings of his warm heart, they appeared deeply affected. Numbers dropped their faces upon their hands, and some wept. The substance of his remarks, as we were afterwards told, was, that we, who had come to teach them, were good people, and sought the good of the Cherokees—that what we had to tell them was important truth, and deserved most serious attention; but it was to be feared that some came to meeting out of curiosity, and some to shew themselves, or their clothes, but this was wrong; they should come to hear, and get good. There were some, who would laugh at these things, which however, were of the greatest importance, and they must attend, learn, believe and obey, for without this they could not be happy.

[April] 13. Br. K. returned having had a prosperous journey. At Knoxville he purchased most of the articles which were immediately necessary for the Choctaw mission. Preached three times in the settlements; and yesterday agreeably to appointment, preached a funeral sermon on the death of a woman, the wife of a half-breed, who holds quite a respectable standing. She was a white woman, and left an infant child a few hours old when she died. His mother, step father, and half brother, who were half-breeds, had come about 30 miles to attend the preaching. After sermon Br. K. had much interesting conversation with the husband and his friends. The death of his wife has made a deep, and we trust, lasting impression on his mind. He could read a little, and since that event, which has been about two or three months, he has improved much, and can now read his Bible with some facility, in which he appears to take great delight. He says he feels very differently from what he formerly did, and that it is his fixed resolution to make religion the great business of his life. His mother said, "some years ago Mr. [Gideon] Blackburn preached to us, but many white people told us not to mind what he said; and we were

ignorant, and knew no better than to listen to them; but we are now sorry we did not hear the preacher." How aggravated must be the ruin of those who will neither "go into the kingdom of heaven themselves, nor suffer those who are entering to go in."[31]

[April] 15. Agreeable to arrangement previously made with Col[n] Meigs and others, this day had been assigned for visiting the school.[32] Col[n] Meigs could not attend in consequence of business with the Arkansas delegates, now returning from Washington. Br. Hicks, and many other Cherokees, both men and women, attended. Our children gave us very great satisfaction, by their prompt attention to order, and very respectful behavior in every particular, as well as by the exhibitions they made of their progress in learning. Several hymns, which they had committed to memory, were sung by the children alone, much to our satisfaction.

The countenances of the spectators manifested peculiar satisfaction on their part, and many afterwards expressed their approbation in very pleasing terms.

We have reason to believe there is among the natives an increasing confidence in our integrity; and that most of them feel assured of the love and good will of those who have sent us among them.

[April] 16. The Old Glass, (a leading chief of the Arkansas party,) who has of late been telling his people that schools would do the Cherokees no good, called on us early this morning.[33] He is now on his return from Washington, where he has been as delegate for the Cherokees, who have gone and are going over the Mississippi. Though anxious to get to his family, he was persuaded to wait and attend our school. He appeared highly pleased with the school, and expressed great satisfaction. He said the white people crowded upon them so much, that they must go over the Mississippi, blaming none, however, but those on their borders. He expressed his confidence in the good will of the general government and the good people, as he called them, at the north, who were sending teachers to instruct their red brethren. He said, schools were very good for them, and added, "As soon as we get a little settled over the Mississippi we shall want schools there."[34]

Brother Hicks, the Christian chief, left us an account of some of the customs of his people, which he had committed to writing at our request. Extracts follow—

"The Cherokee people are divided into seven different clans, or classes, each having a distinct name. No one is permitted to marry within his own clan; the children always belonging to the clan of the mother, without any respect to the father.

"Murder committed by a person of one clan on a person of another clan, is always punished with death; but if the murderer and murdered are both of one clan, it frequently happens that the clan intercede with the head chief of the nation, and a pardon is granted; which pardon is published in the national council when convened. The national council is composed of persons from each clan; some clans sending more, some less, according to their population, though the number is not very definitely fixed.

"Each clan has its separate portion of land, which is held in common, the poorest man having the same right as the richest. Before eating the green corn when in the milk, the people collect in their different districts and villages, at night, the conjurer takes some of the grains of seven ears of corn and burns them in the fire. After this each family is allowed to cook and eat their roasting ears. They observe the same custom before eating the bean, when it begins to fill in the full.

"The green corn dance (so called,) was formerly in high esteem. This is held when the corn is getting hard; and lasts four days.[35] This is held where the national council sits; a quantity of venison being provided to support the assembled people. It is said that formerly a person was chosen to speak to the people on each day, in a language that now is very little known. At such times as the above, a piece of ground was laid off and persons appointed to occupy it; no other being allowed to use it while the feast lasted.

"There is a notion that still prevails among the Cherokees of making new fire every year. This is generally done in the month of March. The fire is made by drilling in a dryed grape vine in the morning, after a dance all night. Several persons are chosen to perform this with the conjurer. After this fire is made, each family in the town comes and gets the new fire, putting out all the old fire in their houses.[36]

"The physic-dance was very much in use formerly, but is partly neglected now. This belongs to the women in particular, except seven men, who are chosen out of each clan to carry the water to boil the physic, and when boiled, to carry it to the people for old and young to drink of. The physic is not drunk until the singer has proclaimed with his song, on the top of the town-house, and sung, He-yauh wah: yauh-eau-mi (repeating the same several times,) and they have painted all the parts of this house white with clay; and danced two of the nights in seven; and in the morning, after the last night, bathed themselves in water.[37]

"They have a similar practice of choosing men or women to represent the clan, in what is called making rain. In making rain, seven men or women are chosen to represent the clan, who keep fast during the time the conjurer is about to obtain rain; and when the rain comes he sacrifices the tongue of a deer which is procured for that purpose. The conjurer himself observes a strict fast, with frequent bathing, during the time he is making rain. On such occasions, the conjurer speaks a language different from the present language of the nation, and which few understand. They who design to follow those practices, are taught the language, by those who understand it.

"The eagle-tail dance is still in use among the Cherokees. The design of this dance is to instill in the minds of the young people the spirit of war; the old warriors rehearsing in the dance, the dangers they have passed through in attacking their enemies, the distance they have travelled, the time they have been out, &c. Some victuals are usually set apart for the boys to eat at day break, and when the boys have eaten, they go out of the town-house and are met in the entry of the house by young men who have a battle with them, which consists in pelting them with mud collected for that purpose.

"It is also a custom to give Eagle-feathers as a token of friendship in making peace among red people. The doctors among the Cherokees suppose that cures are to be made in seven nights. During these cures the doctors are remarkably strict to keep out of the house, where the patient is, such persons as have been handling a dead body, or have any other ceremonial uncleanness."[38]

Brother and sister Williams, and sister Catharine, set out to day on a visit to Father and Mother Gambold's. May the Lord preserve them by the way, make their visit pleasant and profitable, and return them to us at the appointed time.

[*April*] *18.* Brother Butrick went out about 20 miles to fulfill an appointment to preach to-morrow, expecting to go from thence on Monday to Father Gambold's and return with Brother Williams. Our fervent prayer is, that God will grant this brother his gracious presence, and make him the happy instrument of good to some of the poor natives on this tour.

Journal of the Cherokee Mission continued

Sab. Apl 19. The half-breed mentioned in our journal of the 13th, was present for the first time on the Sabbath, as he lives about 30 miles distant. He has been one of the public interpreters, speaks his own language better than most of his people, & ours very well. He gave very solemn attention, & after sermon addressed his people in the Cherokee language, & exhorted them to listen to the Missionaries.

[April] 20. A Cherokee woman aged about 60, who had been a constant attendant on public worship with us for some time, though she does not speak our language and understands but little of it when spoken, tarried with us last night. This morning she expressed an anxious desire to live & die with the people of God. She has for some time been very serious and attentive to preaching. We hope the Lord has opened her heart to receive the truth in the love of it.

[April] 22. Br. W. with his wife & sister Catharine returned from their visit to Father & Mother Gambolds. They bring the pleasing inteligence that there is some increasing attention to the word at Springplace, & our brethren there are rejoicing in hope. Br. B. tarried behind to bring up some cows that had strayed from us.

[April] 23. Br. B. returned with the cows. He had an interesting visit with Br. Hicks—was accompanied by him and some of his family to the place of preaching on the sabbath. After sermon the substance of what had just been said, Brother Hicks repeated in his own language for the benefit of those who did not understand English. All appeared attentive. Br. B. observed some attention among the black people at Springplace. There are many of this class of people in bondage to the Cherokees, & they all speak english. Their masters, so far as has come to our knowledge, are all willing to have them instructed, & generally very indulgent in giving them time to attend meeting. If the benefit of our mission could extend no farther than to these depressed sons of Africa, we should have no cause to regret our being sent to labor in this field, or to apprehend that our patrons who are contributing for the temporal support of this mission will, in eternity, think their money lost.

[April] 30. Two missionaries, viz. Mr. W^m McFarland & Mr. Nicholas Patterson Licentiates from the Theological Seminary at Princeton, being on a mission from the General Assembly to St. Louis, turned

out of their course to visit us in this heathen land. We soon recognized them as dear brethren & fellow laborers in the Gospel.

May 1st Our visiting brethren being with us, for the first time, & probably for the last in this life, we concluded to give information to our little flock that the sacrament of the Lords supper would be administered the next Sabbath; & a lecture preparatory preached tomorrow at 2 Oclk P.M.

[May] 2. Church convened according to appointment. Br. McFarland preached. After sermon Br. Hoyts daughter Anna, & a black woman called Juno, were examined as candidates for admission to the communion. As all the chh members had for some time been well satisfied as to the piety of Juno, & her knowledge to discern the Lords body, & as she had already passed one communion since she might have been admited had she been normaly propounded, it was thought best that these candidates be admitted tomorrow.

Sab. [May] 3. Br. Patterson preached—the two candidates were admited—the Lord was graciously present, & we had a joyful season around the table which our covenant God spread for us in this wilderness. Surely the wilderness was glad for them, & we looked forward with joyful anticipation to the day when this whole desert shall rejoice & blossom as the rose.
Robin Martin, a freeman of colour, was examined, & received to be propounded for admission to the chh.

[May] 4. Our traveling brethren, though in haste to be on their journey, concluded to spend this day with us that we might have opportunity to unite in the monthly concert.[39] It is a great encouragement to missionaries to reflect that the whole host of Israel is at one time wrestling with God for his blessing on their feeble & unworthy labors. Surely a cause this powerfully plead must ultimately prevail, for the God of truth & power has promised. A letter from the Treasurer this day received authorized us to expect his arrival very soon.[40] We anticipate great profit from his visit, & the particular instructions which he may be able to give from personal acquaintance with all the particular & local circumstances of this mission.

[May] 5. The affectionate brethren Patterson & McFarland left us early to prosecute their journey. Though our acquaintance with them was formed in a very short time, such was the union of sentiment and

feeling that it seemed an old acquaintance & parting was hard. As they were about to leave us the family was collected, the brethren gave each an affectionate farewell address to the children, united prayers were offered, a parting hymn sung, & with weeping eyes we commended each other to God & the word of his grace with the full & certain hope of soon meeting in the world of spirits to part no more.

> "This glorious hope revives
> Our courage by the way
> While each in expectation lives
> And longs to see the day."

[May] 8. At the close of this day we were permited to receive to our gladened bosoms our long expected friend & beloved brother in the Lord, J. Evarts, Esqr the Treasurer of the Board.[41] Though unknown by face to most of us, we immediately recognized a friend, a patron, a guide. Though still feeble he says his health has been improved by his journey.

Sab. *[May]* 10th A black man & woman, who live about 20 miles from us, expressed a desire to unite with the chh, & were examined. So far as we could judge from present appearance they gave hopeful evidence of piety, but as we have not had opportunity to be particularly acquainted with their walk & conversation since they date their hope of conversion, it was thought proper to consider them a[s] candidates, but not to be admited untill we should have further opportunity to ascertain their true character.[42]

[May] 14. Our spirits were refreshed by the arrival of our dear brother [Elias] Cornelius. His health is somewhat impaired by his long & fatiguing journey through the wilderness, & exposure to the scorching sun of noon & chilling damps of night; but we hope it will soon be restored, improving by a few days of quiet rest with us. He brought with him to take for the Foreign mission school [F.M.S.] in Conn, a fine looking Choctaw lad aged about 15.[43]

[May] 15. The Governor of Tennessee [Joseph McMinn] called, dined with us, & visited the school.[44] He expressed much satisfaction in the appearance & progress of the schollars, a high opinion of the utility of this institution & the importance of establishing others on a similar plan in other places. Towards evening he went on to meet the commissioners who are a little below us running the line between

Tennessee & Georgia.[45] It is expected this line will pass not far from the mission house.

[May] 16. Having appointed by the will of God, a special communion on account of our brethren being with us, a preparatory lecture was preached.
At evening the governor returned & tarried for the night.

Sab. [May] 17. The governor assigned pressing business as requiring him to pursue his journey on this day, & left us with his attendants after breakfast.
Br. Cornelius preached—22 communicants of different nations & complexions surrounded the table of him who "by the grace of God tasted death for every man", & we trust our spirits were all refreshed by eating his flesh & drinking his blood.[46]

Sab. [May] 24. In the morning Br. Cornelius preached what he considered his last sermon to this people.—Brother Kingsbury's farewell discourse followed in the afternoon. It was truly a solemn & affecting day to us all.

May 25. Ever memorable to us will be the transactions & events of this day. Three of our fellow laborers (Br. Kingsbury & Br. & Sister Williams) left us with the expectation of laboring no more in this part of the vineyard.[47] Br. & sister W. are to descend the Tennessee in a boat, Br. K. to go on business to the settlements & the agency, then to return this way & leave us immediately, & follow by land. The scene was rendered still more solemn & impressive by Brs. Evarts & Cornelius, with the three Cherokee & the Choctaw lads, leaving us at the same time.[48] Though we could rejoice that the Lord had opened a door to extend our missionary labors among the 20,000 Choctaws, & that our brethren & sister were willing to engage in this ardous enterprise, & enter an uncultivated field several hundred miles from us, still our feelings were severely tried on parting with them: perhaps not less so than when we parted with our dear relatives & friends at the north.
The morning was spent in making the necessary preparations, about noon our numerous family was collected, prayers & praises offered, after which Br. & sister Williams took an affectionate farewell of the children & departed. Most of the brothers & sisters accompanied them to the river, where a number of our Cherokee neighbors had collected to testify their regard for those who had been teaching them what

they now consider the best things. Their falling tears manifested their grateful attachment to missionaries. Here we again had the satisfaction of pouring out our hearts in prayer to God & mingling our songs of praise, with the expectation that our next meeting would be around the throne above. Br. & Sister W. departed in the boat, Br. K. crossed the river, accompanying our dear brothers who were going to the north, the rest of us returned to the ~~lonely~~ mission house at Brainerd.

This evening one our largest schollars, who went with his friends to the agency a few days since, returned with a rifle which he had received from government in consequence of having enrolled his name as one who would go to the Arkansas. He appeared very shy—passed the house without calling & stopped at the schoolhouse which was then unoccupied, and went in. One of the brethren observing this repaired immediately to the place, & found him gathering the books which he had formerly used with the intention of taking them & departing without speaking to any of us. He was told that we did not allow our schollars when leaving us, to take, without our consent either the books or clothing which we had furnished them while here; & that we were very sorry he should think of leaving us without first taking us by the hand. He was disconcerted & ashamed; returned to the mission house—shook hands with the family, and departed. It was painful to have this promising lad, who had been well contented with us, was just beginning to understand a little of our language, & nearly forward enough to begin to read, thus enticed away, to return perhaps, to savage life. But as the regulation of this business does not come within our province, we were called only to the duty of our submission.

{The Indians say they don't know how to understand their good Father the President. A few years ago he sent them a plough & a hoe—said it was not good for his red children to <u>hunt</u>, they must cultivate the earth. Now he tells them there is good <u>hunting</u> at the Arkansas; if they will go there he will give them rifles.} Perhaps it will be best not to publish the above which is in brackets.

[May] 26. Extract from the record of proceedings at meetings for business.

"Considering the various duties that devolve upon us in consequence of our numbers being diminished, & particularly the increasing care & confinement of the Teacher, as it is necessary that some one should guide the children from the time they rise untill they go to bed, Therefore, according to the advise of Esqr Evarts, the Treasurer,

Resolved that Br. Hoyts son, Milo enter the school as usher, hoping that in due time he may be prepared to take full charge of this or some other mission school.[49]

[May] 28. Three of the committee appointed by the Board to visit the school, arrived for that purpose[50]—Br. Kingsbury returned.

[May] 29. The committee visited the school, viewed the buildings, farm, & mill.

This day, in a meeting for business, we resolved to purchase certain improvements near the mill, for the purpose of renting to the miller, whoever he may be. These improvements consists of a dwelling house, several out houses & about 20 acres of land. The Treasurer when he was here advised to purchase these if they could be obtained for $150. They were bought for $100.

[May] 30th We were this day called to the painful duty of taking our final leave of Br. Kingsbury as a fellow laborer in this part of the field. He is to preach tomorow at Nicojac [Nickajack]. The assembled children received his last council & admonition in tears. The quivering chin & falling tear witnessed how dear this brother is to us all. May the Lord preserve him. We part with him willingly only for Jesus sake.—The approaching sabbath being the stated time for communion at the table of the Lord a preparatory lecture was preached.

[May] 31. A large number of our friends & neighbors collected for divine worship. Our Rev. brother [Isaac] Anderson preached, after which the sacrament was administered.[51] The assembly was solemn, & some considerably affected.

June 1st This morning the visiting committee, with many expressions of goodwill to us & desires for the prosperity of the mission, took their leave of us. As their report is before the Prud. committee,[52] it is unnecessary for us to communicate any further remarks which we have made in our journal respecting their visit; yet we cannot refrain from observing that it has been very agreeable to us, & we have the fullest confidence that their hearts are with yours & ours in the great work that is before us. We have renewed cause to thank our God & take courage.

[June] 2. A full blood Cherokee, about 24 years of age, who has neither parents nor home, made application to enter the school.[53] It appeared

he had led a rambling live [life], & obtained his living by hunting. From what motives this son of the forest was led to make this application we could not determine. Our fears were that he might think this an easy way to obtain his bread—that if admitted he would, by his slothfulness, injure our other schollars, or if crowded to continual applications might soon leave us, to his & our disadvantage. The duties that would be required of him were stated in a manner calculated to discourage him at once if these were his views. He said he understood all these things, was willing to comply with the terms, & would continue without intermission untill he had obtained an education, except that he should want some time to hunt to get money to buy his clothes. He was told hunting could not be permitted, but we would put him in a better way to purchase clothes, viz., that we would employ him to labor with our men in the field a sufficient time to buy his necessary clothing. He appears well pleased with this—said he must go to the Agency to get some money that was due to him, & would soon return if we would agree to admit him. Though we still had our fears on account of his age & manner of life, it was thought best not to reject him. He was told that we would receive him.

Sab. [June] 7. The African part of our congregation was larger than usual—they came from different directions 10, 12, & 17 miles. Several, who, from the distance they live & other causes, can but seldom attend to hear the gospel & receive instruction at the sunday school, manifested that they had acquired more knowledge of divine truth than we could have expected under their circumstances; & three or four appeared to have such a feeling sense of sin, & their need of a Savior like Jesus, that we could not but hope the Saviors image was stamped on their hearts. One of these, who appears to be not more than 25, remembers when he was brought from Africa, & says he is very thankful that God caused him to be brought, though slave, into this land where he can hear of the Savior. He says he once thought it hard to be a slave, but now he cares nothing about it if he may be a christian.

Another, on being asked if he thought he had been wicked, exclaimed, while his eyes filled with tears, " Wicked! O yes Massa. Wicked! nobody so wicked. Wy Massa, fore des people came here," (meaning the first missionaries) "we all wicked as could be—we do noting but bad bad all e time. An we know noting more an e cattle. O massa! you cant tink how bad we all den be. No sabbaday—no prayer—no tink u God at all—noting but drinken, froliken, fighten, O! every ting bad." But are you wicked now? "Massa, I no more do dese bad tings, but hab berry bad heart." Do you think your heart is now as bad as ever it was? "Hope not massa." How did your heart get better? "I pray to Jesus Christ, an He make it better." Do you think you deserve to be sent to Hell? "O yes massa." How do you think you should feel towards the Savior if he should sent you to that dreadful place of torment? "O! me pray to him for all dat." This man & his wife who also is serious, have been pretty constant attendants at the Sunday school, & have begun to read in the bible. We are told their mistress (who is one of the late Cherokee converts,) is herself learning to read by their assistance & the occasional assistance of her little son; who is one of our schollars; & that she is making considerable progress.[54]

June 11. The mill which has been erected with much trouble & frequent disappointments in consequence of the inexperience and unfaithfulness of the workmen, was this day put in operation. From its motion we are led to believe it will do better than was expected: & if the dam can be so secured as to stand against a flood of water, we have raised expectations that its advantage to the institution & the neighborhood, will soon repay the great trouble & expense of building. The dam that was first made was some time ago found to be insufficient, the greatest part of it has been rebuilt & we think sufficiently strong, but doubts are entertained respecting a part of it which stands on the mill side of the stream, & has not been rebuilt. Should this fail, we think it will not immediately endanger the mill, & may be repaired at a small expense.

[June] 12. Br. Hall was last night taken suddenly ill, we think in consequence of a violent cold occasioned by working hard in the water at the mill.

[June] 13. Br. Halls complaint increases—he is greatly stupefied—at times partially deranged, & his fever runs high.

Sab. [June] 14. Through the goodness of our covenant God the means used for Br. Halls recovery have been blessed; and he is much better, though still very weak, & his lungs oppressed with phlegm.
A gentleman from Raleigh N.C., who lodged in the neighborhood last night, attended public worship with us, & on invitation, tarried for the night.

[June] 15. The gentleman mentioned above said he had formerly thought Indian reform impracticable, & supposed the people of the North who were attempting it were strangers to the character of the aborigines; but having heard a favorable report of this establishment he had turned out of his way to see for himself—that what he had already seen in our congregation & families in this vicinity which he had visited, had led him to believe the northern people understood the indian character better than their near neighbors—that he had already given up his former opinion respecting indian reform, & if he should not be burdensome he would be glad to spend the day with us that he might have opportunity to see the children at their labor & observe their manner & progress at school.

[June] 16. The gentleman from Raleigh, after making a donation for the institution, left us this morning. His visit was very agreeable to us, & he assured us it had been very interesting & satisfactory to him— that he was astonished at the appearance of the children, the regularity of their behavior, their readiness to labor, aptness to learn &c—that he should take great pleasure in using his influence to aid the opperations of the Board. Br. Hall is slowly convalescent, yet we have some fears from the iritable state of his lungs, though he expectorates freely & raises much.

[June] 18. A sudden rise of water has proved that our fears concerning a part of our mill-dam were not groundless. That part of the dam which is on the mill side of the stream is about 30 feet in length, & was built with hewed logs & dirt, without planking. The water found its way through the dirt & carried most of it out, but did no other material injury. We have determined to repair it by planking, & think this will render it permanently secure.

[June] 19. Our family is increasing every week, & we know not how many children it is best to admit under our present circumstances. When Esqr Evarts was here he thought it would not be expedient to admit more than 50 children at a time the present season, if we could avoid without difficulty. We all concurred in this opinion, but the applications are of such a nature that we now think it best to go a little higher rather than refuse any full-bloods, as we have for some time past received all such who have applied. We now think we will try to go as high as 60, though we are not without our fears that the sisters will sink under the accumulating labor that devolves upon them in so

large a family in this warm climate. The continued heat of a southern summer debilitates the nerves of northern people very much—sister Hall is frequently so feeble as to require nursing, & continually unable to labor, except a little at very light work: & some of our children came almost naked.[55]

Surely our dear sisters at the north would gladly take part with their sisters here in the labor of making clothes for these naked sons of the forest, if they knew their need. We trust this will soon be made known to them, and arrangements made for sending clothes ready made for these children. This would be a great relief, & enable us to take more children without any additional female help.

Br. Hall has so far recovered as to be able to ride out a little, & we hope will soon be able to ride to the settlements where he intended to have gone on business about this time if his health had been good. We feel that we have great cause of thankfulness for his speedy recovery.

[June] 21. Our sister, mentioned on the 7th as learning to read by the help of her servants & her little son, was requested to give a specimen of the progress she had made, and, to our surprise & great satisfaction she took the New Testament & read a considerable portion of a chapter very inteligibly. This she had studied. Turning to different parts we found she could very soon find out a verse in almost any place, &, where the words were generally short, read inteligibly without any previous study. All this knowledge of letters she had acquired within a few months of those who learned their letters in this place within a year past. What cause have we to thank God & take courage, when the light of divine truth is finding its way, in such unexpected channels, among a people who have been for ages in darkness & the shadow of death?

[June] 23. Br. Hall, though not perfectly recovered from his late illness, thought himself able to ride a short distance, & left us for the settlements.

[June] 24. Four gentleman from North Carolina made us a short visit. They experienced much satisfaction & some surprise at the appearance of the children, & left a small donation for the benefit of the Institution. We have reason to believe that the sentiment very generally prevails among the white people near the southern tribes, (& perhaps with some farther to the north) that the Indian is by nature radically different from all other men, & that this difference presents an insurmountable barrier to his civilization. We are often very

particularly inquired of on this subject by persons of the above sentiment. ~~& as frequently reminded of the boy who exclaimed, who General Washington was pointed out to him, that is not General Washington! that is a man!~~ We wish those who make the above objections to all endeavors to christianize & civilize the Indians, might be reminded that the Indians are men; and their children, education alone excepted, like the children of other men. Considering the advantages of the children under our care, we think they are bright & promising as any children of equal number we ever saw collected.

[June] 26. Finished the repairs on our broken mill-dam, & think the whole is now permanently secure. We have unanimously agreed that it is best to procure a bolt & prepare the mill for making flour.

[June] 27. Br. Hall returned. It is our practice when any one goes to the settlements to have all the business arranged which can be accomplished either going or coming, so as to do as much as possible in a little time. This arrangement required Br. Hall to take a circuitous rout, in which he found great inconvenience on account of not being acquainted with the roads, or paths; for we have very few roads here except horse paths, & in these we frequently ride from 10 to 15 miles without a house. He was treated, as usual, with much kindness and hospitality by the Natives. Notwithstanding the fatigue which he endured by loosing [losing] his way & wandering in the woods, his health is improved.

At Washington [Tennessee] he received a letter from the Treasurer. We were happy to hear of his welfare & that of the lads with him. Soon after Br. H. arrived at Washington a constable told him he had a special warrant for him, in favor of one James Wilson. Although Wilson had threatened this when in a ~~violent~~ passion, we did believe the moment of sober reflection would bring him to consider our very liberal conduct toward him, & that thus he would be so far from executing his threat that he would be ashamed of having ever uttered it. On settlement of accounts we paid him considerable more than his just due in order to prevent contentions. But such is the depravity of the human heart that some men will sacrifice ease, conflict & reputation, to gratify a malignant passion. The officer had the politeness to suffer Br. H. to go when he pleased untill the hour of trial; & he found no difficulty in procuring friends to render him all the assistance he wanted.

D. Rawlings Esqr, a very respectable magistrate of Washington, was particularly attentive, & ready to render every assistance in his power; without being asked he offered & gave his bond with brothers for his appearance at the time of trial, which is continued to the 3rd Wednesday of Oc^t next.[56] This Wilson was the principal workman employed in building our mill, & from the first has given us much trouble. At the Agency Br. H. was treated with much kindness: the Agent manifested a disposition to do everything in his power to forward our mission. He gave Br. H. authority to purchase, at the expense of government, 4 large & 2 small spinning wheels, 1 loom, 24 hoes & as many axes for the use of our schollars.

Sab. [June] 28. Our black school continues to prosper. The coloured man who has united to the church is a very dear brother, & promises great usefulness to his coloured brethren. His heart is fixed & much engaged to instruct them all he can. Two Cherokee women who have families entered our sabbath school to day according to their promise last sabbath: one of them read well in words of 3 letters.

July 1st We have long felt that it would be a privilege which might conduce to our spiritual profit, if we could have a day for fasting, humiliation & prayer when all the brothers & sisters of the mission family could unite in this duty: but the difficulty of disposing of our children in the mean time presented such an obstacle that we have never untill this day attempted. Some of us have been a little interrupted by the necessary cares of the family, but in general we have enjoyed the day in a good degree of quietness, &, we think to our spiritual benefit. We had, in truth, great cause to humble ourselves before God, for we had become almost dead with lukewarmness, temporal cares, & other evil affections known only to our God, & which we are ashamed to enter in our journal. We found it good to wait on the Lord in this his appointed way and thought it might be for his glory & benefit of his little flock here, to have stated seasons when the whole church might be called to this duty. The friday or saturday previous to our stated communion was talked of as a proper season, & we agreed to set apart the Saturday previous to the next communion for this purpose.

[July] 3. Two Cherokee men & one woman having with them two boys & one girl, came to the mission house. They could not speak a word of english, there was no one at the house that could speak to

them, the children being at school. From their appearance & signs we thought they wished to leave the children with us, & made signs to have them follow one of us to the school house, where were some children who can speak a little in both languages, but our best interpreter was absent. By means of the schollars at school we found they wished to leave their children. And what could we do? We had already admited more than, on a former occassion, it was thought best to admit this summer, & we some time ago engaged to take several which have not yet come, but are daily expected. If we refused these we had no interpreter that could be depended on for communicating our reason for so doing, & we knew not what prejudices might be excited; for these were full-bloods & many of our children are half-breeds. If we received these children we should probably be obliged to clothe them, for the boys were covered simply with one garment which reached about to their knees, having neither shirt nor pantaloons beside. Our sisters were wearing down & ready to faint with the fatigues of providing, in the heat of a southern summer, for the family we already had. But this was not our greatest difficulty. Our expenses are great, most of our provisions have yet been brought 40 or 50 miles, & we may possibly be blamed as exceeding our instructions if we attempt to provide for so many in this infant state of the institution, before we have even finished our buildings. Weighing all circumstances, we thought the danger of rejecting greater than that of receiving, & concluded to receive their children without attempting to state any of our difficulties to those who had brought them as it was probable we could not have made them understand if we had attempted it.[57]

A good interpreter might be of great service if fixed at this station, not only on occasions like the above & others of a temporal nature, which frequently occur, but especially to enable us to speak of the great salvation to this benighted people when they come in our way.

Occasions offer almost every day when we might speak to them if we had a good interpreter, but are now under the painful necessity of sighing over their ignorance & remaining silent. Such an interpreter seems also almost indispensable to enable Br. Butrick to proceed in acquiring the language.[58]

Although we have as yet got along without excluding any children of late that have been offered, there is reason to believe we shall soon be under the absolute necessity of turning them by unless more laborers are speedily sent on to our assistance.

With more help, & a little additional expense, we might establish a separate school for the girls, & let our present schoolhouse be filled with boys. Father Gambold, who has resided as a teacher, more than 12 years in the nation, thinks we shall find it quite necessary to keep the sexes more sepparate. Being himself unable to have more than one school, he has, after repeated experiments of both sexes together, excluded the females entirely.[59]

Sab. [July] 5. Three cherokees, who live a few miles from us & tarried with us last night, took up their horses early this morning for the purpose of going to the mill after some meal that they might have it here in readiness to take home with them after public worship. We stated to them our views & feelings, & the impropriety of doing such business on the sabbath day. They excused themselves by saying they did not know it would be wrong, or contrary to our feelings, but as they now understood it was, they would not do it; very cheerfully turned out their horses, & did not go after their meal untill monday. We were pleased with their readiness to do what we thought was right; & the confidence which they placed in us as teaching the best way. May the Lord ever help us to guide them right.
In the agreement with our miller, as writen but not signed, he engages not to grind on the sabbath day; the above circumstance suggested the propriety of prohibiting also the receiving of grains or delivery of meal or flour on that day: to this he will very readily comply, & thus the mill may assist in establishing a sabbath in this place.

[July] 6. The return of another monthly concert was very refreshing to our languid spirits. O what a mercy is that the solitary missionary (as well as those who are associated in the little bands as we are) may reflect that the circle of christian friends which he has left, & numerous other circles in various parts of the christian world, are, on the same day collected to offer their united supplications for the prosperity of Zion generally, & for a special blessing on every missionary effort! The reflection animated our spirits & quickened us in our united supplication this day.
The bare mention of the monthly concert & its object to our children often excites in them tender emotions & grateful affections, & gives us a precious opportunity advantageously to impress on their minds the importance of eternal things. We felt this day as if the Lord was hearing the prayers of our brethren for us, unworthy as we are and fondly hoped we should no more be left to so cold & lifeless a state as

we sometimes have been. "Brethren pray for us," is the sincere & ardent desire of our souls. And may the Lord ever more pour out upon his people "a spirit of grace & supplication" causing them in fervor of spirit to say with the prophet "For Zion's sake will I not hold my peace, & for Jerusalem's sake I will not rest, untill the righteousness thereof go forth as brightness, & the salvation thereof as a lamp that burneth".[60]

This evening the Rev. Dr Brown of Georgia,[61] returning from Tennessee called on us: and soon after him Mr. Randolph Stone, a Licenciate from Connecticut. Mr. Stone has spent about six months in Georgia and is now on his return to New England by circuitous rout, through Tennessee, Kentucky & Ohio.

We ought to be very thankful that our God is so often refreshing us, in this lonely place, by the company of our very respectable & beloved brethren; and we find it animating to our children to have so much notice taken of them by men of this character.

7. July. Dr Brown did not expect to see such encouraging prospects among the Cherokees—he left us to day, with assurances of his best wishes & readiness to aid us by any means in his power.

The Joiner, who has for some time been expected to assist us in finishing our buildings, arrived; but not in a situation to go immediately to work.

[July] 8. Br. Stone left us to pursue his journey. His visit has been refreshing &, we hope, profitable to us.

[July] 10. Our Joiner left us this morning. He is an intemperate man. Perhaps this was not known to Br. Kingsbury when he engaged him. Br. Hall learned it at Washington, and the man engaged to drink no whisky while here. This promise he kept; he could not have done otherwise unless he had brought his whiskey with him. But it appears he got very drunk when he came down. Soon after he arrived he was violently attacked with cramping fits: after these left him he began to work a little, but soon became crazy. We did for him every thing in our power, & kept him untill this morning, but could keep him no longer. Fearing he would perish in the woods, br. Chamberlain took one of the boys & went after him. His drunken frolic was, no doubt, the cause of his fits & derangement.

Unpleasant as the above occurrences were, we hope they may be overruled for good to the children who have witnessed this awful scene. They saw the man in his dreadful fits—they heard his shouts & screams of terror by night—they witnessed his deranged state by day, & knew it was all the effect of intoxication. We endeavored to improve this season to impress on their minds the numerous evils attending intemperance in this world, & its awful consequences in this world to come. And we hope these impressions at least, with some, may be lasting.

One of our largest schollars, aged about 19, left the school in order to make preparation to go with his father to the Arkansas.[62] This lad needs more school instruction, but we hope what he has received will be of lasting benefit to him. He can read, & writes a tolerable hand.

Br. C. found the deranged Joiner keeping his course direct for home, & thought best to let him go on.

[July] 11. The Rev. John Joyce, formerly of Philadelphia, late from Augusta called to spend the Sabbath with us.

Sab. [July] 12. Congregation as usual. A chapter was expounded, as usual, in the morning—afternoon Br. Joyce delivered a very interesting & animated discourse from Ps. 68:18.[63]

[July] 13. We were under the disagreeable necessity of refusing admitance to three fine looking boys who had been brought near 40 miles with hope of being placed in the school. They were half-breeds and we thought it a very favorable providence that the father of two of them was present, is a white man, & could understand our reasons for not receiving them. He appears well satisfied.

In addition to the above particulars which we have recorded day by day as they occured, we send, for the information of the Prud. Com. a short summary of the Lords dealing with us since our journal was last sent up, viz.

The general state of the church has been prosperous—the new converts (for ought that appears) have walked steadfastly & uprightly in the ways of truth—and (so far as we know) the chh has favor with all the people.

As to the general state of religion in the hearts of your missionaries, we have cause to humble ourselves in the dust before God, & with tears of penitence, to beg your prayers that He would be graciously pleased to increase his work in our hearts, & give us more faith, love & zeal; a greater spirit of self denial & more entire devotedness to him in the great work which He has assigned us.

Our children have been more obedient, faithful & industrious, than could have been expected, considering the depravity of human nature, and the manner of their education before they came to us.— There has been but little sickness among them considering their numbers.

We believe the natives are well satisfied as to the manner in which the school is instructed, & the general treatment of their children. We hear no complaint.

Except Br. & Sister Hall, we have none of us been confined with sickness; but the heat of summer is somewhat oppressive & relaxing to us all. We cannot perform as much labor as we could when at the north; & are more frequently indisposed; yet the climate is evidently healthy, & the summers not oppressive to those who have long resided in this latitude. A cool night in which we can sleep comfortably has as yet succeeded every day. We are told that a sultry hot night, as is sometimes felt at the north, is seldom or never known here.

Br. Hoyt was suddenly attacked, about the last of April, with a local pain in his right arm, apparently of the rheumatic kind, which lasted with some gradual abatement, for more than a month. No great inconvenience, however, was suffered from it except that the arm & hand was so debilitated that he could not labor or write for some time after the pain ceased. The arm & hand are still very weak, but slowly gaining strength.

Br. Hall has been often out of health beside the sickness mentioned in our journal—and sister Hall is constantly in a very feeble state, unable to assist in the business of our large family, & frequently confined almost entirely to her bed; at which times she suffers much.

The seasons of the year have been ordered very favorably in this part of the country. Crops every where look finely. We have about 7 acres of rye & oats (which we are now gathering) something more than 30 acres of corn, about 3 acres of Irish & 2 of sweet potatoes, and a small patch of cotton. All these promise well, except the cotton—It appears, from frequent experiments of others, as well as our little experience, that this part of the country does not well suit the cotton plant.[64]

Our young cattle & hogs increase & grow well, but we can have but little profit from our milch [milk] cows for want of pasture fields.

The committee will unite with us in grateful acknowledgments to our covenant God for his abundant mercies to us his unworthy servants, & accept the assurance of our most affectionate regards for them, the other members of the Board of Commissioners, & all our beloved patrons in Christ.

[signed individually by each missionary]
Ard Hoyt, D.S. Butrick, Wᵐ Chamberlin, Moody Hall

N.B. Br. B. desires to make the following remarks concerning his account of the language, viz.:
1) when a) occurs in any Ind. word with out a mark over it to shew its sound, it has the 4th sound of a, as in part, except in the 5th class of nouns, where is Tā tlō ŭi plural of Tlō ŭi tree.
2) In the 5th class of nouns for ô ye ilŭ leaf tsô ye ilŭ leaves, read ô iŏl lō gŭ — tsô iŏl lō gŭ. Marked according to Perrey's Key.

Continuation of Mission Journal, Brainerd

July 14. The Rev. John Joyce on his way to the westward, left us this morning. We have been edified & comforted by the agreeable visit of this worthy brother who staid with us three days. He expressed great satisfaction in the school, & in the appearance of our congregation; & thought the Cherokee Nation opened as fine a field for the justice or the charity of the people of the United States as was ever presented to the eye of benevolence. He felt no small degree of assurance that if the directors of our national affairs could view the scene as it appears to an eye witness, government would immediately afford a very liberal support not only for this school, but for others to be established on this plan. He said his mind was so impressed with the importance of this subject that he felt it an imperious duty to write to the Secretary of war before he left this place, & delayed his journey half a day for that purpose.

Br. Hoyt & Butrick went out for the purpose of visiting Mr. Hicks to confer with him on the concerns of the schools &c. Br. B. expects to go as far as Father Gambold's, & perhaps spend a few days with a Cherokee in that neighborhood to get some instructions in the language.

[July] 15. Br. Hoyt returned. He found Mr. Hicks deeply engaged for the welfare of his people, & had much interesting conversations with him on the subject of missions & schools, & their national concerns as connected with them. Mr. Hicks says many of the people are very anxious to receive instructions & their anxiety is increased from the

conviction that their very existence as a people depends upon it. The experience of the last 20 years, in which they have turned their attention more to agriculture & less to hunting, he says has convinced them that they can live much more comfortably by tilling their land & raising stock than they can in their old way. They find also that their new way of living tends to increase their population. While they lived in their old way, moving from place to place in search of game through the whole winter, thus exposing their women & children to many privations & hardships their numbers were constantly diminishing: but since they have provided homes for their women & children, where they can be warm & have enough to eat the whole year, they are increasing like the white people.[65] This remark respecting their increase was intended to apply simply to those families that have for several years pursued agriculture. Mr. H. mentioned by name many families of this class consisting each of a large number of young & healthy children. He thinks their increase since Col[n] Meigs estimated their population at 12,000 had been equal to the whole Arkansas emigrations: & if these now wishing to remain in the land of their fathers may be permited to do so in quietness & peace & may also be favored with general instructions on the plan of the Board there is reason to believe that their population will at no very distant period, be sufficient to fill the whole country they claim, with farmers, mechanics &c.[66]

He says our school gives universal satisfaction. They only wish it were in our power to take more children. If school masters could be sent by the Board to teach the children where they could board at home, they would be well received. He also says if this establishment can be so enlarged as to take more children there will be no difficulty in bringing them from every part of the nation.

A full blood cherokee girl was this day brought by her mother for the purpose of entering her in the school. We told the mother (by an interpreter) that the school was full, & we could take no more at present. She said one would make but little difference, & urged that we would receive her daughter, alleging that she had brought her a great way, & very much wanted to have her instructed. We told her we had sent away some children & it would give offense if we should now take hers, as we had told the people we could admit no more at present, except a few that we had previously promised. With great quickness she caught at this, & said one of the missionaries had told her some time ago that we would take her daughter when ever she would bring her. This was probably an artifice, but whether true or false, as we could not contradict her assertion, it afforded us the means of obviating any charge of partiality which might be brought against us for admiting this one after others had been refused; & we consented to receive her.[67] The mother having got over this difficulty was immediately tried with another: the child was unwilling to be left, & with the most bitter cries entreated her mother to take her back. The mother finding that words did not avail to quiet the child, brought her to submission by the rod: & thus commiting her to our care, departed.[68]

[July] 18. Rev. Richard P. Corn [or Carn] of the methodist connection, called to spend sabbath with us.

Sab. [July] 19. Congregation small—in the afternoon Mr. Corn preached from Rom. 1: 15,16.[69]

[July] 25. According to previous appointment this day was set apart by the chh as a day for fasting, humiliation & prayer. Found it very profitable to wait on the Lord in this ordinance.

Sab. [July] 26. A black man servant, of one of our Cherokee sisters, was baptized & received as a member & communicant in this chh. Rev. Mr. Corn was present, preached & united with us in the holy ordinance of the supper.

The members which have been added from among this people, consisting of five Cherokees, three Africans & one white man, were all present, the blessed Savior also made one in the midst of us, & we had a good day.[70]

This evening our hearts were refreshed by the relations of one of our largest girls. She had for some time past been very seriously impressed, & now ventured to state to us that something more than a week ago she felt a great change in her views & feelings, & since that time had entertained a hope that the Lord had begun a good work in her soul. From a variety of circumstances we think there is reason to hope that it was even so—time may enable us to judge with more certainty. This girl has ever been amiable in her deportment, & her talents are good.

O that our gratitude might increase as do the mercies of our God! But in this we are greatly deficient.

Several Cherokees came from a distance on saturday, & kept sabbath with us. We had much conversation with them by an interpreter. A discovery of the thick darkness that shrouds their minds was enough to make the benevolent heart bleed. Whether their expressions were true to feelings of their hearts, or whether they endeavored to deceive us, we cannot tell; but with apparent seriousness & sincerity, they expressed themselves for substance as follows, viz. That they had no expectation of any thing after death—that they seldom or never bestowed any thoughts on these things—that they were not conscious of ever having done, said, or thought any thing that was wrong or sinful—in short they appeared as stupid, ignorant & unconcerned as the hearts that perish ever destitute of that conscience which St Paul speaks of as "accusing or excusing".[71] Nor did all we could say (though they gave us a patient hearing, & answered whenever a question was asked) appear to awaken any anxious inquiries on these momentous subjects.[72]

In respect to these persons, & some others with whom we have conversed, we might say in the language of the prophet "Darkness hath covered the earth, & gross darkness the people".[73] But it is not thus with all the Natives around us. Some of them are considerably enlightened, & feel the importance of receiving further instruction. Darkness itself cannot be seen without some light.

July 29. Father & Mother H. set out for the settlements.[74] He on business, she for her health.

August 8. Fa. & M. Hoyt returned. Her health has been improved by the journey. They were affectionately received & hospitably entertained by the way & in the settlements. Fa. H. preached on Saturday & on the Sabbath in two places both within the bounds of a Presbyterian congregation. The Lord gave good success in all the business contemplated, except in hiring laborers to complete our buildings, dig a well & etc. These could not be obtained.

Sab. [Aug.] 9th We feel ourselves under renewed & increasing obligations of gratitude to the giver of all good for the hopeful appearance among our children. Several of them appear seriously & solemnly impressed with divine truth, & we have hope that two or three of them have been recently born of the Spirit. It is no uncommon thing to hear these dear immortals fervently pouring out their supplications to God when they suppose no one but Jehovah hears & often in their little circles prayer & praise is heard.

This evening one of the brethren passing the house where the girls lodge about 9 ock, perceived they were engaged in social prayer. Struck with the animated voice & appropriate language of the speaker he stopped & on hearing further supposed it to be one of the missionary sisters, & thought she had an unusual spirit of prayer & fervent wrestlings with God. On entering the dwelling house he was astonished to find all the sisters there, and immediately related what he had heard. It was from the mouth, or shall we say from the heart of a Cherokee girl about 14. She is one of the hopeful converts, & has lately returned with a younger sister from a visit at their fathers. They say they do not like to be at home because they have no prayers there. Being detained by rain a day or two at their fathers after they expected to return, the youngest became quite impatient, & told her sister the day before they returned that she intended to set out the next day if it did rain, & the next morning persuaded her father to suffer them to return, although the rain continued & the distance is about 25 miles.

How would it rejoice the hearts of the pious patrons of this institution to see these dear children who but for their benefactors might never have heard the gospel, now rejoicing in Christ Jesus & esteeming it a privilege to leave father & mother to be with christians!

[Aug.] 13. Br. & Sist. Hall set out to go on a visit to Fa. Gambolds. This journey was undertaken with a particular view to sis. H's health which is very poor.

Sab. [Aug.] 16. A mulatto girl, servant of a half breed Cherokee, was received to the chh.[75]

[Aug.] 17. A full blood Cherokee youth applying for admission to the school was found able to spell correctly in words of 4 & 5 letters.[76] He had been taught solely by black people who had received their instruction in our sunday-school.

[Aug.] 19. Mr. John McKinny of Augusta traveling westward, called & spent an hour in the school. He expressed great satisfaction in the appearance of the children; thought those who believed Indian reform impracticable would change their oppinion were they to witness the change already wrought in them, & manifested his goodwill to the Institution by a donation of Fifty dollars.

[Aug.] 20. Br. & Sis. H. returned. Had an agreeable visit with our dear friends at Springplace—and on their way home had an interesting

interview with a number of the chiefs & warriors. ~~who had assembled for a Ball play. This is a celebrated diversion among the indians. Great numbers on these occasions are often assembled from different parts of the nation, merely to look on.~~ They paid great respect to Br. Hall as a missionary—spoke highly of the school as beneficial to their nation, & expressed many thanks to the good people who were thus providing for the instruction of their people. One of them, who had been to Washington [the federal capital] & seen the President, said the President told him the missionaries were good people & they must treat them kindly, adding with emphasis "and we shall".
Sister H. has received little or no benefit from this ride.

[*Aug.*] 25. One of our female schollars, a late hopeful convert, who had been home with her sister on a visit returned. The joy she manifested on geting back clearly evinced that she felt the Lord's people to be her people, & considered that she had returned to her kindred & friends. She left her sister to stay out the time assigned for the visit, but said she could not be contented to stay any longer where they had no prayers.—She had seen a great many kind relatives & friends, but could find no happiness there.—She wanted to get back where she could attend prayer meetings & hear & talk about good things. "Is not this a brand plucked out of the burning?"[77]

[*Aug.*] 28. Br. C. went out for the purpose of visiting some families in Mr. Hicks' neighborhood & trying to collect the people in that quarter for preaching on the Sabbath; the place thought of for preaching is about 20 m. from Brainerd. Sister Chamberlin went with him.

[*Aug.*] 29. Three of our girls went off slily this morning just at break of day. We suppose they have gone about 4 m. for a visit, as they asked liberty yesterday & were refused on account of the distance. We think the two youngest were inticed by the elder, who is about 15. This girl had given us much trouble.[78] She is a mixed blood, but nearly white; speaks english, & has been much among white people. She has been dismissed from Fa. Gambolds, & one other school for her bad conduct.[79] We were on the point of dismissing her last May; but fair promises & a partial amendment, gave us hope that we might do her good without injury to others & on this account have suffered her to remain with us.

Sab. [*Aug.*] 30. The three girls returned soon enough to attend public worship.

[Aug.] 31. All the brethren who were at home met this morning to consider the care of the runaway girls. It appearing that the two younger were inticed by the elder, they were pardoned, & she dismissed from the school. It was very painful to part with one of our schollars in this way, but the necessity of the measure appeared evident. We commend her to the mercy of God, & she parted from us in tears.

Sab. [Sept.] 4. Br. & Sis. Chamberlin returned. They were affectionately recvd in all the families they visited—between 40 & 50, chiefly half-breeds who understand English, attended preaching on the Sabbath—all were attentive, &, by request, an appointment was made for one of us to preach there again in two weeks.

After sermon Mr. Hicks repeated the substance of the discourse in cherokee.

Br. C. was informed that a report that we did not give our children enough to eat had obtained considerable circulation & some credit among the natives.

[Sept.] 5. An uncle of one of the school girls called to day & frankly told us that the mother of the girl, having been informed that the children were not well fed, requested him to come & take the girl away.[80] He said it was his sisters wish that he should say nothing to us about any complaint, but simply take the girl home under the pretense of making a visit, but he had seen & known too much of these things to act in this manner, having lived at Fa. Gambolds, & attended his school, for four years. He said it was there frequently the case when a child became dissatisfied & wanted to get home, that he would go to his parents with some false story as they did not have enough to eat, were not taken care of when sick, or the like, & some would believe these stories & take their children away. He believed the children were well used here & should not take his Niece, except for a few days on a visit. After some further conversation with the girl, he concluded not to take her even for a visit, for the girl said she should like to see her mother here but did not want to go home.

Nearly half the schollars are now absent, having been taken away under pretense, or in reality to visit their friends.

From the above circumstance, & what Br. C. heard, we think it highly probable that these false reports have induced many to take their children away with the design of not returning them: but those who intend to continue their children at school are very fond of taking them home frequently, & for long visits.

We have taken great pains to convince the parents of the importance of keeping their children more constant at school, but conclude that time alone can remedy this evil.

We have also had some trouble from one parent bringing a child & the other taking it away, ~~in cases~~ where the father & mother do not now live together. ~~In such cases the mother has a right to the children in preference.~~

We have now three children who were brought here by their father, a half-breed of some education, who have two mothers & neither of them have for some time lived with their father. He has another wife & they have other husbands. The mother of two of them came for the purpose of taking them from the school & told us the mother of the other was coming for hers soon. The children were sorely grieved at the prospect of being taken from us; & we also were grieved on their account: for the mothers among this people are considered as having the right to the children in preference to the father. One of the two, a girl about 13, we hope has found the Savior. As she wept and asked what she should do, we told her to ask God to make her mother willing to let her & her brother stay. As soon as the idea was suggested she appeared to receive comfort, went out, & no doubt complied with our advise. The next morning their mother said they might stay, she would only take the boy (who is about 9) for a few days on a visit.

Sab. [Sept.] 6. Few people attended meeting—two members of the chh known to be near, did not attend. The cause to us is unknown.

[Sept.] 7. "Without are fightings within are fears".[81] Br. Hoyt went this morning to look after the two brothers that were missing yesterday. He found their minds evil affected toward the missionaries. One of them said he thought he had better stay at home than to go where he should hear what was not true. Being asked what he had heard that was not true he said one of the missionaries when preaching had told them they ought to cover a brothers faults & not spread them abroad in the world. For his part he could not read the bible to know what that said, but some who could read told him the bible said just the other way. He appeared greatly agitated. The other brother who is a black man & was brought up by a Presbyterian in Virginia, said when he joined the chh he thought we were Presbyterians. He had not

inquired, but he knew we talked to him just as his good old master used to say was right: but a white man whom he named, had told him we were not Presbyterians. He therefore, thought we men-pleasers, and did not like to have our sentiments known; & he thought we had better be alone than to be connected with such people, and this was the reason he did not come to meeting.[82]

[Sept.] 12. Br B. went out for the purpose of meeting the appointment for preaching tomorrow at the place where Br. C. preached two weeks ago. Br. Hall went with him expected to return on monday. It is expected Br. Butrick will go on to preach a funeral sermon on account of the late death of the daughter of a chief who is called the Ridge.[83] This is about 60 mi. South by East from Brainerd.

Sab. [Sept.] 13. Several persons manifested their delight in the public worship of God by coming from 2 to 7 miles in a very heavy storm of rain.—Some who formerly attended almost all weather, now seldom attend.

[Sept.] 14. Br. Hall returned. Notwithstanding the heavy rain about 20 persons attended to hear Br. B. & expressed a desire that preaching might be continued at that place. He therefore gave them encouragement that one of the missionaries would attend every two weeks.
We were this day refreshed by a letter from Br. Kingsbury. He & Br. & Sister Williams have been preserved in good health, though many around them are sick.
On the 12th of August the first tree was cut on the place designed for their establishment.

[Sept.] 22. Br. B. returned. He had been kindly received wherever he went—says the field appears white for harvest[84]—He preached the funeral sermon & spent several days in that place. Several families of natives live near together in that place & have a school kept by an elderly white man whom they pay for his services. There are also some white families in the neighborhood. The natives would be pleased to have a mission school established there. The chief called the Ridge, or Majr Ridge, returned with Br. B. & brought one of his sons with him, a lad about 17.[85] At the request of the father & the lad we recommended him to the F.M.S. in Conn, & gave him $50 for traveling expenses. He is to go north with a gentleman from New York now about to return to that city.[86]

[Sept.] 23. Six days ago the father of the three children mentioned on the 5th, borrowed a horse of us to take his two daughters (the son being there with his mother) as he said on a visit to a friends promising to return with them in three days. This morning the horse was brought back with a letter from the father, stating that he was well satisfied to have his children with us, yet he must request us to excuse him for once forfeiting his word to us in not bringing his daughters back as he had promised. The reasons he assigned were his children were dear to him & he thought himself capable of bringing them up better & in a more civilized manner than their mothers were, they being in an uncivilized & heathen state. If the children were to remain with us their mother would soon take them away, & it would then be out of his power to get them. He promised to put them into a good school, & to see that they were well educated. We know not where he has taken them, but probably out of the nation.[87] It is said the girls were unwilling to go with their father. His son has now returned to the school, & will probably be sent for soon.—"The way of transgressors is hard".[88] How much better for this man & his children if he had adhered to the original institutions of marriage; few, however, of the natives pay attention to it.[89]

Sat. [Sept.] 26. Gloomy season in the mission family—This was a fast day for the chh—being the day previous to the stated time for administering the sacrament of the Lords supper and it was said that such feelings existed in the mission family that we were not prepared to unite in that holy ordinance, & it was therefore purposed to put off the communion, though it had been publicly announced for two weeks. This circumstance shewed that we had great cause to humble ourselves before God, & perhaps quickened us in the duty of fasting & prayer. We were grieved & shocked at our situation, & trembled in view of the consequences.[90]

Sab. [Sept.] 27. The Lord in infinite mercy heard; & saved us from the dreadful pit. The proposal to postpone the sacrament was withdrawn, all expressing a willingness to unite in that holy ordinance except one, who was unwell & could not go out. Surely, if any ever needed the application of that blood which cleanseth from all sin, we did: & we trust the Lord made us in some degree sensible of our need. If our hearts deceived us not, we experienced the truth of that declaration by the prophet. "I am the Lord that healeth thee".[91] We had a sweet & comforting season at the communion table; where it is believed every one present was enabled in sincerity to renew covenant with God & his people.

All the new converts present, (tho, ignorant of the dreadful night we had passed through) expressed usual joy in this occasion. One of them said she would not have missed the hapiness of this day for the world.

O the infinite mercy & grace of our covenant God, which prevented us from depriving these children of their bread!

At evening the professors in the mission family had a meeting for thanksgiving & praise to God for his preventing & restoring grace.

[Sept.] 28. This afternoon word was sent that the little Osage captive was at a neighbors 4 miles distant, & would be sent to us the first opportunity.[92] Fa. Hoyt immediately went after her.

On seeing the dear orphan who appears to be about 4 or 5 years old, he directed her to be told in Cherokee (for she does not understand English) that he would be her father. She fixed her eyes with great earnestness upon him for about half a minute, & then with a smile reached him her bonnet as a token that she accepted the offer & would go with him. As he took her on the horse before him, she gave him some nuts she had in her hand, & leaned her head on his bosom as if she had really found a father. She was very playful & talkative for a while & then fell asleep, & slept most of the way to the mission house. When first introduced to the family she seemed a little surprised on seeing so many gathered around her, but the children begining to talk to her in a language she understood, her cheerfulness immediately returned, & she appeared to be quite at home. It is said she speaks the Cherokee language well for one of her age, though it is but little more than a year since her captivity.

It was understood when Br. Cornelius was here that, if obtained, she should be called Lydia Carter, the name of the benevolent lady of Natchez who contributed so liberally for her redemption. We call her by this name. Our feelings on the reception of this exiled orphan may more easily be conceived than described. We feel ourselves bound, not only in duty, but by the feelings of our heart, to train her as an own child.[93]

Ard Hoyt, D.S. Butrick, Wm Chamberlin

Continuation of Mission Journal, Brainerd

1818

Oct. 1. Having failed in several attempts which were made to sink a well last year, & for the want of one been under the necessity of bringing all our water from the creek, or from a small spring under its bank, about 80 or 100 rods from the mission house, we feel it worthy of noticing in our journal that we this day finished our well, which is likely to afford us plenty of good water, though, from the quantity of limestone through which it passes, it is too hard for washing. It is about 28 feet deep, the bottom all rock except a small crevice through which the water rises. We attribute the failure last year to the abundance of rain which fell that season, causing the earth to cave as they dug.

It is believed this is the only well in the cherokee nation: & we feel under increased obligations of gratitude to the giver of all good for this addition to our convenience & comfort.

[Oct.] 7. Fa. Hoyt left us for the purpose of meeting the Presbytery of East Tennessee, which is to meet at Washington [Rhea Co.] tomorrow.

[Oct.] 10. Br. C. went to Mr. Hicks' & expects to preach in that neighborhood tomorrow. We had a prospect of a very lonely time at the Mission house, but the Lord who is ever rich in mercy & goodness was pleased to send us two dear brethren, Mr. Robert Glenn, who had just received a license from the Presbytery of East Tenn. & Mr. Christopher Bradshaw; candidate for Licensure under the care of sd Presbytery, who will spend the Sabbath with us.[94]

Sab. [Oct.] 11. Had a very precious season. Br. Glenn preached. Our congregation was rather thin, but we think we had the presence of the Lord.

[Oct.] 12. Br. & Sister Hall & Sis. Sarah, left us for Knoxville. We have considerable anxiety on their account, as Sister Hall is in such a delicate state of health. We hope it may be improved by the journey. Br. C. returned this morning. He had a good meeting on the Sab. Between 20 & 30 of the natives attended. Some appeared affected on hearing the word of God, & all manifested a desire to have preaching continued at that place.

Afternoon Br. & Sis. C.—the two visiting brethren, & two of our pious female schollars, went on a visit to a cherokee sisters.—They had a very agreeable meeting—the Lord appeared to be with them of a truth. Thanks to our covenant God for the clusters of Eshcol, of which we are permited to task in this wilderness.[95]

[Oct.] 13. This morning Brs. Glenn & Bradshaw took their leave of us, probably to meet us no more till we meet in heaven. We have great reason to bless God for the interview we have had, & hope it will be of lasting benefit to our souls.

It was said to one of our dear native sisters "If it gives us so much joy to see christian friends here, what will it be in heaven, where we shall meet all the christians in the world, never again to part? O,["] said she (with tears starting from her eyes), ["]it will be more than we can bear.["]

A joint letter from the brethren at the Choctaw establishment brings information that most of the brethren & sisters have been visited with sickness, that sister Williams had been apparently on the brink of eternity; but, at the date of the letter, there was hope of her speedy recovery.[96] May the Lord sanctify their afflictions, increase their graces, & spare them all for further usefulness.

[Oct.] 15. Our spirits were refreshed by a short visit from several dear christian friends of Athens, Georgia, viz. Mr. Josiah Newton, his brother & mother; & the wife of Rev. Dr. [John] Brown with one of her sons.[97] These, with others, so kindly administered to the wants of Fa. Hoyt & family when on their way to this station. The zeal they then manifested for the cause of missions was still conspicuous. They expressed great satisfaction in the progress of christianity & civilization among this people, & said it exceeded their expectations. They were peculiarly delighted to hear the children of the forest sing the songs of Zion. Being now on their way to West Tennessee they encouraged another call as they return.

[Oct.] 16. Fa. Hoyt returned from Washington, having through the grace of God, been preserved in health, & enjoyed a very refreshing season with the Presbytery. By invitation he took a seat in Presbytery as a corresponding member & spent four days with them. They had preaching every day, which was well attended by a large number of people. One of the days was the time of general muster for the regiment of militia. The whole regiment when formed was marched to the place of preaching, which was in a grove, & attended with much solemnity. The Lord has recently poured out his spirit in many parts of this Presbytery, & the friends of Zion are looking up with rejoicing. Mr. Robert Glen, a candidate for Licensure lately from the Theological Seminary in Princeton, received license at this meeting of Presbytery. There is now under the care of this Presbytery, six young men, who promise great usefulness to the church as heralds of the everlasting gospel.

After Presbytery had closed Fa. H. waited to attend the unpleasant lawsuit into which we had been drawn by one of the workmen employed last season on the mill. The case was referred to arbitrators, who, on hearing a statement of facts, immediately decided that we should pay nothing, & left the plaintiff to pay cost.[98]

[Oct.] 17. Br. Hicks came to make us a visit & spend sabbath with us. He thinks the people are generally well pleased with our management of the school—says he hears no complaint, & will indeavor to persuade the parents of children sent to school to keep them more constantly with us. He still thinks there will be no want of children to fill the school whatever may be the number we can admit.

We think the greatest difficulty will be in keeping the children steady at school, & retaining them long enough to fix their habits & finish their education. Many of this ignorant people appear to think their children can become learned in a few months.

Sab. [Oct.] 18. Very few of our neighbors attended meeting, though the day was very pleasant. Only two members of the church attended except those in our own family; but the number of blacks was larger than usual.

It appears that some white people have excited prejudices in the neighborhood against the doctrines we profess to believe as they are expressed in our writen articles.[99] We do not learn that they object to any doctrines advanced in preaching.

Perhaps we have been unfaithful in our preaching—possibly they have misunderstood the writen articles; or they may not have comprehended our preaching. We should be sorry to have any thing found in the one which is never brought to view in the other.

[Oct.] 19. One of our girls, who has been with us about six months, & is about 10 years old, being told that her grandmother, (who has the care of her having raised her from her infancy) was coming to take her from the school to go to the Arkansas, replied with a trembling voice "I dont want to go away from here," & immediately burst in tears. She has since wept much, & expressed a great unwillingness to leave us. Her friends would doubtless be glad to continue her in school were they to remain on this side of the mississippi, but we fear they will not consent to remove without her.

The Arkansas emigration has already drawn off a number of our schollars. May the Lord send them teachers there who shall train them in the way of truths, & complete that which we would gladly do for them.

[Oct.] 20. The boy mentioned Sep^t 5 & 23, whose two sisters were taken from us through fear that their mothers would get them, was this day sent for. He manifested a great unwillingness to leave us— would eat no dinner, & went away alone & wept. The man who came after him said the boys father was well pleased with the school, & would be glad to have all his children here were it not for the fear that their mothers would take them away & keep them: and, as the boy felt so bad about going, he would leave him for the present, & if the father could get some assurance that the mothers would let his daughters remain here he thought he would send them back, adding, they were sorely grieved at being taken away.

The little girl mentioned yesterday, finding this boy was left because he cried, said "When they come after me I will cry as hard as I can, & maybe they will leave me too.["]

Br. B. left us to go to Fa. Gambolds, & from there to attend the talk at the Agency.

[Oct.] 22. Br. Peter Kanouse arrived from the Choctaw station, with Israel Folsom, a half-breed of that nation. He is taking the lad on to the F.M.S.[100]

[Oct.] 27. Br. B. returned. Nothing had been done at the Talk when he left the Agency, the Governor having but just arrived. He saw many of the Indians assembled, & great numbers of white people who were selling whisky to them, & also drinking, swearing, gambling, &c, among themselves.[101]

[Oct.] 28. Br. Kanouse left us on his way to New Jersey, with his Choctaw lad. He also took with him from our school a half breed Cherokee, called James Fields.[102] Both these lads are designed for the F.M.S. in Con.

The presence & conversation of this dear brother has been very refreshing to our spirits, & we hope profitable to our dull & sluggish souls. Our communion has been sweet, & parting painful. We have reason to bless God that even in this heathen land we are afforded such precious seasons, with Christ & his servants.

[Oct.] 30. Being informed that the King & Chiefs of the upper towns were convened in council at Br. Hicks' it was thought best for one of us to make them a visit.[103] This was assigned to Fa. Hoyt & he went out to day for that purpose.

Nov. 2 . Fa. Hoyt returned, & gave the following account of his visit. I arrived at Br. Hicks' on the evening of the day I left home. Some of the expected chiefs had not arrived, & on that account the Council had not yet formed. A number of men were standing round the two doors of Br. Hicks' largest room, & others were standing within. I was invited to pass the crowd & walk in. On entering I observed the king [Pathkiller] seated on a rug at one end of the room having his back supported by a roll of blankets. He is a venerable looking man, 73 years old, his hair nearly white.[104] At his right hand, on one end of the same rug, or mat, sat Br. Hicks. The chiefs were seated in chairs in a semicircle, each facing the king. Behind the chiefs a number of the common people were standing, listening to a conversation in which the king & chiefs were engaged. I was immediately discovered by Br. Hicks, & invited to walk round the circle to him. The conversation was immediately stoped. Br. Hicks gave me his hand without rising, & then introduced me to the king, & to those of the chiefs with whom I had not been previously acquainted; each in his turn giving me his hand without rising. A chair was then placed for me in the circle. As soon as I had taken my seat, the king inquired after the health of the missionaries, the children &c. They then resumed their conversation in their own language, continued it a short time, & closed. We were then informed that supper was waiting.

The king & chiefs filled the table, except the clergymans place, which was assigned to me. The strictest order was observed at table, no one moving a hand untill a blessing was asked, or withdrawing untill thanks were returned. The same order was observed at every meal afterward.

The evening was spent in social conversation, which was carried on with the utmost freedom—Br. Hicks being our interpreter. The king & chiefs expressed great satisfaction in the school, & many thanks to those who are engaged for the instruction of their children & people. The king observed, it was evidence of great love to be willing to teach & feed so many children without pay; & he did not doubt but it would be greatly to the benefit of the nation; for though bad men could do more mischief when learned, the good would be much more useful; & he knew we taught the children to be good & hoped many of them would follow our instructions.

Notwithstanding the number of people collected, there was not the least disorder or tumult—all retired to rest at an early hour, & perfect stillness prevailed the whole night. The council was not formed untill late the next day. It was opened by a formal speech, delivered with animation, & heard with great solemnity. I was told that opening the council in this manner is an antient [ancient] religious right, & considered as an appeal or prayer to the Good Spirit, though few if any now understand the meaning of the words used.

Several letters were read in council, by Br. Hicks, respecting the exchange of country, but nothing of importance was done. The council adjourned ~~till the next day~~ a little before sunset, & the same order was observed the second night as the first.

The next morning, being the second after my arrival, I mentioned to Br. Hicks my desire to give them a talk at some convenient time while the council was siting if he thought it would be agreeable to the king & chiefs. He said it would no doubt be agreeable to them; & he would prepare the way by mentioning it as soon as the council met.

The king & chiefs being seated in the council house, & the people gathered around, Br. Hicks told them I had something to say if they were willing to hear; & informed me that they would thus attend to what I had to say.

I immediately entered the council house (so called) which is merely a spacious roof, supported by posts set in the ground, & left open on all sides, except a railing which extends round the whole building, leaving only an opening on one side about the width of a common door. Next the railing on the inside are benches round the whole building, on which the king, old men, & chiefs are seated; the rest of the people stand on the outside of the railing. I stood a little below the center of the house, facing the king, with Br. Hicks on my right as interpreter, my audience surrounding me on every side.

After a short introduction, in which I expressed my thanks that the Good Spirit had permited me to meet them—that they had received me as a friend & brother, & were now giving me an opportunity to speak to them, I endeavored to exhibit the character of the true God as a being of unbounded benevolence—brought to view some of the evidences of this from the works of creation & providence—told them the good book which contained the principles of our religion asserted & confirmed these truths; & also taught us that to be happy we must be good—that to be truly good was to be like the Good Spirit—that He was displeased with sin, & well pleased only with that which was good, & those who did good—yet he did good to all—& would have all men told what they must be & do, in order to be happy—this was found in the good book—& the Good Spirit would have all men made acquainted with it. I endeavored to shew them that the plan for missions & schools among them must have been devised solely for their good—nothing was asked from them; not a foot of their land, or anything else.

I then gave a brief statement of the feelings of the missionaries before they came out, & of others in our own country particularly their ardent desire that their red brethren might enjoy the same privileges they did—enumerated some of these particularly the education of our children, & its advantages—and observed that they need not think it strange that we were willing to do all we were doing for them without pay, as we found our own happiness in seeking to do them good—that we loved the children commited to our care, & found ourselves well paid for all we did for them in the satisfaction the Good Spirit gave us in our work—that the best way to secure our own happiness was to do what we could to make others happy; & concluded by mentioning what had been said to us respecting small schools where the children could chiefly board at home—wished them to communicate their desires freely & fully on this subject; & though we might not be able to do all that they & we could wish, we would do what we could.

I was heard with the most fixed attention, & have reason to believe, from the starting tear on every side, that the warm feelings of Br. Hicks gave an affecting pathos to the interpretation; which was given sentence by sentence as I spake. I continued my discourse much longer than was at first intended, being encouraged so to do from my own feelings & the appearance of the audience.

When I had taken my seat a few words passed between the king & the chiefs in their own language, after which the king said (Br. Hicks interpreting) they thanked me for the good talk I had given them, & were all well pleased with the whole of it. They knew (as he had told me the evening before) that nothing but a desire to do good could induce us to instruct & feed so many children without pay. It was further observed that they must now attend to business of great national importance, & as soon as that was finished, they would attend to what I had said about other schools, & communicate freely according to my request.

I then observed that I must leave them & return to the school, but, if agreeable, I would first take the king by the hand in token of our mutual love & friendship, & of the mutual love & friendship that subsisted between his people & all concerned in the mission. The king most cordially gave his hand as a token & seal of this, while I implored the divine blessing upon him & his people. This being done, the chiefs all rose from their seats, came up to me one by one, & each gave his hand in a most affectionate manner.

This closing scene was to me truly impressive, & I think will not soon be forgotten.

Br. Hicks left the council & accompanied me a short distance on my way. While by ourselves he assured me there was no dissimulation in what I had seen—that they were all highly pleased, & he thought much good would result from the interview.

Br. Hall returned from Knoxville alone. He brings the heavy tidings that our afflicted sister for whose health the journey was taken, so far from gaining by the ride was rather worse, &, on that account, he had left her in Knoxville. Sister Sarah remained with her as a companion & nurse untill his return.

The Lord has various ways to try his people. O may we ever say from the heart "Thy will be done".

Nov. 4. The parents of Catharine Brown called on us. They are on their way to the Agency. The old grey-headed man, with tears in his eyes, said he must go over the mississippi. The white people would not suffer him to live here. They had stolen his cattle, horses & hogs, untill he had very little left. He expected to return in about 10 days, & should then want Catharine to go home, & prepare to go with him to the Arkansas. We requested him to leave his daughter with us yet a while & go to the Arkansas without her, & we would soon send her to him with much more knowledge than she now had. To this he would not consent, but signified a desire that some of us would go along with him.

It is a great trial to think of sending this dear sister away with only one year tuition, but we fear she must go. The Lord can & will order otherwise if, on the whole, it is for the best.

[Nov.] 6. Br. C. went out for the purpose of making a visiting tour, & meeting our appointment for preaching on the Sabbath.

As he will go by Br. Hicks' & Fa. Gambolds, he took Catharine, and another hopeful convert (Lydia Lowrey) along with him.[105] Catharine expects this to be her last visit in that quarter.

[Nov.] 9. Br. C. returned. He brings information that the natives at Yucalooga [Oothcaloga],[106] are very anxious to have one of us reside with them, preach on the sabbath, & teach a few children who will be boarded by their parents. This place is about 60/5m, south by east, from Brainerd. Br. B. spent some time there on his tour last September. It appears his preaching & conversation has, by the divine blessing, excited the attention of the natives.

In a joint meeting of the brethren it was thought best to pay particular attention to this place; &, if it should hereafter be thought advisable, Br. B. may perhaps collect a small school there, & preach on the Sabbath, & still pursue the study of the language: as he may probably board in a family where they speak only cherokee.

At this meeting Br. Hall inquired whether we did not think he might be spared from this station to go to another, if God in his providence should open the way. Considering the great field that appears opening before us, & the prospect of a farmer from the north to assist at this establishment, it was thought he might.

Nov. 10. Br. Hall took his leave of us to return to Knoxville. He expects to continue there several months. Milo Hoyt went with him in a waggon to take his baggage, & to bring Sister Sarah back, if she thinks proper to return.

[Nov.] 14. A poor cherokee woman, whose husband has taken another wife & left her with a daughter about 8 years old, expressed a great desire to put her child into the school if only she could find some way to furnish her with clothes. Ascertaining that the woman was really poor, we proposed to take the girl & clothe her as our own, if she would let her stay with us constantly untill she had acquired a good education. She readily accepted the proposal, promising to let us keep the girl as long as we thought necessary—that she would come here when she wanted to see her, & not take her away at all.

Sab. [Nov.] 15. We think the prejudices which have been excited in the minds of some of our weak brethren are dying away—perhaps are entirely eradicated. They salute us affectionately as formerly—seek instructions—appear humble—speak of having passed through a dark & unpleasant time in which they almost lost the comforts of religion & the hope that they ever had any. All present to-day appeared to enjoy the Sabbath, take delight in the ordinances, & experience the communion of saints. We are liable to mistake in our judgment of characters, & may have admited some to communion that have never experienced renewing grace; but we think these cherokee & african converts give as good evidence of a saving change as is commonly found among more enlightened professors: &, in respect to some of them, we feel almost an assured confidence that they have passed from death to life.[107] Separated as they are from each other, & from 2 to 20 miles from us, & some of them unable to read at all, & none of them good schollars, it is morrally impossible that they should make rapid progress in knowledge, or in so short a period, be able to answer all the sophisms of irreligious men; but they are evidently growing in knowledge, & (if we mistake not) in grace.

[Nov.] 18. Milo Hoyt returned with the waggon from Knoxville. Sister Hall's health is some better than it was. Sister Sarah concludes to stay with her untill after her confinement.

[Nov.] 19. We had this evening a melancholly proof of mans proneness to degenerate into the savage state, & loose [lose] the knowledge of the truths as it is revealed in the scriptures. A mother advanced in life & a son apparently about 25, who would not from their appearance or their language, be suspected to have one drop of Indian blood in their veins, tarried with us for the night. The[y] said they were part cherokee, though the son could not speak the language at all, & the mother but poorly. They were free to converse, & manifested almost a total ignorance of every thing relating to religion or a future state, & differed in nothing but colour & speech from the sons of the forest.

[Nov.] 20. We had a very affecting scene on account of our sister Catharine. Her father & mother, returning from the agency to go to the Arkansas, stopped yesterday for the purpose of taking her along with them. She felt that she needed more information to be prepared to go alone into the wilderness, & entreated them to leave her with us a little time longer.
She is their only daughter, & they would not consent on any terms to leave her behind. The struggle was very severe. She wept & prayed; & promised to come to them as soon as she had finished her litterary

education, & acquired some further knowledge of the christian religion. We engaged that she should be provided for while here, & assisted in going to them. Her mother said she could not live if she would not <u>now</u> go with them—Catharine replied that, to her, it would be more bitter than death to leave us & go where there were no missionaries. Her father became impatient, & told her if she would not mind him & go with them now, he would disown her forever; but if she would now go, as soon as missionaries came to the Arkansas (& he expected they would be there soon) she might go & live with them as long as she pleased. He wished her to have more learning.

Never before did this precious christian have so severe a trial, & never, perhaps, did her graces shine so bright. She sought for nothing but to know duty; & asked for a few minutes to be by herself undisturbed. She returned, & said she would go.—After she had gathered & put up her clothing &c, the family were collected, a parting hymn sung, & prayer offered. With mingled emotions of joy & grief we commanded her to the grace of God, & they departed.

Precious babe in Christ! a few months ago brought out of the dark wilderness; here illuminated by the word & spirit of God, & now to be sent back to the dark & chilling shades of the forest, without one fellow traveler with whom she can say "Our Father"! O ye who with delight sit under the drapings of the sanctuary, & enjoy the communion of saints, remember Catharine in your prayers!

[Nov.] 22. The woman who left her daughter on the 14th with the promise that she should stay with us as long as we pleased, came to take her away. She had heard that the child cried for mother when she was going to bed; which was true. We told her the child would be contented after she had been here a short time—that several of the children who were now unwilling to leave us, were more discontented at first than her daughter. But the poor unenlightened mother, knowing nothing but the feelings of nature, could not be persuaded to leave her. We were very sorry to part with this child & have her taken back to the regions of darkness, perhaps never to see the light of life; but were obliged to submit.

[Nov.] 23. Sister Chamberlin continues very unwell—mother Hoyt's feeble strength is almost exhausted, & sister Anna's health is breaking under the double charge & labor which devolves on her. Some of the poor children that we have agreed to clothe are geting ragged, & we fear the uninformed natives will think we are not careful to do by them as we have promised. The clothing so long since forwarded for our relief, & which at this time would be of most essential service, does not arrive. We have heard that boxes directed to us have been some time in Augusta, but no team could be found to bring them on.—We have need of patience. "Lord increase our faith".[108]

[Nov.] 24. Our friends from Athens, mentioned on the 15 ult, called on their return. Mr. J. Newton gave five dollars for the benefit of the institution.

[Nov.] 25. A white man, who has a Cherokee family, & is himself about as ignorant as most of the Cherokees, brought back his son who has been at home on a visit. He said he was greatly discouraged about trying to give his son an education, & did not know what to do about bringing him back, as he thought the white people were determined to have the country, & it was likely he should be obliged to remove over the Mississippi before his son could learn enough to do him any good. He said many of the cherokees were discouraged & keeping their children at home on the same account. We told him this need not make any difference as to sending their children to school, for in the event of the removal of the nation the school would be removed also; & what was lacking in the education of children admited to school here should be finished there. He seemed much pleased with this, & said he did not before expect we would be willing to go so far—he should never go unless he was obliged to.
This people consider the offer of taking reserves & becoming citizens of the U.S. as of no service to them. They know they are not to be admited to the rights of freemen, or the privilege of their oath; & say, no cherokee, or white man with a cherokee family, can possibly live among such white people as will first settle their country.[109]

[Nov.] 28. The great talk for which the people began to assemble on the 20 Oct was closed [110] yesterday. The U.S. Commissioner proposed to the Cherokees an entire exchange of country, except such as chose to take reserves & come under the government of the U.S. This proposition they unanimously rejected, & continued to reject as often as repeated; arguing that the late treaty might be closed as soon as possible. Nothing was done.[111]

Ard Hoyt, D.S. Butrick, Wm Chamberlin

Brainerd Mission Journal Continued

Dec. 1. Received information by the Agent [Col. Meigs] that a cherokee in the lower part of the nation has an Ossage boy, 9 or 10 years old, who was brought over captive by him on the return of the Cherokees from their expedition against that tribe, a little more than a year ago;[112] —that he was now about to return to the Arkansas, & would leave this boy with us, if any one would go after him. We were also told that in the same family, there was a captive girl, somewhat older than this boy; & that she was a sister of the Osage girl now with us.[113] It was thought probable they might be persuaded to leave both the girl & the boy.

[Dec.] 2. Further inquiry was made respecting these Osage children, & it was thought best to go after them immediately.

[Dec.] 3rd Fa. Hoyt & his Son Milo, set out ~~to go~~ in quest of the little captives.

[Dec.] 12th Fa. H. & his son returned. They had traveled between 2 & 3 hundred miles—lay in the woods three nights—encountered several storms, swam one creek &c—but could not obtain the objects of their pursuit. They found both the children. The girl is indeed Lydia Carters sister, & appears to be about 15. The boy is younger than we expected, perhaps 4 or 5. It was very painful to leave these children to be taken back again to the deep shades of the forest, after being brought so near the light—but nothing could be done to prevent it. The owner of the boy said the Agent had misunderstood him.
In this tour Fa. H. spent 2 nights & a day at Catharine Browns father's. He was received with great cordiality by the whole family, & Catharine's joy was so great, that he says "I felt myself more than paid for the fatigues of the whole journey, by the first evenings opportunity.["] Catharine said it had been very dark times with her since she left Brainerd. All around her were engaged for the riches & pleasures of the world; & because she could not unite with them, as formerly, they were telling her they supposed she thought herself faring good now—that she expected to go to heaven alone—& the like—Her greatest burden was a fear that she should be drawn away from the right path, & at lengths be left to do like these around her. She felt herself too weak to leave the society & instruction of christians, & go into the world alone.

A small roomful of people more than half whites, were collected here for preaching, & gave very good attention. A Cherokee woman wept almost the whole of sermon time.

Sab. Dec. 13. The little company of professors now left at Brainerd were again refreshed at the communion table, which our Lord in great mercy continues to spread for us in this wilderness. Only six communicants, beside the mission family, were present at this time, two of our Cherokee sisters being kept at home by sickness. But though our number were less than on some former occasions, we had the consolation to reflect that none were willingly absent, or excluded for misconduct. ~~& that those present gave satisfactory uncanny evidence of increasing love to the Lord & his people~~. We had a good day—our communion with our Cherokee & African brothers & sisters was sweet, and the little sheaf which the Lord has gathered here appears more & more precious.

[*Dec.*] 25. We were refreshed by a joint letter from our dear brethren at the Choctaw station. We rejoice when they rejoice, & weep when they weep. The Lord has again blessed them with health, & they are going on with their buildings. The Choctaws have held a talk for 20 days with the U.S. Commissioners, & to a man, refuse to give up any of their land.[114]

Br. Chamberlin left us this morning, on a visiting & preaching tour down the river. He has an appointment for the coming sabbath on the Tennessee, 40 miles below Brainerd.

Christmas is a great day among the whites & half-breeds in this country. It has been kept in such a manner, that the cherokees have given it a name which signifies shooting-day. Almost all the slaves have their time from Christmas to the end of the year, & generally spend it in frolicing & drinking. Considering the general abuse of the day by almost all classes of people, we had doubts whether it would be best to take any notice of it; but hearing that a number of blacks were calculating to attend preaching on that day, if there were any, instead of frolicing as usual, we gave public notice of preaching. Several black people, & some of our white & red neighbors attended. A number of the blacks coming in too late for the sermon, we appointed an evening lecture for their instructions. The attention manifested at the evening service induced us to appoint a lecture for the next day.

Sat. [Dec.] 26. About 20 blacks attended with our children to hear preaching. We can scarcely tell how much satisfaction we have taken these two days in teaching this little handful of poor slaves. ~~There is reason to believe several of them are truly of the little ones whom Jesus commands us not to despise.~~

Sab. [Dec.] 27. The little company of Africans were all present again to day, & continued their attention. We hope it will be for their everlasting good, that they have been inclined to leave those diversions of which this people are generally so very fond, to spend so many of their holidays at the feet of Jesus.

One of this company, of whom we entertain a hope that he is truly enlightened by the word & Spirit of God, is soon to be taken over the mississippi: probably before he will have an opportunity to come again to receive instruction from us. He was greatly distressed with the thought that he should probably never see missionaries, or hear preaching again. We exhorted him to put his trust in God, & to live always near the Savior by a prayerful obedience to all his commandments, so far as he knew them; gave him such other instruction as we thought suited to his particular case, & indulged the hope that even by this bondsman the Lord would send some light into the dark regions where he was to be taken. He was greatly comforted when we told him possibly missionaries would be sent into that country, where he would some day see & hear them. The cherokees in general, even the looser part of them, are very willing their slaves should receive religious instruction, for they say it makes them better.

[Dec.] 29. Br. C. returned. He was very kindly received wherever he called, had an attentive audience on the sabbath of about 30 persons, & received as a token of friendship, a number of Christmas-gifts, from different persons on his tour.

There is no place near us where a large audience can be collected. As the people do not live in vilages, but scattered over the country from 2 to 10 miles apart; to collect in any place 20 or 30 who can understand our language, is as much as can be expected.[115] If we could preach in cherokee we think we should have much larger assemblies.

Br. B. went out to day to buy corn. What we raised is nearly spent, & we do not expect our general supply for several weeks.

Sister Anna is just beginning to get about house, after more than three weeks confinement. Her sickness appeared to be in consequence of too hard labor in the kitchen. Sister Chamberlin still continues in a feeble state of health, unable to assist in the labor of the family, or to take charge of the female schollars. Mother Hoyt, with all her bodily infirmities, has been, & still is our main dependence in the female department. What distresses us most is, there is no female able to superintend & keep with the girls while out of school. We see, & very sensibly feel, the want of this. Considering the dark shades of the forest from whence these dear girls have so lately been brot., they do much better, than we could have expected; but they, as well as the boys, need some one with them every hour.

Jan. 1. The old king & one of the principal chiefs, from the southern part of the nation, came to visit the school.[1] They arrived just at evening. Winter evenings our children are collected in one room, where they are exercised in spelling, answering questions, singing &c. When the old king saw the children assembled this evening, he was greatly delighted, & shook hands with them most affectionately. He appeared much pleased during the first exercises, (though he does not understand english) but when they came to the singing, he could not refrain from tears—though evidently endeavoring to repress his feelings, as if ashamed to weep; the furrows of his war-worn cheeks were plentifully watered, & his handkerchief almost constantly applied to dry them. He spoke to the children affectionately, as did also the accompanying chief.

[Jan.] 2. The king & chief visited the school. After the children had passed through their various exercises, the king addressed them in a grave & affectionate manner, sitting: the chief then arose & spoke, as it appeared to us, in a most eloquent & persuasive manner, for some time. By his jestures we supposed he was talking to the children about geting an education at the school,—then dispersing through the nation—doing good through life, & then meeting together above to receive a reward. The children listened with great attention, & most of them were considerably affected. From the children we afterwards learnt that our conjectures respecting the substance of the discourse were correct,—that he told them the missionaries must be good men or they would not be willing to do so much for them without pay; that we knew more than the Indians did, & they must listen to our instructions; keep steady at the school & be obedient untill they had learned all that we wished them to learn; & when they went away from school they must remember & follow the good way they had learned here; if they did so they would do much good to their people while they lived, & when they died they would go above & be happy. After the chief had concluded, the king spoke again to the children for a few minutes, & requested that they might all come round & shake

hands with him, which they did. Both the king & chief then expressed their warmest thanks for the good we were doing to their nation; said they should think much of us, & of the school; & would tell their people every where that it was very good to send their children here where they could learn good things, &c.

This evening Milo Hoyt returned from Knoxville. He brings the agreeable inteligence that sister Hall was delivered of a daughter on the 27 ult. & both mother & daughter were likely to do well.[2]
Milo expected to have brot. down our pork & other articles in a boat, but the cooper having disappointed Br. H. by not making the barrels in which the pork was to be packed, & as Br. H. could now soon be spared to come down himself, he directed Milo to return on horseback, concluding to come himself in the boat after a few days.
Returning, about 30 mi. from Knoxville, Milo's business called him off the main road; in geting on to it again he had to pass several miles through the woods. Within sight of a house, just before he came on to the main road, he was met by a man on horseback, who accosted him as an old acquaintance, & rode up as if he would shake hands; when suddenly seizing his bridle, & turning his horse about, he presented a cocked pistol at his breast, & commanded him, on pain of instant death, to ride back. The boy positively refused to go one step back—the man (being as was supposed afraid to fire his pistol so near the house) then leaped from his horse, drew a large knife, & told the boy to deliver his money, or he would instantly cut his throat; still holding the horse by the bridle. At this critical moment, the boy, giving his horse a stroke with the whip, & twitching the bridle, made his escape. He had with him between four & five hundred dollars.[3]
It is considered much safer traveling any where in the Cherokee nation, than over the line on its borders.

Sab. [Jan.] 3. The place for preaching every second Sabbath in Br. Hicks' neighborhood has by his request, been changed from the house where we formerly met to Br. Hicks' dwelling house. Br. C. fulfilled the appointment there to day. About 25 Cherokees, & a number of black people attended—the meeting was interesting, & Br. C. hopes good may yet be done in that neighborhood.

[Jan.] 4. The corn which was conditionally promised Br. B. does not arrive, & we fear it will not come. Borrowed some of a neighbor, & sent four men to take our perogue up the Tennessee intending one of us to ride up the river untill we could find corn to fill it. They found

the Tennessee had taken a sudden rise, & was so rapid they could not ascend.

[Jan.] 5. Borrowed corn of another neighbor, & threshed what rye we had raised.

[Jan.] 7. Engaged a neighbor who was going up the river on business to go to the man who contracted to deliver us corn some time in this month; & to get him, if possible, to send some down immediately. We consume about 30 bu of corn a week. To live by borrowing would soon drain all our neighbors.

[Jan.] 8. The clothing prepared for our dear children, & forwarded last July, by the pious females of Phil[adelphia] & Lansingburg arrived this day.[4] These clothes have been kept back untill the nakedness of many of our precious charge prepared us to feel the importance & value of the gift. Had we recvd them sooner, we should doubtless have been less thankful for them. O! could these dear sisters know how much good they have done to us, to the children, & to the cause of Christ here, they would feel themselves a thousand times paid for their labor of love. It is not merely assisting us in our labors & cares; it is not merely clothing the naked & relieving the distressed; but it is in fact preaching Christ; & that in a manner calculated to engage the attention, & interest the feelings, of the rudest savage. He beholds his child, the object of his warmest affections, decently & comfortably clad. And who has done this? A ~~christian~~ person whose situation precludes the possibility of his expecting, or receiving, any return from his beneficiary. And what has moved him to do this? His religion—He is a christian. It requires no metaphysical reasoning, no refined logic, to bring the mind to the conclusion, that religion must be good. It is thought christians are not generally aware of the importance of their charities in sending the gospel to the heathens, considered simply as recommending the true religion, & gaining the attention of the untaught, by this act of benevolence. Every dollar given to supply the mission fund, may be considered not merely as going to support missions, but itself becoming a missionary; silently but forcibly declaring, the religion of the gospel as a religion of benevolence, & therefore from that God who "is kind to the unthankful & to the evil."[5]

[Jan.] 15. Hearing that our promised corn would not be down soon, & the Tennessee having fallen, we sent three men with our Perogue after

corn. We expect it will come high to us in this way, but we have no other resource, having lived by borrowing for several days.

Sab. [Jan.] 17. Br. C. preached at Br. Hicks'. The congregation there rather increasing, & people attentive to hear, but no other hopeful appearance.

[Jan.] 18. Bought 60 bu. Corn from a boat in the Tennessee at 75/bushel, by the time we get it home it will cost nearly or quite a dollar.

[Jan.] 21. The three hands who went after corn returned. They have spent 8 days & brought 150 bu. for which they paid 50/bu. The Chickamaugah creek is too low to bring the corn up by water; we shall therefore be under the necessity of hauling it over the high-lands in a waggon.

Sab. [Jan.] 24. There has been so much uniformity in our Sabbath day congregations at Brainerd, for some time past, that we have nothing new worthy of particular notice. They still continue much the same. While there is reason to hope that some are edified every day, there is reason to fear that others are hardening more & more. They attend with decency—hear as if they assented to all as true; & yet remain (like many thoughtless hearers in old congregations) unawakened & unconcerned. But, through the power of divine grace, some appear to hear in a different manner. We have hope for several who have not yet publicly confessed Christ, that they do indeed receive the truth in love.

A slave belonging to one of the old religious men (as their adherents call them) says he should be willing to travel twice as far for the privilege of such meetings, though, he now has to walk 10 miles over a very rough & high mountain, & return the same day. He & his wife of whom we also have hopes, appear much grieved that their Master is about to remove with them to the Arkansas, because they think they shall no more hear preaching &c—He was greatly rejoiced to day when we told him it was possible God would send missionaries there.

[Jan.] 25. We have been looking for Br. Hall to come down with our pork for more than two weeks; our anxiety has been one very great, as we hear nothing from him—concluded if he does not come to-day that we will send Milo Hoyt to inquire after him, & to see to geting down the pork if Br. H. cannot come. (We fear the man who has

engaged the pork to us will dispose of it in some other way if it is not attended to, as we agreed to take it in December.)

[Jan.] 26. Hearing nothing from Br. H. Milo set out early this morning. A Cherokee man who does not know his age, thinks he is about 25, apparently not quite so old, offered himself as a schollar. He spoke english, & his countenance indicated a mind that might admit of improvement; but having the dress & dirty appearance of the most uncultivated part of the tribe, & withal a mind & body for so many years under the influence of these habits, we were sorry to hear him say any thing about entering the school. But after hearing his story, which was somewhat interesting, we thought best to take him on trial. He says he was born & has always lived, near the white people on the borders of Carolina: That when he was small he went to school a short time, learned the letters, & to spell a little. After he left the school he studied his spelling book at times, untill it was worn out; That he had ever since had a desire to learn to read, but being too poor to support himself at school, & having worn out his book, he had given up the hope of geting learning, & nearly forgotten what he once knew. Being at Knoxville last Christmas he saw Br. Hall, & for the first time heard of this school. He there determined he would come, & try to get into this school as soon as he could. He said he was never before in this part of the nation & had been 7 days coming. He readily agreed to our terms of entering & continuing in the school; but said he had no way to get clothes, except by selling his gun, that being all the property he had in the world. He had tried to sell this on the road but could find no one who had the money to pay for it. We had often heard that the people in that part of the nation from which he said he had come, were the most ignorant & uncultivated of any in the whole tribe, & could not tell but he was sent here to obtain light & be the instrument of carrying it back to that corner. His willingness to part with his gun (a piece of property so dear to the Indian) we considered a favorable omen; & agreed to take his gun & pay him for it in clothes as he should want them. With this he was highly pleased; striped off his dirty rags, & we clothed him from the box lately sent from Philadelphia. He says his name is John Arch.[6]

[Jan.] 31. Previous to the administration of the Lords supper, Br. Reese offered for baptism an infant child & three other children, who, untill of late have lived with their mother, a woman not now considered as

his wife, he having parted from her & left the children with her before his conversion.

When separations of this kind take place (which are frequent among this people) the mother is considered as having the sole right to the children, but if she please she can relinquish this right to the father. Since this brother has found the Savior, he has been very desirous to get his children, that he may train them up in the way they should go.[7] A part of them he obtained & offered in baptism some time since. Two of the three oldest baptized at this time he has lately obtained of their mother & taken into his family as his own. One of them, (the oldest,) the mother will not as yet consent to give up entirely; but she has agreed that she shall be educated in the mission family & school, we therefore thought she might be admited to baptism.

With these four children we also baptized Lydia Lowrey, aged about 16. She has been in the school about 12 months, & became a hopeful subject of divine grace last summer. For several months she has been under particular instruction as a candidate for baptism. Her whole deportment since the apparent change has been such as to give increasing evidence that it is real & saving. She will now be considered as a candidate for full communion, in all the ordinances & privileges of the chh of God.

A Cherokee woman, supposed near 70, (the one mentioned in the report of the visiting committee last June as a hopeful convert) this day put herself under our care for special instruction as a candidate for the holy ordinance of baptism.[8]

The wilderness & solitary place is glad for them, & the desert blossoms as the rose.[9] O! how precious are the privileges we enjoy here in this wilderness! We feel that we would not change our place & our employment, for any thing short of that eternal rest which God has prepared for them that love him.

After the above baptisms were administered, the professed followers of Christ, consisting of Black, Red & White, surrounded the table of one common Lord, & found "a feast of fat things."[10]

This day completes 12 months since the first new converts were added to this chh, & it now contains 11 adult members, & 24 baptized children beside the mission family. "The Lord has done great things for us, whereof we are glad".[11]

Feb. 6 [1819]. Br. C. went out this afternoon to meet the appointment for preaching at Br. Hicks' tomorrow. Our regular appointments there have been once in two weeks; this time the appointment was put over to the third week on account of the sacrament.

Sab. [Feb.] 7. Very few attended preaching at Br. Hicks'. Some who saw Br. C. when on his way satturday, said they did not understand the time when he was to come again, & not expecting preaching on this sabbath they had appointed a dance, to which they were then going.[12] They did not feel willing to abstain from this diversion in order to hear the gospel.

[Feb.] 11. Recvd a letter, said to be writen at the request & in behalf of all the people of the district called Battle-Creek, requesting us to send them a schoolmaster to teach their children. This district lies on & near the Tennessee on the north side of the river, about 40 miles below Brainerd.[13]

[Feb.] 12. Agreeable to previous appointment this day was observed as a day of fasting, & humiliation, & prayer, with a particular reference to the state of this people, & their Delegation to the general government.[14]

It was a wet day, & some of the chh members did not attend. We believe they were detained by sickness. We think all that did attend experienced seasonable refreshment from the presence of the Lord, & found it a good day.

The family being assembled at the usual hour of prayer in the morning, the duty, nature & design of fasting were inculcated & explained, & the manner in which a fast day ought to be kept plainly stated. Orders had been previously given that no cooking should be done untill towards evening, all labor of the workmen was stopped, & the children who did not choose to keep a fast strictly were permited to take a piece of such food as had been before prepared. Some of the children abstained entirely, others took a piece.

A special meeting for prayer was appointed to commence soon after family prayer closed, & the children permited but not required to attend. During prayer meeting, which continued untill about 10 ock, we were joined by some of the chh members who had come to spend the day with us. From 10 to 1 the time was spent in conference with these brethren, except a short season allotted to secret prayer. At 1 ock public service was attended. The day appeared short; & it was indeed a good day to our souls, & we hope beneficial to others.

"Wait on the Lord ye trembling saints,
And keep your courage up:
He'll raise your spirit when it faints,
And far exceed your hope."

Having an opportunity this evening to send directly to the people of Battle-Creek, & fearing they would not well understand us if we attempted to write particulars, we sent them a short friendly letter, & told them they might expect a visit from one of us within two or three weeks, & we would then consult with them as to what was best to be done respecting their school.

Feb. 13. Br. B. got on to a horse & rode a few rods for the first time, after a confinement of more than three weeks by an inflamatory rheumatism. There is now a prospect of his speedy recovery.

[Feb.] 15. Milo Hoyt returned & Br. H. with him. The reason Br. H. did not come down with the pork at the time we expected was, he thought the weather was too warm to save the pork if he killed it. Sister H. has suffered much since her confinement, but was more comfortable when he left her. Every individual of the mission family at Brainerd has suffered more or less by sickness this winter, which has been uncommonly warm. At one time the three sisters were all confined at once. But the Lord has been our most gracious helper; & while He lessened our numbers & weakened our strength, He has carried on His own work prosperously—thus shewing that He has no need of help from man.

Through the goodness of God we can now say that we are all able to get about again, & the most feeble to do a little.

Sab. [Feb.] 21. Br. C. fulfilled the appointment for preaching at Br. Hicks' to day. He was well received, but not as many people attended as before they lost the time on account of its being put off one week for the sacrament.

[Feb.] 22. Br. H. set out on his return to Knoxville. It is not expected sister Hall will be able to return soon, but as she has partially recovered. Milo Hoyt was sent to accompany his sister Sarah down.

[Feb.] 25. Having heard that our corn was on the way, we have waited for it untill we have borrowed nearly all that our neighbors have to spare. We now conclude that the report concerning the boat as on the way must have been incorrect; & that it is expedient for one of us to

go immediately to the man who contracted to bring the corn and, if he is not about to bring it, look for it else where.

Fa. H., though in poor health, set out for this purpose.

[Feb.] 27. Fa. H. returned. He had traveled about 20 miles the first day, & found himself unable to proceed. With much pain & difficulty he got back on the third day. Had heard nothing of corn coming for us; but was informed that several corn boats were coming down on the river, & it was expected they would some of them stop for the purpose of selling in this neighborhood. We immediately sent to the river in hope of being able to purchase for our present necessity. In this we were disappointed—the boats had all passed without calling.

While in this suspense respecting our daily bread, not knowing what to do, or in what way the Lord would provide, our spirits were animated by the reception of the annual report of the A.B.C.F.M., & some reviving missionary sermons. The Charge &c, given at the late ordination of the four missionaries, we considered as coming directly from our fathers to us—felt disposed to renew our ordination vows— "Thanked God, & took courage".[15]

March 1. One of our neighbors having a quantity of corn brought to him down the Tennessee, we made application & he cheerfully offered to lend us 100 bu. We expect this will last us about three weeks. And as we had not money sufficient to pay for corn, if one of us should go to the settlements after it, we concluded to wait the return of Milo Hoyt from Knoxville, as he is expected to bring money, & we look for him in a day or two.

Articles of kitchen & table furniture, shoes &c forwarded by the Treasurer last September, & a box of clothing from females in Otsego & its vicinity, arrived in safety. Our heavenly Father knew we had need of all these things, & he has sent them to us. He knows also that we have need of our daily bread, day by day, & we trust he will provide. This box of clothing is in itself valuable, & at this time peculiarly suited to our circumstances & wants.

[March] 4. A boatman called this morning & offered corn for sale. His price was ,75 cents at the boat, which by the time we get it here will be nearly twice as much as we expected to pay for corn; but as this is now the common market price we could not complain. Having brought away but 30 bu. of the 100 we had borrowed, we purchased 130 bu, paid this debt, & expected the remainder would last untill we could probably get a full supply.

Br. C. set out this morning to go to Battle-Creek to talk with the people about commencing a school there.

Milo Hoyt returned from Knoxville with his sister Sarah: both in good health. They left sister H. better; but it was thought not best for her to return at present.

They brought us some money to purchase corn, but not sufficient to obtain a supply for the season if we are obliged to buy at the present price. We hear nothing from the man that agreed to furnish us.

[*March*] 6. Br. C. returned. The people at Battle-creek, though still anxious to have a school, consented to wait untill the return of the Delegates.[16] We had two reasons for advising to this measure. 1st We could not tell what changes might take place respecting their land. If they did not agree to an entire exchange of country, that part contemplated for the school might be given up as the portion of the emigrants, & this might render it advisable to have the school in another place. 2nd We had no one but Br. Butrick that could now take charge of the school, & we were unwilling to hinder him in the study of the language, except from necessity.

Br. B. went to meet the stated appointment for preaching at Br Hicks' tomorrow.

[*March*] 8. Br. C. set out for the settlements to look for corn. Br. B. returned. He found the little congregation at Br. Hicks' attentive as usual—between 30 & 40 present.

[*March*] 13. Br. C. returned. His journey had been somewhat fatiguing. The day previous to his arrival had been peculiarly so on account of his missing his path in the woods, but for this he might have got home yesterday with ease.

He did not see the man who had engaged the corn; but was told that he had left orders to sell the corn of his own raising, which was at first designed for us, & had gone about 60 m. farther up the river after corn which he had purchased to meet his contract with us, & was everyday expected on his return with the corn.

[*March*] 22. Hearing nothing from the expected corn, & having but little hope of receiving it, Br. B. went out for the purpose of purchasing elsewhere if this is not coming.

[*March*] 23. The man who had contracted to deliver our corn, together with wheat & rye, at the mission house, came & stated that he had brought the grain down to the mouth of the creek, (which is by water 12 or 15 miles from the mission house) but that it was impossible for him to bring it up the creek, having, as he said, from necessity, engaged to discharge his hand as soon as they got the boat into the creek. The contractor tells of many difficulties, labor & hindrances— says he has done every thing in his power; & if we should give him the price agreed upon for the grain delivered here & take it at the boat where it now is, he should be a great looser [loser] by the bargain. He states further, that he forwarded for us 200 bu. corn to relieve us in our distress by a boat that was going farther down the river, with a letter stating his difficulties & prospects; & that he supposed we had received this untill when on his way down, he heard that the boat containing the 200 bu., had unintentionally passed us in the night, & did not discover the mistake untill it was too late to leave the corn within our reach. In consequence of this failure the corn he has will fall 200 bu. short of what he engaged us. He pleads that we will excuse him from geting the grain up the creek on account of his many past difficulties & present embarrassments—alleging that he had no conception of the difficulty of ascending the creek with the grain untill since his arrival, & that he could have sold the grain at the price we were to give, without moving it out of the crib.

We also could plead difficulties & losses in consequence of his failure. But still he thought he ought to be excused, as his failure was owing entirely to the uncommon drought & its consequences. We did not know what duty or expedience would require in respect to an abatement from the contract; but the grain we must have, & showed paid the expense of geting it up the creek, there was no alternative but to see to geting it up ourselves. On the whole, to make every thing easy, we agreed to pay the stipulated price, & take the grain where it is, he giving us the boat; which cost 150 dollars. To bring the grain up the creek we expect will cost about 8 days work to every 100 bu. There is 800 bu. corn, & nearly 300 bu. wheat & rye. 88 days work to be performed in this country where help is so scarce, and just at the season of puting in our spring crop; will be to us a very serious inconvenience, & we fear a great loss to the institution in our next crop, but necessity is laid upon us.

There is plenty of good land around us, & we have full liberty to improve as much as may be necessary for the support of the school. Every thing we get from Tennessee might be raised here with as little labor as there if the land was once cleared & fenced. The expense of geting on our supplies this year would have opened & fenced a very large field, if it had been applied for that purpose. If we had a small company of our brethren from the north to assist in clearing a farm here, we might hope soon to be able to live without this great expense and trouble of geting our bread & meat from abroad.

Catharine Browns father brought her & commited her to our care untill her education should be completed; intending to set out with the remainder of the family for the Arkansas immediately on his return. She can assign no external cause for this change in her father's mind & conduct concerning her; but ascribes it all to the special providence of God, & considers it as an evident answer to fervent believing prayer. The time drew near for their departure—she felt that it would not be for the best that she should go, & that God could change the minds of her parents & make them willing to leave her. That their minds might be thus changed was the burden of her prayers, & she felt, (particularly one evening) that the Lord would grant her request; & rose from her knees with a degree of assurance that she should be sent back to Brainerd. Returning to the house, & entering the room where her father & mother were sitting by themselves, he addressed her to the following effect. "Kate, we know you feel very bad about leaving the missionaries & going with us to the Arkansas—we have been talking about it—we pitty you, & have concluded that you may go back."

How unsearchable are the ways of God![17] We thought it a very afflicting providence that this lamb should be snatched from the fold of Christ, to go, as we thought, where she would be exposed to be devoured by wolves: & were ready to say in our hearts, not so, when her father required her to go with him. But in this very way God has given her an opportunity to set an example of filial obedience, by submiting to the authority of a father in the most painful requisition, & of manifesting her love to the Savior in her willingness to forsake all for him, & at the same time granted her the object of her pious & fervent desire.

[*March*] 24 {Br. B. returning from his expedition after corn, arrived on the opposite bank of the Chickamaugah just after dark. He had rode about 40 m, swam two creeks, eat nothing since breakfast, & we had no means of geting him over the creek or conveying to him food for himself or horse.

The highwater had broken & carried off our small canoe, the large one was down the creek after corn, & the stream was so rapid that it was thought unsafe to attempt swimming it, especially with a timid horse in the night. After much agitation, & various unsuccessful plans to get him over, it was concluded that he must spend the night there. His clothes were wet, the ground filled with water, the weather cold, & he had no blanket except a small one which had been used under his saddle. To remain in this situation thro the night without fire, would not only be very uncomfortable, but endanger health if not life, as he had scarcely recovered from a severe turn of inflamatory rheumatism. Various attempts were made by the strongest men, to throw a brand of fire to him, but without success. In this dilemma, an indian boy proposed to fasten a piece of lighted spunk to an arrow & shoot it over.[18] This plan was immediately adopted, & fire very readily sent over to him. Our joy on this success was but transient, for no fuel could be found except green trees & bushes & what had been soaked in the water, so that all his attempts to kindle a fire failed. We built a fire on our side of the creek, which, though it could afford him no heat, served to render the darkness of the night less gloomy, & to keep off the wolves which were howling in numbers near him. Some of us kept watch to prevent his sleeping too long at a time, & hands were dispatched down the creek to get a canoe to bring him over.

By occasionally taking a little rest in sleep, & walking the remainder of the time, he kept the use of his limbs, tho, at times they were nearly stiffened with the cold. After light his horse was turned in & swam the creek safely, but not without considerable difficulty—and about sunrise we succeeded in geting Br. B. over.

His health was so mercifully preserved that no evil consequence followed.}

Apl. 2nd Br. & Sis. Hall returned. They came by water. Sister thinks her health has rather improved than otherwise by the journey.

[*April*] 12. Br. Hicks, having a few days since returned from the seat of government, made us a visit.

This brother, as might be expected, is much engaged for the instruction of his people. While an entire exchange of country was thought of as a measure they might be pressed to adopt, his spirit was often greatly born down with discouragement; but since they have succeeded in geting a part of their country guaranteed to them anew, & so many christian people are engaged for their instruction, that hope which was almost expiring is raised to confident expectation. His heart is overflowing with joy, gratitude, & praise to God; whom he is ever ready to acknowledge as "the giver of every good & perfect gift".[19]

In addition to the plan of introducing pious school-masters to the exclusion of all irreligious & immoral men of that profession, he is much engaged to introduce pious mechanics—such as Blacksmiths, Tanners, shoemakers, wheelwrights, &c. Men of this description, well acquainted with their business, on being recommended to the chiefs by some missionary society in which they have confidence, might be admited under circumstances very favorable. {They might have apprentice boys on good terms, receive a good price & merely pay for their work, & have the priviledge of improving as much good land as they can consistent with this business, not free, with the advantage of keeping cattle & hogs as many as they please.}

The absolute necessity of blacksmiths, in particular, has induced them to permit some of their trade to come in who are much more expert at the whiskey bottle than the anvil & who seldom or never speak of the true God & Savior but by profaning his name. These, Br. Hicks says, are a public nuisance; but unless they can get better men in their places, they cannot clear the country of them, for the people must have blacksmiths. Almost all the men of influence in the nation, perhaps we might say all, are pressing the people to attend more to agriculture, assuring them that this is the only way they can live & keep their country.[20] As this business increases there will be a necessity of increasing the numbers of mechanics, particularly of Blacksmiths.

Br. Hicks hopes their christian friends, who are doing so much for them by sending religious teachers, will also be made acquainted with their wants as it respects mechanics, & send them help in this line also.

[April] 17. Br. B. went down to Br. Hicks' in order to fulfill the appointment for preaching there tomorrow. While there, the beast he rode, which was one of our most valuable horses for riding, died—{supposed to have been killed by batts.}

[April] 19. From Br. H.'s br. B. went to Springplace to visit our dear friends there, & attend to certain proposals for a school at Yoo-killogee [Oothcaloga]. Finding that a Cherokee in that settlement was expected soon to join the chh at Springplace, he thought the United Brethren might possibly wish to establish a school there. This he mentioned to Fa. Gambold, & concluded to wait till the arrival of the

U. Brethren, who are expected soon to the assistance of Fa. Gambold before making any preparations for a school at Yukillogee [Oothcaloga].[21] {We had a little time before ignorantly admited to our school, a boy who had been dismissed from Springplace for bad conduct. Br. B. thought Fa & Ma Gambold, not knowing our ignorance of the fact of his dismission when we received him, had thought we had done wrong.}

The brethren at Springplace together with Br. Hicks, expressed their desire that we should have a sepparate school for the girls at Brainerd, to be taught by one or two of the sisters.[22]

[April] 22. In a ~~joint~~ meeting of the brethren for business, Resolved, that we receive no schollars dismissed from a school of the United Brethren for improper conduct, unless by a writen request from the directors of that school: and that this resolution be made known to the chiefs at the next Council.

Sab. [April] 25. The Rev. Messrs. Saunders & Modderwall, missionaries from the General Assembly, & Mr. Scott, a lay brother from Georgia, called this morning & kept sabbath with us. Mr. Saunders preached in the morning, Mr. Modderwall lectured at evening.

We had reason to thank the Lord for the edifying discourses of these brethren; & for their refreshing company & conversation. We trust the scene will be gratefuly remembered in eternity.

[April] 26. Our visiting brethren, being in haste to pursue their journey, left us early this morning, leaving many tokens of their brotherly love & warm attachment to the cause of missions. May the Lord make them instrumental of much good wherever they may be, as they have been here, & give us grateful hearts for this & the many other like precious seasons of communion & fellowship with his servants; which he is granting us in this wilderness.

May 4. Got up the last of our grain from the boat.

In consequence of the unsteady state of the creek, it being sometimes to high & then again to low, & the expense of keeping one man so long taking care of the boat, it has cost more to get up this grain than was at first expected.

[May] 7. The Cherokee woman mentioned in our journal of Dec. 12, as somewhat affected under preaching at Catharine Brown's fathers came to us, a distance of 120 miles, to hear (as she says,) more about the Savior.

It appears that soon after her first impressions, she sent for Catharine to read & explain the bible to her, & to pray with her: and before Catharine came away she told her she intended to come here for further instruction as soon as she could.

Ard Hoyt, D.S. Butrick,
Moody Hall, Wm Chamberlin

Continuation of mission journal Brainerd.

May 11, 1819. By appointment of the brethren Father Hoyt attended the national Talk & Council. This Talk was for the purpose of making known to the people what the Delegates had done at Washington [the Federal Capital] &c.—The success of this delegation has raised the hopes of the nation. They feel, more than ever, anxious to make improvement; & are convinced that the instruction of their children is very important for this end. The Missionary [Herald] is received & treated as an old tried friend.

Dr. Worcester's parting Address to the Delegates when at Washington was read in open council, & interpreted as read.[23] All appeared much pleased with the Address; & as the way of their improvement was pointed out, & the blessings would follow described, all seemed to say, we will follow this advice, & shall experience this good.

They want mechanics & school-masters; & wish to have them come from one of the two societies that have already begun to help them, as they say they are acquainted with these, & can trust the men they will send.

Application was made for local schools in several places; but as we can establish but one at present, it was thought best that this should be somewhere in Etowee [Etowah] district, & that we should some of us go & select the place.

[May] 12. On receiving a letter from the Rev. D.A. Sherman, informing us that a draft we sold in Knoxville had not been honored, a meeting of the brethren was called.[24]

At said meeting resolved that Fa. H. go to Knoxville without delay, & attend to this business.

[May] 20. Fa. H. returned from Knoxville. The cause of our draft being at first refused, was a mistake in the Clerk of the Bank entering our

deposit in a wrong name. The mistake had been discovered, & the draft honored.

On his return from Knoxville Fa. H. visited the Agent Col^n Meigs. He found him more than ever engaged for the instruction of the natives.

The Agent had received instructions to pay the balance of our acc^t for expense in building so far as it had been rendered; & he did not doubt but other accounts for necessary expense in building, either additions to the present establishment, or for a local school, would be allowed when presented; but he did not think his instruction authorized him to put up more buildings without first consulting the Sec. of war. He advised, however, that, if we should think best on visiting the people in Etowee, to commence buildings immediately for a school there, that we proceed without delay, stating to him our reason for so doing. These reasons he would transmit to the Sec. with the expectation that he should be directed to pay the expense.[25]

May 24. Resolved, that it is expedient for one or two of the brethren to go as soon as may be convenient, visit the people at & about Etowee and see what can be done & do what they shall think expedient, relative to a local school there, so far as shall be agreeable to instructions received from the Prud. Com.

Resolved that Father Hoyt & Brother Hall go.

Resolved that measures be taken to obtain a riding horse as soon as may be convenient.

[May] 27. The President [James Monroe], accompanied by Gen. Gaines & Lady, stopped to visit the school.[26]

We had expected the President would call as he passed, but thought we should hear of his approach in time to make a little preparation, & to meet & escort him in: but so silent was his approach that we had no information of his having left Georgia, untill he was announced as at the door.[27]

In thus taking us by surprise he had an opportunity of seeing us in our every-day dress, & observing how the concerns of the family & school were managed when we were alone: & perhaps it was best on the whole that he should have this view of us. If we had tried to appear a little better than common, we might only have made it worse.

He looked at the buildings & farm, visited the school, & asked questions in the most unaffected & familliar manner: & was pleased to express his approbation of the plan of instruction; particularly as the children were taken into the family, taught to work &c. He thought this the best, & perhaps the only way to civilize & christianize the indians: and assured us he was well pleased with the conduct & improvement of the children.

We had just put up, & were about finishing a log cabbin for the use of the girls. He said that such buildings were not good enough, & advised that we put another kind of building in place of this; that we make it a good two-story house, with brick or stone chimneys, glass windows, &c, & that it be done at public expense. He also observed, that after this was done, it might perhaps be thought best to build another of the same description for the boys; but we would do this first.

Giving us a letter directed to the Agent, he observed, I have writen to him to pay the balance of your account, for what you have expended on these buildings; & also to defray the expense of the house you are now about to build—make you a good house, having due regard to economy.[28]

[May] 28. The President left us this morning after breakfast. Before his departure he, in the kindest manner, requested Fa. H. to write to him unofficially from time to time, & give him a free & particular statement of the concerns of the mission, & of our wants.

We feel ourselves under great obligations of gratitude to the supreme giver of all good, & to the chief magistrate of our nation, for this friendly visit.

[May] 29. Rev. Erastus Root, with his wife, on a missionary tour from Georgia through the western states, called on us. Br. B. went to fulfill the appointment at Br. Hicks'. The Grandfather, Grandmother & mother of two of our girls came & expressed great dissatisfaction that one of the girls had been whiped. They took them both away though one was very unwilling to go, & both said they would choose to stay.[29]

Sab. [May] 30. Br. Root preached. Br. B. returned at evening. He found a good number of Cherokees assembled, & they were attentive to the word.

[May] 31. Fa. Hoyt & Br. Hall set out for Etowee, to make arrangements for a local school.

Having submitted our difference with the Miller to arbitrators, & they having decided that we pay no part of his demand, & that he leave

the premises by the 18th of June next, & he, on that account requesting us to take the mill immediately, therefore
Resolved, that we release Mr. Robison the miller, from any further charge of the mill.
Resolved that we endeavor to purchase from Mr. J. Ross the 40 bu, of corn we borrowed of him.

June 1. Brother & Sister Root left us. We feel ourselves under great obligations of gratitude to our blessed Lord for sending this dear brother & sister to visit us. We have been refreshed by their company. Br. B. received a heavy fall from a building he was helping to raise. No bones were broken, & he did not sustain so great an injury as was at first apprehended. He is confined to the house, & probably will be for several days, if not weeks.

[June] 7. The Rev. Job P. Vinal & Rev. Epaphras Chapman, Licenciates on an exploring mission under direction of the United Foreign Mission Society, called on us.[30] They are instructed "to perform an exploring tour among the Indians on the western side of the mississippi (chiefly between Raccoon & Red Rivers) with a view to ascertain whether a mission can be introduced among them, & to select the most suitable spot for commencing the opperations." They are restricted to no tribe, & are expected to bring back information which will govern the ultimate decisions of the Board respecting the spot where to begin, but are to bear in mind that the board have their eye particularly on the Cherokees upon the Arkansas, & have voted to attempt a mission there.

[June] 8. Mr. Isaac Fisk & Dr. Wm W. Pride, on their way to join the brethren at Elliot, arrived, in good health.[31]
Fa. H. & Br. H. returned. An ample field for opperation appears to be opened in that section of the nation. They determined on the place for a local school, & made arrangements for puting up the necessary buildings. They gave short notice of preaching on the Sabbath near where the buildings are to be erected. About 80 persons assembled, & gave good attention. This place is about 65 miles Southeast from Brainerd, near the waggon road that leads to Georgia.[32] Springplace will afford a halfway house between Brainerd & the new school.

[June] 11. A lecture preparatory to the Lords supper was preached by Br. Chapman.

Mr. Job Bird of Putnam County, Georgia; aged 52, traveling through the nation with his family, deceased last evening, about 7 miles from this place.

By request of the widow, his remains were this day deposited in our burying ground.

June 12. Col.ⁿ George Gillespie, the farmer who offered last year to supply the establishment constantly with meat & grain, having called to see if we could agree for another year, & now offering what we need for the present, wishes to know before he gives his terms how much we shall need. Therefore the brethren gave it as their opinion that we shall want in addition to what we now have, 300 bu, corn this summer—and for another year 1500 bu, Corn, 300 Rye, 200 of wheat, & 8000 lb pork. And that we receive Col.ⁿ Gillespie's proposals but do not at this time complete the contract with him, except for the corn that is wanted immediately.[33]

Resolved that we cover the barn we are now building with long shingles.

Sab. [June] 13. Br. Vinal preached. Our aged Cherokee sister, Anna McDonald, having given satisfactory evidence of her knowledge to discern the Lords body & of her faith to feed upon him, was admited to full communion.[34] The sacrament of the Lords supper was then administered to 23 communicants, all members of this chh, except the 4 visiting brethren. Br. Chapman lectured at evening. We have great cause to bless our God & Savior for this precious season.

[June] 14. Resolved that Fa. H. prepare a joint letter to the Cor. Sec. & that Br. H. prepare one for the brethren at Elliot. Br. B. being under the necessity of going from home this morning, voted to adjourn this meeting to thursday next.

June 16. In regular chh meeting, two of our schollars, viz. Mary Burns, aged about 16 & Nancy Melton, aged about 15, offered themselves for, & were examined & received, as candidates for baptism.[35]

Doings of the brethren in meetings for business. Our miller proving to be a profane & intemperate man, & we having told him that we could not, on that account, employ him after the expiration of the term for which he is engaged, demanded that we give him the privilege of continuing with his family where he now is untill after next corn harvest, or pay him what he considered damage on account of his not having the privilege of raising a crop of corn. We considered this demand altogether unreasonable, but thought if we dismissed him without paying any attention to it, he might, by misrepresentation, injure us in the view of our neighbors.

Therefore, Resolved, that Br. H. make a statement of the circumstances to our most influential neighbors, & get their advise.

June 17. Our dear brethren Vinal & Chapman left us to pursue their long journey to the west. Our communion has been sweet, & parting painful. May the God of Israel go with them, & make their way prosperous.

As sister Chamberlin expects soon to be confined, & there is no help of the faculty to [be] obtained here the brethren thought it duty for Dr. Pride to delay his journey for the purpose of rendering the necessary assistance.

This oppinion being expressed to the two brethren, they concluded to tarry with us for the present, though they are very anxious to get to Elliot, the place of their destination; & if they went on at this time, according to their first arrangement, might have the company of Brs. V. & C. most if not all the way.

Met according to adjournment.

Resolved, that considering the case of sister Chamberlin we think it the duty of Br's. Pride & Fisk to continue with us a few days longer; & that they be invited so to do.

Having received, (a present to this establishment) the History of the United Brethren's missions in North America from the Rev. Mr. Van Vleck.

Resolved that a letter of thanks be writen to him, & that Fa. Hoyt write this letter.

~~Resolved that Br. Hall pay all necessary attention to the buildings &c.~~

Resolved that we approve of what Fa. Hoyt & Br. Hall have done relative to begining a school near Etowee at a place called Talloney that Br. Hall pay all necessary attention to the buildings &c at the place, and therefore that he be released from his particular charge as steward of this establishment.

In view of a branch of this school soon to be established, Resolved, that no individual or individuals of the mission family take any measures, either directly or indirectly, to persuade or cause any member of this school to leave this school & go to another unless requested or authorized to do so by a vote of the brethren in a regular meeting for business.

Resolved, that no schollar, dismissed from this school for bad conduct, shall be received at any branch school, & also that no schollar, dismissed from any branch school for bad conduct, shall be received at this without a mutual understanding of the managers.

Considering the great increase of our cares and labors, both in the male & female departments; & that no additional help is sent on (though long expected) Therefore, before signing these minutes, we have agreed to make it a special subject of prayer that our dear Savior will be pleased to incline the hearts of some dear faithful brothers & Sisters to offer themselves to the Prud. Com., and that they may be sent out for our assistance.

Ard Hoyt, Moody Hall, Wm Chamberlin

N.B. As Br. B is to preach tomorrow at Br. Hicks he wished to go before the above resolutions &c could be coppied, he requested us to mention that this is the reason why his name is not with ours on this, as in the letter writen this day & signed before his departure.

Journal of Mission at Brainerd

1819

June 21. In meeting for business the following resolutions were passed viz.

Resolved, That we write to the Agent (Colⁿ Meigs) informing him what we had done respecting a school at Taloney, & making the necessary inquiries respecting aid from government in puting up buildings there—& that Fa. Hoyt prepare this letter.

Resolved, that inquiry be made immediately respecting the best way to procure materials for building the house ordered by the President for the girls.

Resolved, that Br. Chamberlin prepare a letter to the Treasurer stating the articles that are wanted for the use of the school.

[June] 28. In meeting for business Resolved, that Br. Hall, on his tour to the Agency &c, endeavor to engage Mr. Joseph Utter to make brick for the girls house.

Resolved, that Br. Hall take the sorrel horse, lately bought, for the use of the school at Taloney, & also the little waggon.

July 4. We have renewed cause to sing of the mercies of our covenant God. Sister Chamberlin, whose confinement has been looked for several weeks, was this day safely delivered of a daughter. Mother & child both likely to do well.[36]
We think we shall not be blamed for detaining Dr. Pride to assist on this occassion by any who know how much he was needed.

[July] 6. Brs. Fisk & Pride left us to pursue their journey to Elliot. May the God in whom Elliot trusted make their way prosperous & prepare them & us to meet again in this or a better world. Our communion with them has been sweet & parting painful. Brethren met for business. Br. Hall having considered his relation to this mission family dissolved by his appointment to take charge of the local school now contemplated, did not attend.
Resolved, that we finish 5 acres of the clearing now begun, & prepare it for turnips. Adjourned till tomorrow morning.

[July] 7. In meeting for business Resolved that a joint letter be writen to the Corresponding Sec. respecting an usher to assist in the school & in taking charge of the boys out of school, & that Br. Chamberlin prepare this letter.

[July] 12. In meeting for business Resolved that we let Br. Hall have fifty dollars in addition to the fifty-seven he has already taken, for the school at Talloney.
The question was asked, Shall we send to the Agency for money & to Col^n Gilespie for corn. Resolved that we wait for a few days & if the corn does not come it will be necessary to send.

July 14. The boat which was expected with 300 bu. corn arrived at the mouth of the Chickamaugah with 212 bu. The man with whom we agreed for the corn writes that when he purchased the boat he thought it sufficient to bring the 300 bu. but on trial thought it not safe to venture more than 212 bu. The Creek being to low to bring the corn up by water & there being no place of depositing where the boat lay, we were obliged to take it down the river about 4 miles to Mr. Ross' Warehouse.

[July] 19. The boat in which our corn came being old; & the men who were taking it to the ware house probably very negligent, running upon a sand bar the boat sprung a leak, & sunk, & most of the corn got wet. In this hot country wet corn spoils very quick in the summer. Twenty or thirty bushels in the bottom of the boat was entirely

spoiled, & more than twice that quantity so injured that it will not do for bread—We do not expect more than half the corn will in any way do to eat; & to receive it as well as we have has cost us in geting it out of the water, spreading, drying &c, about 11 days work; & we now have to haul it about 7 miles over a very tedious hill or mountain. Every renewed difficulty & loss of this kind, in obtaining supplies from the Tennessee farmer, more clearly evinces the importance of raising them here.

[July] 20. Three days ago the father of the fine full-blooded boy whom we called Jeremiah Evarts, came with Jeremiah & a younger son.[37] It is now about 10 months since he took Jer^h home on a visit expecting to return him in six weeks. He remained with us untill this morning saying little, but attentively observing every thing that was done. This morning he told us he wished to leave his two sons with us untill they were well learned, & should only want them to go home on a visit once a year: adding that he had been brought up in ignorance himself, & once thought as he had but little time to live he would spend it in idleness, drinking, frolicing, &c—but finding this to be a bad way he had left it & gone to work which he found a much better way to live. He did not wish his sons to be brought up the way he had been, or to do as he had done. He was now to old to go to school himself & learn but he thought if his sons were instructed they might teach him, & he would be glad to learn from them.

The reason he did not bring Jer^h back at the time appointed was, he was told he could not learn so fast here where there were so many in school as where there were but a few, & as he wanted his son to learn as fast as possible he had assisted in making up a small school near home. But he soon found his son who was becoming a better boy when here was geting worse there, but having engaged him in that school he could not get him out at once. When he talked of bringing him back here, he was told that we kept the boys to work in the field & that was no way to learn them. On the whole he had concluded to come with his two sons & stay till he could see for himself. That he had been looking at every thing & was well pleased with the whole. Observing in a particular manner that it was very good for them to work a part of the day, for he wanted his boys to work for a living when they left school, & if they worked none here they would not know how. These ideas were communicated by an interpreter—he speaks no English.

What the father observed in respect to the boy's loosing in morals, he might also have seen in respect to letters, if he had been learned himself. This boy, though one of our most promising schollars in learning & behavior has lost much in both since he left us. We hope the time will soon come when this people can no longer be imposed upon by these sham school-masters who, by idleness or disipation, have been driven from civilized society to be a nuisance among the Indians.

[July] 22. Meeting for business. Br. Hall having been to Taloney & returned requested the brethren here to advise respecting his purchasing a farm for the use of the school in that place.
After long conference with Br. Hall on the subject we unanimously advised that the farm should not be purchased untill the mind of the Prud. Com. could be known on the subject.

[July] 23. Br. B. set out with Br. H. to go to Taloney.

[July] 26. A sepparate school for the females was commenced under the particular charge of Sis. Sarah [Hoyt]. This school would have been in opperation sooner, but we had no building for the purpose. The one now occupied is only a temporary log cabbin, but we hope it will answer the purpose untill a house can be built according to the Presidents directions.
We think it highly expedient that a saw-mill should be errected in this vicinity before this building is put up; & have concluded to put off this building for the present, in hope that a mill will soon be built. Our neighbor, Mr. John Ross, would build one immediately on the nearest mill seat to the establishment if he could obtain workmen.

[July] 28. Brs. B. & H. returned from Taloney.

[July] 29. Meeting for business. Br. Hall being invited came in.
Br. Butrick stated what he had seen & heard in relation to the school at Taloney. Whereupon Resolved,
That we advise Br. Hall to proceed with that school according to the original plan as proposed to the Prud. Com. viz. That he procure, by building or otherwise, a cheap cabbin for himself & wife, and, as soon as a school house can be in readiness, commence a school with & for the children of that neighborhood, & such as may at the expense of their parents be boarded in that neighborhood, & that he be at no expense for buying or clearing land, except for a garden spot, without special directions from the Com. And that if he take any children into

his family to board, the number should be small, not exceeding the number proposed to the Com. And furthermore, should Br. Hall decline this, we advise that he, for the present, teach the boys school here, & that Br. Chamberlin go & commence the school at Taloney on the above plan.

Our reasons for the above advise are,

1st In our remarks to the Com. respecting local schools, we said, The teacher may have a garden from which he can receive some support, or if the Board think proper to send a missionary farmer to each of these schools, he can support his own & the teachers family. Whether the Com. expect the teacher at Taloney to have a garden only, & receive what support he can from that, or whether they expect to send a farmer to support the teacher we know not. Therefore, we cannot advise to purchase a farm at present, especially as we think a convenient place may be had for a house & garden, & that a farm, if the Com. advise to purchase one, can be obtained to as good advantage, hereafter as now.

2nd We also stated to the Com. that log cabbins, of little expense, would answer every purpose for these local schools. We therefore cannot advise to errect buildings of considerable expense, without further instructions from the Com.

3rd We believe if a teacher should go to Talloney according to the above advice, & be faithful to his charge, it would not be more than 3 or 4 years before the Cherokees themselves would support him.

4th Unless the health of Br. & Sis. Hall should be much better than it has been the year past, we think he would not be able to do more than attend faithfully the school, congregation & a garden.

5th When the subject of another school was mentioned to the President He said, We will first erect all the necessary buildings here—get this school into complete opperation, & make a full experiment here. If we succeed we may then think of more schools as circumstances may justify the expense—but at present it will be best to confine our opperations here, or words to that effect. We felt a delicacy in proceeding even on the small scale, after this declaration of the President; but thought, as he had not time then to hear a full statement of our views respecting local schools & had taken a sketch of this from us on paper for further consideration, the circumstances of our having previously pledged ourselves to the natives of one such school, would justify us in the eye of the President for making the trifling expense then contemplated. But if we should proceed on the enlarged plan, & ask government to pay the expense of the buildings, or pay the expense out of the society's fund without asking government it might tend to lessen if not destroy the confidence of the President, & in the end be a great injury to the cause.

6th If we were sure the business could be satisfactorily arranged with the Com. & with the President, we thought there was danger of exciting unpleasant feelings, if not jealousness, on the part of the natives themselves, if a farm should be purchased, a stock collected &c at that place.

We had told the natives that we could not at present give them another school on the plan of the one at Chickamaugah: but if they desired it we would furnish a teacher for some place where the children could board at home.

In selecting the place for the school now contemplated, this plan of the school was kept distinctly in view, & the natives understood that only a small piece of land would be wanted.

They said if we wanted to improve land & keep stock, they could select a much better place—mentioning several, particularly one about 6 or 7 miles from this place where there was plenty of good land, & a good range for cattle. But if one could do little more than to teach such children as could be boarded by their parents, & did not want a farm, this would be the best place.

As nearly or quite all the good land in this neighborhood is improved by men who value property, & as they think much of the range for their cattle, which is already to scanty for them, we think, if they should now for the sake of the school, consent to have us occupy a farm & keep stock there, they might look with a jealous eye on one who should have a stock to eat what they wanted for their own cattle, & be raising crops of grain on land which they themselves wished to occupy: and instead of feeling under obligations for the school, they would probably think the teacher under obligation to them.

July 31. There are now 83 schollars belonging to the school. 50 boys & 33 girls. Among these are 4 or 5 besides those that have been admitted to the chh & as candidates for baptism, who have serious impressions which we hope may be lasting.

The Prud. Comm. & all acquainted with our circumstances
will see how much we need their prayers.

Ard Hoyt, D.S. Butrick, Wm Chamberlin

Journal of the mission at Brainerd Continued

1819

August 4. We were greatly surprised on missing one of the schollars this morning & to learn that he went off the evening before & had not been seen since.[38] This appeared the more strange as he was very steady in his habits, had attained the age of manhood; & might have gone openly at any time. It was very painful to think he had left us in this manner, as he had appeared much attached to us, was seriously inclined, & we had hoped savingly converted to God.

In the most diligent inquiry we could find no cause for this abrupt departure, except that some of the boys had accused him of stealing a peach, which, it was said appeared to hurt his feelings, & had excited a little warmth: though we could not learn that he had said any thing more to his accusers than that the charge was false, & that he would not do such a thing for a thousand peaches.

About school time in the morning, to our renewed surprise, he came in, with a serene & pleasant countenance, & seemed to suppose he could not have been missed. On being asked the cause of his absence he said he did not think as we should miss him—that his heart got bad when they accused him of stealing a peach—& the Good Spirit went away from him—& he had been out to pray & seek his God—His very countenance indicated that his all night prayer had been heard & answered—On being asked if he had found relief, he answered Yes: & in the afternoon conference he spoke feelingly of the peace of mind he then enjoyed.

[*Aug.*] 6*th* Mr. Alfred Wright, a licensed preacher, on a mission from the South Carolina Presbyterian & Congregational Missionary Society, called on us.[39]

As the next Sabbath was our communion season, we constrained him to stay & preach to our little flock.

August 7. Preparatory Lecture by Mr. Wright.

We learn that the Cherokees who had the little Osage boy did not go to the Arkansas last winter as was expected, & it is thought probable will not go at all: we also learn that the boy has been sold to a white man, an intruder in the nation.

Br. C. in the tour which he is soon to make in that part of the nation will inquire after the boy.

Sab. [Aug.] 8. 8. Mr. Wright preached. Br. Chamberlin's infant, called Catharine Brown, was baptized. Our little company of professors which the Lord hath gathered in this wilderness, then surrounded the table of our Lord—none were absent except one sister who was kept at home by a sick child.

Love to God & his people appear to increase in all the new converts: & our souls were fed with living bread. O how unworthy are we who are called missionaries of these abundant mercies!

[Aug.] 9. Our dear brother Wright took an affectionate leave of us this morning to prosecute his mission in East Tennessee. May the Lord go with him, & bless his labors there.

From the commencement of the school many parents have fixed on this season of the year to take their children home to visit, it being a time when green corn & watermelons are plenty—a sort of feasting time with many among this people—We therefore thought best to have something like a vacation at this time, & give liberty for all the children to visit their friends, if they choose, for three weeks. In consequence of this arrangement, Br. Chamberlin appointed a visiting & preaching tour to the western part of the nation, keeping down by the Tennessee river. For this purpose he left us to day expecting to be gone two or three weeks, & to go nearly or quite to the west line of the Cherokees. Catharine Brown will go with him as far as her fathers, which is about 100 miles, & nearly as far as he expects to go.

It appears that notwithstanding the general leave to go home, from 20 to 30 of the children will continue with us, & we expect to keep the school regularly for them; as we think it will not do to urge them away or to suffer them to continue here without a regular school.

[Aug.] 19. Raised the barn; which is 36 feet by 40, 14 feet posts.

We were under considerable apprehensions that this barn would not be raised without injury to some one, as those who assisted were entirely unacquainted with puting up a frame, & most of them had perhaps never seen one of this kind—The workmen themselves had never assisted in framing or raising a barn. In geting the timber, laying off the frame &c, Br. C. assisted as master workman. There being no mechanic to be found who understood the business.

Our reasons for attempting a frame rather than a log barn, under these circumstances were; a log barn at the best is but a poor thing, & will soon rot down & we had put up so many log buildings on this place that we should have been obliged to haul our logs so far that it was thought a barn of that discription would cost nearly as much as a framed one.

The whole came together very well, appears to be a good frame, & was put up without injury or accident to any one, except a slight wound in one finger.

Sat. [Aug.] 20. Br. B., according to previous appointment made by request; went out for the purpose of preaching tomorrow, near the Tennessee river, about 15 miles above us.

Sab. [Aug.] 21. Br. B. returned at evening. The day was very wet & uncomfortable, yet about 40 persons assembled who understood English, & gave good attention to the sermon, which is supposed to be the first ever preached in that neighborhood. At the request of the people an appointment was made to meet them again at that place on the fourth sabbath.

Aug. 25. Br. Chamberlin & Sis. Catharine returned. He found in every place a number of whites & half breeds, who understand English— These were generally disposed to attend preaching. In one instance where he stoped for the night, without thinking of being able to collect any for religious worship & instruction word was sent out without his knowledge that he was there, & he was surprised to see people coming in; but knew not the cause untill they requested him to preach to them, saying they had come in for the purpose of hearing him.

A decent attention to the preaching of the word was all the encouraging appearances he saw in this tour. No serious convictions of sin & exposedness to the wrath of God were discovered nor any anxious inquiry after the way of salvation heard.

Br. C. visited two girls, that had been a while at school, & when here were under serious impressions & desirous to continue with us, but were taken away against their will by their father, a half breed of some education who has been much among the whites.

The girls had lost their serious impressions, & frankly told Br. C. they did not now pray to the Savior or mind any thing about these things, as their father had forbidden them. it was all unnecessary & had better be left alone. That part of the country appears much infested by lawless whites, who are stealing horses &c from the Indians.

Br. C. on his return reported that he had ascertained the fact that the Osage boy had been sold—that the price was about $20, but was not able to see the boy.

[Aug.] 28. While we were exerting measures with Mr. John Ross & others to rescue the Osage captive, news came that the man who first bought him had sold him to another white man, for $150.[40]

It now, more than ever, appeared that a plan was laid to take the boy into perpetual slavery, & no time was to be lost in taking measures to counteract that nefarious design.

Mr. Ross agreed to apply to Mr. Hicks, & the U.S. Agent, for directions, & authority to rescue the boy, whenever he might be found.

[Aug.] 31. {Special meeting for business. The brethren considered a letter handed them by Br. H. bearing date Sep. 1st. As a desire to improve the character of Br. H. among other persons, was no cause of our writing the letter referred to in his, & as we cannot yet see wherein we made a false representation to the Prud. Com. Therefore Resolved, that we consider his said letter unreasonable.}[41]

Sab. Sept. 5. Br. B. according to previous appointment, went out to preach at the house of a white man who has a Cherokee family about 10 miles south of Brainerd.

Br. Reece, & John Arch (the young man who went out for the night to pray) went with him.

A number assembled, part of whom could understand English, & part not. Br. Reese interpreted.

An appointment was made to preach there again in four weeks.

Sept. 6. Meeting for business.

Resolved that we improve the first opportunity of low water to clear the Creek, to make a more convenient passage for boats bringing up supplies. Resolved that we build another cabbin for the boys as soon as convenient.

Sept. 7. Br. B. who has been unwell for a day or two was this day confined to his room.

[Sept.] 14. Br. B. got into the light waggon & rode a short distance, having been confined to his room since the 7th. He has had considerable fever, & taken much medicine—we hope he is now in a way soon to recover.

[Sept.] 15. Four boxes from our fellow helpers at the north came to hand safe & in good order. They came by way of Baltimore & Knoxville, & contained cloth & clothing for us & for the children.

One was from three Sisters in Worcester, Mass. & one from the female society for retrenchment—Reading Mass. Aux[ilary] to the A.B.C.F.M. The other two boxes contained neither letter nor mark by which we could know from whence they came, only that they were directed first to Baltimore. One of them was filled with clothing for children, & contained a letter to Mrs. A. R. Gambold, wife of Rev. John Gambold from one who was her pupil in Pennsylvania, writen at Windsor, N.Y. but Mrs. G. says there is not a word in her letter respecting the box or its contents. The other box contained clothing for men, women & children, with a number of New Testaments. Whether a letter giving an account of these boxes has miscarried, or whether it was the design of the donors to keep their charity a secret, we know not: but we think it of some importance that notice should be given of articles sent, & that we should acknowledge the receipt of them when they arrive. Without this precaution valuable boxes may, by some casualty, be stopped by the way—never missed, & never found. We have already, in our short experience, found special advantage by knowing what was forwarded & on the way to us. It might be of service. {If each box contained a bill of its contents, ~~with the cost a supposed value in the form of a merchant's bill, it would be a great help to us in fixing the price, of them when we sell for the benefit of the institution to those who are able & disposed to pay.~~}

[Sept.] 16. Meeting for business. Enquired whether we should continue in our employ a man who has been laboring for us a short time for the purpose of putting him at the mill. We knew not what to do with the mill. It is too far from us for one to tend it & be kept at the same time under our eye; we were afraid this man would be unfaithful if out of our sight; & we knew of no other person we could get to take charge of the mill. On the whole, Resolved not to employ him.

[Sept.] 17. Mr. J. Ross returned from the Agency, & showed us a precept issued by the Agent in the name of the President [of the United States] authorizing him to take the Osage boy wherever found, & place him under our care untill further orders from the President. Br. Kanouse & wife arrived on their return from Elliot.[42] They have had a prosperous journey thus far, but their horse is lame.

Sept. 23. Fa. H. who has had frequent ill turns for several weeks past was this day confined with a bowel complaint, attended with fever. We have reason to be thankful that Br. B. has recovered strength, so as to be able to attend to the business before this confinement.

[Sept.] 27. As the horse Br. Kanouse brot with him appears too lame to perform the remainder of the journey, therefore Resolved, that he be permited to leave that horse with us, & take the best black horse now belonging to this station.

Resolved, that the girl called Anna, whose father's name is John, be named Ann Porter, in compliance with the request of a Society of Ladies in Wilmington, Delaware.

[Sept.] 28. Br. & Sis. Kanouse left us to pursue their journey home. They appear to be well qualified for usefulness on mission grounds, if God in his providence had seen best to continue them at this work.

[Sept.] 30th Special meeting for business, Br. H. present. Read a letter from the Corresponding Sec. of August 26. Also his letter of May 6th with the rules accompanying it, Adjourned for family prayer.

Met according to adjournment—after some conversation on the subject of the forgoing letter,

Resolved that each brother be requested to write his views respecting the letter from the Cor. Sec of May 6th, & of the rules accompanying it. And also the letter from the same of August 26. & present the same our next meeting.[43]

Resolved that the buildings for the Local School at Talloney, be errected at the place last selected by Br. Hall.

Resolved that the following building be errected at the above place, viz.

A building of hewed logs 29 ft by 17-1/2 feet; cabbin roof to be divided so as to make two rooms: to have 2 glass windows in the dining room & 1 in the kitchen, & a chimney at each end, for the dining room of stone, for the kitchen of wood; with suitable under floors, a floor over the dining room & a cellar under the same. A building for schools & meetings 22 by 28 feet, hewed logs & shingle roof & stone chimney, with 5 glass windows, with suitable floors & seats.

Resolved that Br. H. take from the treasury $30 dollars in addition to the $30 he took 2 weeks ago.

Oct. 4. Meeting for business. Resolved that we spare our hired man Shelton 6 or 7 days to fulfill an arrangement made by Mr. Gentry, that the said Gentry may be at liberty to go, & work upon the building at Talloney.

Oct. 6. Br. H., with two hired men, set out for Talloney, with a view to commence buildings there for a Local School. He expects to be able to hire more help in that neighborhood.

Oct. 10. Mr. Ross brought the Osage boy & placed him under our care according to the direction of the Agent. He is not quite so large as the Osage girl, & is thought to be under 5 years—he is quite active & appears to have a good natural genius—has forgotten his native tongue, & speaks only English, except occasionally a cherokee word.[44] Mr. Ross left home, with two assistants, after this boy on the 24 of Sept, not knowing where he was. He found him within 15 miles of the mouth of the Catawba, about 250 miles from Brainerd.

Having ascertained where the boy was, he took the precautions when near the place, to leave his horses behind & approached silently on foot. He found the boy entirely naked in the yard before the house, & took him in his arms before he made his business known to the family. The man disclaimed all intentions of keeping the boy in slavery, & wished Mr. R. to leave him a short time untill they could prepare him some clothes. But he refused to leave the boy a moment, or to suffer him to sleep from him a night.

The neighbors told Mr. R. the man said the boys mother was a mulatto, & that he was born in slavery—that he had said he was going in a few days to take him on to market, & sell him. It was also said that this man had endeavored to persuade another to join him in this business, stating that there were a number of captives in the Cherokee nation which he thought he could obtain at a low price. O when will this highly favored land, called the land of freedom, cease to trafic in human blood!

[Oct.] 11. The Osage boy appears delighted with his new situation. On observing to him that he would find a father & mother here, he answered with quickness & animation, Yes, and <u>bread</u> too.

[Oct.] 13. Five boxes of clothing came on from Knoxville by way of Baltimore, sent (as appears by letter & bills in them) 1 from Ladies of Woodstock, V^t & forwarded May 20th. 1 from Gentleman & Ladies Pawlet, V^t forwarded March 6th. 1 from Portland, Maine, forwarded March 27th. 1 from Dorcas Society, Hawley, forwarded May 11th. 1 from Hatfield, containing some articles from Ashfield & Hadley forwarded May 3rd.

We ought to be very grateful to that God "who hath mercy on whom he will have mercy, & compassion on whom he will have compassion" for putting it into the hearts of his dear children to send, from the most remote parts of the U.S. these seasonable supplies of ready made clothing to cover these naked children of the forest; & in this way to evince the power & excellence of that gospel which he has commanded to be preached to every creature.[45] To him be all the praise—& from him may each & every donor receive a munificent reward. Our best thanks, which indeed are but poor, is due to every one of them.

It is not known to us that this mode of supplying the missions was early expected or even thought of by any one; but now we see not how we could well have proceeded without it. We hope, & trust, that these who have begun to afford this help will not become weary of it, & that these donations will be enlarged as the mission increases by the formation of other establishments.

[Oct.] 18. Meeting for business. Resolved that Fa. H. prepare a letter to the Cor. Sec. in answer to his of August 26th.[46]

As the national council is to meet in one week, Resolved that Br. B. go to Br. Hicks' & make known to him the late communications from the Prud. Com. respecting the help that is coming on, & respecting the Local Schools.

Resolved that we keep over as many swarms of the bees as it is thought have honey sufficient to keep them through the winter.

[Oct.] 22. Br. C. Washburn, wife & child, arrived, all in good health.[47] By the good providence of God, they have had a very quick & prosperous journey from Georgia to us. They left Jackson County on monday—crossed the Chatahooche into the Cherokee country Tuesday, & arrived at Brainerd on friday evening.—

Sab. Oct. 24. Fa. H. attended public worship for the first time since his confinement. He has been absent 4 weeks.

Br. Washburn preached. Br. B. went out this morning to fulfill our apointment for preaching at Mr. Rackley's 12 or 15 miles above us on the Tennessee. He rode Br. Washburn's horse, which died at the place of preaching—cause unknown.

[Oct.] 27. Rev. Mr. [Robert] Glenn, who is preaching as a missionary ministering under the direction of East Tennessee Presbytery, called on us.

[Oct.] 28. Mr. Glenn preached in the afternoon.

[Oct.] 29. Mr. Glenn left us to prosecute his mission in Tennessee. We have taken sweet council together, had much satisfaction in his visit, & hope the whole family have been profited.

Two of the schollars are down sick with the dysentary, others complaining with ~~a diarhoea~~ symptoms approaching to it. Lydia ~~Carter~~ Lowrey, one of the two, is very sick, we think dangerous. It is said many have died in Knoxville and other places with this disease.

We have reason to be thankful that the Lord is sending so many of the children of this ignorant people to receive instruction from us, & that the parents are disposed to leave them with us so great a portion of the time; but we have to lament that the education of many of them is greatly retarded by their frequent & long visits at home. We have not yet been able to devise any effectual measures to get the children sufficiently under our control in this respect, & perhaps shall never be able untill the parents are more enlightened. We think, however, that we are gaining ground. When the children enter school the parents assent to all we say on this subject, & promise (perhaps with an intention to fulfill) to comply with all our terms. But their attachment to their children is so strong, & their desire to have them with them so great, that most of the parents will devise means to get their children home too frequently, & then retain them too long.

In some instances, where the children have been seriously inclined, & have manifested a desire to be more constantly with us, they have been detained a long time, or kept away entirely.

The two girls aged 15 & 16 mentioned in our journal of June 16 as received candidates for baptism, were not long after that taken home by their relatives as on a visit, but have not yet returned. We suppose it would be perfectly agreeable to their relatives that they should be trained for, & if thought proper subjects, be admitted to the chh of Christ, as had been the case with Catharine Brown & Lydia Lowry; nor has any thing to the contrary ever been manifested to us, except that they do not return. Br. C. saw one of them when he was in the lower part of the nation last August—she still appeared attached to the Savior, & manifested a great desire to get back to Brainerd. Her mother, who is a widow, said she would send her back in a short time. Two days since her mother came for the clothing she had left here, & said she was going to the Arkansas with her daughter to visit some relatives there, & when she returned, she would bring her back to the school.

The other girl we have none of us seen since she was taken away. As often as we hear from her, the word is "she is coming back soon."

Whether we shall ever see either of them untill we meet at the bar of God, is known only to him "who worketh all things, after the counsel of his own will";[48] and "who hath his way in the deep, & his path in the great waters,"[49] but we are admonished to "do with our might what our hands findeth to do",[50] not only as our lives are short, but as we know not how soon those under our instruction will be removed beyond our reach forever.

Nov. 4. Hearing of three boxes of clothing sent on within 40 miles of us, without charge to the mission, we sent a light waggon after them; & this day they arrived safe.

It appears from accompanying bills & letters, that one box is from Danbury, Con. & towns adjacent, by Dean. Thomas Tucker, Agent. This box contained a little more than 200 articles of various kinds down to pocket Hkfs [handkerchiefs], binder tape, cotton-balls, thread, needles &c with some pamphlets & tracts.—

One box was from members of the Female Academy at Litchfield, Con. containing 13 shirts, 4 pr pantaloons, 6 frocks, & 3 hunting shirts.

One from females in Northampton, Mass. by Mary Williams Agent, containing 182 articles of clothing, including caps, handkfs, aprons &c—1 towel, 1 pillow case, 39 yds cloth of various kinds, 1 penknife, thread & pins, 1 Bible & a quantity of Tracts.

In a letter found in the box, they say "The coats & cravats were designed for the missionaries—the calico & gingham which is un-made, the caps & collars, with some other articles which will be found with them, for their wives & daughters which they will with any other articles in the box they may find necessary, appropriate to their own use.

The Broadcloth coat is designed for Mr. Hoyt".

By what means our unknown sisters, or their tailor, could have known how to cut this coat we know not, but it could not have been better fitted to the person for whom it was designed if he had been measured in the Tailor shop.

[*Nov.*] 6. Our Sister Lydia Lowry (one of the schollars mentioned as sick with the dysentery on the 29 ult) has been brot. apparently near the grave, but is now in a hopeful way to recover.

The report of the sickness prevailing among our children, probably with some exaggeration, has allarmed many of the parents, & they are coming to take their children home. The disease has however, through the mercy of God, subsided. Only two have been thought dangerous at any time, all the others are now nearly well & no new cases; yet we fear the allarm will keep many from the school for several weeks.

The father of John Arch, has been with us two or three days. We learn that he came for the express purpose of taking his son home with him, nor does it appear that he can easily be turned from his purpose. If it is best for him to continue longer in school, the father thinks he can find a school nearer home—He is unwilling to have his son so far from him.

It is a time of trial with John—he loves his father & desires to please him—He thinks he loves the Savior, & is willing to forsake all for his sake. We advise John to persuade his father to stay a few days—to comit the case to God—& trust in him to make duty plain in due time.

[Nov.] 9. The Rev. Abraham Steiner, of the Society of United Brethren in the southern states made us a friendly visit.[51] He brought an affectionate letter to us from the Directors of that Society. They desire that no sectarian differences may be known among the heathen; & propose a reciprocal communion & fellowship between their chh & ours among this people, & a mutual interchange of members if any should change their place of residence as to render such a change convenient & expedient—

They also desire that no children dismissed for bad conduct from one school may be received to the other, except by request of the Directors of the school from which they are dismissed.

We replied that these proposals were agreeable to the views & desires of our Directors, so far as we understood them, & were in perfect accordance with our wishes.

Mr. Steiner has, for a number of years been warmly engaged for the Christianization of this Tribe.

In 1799, he was sent out by the Directors of that Society to ask permission to establish a school in the nation. He pressed the subject with great zeal in the national council, backed by the officers of government, but was utterly refused.

In 1800 he came out again, & renewed his application—was again refused—but before the close of the council two influencial Chiefs agreed to patronize the school independently of the national council, & offered a place near the residence of one of them on land which he had cleared.[52] The other chiefs did not, after this, press their opposition—& shortly after the mission & school at Springplace was commenced, which has continued without suspension; though at times with great difficulty, ever since.[53]

Mr. S. says that no waggon road had ever been cut, or waggon entered the nation untill some time after this. The chief on whose land the mission was established built the first waggon—for which he was severely censured by the council, & forbiden to use such a vehicle. But he did not regard their mandate. Their objection was, "if you have a waggon there must be waggon roads—& if waggon roads, the whites will be in amongst us."[54] Mr. S. has been absent from the nation 16 years. The improvement, he says, since that time has been most delightful & astonishing.

Having heard that the brethren destined for this station & for the Arkansas were near, Br. Washburn & Milo Hoyt went out this morning to meet them.

[Nov.] 10. Br. Conger arrived about 3 ock in the light waggon, & told us we might expect the rest of the company next morning.[55]

At evening, after dark, one of the double waggons arrived with Br. Congers family. They left the other waggons on the opposite side of the Tennessee, expecting they would all get over the river before dark, & come on to breakfast with us in the morning.

It is a time of great rejoicing at Brainerd. We feel that the Lord has heard our prayers for help, & it is now our duty to render praise.

[Nov.] 11. The remainder of our brothers & sisters, with their children, arrived this morning in health.

Their journey has been, on the whole, prosperous, & attended with few disasters. Two horses died suddenly on the road, but were immediately replaced by purchase. Sister Vail was for a time sick, & unable to travel, but it was thought not best to detain the whole company on her account. Br. Vail & their two little ones, remained with her, & kept the light waggon, by means of which he was able to overtake the company after her recovery—so that the general progress was not in the least hindered on that account. The whole journey from N. Jersey to Brainerd was performed in Six weeks.

O that we could be sufficiently thankful to our gracious Savior for the abundant mercies which we have experienced & the sweet consolations now afforded us!

Meeting for business.

Resolved, that when any brother goes out to take charge of a Local School, he takes with him from the original establishment, such articles as he shall think necessary, with the consent of the brethren in regular meeting; & that a list of all these articles, with their supposed value, be left at the original establishment.

As our expected help has arrived, therefore, Resolved, that we consider Br. Butrick as relieved from the temporal concerns of this mission to return to the study of the Cherokee language.

[Nov.] 12. Br. Hicks writes that the late council forbid their own people to employ whitemen to till their land, or oversee their farms, but that missionaries may employ what help they need. The chiefs in council were well pleased that farmers & mechanics were coming to our assistance at Brainerd.[56]

Meeting for business—all the brethren present.

Resolved that the brethren who are going on to the Arkansas, take for their journey Three horses from this station: & that Brs. Hoyt, Finney, & Conger select the horses.[57]

Resolved that the above mentioned brethren select also a waggon for the Arkansas mission.

[Nov.] 15. Meeting for business.

Having experienced much difficulty & inconvenience in tending the mill for some time past.

Resolved that we let the miller, Raney—take the mill & have all the profits of it for tending, on condition of his grinding toll free for the mission family.

Resolved, that Br. H. take for the use of the school at Talloney the articles mentioned in the bill presented by him at this time.

Resolved that a joint letter to the Prud. Com. be prepared, respecting a Mr. Gahagan, now at Taloney, that Br. Hall prepare this letter, & that Mr. Gahagan continue with Br. Hall at Talloney untill an answer can be received from the Com.[58]

Resolved that the management of the farm, & directions of the mechanical business, be assigned to Br. Conger.[59]

[Nov.] 16. Adjourned meeting for business. Sisters all present.

Resolved that Br. Vail be an assistant to Br. Conger in the farming & Br. Talmage in the mechanical business.

Resolved that Sister Talmage take the charge of the kitchen—Sister Conger oversee the washing—Mother Hoyt the making of soap, & Sister Vail the Ironing.

Resolved that the cabbin next the lumber house be prepared for a Tailors shop.

[*Nov.*] 18. Meeting for business.
Resolved that Br. Hall take 100 dollars in money for the use of the Talloney school.
Resolved that Fa. Hoyt prepare a joint letter to the Postmaster-general respecting a post office at Talloney; & another to Col^n McKinney.
Resolved that Br. Hall take a double waggon & harness for the Talloney school.

[*Nov.*] 22. Meeting for business.
Br. Hall having added some articles to the bill presented on the 15th
Resolved that he take such articles as are contained in the bill now presented, bearing date Nov. 22, 1819.
Resolved that we assume the debt against Br. H. for articles purchased for the Talloney school, in favor of A. J. Huntington of Augusta.
Resolved, that George W. Halsey go to Talloney & work on the buildings there untill Br. Conger returns from Augusta.
Br. & Sis Hall, with their household goods, left us for their station at Talloney. Br. Vail went with them to drive the waggon that carried most of their goods, George W. Halsey (Br. Congers apprentice) to assist on the buildings for a few weeks, & Sister Anna to assist Sister Hall untill a girl can be hired.
May a divine blessing attend them, & ever rest upon their labors.
A box containing 100 Bibles & 100 New Testaments forwarded to us, for gratuitous distribution, from the Phil. Bible Society, by our precious brother Robert Ralston Esqr, last May, reached us in safety. A part of these have been much needed here for several months, & we trust the remainder will ere long be distributed to those who will be able to read them. These volumes are, therefore a very seasonable & precious treasure; They have come without injury. With these we recd a large box from the Brainerd Society of Females, Phil^a & a small one from Windsor & Deposit N.Y., of very valuable clothing, cloth, thread &c, all in good order.
O! what are we, that our God should incline his children to make us their Almoners, in a matter of such disinterested liberality! May his grace direct us to dispose of these charities as shall be most for his glory. And may a divine reward be granted to the benevolent givers, an hundred fold in this life, & in the world to come the unspeakable

satisfaction of mingling souls with many whose salvation they have furthered.

Nov. 25. Br. Conger has been confined with a slight fever for 5 days. We hope he is now, through the mercy of God, on the mend.

Last week we were busily employed in preparing for the departure of Br. & Sis. Hall. This week we are reminded that Brs & Sisters Finney & Washburn expect to leave us early next week.

We meet—by the grace of God our hearts are united. The command of Christ requires us to sepparate—but we trust his love will bind us, unworthy as we are, in bonds stronger than death; & after we have been supported to sustain a few days labor here on earth, perfect us forever in that blessed society above, where friends never part.

[Nov.] 27. Br. Conger becoming more unwell it was thought best to send to Washington (Ten.) for a Physician.

At a church meeting after preparatory lecture, John Arch, a full blooded Cherokee who came to us last January, was examined as to his experiential acquaintance with the religion of Jesus, & being judged a hopeful convert, was accepted as a candidate for baptism.

We hear from Springplace that they have lately baptised three adults, hopeful converts of our red brethren—& that they have hopes for one or two more.

Sab. [Nov.] 28. Another precious season was granted of renewing covenant at the Table of our Lord. In respect to numbers of us it was the first, & will probably be the last season of communing together in this sacred ordinance.

Brs. Finney & Washburn officiated, & it was, we trust a refreshing season to us all.

[Nov.] 29. Meeting for business.

Resolved that the brethren destined for the Arkansas have liberty to take from this establishment certain articles mentioned in a bill presented to this meeting, value $29,21-1/2.

Resolved that John Arch, together with David Brown,[60] assist Br. B. in the intervals of school, as interpreters for writing the Cherokee language.[61]

Resolved that our meetings for business be not, in ordinary cases, prolonged after 9 ock.

The father of John Arch, after continuing with us a few days, appeared perfectly willing to leave him with us; & took an affectionate leave of us all to return home about 12 days since.

[Nov.] 30. We were this day called to the painful duty of parting with the dear company who are, by the will of God, to penetrate the forest & seek a place to labor far West.[62] Our communion has been pleasant, & parting painful; but we have reason to bless God for the precious interview we have had, & for those delightful ties which have been strengthened here, & which, we trust, will bind our hearts forever.

May the good providence of God protect them, & the presence of him who dwelt in the bush be their comfort & their stay; and the giver of every good & perfect gift grant them the desire of their hearts in making them the happy instruments of imparting the blessings of salvation to multitudes, who shall be their joy & crown of rejoicing in the day of the Lord Jesus. And at the establishment now to be formed at some unnamed place in that dark region, may they have the satisfaction of entertaining missionaries destined to carry these glad tidings as far to the west of them as they are now going west of us.

Dec. 1st Br. B. who went yesterday to accompany the brethren a short distance, returned.

In assending the river bank after crossing the Tennessee, one of the horses in the double waggon refused to draw—after considerable delay & difficulty, this horse was taken out & the one belonging to the single waggon put in, & the Load taken up. It was now to late to get to the house where they expected to lodge, & they camped in the woods.

The horse that refused to draw was never known to do the like before but on being harnessed again in the morning to the double waggon he refused to proceed on level ground—he was then taken out & put to the single waggon, but with no better success. At length they concluded to take the horse that Br. B. rode, & send the other back. It is said the horse they took from Br. B. has repeatedly refused to draw in steep places, & we fear they will not be able to go on with their loads.

Dec. 3. We were again called to the pleasing duty of opening several boxes containing clothing for the children & missionaries, furnished by the charity of our sisters at the north. It appears that one box was from East Hartford Con. 1 from Rindge N. H. 1 from Bath N. H. & Barnet V^t & one from the western Soc. Worcester & 1 from Greenfield.

These boxes, together with a Trunk from the Treas^r, containing Books, Slates, Pencils &c for the schools, & some clothing for the children from Holliston, Mass. were forwarded by the Treasurer from Boston about the middle of August last, by way of Baltimore & Knoxville.

These repeated donations coming into our hands from the friends of Jesus & his cause among the heathen, increases our responsibility, & ought to excite increasing gratitude to Him who has promised his Son the heathen for his inheritance, the uttermost parts of the earth for his possession. Our warmest thanks are also due to those our fellow helpers, who with so much labor & care, & we trust with many fervent prayers, have prepared & sent these useful things. May God grant us grace to feel & to act in character.

Sab. [Dec.] 5. Br. Conger, though still feeble, was able to attend the public worship of God, in the little sanctuary which he has graciously afforded us in this wilderness. Br. B. who went out yesterday to attend an appointment 10 miles south of us, returned this evening. Preaching at that place is once in four weeks, & Br. Reece generally attends as interpreter.

The attention of the people in that neighborhood is not abated. Four came to the place of meeting last evening on foot, a distance of 10 miles, 5 of which they walked after dark, fording one large creek. It being to dark to see any thing that was not white, one went before, feeling out the path with his feet, & the others followed in succession by observing each the blanket of his leader.

Br. C. is out to preach at Br. Hicks'. It is our intention to have but one appointment out on each Sab. but in consequence of one appointment being put over to attend the sacrament here, we had two this day.

[Dec.] 6. Meeting for business.

As there has been some dissatisfaction among the natives on account of clothes sold to the children,

Resolved, that we take no more pay for clothes: but if the parents are willing to give any thing it shall be considered as a Donation.

Resolved, that a joint letter be writen to the Com. respecting the sending of John Arch & David Brown to the F.M.S. Cornwall.

Convened respecting the Resolution passed Nov. 10th.

The brethren gave it as their unanimous oppinion that the above mentioned resolution extends to all articles not originally private property, as they consider all donations made to an individual as coming into the common stock of the mission.

Resolved that Br. Hall be requested to give an account of the several items already purchased for the Taloney school, & how much money he will want immediately & for what purposes.

[Dec.] 9. Br. Conger rode out about 4 miles & returned without any apparent injury from fatigue. He hopes soon to be able to set out for Augusta after the machinery, tools, &c.

Mr. Andrew Ross, who, in connection with his brother John Ross, has lately established a Store at Fort Armstrong, about 60 miles from Brainerd, says the people there appear very anxious to have a school in that neighborhood.[63] He thinks 30 schollars might be collected; who would board at home, or in the neighborhood at their parents expense.

We have had repeated applications for a school in that place.

[Dec.] 10. Rev. Messrs. Donald & Anderson of the visiting Com. & Rev. Mr. Eagleton of Kingston E. Ten. came this evening for the purpose of visiting the school, & looking into the state & management of the general concerns of the mission.[64] Others of the Com. had contemplated coming but were prevented by sickness & other causes. We can hardly expect a general attendance of the Com. at any one time, as all, except one, live more than 100 miles distant.

[Dec.] 11. The three visiting brethren attended the boys school in the forenoon. In the afternoon Mr. Donald preached a preparatory Lecture.

Sab. [Dec.] 12. This we trust was a precious day to us all. Mr. Anderson preached the Serm. before communion—The Osage boy, whom we call John Osage Ross, was offered for baptism as the adopted son of Fa. H. & was baptised by Mr. Donald. After which the sacrament of the Lords supper was administered to Red, Black & White, the professed followers of him who "by the grace of God, tasted death for every man".[65] Mr. Eagleton preached in the evening.

[Dec.] 13. The visiting Com. confined their attention to the girls school during the forenoon exercises.

In the afternoon both schools were brot together. In the evening the children were assembled as usual, for Catechizing, singing &c—the Com. still attending their exercises.

The behavior of the children was satisfactory to us, & we believe to the Com. We only have to regret that numbers of them were absent, having been taken away in consequence of the frights of their parents on the appearance of Dysentery, & not yet returned. Only 67 besides the children of the missionaries, were present.

Meeting for business. Visiting Com. present by request.

Br. Butrick presented in manuscript a Cherokee Spelling Book. The opinion of the Com. being asked, they decided that it was best to have it printed. Whereupon Resolved, that measures be taken immediately to have the s^d Spelling Book printed.

Resolved that Br. B. go to Knoxville to superintend the printing of the s^d book, & have leave to take with him David Brown.

Resolved that 600 copies of s^d book be printed.

Mr. Eagleton having expressed a desire to take John Arch into his family, & give him the benefit of his private instructions, & of the Academy which is near his door,[66] & John having expressed a willingness to go, at the same time refering it entirely to our judgment, saying he looked upon the missionaries here as his fathers, & would follow our direction—It was thought best for John to go with Mr. Eagleton for the present.

[Dec.] 14. The Com. took an affectionate leave of us early this morning—Mr. Eagleton took John with him. Br. B. also left us in their company for Knoxville, taking with him David Brown.

This visit has been very agreeable to us, & we think will be productive of much good to the School.[67]

Meeting for business.

Resolved that we purchase 4000 lb. Pork, & 1000 bushels corn, in addition to what we have already engaged. Also, that we purchase 500 bushels of oats, if they can be obtained on reasonable terms.

[Dec.] 16. Br. Conger took his departure for Augusta, expecting the teams to follow him next week.

It was his intention at first to have had the teams set out when he did, thinking he could gain time by traveling faster than they could to do the business in Augusta before their arrival. But in consequence of his feeble health at this time he thought he should not be able to travel faster than the empty teams.

Br. Reece gave us 21 bushels of corn for the benefit of the Institution. It is supposed he has raised this year, with his own hands 200 bushels more than will be wanted in his numerous family.[68]

[Dec.] 23. Br. Talmage set out with a hired man & two waggons for Augusta, after the machinery tools &c—Br. George W. Halsey & sister Anna returned this evening from Talloney.

[Dec.] 24. Special meeting for business.

Resolved that a joint letter be writen to the Prud. Com. giving a statement of certain facts so far as they have come to our knowledge, concerning the School at Talloney.[69]

[Dec.] 27. Meeting for business.

Resolved that we proceed immediately to erect a Ware-house on the bank of the Tennessee 24 by 20 feet, having a crib for corn, 6 feet wide, on each side, leaving a space of 8 feet between them.

[Dec.] 28. Br. Vail went out with three hands to cut a road to the Tennessee & put up a ware-house.

[Dec.] 29. Two teams arrived with machinery, tools &c from Augusta. They brought two valuable boxes of clothing, one from Morristown N.J. & one from Durham, Green Co. N.Y. These clothes are well calculated for service & convenience in a warm country, & we can never be thankful enough for the abundant supply which our dear Sisters, by the will of God, have sent us from time to time, since the wants of these children were made known to them. We receive it as a pledge of their ardent desire to advance the Redeemers Kingdom among the natives of our land, & of their faithful coopperation in this work, so long as the Savior shall graciously permit us to be engaged in it.

We think it would have been well if we had anticipated this cold winter, & asked in due time for some blankets, & perhaps, (if it would not have been too expensive,) for some warm clothing for the children.

We believe few, if any, of our dear sisters at the north imagine that the winters here call for the same kind of clothing that they do there, but we, who have experienced both climates, see but little difference. The cold here is not indeed so intense, but the weather being more variable, the same degree of cold is more sensibly felt here than there.

We are this day shrouded in our cloaks when we go out, & shivering over the fire when we come in, expect a storm of snow.

[Dec.] 30. A very considerable snow fell last night, & is driven from the trees by the wind to day; which is cold & piercing. The cattle run up to us from the woods, lowing for their fodder, & the men who went out to build the warehouse have returned, leaving their work for milder weather.

[Dec.] 31. A very cold day—Though clear, the snow does not melt on the south roof of buildings.

1820

Jan. 1, 1820. The cold has in some degree abated—the snow melts a little on the south side of buildings, but it has wasted but little even on the roofs,—though the day is perfectly clear.

Jan. 3. The nights are still very cold, but the days are a little warmer, & the snow becoming thin in places in the opened land. Br. Vail, with the three hired men, returned to their work building the ware-house.

[Jan.] 4. We have corn sufficient only for two or three days—have been expecting our supply according to contract, before the end of last month. We now learn that the Tennessee is too low for the heavy corn boats to run, & have concluded to send out tomorrow to see if we can purchase a few bushels at some place on the Tennessee from which it can be brought in a canoe or light boat.

[Jan.] 5. Milo Hoyt went out after corn, with instructions to proceed untill he can get it.

[Jan.] 7. Br. V. and the men returned from their work on the warehouse. They have put up the body of the building (which is 24 by 20) made the shingles & covered it. The door, floor, & cribs, are left for the arrival of the corn boat, from which we expect to get boards for this part of the work.
Only about 20 days work, with the addition of a little help in raising; have been spent on this building. Four or five days have cut the road to it, & we now expect to get our corn from the Tennessee much cheaper, & with less waste, than heretofore. The place where we have built this house is thought to be about six miles, following the course of the river, above Mr. Rosses Warehouse, & about the same distance from the mission house; being, as is supposed, the nearest point at which we can strike the Tennessee from Brainerd. This way to the Tennessee; which runs in a narrow valey, between high & rough hills, was not discovered by us untill of late. We have heretofore supposed there was no alternative but to bring our supplies that came from the Tennessee, up the Chickamaugah, or over the high ridge, which, from

its height & steepness towards the river, may be called a mountain:
but in this new way, through the valey, we find a convenient, &
comparatively easy road.

[Jan.] 8. We hear nothing from Milo, or any corn coming to us, & were
this morning about to send out to see if we could buy or borrow
among our neighbors. Just as a horse was brought up for this purpose
a man came from one of our neighbors for the sole purpose of telling
us, he would lend us corn if ours did not arrive in season.

[Jan.] 9. Milo returned. On his way out he engaged a man to bring us a
temporary supply of corn, which he expects will be at the new
warehouse tomorrow. He went to the contractors, who told him the
water was rising, & he expected to be able to start the corn boats by
the 9th, which is this day.

By the advise & consent of all the brethren, the gristmill was sold
about the 1st of last month for three hundred dollars—One hundred
to be paid on or before the 1st of March next, & the remainder in the
course of the year. The reasons for selling & it not being mentioned in
our meetings for business at the time are briefly as follows.

We found it impracticable to get a miller to tend it, of suitable
character, on reasonable terms. It was frequently geting out of repair,
& not likely ever to be profitable to the mission—It was thought
probable that a time of high water would make breaches in the dam, if
not carry the whole off, & thus cause much expense to repair it, as it
has done heretofore. If we build a dam for a saw-mill, as we now
expect, on the Chickamaugah it is thought it will be best to build a
good gristmill at the same place, even if this present mill is not sold—
A responsible neighbor was willing to buy the mill, & engage to keep
it in repair & grind for the mission family as long as we chose to have
our grinding done there—The brethren in regular meeting thought it
would be best to sell it, but did not pass a resolution on the subject, as
it was not known whether the buyer would accede to terms which we
should accept. The above mentioned terms were proposed by the
buyer at the mission house, & most of the brethren being present
agreed to accept them when not in meeting, & we were not careful to
have this entered on our journal in its proper place.

Ard Hoyt, John Vail, Wm Chamberlin

Journal of the Cherokee Mission, Brainerd

1820

Jan. 11. John Arch, having continued about two weeks with Mr. Eagleton in Kingston; & then visited some of his relatives in the nation, returned to us. His joy on geting back to Brainerd, the place where he found the Savior; was very great. He said he did not want to see his father, or any of his relations, half as much as he did to come back & see us.

It was suggested; before he went with Mr. Eagleton, that possibly his father might object to his going out among the whites—& we concluded that he should after a short stay with Mr. Eagleton, go & see his father & other relatives, & learn their feelings. He had been about halfway to his fathers, saw some of his relatives, who he says advised him to continue with us if we would keep him, & he wanted to get back so much, he thought he would not spend time to go to his fathers.

He speaks very highly of Mr. & Mrs. Eagleton, & of their kind attention to him while there. Says he will go back if father Hoyt thinks it is best—he is willing to do that which will tend to the greatest good—but if we think it will do as well, & are willing to keep him, he had much rather stay here. We therefore concluded to let him stay.

[Jan.] 15. Brothers Conger & Tallmadge returned from Augusta with the teams. By the blessing of God they have had a very quick & prosperous journey—the teams having been absent but three week & three days.

Machinery for the Saw-mill—blacksmith tools &c—are all now here, & we hope to have at least some of them in opperation soon.

They brought with them six boxes & one package of clothing, donations to this mission from the following places viz. Lansingburg, N.Y. containing some articles from Troy—Tyringham, Berkshire Co. Ms. York-town Westchester Co., N.Y. [Ashbu?] N.Y. Dorcas Soc. of South Salem Westchester Co. N.Y. Hartford Con. & Oglethorpe Co. Georgia. Thus have the charities of the friends of missions, from north to south, run together like the hearts of christians, & in one waggon found their way into this wilderness. O may they be as the messenger of the living God, testifying that the religion of Jesus is from him whose nature is love!

Jan. 16. Two boats containing 1500 bushels corn for the mission, arrived at the new warehouse.

The delay of this corn, which was expected more than a month sooner, has occasioned some trouble & additional expense, but, through the kind providence of our God, we have not lacked bread.

[Jan.] 17. Br. Vail, with the hired men & several boys, went for the purpose of unloading the corn boats. He found the corn very wet, &, as he supposed, much injured. The owner was not with it. The boatmen did not choose to deliver any unless he recvd the whole as good according to contract. This he thought he could not in justice do, & all hands returned, leaving the corn as they found it.

[Jan.] 18. Br. Conger, with two men who had often seen corn wet in boats & had experienced both of saving & loosing it when in that state, went to examine the corn. They are all of opinion that the corn is much injured, & advise not to receive it as it is, but think if the owner were present, & would consent to sort it, there is at least some part of it uninjured.

[Jan.] 20. The owner of the corn arrived, brought a drove of fat hogs which we had agreed to take of him. They are to be killed & weighed here. He speaks well on the subject of the corn—says if any part of it is damaged he has more at home, & will make his contract good. He does not wish us to receive an ear of damaged corn.

Br. Butrick & David Brown returned from Knoxville. They had been detained longer than they at first expected—had made some additions to their manuscript for the Cherokee spelling book & got it printed. The people of Knoxville & Maryville received them very kindly, & entertained them free of expense while there. Rev. George Erskine (a man of color) belonging to the Presbytery of E. Ten. came from Knoxville with Br. B. to make us a visit.[1]

Br. Chamberlin left Brainerd this morning to visit Br. Hall at Taloney, & attend to some business relative to preparations for a school there.

The U.S. Agent, by letter recvd this day, informs that the Osage boy is placed with us by order of government, & cannot be removed except by the same authority. He also says there is a fine Creek boy in the upper part of this nation who was captivated by the Cherokees in the late Creek war; & he will obtain him for us if we will take him.

[Jan.] 21. On examining the corn in the presence of the owner it was agreed to take it into the warehouse (sorting out the poorest) & see

what effect time will have upon it: he engaging to make good all loss.

Sab. [Jan.] 22. Our colored brother preached to great satisfaction, & we hope not without profit to the hearers.

[Jan.] 23. David Brown left us to visit his father, who sent for him & Catharine last week because he was sick. Catharine went with the messenger, who left word for David to follow as soon as he returned. David seems unwilling to leave us, & says he shall return as soon as he possibly can. He was very thoughtful, for some time before he went to Knoxville, & at times appeared exercised with pungent conviction—now he thinks he has found the Savior, & we hope he is not deceived.

[Jan.] 24. Br. Erskine left us early this morning to return to Knoxville. Br. Chamberlin returned this evening from Taloney. From various causes the buildings have not progressed so fast there as we could have wished, but the people appear still anxious for a school, & Br. Hall wishes us, if practicable, to send some workmen to build the school house.

[Jan.] 25. Had considerable conversation (by an interpreter) with a Cherokee who had come about 60 miles to place his son under our care.[2] From his dress, general deportment & conversation, he appears to rank high in natural intellect, & much above the ordinary class of his people in improvement. He gave very serious attention while we talked to him on the subject of religion, & a future state. On being asked what his past views had been on these subjects, He answered that he was a child; &, untill he had now heard from us, he had never attained any ideas more than he had when a little child. He was then asked what had been his thoughts respecting the Good Spirit, our Creator: He answered, the same that they had been on the other subjects of our conversation. He had thought but little about it, & knew no more than he did when a child. Said he was very glad to hear what we had told him, should think much upon it, & never forget it.

Similar to this is the statement of most with whom we have conversed, so far as they appear to give us a frank statement of the darkness of their minds.

How deplorable must be the state of an immortal mind under such darkness! Quick to perceive & distinguish in all things that come under the sight of the eye—sagacious in all things pertaining to time

& sense—yet hastening to an eternal state of existence, with scarce a thought about it, & not one correct idea concerning what that state will be, or what constitutes a hapy preparation for it. Thousands of these are in the bosom of the United States, surrounded on every side by a white population, called christian.

It has been said & thought by many that it is not in our power to instruct them. This is now demonstrated to be incorrect. They are willing to be taught—they ask for instruction—& if we do not teach them, their blood may justly be required at our hands.

Jan. 30. Our hearts were gladened by the reception of a fine looking Creek boy, apparently about 10 or 11, who has been for several years a captive in this nation, & is now liberated by the U.S. Agent, & by him placed under our care.[3] The Agent writes "He is a very fine child of nature. I find that he has a sound mind in a sound body, which only wants cultivation to make him one day a very useful member of the great community; & especially to the tribe he belongs. His Indian name is very difficult to pronounce or to write—And as he is now beginning a rational existence, I have given him a name which in time may be found to be appropriate—I have named him Joseph. If agreeable to you I wish he may retain that name; to which you may perhaps think proper to add a Sirname. It is not improbable that I shall obtain one or two more Creek children." Thus in the good providence of God, are collected in this one family the children of three different tribes. The Lord grant that they may yet be instrumental of bringing these several tribes to the knowledge of that one & only Savior, in whom the whole family of the redeemed in heaven & earth are named.

Feb. 7. Br. Conger set out for Rhea Co. to hire laborers, & do some other business for the mission.

[Feb.] 9. A respectable Cherokee called to invite one of the missionaries to ride out tomorrow about 10 miles, & officiate at his weding. He, & also the intended bride, have both been taught to read—are very decent & respectable in their moral deportment, & at times manifest a serious attention to the things of religion. We readily accepted the invitation.[4]

[Feb.] 10. Br. Butrick, accompanied by some young people of the mission family & school, went out & attended the wedding.

[Feb.] 14. A messenger arrived from Br. Hall's, stating that the black woman they had hired in the kitchen, was taken away; & they could get no person there to take her place. They wish us, if possible, to send them help.

[Feb.] 16. Br. Conger returned—He has engaged two carpenters & two common laborers, who are expected on soon. He saw the Agent, & mentioned to him that we had proposed to add the Sirname Meigs, if agreeable to him, to that of Joseph, which he had given the Creek boy. The Agent was pleased with it. We shall therefore call the Creek boy Joseph Meigs.

Sat. [Feb.] 19. After preparatory lecture John Arch, who has continued to give increasing evidence of piety, was examined in respect to his general knowledge of the christian doctrines, & especially of the nature & design of baptism. The chh being satisfied on these points voted unanimously that he be admited to baptism tomorrow, previous to administration of the Lords supper.

Sab. [Feb.] 20. After sermon, John Arch was baptised, agreeable to the vote of yesterday. He recvd the ordinance with great solemnity & apparent joy.
When we consider the manner of his coming to us, but little more than a year ago, from the most distant & most ignorant part of the tribe, without any one to encourage him, having barely heard that there were people here that would teach him; added to his diligence in the study of science & theology, the progress he has made, & his apparent devotedness to God, we are led to hope that he may in due time prove a blessing to the chh, & his people.

[Feb.] 22. Being unable to get any help for Sister Hall in this neighborhood, & hearing that a black man, used to kitchen work, whose master resides near Washington Rae [Rhea] Co. might probable be obtained, if one of the missionaries would see his master, & become responsible for the pay &c, Br. Conger, by direction of the brethren, set out this morning to go after him.

[Feb.] 24. At 3 ock. P.M. Milo Hoyt & Lydia Lowry were united in the solemn bans of matrimony, at our usual place of public worship, in the presence of the mission family, children & some neighbors.[5]

[Feb.] 26. Br. Conger returned having engaged the black man he went after. Dr. Strong, of Knoxville, came down with him to visit the school.[6]

Feb. 28. Dr. Strong left us having expressed much satisfaction in the progress of the children, & the general concerns of the mission.
The man we sent about the first of this month to build the school house at Taloney, returned. Most of his time has been spent on the dwelling house, as there were no boards prepared for the school house. He says they have put up most of the logs for the body of the house, & made shingles for the roof, but it was not thought advisable to proceed any further untill they could get boards.
Sister Hall was very unwell, & could get no help in the kitchen.

March 3. Rev. Mr. Stewart, a Licentiate of the South Carolina Presbytery, now on his return from a mission in Alabama, called to make us a visit. He preached yesterday in the nation near Ft. Armstrong—found the people very attentive to a missionary, willing to hear, & very anxious for a school. They told him they had applied to us several times for a school, & intended in a few days to send again. He thinks that a very eligible situation for a Local School.

[March] 4. Br. & Sis. Conger left us early this morning to go to Father Gambolds, partly a visit & partly to get some fruit trees. Br. Vail is expected to go after them on monday with a waggon to bring on the trees.
Sis. Catharine & her brother David returned. Their father, whom they went to visit on account of his ill health, has so far recovered as to be able to come up with them. Catharine says David seized his bible as soon as he got home; & began to read & interpret to this father & mother & other members of the family, exhorting them all to attend to it as the word of God; to repent of their sins, which he told them were many & very great,—to believe on the Lord Jesus Christ, & become his followers &c. By his fathers consent he maintained the worship of God in the family morning, evening & at table. That he conversed freely with their friends & neighbors, & was not ashamed to own himself a christian; or afraid to warn them to flee from the wrath to come. Several in that neighborhood appear serious & disposed to inquire after the way of truth & life.
Their father brought us a letter, signed by himself & other Head men & Chiefs in that district, in which they say, they are daily witnessing the good effects arising from education, & have held a council to

devise means for a school in that neighborhood, & wish our advice & assistance on the subject.

Mr. Brown states verbally that they said if we could only furnish a single man to teach their children, they would be very thankful for the favor. That they had been trying to begin a school themselves, & had engaged a teacher. But before the time of commencing the school he stole a drove of hogs, & run off.

David Brown appears very anxious to get an education preparatory to becoming a minister of the gospel. He has obtained his fathers consent to go [to] the north for this purpose.

Sab. [March] 5. Mr. Stewart preached to our satisfaction, & we hope edification.

[March] 6. Mr. Stewart left us early to pursue his journey homeward. He said he had come 60 miles out of his way to visit this establishment, & felt well paid.

Br. Vail set out with a waggon to go to father Gambolds after trees &c. In the monthly concert of prayer John Arch & David Brown, both prayed in their turn. Their expressions were appropriate, fervent & devout.

March 7. Meeting for business.

Resolved that Br. Butrick prepare a joint letter to the Cor. Sec. & also to the Principal of the F.M.S. relative to the character & circumstances of David & John Brown—inquiring whether they can be admited to the F.M.S.[7]

Father H. read a letter prepared as answer to the request of the Chiefs at Creek Path for a school, which was approved.[8]

Resolved that Br. Butrick & Sister Sarah accompany Fa. Hoyt to Taloney.

Resolved that we send the following communication to Br. Hall, viz,

Dear Brother, We think your reasons for not coming with Br. Chamberlin at our request, were not sufficient. We think that your delay to forward your account, & tell us for what purpose you wanted money, & your entire refusal to send us a list of articles you took from this establishment, not stated on the list which you left, are censurable, & that you ought to acknowledge your fault in these respects.[9]

[March] 8. Many anxious thoughts respecting the school at Creek Path. Concluded to call a meeting of the brethren, & inquire whether we

shall not reconsider our answer to the letter from that place, as we still have it in our hands. A special meeting was called, records of S^d meeting as follows.

After some conversation on the subject,

Resolved to reconsider our answer to the request of the Chiefs of Creek Path for a school at [that] place.

In a reconsideration of the subject the following particulars were brought in review.

Last June, encouragement was given in the national Council that teachers would be furnished for such schools—

They were told that one school, if desired, would be put in opperation immediately: and soon after it was determined to have this school at Taloney—It is known through the nation that that school is not yet in opperation—but the causes of the delay are unknown. Some are telling the natives that we are deceiving them, & never will give them schools according to our promise.

If, under these circumstances, we barely tell them of Creek Path, that we will write to the north for a teacher, & get one as soon as possible, they may be discouraged, & we cannot tell what evil may follow.

And further, there appears to be some serious inquiry after the way of life amongst adults in that neighborhood, & this may be a favorable time in that respect. Therefore, Resolved, That Br. Butrick go to Creek Path, & if he find[s] circumstances for begining a school as favorable as have been represented, & the people will prepare a house, that he commence a school as soon as practicable; with the expectation of being relieved from this charge as soon as a proper person can be found to fill the place.

Also Resolved that he have leave to take John Arch with him.

March 9. Recvd, by way of Baltimore & Knoxville, 5 Boxes & 2 Trunks, which were shiped at Boston by the Trea^r about the middle of Nov. last. The boxes were from Greenfield, South Hadley & Bridgewater Mass. & from Middlebury & Windsor V^t.* The Trunks contained various articles from Boston, Salem & Cummington Mass. with Paper, Slates &c, purchased by the Treasurer in Boston.

Opening these boxes & trunks we find them filled with valuable articles which we look upon as testimonials of love to Christ, & sure indications that many prayers are offered for the success of this mission. These prayers have been heard, & we trust will continue to be heard, untill those who now receive these charities will join their benefactors in the mission ranks, & aid in spreading the trophies of the cross to the western ocean. We cannot but consider our situation as almoners of such ample funds to be highly responsible; and do humbly beg an interest in the prayers of Gods people that He will grant us grace to be found faithful.

*a letter from the Trea^r states this box to be from Windsor, V^t: a note in the box seems to imply that the articles were from Clairemont N.H.

March 11. Br. Butrick, having John Arch in company, left us expecting to preach tomorrow at Br. Hicks', & then go down to Creek Path, &, if circumstances there appear as favorable as represented to make preparations for & commence a Local School as soon as practicable. As Br. Butrick has spent much time, & made very considerable progress, in the study of the language that he might be the better prepared to act as an evangelist among this people: & as a great door is opened for his usefulness in that office, we hope & pray that someone qualified with gifts & grace for a school teacher, & who is willing to devote himself to that service; will soon be sent to occupy the place he is now taking. Nor is it one school-master only that we desire. Numbers might now find immediate employ in eligible situations, were they disposed to enter the whitened field.

Br. Vail returned from father Gambolds, having been detained there by highwater from the 5th inst.

He left Br. & Sis. Conger there, they being detained by her ill health. Before her departure she had had several ill turns, & had not fully recovered from the last of them when they left us. Br. V. left her geting better, & they hoped she would be able to return in two or three days.

Sab. [March] 12. In the morning prayer meeting we were enlivened by the fervent supplications of David Brown. After prayer meeting, he, together with Catharine, & our aged sister McDonald, gathered a little group of their people who had come to spend sabbath with us, & held a religious conference, with prayer & praise, all in the Cherokee tongue: none but David & the two sisters understanding the English.

Mr. J. Ross, who has lately returned from Ft. Armstrong, says the people in that vicinity again spoke to him on the subject of a school for that neighborhood. They are quite anxious for it, & he thinks a number sufficient for a good school might be collected who would board with their parents or friends.

We know not what to do with this place—They may think their claims quite equal, if not superior to those of Creek Path. We have no one that can possibly be spared to go to them, except Milo Hoyt, & his assistance here as a Tailor &c is much needed.

March 13. Meeting for business.

Took up the subject of a school to be located somewhere in the vicinity of F^t Armstrong. As Milo Hoyt & his wife are willing to go & commence a school there if it is thought best, Therefore

Resolved, That Br. Chamberlin go and visit the people in that vicinity, &, if the prospects appear favorable, make such arrangements for a school as he shall think proper.

Resolved, that Br. Talmage have the care of the Flat & canoe, for the express purpose of keeping them so fastened that they shall not be taken off in time of high water.

Resolved that the Bell be rung half an hour before sunrise, & tolled at sunrise for prayer: that it be rung at 7 ock for breakfast & again a quarter before 9 ock & tolled at 9 for school—rung at 12 ock for dinner, a quarter before 2 & tolled at two for school, rung at sunset for supper, & tolled an hour after for evening prayers, & rung again at 9 in the evening.

March 15. Crossing the Chickamaugah with a waggon load of corn the boat was driven by the current with such violence against a tree as to throw the horses out of the boat. Their hinder parts being kept upon the edge of the boat by the harness which was fastened to the waggon their heads were plunged under the water, & before they could possibly be extricated, one of them, a fine mare from N. Jersey, was drowned.

Ard Hoyt, John Vail, Wm Chamberlin, John Talmage

Journal of the mission at Brainerd Cherokee N.

1820

March 16. Fa. H. & sis. Sarah left Brainerd on a journey to Taloney— He on business relating to the projected school there—She chiefly as a nurse, he being in a very feeble state of health.

[*March*] 18. Br. Reece being invited into the little room where we keep the clothing sent on for the use of this mission, looking round upon the articles as they were laid up on their several appartments, was soon observed to be suffused in tears. Observing that he was noticed, he said, with a heart so full that he could scarcely speak "I cannot keep from weeping when I see what the good people are doing for us poor heathen. It makes me astonished to think we are so hard hearted & stupid, when others are thinking & doing so much for us".

Another boat load of corn arrived at our warehouse containing about 1000 bu. This is from the same man that brought us the 1500 bu. last winter what got wet in the boats: & is designed to make up the deficiency of that, the greatest part of which was so damaged as to be unfit to eat immediately after the warm weather commenced.

[*March*] 20th Br. Chamberlin went out for the purpose of enquiring into the expediency of immediately commencing a Local School in the vicinity of F^t Armstrong—with instructions to make arrangements for S^d school, if, in his oppinion when on the spot, appearances are as favorable & the case as urgent as has been represented.

[*March*] 24. Br. & Sis. Conger returned from Fa. Gambolds. She has been very low, for a time apparently near the grave, & is still very feeble; but, through the mercy of God, she is so far recovered that she appears to have sustained no injury from riding home. They were two days in returning.

This evening Br. Chamberlin returned from F^t Armstrong. In his oppinion it is a very favorable & important time to establish a Local school there.

In an interview with the principal chief of that district Br. C. enquired if the people wanted a school. He answered, by the interpreter, that they did not merely want a school but they wanted one very much. He said they would be very glad of a large school, like the one at Brainerd, & proposed a place for it on the Coosa river, where he said suplies of all kinds might be brought by water.

On being told that we were not able to give them such a school at least at present, but could only furnish a teacher for such children as could board themselves, he said they would be very thankful for such a school—that he had a small cabbin just where they wanted the school which he would give for the use of the teacher, & that himself & neighbors would build the school house:

So far as could be assertained the chief spoke the mind of the whole district. All were agreed that it would be best to have the school at the place named by the Chief which is on the Chatooga creek about 6 or 8 miles from F^t Armstrong. And Br. C. gave encouragement to send a teacher in a few days. He also understood that the Path Killer intended soon to ask for such a school in his neighborhood. This aged warrior & king is telling his people wherever he goes that schools are very good for them, & they must keep their children at school untill their teachers say they have learned enough, which he tells them will take at least four years. This venerable old man, who is now so much engaged for the instruction of his people, we understand has never had the least degree of school learning himself.

Sab. [March] 26. Fa. H. & Sis. Sarah arrived this morning from Taloney. Being unable to reach home last evening, they lodged four miles back with one of our Cherokee sisters.

They found Sister Hall in a feeble state of health, but better than she had been. The people appeared very anxious to have the school begin. Boards were sawed to finish the school house, & would be ready to work in a few days.

March 27. Meeting for business.
{Resolved that we send the two carpenters, Shelton & Leuty to finish the school house at Taloney; & that they set out next monday.[10]
Resolved that we send to Br. Hall for the use of the school $50.}
Having heard Br. Chamberlins report respecting the prospects for a Local School on the Chatooga Creek near F^t Armstrong,
Resolved that preparations be made to send Milo Hoyt immediately to commence a school there.
Resolved that Br. Talmage make out a list of prices of the several articles of blacksmithing, & present it at our next meeting for business.
Resolved that the hired men be discharged from their labor on satturdays at 4ock P.M.

[March] 29th {About 4 ock} this morning sister Talmage was made the joyful mother of a promising Son. Circumstances favorable.
This is the first male child born in the mission family at Brainerd. May he live to become a faithful missionary of the cross.
Special meeting for business.
Resolved that Milo Hoyt be permitted to take, for the use of the projected school at Chatooga certain articles of household furniture, as by bill presented at this meeting.
Resolved that he be permitted to take Darius Hoyt with him to assist at Chatooga for a few weeks.[11]

Apl. 1st In church meeting after preparatory lecture David Brown gave a relation of his religious experience & answered such questions as were put to him relative to his supposed gracious change. His relation & answers were satisfactory, & he was admited by unanimous vote, a candidate for baptism.

[April] 3*rd* Milo Hoyt & his wife, set out for their new station on Chattooga Creek; & took Darius Hoyt with them to assist for a few weeks.

Br. Vail went with them and took such articles of household goods & provisions as is it was thought best to send from this place.— Chattooga is about 60 miles, south by west from Brainerd, & about the same distance from Creek Path & from Taloney.[12]

Meeting for business.

Resolved that the bill of prices for Blacksmithing as presented by Br. Talmage be accepted.

As it appears there will be much more work in the blacksmith line than one man can do, & as the poor natives frequently get more orders from the Agent for work in that line, for which government will pay, than they can get smiths to fill, & as a blacksmith offers to hire to us, who is approved by the natives, & has a permit, therefore

Resolved, that Br. Talmage be authorized to hire this blacksmith at price not exceeding 30 dollars a month.[13]

Resolved that Br. Talmage have the management of the blacksmithing business.

Apl. 5*th* Recd as letter from Br. Hall dated March 30th informing us that Sister H. was that day confined in childbed—child was very feeble, & not expected to continue long.[14] He wishes one of the sisters to come to their assistance. It would doubtless be very agreeable to have one of the sisters with them at this time; but if one were to set out, from Brainerd immediately it would be a least 10 days after the birth of the child before she could get to them. They have a black girl in the kitchen & a white one, though young & inexperienced to nurse. We know not what is duty.

Sister Conger & Sister Talmage are both confined, Mother Hoyt is able to do but little, sister Chamberlin is also almost reduced to a skeleton, & but just able to keep about the kitchen & others appointments to which her charge leads her; & Sister Anna's health is still feeble & precarious, so that it is only with the utmost exertion that we can get along with our necessary daily business: the family consisting of about 130 persons; besides many coming & going. On the whole concluded to write to Br. Hall, & not send any one untill we can hear from them again. May the Lord comfort this brother & sister in this time of trial, & grant a speedy restoration to health.

[April] 8th Br. Vail returned from Chattooga. He had, on the whole a prosperous journey, tho, somewhat hindered by the hardness of the road & breaking a waggon.

He left all well & cheerful. Their dwelling house, or cabbin, is entirely in the woods & rather small, being about 12 x 14 f. perhaps not quite so much on the inside. But they can soon build an addition for their lumber, meat, meal &c.—There is one small cabbin in sight—but no village in that part of the country. The inhabitants are scattered thro the woods; each family on its own little plantation.

The news of their arrival soon spread, & numbers came to welcome their new friends, manifesting great joy that one had arrived to teach their children. They had not begun the school house, having been waiting, as they said, for their teacher to come & tell how & where he would have it built. They were all now ready to set immediately about it, & said they would soon have it ready for the school.

Mr. Espy, the millwright, from Athens Georgia, arrived this evening.[15]

[April] 10th Meeting this evening.

The millwright having this day examined the several places that have been thought of for the mill, gives it as his decided oppinion that there is but one place where a dam can be made to stand. At this place the creek is not wide, & a firm rock extends from bank to bank rising on each side of the Creek. The only objection to this place is there is not sufficient fall to place the mill near the dam, & we must be at the expense of digging a canal about three quarters of a mile. But when done it is thought the whole will be permanent. And a sawmill, gristmill, or any other water works that may at any time be wanted may be built within a few rods of the mission house, with plenty of water at all times, & without the least possible danger from the flood; which in this creek, is at times very powerful. If a mill race is cut here it will enclose in the bend of the creek about 300 acres of good farm land, which will require but very little fence on the bank of the creek to make it secure from all encroachment.[16] Although we greatly regret the necesity of so much expense at this time, yet considering the above advantages, & the great risk of building at any other place, Resolved, that we build the mill dam at the place recommended by the Millwright.

[April] 12*th* Meeting for business.

As it will be wholly impracticable to do our cooking as it out [ought] to be done in one small kitchen, if we bring into our present family all the laborers that it will be necessary to employ in order to proceed with our enlarged business; & as it is of some importance that the laborers should have their own time for eating, prayers &c; & that their tools should be kept quite sepparate from those of the boys, therefore,

Resolved, that we put up two small log houses, between the mission house & the creek; & that a part of the mission family live there, & cook for the laborers.

Apl. 13*th* Recvd a letter from Br. Butrick dated 8th inst. It was truly welcome, as we had not before heard from him since the 3rd day after he left us, which is now a full month.

The prospects at Creek Path are hopeful. He writes "When we left Brainerd we lost our path, traveled till some time after dark, & came to the road near Little Meat's. We stopped, & were greatly refreshed by the kindness of our dear Cherokee friends. We left there early on Sabbath morning & went to Br. Hicks'. The congregation there was not large. Old Mr. Hains of Shoemake gave me one dollar & Br. Hicks 2,37 cents, which enabled us to pay 25 cents for corn, 50 cents for a pair of mocassins & our expenses on the way, & retain 25 cents.[17]

On monday we traveled to Mr. Pardue's, visited Three killer on the way. Tuesday to Mr. Burns'. Got a recruit of provisions. Wednesday to a large hickory blown down by the wind, where we had a very comfortable lodging. Thence to a Mr. Scotts. Friday to a large white-oak log in the woods between Shoat's & Cox's. Saturday to Capt J. Browns". (This Capt Brown is a brother of David & Catharine, & lives about 5 miles from his fathers & in the neighborhood of the school.) "We told him our business, & he informed others &c. Sabbath, to his fathers, where we were kindly recvd, but it being late in the day we had no meeting. Monday Capt J. Brown came—told me he had seen the chiefs, they were glad we had come, & wished me to accompany him the next day, look out a place for the school-house, & meet them at an appointed place. Tuesday I went with Capt Brown, but referred it to him to say where the house should be. He selected a place, we met the chiefs, I told my errand &c. They told me they would do as I had stated, & appointed the next Friday to begin the house—Friday they assembled, Old men & children. They cut the timber, & put up the house, making the inside 22 f by 17. Saturday they made the boards (without a saw), covered the roof, put up most of the Chimney, cut out the door, split part of the puncheons for the floor, put in the steps, & hewed down the house inside. I think the house is nearly or quite as high as that at Brainerd. We appointed a meeting in the new school house the next day. Sabbath we met—perhaps 30 Cherokees, & a number of black & white people.

Monday, Tuesday & Wednesday, a less number worked on the house, & made a good floor, door, hearth, back, finished laying up the chimney, chinked the house, made the benches &c. Thursday we began school. 8 schollars the first three days.

Sabbath, we attended meeting, perhaps 60 or 70 Cherokees attended. I began a sunday school for the blacks, 10 or 15. Monday about 20 schollars, after that, this week we have had about 27, upwards of 30 different schollars, & old Mr. Gunter told me to day he expected to send 10 in a month from this time.[18] Last night the people had a talk. The Path Killer advised them to be attentive to our instruction, & to give their children into our care; telling them that they must continue their children with us at least 4 years in order to profit them. This morning they desired me to meet them at the Store. I went. Saw the dear old Path Killer. I can not but love him. The people agreed to send an express to Brainerd when necessary. I stated to them the propriety of benches prepared as at Brainerd in order to accommodate all the children, & expect they will get plank & prepare them next week.

The people here, from the oldest to the youngest, appear anxious to receive instruction, both religious & scientifical; & some appear really inquiring after the truth.

All the people we see receive us as their nearest friends. So we say now; but how long we shall receive these undeserved marks of attention the Savior knows. It is not for any thing we are, or do; but because they wish to learn, & desire & have a disposition to be kind. We have our board free of expense, & our dear old Mrs. Brown does our washing. I have writen this letter in the singular, as if no one were with me: but our dear Br. John has done much more than I have. He has not only done all that I have by interpreting, but has done much himself." Speaking of the progress the children have made in these few days he says, "About 14 who knew none of their letters, have learned them, & read in two letters, some in three. If the people continue pleased with the school, I think there will in a few days be 40 schollars. You will not be surprised however, if there should not be ten." The above appears to have been writen on Saturday. Sabbath evening he adds "To day we have had a large collection of people for this country. About 100 Cherokees & blacks."

[April] 15. Br. Conger left us to take his eldest daughter to Fa. Gambolds.[19] She expects to continue there a while for the benefit of instruction. Br. Conger thinks it highly necessary that she should have more school learning, & that the business here is so constantly crowding upon the female department, that it will be best to take her where she cannot be taken off from her school.

Milo Hoyt came up from Chattooga to get a horse & some other articles which are found necessary there. The people are very friendly, & he expects they will have the school house ready for the school next week.

This evening we were refreshed by a letter from the dear brethren at Elliot. Brs. Finney & Washburn were still there. They had made one attempt to get over to the Arkansas, but were obliged to turn back on account of high waters. A desire to have their children instructed appears increasing among the Choctaws; & Br. Kingsbury has gone to commence another Establishment in that nation near the Tombigbe.[20]

Sab. [April] 16. Milo Hoyt offered himself to be examined with a view to be propounded, if the chh should think proper for admition to full communion in the chh. Hopes have been entertained of his gracious renewal for perhaps more than a year: but owing to occasional darkness & doubts, he has hitherto been kept from making a public profession, through fear that his heart deceived him, & his profession would prove unsound. His supposed evidences have, in his view, been of late renewed with additional clearness. His relation & answers were satisfactory, & he was, by unanimous vote received to be propounded.

[April] 17th Meeting for business.
Resolved that the Sorrel horse, with such Harness as will be wanted with him, be assigned to the school at Chattooga.
Resolved that Robert Step, one of the laborers, be dismissed from our service tomorrow morning for his bad conduct.
Milo Hoyt left us this morning to return to Chattooga.

[April] 22. Some of the laborers have been employed the week past, hauling timber for the saw-mill & other buildings with steers raised at

Brainerd. Four pair already work very well; a fifth & perhaps a sixth may soon be added.

Few people in this part of the country, either red or white know any thing about working oxen. A few pair well broken, introduced into different parts of the nation, may do much toward teaching the people that "Much increase is by the strength of the ox."[21] Cattle are so easily raised in this country that the natives might easily furnish themselves with oxen, did they but know their use & how to train them for work.

Sab. [April] 23. The members of the chh being detained after sermon, David Brown was examined as to his knowledge of the nature & design of baptism, what constitutes a due preparation for receiving holy ordinance, & what are the special duties & relations of the baptised. He giving satisfaction on all these points, next sabbath was assigned for the day of his baptism.

[April] 24. Mary K. Rawlings, a member of the Presbyterian chh in Washington Rhea Co. having offered her services gratuitously, for our assistance have for a time, & she having no convenient way to get to us unless we can send for her, we sent David Brown with a horse to assist her in coming.[22]

We think the help of this devoted young woman will be of great service here at this time, as the labors of the female department are increasing, & our Sister Anna Hoyt continues in such feeble state of health that it is not probable she will soon be able to render much assistance, either in the school or in the kitchen.

Meeting for business.

Some of the laborers asking for more wages if they continue, Resolved that we will not raise the wages of common hands.

Resolved, that Br. Conger with his family remove into the new cabbins as soon as they are in readiness.

[April] 27. David Brown returned with our beloved sister Mary K. Rawlings.

Mr. Dawson, who is engaged as a teacher in the mission school projected by our Baptist brethren in the eastern part of this nation, called to make us a short visit. Mr. Dawson & the Rev. Mr. Posey & family, have commenced their opperations on the bank of the Highwasse [Hiwassee] creek, about 20 miles from the Tennessee river & about 120 from Brainerd, in the valley called Peach Tree.[23]

They do not expect to begin their school untill corn is ripe.

[April] 28. Br. Dawson left us, on his return, about noon. He appears much engaged for Indian reform, & truly devoted to the work.

The laborers sent from this place to work on the school house at Taloney returned. They say the house is nearly finished, but, the plank failing, they were obliged to leave about three days work, which can be done by a carpenter in that neighborhood. Br. Hall writes that he hopes to commence school in about 2 weeks.

Ard Hoyt, Abijah Conger, John Vail, Wm Chamberlin

Journal of the Mission at Brainerd continued

1820

April 30. The church opened her gladened bosom & by baptism admited David Brown to visible membership.[24]

May 1. We were greatly surprised this evening to learn that Br. Talmage had made up his mind to leave the Mission & had even concluded to go, with his wife & child, in the waggon we were about to send to Augusta for Iron & steel which was expected to start tomorrow.[25] On learning this the brethren concluded it would not be duty to send a waggon after this iron if Br. Talmage were going with it not to return, as the iron would not be needed unless he remained to work it.

Br. T. says he has nothing against any one of the Mission family, but as he cannot feel contented here, he thinks it not his duty to stay.

O how misterious are the ways of Providence! O what cause have we to be humble before our God. Surely it is the Lord alone who can save the Mission. This we have always known, may we now feel it more & more.

Resolved that Br. V. in addition to his present charge take the oversight of the temporal concerns about the Mission house.

Resolved that Br. George [Halsey] take the little waggon and go to Taloney for Nancy Brow[n?]

Resolved that Father H. prepare a joint letter to Br. Hall.

As Br. Talmage has stated that he thinks it his duty to leave the Mission as soon as convenient, Therefore Resolved that Br. T. be released from the Blacksmithing business. Resolved that Father H. prepare a joint letter to the Cor. Sec. reporting the intended departure of Br. T. & also respecting another Blacksmith.[26]

[May] 3. Our distressful feelings respecting the designed departure of Br. Talmage are quite indescribable. All we can say & all the reasons we have to offer do not appear to alter his views or opinion on the subject—He still maintains the position that as he is not satisfied or contented to stay he has a right to depart, & that immediately without giving time even to notify the Pru. Com. Under these circumstances we thought it duty to set apart a day for fasting, humiliation & prayer, & appointed Saturday the 6th inst. to be observed & kept as such by this mission family.

> O dearest Saviour intercede.
> For us in this our time of need
> Thou see'st O Lord each asking heart,
> Which mourns & bleeds with inward smart.
> Thou also see'st thy little band
> All helpless leaning on thy hand,
> To thee we look, to thee we pray
> O help us in this trying day.

[May] 4. Br. Conger removed into the new house. It has two rooms about 14 by 16 in the inside with a chimney to each room, being made each with a separate pin of logs as high as the eves & placed 14 feet apart—A roof near 50 feet in length extends over the hole leaving the space between covered, but open in front & rear. The Kitchen & pantry are left without a floor. The other room floored with split timbers. The logs are hewed down on the inside & split boards nailed over the open places in the logs, & laid loose as a floor or ceiling overhead, making on the whole pretty nice & comfortable dwelling room.[27]
In the evening after early family prayers at the Mission house, the mission family with some of the schollars attended a prayer meeting in the new house. It was a refreshing season to our drooping spirits: which had in some degree been previously prepared by the arrival of our dear John Arch with good news from Creek path. Br. Butrick writes that the school has increased to 45, & more would be glad to enter soon if there could be room for them. Br. B. wishes it possible to have an assistant. The schollars being chiefly new beginners require much more attention than they will when further advanced. He is now obliged to employ Br. John the whole time as a teacher & can do very little towards bringing him forward. It is thought John ought not so soon to be hindered in his studies if it can be avoided. The natives

say if a female teacher can come to instruct the girls they will build another house for them. The whole expense including board, washing &c for Br. B & his assistant has been sustained by the people except a few books, slates & some other trifling contingencies.

The Sabbath meetings are well attended—numbers thoughtful, some under more deep convictions, & one or two hopeful cases of conversion. One of the girls received as a candidate for baptism here about a year ago and soon after taken from us, has found means to get to that school. She began to write some before she left us, & by a letter now received from her it appears she has lost nothing in writing, but has rather improved since she has been by herself. She now hopes to find her way to Brainerd, & to the chh. The woman who came more than 100 miles last May to seek instruction here, as she said about the Savior, is among the serious inquirers at Creek Path. O that the Lord of the harvest would thrust labourers into this whitened field.[28]

May 6. Agreeable to previous appointment, this day was set at hand by the Mission Family for fasting & prayer. It is with us a day of trial & affliction,* and a day of rejoicing–We have truly a mixed cup. Blessed be God that it is not an unmixed cup of anguish & dismay as our sins deserve.—After preaching, the two candidates for communion at the Lords table (John Arch & David Brown) answered questions relative to their preparation for admission to that holy ordinance. Their answers gave full satisfaction to the chh that they had "knowledge to discern the Lords body, & faith to feed upon him"; & the chh unanimously agreed that they be admited tomorrow.[29]

The painful case of Br. Talmage was brought up by the question whether it be proper to admit him under existing circumstances to communion at this table tomorrow. He was not present & has not been with us through the day. On inquiring it was found that he went out with a gun in the morning.

The chh considers the case of Br. Talmage a difficult one. Although we think he is altogether wrong in leaving the Mission, especially at this time & in this manner, yet he says he thinks he is doing right: & all we can say individualy & collectively, appears to have no convincing weight upon his mind. As the case has not been legally brought before the chh in the form of a charge it was conceived that the chh as such could not properly act upon it at this time, yet considering our circumstances here before the heathen it was thought best to request Br. Talmage not to unite in the communion. Sister

Talmage says it now is, and ever has been, her desire to continue in the Mission, according to their first engagement.
Br. George returned from Taloney with the girl we had hired here & taken there to assist Sis. Hall, we having promised to see that she was brought back whenever she became unwilling to stay, or was no longer needed there.

* These expressions refer to the departure of Mr. Talmage from the mission. See the last annual report of the Board, under the head of the Cherokees, pg. 35.[30]

[May] 7. We have had great cause of joy & of sorrow on this holy day. Br. Talmage's absence with the cause was calculated to excite the most painful sensations while the prosperity of the chh in other respects called for the warmest gratitude & praise to the giver of all good. With the exception of Br. Talmage & his wife (she being unwell) all our Cherokee & African brothers & sisters with all the chh. members of the Mission Family (except those at Local schools & one black Br. who is far off on business) were asembled before the table of the Lord, and there witnessed the admission of John Arch & David Brown to full communion of all the duties & privileges of the followers of Christ.

[May] 8. Received boxes of clothing &c from the following places viz. Otsego N.Y. containing several bundles from different societies & individuals viz. one from a female society in Newberlin, one from Burlington female Benefficent Society, one from a number of Ladies in Hardwick Village & one from Ladies in Bloomfield, also some articles from the Kendwick & [Fly?] Benevolent Society. The last of which sent clothing for the school last year.—One box containing hats & medicine from Mr. George Pomeroy Cooperstown N. York, one from Griswold Con.—one from Rupert Vermont, one from Granville Vermont. All containing very useful clothing. We have now a very good supply for the Summer. Most of the clothing now on hand is of thin cloth, too thin to be serviceable in winter.
A kind providence appears still to smile upon the Mission, & amidst sorrows, & afflictions, sends consolations & encouragements.

> In thy strong arm Lord we'll confide
> Through the rough storms thou art our guide
> O'er all the host which Satan brings
> Thy army still its victory sings.

May 8th Meeting for business.—

Resolved that we recommend to Sister Catharine Brown to go and take the charge of a female school in her Fathers neighborhood, as soon as the people will put a house in readiness.—

[May] 9. A gentleman & his{Mr. John M. Foster &} wife from Frankfort, Kentucky, who called on us last evening, left this afternoon. She is traveling for her health, & had a desire to come this way, in order to visit the school. They appeared much interested in the children, & expressed great satisfaction, on account of the brightening prospects among this people. Though our interview was short, parting was painful. They both appear to possess a true Missionary Spirit. {He left a donation of $20.— When he understood it was to be entered as a donation to the Mission he requested that his name might not go with it, but consented that it should be entered as a donation from a Gentleman of Frankfort, Ky.}

[May] 11. David Brown set out this morning on his way (if the Lord will) to the F.M.S. He goes by way of Savannah & Boston. We did expect Mr. Elijah Hicks to accompany him.[31] He has waited several days, but finding that Mr. Hicks could not go soon he interceded that we would let him go on alone. It is indeed a long journey for a lad of 19 to undertake alone among strangers & a people of another Nation. But no difficulty appears to him insurmountable or even great which comes in the way of his being prepared to preach that gospel which he has found so precious & powerful in his own case. By the assistance of his friends he has obtained money sufficient to defray the probable expense of his journey, and then he will be under the necessity of casting himself upon the charity of the friends of Jesus. And he appears not to entertain the least doubt but a competency will be obtained from this source. We hope & pray that He who hath promise of the heathen for his inheritance will so replenish the funds of that school, that the directors of it will not feel themselves obliged to exclude this our dear brother from their patronage. We often think, if we could only have access to the individuals who possess the property of the N. States we could willingly on our knees, beg of every one that had a sixpence to spare. But we reflect again the treasure & the hearts of all are in the hand of the Lord & we prostrate ourselves before him & beg that he will not suffer his people to shut their hand against the poor heathen whose souls are perishing for lack of that knowledge, which, through their benefficence, might be imparted unto them. May the dear Savior vouch safe his gracious presence with this our dear red brother & fulfill his desire according to his enlarged faith.

[May] 13th Milo Hoyt having left the school in the charge of Darius came up from Chatuga [Chattooga]. He performed the journey in one day. Cows for milk, & certain other articles of food cannot be obtained there as was expected & he was under the necessity of returning for supplies. Appearances there at present are very different from those at Creek Path.

When the people assembled to build the house according to the agreement which their chief made with Br. Chamberlin, they appeared evidently dissatisfied. They went about the building very reluctantly; though they had before expressed great anxiety for a school. They put up the body of the house, & then left it without assigning any reasonable cause. The chief, with the assistance which Milo & Darius could render, proceeded with the house, got it sufficiently forward to admit a school, & word was given out that the school could commence on the 25th of April. No children attended. After waiting several days he sent for the chiefs and told them he came for the sole purpose of teaching the children, & if they did not attend he should immediately return to Brainerd. They assured him it was their wish to have a school and the children should attend. The next day (Wednesday) 8 children attended. Thursday & friday 15. Saturday, he left Chatuga early in the morning & came to us. None of the children knew a letter & but one could speak English. This one learned the whole alphabet and began to read in words of two letters in those three days.

[May] 14. Received a very affectionate letter dictated by the Father of the boy we call Jeh [Jeremiah] Evarts interpreted & written by sister Lydia Hoyt & directed to Father Hoyt & Br. Chamberlin. He has no knowledge of letters or of the english language. The following is an extract from the letter. "We have been separated a long time from each other, but I hope you have not forgotten to pray for me & my nation. My Dear Friends, you told me much about our Dear Crucified Savior & I hope I have not forgotten what you said. O no! my dear friends, I cannot forget the great Redeemer who has, as I hope, redeemed my immortal soul from eternal destruction. I hope you will instruct my dear children in the right way, & that the Lord may have mercy on them, & turn their wicked hearts to himself. Give my love to them."

Enclosed in the above was an open letter directed to two persons in this neighborhood, whom, it seems, he considers as fellow converts to christianity. One of them is a member of the Chh. The following is an extract from this enclosed letter. "My dear friends, though we do not now see each other, yet I hope our hearts are still united in Jesus. Let us go on the way we have begun, for it is not a tedious way. May the Lord of love be your father. I have talked to my poor parents, but I cannot convince them of their sins. I know that God is able to change their wicked hearts."

Do not these sentiments appear to flow from a heart enlightened by the word & Spirit of God? Andrew, when he had found the Savior immediately sought his brother Simon to bring him to Jesus. Philip did the same for Nathaniel. And Moses said to his father in law "Go thou with us and we will do thee good, for the Lord hath spoken good concerning Israel."[32] This man seeks to bring his relatives & friends to Jesus, & is assured that he is able to do them good. His daily walk and conversation, so far as we can learn, is in unison with the sentiments expressed in these letters. And yet it appears this man has received but little instruction except what he has picked up here in his short visits to his children. And these have been at long intervals as he lives about 60 miles from us, & is busily occupied in domestic concerns.

[May] 15. In meeting for business.

As the object we had in view, in dismissing the laborers at 4 oclock Saturdays does not appear to be answered, Therefore Resolved that the vote respecting their being so dismissed be rescinded.

Resolved that a cheap cabin be put up for the use of the school at Chatuga.

Resolved that Milo Hoyt take $30 for the use of the school at Chatuga.

[May] 17. Br. Hall arrived this evening from Taloney. Br. David Brown arrived there last Saturday & spent the Sabbath with Br. Hall. On monday morning David's horse left him, in the course of the day they heard of him coming towards Brainerd. As David did not like to turn back & as Br. Hall wished to attend to some business here, it was concluded to leave the school with David while he came for the horse expecting to find him here. We have seen nothing of the horse, & hear our dear brother will have much trouble in looking after him.

The school was begun the day before Br. Hall left home on the 15th inst. 14 schollars the first day. [About?] 20 had come in the second day

in the morning before his departure. There is a prospect of a full
school. Sister Halls health is improving.
In meeting for business B. Hall present.
Resolved that Br. Hall take $25 for the use of the Taloney school.
Resolved that the white mare be assigned to the Taloney school in the
place of the sorrel horse first taken by Br. Hall.

[May] 18. The most solemn day Brainerd ever saw. O! "Tell it not in
Gath; publish it not in the streets of Ashkelon, lest the daughters of
the uncircumcised triumph."[33] One whom we had been in the habit of
calling Brother, one who had covenanted with us to spend & be spent
in the Mission, left us without assigning any satisfactory reason, and
without any apparent remorse. "Let him that thinketh he standith,
take heed lest he fall."[34]
Meeting for business.—Resolved that we jointly write to the Pru.
Com. for direction relative to clearing a few acres of land at Taloney
for the benefit of that school & also that we inquire of them relative to
assistance being sent there—Resolved that we approve of Br. Halls
having built a cheap chimney to the dwelling house & also that we
recommend that he build a similar one for the school house.

[May] 19. Br. H. left us on his return & took Sister Catharine for a visit.

[May] 21. A complaint was brought before the chh. against Br.
Talmage for leaving the Mission. As it appears he is still in the
neighborhood & probably will be for some days. The chh. appointed
Wednesday next to hear this case & directed that Br. Talmage be cited
to attend. Sister Sally McDonald being about to remove into the
neighborhood of the chh. of which the kind Mr. Gambold is pastor at
Springplace, a letter was directed to be given recommending her to
the fellowship of that chh. & authorizing a dismission from this chh.
to that. She appeared much affected at the prospect of removing from
us, though it is but a short distance & she knows it is to go amongst
dear christian friends, & natural relatives. The ties that bind these
dear converts to us, & us to them, we trust are such as will never be
broken.

May 22. Meeting for business. Resolved that we clear a field for
turnips over the creek opposite the fish trap.

[May] 24. Br. Talmage attended agreeable to citation. He plead as a
justification of his conduct in leaving the Mission, that he never
considered that he had engaged to continue in the mission unless he

should be pleased so to do after making trial. He stated as a reason of his dissatisfaction, boarding in common with the children on such coarse food, & also that the brethren previous to the building of the blacksmith shop, had assigned to him the care of getting up wood & salting meat. The instructions given to him from the Pru. Com. before he left New Jersey were read. They say "you are considered as engaged for life."[35]

The chh. by unanimous vote decided that his plea of justification was inadmissible, & unightedly [unitedly] endeavoured to convince him of his error.

Although this decision & labour appeared to have no good effects as there was a possibility that further exertions might be blest & it being expected he would continue some time in the neighborhood, a final sentence was defered.

Catharine Browns father came from Creek Path with a letter from Br. Butrick. He writes "The people after hearing that Sister Catharine was willing to teach the girls as soon as a house could be prepared, & that the Missionaries thought well of it, immediately resolved to build a house the same size as the other & appointed the next friday & saturday to build it.

On friday about 50 cherokee men besides boys & blacks asembled, built the house, covered it & almost completed the floor. Saturday they finished the floor, hewed it down inside, & chinked it & put in the beams. They expect to make the door & benches this week. I told them it was not absolutely certain whether Sister Catharine would come or another person though I expected she would come. I think it would be well for her to come as she can talk & there will be no good interpreter. If she teaches a few months and then continues a schollar, she may do great good. Her Mother is peculiarly anxious to have her at home."

Mr. Brown says he did not come to take Catharine from us or from the school, & he does not wish her to go unless we think it best. He appears seriously impressed with divine things. Catharine is still at Br. Halls, he will wait her return.

[*May*] 25. Rev. Remembrance Chamberlin on a missionary tour under direction of the General Assembly called on us. He brought a letter from Dr. Waddel Pres. of the college in Athens Georgia enclosing $77 a donation from the auxiliary Missionary Society in Madison, Morgan County, Georgia.[36] He also brought from the charity box of the Theol

Sem^y Princ [Theological Seminary Princeton] a donation of Twenty dollars. This money came truly in a time of need. Our Treasury was drained & we could not tell how we were to answer our money calls, for tomorrow. "Our heavenly Father knoweth that we have need of these things."[37]

We learn that Br. Talmage with his wife & child, left the neighborhood this morning in a waggon that was going to Augusta.

[May] 29. We have been edified by the conversation & preaching of our visiting Br. Mr. Chamberlin. He left us this morning to pursue his mission to the west & North. Recvd by way of Baltimore & Knoxville the following boxes, chest & trunk; shiped by the Treasurer at Boston on the 19th Feb. viz.

No. 7. Containing clothing &c from Newton, Mass. Concord N.H. Conway Mass. North Yarmouth Me. & New Ipswich N. H.

No. 8. Clothing from Southampton, Mass. & the residue from New Ipswich N.H.

No. 9. Containing shoes purchased by the Treasurer, & clothing from shburnham, North Yarmouth, & Sharon V^t As this box was broken and contained no bills—we give a bill of all that was found in it, that it may be known, whether all came safe. It is as follows 60 pr of shoes, 26 pr of stockings, 1 pr mittens, 1 pr suspenders, 11 shirts, 6 pr pantaloons, 2 boys great coats, 4 vests, 8 shifts, 9 skirts, 4 dresses, 1 apron, 1 pocket handkerchief, 12 pieces cloth, mostly remnants.

No. 10. Clothing from Greensborough & Hardwick V^t, box somewhat shattered, but the articles appeared not to have been moved since the first packing.

No. 11. Clothing from Townsend, Mass.

No. 12. A trunk given to the Osage captive girl by Mrs. Carter, with some articles in the bottom for her also. The upper part containing articles from other sources. The hasp of this trunk was loose. It contained for Lydia Carter 5 dresses, 4 remnants of the same kind of cloth, 3 shifts, 2 aprons, 1 skirt, 1 towel, 1 thread case, Pocket handkerchief, bunch of tape, paper pins & 2 rolls of cotton ferret. For the Juvenile Cherokee library at Brainerd two hundred books & cards.

No. 13. A chest of clothing from Buckland, also woolen blankets, this last article is very much needed here.

No. 14. A box from Bridport, V^t.

Through the very kind and benevolent attention of the friends of missions principally of our unknown sisters in Christ, we have a present supply of clothing for the children excepting some garments for our largest boys, which may be supplied from cloth which has accompanied the clothing. We feel ourselves bound to praise and adore the bountiful giver of all good, that he has opened the hearts of our dear sisters so amply to supply our needs. We trust that he who has excited in them this benevolent spirit will pour upon them his blessing & enable them to supply the future wants of these dear children.

[*May*] 31. Sister Catharine having returned from Taloney, left us in company with her father to go to Creek Path, to teach a female school. How very different the scene from one that passed here not quite two years since, when her father required her to leave the society of christians and accompany him to the then dark shades of the Arkansas? Now he does not ask her without our consent, will not take her except by our advise: and she is going not into the wilderness unprepared to teach others or even to improve her own mind, but into a place where divine light has already begun to spring up, prepared, as we think to teach. Yet it is highly probable that this removal will not be productive of so much good as the former. So unsearchable are the ways of God! So incompetent is man to judge. It now appears that her first removal was the means of sowing the seed which is now springing at Creek Path with such hopeful promise. Catharine was received to this school July 9th 1817; Baptized Jan. 25th 1818 and admited to the communion of the Lords supper March 29th 1818. Her father with great apparent tenderness appears anxiously inquiring after the truth.

In meeting for business, As George W. Halsey has expressed a desire to spend his days in the mission & it is thought he may be better prepared for future usefulness & also be of more immediate service to the Mission by going into the school as an assistant teacher & to labour with the boys, Therefore Resolved that G.W. Halsey enter as an assistant for the above purposes immediately.

June 1st Mr. Adam Hodgson Esq. merchant recently from Liverpool England called on us with an introductory letter from Br. Kingsbury.[38] He left Elliot on the 20th ult. having been traveling only 10 days from Elliot to this place as he rested on the sabbath. He left the Mission family and schollars at Elliot in a general state of health: & speaks highly of the improvements & present state of that establishment.

Br. Kingsbury writes "Appropriations have been made for a third establishment in this Nation, & we are urged to commence it immediately.[39] It is a source of deep regret that our means will not admit us to extend our opperations with that promptness, & alacrity, which the exigencies of this nation require. You will unite with us in beseeching the Lord of the harvest to send forth many more laborers and to raise up the means for their support."

Brs. Finney & Washburn had left their female companions at Elliot & gone to the Arkansas, expecting to spend the Summer in making preparations there.

[June] 2nd Mr. Hodgson left us early this morning to prosecute his journey, leaving many tokens of his good wishes & ardent Zeal in the cause of Missions. {He gave $10 to the common fund of the mission & $5 to be appropriated to our Juvenile library.}

June 5. Brother Ch. set out for Chatuga for the purpose of spending a short time in visiting the people and preaching in that neighborhood.

[June] 6. Raised the building intended for the female schollars. It is 40 feet by 20, two story and to have a chimney at each end. The upper story is intended for lodging, the lower to be divided in the middle— one room for the school the other for work.

[June] 10. Br. Ch. returned from Chatuga he found the people very ready to assemble to hear preaching. Many more attended than could get into the house & heard with the strictest attention. It now appears that the reason of their leaving the school house before it was finished and being so backward about sending their children, was, they were dissatisfied with the place their Chief had selected for the school. This they did not make known, even to their teacher, or any other person who would inform us. Br. Ch. providentially discovered it while among them. Br. Ch. took a more particular survey of the country & found that their dissatisfaction was not without ground, as the house was entirely on one side of those who wished to be benefited by the school. He informed them that the school was not intended for any individual, but for all of them & they should have the privilege of fixing it in the place which they should judge most convenient for the settlement. On hearing this they consulted together a few moments & unanimously agreed to remove the school about three miles, & across

the creek: that they would send their children to the present place until they had built a school house & one for the teacher. Appearance for preaching are favorable.

Br. Gahagan came back from Br. Halls. He has 37 schollars on his list, & more coming in: Sabbath meetings are well attended.

[June] 12. Received a letter from Br. Hall requesting us to send him money.

In meeting for business

Resolved that Br. Ch write to Br. Hall & inform him that there is no money in the treasury & we have no means of getting any at present.

{Resolved that Father H. prepare a letter to the Postmaster Gen. respecting the post office being removed here in case Mr. Ross should leave the neighborhood.}

Resolved that we get 20,000 brick made this season.

Resolved that Br. Conger be authorized to buy a boat of Mr. Slover.

Resolved that Br. Butrick be authorized to purchase 20 bushels of corn for the use of the school at Creek path.

[June] 20. Resolved unanimously that we consider it contrary to the expectations of the Prud. Com. and injurious to the mission to hold private property on mission ground. And if any member of this family has brought or may hereafter bring private property with the expectation of retaining it as such, or of selling it as private property on mission grounds, he or she be requested to consolidate it with the mission property or to take it away & in no case to offer it for sale as private property within the precincts of the mission family.[40]

[June] 22. Received a box with articles of clothing from Conway & Newton Mass. Some valuable Blanketing which will be very useful the coming winter. Besides a number of made garments & several pieces of cotton and linnen cloth.

[June] 23. Received interesting communication from Creek path. Sister Catharine arrived safe & commenced her school with very flattering prospects; she has about 20 schollars & expects more soon. Both children and parents appear much engaged to receive instruction, & many are earnestly inquiring the way to life & salvation. Several of the schollars are now able to read in the Testament having had some instruction before, but most of them began anew.

We have great hopes that a little church will soon be established there. One woman who appears to give evidence of a real change of heart has been received as a candidate for baptism. Her husband appears very susceptible on the subject of religion and expresses an ardent desire to be prepared to come with her. Dear Sister Catharine who was lately mourning on account of her dear friends, covered with thick darkness & sin, & unmoved by all her conversation and exertions to bring them to the light, now with great joy beholds her dear parents, brothers & sisters unitedly weeping for their sins, & earnestly inquiring after the good way which she has found. O how great the power! how rich the grace of our God! The work is his and he will accomplish it in his own best time & way.

Meeting for business Resolved that Br. V. prepare a letter to Br. B in answer to his of June 4.

Resolved that we send $20 to Br. B. for the use of the school at Creek Path.

Resolved that we think it best to build a grist mill this season & that a statement of the probable expense be forwarded to the Com. for their approbation.

Resolved that Marly [or Manly] be dismissed from our employ immediately, for bad conduct.

June 24th Br. Ch. went to Br. Hicks' for the purpose of conversing with him on the subject of apprentices to the blacksmith trade, & to see if some plan could not be devised to recover the expense which may hereafter be incurred by schollars who leave the school before they have finished their education.

[June] 26. Br. Ch. returned. He had a very interesting meeting with a number of the chiefs who were providentially present. He preached twice on the sabbath to a very attentive audience. The chief who visited us with the Pathkiller last season (called the Boot) was present.[41] He told Br. Ch. he believed all he had heard was true. He said when a person fell asleep & had an interesting dream he would remember it and tell it to his friends & now he had heard these things he would remember them & tell them to his people. He would tell the Pathkiller how he providentially & happily met with the missionary and heard his talk. He said neither he nor the Pathkiller understood what the motives of the missionaries were until they visited us last season, that when they found we were teaching the children about the things of another world they were very glad, & from that time they had both been convinced that the motives of the missionaries were good, and he hoped their children would all grow up in the

knowledge of those things which he had been hearing. On the subject of apprentices to the blacksmithing business, the Chiefs gave it as their decided opinion that the boys should be bound to us for a certain time & that the chiefs should see that they were not taken away in that time.

On the subject of children leaving the school before they had received their education, They said it was a loss to the nation & to the society, to have children go to school a while and then leave it, before they were sufficiently instructed to be useful to themselves & others. It was their opinion if any should take their children away before they finished their education they should pay the expense which shall have been incurred. They said the arrangement should be entered into at the next council.

July 2. Milo Hoyt was admited to full communion with the chh.

[July] 3. In compliance with the request of a society of young gentlemen in Southampton, Mass. a boy has been selected to bear the name of Vinson Gould, to be educated by them & at the request of a society of young ladies in the same place a girl has been selected to bear the name of Mindwell Woodbridge Gould, to be educated by them. The children are called after their pastor & his wife. The boy is between six & seven years of age, his father has emigrated to the Arkansas and left him with his mother. She is poor and wishes us to take the charge of the boy till he is educated.

The girl is between five and six years of age she came here last fall with her parents on a visit to see their other children. The little girl was unwilling to go back with them and we concluded to let her stay.[42] She has called sister Sarah Mother & being destitute of a name that we could conveniently pronounce, she has been called baby till the present time.

In meeting for business, At the request of Br. Conger, Resolved that Br. V. in addition to his present business have the management of the farm.

[July] 5. One end of the mill dam gave way. The millwright supposed he had driven the timbers to the rock. It now appears that what he took to be a rock was only gravel. The water found its way under this and carried away the bank about one rod wide. This is a painful disappointment, & will necessarily be attended with considerable additional expense. It is however a favorable circumstance that the

mistake has been discovered so early. The water is now low, and we hope to be able to guard against the like disaster in future.

[July] 6. Our heavenly Father who has always been rich in mercy towards us, has this day given us fresh tokens of his parental care. Our treasury was empty & several demands came against us which we knew not how to meet. We have just received a line from Colo. Meigs giving us information of two hundred & fifty dollars he has for us from the Sec. of War. This will help us out of our present difficulty—& we hope teach us to put our trust in God for the future.

[July] 7. Received a letter from Dr Worcester giving the joyful assurance that more labourers will be sent into this field as soon as the season of the year will safely admit. May the Lord give our brothers & sisters now at the local schools grace & strength to hold out until this relief shall arrive.

[July] 11. Received in a letter from the Rev. Mr. Murphey of Medway, Geo. Fifty dollars, a donation from a Juvenile society in that place and its vicinity.[43] The Society being constituted for the purpose of aiding in the education of Indian children at Brainerd. Mr. M. observes "the sum is small & will probably increase." This again was a very seasonable and needful supply. The two hundred & fifty dollars being only sufficient to supply an urgent call of the moment.

[July] 12. Br. B. arrived from Creek path, having left the two schools in the charge of our dear Br. John & Sister Catharine. The gracious opperation of the Spirit appears to be still continued at that place. Catharines father & mother, one brother & his wife, two sisters & several others it is hoped have experienced a saving change.[44] Time will probably enable us to judge with more certainty. Others are under serious impressions & the general attention to the word continues.

[July] 13. Br. B. left us this afternoon being anxious to return to his charge at Creek path. Sister Ann, having for some time been in a feeble state of health & frequently suffering injury from engaging too much in the laborious concern of this large family. It was thought it might contribute to her health to spend a few weeks with Sister Catharine: and also that she might be useful there among the female converts & assist Catharine in pursuing the study of grammar. She therefore accompanied Br. B.

[July] 19. Meeting for business. Having heard that our millwright will not be able to return soon, Resolved that we take measures to mend the dam immediately.

Wm Chamberlin, Ard Hoyt, John Vail

Br. Conger is absent.

Journal of Brainerd Mission

July 20th 1820. Brother Thomas Stewart & David Humphries called on us, being on their return from a circuitous Missionary tour under the direction of the Domestic & Foreign Mission Society of the Synod of S. Carolina & Georgia. The object of their Mission was to find a proper place to commence an establishment in some of the Tribes east of the Mississippi, on the plan of the Mission here. They first visited the Creek nation, found many individuals disposed to receive such a Mission, but in the National council it was rejected. From the Creeks they passed through the Chocktaw Nation, visited Eliot, & went on to the Chickasaws. Here they found a very favorable reception, fixed on a site for their Mission establishment, & expect it will be commenced next fall or winter.[45]

[July] 24. In meeting for business, Resolved, that we send to Br. H. $124.00 for the use of the Taloney School. As we are directed by the Treasurer to calculate our necessary expenses beforehand, & to state them to him before we have permission to draw, Therefore, Resolved, that the Manager at each Local School, transmit to the Treasurer at this place, an estimate of money that will be wanted, & for what purposes, soon enough for us to transmit the same to the Treasurer of the Board, & receive returns, before said money will be wanted.

Our visiting Brs. Stewart & Humphries having spent the Sabbath with us, & preached to our little congregation, left us this morning with the expectation of returning with a number of assistants after a few months on their way to the proposed place of their establishment. This however depended on the decision of Synod.

[July] 25. Br. Milo H. finding that he could not purchase provisions at Chatuga for the support of the family and that the school continued small, returned for instruction. Considering the great expense of purchasing and transporting provisions from this place to Chatuga at

this time, the need of br. Milo's labours here, & that we had reason to expect a permanent teacher for that school soon, Therefore, concluded that he go to Chatuga & inform the people that there will be a vacation in that school until they finish the house at the new place.

The Father of the boy called Jerh Evarts made us a visit. He appears very thoughtful on religious subjects; warmly attached to Christians; & anxious for further instruction. He expressed a great desire to live near us, but said the support of his family required that he should continue to live & labor where he now is.

[July] 27. Rev. Mr. Simmons of the Methodist connection, & a Mr. [William] Carr one of Mr. Blackburn's former teachers, called on us, visited the schools, expressed their approbation, & left each a donation.

Agreeably to instruction from the Treasurer, a child has been named Samuel Newel, provided for by the Juvenile mite Society & the Female mite Society of Augusta, Maine.

[July] 30. Mr. John Lawson of North Carolina traveling in company with his wife & her father, Mr. Howard, attended public worship with us today. They stoped in the neighborhood early yesterday for the purpose of spending Sabbath with us & taried a while after meeting. They appeared to take a lively interest in the children, & the concern of the Mission generally. Mr. Lawson left a donation for the benefit of the Mission.

[July] 31. Meeting for business. Resolved that Br. Chamberlin take the charge of repairing the mill dam.

August 14. Resolved, that we stop the crossing places in the bend of the creek by felling trees, so as to enclose a large tract of wood land within the race, for the purpose of keeping our cows.

[Aug.] 15. Received a letter from Br. H. mentioning that they are again destitute of female help & know not where to hire any, enquiring if help can be obtained here. After, considering the subject not withstanding we are much crowded here, concluded, to write to Br. H. that if he cannot obtain help else where Sister Mary will go.

[Aug.] 21. Mr. Gahagan arrived from Taloney stating that he had been to Georgia in search of help for br. H. but could not obtain any & requesting that Sis. Mary go. Accordingly Sis M. left us for this purpose.

[Aug.] 22. Received a letter from Colo. Meigs requiring the Osage Captives.[46] He writes as follows: "Gov. [James] Miller of the Territory of Arkansas,[47] having been authorized by Government to adjust a difference between the Arkansas Cherokees & the Osage Nation to prevent a destructive war, apparently on the very point of commencing, met the chiefs of both these tribes in a conference, & having heard the parties, brought them to promise to suspend the stroke of the war hatchet, on the following terms, (viz.) The Arkansas Cherokees, to collect & return to the Osages all the prisoners that were taken in a late war between the parties; and the Osages on their part to give up certain men of their Nation, who had murdered three Cherokees, since a peace had been made. These stipulations were solemnly made in the presence of Gov. Miller, Acting Arbiter in behalf of the Government, who feel their duty to compel the parties to act, with mutual good faith. The Gov. therefore in his capacity as Gov. & ex officio Superintendent of all Indian affairs, in that section of our Country, demands the delivery of the prisoners on one side & of the murderers on the other side."

In Gov. Millers letter to me, requiring these young prisoners, he has promised that his influence shall be used to have the two Osage Children under your charge returned again to your care.

I am sensible, it must be painful to you to part with them: but it seems the only measure to be adopted, to prevent the sheding of much Blood.

Mr. John Rogers a kind & humane man will take the best possible care of them—I request that the Children may be comfortably furnished with every thing necessary & proper for their journey, & I will pay your Bills for the same.[48]

I have stated to the Secretary of war, all the expenses that have been incurred hitherto, on account of those children, & that all that expense, or other expenses that may be properly incurred on their account, ought to be deducted from the Arkansas Cherokees Annuity.

I request you to deliver the two little prisoners to Mr. Rogers. I am confident that he will be governed by your advice, & will in every respect act towards them kindly & tenderly."

This message was inexpressibly distressing to all the Mission family, especially to those who had adopted these children as their own. We had some days since been informed that the children were demanded, & had reason to expect they must be given up, but still were not without hope that by some means they might yet be retained until they should be prepared to carry the knowledge of the Savior to their people. All hope is now taken away. They must be given up: not to the arms of death to be taken to the Gracious Savior, but to a call from the wilderness to be taken back probably to a savage life, or a premature death. We can only commend them to the care of that Gracious Redeemer to whom they have been devoted in baptism, & who is still able to preserve them & bring them where they can receive that instruction, which we would gladly have given, & by means of which, they may still be prepared, for usefulness in life, peace in death & happiness beyond the grave.

John Osage Ross, being younger & not having been as long with us, was not so much affected. But Lydia Carter had become strongly attached to us all, especially to br. & Sr. Chamberlin, whom she called Father & Mother. She knew no other parents, consequently the thought of a separation was peculiarly trying to her, as well as to us.

When she heard that Mr. Rogers, had come for her (which was early in the morning) she, in company with another little girl took to the woods. All the persons about the house including the children of the school, went in pursuit of them, but without success. A little after noon one of our neighbors came and informed us, that he had seen them, about three miles from this place on their way to the little girls fathers. Milo Hoyt was immediately sent to fetch Lydia. When he came to the little girls fathers, he found that Lydia had been there, but fearing some one would know where she was & come for her, she could not rest contented, until she went two miles farther making in all nine miles which she traveled through the woods, to avoid being taken. When she first saw Milo, she appeared somewhat frightened & began to cry, but he soon consoled her by telling her some pleasing things about the man who had come for her & what she would see on the way. On returning she appeared cheerful, & learning that we thought best for her to go, she said she was willing. This releaved our feelings very much, as we could never before make her consent to go away on any terms, and we now feared she would have to be forced away from us. She remained very cheerful, & sung in family worship with her usual animation.

[*Aug.*] 23. The morning was spent in preparing our dear children for their departure. Lydia having a trunk & some other articles that had been presented to her at different times, which she could not take with her, desired her mother to keep them for her little sister Catharine, if she should not return adding "here is a little handkerchief too small for me. I wish to give this to Catharine whether I come back or not."[49] She remained composed until just before they started. She then appeared in deep thought. She then looked around on those she loved for the last time & then droped her head & the tears flowed profusely. She walked out to the horse without being biden, & not withstanding her evident grief, she was not heard to sob aloud except when taking leave of her little Sister Catharine. Her whole appearance through this trying scene was like that of a person of mature age in like circumstances. It is the Lord let him do as seemeth him good.[50]

Little John having been told from the beginning, that if he would go willingly without crying he should have the little horse on which he was to ride & the saddle & bridle, for his own, went off smiling & was apparently much pleased with his newly acquired property. We have great hopes that these dear children will be taken into the Mission family at Union.[51]

[Aug.] 29. Resolved that Br. Conger go and look up some mill stones. Resolved, that we contract for 3000 bushels of corn for the ensuing year.

Sept. 4 1820. Resolved that we send $40. to Br. B. for the use of the school at Creek path.

Received $32. from the Bardstown Baptist Missionary Society, Remited to us through the agency of the Rev. Wm Eagleton. We think we feel thankful, that our dear brethren from different parts of the country, are thinking of, and affording us, such seasonable aid. And we feel the more thankful as we have reason to think, we have the prayers of those Societies, & Individuals, who are aiding in the pecuniary concerns of this institution.

[Sept.] 9. Br. C. went out for the purpose of preaching tomorrow, where we have an appointment once in four weeks, about fourteen miles up the Tennessee.

Sab. [Sept.] 10. Br. C. returned this evening, had more than an ordinary number of hearers several appeared affected.

[Sept.] 11. Meeting for business. As Br. & S. Conger are to be absent one or two weeks, therefore Resolved that Br. & Sr. V. go to the farm house and take the charge of that part of the family until they return.

[Sept.] 16. Br. C. went to Br. Hicks' to spend the Sabbath. We formerly had an appointment at Br. Hicks once in two weeks but since Br. B.

left us we have not been able to attend these oftener than once in four weeks & some of our preaching stations we have been obliged to abandon altogether.

[Sept.] 17. Br. C. returned, had a pleasant meeting with that dear people, some in that neighbourhood appear to rejoice in the blessing of the gospel.

[Sept.] 20. A Cherokee woman called and left two girls in the school.[52] They were very unwilling to stay. They clung fast to their mother who seeing she could not well get rid of them desired Mother H. to take them away out of her sight. The children screamed & cried very much, but the mother put on the fortitude to leave them in that situation. When we consider how much parents indulge their children in this country, we are surprised that they appear so willing to leave them at school so much against their own will.

[Sept.] 22. Sister Ann returned from Creek path accompanied by Susan Brown a sister of Catharine, she has lately experienced a hope in Christ. God grant that she may adorn her profession as her sister has done. Sister Anna informs us that the work of grace appears to be going on at Creek path. She also informs us that she saw our dear little Lydia on her way to the Osages. Lydia told her she wished she could write to her father & mother. Sister A. told her she would write for her if she would tell her what she wanted to say. She appeared pleased with this & began, but was able to say only a few words, before she was so much affected that she could not proceed. She said she wanted her father and mother to come to the Osage country and get her.

[Sept.] 23. Br. & Sr. Conger returned from Knoxville having been absent two weeks.

[Sept.] 25. Resolved that Br. Ch. prepare a joint letter for the brethren at Eliot.

Oct. 1. Completed the repairing of the mill dam. Br. Chamberlin will now return to the school. This has been a long and fatiguing job. We found on commencing this work that there was no solid rock to build upon & it was the opinion of most people who examined it, that a dam could not be made to stand in that place. We were sensible it would be very difficult to make it sufficiently strong; but all who examine it now have the utmost confidence that it will never give way. The foundation is laid upon the gravel about four feet below the bed of the creek. On this is built a wall of large stone compactly laid, about forty feet in length, ten feet broad at one end & six at the other. About ten feet of the broadest end of the wall is raised twelve feet on the bank side, slopes off in front with the wood dam & is raftered & planked. The remainder of the wall (which is a little more than thirty feet) rises perpendicular about sixteen feet. In front of the wall are plank driven for considerable distance into the gravel. In front of these a bank has been made of lime gravel & clay, as high as the wall & about three rods wide at the bottom.

We have abundant reason to be thankful to our Heavenly Father that the health of our br. & the hired hands has been preserved through this fatiguing job especially as in the first part of the time they were obliged to work almost to their necks in water.

[Oct.] 4. Meeting for business. Resolved that Betsey Michel [or Nickel] be dismissed from our employ immediately.

Resolved that Mr. Slover be notified immediately to come and finish the race.

Resolved that Milo Hoyt go and give Mr. Slover the above notice, & attend to some other business in that neighbourhood.

Resolved that we deem it expedient for various reasons not to pay our monthly hands any money oftener than at the end of every month, & the daily hands every saturday if called for.

Resolved, that no brother shall leave Brainerd to go over ten miles unless a majority of the brethren be in favor of it.

[Oct.] 5. One of our white neighbours came to get some work done in the blacksmith shop. While he was waiting for his work, he and the blacksmith entered into conversation, They soon became angry & came to blows. One of the brethren heard the noise and ran into the shop, & although he forced himself between two angry men armed with clubs and tongs, suceeded in calming them so as to get them both to the Mission house.

Here they both told their story before the brethren. It appeared that the blacksmith gave the first blow. He had been guilty of so many misdemeanors before this, that we had found it necessary to admonish, & forewarn him that he could not be continued without amendment but notwithstanding all this, he was evidently getting worse & worse. Although the mission must suffer very materially for want of the labor of this blacksmith, yet it is thought it will suffer more by continuing such a man in our employ. Therefore, Resolved that Nimrod O'Kelly the blacksmith be dismissed from our employ immediately.

Every instance of this kind of which we have had many may perhaps be considered as an indication that none but the servants of God should be employed ever to labour on mission ground. O that the time may come when the business of this mission can all be done without employing white people who know not the Lord.

[Oct.] 7. Br. C. went to fulfil the appointment up the river.

[Oct.] 9. Br. C. returned. In consequence of a heavy rain on the Sabbath he did not get to the place of his appointment.

[Oct.] 10. Resolved that Br. Chamberlin be directed to attend the council which is to be convened the present month.

[Oct.] 11. We have renewed trouble and difficulty from Nimrod O'Kelly the dismissed blacksmith. The Cherokees have a law that anyone who employs a white man must be accountable for his conduct, & with some limitations liable for his debts.

A small ballance was due to O'Kelly which we declined paying unless he would give security (which he might have done without any trouble) for the payment of a certain debt which he owed in the neighbourhood & for which we had made ourselves responsible. He became enraged, refused to give one cent in security for the debt & threatened if we did not pay him, he would whip some one of the Missionaries all most to death. This was yesterday. Today he asked Br. Conger if he would pay him, he answered, that he could not under present circumstances upon which O'Kelly jumped upon him pressed him down into the mud, & we know not how far his rage would have carried him had he not been taken off by one of the hired men who stood by.

Our millwright returned from Georgia.

Oct. 12. O how sweet it is to meet with Christian friends in a heathen land. Our hearts were made to rejoice by the arrival of our dear brothers Butrick, John Brown sen^r & John Brown jun., his wife and sister Catharine.

[Oct.] 13. Meeting for business. A letter was received from the Chiefs at Creek path, handed by br. John Brown Senr as follows: "Friends & Brothers, We are glad to inform you we are well pleased with Mr.

Butrick who has come forward as a teacher to instruct our people. We believe he does discharge his duty & we hope the cause will be of great advantage to our people. Our wish is, you may prosper throughout our nation in your laudable undertaking. It is out of our power to see you in any short time, on account of the National Council & other business we are obliged to attend at this time. It is our wish the school should continue at this place. Mr. John Brown (Sen[r]) will hand you this who will present you our hands in friendship. We hope we shall see each other before long. We are glad to see our children progressing so well. We conclude with our best respects."[53]

> Speaker
> Wau sau sey[54]
> Bear Meat

Resolved that Br. Chamberlin be directed to write an answer to the above letter.

Resolved that br. B. be instructed to hire Dempsey Fields to assist him in the school until another teacher shall arrive.

Resolved that we send to Creek path for the school house five, six light sashes with glass to fill them.

[Oct.] 15. Had a precious season in commemorating the death of our Blessed Immanuel. O how merciful is our Heavenly Father in furnishing such a table in the wilderness.

[Oct.] 16. We were disappointed in not seeing any of the examining Com. But we had the pleasure of meeting several of our Cherokee friends. We proceded to examine our schools as if the com. had attended. All who were present expressed the highest satisfaction in the improvement of the children.

One of our little girls got very badly burned. Her clothes caught fire & nearly consumed on her back. We feel very thankful that both her parents were here & the burn was not so bad but that they could carry her home with safety.

[Oct.] 17. Br. H. arrived. The straying of his horse prevented his coming last week. The school under his care is doing well. About thirty six attend constantly and learn well.

Meeting for business. Resolved that the principal teachers of the schools at this place have charge of all clothing, Books &c sent on for the use of the Mission, & that all applications for any of the s[d] articles by any member of the mission family either at Brainerd or at any of the local schools, be made to one of them & that they keep an account of all articles given out, in a book kept solely for that purpose & that a coppy of articles sold or given out to any member of the Mission family or to the local schools be given to the Treasurer of this Mission to go up to the Treasurer of the Board, with our regular account.

Resolved that the Treasurers account be examined by the brethren after being prepared for the Treasurer of the Board.

Resolved that it be left to the discretion of the teachers at the local schools whether they admit black children into their schools or not.

Resolved that we deem it important that a female teacher be provided for the school at Taloney to take charge of the girls.

Resolved, that at each general meeting, the teachers of the local schools shall report to the brethren, the whole & average number of schollars at their several schools, their classes and improvement from the last general meeting, & that the same be entered by the secretary in a book kept for that purpose. Also that each teacher report at the same time the general state and prospects of religion & civilization at his station.

Resolved that the mark of the live stock at the local schools be the same as at Brainerd, & that the number be annually reported & recorded as above.

Resolved, that no brother having charge of a local school shall contract any debt without first obtaining the consent of the brethren at Brainerd except in cases of absolute necessity & in all such cases he shall give notice of such debt to the Treasurer at Brainerd as soon as may be. Resolved that br. H. prepare a joint letter to sister Mary K. Rawlings on the subject of her being recommended to the Pru. Com. as an assistant Missionary.[55]

Resolved, that a supposed value be assesed to each article of clothing delivered to the Missionaries.

Resolved, if practicable, that we obtain, immediately $100. for the school at Taloney.

Resolved, that Br. H. have liberty to purchase a new log cabin in his neighbourhood, which can be obtained for about five dollars & be paid for in clothing.

Resolved that our general meetings be hold semiannually viz. On the saturdays after the second Wednesdays in October & April, & that the order of s^d meetings shall be as follows:

1st Preparatory lecture on Saturday.

2nd Sermon & Communion on the Sabbath.

3rd Examination of the schools in this place, on Monday.

4th Meeting for business conducted as follows,

> 1st Read all communications relative to the concerns of the Mission from the Cor. Sec. & Treas. of the Board, which may have been received since the last general meeting, & all resolutions past in meetings for business at Brainerd.
>
> 2nd The teachers of the Local Schools make their reports.
>
> 3rd The business of each Local School, in alphabetical order.
>
> 4th General business of the Mission.

Resolved, that with the approbation of the Pru. Com. there be a semiannual vacation of three weeks: to commence at the Local Schools Saturdays after the first Wednesdays in October and April, & at this place the day after examination.

[Oct.] 18. Our dear Brothers & Sisters from Creek path left us, to return. We have had a sweet season with them and parting was painful. How sweet will be the time, when all the children of God, will meet in their Fathers Kingdom to part no more.

[Oct.] 19. Br. H. left us to return to Taloney.

[Oct.] 20. We have just heard of the death of our dear Sister Crutchfield at Springplace.[56] She was the first fruit which the Lord granted to our dear father & mother Gambold & she is now the first which He has taken to Himself.

[Oct.] 24. Br. & Sr. Chamberlin set out for father Gambolds where she expects to remain until he goes to the Council & to Taloney.

Sr. Anna Hoyt has been confined to her room for several weeks, with an ulsurated tooth: her face and throat were so swolen that for nine days she was unable to swallow any thing but a thin drink, & that with difficulty. For one or two days the passage was so nearly closed, that she found much difficulty in breathing, & we were alarmed lest it would prove fatal, but the Lord sent relief in due time. She is now recovering fast.—

Advance of the Cherokees in civilization.[57]

Nov. 1st Br. & Sr. C. returned. He left Sister Chamberlin at Father Gambolds, while he went to the Council. While there he put up at Majr Ridges, where he had an opportunity of preaching to a large number of our Cherokee Brethren. The Ridge says he can never be thankful enough to the Missionaries, for providing a way for his son to receive an education. He says he wishes him to stay at Cornwall until he gets a great education, & he hopes the Lord will give him a good heart, so that when he comes home he may be very useful to his Nation.

The Council have made a law to compel parents to keep their children at school, when once entered, until they have finished their education, or pay all expense for clothing, board, & tuition. They have also given the Superintendents of each Mission authority to take out of their schools such children as they shall think proper, & with the consent of their parents, put them to such trades as are attached to their Missions, & when such children have learned a trade they are to be furnished with a set of tools at the expense of the Nation.[58]

They have also divided their country into eight districts or counties, laid a tax on the people to build a court house in each of these counties & appointed four circuit Judges.[59] The cherokees are rapidly adopting the laws and manners of the whites. They appear to advance in civilization just in proportion to their knowledge of the gospel. It therefore becomes all who desire the civilization of the Indians to do what they can to send the gospel among them.

Br. Chamberlin after leaving the Council went to Taloney, where he spent the sabbath. The people there were very attentive to preaching; some shed tears. One black man appeared to be under pungent conviction. The children of the school most of them attended meeting. They were very neatly clad. They appear to be very bright children, we hope some will be raised up there to be ornaments to their Nation.

[Nov.] 4. Brother John Arch returned from a visit to his fathers. He has in his absence attended a meeting of the Presbytery, & Missionary Society in North Carolina. He had an opportunity of siting down to the table of our Lord, with above five hundred brethren. The good people there gave him better than fifty dollars worth of clothing, & made him member for life of the Missionary Society.

[Nov.] 6. Br. C. went to fulfil the appointment up the river.
Meeting for business, Resolved that we send Br. H. $100. if we can obtain it before the next mail.

[Nov.] 7. Br. John Arch has concluded to stay here and attend school. He told us he would go to Creek path if we said so, but it was his choice to stay here. He feels very anxious to be prepared to instruct his people.

[Nov.] 16. A Brother of the Methodist connection called on us & gave us a sermon this evening.

[Nov.] 18. Br. Chamberlin's little daughter got to some Arsenic which was mixed with butter for the purpose of destroying rats. We know not how much she eat, but have reason to think the quantity was considerable. It created in her a burning thirst, & she had one severe spasm. We gave her a large portion of sweet oil, which in a few minutes counteracted the affects of the poison. After this we gave her antimonial wine, which provided a vomiting. But we have no doubt it was the sweet oil under God that saved the child's life. It would be well if this remedy against poison was more generally known.[60]

We have now 11 boys and six girls in the school supported in whole or in part by different Associations viz.

Ann Porter	beneficiary	of the Female Praying Soc. Willmington, Delaware.
Samuel Newel	Do	of Female Mite Soc. & Juven. Mite Soc. of Augusta Maine.
David Paxton	Do	of Juven. Missionary Soc. in 2nd Dutch Reformed Church Phil.
Samuel Spring	Do	of the Young Ladies Beneficent Soc. New Port.
Mindwell Woodbridge Gould	Do	of a Soc. of Young women Southhampton Ms.
Vinson Gould	Do	of a Soc. of men Do Do.
Manassah Cutler	Do	of a Female Soc. Hamilton Ms.
Hariet Newel	Do	of first Adult School Soc. Phil.
Mary Mason	Do	of Several Ladies in Boston.
Eliphalet Wheeler Gilbert	Do	of Sab. School in 2nd Presbn Church Willmington Delaware
Betsey Mayhew	Do	of Heathen school Soc. Newbedford, Ms.
Bethuel Dodd	Do	of Ladies in Utica New York
John D. Paxton	Do	of Assoc of Ladies in Presbn Church Norfolk, Virginia
Edward Hop Ful	Do	of [Tlohos?] of Baltimore.
John C. Latter	Do	of Juvenile Soc. in connection with a Sab School, Newcastle Del.

Caroline Smelt	Do	of Female Mite Soc. Franklin street Baltimore.		
Nicholas Patterson	Do	of Male Do	Do	Do[61]

All these are promising children & may hereafter by a divine blessing, do honor to the Societies & individuals by whose benevolence they are now supported.

We should have mentioned in our Journal of Feb. last that Dr. J.C. Strong of Knoxville very generously vaccinated a large number of our children & gave instructions for vaccinating the remainder should the matter opperate in these by which means the whole school have received that sure preventive of the small pox.[62] We did not notice this omission until we saw that part of our Journal in print.

Ard Hoyt, Abijah Conger, John Vail, Wm Chamberlin

Journal of the Mission at Brainerd

Nov. 21. Br. Conger returned from the Agency accompanied by the Rev. Mr. [William] Dickinson, on a missionary tour soliciting funds for the Western Theological Seminary.[63]

[*Nov.*] 22. Resolved that br. Halsey go to the agency tomorrow, for some money.
Our dear br. D. preached to us this evening.

[*Nov.*] 23. Br. D. left us to proceed on his journey.

[*Nov.*] 24. Br. C. left us for the purpose of spending the Sabbath and preaching at br. Hicks'.
Richard Fields came and brought us letters from Creekpath.[64] The brothers & sisters are all well at that place & appear to be growing in grace. They have sent an urgent request that br. John Arch should come back, he has concluded to go.

[*Nov.*] 26. Br. C. returned. The weather being unfavorable his congregation was small.

[*Nov.*] 27. Commenced sawing with our new mill: but find the water insufficient to keep it in constant operation, on account of a certain rock in the race, which must in part be removed.
Resolved that next Thursday be observed as a day of fasting & prayer by the Mission family.

Dec. 1. Our millwright having finished the sawmill left us to return to his family in Georgia. We would gladly have retained him to put up the gristmill, but he thinks duty calls him away. He is a dear man, & with reluctance & grief we part with him.

[Dec.] 3. This day Mr. John McPhaerson was received to the communion of the church. He is a white man who has a Cherokee family.

[Dec.] 4. Resolved that father Hoyt write rules & regulations respecting the ferry & hand them to the ferry master.
Resolved that we put up our hogs for fattening tomorrow.
Resolved that we build a smoke house 16 feet square & 12 feet posts.
Resolved that Br. Ch. go to the agency this week on business.
The father of the boy called Jeremiah Evarts, having spent the sabbath with us, stayed today to have some farther conversation. He appears thoroughly convinced of the truth and excellency of our most holy religion, & of the great advantages of civilized life. He says he sees a very great & pleasing change among his people, since the missionaries came, & is sure from these good effects that the whole is from God. He speaks very feelingly of the deplorable state he was in before he received instruction, & expresses a great desire that his own children & others should be trained up in a different way from what he has been. He now sees that every thing around him declares the Being & Providence of God, but this he did not see while in his former state. He has found his heart to be exceedingly depraved, but thinks it is made some better, yet is still sinful, and he is often lead to do, & still oftener to feel & think what he now hates & knows to be wrong. He has experienced many evident answers to prayer, & thinks God will hear his prayers, & sometime give him a better heart. He often speaks to his neighbours of these things, and against their bad conduct. Many of them laugh at him, & tell him he cannot know anything about religion, because he cannot understand English. But he does not care for that. He knows God can understand him in his own language, and he shall continue to pray for them.
After much conversation of this kind in which he gave a particular account of his own experience, he said he had told us all his heart, & wished to know what we thought of it; and whether there was any reason to hope that God was bringing him in the right way. He said if he could be prepared for it, he should be glad to come & be one of the children, meaning a member of the church, he said it gave him great satisfaction to meet with christians & to hear them talk, it seemed like

coming into great light. He should be very happy if he could talk with us in our own language. He could then express himself more fully, & receive more instruction. But he should never forget what we had told him: he thought of it every day. Being told what was doing for the red people at the West, & especially what the Osages on the Missouri had done to obtain a mission among them; he said it made his heart glad. It was the work of God & He would carry it on.

[Dec.] 11. Resolved that as Sleeping Rabit was not acquainted with all the regulations of this school, when by the request of the teacher at Creek path he left that school to come here, & as he has acknowledged his fault in leaving as in a private way, the teacher there be permitted to receive him again as a schollar.[65]
This day a boat with a thousand bushels of corn arrived. The warehouse being nearly full, and the road to it becoming muddy by the recent rains, we thought best to bring this boat into the Creek, and convey the corn by water to the Mission.

[Dec.] 12. Resolved that the price of boards at the mill shall be as follows viz: one dollar per hundred for 3/4 & all under, and one dollar twenty five cents for inch planks & twenty five cents for every additional 1/4 inch.

[Dec.] 14. About 10 O'clock this evening our sister Lydia [Lowrey Hoyt] was made the joyful mother of a daughter.[66]

[Dec.] 15. Last night & today the rain fell in torrents.

[Dec.] 18. The Chickamaugah is said to be higher than it has been in ten years past. Our fields on the Creek are under water & the rails mostly on float.
Resolved that by permission of the Chiefs we hire Mr. Hooper to labour one year, provided he will labour for $120,00, with the privilege of a cabin for his family & of keeping two rows.

[Dec.] 19. Resolved that in addition to the mechanics, Hewbert [or Shewbert], & Wm Carr, be under the direction of br. Conger, & that he see to chopping & hauling logs for the mill. And that the rest of the common labourers be under the direction of br. Vail, and that he make enquiries for some more good labourers.

[Dec.] 20. We hear of much damage done by the flood but through a kind Providence our dam & sawmill, erected at so much expense of

labour & money remain unhurt. Thanksgiving & praise are due to God.

About 8 O'clock this evening our dear sister Pain & her children arrived in good health.[67] Their journey was fatiguing & in some respects hazardous, but through a kind providence they have arrived safe to this desired home. May the infinite mercy & grace of God prepare them & us for all trials yet to come.

[Dec.] 25. Through the mercy of our God we are permitted to see another Christmas eve, and a table spread for our refreshment with such provisions as our kind, & indulgent Father, through the death of his Son Jesus, has provided: 133 sat down at the first table, and twenty at the second, making 153 in the whole. O that all these dear souls were prepared to sit down at the marriage supper of the Lamb.

[Dec.] 26. Considered a letter from br. Hall in which he states his inability to get his wood, & attend to all the concerns of the family & school, & requests permission to hire a man constantly untill other help shall be sent on for that station, proposing to employ him a part of the time in clearing land.

Resolved that we deem it expedient for him to hire his wood got, but think we are not authorized to hire for the purpose of clearing land without direction from the Prudential Committee.

[Dec.] 30. Recvd by way of Augusta seven boxes & one trunk containing articles for the Mission as follows, viz:

1. One trunk from the Brainerd Society, Philadelphia, containing about 100 yds valuable cloth, consisting of Casimer, bedticking, flannel, 58 garments, 20 best quality pewter plates, 8 doz, brushes, 1 doz. Clamps, 7 Octavo Bibles, 1 doz. Testaments, & 800 tracts.

2. One box from the Female Reading Society, & other ladies of New London, containing 137 garments, including bedding, caps, shoes, bonnets &c, 35 tracts, 6 primers, 1 gross buttons, 1 doz. pair scissors, 1 doz. tea spoons, 1 doz. boxes, 4 pr knitting needles, silk, cotton thread, buttons, thimbles, [p?es] &c.

3. One box from Woodbridge, Con. containing bed quilts, comfortables &c valued by donor, $24. In our opinion very low.

4. One box from ladies in New Milford containing 88 garments, 93 3/4 yds cloth—various kinds, 5 remnants, tape, pins, needles, thimbles, shears, scissors, thread, tracts. Also in the same box articles by ladies in New Preston Society, viz: 26 garments, 5 yds nankeen, 1 remnant

flannel, & one skein stocking yarn. Also articles given by individuals in Sherman viz: 3 yds cloth, 7 garments, 5 primers.

5. One box from the Female alms Society Benson, Vermont, containing a great variety of useful articles of clothing, flannel, blankets &c. Estimated value annexed to each article Total valuation $76,73.

6. One box from ladies in Whiteboro & Lenox viz: from Whiteboro 53 articles of bedding & clothing, one remnant of flannel, pins & thread. From Lenox 70 articles of bedding, clothing &c.

7. One box from ladies in the village of Waterford, viz: containing 79 garments, 15 yds factory & a variety of thread, articles as cambric, leno, [?hum], shears, thread, pins, needles, tape, school books &c.

8. One box from the Elliot Society Philadelphia, for the mission at Elliot, directed to our care. From a letter to us it appears that this box is valued at $110,00. We think that boxes to Elliot had better be directed by way of New Orleans, as there are no waggons going to that station, nor is there any regular convoys by water.

We have great cause of gratitude to God, & many thanks are due to his dear people for this seasonable supply. Some of our poor children began to be in want, and without this aid, must soon have been in a suffering condition. The comfortables, bed quilts, blankets, & woolen clothes, are of peculiar service at this time. If it would not be too much trouble to the donors we should be glad always to receive a bill of all articles with the value of each annexed. This would enable us to fix a fair price to those we sell.

1821

Jan. 1. Resolved that we request Mr. Huntington not to send any more sugar or Coffee at present.

Resolved that we send Mr. Guess to labour at Taloney for a time if he is willing.

[Jan.] 6. Last night the snow fell about 10 inches deep.

[Jan.] 8. Resolved that Wm Rices wages be reduced to five dollars per month.

[Jan.] 9. Last evening br. Chamberlain & four of the children were taken very unwell. Their illness is probably occasioned by the late sudden change of weather. The snow still continues [uninterupted?]. We cannot be sufficiently thankful for warm clothing for the children during this cold season.

[Jan.] 10. For sometime past we have had no hired help in the female department except one hired girl. Her master has sold her, & this day taken her away. To avoid expense of hiring the sisters resolve on endeavouring to perform the labour of the kitchen & of the whole female department themselves.

This afternoon we were permitted to welcome, as fellow labourers in this field, the Rev. Wm Potter, Dr. Elizur Butler, with their wives.[1] Their journey on the whole has been prosperous, though considerably retarded by the badness of the roads, & inclemency of the weather. Journies from the northern states to this country are performed with more convenience (by land) as early as the first of September.

[Jan.] 11. Resolved that we hire James Carter one year at $10 per month.

Resolved that br. Potter take charge of the school at Creek path & that br. Butler remain here.

[Jan.] 15. Br. Potter left us for Creek path in company with a Cherokee boy from that place, to make arrangements for his removal. The sick in the family are nearly recovered.

Resolved that a man be sent tomorrow to br. Halls, to assist him in getting wood.

Resolved that we send to br. Hall for the use of the Taloney school a draft on Mr. Schank of Savannah for $60.

Resolved that James Carr be sent to br. Halls to get wood.

Resolved that br. Butler make choice of a horse and take charge of it.

Resolved that br. Butler take the office of Steward and Treasurer of this Mission.

Resolved that father Hoyt prepare a joint letter to the Prud. Com. on the following subjects, viz: Chattooga school, Blacksmith, Physician's charge, &c.

Resolved that if we sell corn to our hired hands we charge $0,50 per bushel.

[Jan.] 16. James Carr left us for Taloney.

Resolved that we hire Lying Rock, a Cherokee[,] three months.

Resolved that br. Butler if called to visit the sick be authorized to ride over ten miles without particular leave from the brethren.

[Jan.] 22. Resolved that br. Butler prepare a joint letter to the Prud. Com. in answer to Dr. Worcester's of Nov. 13.[2]

Resolved that we hire Clinging no longer.

[Jan.] 25. Very clear but excessive cold. We were obliged to divide the boys into small parties, & send them into the cabins to be instructed by monitors, except what could sit near the fire in the school house. We feel the cold as sensibly as we should in the northern states.[3]

God is still remembering us in mercy. This day we received $50 collected by Rev. E. Smith, in Frankfort, Kentucky, $50 from the Transylvania Society Kentucky.[4]

[Jan.] 26. Brs. Butrick, Potter, & John Arch arrived from Creek path.

[Jan.] 27. Resolved that br. Butrick have leave to board at br. Milo Hoyts, for his convenience in studying the language & that he have liberty to take br. John Arch with him.

[Jan.] 29. Read a letter from br. Hall, in which he asks for help. As we do not think the brethren here have a right to hire men to clear land at the local schools, without special permission from the Prudential Committee, therefore,

Resolved that so much of br. Hall's letter as relates to this subject be copied & sent to the Committee.

Resolved that brs. Butrick & Chamberlain draft an instrument, stating what shall be required of children at the local schools.

Resolved that br. Potter be directed to build a house at Creek path, of the following description, viz: one cabin 16 by 22 feet, divided by partitions, making 2 bed rooms, 8 by 10 feet. Another cabin 16 feet square, with upper & lower floors to both. The cabins to be placed 10 feet apart, & the roof to extend over the whole, wooden chimnies, two 6 light windows in one & one in the other cabin.

Resolved that brs. Potter, & Vail select a horse for Creek path.

[Jan.] 30. Resolved that br. Potter be permitted to take the articles contained in the bill he presented this evening.

Resolved that we think it best for br. Potter to take two horses and a waggon to remove with sister Potter to Creek path, & that he take with him John Campbell to assist in building a house.

Resolved that brs. Potter & Vail select the horses to go to Creek path.

Resolved that br. Potter have liberty to purchase for the use of the school at Creek path, cows not to exceed three.

Feb. 1. James Carr having returned from Taloney on business for br. Hall, and as he is our waggoner, & our business has suffered considerably for want of a proper person to drive the team, therefore,

Resolved that we retain him & send another hand one month to assist br. Hall in getting his wood.

Resolved that the first sawing that is done be for the girls house & that the building be finished as soon as possible.

[Feb.] 2. Br. Butler went to the warehouse yesterday to purchase flour for the Mission. Before he accomplished his business it was dark. He endeavored to return but found it impracticable, as he could not see the road himself, & his horse would not keep it. Finding himself lost in a wet, & swampy place, where it was not convenient either to sit or lie on the ground, he sat on his horse during the night, & this morning finding the road some distance from him, returned; having been permitted so soon after his arrival to witness the loving kindness & protecting power of God, in preserving his children when passing through perils in the wilderness.

[Feb.] 5. Sister Conger was delivered of three children, two daughters & a son. The son scarcely entered on this stage of life before he was called into eternity.[5]

Resolved that the school girls be not taken out of school during school hours to labour.

Resolved that the hired men who board at the mission house be under the immediate care and direction of br. Vail.

Resolved that sister Catharine be requested to teach the girls school at Creek path till the other teacher goes to that place; & that she be supported as a missionary while thus employed.[6]

Resolved that the boys for their steady work out of school chop wood for the summer.

Resolved that br. Chamberlain prepare a joint letter to sister Catharine.

[Feb.] 6. This day the Mission family including the children of the school, attended the funeral of sister Conger's child, committing its remains to the grave.

[Feb.] 7. Resolved that br. Chamberlain go to Creek path with br. Potter to assist him in making preparations for his family.

Resolved that br. Butrick take charge of the boys school during the absence of br. Chamberlain.

[Feb.] 8. Br. Vail set out for Taloney in company with sister Sarah Hoyt, & a hired man.

Br. Potter set out for Creek path, accompanied by br. Chamberlain, & a hired man.

[Feb.] 9. Received by way of Augusta 17 boxes & one Tierce containing as follows viz:—[7]

1. One box from the towns of Griswold, Dorsett, Hampton, Preston, Lisbon, Windham, & Litchfield Southfarms, containing 85 garments, 17 yds cloth, 1 doz. thimbles, &c.

2. One box from Newhaven, Vermont, containing 49 garments, 15 yds cloth, thread, books &c.

3. One Tierce from Mansfield, containing 79 knots stocking yarn, 72 yds cloth, 161 garments, 38 knots thread, 56 skeins silk, gimblets, needles, combs, pins, awls, knitting needles, ink stand, books, tracts &c &c.

4. One box from Middletown N.Y. containing 37 garments, 34-1/2 yds cloth, yarn, cotton, thread &c.

5. One box from Cooperstown & Burlington containing one small trunk for father Gambold, 5 skeins yarn, 45 yds cloth, 36 garments,

testaments, spelling books &c, & some valuable presents to individuals.

6. One box from Westford Con. containing 75 garments, needle books, work pockets, Bibles, other small books &c &c.

7. One box from Paris N.Y. containing 49 garments, 1 piece red flannel, thread, books &c, & a part of two sets of Lancasterian lessons.

8. One box from Ludlowville N.Y. containing 23 garments, knitting needles, books &c.

9. One box from Philadelphia containing 6 garments, & a number of valuable books, & tracts, tape, scissors, needles, thread, buttons, &c.

10. One box from Gt. Barrington, Mass. containing 74 garments, 25 yds cloth, yarn, thread, needles, thimbles, buttons, books, tracts. &c.

11. One box from Elmira N.Y. containing 112 Garments, 13 yds fulled cloth, $1,50 cash. Estimated value annexed [$]102,81.

12. One box from Salisbury, Vermont, containing 91 garments, stocking yarn, thread &c.

13. One box from Madison N.Y. containing 52 garments, 7 yds cloth, tape, paper, yarn, thread, books &c.

14. One box from Genoa, N.Y. containing 39 garments, 12 yds cloth, thread, & annexed value $52,00.

15. One box from Newhaven Con. containing a number of Bibles, testaments, & many valuable articles, of clothing which were unfortunately mixed with other clothes, before an account of them was taken, & as we found no bill, we are unable to enumerate the articles.

16. One box from East Bloomfield N.Y. containing 124 garments, & 25 yds cloth annexed value $146,84.

17. One box from Upton containing 25 garments, 20-1/2 yds cloth, books, tracts &c.

N.B. By some means one box of clothing is lost from this account. 17 boxes & 1 tierce received; & 16 boxes & 1 tierce found in the account. The articles of this box must have been, either accidentally mixed with others, before an account of them was taken, or the bills were lost before they were placed on the journal. $4,50 lost not found on the account.

Feb. 12. Resolved that we hire Perry Brown for one month.

[Feb.] 13. Br. Butler left us for the Agency on business.

[Feb.] 15. Br. Butler returned.

[Feb.] 16. Br. Milo Hoyt this day removed to his new dwelling about half a mile distant. May the blessing of God & the prayers of his people attend him & his, & render them useful where, & as long as they live in this vale of tears. Br. Vail returned—brought sister Mary Rawlings from Taloney & Ann Conger from father Gambolds.[8] He brings intelligence of the sickness of mother Gambold.

This day received 11 boxes containing as follows, viz:—

1. One box from Woodstock, Con. containing 52 garments, yarn, clothes, paper, ink powder, books, silk &c &c.

2. One box from Springfield, Mass. containing many valuable articles of clothing, thimbles, needles, thread, books.

3. One box from ladies in Nelson containing 50 garments, 39 yds cloth, yarn, paper, pins, thimbles, wool &c. Annexed value $127,76-1/2.

4. One box from Bridge Water, containing 87 garments, tape, pins, books, &c.

5. One box from District of Maine, containing first, from Gorham, 30 garments, 2 hats filled with articles for Mr. Hoyt, canister, & bundle for Mrs. Williams, Choctaw nation. Second, from Croydon, 13 garments, 29 yds cloth, buttons, silk, thread, tracts, &c. Third, from Greenville, 76 garments, 35 yds cloth, yarn, thread &c. Fourth from Reading 59 garments, 2 remnants gingum.

6. One box from Williamsburg containing 58 garments, 20 yds cloth, buttons, pins, thimbles, thread, silk, yarn, pin ball &c.

7. One box (place unknown) containing 20 garments, 23 yds cloth, books &c.

8. One box from Brooks containing 6 garments, 6 large tin basins, 3-1/2 doz. scallops, one bundle for Mr. & Mrs. Hoyt, 19 yds cloth, thread, buttons &c.

Together with the above mentioned boxes came one empty trunk, which, unfortunately had been robbed. One of the above boxes had been broken open. Some of the articles was taken from it. This is the first instance of boxes of clothing being injured on their way to this place.

9. One box from Bedford, Milford, Newburyport, Kingston, Goffstown, & Westford containing 226 garments, paper, quills, pins, needles, thread, silk, & a bundle for Mr. Hoyt.

10. One box from Paxton, Mass. containing 125 garments & many other valuable and very useful articles. Annexed value $140,00.

11. One box from Yale college containing 113 garments, 40 yds cloth, pattern for a dress for sister Catharine Brown, 4 doz. inkstands, some valuable books &c.

All these precious goods have arrived safe. From whence? From a far distant land. We look at them—we recognize the features of our dear fathers & mothers, brothers and sisters & friends, whom we had bid farewell, expecting to see them no more in this world. We do not see them, but blessed be the Name of our God, we see the work of their kind, beneficent hands; and say, do our dear friends remember us still? Do they see our tears? Do they hear our groans? Do they bear us, & the dear heathen, in their hearts before God? And what can we do for them? How can we repay this kindness? This unexpected attention to all our wants? We can do nothing. No, dear friends, we can do nothing. ~~Our treasures in this world are small; in the world above, almost nothing.~~ We are indigent beggars before God, & men. We fear grieving the Holy Spirit, through the depravity of our hearts. We fear erring from the path of duty, through the blindness of our minds. We fear the children of God will grow weary & impatient,—let their hands hang down, & leave us to stumble & fall alone; with this infinite weight of responsibility upon us. We know that through this multiplicity of our cares, & the infirmity of our bodies, we are unable to answer their kind & affectionate letters as we would wish, or to give them that information they long for, & have a right to expect. And we are frequently grieved, fearing they will consider us ungrateful, inattentive to their requests, & utterly unworthy their farther attention. But why these fears? Do they not know we love them, & long to unbosom our hearts, & make known every thing would be pleasing or interesting to them? And farther, it was not our love or attention that opened their hearts and unlocked their treasures. No: it was a zeal for the glory of God,—a desire to do good,—a love for immortal souls. As long then as God continues to be that fountain of excellence,—as long as their hearts glow with benevolent & grateful sensations, as long as heathen can be found on the footstool of our God, so long will his children remember & ardently pray for those who they send as heralds of salvation to a benighted world. Yes, dear friends, with confidence we cast ourselves at your feet, believing, knowing that your sympathetic tears will not cease to flow, nor your hands be shut when we cry for help. You will not cease to pray that he who took up the fragments that nothing should be lost, will enable us to make the best possible improvement, of all the tokens of your remembrance of us,—your love to God & the dear though benighted heathen. Them you will always carry in your hearts before God. But a few years since, not a star glimmered in all this dark region. Now more than 30 bright luminaries are diffusing their light, & guiding immortal souls to Jesus. These dear Cherokee & African converts, you will not, you cannot forget. They are your treasure. They will be your crown of rejoicing in the day of the Lord Jesus.

Feb. 19. Resolved that we sell the bay mare for $30. Resolved that we build a cabin near br. Milo Hoyt's for the convenience of br. B. while attending to the language.
Br. Butler left us to visit mother Gambold.

[Feb.] 20. Br. Butler returned—brought the mournful tidings of the death of our dear mother Gambold. She died about 10 minutes before his arrival. That pious, humble, devoted Missionary is no more. We weep, we mourn, we rejoice. O that a double portion of her spirit may rest on many daughters in Israel, & prepare them to fill her place.

[Feb.] 21. Br. John Arch left to attend the funeral of mother Gambold.

[Feb.] 22. Sister M. Rawlings left for Washington.[9]

[Feb.] 24. Br. John returned accompanied by br. Baskum.

[Feb.] 25. Br. Baskum gave us a very interesting sermon on closet duties.[10]

[Feb.] 26. Resolved that we endeavour to hire a female to labour at br. Halls.
Resolved that br. Butler have charge of the garden this season.
Resolved that the lot near the schoolhouse be devoted to fruit trees, & that br. Butler have charge of it.

[Feb.] 28. Br. Baskum preached to the mission family and a few of the neighbours.
Resolved that br. B. be released from the charge of the boys out of school; instructing them school hours only till br. Chamberlain's return.
Resolved that brs. Milo Hoyt & Charles Reece have leave to get the corn on the Chickamaugah & save what corn they can.
Another of sister Congers infants died this day.

March 1. The Mission family attended the funeral of sister Conger's child.

Br. Baskum left us for Georgia.

Br. Chamberlain returned from Creek path. He and br. Potter found the dear lambs of Christ in that place walking in the fear of God. They administered the communion, and baptized one Cherokee woman. The other candidates for baptism generally appear well. Before br. C. left they had put up one cabin 16 x 22 feet, and another as far as the roof 16 feet square. Next Saturday is appointed for the Cherokees to meet & finish raising & put on the roofs.

[March] 5. Resolved that sister Potter go to Creek path this week with Mr. Ross if she chooses.

Resolved that br. P. be directed to purchase plank at Creek path to finish his house.

Resolved that we endeavour to obtain $100 ~~of Mr. Ross~~ for the Creek path school & send it by Mr. Ross.

Received 11 boxes of clothing as follows viz:—

1. One box from Bristol, containing 21 yds dressed flannel, near 70 garments, 14 yds white flannel, Brass hair combs, Bibles, Psalmbook, yarn, thimbles, needles, &c &c.

2. One (place unknown) containing 82-3/4 yds cloth, 125 garments, yarn, thread, pins, knitting needles, &c.

3. One box from the Cherokee Society of South Hadley containing 160 articles.

4. One box from Glastenbury 44 yds cloth, 103 garments, including shoes, bedding &c.

5. One from South Granville containing 17 yds flannel, 37 garments.

6. Six other boxes, two from places unknown, one from New Hartford, one from Sommers, one from Stratford, & one from Sangerford. These boxes are valuable, containing many very useful articles.

March 6. Resolved that br. Butrick be directed to prepare joint letters to br. Hall & br. Potter.

Resolved that we give Mr. Shelton a garden spot at the lower end of the field, by the farm house.

Resolved that Wm Carr be under the direction of br. Vail. As father Hoyt requests the brn. [brethren] to look over the articles taken by him for br. Milo Hoyt, from this establishment & make an estimate of their value; and as it is not convenient to attend to this business in meeting, therefore, Resolved that brs. Vail & Butler be a committee to attend to the above business, & present the same at our next stated meeting.[11]

[March] 8. {Read a letter from br. Hall requesting that br. John Arch be sent to his assistance. The question was asked shall we endeavour to send John Arch to assist br. Hall for a time? Answered in the negative. Br. John having previously expressed an unwillingness to go.}

[March] 10. Father Hoyt received a letter from New Orleans requesting him to meet Dr. Worcester at Mayhew, in the Choctaw nation, between the 20th & 25 of this month.[12]

[March] 12. Resolved that br. Vail accompany father Hoyt to drive, and take charge of the horses, & sister Anna Hoyt to assist & pay all necessary attention to his food &c, on account of his ill health.
Father Hoyt, br. Vail & sister Anna Hoyt left us for Mayhew. Sister Potter goes with them to Creek path.

[March] 13. A horse belonging to the Taloney school, & one belonging to a hired man, were stolen from the stable last evening.

[March] 18. A cold freezing day. Had a happy season today in celebrating the supper of our blessed Redeemer.

[March] 22. The stolen horses were returned by a Cherokee. He found them hobbled on the mountain, about 20 miles from this place.
Darius Hoyt, who has been dangerously ill considerable time we hope is some better.

[March] 23. Br. Potter arrived from Creek path to make arrangements for removing his household furniture.

[March] 27. Resolved that we hire Alexander & Joseph Hannah to work in the smith shop six months.[13]
Resolved that we hire Mr. Lenox two weeks at $0,50 per day.

[March] 29. Br. Potter left us for Creek path. The weather continues cold. During 3 or 4 days the ice has remained about the saw mill.

[March] 30. Br. Butrick is confined to the house with the rheumatism.
Sister Sarah returned from Taloney. Sister Hall is still feeble, but her health is improving.
By an unusual rain the Tennessee has arisen much higher than it was in Dec. last. Several hundred bushels of our corn in the warehouse & a

crib have been some time under water. This corn we thought secure, as no flood to our knowledge had ever covered the ground where it was stored. But to our great grief & disappointment, we find most of it spoiled. We are led anxiously to enquire, Why this waste of mission property? Why should an infinitely wise & Holy Providence tear from the funds of the mission & destroy at once so much, obtained by the prayers, tears & labours of his own children: Have we been prodigal with that precious article of provision? Have we abused the indulgence & wearied the patience of our Heavenly Father? and obliged him thus to chastise & afflict us? O that he would thoroughly reform us, & turn even this dispensation to the furtherance of the gospel. We are now obliged to purchase more corn.

April 2. Mr. Pain, being in a low state of health and unable to come to Brainerd as was expected, has sent for his family.

Sister Pain after taking a solemn & affectionate farewell of the Mission family, left us with her children for Pennsylvania.[14] It is a great trial to part with this dear sister; and we hope and pray that her God and our God will ever protect, guide & support her while in this world of sorrow & disappointment.

[April] 4. Mother Hoyt was taken very sick and thought by some to be dying. The family was called in; but she appears better this evening. Her sickness is doubtless occassioned in a great measure by her great fatigue, & care with Darius.

Darius is mending very slowly. Br. Butrick is confined to his room & mostly to his bed. We have now but two brothers & two sisters able to take any part either in nursing the sick, or providing for this numerous family. Thus far the Lord helps us, & we have great cause to adore his holy Name. We cannot be sufficiently thankful that a physician is provided against this time.

[April] 9. The little boy we call <u>Vinson Gould</u>, while playing with the saw in the saw mill, had a piece of his thumb, & his forefinger cut off, & his middle finger mangled in a most shocking manner. We forbade the boys going into the sawmill; but this boy ventured to disobey because his father was with him. His father is here on a visit.

Resolved that we hire Renolds to tend the mason while putting up the chimneys in the girls school house.

[April] 11. Mr. Foster a lecturer from Virginia called on us in company with Mr. Ross & his daughters: & in the evening delivered a lecture on union & forbearance.

[April] 12. Mr. Foster left us for Georgia.

[April] 13. Mother Hoyt & Darius very sick.—br. Butrick still confined with the Rheusmatism. The rest of the family including the children unwell with bad colds.

[April] 16. This being the day appointed for the examination of the schools, most of the parents of the children were present, & several others. We dressed the children decently and then, first, examined the girls school, second, marched in procession to the boys schoolhouse, & examined their school. We thought the children appeared well. All present seemed highly pleased with their improvement. After examination most of the children left us to return home to spend the vacation.

[April]. 17. We have now with us only 5 boys & 2 girls. We feel lonesome, not seeing the dear children about us. O that the blessed Saviour would keep them from all evil during their absence from us.

[April] 19. Resolved that we hire Mr. Hibs a short time.
Resolved that br. Conger be directed to hire Mr. Long at $1,00 per day to finish the girls school house.

[April] 21. Received a letter from father Hoyt. He states that Dr. Worcester had not arrived at Mayhew; but was to set out the next day to meet him, thirty miles from that place.
Mother Hoyt, br. Butrick & Darius are still confined with sickness. We should not be surprised if Darius should not survive till his fathers return. He is in the hands of a gracious God.

[April] 30. Br. Butrick is far recovered as to be able to preach to us to day. Mother Hoyt is gaining. Darius as he was.

May 5. Received a letter from Mrs. Ann Shipman Livingston, of Philadelphia inclosing a ten Dollar bill.
We think we feel thankful to God for raising up so many friends to this mission, who are willing to sacrifice their temporal interest for the spiritual good of these perishing heathen.

[May] 7. Br. Butrick so far recovered as to return to his study at br. Milo Hoyts.

A Cherokee woman brought two children to the school.[15] She said her husband (a white man) had burned up her house, destroyed all her furniture, sold her cattle & horses, & she was left destitute. She appeared thankful that she could find so good a home for her children.

[May] 8. The children begin to return. The school commenced today. A Cherokee man brought four children to the school.[16] We felt under obligation to received them as we had told him we would last fall.

[May] 17. Resolved that we take a cow of Mr. Burns for smith work, & clothing.

As the persons have been detected who broke open the box, & trunk last winter, & the Captain of the light horse wishes to know what articles were missing, therefore,

Resolved that br. Chamberlain & br. Butler make out a bill of them, & forward it to br. Hall by the next mail.

[May] 19. Father Hoyt, br. Vail, & sister Anna Hoyt, arrived from Mayhew. We were surprised to see them without Dr. Worcester. They left him at Mayhew on the third inst. in a very feeble state of health. They had awaited considerable time in expectation of his returning with them. It was at length determined that if ever Dr. Worcester were able to leave that place, which to many appeared doubtful, it would be necessary for at least 2 persons to come with him from Mayhew as attendants, even if father Hoyt & br. Vail waited to come with him,—that these two would probably be sufficient to do every thing for him by the way that he should need,—that it would be difficult for so large a company if they all traveled together, to find accommodations by the way, & therefore as it seemed important for father Hoyt & br. Vail to return soon, having already been much longer from Brainerd than was expected, it was thought advisable that they should come on, leaving Dr. Worcester to follow at any time when he should think himself [able].

They made a short stay at Creek path. Br. & sister Potter were in good health. The people in that neighbourhood were assembled, & listened attentively to a discourse on the subject of religion, & the importance of school education. All appeared well pleased with their teacher,— the school, & the great concerns of the mission. The church members appeared to be walking in love, & the fellowship of the Spirit. One of the principal Chiefs assured them that he would always do every thing in his power to promote the welfare of the school, & the comfort of the teachers.

[May] 22. Resolved that we endeavour to hire a man to assist br. Potter in finishing his house.

As sister Vail's health is poor & she wishes to be more retired than she can be in the mission house, therefore, Resolved that we repair a cabin for her use.

[May] 25. Dr. Worcester this day arrived. He left Mayhew on the 7th inst.—was detained 3 days at Russellville, a small village in Alabama, about 118 miles from Mayhew, partly on account of his own feeble health, & partly on account of the sickness of Dr. Pride, his attendant, who was attacked with an intermittent fever.[17] Dr. Pride being unable to proceed, a man was hired to take his place, & Dr. Worcester notwithstanding his extreme debility, traveled without farther intermission, till he reached Brainerd, a distance of full 200 miles. It appears to him & to us almost a miracle that he has been sustained to perform such a journey, being at the time of his arrival unable to support himself on his feet, or even to stand by leaning on another. He was brought in the arms of two of the brethren from his carriage to the house. For a few moments he was supported in a chair, but was soon obliged to take a bed. It was observed to him that he had got almost through the wilderness. He replied, "This may be true in more respects than one. God is very gracious, he has sustained me, as it were by miracle thus far, & granted one great desire of my soul in bringing me to Brainerd; & if it be agreeable to his holy purposes that I should leave my poor remains here, his will be done." He said further, "I had rather leave my poor remains here, than at any other place." We hope, however, that after a little rest from the fatigues of such a journey, with such medicines & cordials as will be found here, his strength may be recruited, & in due time, his health restored.

[May] 26. Dr. Worcester's complaints appear more complicated & difficult than we at first apprehended. Strictures in various parts give him much pain, & he is unable to rise from his bed without help.[18] A Mr. Pharr from the Chickasaw Nation, who had been assisting the Rev. Thomas Stewart in making preparations for a mission establishment among that people, called on us this evening. He informs [us] that the prospects are favorable with support to the Natives, though a want of sufficient help retards the work in some measure.

[May] 27. Sabbath. At the request of Dr. Worcester, the members of the church & some of the Congregation, were introduced to him; and being raised in his bed, he addressed them in few words. His address, though short, was peculiarly feeling & interesting. As these people left the room, Dr. Worcester overheard one saying to the children, "He is very feeble, you cannot see him now: You shall see him another time;" and immediately replied, "Oh! they want to see me; let them come in." One said, "You are very feeble, it may be injurious," he replied with tears, "I want to see all my dear children & take them by the hand." The children were then called in. He took each by the hand as they passed the bed. Having all passed round in procession, they stood & sung an hymn. He was affected to tears, most of the time. After the hymn, he addressed them in a most affectionate manner, which in return melted them to tears.

Dr. Worcester has been since his arrival afflicted with strangury, flatulency, & Diarhea, ~~we have been and still are using various means to relieve him~~.[19] The best medicines we could obtain have been given. The warm bath used, & emollients applied for the strangury with little effect. It was proposed to him to send to Tennessee for additional advice, but he objected, & put himself, under the direction of heaven, into the hands of his friends here.

[*May*] 28. About as yesterday. The strangury has terminated in a total suppression of urin[e]. As the last means, tobacco leaves, moistened in warm water, were applied to the region of the bladder. This caused a general relaxation and perspiration. But the desired effect was not produced. Toward sunset the catheter was introduced & eleven gills of urin extracted. This gave him much relief, but increased his debility. He has been in the habit of using bark, Opium, & other medicines on his journey for spasms, diarhea & debility.[20] And as we found the least omission had a bad effect, we continued them.

Resolved that if any brother have business to bring before the brethren in regular meeting, that he present the same in writing.

Questions by br. Conger. 1. Shall we hire the men who came yesterday? Ans. yes. 2. Shall we hire Mr. Hog? Ans. No. 3. Shall br. Conger have leave to go to Kingston on business concerning his lands? Ans. Yes.

[*May*] 29. Our dear friend is rather more quiet, we can hardly say better. Br. & sister Conger left us for Kingston.

[*May*] 30. Dr. Worcester was desirous to ride out, thinking it might be beneficial. His debility was such that a moments consideration prevented it. At his request he was removed into the Piazza; and was refreshed with a mild breeze. This was the first time he left his room after his arrival.

May 31. In the morning we were somewhat alarmed, fearing he had but a few moments to stay. He however revived considerably, but was evidently on the decline.

June 1st He requested br. Chamberlain to look over his bills of expense from Natches to this place & put them in order on his memorandum book, that his accounts might be left intelligible to his friends. He was able to direct their entry, & having kept no account for the last 60 miles, was able to give particulars from memory. This is the only business he has been able to attend to since his arrival except to settle with the man who accompanied him from Russelville.

[June] 2. This morning he requested father Hoyt to write to Mrs. Worcester. Being asked if he would direct what should be written, he mentioned the time of his departure from Mayhew, & some occurrences by the way till the time of his arrival here; and added, "For the rest write as you think proper." Towards evening two chiefs arrived, & informed us that by appointment the chiefs from the different parts of the nation, were soon to meet here & welcome their friend. He was too feeble to see them today.

[June] 3. Sabbath. This day we were again permitted to meet around the table of our Lord. After meeting the chiefs who called on us yesterday were introduced to Dr. Worcester. He spoke a few words, which was interpreted to them. We hear nothing from the chiefs which were expected. Br. Hicks being afflicted with a [excarius? or exarius?] of the thigh bone, & the first symptoms of the Hectic fever, sent for br. Butler to visit him.[21] He has long been afflicted with lameness,—has applied to many physicians, & from time to time obtained a temporary relief, but is at present nearly confined.

[June] 4. Dr. Worcester is still failing & we fear will never recover. Resolved that we endeavor to hire hands to clear out the mill race. Resolved that we do not employ Wm Carr, unless he pay the damage, that has accrued in consequence of his leaving our business, contrary to contract. Resolved that br. Butrick prepare the journal to send to the Cor. Secretary.

[June] 5. Our dear friend is evidently fast going to the eternal world. In the morning we gave up all hopes of his recovery. For short intervals during the day he has been in a state of mental derangement. But even in this state his mind was employed on the great subject of building churches, & extending the dear Redeemers kingdom.

[June] 6. During the day he has been insensible to pain, & to appearance spent much of his time in prayer. He said if he were to choose, he had rather go & be with Jesus, than dwell in the flesh. He did not regret engaging in the missionary cause, but rejoiced that he had been enabled to do something towards this great object.
We learn that the chiefs generally delayed their appointed visit to Dr. Worcester on account of information that he was unable to converse.

[June] 7. With reluctance we enter upon the events of this day. Our thoughts recoil. Our pen stops. Involuntary tears darken our eyes. A rising sigh, a bursting heart, impatient of restraint, demands our attention. We seek where to weep, we enter into our closets & weep there. We resolve to be men and not children. We resume the task. Our weakened hands recline & refuse to perform their office. We look at each other, and say, who shall bear the doleful tidings. A solemn silence casts a still darker shade on the gloomy scene. Every heart is faint. Every head is sick. Every hand is weak, and the secret response of each is, " I cannot do it." Could I see my dear—on his knees before God, pleading for me, O could engage in the most arduous labours, I would not shrink from pain or from death. But where is he? O look to Salem, that dear place of his former abode, but he is not there. O ask the companion of his bosom. A silent tears answers, he is not with thee. His closet mourns in silence. That fountain, which from thence made glad the city of our God, and watered the parching deserts of America, is now dry. His study, that bright luminary, which diffused its reys over christians & heathen lands, is now eclypsed. And what have I left in all this vale of tears? Or, who will hold up my hands before God? O ye daughters of Israel, weep for the heathen. Let the shores of Asia be clothed in sack cloth. Let the wilds of America be bathed in tears. Let the friends of missions hang their harps on the willows, & for a moment suspend their songs. Thus of feelings recoil & our eyes turn from the scenes of this dark day. But why indulge these despairing thoughts? Will not some Elisha be found to seize the mantle of this departed Elijah, and with a double portion of his spirit, revive the hopes of the heathen world? Is not our Immanuel still head

over all things to the church? And will he not accompany the heralds of salvation, the missionaries of the cross, even to the end of the world till all the heathen are his inheritance & the uttermost parts of the earth his possession? Why not then, leaning on the bosom of Jesus,— reclining in the arms of the church of God, announce the death of that great champion of the cross, that friend of God & men, the Rev. Samuel Worcester, D.D. He is dead.

This morning about 7 O'Clock, he cast his eyes towards heaven, and smiling resigned his spirit to God. Without the least apparent pain or strugle, he fell asleep in the arms of Jesus.

The funeral exercises are to be attended day after tomorrow at 10 O'Clock.

Br. Butler left us to visit br. Hicks.

[June] 8. Br. Butler returned.—found br. Hicks much better than he expected. Br. & Sister Conger returned, having accomplished their business at Washington.

[June] 9. Many of the Cherokees, some from considerable distance, came to perform the last act of kindness for their friend & benefactor. We first walked in procession to the grave, & consigned to its last rest, till the great rising day, the body of the dear deceased. We then repaired to the school house, where a letter from br. Hicks to the cherokees present concerning Dr. Worcester was read, and an appropriate sermon preached by father Hoyt, from Ps. 112.6. "The righteous shall be in everlasting remembrance."

> Ard Hoyt, D.S. Butrick, Wm Chamberlin
> Abijah Conger, John Vail, Elizur Butler

Mission journal Brainerd 1821

June 11th Meeting for business.[22] Br. butler inquired respecting the purchase of wheat, rye, & corn. Answer deferred to next meeting. Resolved that the old grey horse be assigned to br. Butrick for his particular use and under his direction.

Resolved that we let Milo Hoyt have a saddle on his fathers account.

[June] 12th From the beginning of this year we have been expecting to receive money from Government through the Agent, partly on account of the annual stipend which was to have been paid quarterly

& partly on account of the house we are building for the female schollars. Some months past the Agent told us he believed his letters to the war department for money must have miscarried—he had written a second time—and as soon as the money should arrive he would give us notice—We have now heard that the money has arrived but the Agent is unable to do business, having lost the use of his speech and his hand almost entirely, and that he is not expected long to survive. Br. Butler therefore left us this morning to go to the Agency for the purpose of getting this money if it can be obtained, this being all our dependence for paying workmen who labor on the building, and for other supplies for the summer; as the state of the treasury at Boston will not admit of our drawing from them at present.

[June] 13th A Cherokee man and his wife came with 5 children, two sons and three daughters. They took them home at the time of the vacation & state as the reason why they did not return them at the time that 4 of the children, and the father have been sick. That they wished to bring them and the children were very anxious to get back as soon as they could. They say they met a man on the road who told them it would do no good to send their daughters to school—it would be well for their sons to have learning and would be a great benefit to the nation, but it was not good to send their sons to this school. That Mr. Hicks spoke well of it because he got money for every thing that was done here—That the boys would be sent away among the white people & never be returned. And that Mr. Hicks had a sum of money for every boy that was thus sent away. He further said, that he had once thought well of these schools, and had sent some of his children to the school at Taloney, but had taken them away and would send them there no more. He advised them to keep their girls at home, & to send their boys to school where they would not be stolen.
They said they should believe the missionaries, & keep their children at school—they knew we loved them and treated them as our own children, and both they, and their children would do just as we told them.
We have repeatedly heard of a story in circulation for substance the same as the above and many equally foolish, & wicked, all put in circulation by men whose knowledge would have engaged them sincerely in the mission cause had their hearts been moulded according to the spirit of the gospel.

Br. Butler returned. He found the Agent considerably better & obtained some money, which, though not as much as we had reason to expect will enable us to proceed a little longer without great impairment. Two other children returned to day who have been absent since the vacation. They bring various excuses for not coming at the time, chiefly that they have been sick. Two small girls say they could get no one to come with them—they came today alone a distance of more than 40 miles. There are still some who left at the vacation and have not yet returned.

June 16th Br. Butrick went out to day with br. Reece for interpreter with the expectation of preaching tomorrow at a place where we formerly had regular appointments, but which for sometime past we have been unable to attend to.

Sab. [June] 17. The Rev. Mr. Wood formerly of Massachusetts who is now teaching an Academy in Powelton, Geo. came in very early this morning.[23] Having at this time a short vacation in his school, he came out for the purpose of visiting Brainerd. He expected to have got in last evening but it growing dark he feared he should lose his way and put up at a house about 6 miles from this place. In the forenoon Mr. Wood preached from Isaiah 45:22.[24] In the afternoon our services were adapted more particularly to the instruction of those who understand only the Cherokee language, the whole of the discourse being interpreted as spoken, and the singing in Cherokee. It is our intention to continue these exercises every Sabbath, br. John Arch being interpreter.

Br. Butrick and br. Reece returned this evening. They held their meeting about 11 miles distant from Brainerd where the Cherokees have lately built a council house, which makes a very convenient place for public worship, particularly in the warm season.[25] Nearly or quite all the people in that vicinity were present and gave very good attention. More than a year ago br. Butrick learned some of them a Cherokee hymn. These placed themselves on a seat together and delighted the ears and hearts of our brethren by singing that hymn with great accuracy and melody.

[June] 18th Meeting for business.
Br. Conger inquired shall the running gears to the grist mill be painted and the water wheel be hitched. answered in the affirmative.

Mr. Wood continued with us, visited the school, surveyed the premises &c. We are sorry to hear him say that an appointment to preach in Georgia renders it necessary that he should leave us tomorrow morning.

[June] 19th Mr. Wood left us early this morning on his return. His visit has been very pleasant and edifying to us, and we hope beneficial to our precious charge.

Two sisters from the church of the united brethren at Yew-ca-lu-ga [Oothcaloga] came to make us a visit.[26] One of them was formerly a member of this church but removing into the neighborhood of that church was dismissed from our particular care and received into the other church. They appear to be growing in knowledge and grace, and bring a pleasing account of the peace and prosperity of the little flock there. The number of communicants in that church at Yew-ca-lu-ga and Springplace so far as we have been informed is 12 besides the missionaries. Several others are considered as hopeful converts but have not as yet been admitted to the communion.

[June] 21st Meeting for business. Concluded that we purchase certain cattle of sister McDonald provided we can agree on the price and terms of payment. Concluded that the Chattuga sorrel be assigned to br. Butrick for his particular use in the place of the old grey.

Br. Butrick set out for a south-eastern tour in the nation. He expects to spend the sabbath with br. Reece near the Ridges about 60 miles from Brainerd and will probably visit Taloney before he returns.

[June] 23rd Received a letter from the Rev. E. Smith of Frankfort, Kentucky containing $100, a donation from Gen. M.D. Hardin a member of his congregation.[27] This liberal donation from an individual unknown to us calls for our grattitude not only to the donor but also to the God of all grace who, has given him a heart to feel for the poor perishing heathen; and especially coming at a time like this when without such aid we should soon be under the necessity of curtailing our opperations & that at a time when the disposition of the natives calls loudly for their enlargement. We are under great obligations to our dear brother Smith—to many of his congregation and many other friends of missions in Kentucky for the repeated and seasonable aid which they have given to this mission. While the alms and prayers of Gods people continue thus to ascend as a memorial before him, we trust he will not suffer their labor of love to be in vain.

[June] 25. Meeting for business. Resolved that we prepare a piece of ground for turnips adjoining the Timothy meadow.
Resolved that br. Conger be permitted to lay a floor in the kitchen and space way of the house he occupies.
Resolved that we purchase 20 bushels of wheat and 20 bushels of rye.

[June] 26*th* Br. Butrick returned. He was kindly received wherever he went but did not make so long a tour as was expected on account of the lameness of his horse.

[June] 27*th* Br. George W. Halsey having come out a minor in the family of br. Conger and consequently not permanently attached to the mission left us this day on his return.

[June] 29*th* Received a letter from br. Hall, Sister Hall has been more unwell than usual. They have no female help for the kitchen and know not where they can obtain any. Br. Hall has been obliged to nurse, cook, wash, &c, and had been obliged to limit his school for several days. He has resumed it again this week. He wishes a br. and sister to go out at least for a short time. We sympathize with this dear brother and sister in their trials and know not how they will get along. It was never expected they would be able to take care of a family & teach a school without someone to assist Sister Hall in the house; but it was expected such help could be hired unless it should at some time be thought best by the Com. to send a female assistant to that school. A meeting of the brethren was called to consider br. Halls letter. Resolved that br. Butrick prepare a letter to br. Hall, to be signed by us jointly, stating our utter inability to afford any assistance to that school at present, and proposing, if help cannot be obtained now to enable them to continue there, to remove them back again to this station. It is painful to think of leaving or suspending that promising school and we hope that in some way help may be obtained, but when we consider the smallness of our number here and the great labor which must be performed here every day in order to keep our hundred children with us, there remains not a doubt but it would be better to suspend that school than to spare help from this, even if our younger sisters were in usual health, but at present there is not more than one in this family who would be able to do the work at Taloney if she was there.

July 2*nd* Meeting for business, resolved that we endeavor to obtain two men to cut and draw logs for the saw mill untill there is a large

supply, and that they be under the direction of br. Conger. Resolved that the mill house be built one story and a half above the husk.[28]
Last fall we sowed about 4 acres, on the margin of the Chickamauga creek with Timothy and are now well satisfied that fine meadow may be made on the low land near this stream. We have gathered a fine bunch of hay from this little piece; the grass was waiste high and very thick. But unless we can have more help as assistant missionaries we despair of ever extending the agricultural business to much profit, any farther than labor can be performed by the children of the school. These do exceedingly well for boys of their age and opportunities, but we greatly need one or two pious men to labor with them and direct this important branch of their education. We find it quite too much for any one man to teach the school, and labor with, and instruct, such a number of boys out of school. Br. Chamberlin has taken most of this labor upon himself untill his health has so entirely failed that he is scarcely able to teach the school, and the other brethren are necessarily as much engaged in their several departments that it is impossible for them so to attend to the labor of the boys, as to do them justice or to render their labor as productive as it otherwise might be. We are therefore extremely sorry to hear from the Treasurer that the funds of the society are too low to admit of sending more help at present. We are often obliged to send this large company of boys out with their hoes or their axes, without any one to teach or direct them, and as often think if all the attendant circumstances and consequences were known to the pious young men in our church there are at least two or three who would gladly come out to assist in this business though they should be obliged to lay their bread by the way. Two or three such men having health and strength of body and taking each twenty or thirty of these boys under his direction while out of school might with their assistance perform much labor, in clearing and improving land, and at the same time render a most essential service in training these children to habits of industry and good management; and while the boys were in school they might be very usefully employed in putting tools in repair, or by pursuing their other labor as health and strength should permit. If we are not greatly deceived we do not desire this help for the sake of lessening our labors or cares but because we think it would tend to the more rapid improvement of the children and ultimately, with the divine blessing; prove a saving of expense to the mission.

Ard Hoyt, Wm Chamberlin, Abijah Conger,Elizur Butler, John Vail

Journal of the mission at Brainerd 1821

July 5*th* Br. Butrick set out to go to Taloney for the purpose of visiting br. & sister Hall & if possible divising some means for obtaining permanent kitchen help.

[July] 10*th* This day the remains of a child of sister Naves, aged about 11 months was deposited in the mission burying ground. Both the father and the mother behaved with great propriety on this trying occasion. The complaint of which the child died was the dyssenterry which prevails considerably in the neighborhood and we are told to a very alarming degree in many places around us. Hitherto our large family have all been preserved from this disease.

Br. Butrick returned from Taloney this evening. He found br. & sister Hall in great want of help; their black man and woman had both left them; their youngest child is very feeble & requires constant attention night & day. They had no assistance except a man from Georgia who had agreed to stay with them & teach the school for a short time untill we could see what might be done for obtaining permanent help.

Special meeting called to attend to business relative to the school at Taloney. The question was asked shall a general meeting be appointed to take place before the semi-annual meeting in October and brothers Potter and Hall be notified to attend? answered in the negative.

Question. shall we pay to Mr. Alburtty [Alberty] good money for a 20$ counterfeit bill which he thinks he took of br. Hall?[29] As there is very good evidence that br. Hall did not let him have the counterfeit-bill answered in the negative.

Br. Hall having hired a waggon to a white man to remove his family into Tennessee. He having returned the waggon part way and left it, br. Hall inquires shall I endevour to compel the white man to return the waggon or go after it myself. Answered that br. Hall go after it. ~~himself~~.—Resolved that we send two or three barrels of flour to br. Hall by the first opportunity. The question was asked shall we send the little waggon to br. Hall? Answered in the negative.

Resolved that we endevor to hire Jinny[,] Mr. Sheltons black woman[,] to labor a few weeks at br. Halls.

Resolved that br. Butrick attend to the concerns of the family and school at Taloney while br. Hall shall go out to seek for permanent help, and that he prepare a joint letter to the Pru. Com. on the subject of that school. The question was asked shall br. Butler act as a physician? Answered in the affirmative. The question was asked shall this be his first business? Answered in the affirmative. The question was asked shall the br. in the chair be allowed to vote as if not in the chair? Answered in the affirmative.—Resolved that br. Butler take charge of the sorrel mare untill the horse assigned to him be fit for use.

July 13. Br. Congers second son was taken with dyssentery.

[July] 14. Br. Butrick went out with br. Reece for the purpose of preaching tomorrow at the new Court House about 11 miles from this place.

[July] 15. Sab. Br. Butrick returned this evening. Most of the people were present and gave very good attention. The principal chief of that district told br. Butrick that his people had got whiskey among them;[30] he had told them they must leave their drinking and be prepared to attend meeting on the sabbath. It appeared that most of them had done so but as some did not attend meeting it was feared that the effects of the whiskey had detained them. The chief said he thought it good to keep the sabbath and when he could have no preaching he invited the people to meet at his house & sing the hymns the missionaries had brought them. It is supposed that not a person in the assembly except the preacher and interpreter could understand english.

[July] 16. Meeting for business. Br. Butler inquired shall we purchase a large waggon now offered for sale and harness for the horses. Answered in the negative. Considering the great importance of having some one continually to take charge of things about the mission house, & barn to see to meal, flour, corn, & corn meal, wood, fires, &c to look up & feed hogs, salt cattle, & keep them in their place, See to calves, pigs &c feed horses, and take charge of them and their driver except such as may be employed on the farm, and see that nothing is unnecessarily wasted or neglected about the house and barn, we think it best that the charge of these things be [ascribed?] especially to br. Vail—& that he shall not be held accountable for any other business.

Resolved that Wm Carr and the ox team be under the direction of br. Conger.

Having failed in all our attempts to obtain help for Taloney in this quarter, and their being no one who could possibly be spared from this mission except br. Butrick, he again set out for Taloney. We hear that br. Halls infant died last week.

[July] 19. {Received a line from Mr. Hicks stating that br. Hall had written to him requesting that his daughter and his niece, two small girls who are members of this school might be sent to assist Sister Hall three or four weeks. He expresses a willingness that they should go and stay through the summer and fall. We are not a little surprised that br. Hall should have taken this step without first advising with us on the subject as the girls cannot be expected to supply the place of kitchen help or render them any essential assistance in any way and especially as we have a resolution passed when br. Hall was here that no member of the mission shall take any measures either directly or indirectly to persuade or cause any member of this school to leave this school & go to another unless requested or otherwise to do so by a vote of the brethren in a regular meeting for business, but considering all circumstances we thought best to permit the girls to go.}
A Cherokee woman at a distance hearing the people in this vicinity were afflicted with the dysentery and supposing it might be among the children of the school sent for her son & daughter. As there had been no case of it among the Cherokee children in the school, and as br. Butler had just received a call to visit a sick woman in that region it was thought best to keep the children. Br. Butler left us in company with the man who came after the children and a white man who has lately with his brother & brothers wife moved into the Nation as blacksmiths.

[July] 20. Br. Butler returned. After riding 20 miles he arrived where the sick woman was at sun down. He tarried with them through the night and in the morning found her so much better he left early and called on the woman who sent for her children. After hearing the children were all well at B. and the reasons why the brethren did not comply with her requests; she was not only satisfied but extremely glad that the children were kept back. ~~At 6 oclock he left her and reached br. Hicks' 10 miles a little before 9. He spent two hours with~~ On his return he visited br. Hicks who seems sensible that his complaints are such, that it would be presumption to flatter himself of ever enjoying sound health. He says he is in the hands of a just God who will do perfectly right; and would at all times be entirely submissive to the dear Savior. When any of us are riding in different parts of the Nation we often think how it would animate & encourage

thousand of christians, to see the pleasant families we pass and visit, to see the marks of their industry in the house and out, to see fields of corn of from 10 to 40 acres, to see droves of cattle and swine and above all to hear these dear people converse on the subject of Redeeming love, and some of them give delightful evidence of growth in grace, and others who show an ardent desire to be instructed in the way of eternal life.

[July] 25. As some of our children have not returned since they left us at vacation we thought it best to send for them. Br. Butler accordingly left us this morning for the purpose of getting two girls and returned at evening with them. On his way after them he met a man who had heard that many of the children were sick & that they were all going home. He expected to take his son home on account of the sickness & said others in his neighborhood were calculating to do the same. When he was told the children were all well and none of them were leaving us he seemed well satisfied & returned home. We know not how such a story came into circulation; but it is very evident that when Satan is loosing his strong hold in heathen lands he will make every exertion in his power to present the triumph of the crass and if possible to recover all lost ground. ~~Oh! that such things might tend to increase the faith of missionaries, and settle them more firmly on the work Christ Jesus.~~
~~Having rode the distance of 40 miles br. Butler returned at evening with the girls and their parents who said the reason of their not bringing the children was the oldest had been quite unwell.~~ As br. Hall has succeeded in obtaining a black girl & sister Halls health is somewhat better, br. Butrick returned, and br. Hall accompanied him.

[July] 26. Meeting for business. Br. Hall present.
Resolved as the set of Scots Family Bible which was purchased for Creek Path is not wanted there that it be assigned to br. Hall for the use of the Taloney school. Resolved that James Carr be sent to Taloney with a horse to labor for a short time. Concluded that under present circumstances it would not be expedient for br. Hall to take more than 4 children into his family.
Resolved that we consider it advisable under present circumstances that Polly Hicks & Darcas Fields go to the school at Taloney. Br. Hall requested the opinion of the brethren respecting the best method of conducting meetings on the sabbath when no minister is present.

As the duties and responsibilities of a Minister among the heathen are peculiarly great—as the heathen should be taught that ministers are sent to them by the special direction of our Savior & are qualified to instruct them in all the great truths of our holy religion & to guide them as a Shepherd to the fold of Christ—as many important qualifications are necessary, to the right of discharge of these duties—as the heathen consider all public teachers of religion as ministers, and as many not qualified may be disposed to act as public teachers without licence, to the disadvantage of the cause of religion:—therefore resolved that we consider the example not good for teachers at local schools not licensed to preach to attempt to expound the scripture or speak as a public teacher from the desk. We think it more prudent for them to confine their public exercises to singing, praying, and reading. The residue of the sabbath can be spent either in private conversation, leading the people to a knowledge of the Savior or instructing children.

Resolved that we furnish br. Hall with $75. as soon as we can get such money as will answer his purpose.

The question was asked shall br. Hall be directed to put a shingle roof on the dwelling house at Taloney? Considering the present situation of our funds answered in the negative.

July 27. Br. Hall left us for Taloney in company with Ann Conger and a hired man.

This evening the Rev. Francis McFarland arrived to make a short visit. He has been on a missionary tour thro. the western states, under the direction of the General Assembly—was up the Missouri about 200 miles from St Louis, which place he left on the 7th June. It was expected the Osages of the Missouri would join the Osages of the Arkansaw, to war against the Cherokees of that country.

Br. Butrick went again to preach at the court house.

Sab. [July] 29. This morning a daughter was born to Br. & Sis. Vail—the child appears strong & healthy, & Sis. Vail more comfortable than we had reason to expect considering the very feeble state of her health for months past.[31]

Mr. McFarland preached to our little flock from Isa. 55:6.

Br. Butrick returned this evening—Nearly or quite every person in the vicinity attended preaching, & appear desirous to have it continued.

[July] 30. Meeting for business—Resolved that br. Vail be permitted to hire a man to assist him in his particular charge.—

Concluded to raise three sides of the gristmill as high as the husk frame with stone and that they be laid in lime mortar.—

August 2nd Fa. Hoyt & br. McFarland returned from a visit to Mr. Hicks—~~he has been a long time afflicted with a lameness, in one leg occasioned by a white swelling—it inflates much more than formerly.~~ —His lameness confines him at home entirely, & at times he ~~is attended~~ is exercised with much pain. It is a grief to him that he cannot attend councils and ride about among his people to guide them in the right way, but he bears it with the patience & resignation of a christian. He has great difficulty in counteracting the influence of a certain class of white men who are persuading the more ignorant class of natives that the missionaries are about to take large tracts of land as pay for teaching the children. It appears that a very considerable number have been led to believe that heavy charges are laid against the nation for the expenses of these schools, and that soon the President will compel their payment in lands. Mr. Hicks thinks it necessary to proceed with great caution, & that all persons who come in as missionaries or assistants should be named to the council, & the reason of their coming particularly stated—if this could be done before their arrivals it would be still better. Single persons do not excite those jealousies near as much as families—But notwithstanding these things Mr. Hicks advises if possible to obtain as many assistant missionaries as will be necessary to perform all the labor without hireling—the council will be glad to receive them—& the consideration of laborers being <u>hired</u> will not obviate any objection. A blacksmith all would be glad to have stationed at Brainerd—men also to tend the mills—work the farms—and men and women to assist in the family & schools as many as are needed he says will readily be granted. And as to these groundless jealousies, persevering prudence with the divine blessing, will soon do them all away—

Perhaps it will be some satisfaction to the Com. to have in this place a brief view of the present state of the mission family & school—what attention is paid by the schollars & others to religious instruction, & how we succeed in temporal concerns—

We have at this time 57 Cherokee boys and three boys belonging to the mission family in the boys school—there are belonging to the school 8 cherokee boys who are absent not having returned since the vacation—of girls we have 30 cherokees and three belonging to the mission now in school & seven cherokee girls absent since vacation making in the whole 87 cherokee children now in school & 102 belonging to it. The two girls lately sent to Taloney are not included in this number. Among the absent schollars are Samuel Spring Ann Porter Mary Mason and Betsey Parker. The parents of these named children having no permanent residence it was sometime before we could hear from any of them. We have lately heard that the parents of the 3 girls have gone with them back to the mountains about 100 miles from us. We know no cause for this as both parents and children appeared always to be well pleased to have them with us. We hope to get them again as they were very fine children and as their patrons must feel a particular interest in them. The schollars have in general been healthy and no particular disease has prevailed in the mission family, for the last six months, yet our efficient strength on which the various labors depended has been greatly weakened by sickness and constitutional debility particularly in the female department so that of the 6 sisters residing at the mission house we have seldom had more than 3 and often not more than 2 that have been able to attend to the school or the labors of the family, except very light work. This has rendered it very difficult and at times utterly impossible to do justice to the female school and domestic concerns of the family. The boys also have suffered very materially during their working hours for the want of suitable persons to direct them in their labors. We find it impracticable to hire help in this part of the country to make up these deficiencies. In other respects the prospects of the mission were perhaps never more flattering than at the present time. Several of our oldest boys appear to be under very serious religious impressions, more of the natives attend to religious instructions than formerly, we have hope for at least 2 of them that they have recently been born of the spirit—

In respect to temporal concerns we are sorry to say (especially in this time of pressure) that it appears to be necessary to be at considerable more expense with the saw mill. The foundation on which it was placed proves insufficient and also some of the under works of the mill. We shall be under the necessity of taking the whole building down and removing it to another place. For the grist mill we have no fears. It is founded entirely on one solid rock and performs well[;] the house over it is not yet completed. We expect to find a similar foundation for the saw mill and still hope that these mills will prove an essential service to the mission. Having done but little at farming the present season, but little can be expected from that quarter.

Ard Hoyt, Wm Chamberlin, John Vail, Elizur Butler

July 5th 1821

Dear Sir,

As it will be necessary to have a supply of medicine in the fall we would enquire where we shall obtain them. They can be purchased at the North about two thirds cheaper than at the south, and the quality will be far superior. They might come with safety in a water proof cask. They may be purchased in New York of a person who takes great interest in the missionary cause. Should they come from the north Dr. Butler would wish to send a list; also mention some surgical instruments. Whilst Dr. Worcester was with us he thought it highly important that we should have a set of maps, and globes; especially a territorial globe; also a thermometer.

It seems very necessary that we have a microscope. One that would cost fifty cent would answer as our purposes.

Yours affectionately,
Ard Hoyt, Elizur Butler

Journal of the mission ~~family~~ at Brainerd

1821

August 4th A Cherokee man who speaks no English came to day (bringing his wife and mother with him) to spend a few days with us in order to be further instructed in the things of religion—He has two boys in school, one of them called Jeremiah Evarts, having no English name he is known by us as the father of this boy, & as such has been mentioned several times in our journal. As it is probable from his appearance, that we may have occasion to speak more frequently of him we shall for the present call him the Enquirer.

Sab. [Aug.] 5. Br. McFarland preached and the sacrament of the Lords supper was administered. A number of the communicants both in the mission family and out were absent from ill health. Those who were able to attend we trust found it a season of refreshing from the presence of the Lord. Our little house was not sufficient to contain the congregation; numbers stood about the doors and windows. The afternoon service, which is now in Cherokee, excepting the prayers, was attended by a number who cannot understand our language. After the usual discourse by br. John as interpreter, br. Reece made a short address and the congregation was dismissed in the usual form, when the Enquirer whose countenance has indicated the most serious and solemn attention through the whole exercise, immediately addressed his people, and spoke at considerable length with great apparent ease and animation. All who could understand his language appeared to pay very serious and solemn attention.

[Aug.] 6. Mr. McFarland having tarried with us longer than he at first expected took an affectionate leave of the children and mission family & left us early this morning to pursue his journey to the north by way of Knoxville. We have been edified, both by his preaching and conversation. May the divine blessing attend him and his labors through life, and at last may we meet in our Father's kingdom above. The Enquirer expressed a great desire to receive further instruction and intends to stay with us, and christians in this neighborhood, untill after the next Sabbath.

[Aug.] 7. Meeting for business. Resolved that Mr. Clark be steadily employed with Mr. Long on the girls house.—Resolved that a man be hired and take a span of horses to work continually on the farm untill the wheat is sowed.—Resolved that br. Chamberlin have charge of the meat stock and hogs. As the foundation of the sawmill cannot be supported where the mill now stands therefore resolved that means be taken to remove it as soon as practicable onto a solid foundation.

[Aug.] 8. Br. Conger left us to go into Rhea county on business.—

Sab. [Aug.] 12. More attended meeting today who cannot understand English than perhaps on any former occasion except at the funeral of Dr. Worcester.—
After the public exercises the church was stayed for conversation with the Enquirer and to decide on the expediency of admitting him as a candidate for baptism. Most of the members had become well satisfied with him from former conversations particularly during the week past. In relating his experience at this time he observed that what was told him here sometime since (supposed to be about 18 months) sunk down into his heart—he carried it always with him, and it had appeared to be growing ever since—that he had from that time found himself to be a great sinner, and been determined to seek further instruction concerning the things which had been told him—

that he had found he could do nothing to make himself any better, but Jesus would take away his sins and give him a heart to do right—that he believed all he had heard from the good book about the Saviour & felt that He was able to keep him in the right way, and bring him to heaven at last—that it was his desire to obey all the commandments of Christ and to live with the people of God—that he felt a great love for christians, was happy in their company and conversation, and that it gave him great pleasure to hear such things as were told him here. Br. Reece observed that from conversations he had had with him the week past he believed the Enquirer had got before him in religion, for he found him able to answer in every thing correctly as far as he himself knew. He was by unanimous vote admitted as a candidate for baptism, as was also the wife of our white br. McPhearson who is the mother of br. Reece.

The wife and mother of the Enquirer who have been with him during the present visit, appear to possess none of his feelings, yet they pay decent attention to instruction when spoken to and manifest no disposition to ridicule or oppose.

[*Aug.*] 14. The Enquirer expressed a desire to remain with the christians here much longer but said he had much work to do at home and must return. After receiving some further instruction and leading in prayer in his own language, (for he speaks no English) he took a most affectionate leave of us and departed.

[*Aug.*] 15. A grey headed man and his wife who have one son in the school came last evening a distance of about 60 miles.[32] They had never been here before and we thought they might have come for the sole purpose of seeing their son. As neither of them understand English we instructed br. John to tell them we would have a talk with them this morning if they desired it. They said that was what they came for; they had not come to see their son but to get religious instruction—some of their relatives they said had become pious and were always talking to them about these things. They believed they were very good and wanted to learn more about them. It appears the man is an uncle of the Enquirer who left us yesterday, and the woman has a sister belonging to the church at Springplace. They appear to have received considerable instruction from their pious relatives and to be somewhat alarmed about their situation.—As is common for persons in an unrenewed state they appear inclined to depend somewhat on their own works and to think they have not been so bad as some others, but from the great change which is apparent in their relatives who have professed religion, they appear convinced of the absolute necessity of a change in themselves beyond what is in their power to effect. They listened with solemn attention to what was said to them and their moistened eyes manifested they were not without some feeling on the subject, and they expressed a determination to make religion the great object of their inquiry and care.—

We feel it an unspeakable blessing to have a pious interpreter to assist in teaching this people, and especially to have one who is able of himself to teach them many things: and we consider it no small token of good designed for this people that God is graciously and wonderfully raising up teachers from among themselves not only here but also in many other parts of the nation.

Br. Conger returned—he has engaged the man who built the grist mill to come sometime next month to put the saw mill upon its new foundation.

[Aug.] 16. {Meeting for business. As br. Hall has promised to be one of 8 to build a saw mill in the neighborhood of Taloney, therefore resolved that he be permitted to give 12 dollars (which is the estimated sum for each proprietor) for that object provided the mill is built but that neither he nor the mission be considered as owning any share in the mill.}

[Aug.] 17. Br. John Brown and his wife [Susannah] came up from Creek path. Having been for sometime in a feeble state of health and continually declining he has come by advice of his friends to spend a little time in the neighborhood for the purpose of being under the immediate care of br. Butler. Both he and his wife appear to be lively growing christians. The christians at Creek path are walking in the love and fellowship of the spirit.—

[Aug.] 18. Finished the walls of the grist mill so far as they are built with stone, for the first story.—

[Aug.] 20. The man and woman mentioned on the 15th left us this morning to return home. The 5 days past they have spent either with us or visiting christians in this neighborhood. Religion seems to be almost the sole object of their attention. Seriousness and solemnity are visible in all their deportment, and before they departed they expressed great satisfaction in the things which they had heard, and declared their determination to walk in the light which now shone

upon them, and to seek further instruction by all the means in their power. We learn that the man is called Fields, probably from his supposed father, he being part white; the woman appears to be a full Cherokee.[33] Neither of them understand English.

Began to frame the grist mill house.

Meeting for business, Resolved that an additional span of horses be assigned for the farm.

[*Aug.*] 22. Received a letter from the Arkansaw Cherokee mission by a Mr. Owen direct from that station.

Brothers Finney and Washburn with their wives, and little ones and sister Minerva Washburn had a quick and prosperous passage from Eliot to Dwight. They left Eliot on the 22nd March descended the Yazoo from whence their keel was towed by a steam boat to the Arkansaw. Last at which place they arrived on the 11th April—left that place on the 19th, ascended the river with their keel boat about 450 miles, and arrived at their establishment on the 10th of May. They were all favored with general health on their passage and after their arrival untill within a few days of the date of their letter, which is July 24th, at which time the whole family were sick with fever and ague except br. Washburn and his little boy: At the time of writing all appeared to be on the recovery except br. Finneys little girl. They had planted about 22 acres of corn, 18 of which on new ground which they had cleared— prospect of a good crop—had built 4 cabins and commenced a school house which they expected to finish by the 1st of October, and expected to be able to open their school sometime in Autumn.

By this letter we have the melancholly tidings of the death of our dear Lydia Carter. She with John Osage Ross and the other captives, it appears had been sent forward to their people but the Osages refusing to give up the murderers in exchange as they had promised, the captives were again brought back, and Lydia and John committed to the care of Gov. Miller. The Gov. being about to journey to New England took little John with him intending to take him to his great father the President, leaving Lydia in the care of a Mrs. Lovely,[34] untill they should be able to take her into the Mission family where he wished her to remain untill an opportunity should offer for her return to Brainerd. But it pleased a wise and holy God that her wanderings and earthly captivity should be ended in the hospitable house of Mrs. Lovely. The brethren say "She was taken with fever and ague before she arrived in this Nation and was never well after it. She had no fever after she came to Mrs. Lovely's but appeared to have been worn out by her exposure while she was weak." This intelligence is indeed trying to our feelings. By her mild disposition and affectionate manner and by the care and responsibility which had devolved upon us on her account she had become very dear to us; but he who always had best the only right to her has done all things well.

The brethren in their letter say nothing of the war between the Cherokees of that Territory and the Osages, but the bearer of their letter states that the Cherokees have as usual been engaged in their corn fields during the season of planting and hoeing corn but were preparing for an expedition against the Osages which they expected to commence in the month of August; and he understood that the Osages of the Missouri had joined their brethren on the Arkansaw for the purpose of meeting the Cherokees in battle. It was generally expected there would be some fighting before their unhappy differences would be settled, but no apprehensions were entertained for the safety of the Missionaries on either side.[35]

August 25th. We have the pleasure of recording, with thanks to Almighty God, the birth of a son; born to br. & Sis. Butler between 5 and 6 ock. this morning. A fine healthy looking babe, and the mother under comfortable circumstances.[36]

[Aug.] 31st Raised the frame of the mill house. It will probably appear strange to the Pru. Com. that we have built a grist mill and put it in opperation before we had siding to cover it. In ordinary circumstances this would (to say the least) be very incongruous. It may be well therefore to observe that the old mill was not likely to be sufficient to grind for our family during the summer had the mill house been the first object, and the mill itself been omitted till the present time we know not where we should have obtained meal, as the old mill, according to our anticipations, has proved insufficient. As the frame which supports the running gears of the mill is entirely independant of that which covers it[,] it was as cheap and convenient to build that part first as last except as it was necessary to throw a temporary shed over the mill to preserve it from the sun and rain while the house was in building, and by doing this we have been able to keep the family in meal, and also to assist some of our neighbors.

Ard Hoyt , Wm Chamberlin, John Vail, Elizur Butler

Brainerd Mission journal

1821

Sept. 1st Sowed about 6 acres of newly cleared land with turnips and timothy. This piece is joining that which was sowed in like manner last year, and now enclosed in the same common field. It is generally thought best to sow turnips at least 2 or 3 weeks earlier, but having been for a long time without rain the earth had become so exceedingly dry that it was thought best to wait untill there was appearance of rain. This day there is such appearance, and we have committed the field to the dry and barren earth to wait the blessing of him who giveth or withholdeth the rain of heaven according to his will.

[Sept.] *2nd* Refreshing showers of rain water the thirsty earth. May the seed we sewed yesterday spring up and bring forth fruit to nourish the bodies of these poor heathen children, and may the dew on Zion fall and cause the seed of divine truth thus to spring up and bring forth fruit unto eternal life.

Received a letter from the chiefs of Wills Valley which place is from 40 to 50 miles S.W. from Brainerd. They have had a meeting of their people, and all are anxious to have a school established in that neighborhood, and wish us if possible, to send them a teacher and particularly one who can instruct them in religion. The majority of these are the same persons who requested a school at Battle Creek more than 2 years ago. Such was the urgency of their request at that time that a brother was sent to them to explain the reasons why they could not have a teacher immediately; and to encourage them (as we were then authorized to do) that an additional number of teachers would soon be sent out, when they might probably be supplied. Soon after this, that part of the country was ceded to the U.S.[37] Without losing sight of the expected school, and religious instruction they have resettled themselves at Wills Valley, and renew their request.—And what shall we say to them? Must we return an answer which will not only dash all their hopes, but give them reason to suspect that all our proffessions of friendship were delusions; and that Government and the christian public are not as anxious for their instruction as they have been told they are?—And how can we give them the least encouragement when we have been obliged to suspend one school for want of means to continue it, & the state of the general Treasury, indicates that we may soon be under the necessity of abridging still more? We know not what to say. If no more schools are to be established we have said too much already. We must tell the truth and leave events with God.

[Sept.] 6. Br. Chamberlin went to the Agency after money.

[Sept.] 7. Br. C. returned. He obtained the second payment towards the girls house; but this was less than half the sum we expected. There are two quarters of the yearly stipend from Government yet behind and more than $100 for blacksmith work. The Agent (who is always disposed to do every thing in his power for the mission) would gladly have paid the whole, but he has not the money. It will probably be 6 or 8 weeks, maybe more, before he can get it. We fear the mission will be embarrassed by this delay.

[Sept.] 10. Meeting for business. The question was asked shall we write for the blacksmith recommended by Rev. Mr. Morrison to come and work for the mission a short time? Answered in the affirmative.
A number of the oldest boys of the school have for sometime been in the practice of holding religious conferences and prayer meetings by themselves. Some of them say it appears as if they were coming out of a dark dungeon into the light of day.

[Sept.] 17th Meeting for business.—Resolved that we draw stone to build an ash house.
Our feelings have been again tried by the painful necessity of rejecting two fine, promising boys of suitable age because our school is full. The parent after finding they could not now be received urged with importunity that we would fix on some future time when we would take them, but it was not in our power even to do this, as there are numbers now waiting to fill the places of any who may be prepared to leave the school. We could only say we wish it were in our power to teach all the children in the nation; will take yours at some future time if we can, and when you come again we will talk more about it. We hear of many who wish to bring their children but who do not apply because they know the school is full. Under such circumstances how can we think of lessening the number of our schollars, and yet it is reduced to a certainty that we must unless the Lord send us more helpers, or give additional strength to these that are now here. We know the Lord can do every thing, and hope he will not suffer our dear patrons to let this mission decline for want of a little additional help.

[Sept.] 20. Received a large and very valuable box of clothing together with a small box of shoes from New Haven chiefly from the students in Yale College, the shoes mostly from shoe makers in the city. A letter accompanying the box states that an approved Merchant Tailor had valued the clothing at $308,50. In looking over these articles we think the valuation would be considered quite low here, after adding the expense of transportation.

With the above articles we received a box from Burk County Georgia directed to Eliot. Did the friends of missions in the Atlantic states know the difficulty of transporting such articles from this place to Eliot they would see the propriety of being requested to forward them by way of New-Orleans.

[Sept.] 24. Meeting for business. Resolved that a room be prepared in the S.W. end of the upper piazza for clothing.
Resolved not to sow the large field with wheat as the season has been too dry for plowing.
{Br. Reece did not attend public worship yesterday. We learn that there were so many Indians drunk in his neighborhood that he thought it unsafe to leave his house alone, or to leave any part of his family to keep it in his absence. Not on account of any ill will they bear to him or any of his, we believe br. Reece is on very good terms with his neighbors and all his acquaintance, but when this people are filled with intoxicating liquor their best friends are afraid to trust them. Through the influence of christianity and civilization there are many among this people who have abandoned this horrid practice, but drunkenness is still the crying sin of a great portion of this people, and many lives are annually destroyed by it.
It is perhaps generally believed that Indians have naturally a greater thirst for ardent spirits than almost any other people, but the sobriety of many families which have become civilized and live after the manor of white people, seems to render this hypothesis at least doubtful. So far as our acquaintance extends, the well informed Indians have as few intemperate men among them, in proportion to their numbers, as the white people. But so long as multitudes of them are suffered to remain in their ignorant state, and the cupidity of their white neighbors is pouring floods of whiskey among them; there is reason to believe they will continue to be cut down by this fell destroyer of life and peace.}[38]

[Sept.] 29. Received a letter from the Treasurer which made our hearts glad by the information that two brethren with their wives and a single sister were expected to join this mission after a few weeks.

Ard Hoyt , Elizur Butler , D.S. Butrick,
Wᵐ Chamberlin , John Vail, Abijah Conger

Brainerd Mission journal

Oct. 1. Resolved that preparations be made to put up more hogs & beef to eat.[39]

Oct. 4. Recd 7 boxes of clothing Viz. One from the Dorcas Society of Becket, Mass. valued at $38,40. One from Female Cent Societies in Barnet, Vermont valued at $82,98. One from Belchertown, Mass. One from ladies & a Juvenile Mite Society in Augusta, District of Maine, including 3 bundles of clothing from Newbrunswick; one from Marlboro, Plymouth & Campton, and one from Cambridge, Mass. containing some valuable & useful books & clothes. These boxes were all valuable & useful, but the estimated value was not given.

[Oct.] 8. As br. Vail thinks he can perform two thirds of the labour of his charge, and as br. Butrick thinks it will be for his health to labour considerably this fall, and proposes attending to the other third, therefore, Resolved that we do not hire a man at present to labour under the direction of br. Vail.

[Oct.] 12. Brother and sister Potter arrived from Creek Path. Sister Catharine Brown and her mother accompanied them most of the way, and are expected here tomorrow. They left the members of the church there in a favorable situation, walking in love, and in the fear of God. One man has lately been received as a candidate for baptism. The school is not large. The average number this year has been eighteen. Most of these have made good proficiency in learning. Eight board in br. Potter's family.

[Oct.] 13. Brother Hall arrived from Taloney. His report is favorable concerning the school under his care. The average number of schollars has been between 20 and 30. From some specimens of writing, and from his report, it appears that they have in general made good improvement. He expresses a hope, that one of his Sunday school schollars, a black man, has lately become a new creature.

Sister Catharine and her mother, the Enquirer, & two Sisters, David Brainerd's parents, mentioned in the journal of Aug. 15th together with several others arrived.[40]

[Oct.] 14. Lord's Day. At our usual prayer meeting, the Enquirer, and Mrs. McPhearson, candidates for baptism, were present. Father Hoyt enquired if their feelings and determinations respecting the service of God were as formerly, and whether they now desired to be admitted to the holy ordinance of baptism? Both answered in the affirmative, and the man expressed his determination to serve God. He told us that since he was here last August he had called together his family mornings and evenings and prayed with them, and had invited his friends and neighbours to meet at his house on the Sabbath when he prayed and talked with them, as far as he was able, and that he had brought some of his friends with him, that they might receive further instruction from us. He said also that he had brought his children except two he left sick to dedicate them to God in baptism according to former instructions. Father Hoyt then enquired of the church whether the candidates for Baptism should this day be admitted to that ordinance, and also whether Darius Hoyt, a candidate for the communion, should be admitted to the Lord's Table?—and was answered in the affirmative. We then repaired to the house of worship, where, in due time, the candidates for baptism, in the presence of many of their poor benighted people solemnly received that holy ordinance, the man taking the name of Samuel J. Mills.[41] Four of his children (all present) he dedicated to God in baptism, viz. Jeremiah Evarts, Daniel, Anna & Nancy. Brother and Sister Butler also presented their infant, William Smith, for baptism. After the aforementioned exercises, we were invited to the Table of our Lord, where we had the pleasure of receiving, for the first time, our dear brother Darius Hoyt.

At early candle lighting br. Chamberlin collected the parents & children in the girl's school room for religious exercises. After singing a Cherokee hymn and prayer br. C. spent a short time in teaching them some of the essential truths of the Bible. After this br. John Arch addressed them in his own language, and then br. Samuel J. Mills, in a most moving & affecting manner, made a lengthy address, and the concluding prayer. Our meeting, we thought on the whole more interesting than those we have seen at Brainerd.

[Oct.] 15th Proceeded in the usual method to examine the schools. This exercise occupied most of the day. All present appeared pleased with the appearance and improvement of the schollars. After examination some of the children left us to spend the vacation with their friends.
General Meetings for business. The communications from the Cor. Sec. and Treasurer of the Board were read, together with the minutes of meetings for business at Brainerd. Adjourned till tomorrow morning.

[Oct.] 16. Meeting. Brothers Potter and Hall reported concerning the schools under their care. Br. Potter presented a letter from the church at Creek Path, requesting us to send br. John Arch to that place as an interpreter. Resolved that their request be granted.
Resolved that br. Potter be permitted to hire a man, not exceeding two months.
Resolved that a desk, book case, small table, butter tub, meat casks, & vinegar cask, be made and sent to Creek Path, together with glass &c as soon as convenient.
Resolved that br. Potter see to the preparing and forwarding of the aforementioned articles.
Resolved that we hire a man to assist br. Hall in getting wood, securing corn & making necessary preparations for winter.
Resolved that a horse be sent to Taloney to work in a waggon with the one br. Hall has while needed in getting wood &c.
Resolved that br. Conger be released from all business untill it shall please God to restore his health, & thus enable him to resume his labours.
Resolved that br. Potter have $200 for the use of the school under his care.
Resolved that br. Hall have $100 for the use of the school at Taloney.
Most of the schollars left us today. Four, two boys & two girls, intend staying with us during vacation. These dear children are our present joy, & our future hopes. Their presence is delightful, & their absence painful to us. For them we rejoice to labour, & for them we entreat the prayers of Zion.

[Oct.] 17. David Brainerd's Parents left us. They appear still anxious to know more of God our Saviour, and seem determined to seek till they find.
Brother Hall left us for Taloney.

[Oct.] 18. Brother Samuel J. Mills & his company left us. Our prayer and our hope is that God will perfect his work of grace and render him a bright luminary in the dark region where he lives. Before he left us, being ready to depart, father Hoyt enquired if he could wait for two prayers, and make one himself. He said he could, for all his happiness consisted in praying & thinking of God.

Brother Morrison a clergyman from Tennessee arrived. He had intended being here at examination, but not knowing the exact time it would take place, was too late.

[Oct.] 19. Br. M. left us to return to his family. A luxury indeed is the company and communion of saints in this wilderness land.

[Oct.] 20. Resolved to take down the old stable.

Resolved that br. Potter take measures to get the cows and other cattle from Chattoogi to Creek Path for the benefit of that school.

Resolved that br. Potter name a boy living with him Thomas Harvey Skinner.

Resolved that the library be removed into the room occupied by br. Butler, and be under the care of sister Butler.

Resolved that br. Butrick perform all the writing for the Mission at Brainerd, except such as belongs to the department of the steward and Treasurer.

[Oct.] 22. Resolved that we hire Wm Carter to labour one year in kitchen & on the farm as needed.

Brother and sister Potter, Mrs. Brown and sister Catharine left us for Creek Path.

[Oct.] 24. D.D. Coffin, President of Greenville College, Tennessee, Rev. Isaac Anderson & wife & Mrs. Rawlings arrived.[42] They expressed much regret at not being able to be here before vacation.

[Oct.] 25. Our visiting friends left us, having an appointment for preaching on the other side of the river this evening. Their visit has been truly refreshing & profitable to us.

[Oct.] 29. This morning br. Butler was called to visit a wounded boatman. Last evening one of the boatmen, partially intoxicated, took a large hunters knife from a Cherokee then in the boat, ~~threw him into the river,~~ and without any provocation, stabbed a fellow boatman, so that it was feared the wound would prove mortal.

Nov. 5. Br. Conger requests permission of the brethren to go to Salem with his daughter to the Female Institution there that she may finish her education, & be prepared for more usefulness: he also wishes the light wagon & a horse for that purpose.[43]

Resolved that the vote respecting br. Conger's release from business be reconsidered. As that resolution may be understood as implying the entire release of br. Conger from missionary service; therefore, Resolved, that it be amended as follow, viz: That he be released from the particular charges assigned him by the brethren, untill his health be restored.

The brethren gave it as their opinion that they had no right to give br. Conger permission to go to Salem.

Resolved that we hire a horse, saddle and bridle to Mr. Clark to go to Georgia.

Resolved that our schools be kept but five hours each day the ensuing winter.

Concluded that the kitchen and dining room be repaired.

[Nov.] 6th This day the schools commenced after a vacation of three weeks. We are pleased to find the children more punctual in their return than ever before after vacation.

[Nov.] 10th Resolved that we hire Wm Carr, Six months to tend the saw mill from sun set to sun rise, provided he will do it for twelve Dollars per month.

[Nov.] 14th Resolved that a stall be built for the oxen.

Resolved that br. Butrick be released from that part of br. Vale's charge which he took Oct. 8th.

[Nov.] 15th Through a kind Providence br. Conger is enabled to resume the labours from which he was released Oct. 16th.

Ard Hoyt, D.S. Butrick, Wm Chamberlin,
Abijah Conger, John Vail, Elizur Butler

Brainerd journal

Nov. 15. A schollar, half white, man grown, went out of school without leave.[44]

[Nov.] 16. The schollar above mentioned attended school to day. When his class took their places to read, he reluctantly sat down with

them and read, but would not spell, though repeatedly required to do so. Br. Chamberlin conversed with him respecting his conduct. He wept, and soon left the house. Br. Chamberlin followed him to his cabin, went with him to father Hoyt's room, and spent some time in conversation with him alone. He did not appear angry but much distressed. He said he wished to leave this country, and go to war against the Osages. Br. Chamberlain enquired why he violated the rules of school, by going out as he did,—why he did not ask permission? he said he thought of it, but his heart was so bad he could not. Br. Chamberlin, after pointing out the danger of attempting to run away from God, told him he might either go or stay as he chose.

[Nov.] 17. The schollar mentioned yesterday told us this morning he had made up his mind to leave the school and go to the Arkansas. When br. Chamberlin gave him his clothes, he said he wished to ask forgiveness for his conduct. When br. C. replied that he would freely forgive him, he immediately burst into tears, and wept sometime and went away much affected. He is now gone and our opportunities of instructing him are probably forever past. After leaving us, he met br. Butler, and told him he was very sorry he left the school, and would go back but feared he could not be received. As br. Butler knew not what he might have done to occasion his leaving the school, he did not urge him to return.[45]

[Nov.] 18. This evening John Rackley, a schollar of about 14 years, was taken with a pain in his head, vomiting, and a high fever.[46]

[Nov.] 19. Resolved that br. Conger and br. Chamberlain determine what shall be the dimensions of the wash house we think of building.
Resolved that measures be taken to hire Mr. James, to make meat casks.
The question was asked, Shall a copy of br. Hall's report respecting the school at Taloney be forwarded to the Committee.[47] Ans^d negative.
Q. Shall some men's coats and pantaloons be sent to Taloney and exchanged for corn. And shall the waggon there be offered for sale? Ans. As we have but few coats suitable for men, & none which will not probably be needed for the large boys, and as we know not what waggons the brethren on their way will fetch, therefore, we think it inexpedient to exchange the above mentioned for corn, or to offer the waggon for sale at present.
Resolved to hire br. Thompson to labour one year in the Smiths shop.

[Nov.] 20. The sick boy was removed into the Mission house for his comfort, and our convenience in attending him. Before night he became delirious. Some of the other are unwell,—generally taken with a severe headache, and vomiting.

[Nov.] 21. Last night the sick boy was in extreme pain, and a continued state of derangement. About 4 O'Clock we sent for his grandmother, about 20 miles, who is his only surviving near relative in this part of the country, except a sister four or five years of age. But we sent too late to give her an opportunity of seeing him alive. A little after sun rise he died. This dear child was almost the only hope of an aged grandmother, whose earthly friends have fled to the world of spirits, and left her grey head to go down with sorrow to the grave. This is the first instance of mortality among the schollars since the commencement of this school. The old lady above mentioned arrived about sunset, inexpressibly borne down with grief.

[Nov.] 22. The remains of the deceased child were committed to the tomb.

[Nov.] 24. Br. & sister Elsworth, and sister Harriet Elsworth arrived in good health, after a long, though prosperous journey of 8 weeks & 4 days.[48] We rejoice in the goodness of God to them and us, and especially to the children and people of our charge in continuing to furnish them with the means of literary and religious instruction.

[Nov.] 26. As br. Hall seems anxious to have the Report of the school at Taloney forwarded to the Committee, therefore
Resolved that it be forwarded according to this wishes.
Q. Do the brethren think it expedient for br. Vail to go to Newjersey for his son? If so, Can he be furnished with the means? Ans. Affirm.

[Nov.] 29. Last night Father Hoyt was violently seized with the Peripneumony and was in extreme pain during the night.[49]
This morning about 3 O'Clock sister Chamberlin was delivered of a son.[50]

[Nov.] 30. Father Hoyt continues in great distress, and considering his former weakness, we consider his situation very precarious.[51]

Dec. 1. Br. Butrick went to Mr. Coodey's to visit a white man, sick with the consumption.[52] As the sick man said he thought he should die tonight, and the family wished it, br. B. concluded to spend the night with them. This man, though frequently warned of his danger, and entreated to prepare for death, told sister Coodey but 2 or 3 days ago, that he had not thought much of dying. And could not even now, when sensible of his near approach to death, say he was sorry for all his sins. About 9 O'Clock he expired.

[Dec.] 2. The corpse of the man who died yesterday was brought to this place, and conveyed to its last earthly home. The funeral exercises—attended about 12 O'Clock.

[Dec.] 3. Last night, as br. Chamberlin was at the well, a large dog that has been here sometime, and has appeared strangely a few days past, came by him, so as almost or quite to touch his clothes, went into the hall, & appeared evidently in a fit of madness. Br. C. through the kind Providence of God, was enabled to escape. After a short time the dog howled, & ran. Peculiar gratitude is due to God, for this deliverance.
Resolved that br. Elsworth have charge of the bell.
Resolved that a new book case be made for the library.
Q. Can br. Hall have $95? Answered in the affirmative as soon as such money can be obtained as will answer at Taloney.
Resolved that the milling, barn and drawing wood be assigned to br. Chamberlin, during the absence of br. Vail.

[Dec.] 4. The mad dog was this morning killed. We know not what, if any creatures are bit.
Br. Vail left us for New Jersey. We should regret his undertaking so long a journey at this season of the year, especially as his labours are so much needed here, were it not so evidently a parental duty. His son, though formerly obedient, has, since the departure of his parents by some means been turned into a dangerous course, which will probably lead to ruin without the restraint of parental authority.
This evening br. J. Hill arrived from Taloney. He left his native hall the first of October, and arrived at Taloney the last of November.[53] He wishes to devote himself to the cause of missions, and not knowing but we had authority to receive him, and feeling unwilling to spend a year or two more in study as some of his friends advised, he came without credentials from the Pru. Com. expecting to be examined as to his qualifications on his arrival here.

[Dec.] 5. As Mr. Jeremiah Hill from the state of Maine, desires to be united with the Mission, and has no credentials from the Board but satisfactory commendations from the minister and private gentlemen respecting moral character therefore,

Resolved that we employ him as a labourer untill advice be received from the Prud. Committee.

Resolved that br. Butrick prepare a joint letter to the Prud. Com. respecting the case of br. Hill.

Resolved that br. Hill be sent to Taloney to assist br. Hall untill these directions from the brethren.

Resolved that we keep up four yoke of young oxen this winter.

[Dec.] 8. Mr. Little from Philadelphia called on his way to Huntsville. Father Hoyt is still confined to his bed, but we trust recovering.

[Dec.] 10. This morning br. Little left us to pursue his journey. He seems truly interested in the service of Missions, and devoted to the service of God. His stay has been short, but his truly christian company & conversations has been refreshing to our hearts. On his departure, he expressed his good wishes and desires to promote the Redeemer's kingdom among the heathen by a donation of twenty Dollars.

One of the horses belonging to the widow Worcester strayed or was stolen last evening. We have not yet been able to find him.

Resolved that br. Butler be permitted to sell a horse to Wm Carr on trust provided he give good security.

[Dec.] 11. Through the kind Providence of God, father Hoyt is so far recovered as to sleep last night without a watcher. We trust that though the Divine blessing, on the means used he will soon be enabled to attend in some measure to the important duties of his station.

> Elizur Butler, Ard Hoyt, J.C. Elsworth,
> D.S. Butrick, Abijah Conger, Wm Chamberlin

Brainerd Dec. 14th 1821

Beloved Sir,

I would just mention that the last communication recd from you was dated the 30th of August. We fear that in some way letters have been misserved or stoped. Mr. Stewart on his way to the Chocktaws arrived here yesterday in good health, having had a prosperous journey.[54]

> Yours, Elizur Butler

Jeh Evarts, Esq.

Brainerd Mission journal Dec. 1821

Dec. 15. Br. Chamberlin dismissed the boys school, and sent the large boys in pursuit of the widow Worcesters horse, while he and br. Ellsworth spent the day in riding for the same purpose. But all were unsuccessful. We fear he is stolen.

Br. Samuel J. Mills and David Brainerds father, whose English name we learn is Fields arrived. The latter brought two girls, one of which has not before attended school. Br. Potter arrived from Creek Path. He brings favorable news concerning the church and people there. Since he was here before, he has baptized one of his dear charge. ~~Br. Samuel J. Mills we think is a growing christian.~~

[Dec.] 16. We had the privilege of coming again to the Lords table. Here the master and the servant are alike, the rich and the poor meet together—The Lord is the helper of them all. We lament the continued debility of our dear father Hoyt, and some of the sisters which keeps them from the house of God.

[Dec.] 17. Meeting for business. Resolved that 3 Vols. of the Christian observer, 2 Vols panoplist, Williams sermons, Henry on prayer, Baxters Sts [Saints'] Rest, & the Rise and progress of religion in the soul, be assigned to the school at Creek Path.[55] As br. Stewart has arrived here on his way to Mayhew and as his horse is taken lame so as not to be capable of performing the journey, therefore, resolved that the black mare be exchanged for his. Concluded that a waggon be provided for Creek Path. Resolved that an axe be sent to Creek Path for br. John Arch to use.

Mr. Day arrived with 50 fat hogs which he had previously engaged.

[Dec.] 18. Our dear brethren Potter and Stewart left us this morning for their respective labors.

~~Killed 29 hogs weighing~~

[Dec.] 19. Br. Parker arrived.[56] He came by water to Nashville, and from thence to Winchester in a hired waggon. At Winchester he left his family and came here on foot, about 60 miles, for a waggon to convey his family to this place. Although he has found some trouble since he landed at Nashville, yet he has generally been prospered and we have great cause to rejoice in the goodness of God, in bringing him in safety to the place of his future labors, and we trust through the

grace of God he will be instrumental of building the house of God in this benighted land. As some of our horses were sick and others wanted for the more immediate labors of the Mission, & as one of our hired men offered to go with a four horse team, cheaper we think than to send the mission team, we hired him, and he left us to go for his team, and meet br. Parker at Winchester.

Mr. Burns a white man with a Cherokee family arrived with 41 fat hogs, most of them had been previously engaged.

~~Killed 16 hogs weighing~~

[Dec.] 24. Br. Parker left us to go for his family having been detained here by rain & high water a number of days. This evening through the kindness and mercy of God our dear father Hoyt was able to be present at our meeting for business, after an absence of 4 weeks.

{Meeting for business. Resolved that we think it advisable provided a suitable interpreter can be obtained, for br. Butrick as an evangelist to visit every town and as far as practicable every family in this nation, forwarding his journal to the brethren here as often as convenient, and when prepared to begin this labor that he be released from the writing lately assigned to him.}[57]

{Resolved that we endeavor to employ br. Reece to ride with br. Butrick as interpreter.}

[Dec.] 28. At the request of the black people in the neighborhood we had preaching. O how delightful it is to the Missionary to see people seeking after instruction.

[Dec.] 31. Meeting for business. {As br. Reece cannot conveniently leave his family this winter, therefore resolved that we request br. John Arch to go with br. Butrick. Resolved that br. Butrick prepare a letter to br. John Arch and the church at Creek Path on the above subject. Resolved that the poney at br. Congers be taken for br. John to ride.} Resolved that a copy of Dr. A.B. Grubbs letter be sent to the Pru. Com.

As assistants have lately arrived and we have heard of others on their way, therefore resolved that the vote respecting the hiring of Shelton be reversed.

1822

January 2nd 1822. A day of fasting and prayer by the mission family. We found it good to seek after our God in this way. We all seemed to feel the infinite importance of enjoying the presence of God, and our utter inability to do anything for his cause without the aid of his Spirit.

Br. Hall arrived this evening from Taloney. His family is enjoying a good degree of health, and the school continues to prosper.

Five of our children returned to the school. They give as a reason for their not returning sooner that one of them has been sick.

[Jan.] 3. Special meeting called br. Hall present. Resolved that br. H. be permitted to purchase a field containing 5 or 6 acres (together with a cabin for fodder) lying near the school house at Taloney, provided he can obtain it for twelve dollars.

Resolved that the brown horse with as much harness as is needed to complete a set for two horses be sent to Taloney for the present.

Resolved that br. Hall be permitted to increase the number of schollars in his family supported by the board to six and that he be permitted to take boarders for pay.

Resolved that br. Ellsworth have the charge of the boys tools, and the boys during their working hours. Resolved that br. Ellsworth have the charge of the barn, getting wood, and meal. Resolved that all the writing of the Mission be assigned to br. Chamberlin except such as belongs to the steward and treasurer.

Br. Hall left us to return to Taloney.

Br. Butrick left us to spend some time in visiting the people in different parts of the nation. He will go first to Creek Path for the purpose of obtaining br. John Arch to accompany him as interpreter. May the Lord go with, and enable him to impart the knowledge of salvation to many perishing souls.

One of our full Cherokee boys reviewing Murrys grammar recited the whole of Orthography, Etymology, and Syntax, at one lesson without missing more than three or four words. Two of our small boys who went home at vacation returned.

[Jan.] 4th Being cold and as a large number of our boys have no shoes we were obliged to let them stay in their cabins. We feel disposed to take this blame on ourselves for their being this destitute. For we have reason to believe, from the known liberality of the christian public, that if we had made our wants more fully known, they would have been supplied.

The Rev. Mr. Martial of the Methodist connection, & Mr. Jack called on us.[1] This evening the family were collected and br. Martial gave us a discourse on the goodness of God in sending his into the world to save sinners. We desire to bless God for sending this dear brother to visit us. We think we have been edified by his preaching.

[Jan.] 5th Brs. Martial and Jack after visiting the school and expressing great satisfaction left us to fulfil an appointment for preaching in the neighborhood.

Br. Thompson a blacksmith whom we have hired for a year arrived with his family. We hear nothing yet of br. Parker since he left us, we begin to feel concerned about him.

Monday [Jan.] 7th Father Hoyt and br. Chamberlin were sick, and brs. Butler and Ellsworth being engaged in killing hogs, the Monthly concert was not attended.

Meeting for business. Resolved that Mr. Shelton be hired to assist in putting up the ox house. Resolved that br. Chamberlin and br. Ellsworth be a committee to prepare rules and regulations for the library.

[Jan.] 8th Br. Parker arrived with his family, after a long and fatiguing journey; but the Lord has sustained him. He brought with him two boxes of clothing donated to the mission, and one from his neighbors and friends in Ohio, and one which he found at Nashville, forwarded a year ago from Meadville Penn. We had notice of this box being at Nashville some months ago but had not before an opportunity of getting it brought on. The articles were all safe and in good order.

[Jan.] 12th Through the goodness and mercy of God our dear br. and sis. Dean from Vermont arrived.[2] They have been prospered on their long journey and are now blessed with health.

[Jan.] 16th Some Cherokees living about 35 miles off having heard that we wished to buy pork brought 25 hogs. The Cherokees think they can hereafter raise all the corn and pork we shall want to buy.

[Jan.] 17th Meeting for business. Resolved that br. Parker be assigned to Taloney.

Resolved that br. Dean have charge of the blacksmith shop. Concluded that we let Mr. Harris tend the grist-mill on shares while he tends the saw-mill. Resolved that Father H. and br. Chamberlin select two boys to be named Wm Kirkpatrick and Eli Smith, and that they declare their decision at the next meeting.

[Jan.] 20th Sabbath. Had our meeting in the girls school house, and through the goodness of God, father Hoyt was able to be with us and lead in our devotions.

[Jan.] 21st Meeting for business. Resolved that brs. Conger, Chamberlin and Ellsworth, be a Com. to draft a plan of a dining room and kitchen, calculate the probable expense, and present it at our next meeting.[3]

[Jan.] 22. A special meeting called. Concluded that br. Butler be permitted to go to Knoxville to obtain money. Concluded that we endeavor to hire a black girl. Concluded that we endeavor to obtain leather for a blacksmith bellows. Resolved that br. Parker set out tomorrow for Taloney and that br. Hill who this day returned from Taloney, now labor here.

[Jan.] 23. Br. Parker set out with his family for Taloney. May the God of Jacob go with them and make them useful in that part of his vineyard.

[Jan.] 25. Received 12 boxes of clothing and cloth by way of Augusta, Ga. One from Otsego county valued at $24,25.

One from Benson Vermont Value $114,61

One from Danbury Con. and adjacent towns. Bills of the articles were forwarded in this box but no valuation annexed. One from Sangerfield, N. York valued $124,62. One from place unknown containing one shirt, 3 quilts, two pr. stockings, not valued. One from Long Meadow, Mass. valued $102,89. One from Southington valued $65,12. One from Turin, Lewis County, N.Y. valued $53,00. One from Weathersfield valued $41,61. One from East Hebron N.Y. estimated $66,47. One from Cooperstown N. York value $50,89. One from Bath N.Y. value $29,50.

[Jan.] 28. Meeting for business. Resolved that br. Ellsworth have charge of the boys except in school hours—and also that charge of the clothing which has been given to the teacher of the boys school.

[Jan.] 31. A half breed Cherokee, one of the head men of Wills town called on us.[4] He says the people of that place had a meeting and sent by him to know whether we would send them a teacher according to their former request.[*5]

Feby. 2. Sabbath. The half breed mentioned above called to spend the sabbath. ~~After meeting br. Hill took him out one side and spoke to him about the school.~~

[Feb.] 3rd Mr. Rawlings arrived with 6 or 7 hundred bushels of corn in a keel boat. He has about as much more 7 or 8 miles below in a boat that cannot come up the creek. We dismissed the school and employed all the boys in unloading the boat.

Feb. 4. Br. Butler sat [set] out for the Agency.
Br. Samuel J. Mills came bringing his younger children to receive baptism. His wife, his neighbor Fields, and six others came with him, as he says to receive further instruction in the good things contained in the word of God. They purpose to stay untill after the sabbath. Mr. Fields returned the W^d Worcester's horse.[6] He came to his house 60 miles from Brainerd, about three days after he was stolen.

[Feb.] 5. Having no pious interpreter at the Mission house, we sent for sister Lydia.[7] Br. Mills and his company gave very serious and solemn attention to the word. The first part of the Saviours sermon on the mount was read and interpreted with expositions and remarks. Exercises closed with prayer, the substance of which was interpreted. Br. Mills says one of the men and two of the women are from a remote part of the nation about 100 miles from his house—that they heard nothing of the Saviour untill he told them—that they have concluded to remove and live near him in order to receive further instruction and unite with him in the worship and service of God.
Received a letter from br. Butrick dated Turnip Town Jan. 28th.[8]
He writes "While at Chattoogy & at this place I have had many sorrowful thoughts at the prospect of leaving these dear people generally born down with an over whelming torment & no helping hand to save them from impending ruin. This is peculiarly the case at Chattoogy. Here our dear Br. Mills weeps, & prays, & mourns, alone.

He says he sees his people as if walking on the last pole over everlasting [woe?], where the least jar would throw them beyond the reach of mercy. He thinks that some of them are seriously enquiring. Br. Mills & the people here are apparently very anxious to have a school & religious meetings. He holds meetings in his own house where many of his neighbors meet to spend the Sabbath. He exhorts and prays with them. He says if they could have a school but one year accompanied with the gospel it would be a great help to them."

> Ard Hoyt, Wm Chamberlin, J.C. Elsworth,
> A. Conger , E. Dean

*This man states that they have been trying to hire a teacher but the man would not take any thing but money, which they could not raise. We think it is very important that the wants of these people be attended to, if possible.

Brainerd Mission Journal 1822

Feb. 5th Meeting for business. Resolved that a plow and set of harrow teeth be sent to Taloney. Resolved that the brethren at Taloney be permitted to build a small cabin for the accommodation of br. Parker. Resolved that the waggon br. Dean brought on, and a set of harness be assigned to the school at Creekpath.

[Feb.] 7. Mr. Rawlings' keel boat returned with the corn that was left down the creek.

[Feb.] 8. Put 7 thousand feet of boards on board a boat to be taken down the river to Creekpath for sale together with articles for br. Potter. Br. Reece being sent for to interpret came and expects to stay till after the sabbath. Had our Cherokee friends together. Father Hoyt spent the most of the afternoon in reading, and explaining to them select portions of the sermon on the mount.[9] In the evening they were again collected. The children of the school were present—We sang a number of Cherokee hymns, and to our astonishment all our visiting friends joined with us—They sang very correctly. A part of the Saviours last words to his disciples were read, after which br. Mills made a long and animated address. How thankful we ought to be that our God is raising up of themselves instruments to communicate his

word to this people, and such too, as are able to declare the love of God from their own experience.

[*Feb.*] *9.* This forenoon was spent in instructing our visiting friends. Br. Reece went home this afternoon to see to his family. He said he would return in the morning.

[*Feb.*] *10.* Sabbath. Br. Reece did not return, we fear some of his family are sick. After our usual exercises the nature of baptism was explained, and the two youngest children of br. Mills were baptised. Sister Lydia Hoyt interpreted. In the evening had a meeting with our visitors. Conversed with each one separately. They all said they maintained secret prayer, and felt anxious to spend the remainder of their days in the service of God, except one woman—who was not of br. Mills' company. She came here to see her son who is in school. When asked if she prayed she laughed and said she could not pray at her house—her husband was a wicked drinking man, & there was nothing good there. She said she had two sons that could read very well and they had never told her anything about the Saviour—they could understand very well and when they come here we must talk to them. After telling her the danger she was in, & showing her the importance of making her peace with God immediately, she appeared more serious, and said she thought religion was a good thing, & felt anxious to know more about it. She promised to make it her business to seek the Saviour.

Heard the melancholy news of the death of our dear br. John Brown Jun. of Creekpath. He died last week with the consumption.[10] Two years ago this dear brother was in heathenish darkness. About that time his br. and sister told him of the bible, and some of the important truths it contained, & he soon felt an unconquerable desire to read it. He would talk and understand familiar English. Soon after a school was opened in his neighborhood he applied himself with the most unwearied diligence to study. In the course of 6 months he learned to read intelligibly—read the New Testament through once and about half through again—wrote a number of legible letters to his friends—became a hopeful convert to the christian religion, and a member of the church of Christ, which he continued to adorn by an exemplary life, till his departure from these dark and afflictive scenes, to join as we trust the church of the first born in heaven.

[Feb.] 11th Br. Mills and his company left us to return home. We fondly hope their visit will not be altogether in vain.
Meeting for business. Resolved that the waggon and harness brought on by br. Ellsworth be offered for sale.

[Feb.] 12. Br. Butler returned. Not being able to obtain the money expected at the Agency he found it necessary to go to Knoxville.

[Feb.] 14. Received 2 boxes by way of Knoxville viz. One from Vernon Con., containing cloth, and clothing: & one from Dr. Cain Rogersville Tenn. containing medicine.[11]

[Feb.] 15. Meeting for business. Resolved that br. Chamberlin have charge of the garden this season. Resolved that we endeavor to hire a man for one year.

[Feb.] 18. Meeting for business. Resolved that Sis. Dean assist Sis. Sarah in the charge of the girls for the present.

[Feb.] 19. Through the goodness and mercy of our God, Father Hoyt was able to attend with us in the dining room and lead in our family devotions.

[Feb.] 20, 21. A very heavy rain. The Chickamaugah very high. Our cattle that range near the creek are in danger of being swept away by the high water.

[Feb.] 22. Heard that a number of our cattle were in the water about 2 miles above us. Two of the brethren with three hired hands set out immediately to try to save them.

[Feb.] 23. The brethren returned. Before they got to the place where the cattle were one of our neighbors had succeeded in getting them all across the creek with the exception of one young calf. This they found lying upon a log surrounded by water. They succeeded in catching it and bringing it across. One of the cows was so chilled that she died soon after they got her out.

[Feb.] 24. Br. Dawson arrived from the Valley towns.[12] He says the school there is in a prosperous situation.

[Feb.] 25. Meeting for business. Resolved that the land cleared for pasture north west of the mission house be enclosed with a good fence as soon as may be without infringing too much on other business: and that a part of the clearing by the boys school house and

some of the land uncleared be included in the same field—And that brothers Butler and Ellsworth examine and stake out the line where the fence shall run through the clearing, and cause a clearing to be made of sufficient width where the line passes through the standing timber. Resolved that as soon as the aforesaid fence shall be completed a gate of sufficient width for waggons, be placed in the centre of the lane or road near the north west corner of the garden & so constructed that it will always close itself except when fastened open. Resolved that br. Dean have charge of the ferry, and privilege of calling on some one for help when needed. Resolved that the rules of the Pru. Com. be read.

Resolved that br. Butler be permited to sell the old white horse to Mr. Harris. Resolved that the Superintendent appoint two brethren to visit the school at Taloney previous to the general meeting.

[Feb.] 27. Br. Dawson left us to return to the Valley towns. Mr. Rawlings boat arrived with corn.

[Feb.] 28. Brs. Butrick and John Arch arrived, having been absent about 2 months.[13] They have visited the most important places in this part of the nation but for certain reasons which we deem sufficient, they deferred going to the Valley towns at present. They were everywhere kindly received; and heard with attention especially by the chiefs—And though we rejoice in the goodness of God to them, yet we also mourn for the many precious immortals they have seen inquiring after God, and been obliged to leave in darkness, having no one to guide their wandering steps.

A half breed and his wife who have children in the school called on us. They have lately buried their youngest child. They said they wished one of us to come sabbath after next and preach a funeral sermon. We told them we would indeavor to comply with their request.

March 1st {Special meeting called. Resolved that posts be put in our ox house with rings on them to slip up and down, so that the oxen may be chained or tied. Resolved that a tight floor be laid in the upper part of the ox-house large enough to hold the corn that will be needed there.} Resolved that a letter be prepared in answer to one received from Br. Hicks on the subject of a school at Hightower, & that one be prepared for the Pru. Com. on the same subject.[14]

[March] 3. *Sabbath*—Had the unspeakable privilege of sitting down to the table of our Lord. Twenty six communicants were present. Five sisters of the Mission family were prevented from participating with us in the feast of love, by ill health. When we think of the expense which is necessary to keep this mission in operation, the dificulty of obtaining adequate funds, and above all our own unworthiness, to be entrusted with the alms of the christian public and the instruction of this people, we are ready to faint. But when we sit down to commemorate the love of our dying Saviour, & see uniting with us these precious souls just plucked as brands from the burning, with countenances glowing with the hope of eternal life; the expense, the difficulties, and our own unworthiness vanish to nothing. We feel that the work is the Lords, the means and the instruments are all in his hands, & he can employ them as he pleases.

[March] 4. Meeting for business. Resolved that br. Dean keep an account of the money received for smith work and ferriage separately, & render his account to the Treasurer the first monday in every month. Resolved that br. Conger keep an account of the expense and income of the mills and render it to the brethren in meeting, the first monday in every month.
Resolved that br. Butler be permitted to write to the Treasurer relative to the duties of Steward, Treasurer, and Physician—asking for advice and instructions.[15]

[March] 6. Our hearts were made glad by the arrival of our dear br. Vail. We have reason to bless God for his goodness to our brother on his long journey to New Jersey and back, and that he has returned him to us with his dear son, both in health. The horse br. Vail set out with became so lame that he was obliged to leave him about two hundred miles from this place. On his return he found that the horse died in about six weeks after he left him.

[March] 7. Brs. Ellsworth & Butler having been appointed to visit the school at Taloney sat out with their wives for that purpose.

[March] 9. Twenty seven packages arrived by way of Augusta.

[March] 14. Nineteen more packages arrived by way of Augusta which (except one belonging to br. Ellsworth that was left in Augusta,) complete the number shipped by the Treasurer on the 23rd of Dec. 1821, including two boxes of medicines shipped afterwards. The articles came safe. In opening these precious treasures collected

by the benevolent exertions of our dear Christian friends and seasoned by their prayers, our thoughts are naturally directed to the supreme disposer of all hearts, & giver of all gifts. And we would devoutly implore the divine presence and direction, that these articles may be disposed of with as much christian zeal & prudence as was displayed in their collection. We do not mention the particular places from whence the articles came, as the Treasurer has an account of them and will be able to inform the donors of their safe arrival.

Brs. Elsworth & Butler with their wives returned from Taloney. They found the family in health & the school in a flourishing situation.

[*March*] 18. A Cherokee man living about ten miles from us and being very low with the consumption sent for one of the missionaries to visit him. Br. Chamberlin went and found him apparently very near his end. He was very anxious for the salvation of his immortal soul.

March 19. Br. Butrick went to see the sick man, & found he died last night. Br. Butrick stayed and attended his funeral.

One of our large boys (to whom we had given the name of John D. Paxton) knowingly and willingly disobeyed the orders of the school, and persevered in his disobedience untill forcible measures were used.

[*March*] 20. John D. Paxton left the school. We had reason to hope a few months ago that this boy would be a credit to the school, and honor to the benevolent people who gave him his name. He appeared very serious, & we hoped that he would give himself to the Lord. And although his late conduct has evinced the depravity of his heart, still we do not give him over—he is in the hands of God who is able to bring him, like the prodigal son, to himself, and cause him to return to his father who is in heaven.[16]

[*March*] 22. A request was sent us from a settlement about 30 miles from this place to supply them with preaching a part of the time. Most of the people in that settlement understand some english. They say they have never had but one sermon preached in the place. Since the people heard that discourse they have frequently been trying to get some one to preach to them. We regret that there has hitherto been a necessity of keeping a minister of the gospel in the school at this place instead of giving him his whole time in the work of the ministry especially as there is such a great field opened for preaching among this people. We hope this necessity will soon cease; and most ardently pray that the Lord of the harvest will send forth laborers untill every Macedonian cry around can be answered.—

Ard Hoyt, Wm Chamberlin, Abijah Conger, John Vail
J.C. Elsworth, Elizur Butler, Erastus Dean

Brainerd Mission Journal 1822

April 6. Br. Thompson & wife, his mother & sister were received into the church by letter.

[April] 8.—Received intelligence that Mr. Evarts had set out on the third ult from Boston with the expectation of coming to Brainerd. Whilst we regret that ill health was the cause of his leaving home we rejoice in the prospect of seeing him once more in this place.
  Meeting for business. (Concluded that Hezekiah Shelton, & Wm Carter be dismissed from our employ for bad conduct.) Concluded that br. Vail select 6 horses for the team; & that they shall not be [rode?]. Concluded that Mr. Suttons son be sent for, to labor for one year. Concluded that the price of corn (if sold) be ,75 per bushel.

[April] 10. Br. Ellis from Vermont arrived.[17] He has been very unwell on the way but the Lord has been very gracious to him & to us in bringing him in safety to the field of his labors. He left br. Blunt at br. Halls on account of lameness.[18] We shall expect him here this week. We trust our hand will be very much strengthened by the arrival of these two brethren.

[April] 11.—Br. Potter arrived from Creek path. Sr. Potter could not conveniently accompany him. Special meeting called. The question was asked shall a horse be sold to br. Milo Hoyt. Answered in the affirmative. Concluded that br. Vail & br. Potter make choice of a horse for Creek path.

[April] 12. Brs. Parker, & Blunt arrived from Taloney. Br. & sis. Hall waited to accompany Mr. Evarts.

[April] 13. Brs. Parker & Blount [Blunt] were received into the church by letter. Br. Ellis having omitted bringing a letter from the church to which he belonged chose to wait untill he could send for one before he [severed?] his relation from that church.
Mr. Fields & his wife arrived. They tell us br. S.J. Mills will not be here at this time. He sent word that he had a large family to support, & he

had to do his work alone, he therefore thought it would not be his duty to leave home untill he got in his crop. Mr. Fields and his wife still appear anxiously enquiring what they must do to be saved. The woman thinks she does love the Saviour. Rev. Mr. Crawford of the Methodist connexion called on us this evening.

[April] 14. Our brother who called on us yesterday preached, after which we sat down to the table of our Lord. (34 in number). Father & Mother Hoyt, sisters Vail, Chamberlin, & Anna Hoyt were kept from this feast of love by sickness.

[April] 15. Our schools were examined.

[April] 16. Most of our schollars left us to visit their parents & friends. General meeting for business. Brs. Parker & Potter present. Communications from the Pru. Com. were read. Reports from the Local schools exhibited & read. Resolved that brs. Vail, Butler, Parker, & Potter examine and say which waggon shall be assigned to Creek Path. Concluded that br. Milo Hoyt, have the lame sorrel horse for $45,00. Resolved that br. Ellsworth have charge of the boys school when it shall be again commenced. Resolved that br. Ellis have charge of the cattle, hogs, & sheep. Resolved that br. Blunt have charge of the ox team.

A letter was received from Mr. John W. Tilford requesting that a boy in the family of br. Potter at Creek path receive the name of John Washington Tilford with a promise of the payment of the sum required by the Pru. Com.[19] Resolved that br. Butrick prepare a joint letter announcing the cordial acceptance of the offer. Resolved that br. Potter select a boy and give him the name of Henry Valleau as soon as a suitable one can be found, to be supported by the Male & Female Mite Society, Baltimore. Resolved that two children of sis. Davis be permitted to come to this school. In consequence of the disagreement of a former committee, Resolved that brs. Potter, Dean & Ellsworth be a committee to decide what waggon & harness be sent to Creek path. Resolved that Father Hoyt, brs. Chamberlin & Ellsworth be a committee to select boys to bear the names mentioned in the Treasurers letter of last July, and that they report as soon as convenient.

Resolved that br. Potter be added to the Com. to make regulations for the library and report tomorrow evening. Resolved that brs. Butrick, Elsworth, Butler, Ellis & Blunt be appointed to form a plan for the residence of br. Parker at Taloney, & report tomorrow evening. Resolved that we adjourn till 2 oclock tomorrow.

[April] 18. Met agreeable to adjournment. The Com. appointed to form a plan for the residence of br. Parker at Taloney, report—On mature deliberation we are of opinion that br. Parkers residence at Taloney be prepared according to the vote of Feby 5, 1822. Regulations of the Pru. Com. read. Will the brethren advise that Cherokees be hired to cut coal wood? Answered in the affirmative. Resolved that brs. Vail, Dean, & Conger select a place for burning the pit. Considering the distance from Creekpath to this place resolved that br. Potter be at liberty to vacate the school at that place 4 weeks, at the end of next term.

The committee to whom was referred the regulations for the library made their report as follows.

1st This library shall be known by the name of the Cherokee Mission Library.

2nd All books at Brainerd, and at each of the Local schools, including such as have been or may hereafter be bought by the money of the Society; given as donations to the mission or to individuals, & such as have been or may be brought on by individuals, shall be one common library and shall be classed, & numbered under the following heads Viz. Theology, Medicine, classicals, History, Biography, Mechanism, Agriculture, Religious Periodical Publications Bound, Poetry, & Miscellany, except bibles, psalm, & hymn books, & common school books.

3rd The books shall all be carefully preserved in a case or cases, & excepting such as are at the local schools, and such Theological, Medical, Classical, & Mechanical ones as shall be necessary for the use of the professional brethren, shall be under the care of a librarian.

4th A librarian shall be chosen annually by ballot whose duty it shall be to keep a catalogue of all the books belonging to the library, with the number of each, and the place to which it is assigned. It shall also be the duty of the librarian between the hours of 12 & 2 on the first & third fridays in every month to hand out books not exceeding the number of 6, to any member of the family who shall make application, & all such books shall be returned on each suceeding drawing day.

5th A Committee of three brethren shall be appointed by ballot at each stated general meeting, to report at the next general meeting the state of the library, & assign to the professional brethren, and the local schools, such books as shall be deemed expedient.

6th When there is more than one brother at a local school the brethren at the general meeting shall designate the librarian for that place whose duty it shall be to report at the next general meeting the state of that branch of the library.

7th No book, shall be lent to persons not belonging to the mission family for any term of time exceeding three months, & if any person shall neglect to return a borrowed book within the above term, the librarian shall not be allowed to lend any book to such person without special leave of the brethren in regular meeting for business.

Provided that nothing in these articles shall be so construed as to affect the Juvenile Library.

Resolved that the foregoing report be accepted. Br. Butler was appointed librarian. Father Hoyt, br. Elsworth, & Butler were appointed examining Committee. Resolved that brs. Butrick, Potter, & Elsworth assist the Librarian in arranging the books.

Our visiting brother left us.

[April] 24. Br. Parker left us this morning for Taloney, and br. Potter this afternoon for Creek Path. We have had a pleasant season with these dear brethren. How animating the thought that all who love our Lord Jesus Christ will soon meet to part no more for ever.

[April] 25. A special meeting called. As we have assigned one horse to Creek path, & sold another therefore Resolved that the vote assigning six horses to the team be rescinded.

[April] 29. Meeting for business. The question was asked what is the horse last assigned to Taloney worth? Ans. $40,00. What is the price of the horse assigned to Creek path? Ans. $40,00. What is the waggon assigned to Creek path worth? Ans. $70,00.

[April] 30. Two women who live about thirty miles distance, called to know if we would take their children. We were obliged to put them off to some future time as it is not thought expedient, to take any more at present.

May 3. Brs. Kingsbury & Goodell arrived.[20]

[May] 4. Br. Posey from the Valley towns called on us & about 9 Oclock this evening Mr. Evarts arrived accompanied by br. Hall.[21] Through the goodness of God the health of the Treasurer is very much improved by his journey.

[May] 5. Br. Kingsbury preached in the forenoon & br. Posey in the afternoon. There were a number of Cherokees present to whom our address was made by br. Kingsbury through br. Reece.

[May] 6. Our children begin to return. {Account of the monthly concert omitted.}

Meeting for business. Mr. Evarts, & Brs Kingsbury, Hall & Goodell present. The subject of planting the large field was proposed by Mr. Evarts. Brs. Vail, & Elsworth were appointed to examine the field and report tomorrow morning.[22] The question was asked shall a br. be appointed to assist the sisters in the kitchen? Concluded that br. Blunt be assigned in the kitchen. Adjourned till tomorrow morning.

[May] 7. Met according to adjournment. After the report of the Com. the question was asked will it be for the benefit of the mission to plant the large field? Answered in the affirmative. Concluded that br. Vail take charge of the above mentioned field, and that he be released from all his other charges. Adjourned untill evening. Met according to adjournment. Took up the subject of the local schools. Resolved that Father Hoyt and Br. Kingsbury be a committee to express their opinion whether communications shall be held directly between the Board and the local schools. Conversed on the manner of holding meetings for public worship at the local schools. Concluded that br. Chamberlin be added to the above Com. to consider certain questions brought forward by br. Hall.

Our schools commenced to day with 30 boys, and 12 girls.

[May] 8. Br. Goodell preached.—Meeting for business continued.— Enquiry was made whether sis. Harriet Elsworth might be spared from this place for Taloney? Answered in the negative.[23]

[May] 9. Mr. Evarts & br. Kingsbury left us to visit br. Hicks, & brs. Vail & Goodell for Taloney.[24]

[May] 10. Mr. Evarts & br. Kingsbury returned.

[May] 12. We sat down to the table of our Lord, & through the goodness of our heavenly Father all the members of the mission family were able to be present.

[May] 13. Meeting for business. As it is understood to be the pleasure of the Pru. Com. that a blacksmith's shop with a trip hammer &c be erected on an estimate of a little more than $200, made by Messrs. Conger & Dean, resolved that the shop be erected as soon as

convenient.[25] Resolved that the wood work of this shop be assigned to br. Conger, & the digging and other work to br. Dean. Concluded that we have three meals on the sabbath during summer.

[May] 14. Br. Goodell returned from Taloney. His audience last sabbath was quite numerous, and attentive. One Cherokee man at Taloney has set apart a corner of his field as he says for the Lord. Surely christians may be encouraged if the heathen begin to devote their property to the Lord for the purpose of spreading the gospel.

[May] 16. Meeting for business. Resolved that it is expedient to obtain Mr. Rogers if practicable to make the guns to the blacksmith shop, if not practicable that we endeavor to obtain Mr. Alexander.

May 19. Br. Goodell preached in the forenoon to those who could understand English, & in the afternoon to the Cherokees through br. Reece.

[May] 20. Meeting for business. Resolved that br. & sister Dean be permitted to live in the house with br. Conger.
Br. Kingsbury left us to return to the Choctaw Nation. Br. Butrick is to accompany him as far as Creek path. The visit of this dear br. after an absence of 4 years has been very refreshing, & gratifying, & we trust profitable to our own souls, and to the souls of many of our precious charge. May the Lord reward him an hundred fold for his labors of love, and make him a rich blessing to the poor heathen for whose good he is daily laboring and give him many souls as seals of his ministry and crown of rejoicing in the day of the Lord Jesus.

[May] 21. Mr. Evarts & br. Goodell took leave of us this morning, the former to return to his family, & arduous labors in Boston, the latter to act as an Agent of the Board in E. Ten. & other places untill God shall prepare the way for him to join the Palestine mission to which he is appointed.—They took with them a Cherokee lad about 16, who is expected to take the name of W[m] Kirk Patrick, & to finish his education under the patronage of the benevolent man of that name in Lancaster Pennsylvania. We have cause of much gratitude to God for this visit of the Cor. Sec., for his improved health, for the sweet seasons of christian communion we have had together, for his seasonable instructions, & exhortation, & for the pleasing prospect of having more schools soon established among these needy people.
Meeting for business. Resolved that our morning prayers be immediately after breakfast, & our evening prayers immediately after supper.

Resolved that the time of supper be half an hour after sun set. Resolved that the children of missionaries be under the same regulations while in school, & laboring hours, as the Cherokee children—unanimous.

[May] 23. Mr. Chamberlin being released from the charge of the school is expected now to devote his time to ministerial duties, and to visit different parts of the nation particularly where they have most desired instruction & wish for local schools. This day he went into the neighborhood of br. Reece and returned at evening. Mr. Hoyt also rode a short distance & visited one family for the first time since his severe illness last December.

[May] 24. Mr. Hoyt went out again to visit among the people. Admitted two schollars to the girls school making three girls, and two boys admitted since vacation.[26] Some have not yet returned who are expected soon—we have now with us only 37 boys and & 22 girls. The children do not all return as soon as we could wish but considering the distance many have to come, & how much their parents need their assistance at this season of the year in putting in their corn, the schools are filling up perhaps as fast as we could expect.
Br. Elsworth, & boys planted 8 acres of corn after school this evening.—

[May] 25. Mr. Chamberlin went out this morning expecting to preach tomorrow at Mr. Hicks', & thence to proceed to Hightower, look out a site for a local school, & make arrangements for putting up a blacksmiths shop immediately—taking time to preach to the people on his tour whenever opportunity shall present. He hopes to get an interpreter at Mr. Hicks to go with him.

Col^n Arthur B. Campbell of Blount Co. Ten. called this evening to spend sabbath with us.

[May] 27. Mon. Col^n Campbell tarried with us, & visited the girls school in the forenoon & the boys in the afternoon. He appears to possess a true missionary spirit, offers his agency at any time and in any way the mission may need it, & thinks something may be done in his neighborhood, & its vicinity towards furnishing supplies of corn-Meat-Iron &c for the use of this station.
Meeting for business: Resolved that br. Elsworth be clerk of meetings for business. As it appears that many of the natives are not able to pay for their blacksmith work untill fall—Therefore resolved that such

persons as may be recommended by Mr. Ross, br. Reece, or other influential men (with whom we are acquainted) as proper subjects of such indulgence, may have credit untill the aforesaid time.

Resolved that corn be sold at 62-1/2 cts. Resolved that br. Blunt have charge of the garden. Resolved that the vote respecting time of supper be rescinded. Resolved that the charge of oxen which was given to br. Blunt, be given to br. Ellis, & that br. Blunt have charge of feeding the hogs.

May 28.—Loaded a boat, at the saw-mill, with boards, plank, and other articles for Creek path. The boards & plank, being about 7000 feet, are to be sold there,—other articles for the use of the family. Br. Butler set out with the boat as it started down the creek, but if the hands appear able to manage it will soon return.

Mr. Hoyt went out again on pastoral visits. He had a very interesting interview with one family—the parents both members of the church. They expressed great joy, and thankfulness that their pastor was once more enabled to visit them. All business was immediately suspended, & the family collected—two black people belonging to another family being near came in. Religious instruction, prayer, praise, & conversation were listened to with such attention that two hours quickly passed in these exercises, after which about an hour was spent in conversation with individuals—There are several young people in this family under serious impressions, but none of them entertain a hope.—In this family are sheltered and fed a poor desolate woman, & her young son of about 10 years.—A little before the birth of this son all her near relatives were slain for the supposed crime of witchcraft, & she was spared only on account of her situation.[27] She appears a poor, feeble, harmless creature: & our sister is laboring assiduously to teach her the christian religion.

[*May*] 29. Br. Butler returned this evening. He lodged in the boat last night, and after assisting untill they had passed the most difficult parts of the creek, he left the boat, visited a sick woman who is under his care, borrowed a horse and returned.

[*May*] 30. Mr. Hoyt again visited families. He found a striking, and an affecting contrast between two families visited to day—One a Cherokee (mixed blood) children instructed in letters, and religion, acquainted with family prayer, decent and orderly in all family duties, christianized and civilized.—The other a white family, raised on the borders of the nation, and now residing in it—children totally ignorant of letters, & of religion—not one could tell who made them; who made the world, or who is the Saviour—unchristianized, and sinking into the savage state, if not already there. Such a difference does the blessed gospel make even in the time of one generation: & (in the former instance) within a very few years.

Br. Butrick returned this evening from Creek path. He found the mission family there all in health, & the church thriving—The brethren hold weekly conferences at different places in the neighborhood, which are well attended, and several persons (not members of the church) are under serious impressions.

Special meeting called. Resolved that br. Milo Hoyt be fully satisfied for the damage he supposes he received, on account of some logs lying on his cornfield over the time that he expected the brethren would remove them.

May 31. Frequent and heavy rains are a great hindrance to the farmer in planting and working his corn. In this climate he may continue to plow and plant piece after piece of his corn field untill the first planted calls for the return of the plow and hoe, and if circumstances require, the same process may be even longer continued without endangering the crop.

We have planted something more than thirty acres, and hoed a part of the first planted, but owing to the repeated rains, we have yet several acres to plow and plant.

As by advice of the Cor. Sec. we now mention in our journal many small matters which were before omitted (as pastoral family visits &c&c) if any part of our journal is printed we trust care will be taken to leave out such small things as might be interesting to the Prud. Com. but not to the public. If at any time we think proper to assert any particular fact, which we think might do injury if sent back in a public circulating from as extracts from our journal are, we shall enclose such in Brackets as heretofore.

Ard Hoyt, Abijah Conger, Jno C. Elsworth, E. Dean, E. Butler

Will you forward to Daniel McPhearson regularly the Herald? He will account with us for it. Please direct it to Rossville Post Office Cherokee Nation.

Yours, Elizur Butler

J. Evarts, Esq.

Brainerd May 30, 1822

Dear Sir

Agreeably to your directions we send you our estimate of the expense of building a kitchen, Boys house, & a dwelling house.— Items for the kitchen with the prices are as follows.

2100 ft. square timber 1 cts ————	$21,00
2000 " ¼ Inch flooring ————	25,00
4100 " Roof and siding ,75 ————	30,75
600 " Window frames, Doors, sashes &c. —	6,00
Glass, Puty, Nails, Hinges, Handles, Bolts –	100,00
Carpenters work ————	$50,00
	$332,75

This estimate supposes the kitchen to be 24 ft. by 28 containing cooking room, small pantry, and meal house 1/2 story high. We have made no calculation for a cellar, or new chimney—It seems desirable that we should have a cellar for milk, so near the well in order that the milk may be benefitted by the cool air.

Boys house 30 ft. by 14—

1000 ft. Sq. Timber 1 ct. ————	$10,00
525 " flooring 1,25 ————	6,56
2400 " Siding, Roofing &c. ,75 ————	18,00
Hinges, and nails ————	25,00
Carpenters work ————	50,00
Chimney &c ————	60,00
	$169,56

You will recollect sir that the Question was asked whether we should have permission to build, a dwelling house or houses for some of the families here—Your answer was that it was not probable the Pru. Com. would grant permission to build more than one small house. You doubtless recollect the crowded and irregular situation of our store room. Our proposition is to build a house 32 x 29 with two rooms—One sitting room, bed room, & closet—The other part is proposed as a store room.—In this case the danger of a loss of some thousands of property by fire would be much less.—We could then convert the old store-room into Bed rooms which would render it much more comfortable on many accounts. The cost would not be far from $111,—A store room might be built separate from all other buildings without a chimney similar to the Tool house which would answer all the purposes necessary. The cost of this would not probably be more than $100,00.—

In addition to the list of articles sent to the Board needed here as donations, we add the following—Viz. Bed ticking, Pressed flannel, Clover and Timothy seed, Garden Seeds, especially Beets—shaving soap, Field peas:—An Ear trumpet for Darius Hoyt.

Ard Hoyt, Abijah Conger, E. Butler, E. Dean

J. Evarts Esqr.

June 1st After preparatory lecture, had some conversation with Br. Reece on his going out as interpreter with Mr. Butrick to the Valley towns, and to make a general tour thro the eastern part of the nation. He is much engaged to do all he can for the instruction of his people, but thinks there is a fine prospect here if we have a stated interpreter on the sabbath, & can visit & preach in the different families & neighborhoods. He thinks much good might also be done by his occasionally going out with a preacher to those places which lie in a circle round us from 10 to 20 miles, always returning here to spend the sabbath. He has been conversing with our aged sister McDonald on the subject. She would be very sorry to have the interpreting here suspended—says she learns many things greatly to her edification which she cannot understand in English.

[June] 2d Communion season. Previous to the administration of the ordinance, its institution, signification, and design, and the requisite qualifications of a worthy partaker were set forth in the form of a preparatory discourse, & interpreted by Br. Reece sentence by sentence.—Afternoon service in Cherokee as usual; directed by Mr. Butrick, and interpreted by Br. Reece.

[June] 3d Monthly concert for prayer. After which a church meeting was called (as by previous appointment) & Brs. Elsworth, & Butler were chosen to the office of Deaconing.

D[r] Butler again visited the sick woman in br. Reeces neighborhood and whose disease was supposed by the Cherokees to be incurable.—

She is much better and in a hopeful way to recover. As Br. Reece has frequently been called to interpret for the D[r] in prescribing for her bodily complaint he has thus had repeated opportunities to prescribe for her spiritual maladies. May the Great Physician bless the means & heal her soul and body. In that neighborhood Br. Butler has visited (a few times) a boy in the last stages of a Scroffula; it appears the disease had been beyond the reach of medicine before he was called.[28]—The boy died to day.

[June] 4th Mr. Butrick went early this morning to attend the funeral of the boy who died yesterday.—

D[r] Butler and wife went out to visit some of the neighbors, and he to transact some business. As the population here is thinly spread over an extensive country (our nearest neighbors, excepting Milo Hoyt, being two miles from us) the distance to be travelled in visiting neighbors is like going from one Parish to another in New England. It is thought it will be too much for Sis. Butler to go the round and return to day. He will probably leave her to spend the night at Mr. Ross' 7 miles from Brainerd.

Business meeting. Br. Dean rendered the blacksmith shop account since April 1st.

Amount of work done for Creek path is			$24,19
dto	dto	Taloney "	22,75
dto	dto	Brainerd "	99,11
dto	charged to customers		10,37
dto	pay received in produce		26,64
dto	pay received in money		30.00
The shop is D[r][29]			213.06
1000 bushel coal			50,00
350 lbs steel			63.00
Balance (exclusive of labor done in			100,06
the shop and stock previously on hand)			

Br. Conger rendered an acct for the mills since the first of March at which time there were about 56 logs at the mill, none on hand at this time.

Amount of C[r] for toll corn, & boards, timber &c sawed is	$222,33
D[r] for tending mills, getting logs &c	56.59
Balance (exclusive of logs on hand March 1st)	165,74

No account has been kept of the expense of the Mills previous to March 1st. Since the first of Jany 1822 the saw mill has sawed 38,800 feet.

At this meeting, resolved, that Brs. Vail, Ellis & Blunt be a Com. to select such oxen and steers to work this summer as they shall think best and make their report at the next meeting.

June 6th Mr. Chamberlin returned. He found the people at Hightower still anxious for a blacksmith, and a school, & made such arrangements as were thought necessary for the blacksmith to go as soon as possible. By inclining a little to the East as he went out, & to the west as he returned he took Springplace, Yookalooga [Oothcaloga], & Turnip town in his rout.[30] He found our beloved fellow-laborers at the two former places in good health, and the church prosperous. They expect to open a school at Yookalooga next Autumn. At Turnip town he found Br. Mills and his little company much engaged in the things of religion, and spent a sabbath with them. As there was no interpreter, & a part of the congregation could understand English, Mr. C. first went thro' the usual exercises in English, & then Br. Mills addressed the people with his usual fluency and animation, for half or three quarters of an hour, prayed and concluded by singing a Cherokee hymn. The utmost propriety and decorum was observed by the whole congregation during all the exercises, and a striking solemnity appeared in every countenance while Br. Mills spoke and prayed. Here is a youth who has been sometime in the school at Brainerd, and left us under serious impressions.[31] He still appears well. Mr. C. heard of him as having been at Hightower and other places, talking to the people on religion, &, as one informant expressed it, preaching Cherokee Hymns. Br. Mills and his little company of seekers, had agreed that they would all come together to Brainerd to receive instruction, as soon as they could leave their corn. They are very anxious for a school in this place, and if we cannot furnish them a teacher they will try to get one from some other quarter. It appears to be of great importance that we should have schools very soon at Wills Valley, at Turnip town, (which is near Chattooga) and at Hightower. These places including Creek path, and Yookalooga lie nearly in a line which at the nearest place is about 50 miles south from Brainerd, and distant from each other about one days ride. Should Mission schools be established in all these places, a preacher might go out from Brainerd to Springplace, Taloney,

Hightower, Yookalooga, Turnip town, Wills Valley, & Creek path, encircling most of the lower part of the nation, & lodge at a mission school every night.—The Cherokees and Creeks have amicably settled the boundary line between them, and lately run it. As by agreement it should be a straight line west from a given point on the Chatahooche [Chattahoochee], to the mouth of Wills Creek (a distance of about 140 miles) they having no surveyor, a hunter standing on the boundary at the Chatahooche pointed out the supposed course to the mouth of Wills creek, on this course a strait line was run by ranging, and they came out at the end of 140 miles within 80 rods of the intended place.

Four Children were returned to day, having been absent since vacation. The father says they were detained a while in consequence of the sickness and death of an elder brother, and afterwards he was so much engaged in his corn, that he could not, until now, spare time to bring them.

[June] 7. The boy called Benjamin Tappan returned to the school, having been absent since vacation. He has heretofore been punctual in his attendance since he first entered. Nicholas Patterson, who return-ed in season after vacation but has had leave of absence to visit a sick mother, also returned to day. His mother is dead.

[June] 8. Mr. Chamberlin went out expecting to preach tomorrow about 15 miles up the river.—The boys planted with corn and beans the three acre lot south of the Carpenters shop. This finishes planting for this year. Some of the first planted corn (seeds bro^t from Vermont) has been set for ears and in blossom several days. If this corn had been planted as early as it might have been, we think it would have produced two crops in the season.

Sab. [June] 9. The two brethren chosen for Deacons last monday, were this day appointed to that office by prayer and imposition of hands. A number of natives who cannot understand English assembled this afternoon, but Br. Reece not being with us we could only sing Cherokee hymns and say a few words to them by one of the boys. This being done the service was conducted in English without any further attempt to interpret. We hope Br. Reece will be here most of the sabbaths—Mr. Chamberlin returned this evening. Saturday on his way out he was informed that the people in the neighborhood where he intended to spend Sabbath, not expecting him had appointed to attend a religious meeting this day over the river. He therefore gave notice that he would preach at a place about 7 miles from Brainerd. A very considerable congregation for this country, collected, and gave good attention.

[June] 10. The men who went to Creek path with the boat, returned. There appears to be a good market for boards in that region, particularly flooring plank. It appears the saw mill might be profitable if we could keep it running—but we were obliged to send the sawyer down with the boat, & now he must return to his family & spend some time on his farm. Thinks he cannot return untill about the first of Sept. We shall try to get another man to tend the mill, but know not where to find one.

—Meeting for business—The brethren appointed last week to select oxen & steers for the team, gave it as their opinion that 4 yoke of oxen that have recently been worked be continued—that the old ox and one large white one be turned out to fat, and that 2 yoke of steers be added.

Question, Will it be thought advisable to stop the boys school and take them into the field to hoe corn one or two days? Answd with affirmative provided we cannot keep up with the ploughs and also continue in school.

[June] 11. Mr. Butrick went to Br. Reeces to get him to assist in examining some translations and to correct if not found right.

[June] 12. Hearing that Mr. Rawlings of Washington is willing to have two of his black people (a man & his wife) come and labor here a given time and obtain their freedom by so doing—Dr. Butler set out to go to Washington & engage them if the terms are such as he shall think reasonable. He will also endeavor to engage a Millwright to make the running gears for the trip hammer shop, & a man to tend the saw-mill.

[June] 13.—Dr. Butler returned, having found means to put the business on which he went in a train to be accomplished without his going to Washington.

The boys having got behind the ploughs in hoeing, by having many other things to attend to, their school was stopped this day and they got up with the ploughs.—They will now be abundantly able to keep up without hindering the school anymore. One cause of their getting behind is, Br. Elsworth with some of the boys, had been engaged a part of the time for several days in preparing a place for the boys to sleep during the heat of summer, the cabin being too much confined to met their habits. The roof is composed of reffuse boards from the saw-mill, the joints broken with slabs; and supported by five rows of posts set in the ground—covering an area of about 18 by 35 feet. Under this is a floor 12 feet wide, elevated about two feet from the ground, divided in the middle lengthwise by a single board. On each side of this division the boys sleep upon their blankets, [hole in ms] the rain, and having a free circulation of air from all sides.

[June] 14. Br. Elsworth and wife, went out to visit some of the neighbors. As it was not convenient for any one of the mission family acquainted with the roads, or paths, to go with them, they took one of the schollars for a guide. Darius Hoyt takes charge of the school during his absence. One of the large boys (Horace Loomis) being permitted to go after Whirlleberries left his companion, saying he would go home. Br. Reece came with 9 or 10 of his neighbors to get work done at the blacksmith shop. He introduces them as needy industrious persons whom it will be safe to credit.—

Sab. [June] 16. Br. Reece attended, & interpreted the afternoon discourse. A letter from Br. Hall mentions some very hopeful appearances in a part of his neighborhood.

[June] 17. Mr. Chamberlin set out for Wills Valley. If he can obtain an interpreter he will probably visit Turkey town, & other places in that part of the nation.[32]

[June] 18. Br. Conger left us to journey for his health. He expects to go to New Jersey. As his health is not sufficient to enable him to continue his charge here, & sister Conger's health has not been generally good since she came to this place, & as he has property sufficient for the support of his family, he thinks it may be duty to take measures for removing his family from the mission. He travels on his private expense.

[June] 19. Sister Sarah went to assist in cooking &c at Br. Congers; sister Conger being unwell, & her daughter Anna not able to do the work.

[June] 20. As sister Sarah cannot well be spared from the girls, the servant maid who has been employed in the kitchen at the mission house, was sent to Br. Congers for a day or two. The schollar to whom we had given the name of John D. Paxton returned, and was again admitted to the school.[33] A little before the last vacation he violated a

rule to which a certain penalty had been annexed, & being compelled to suffer the forfeiture he took offense and left the school without permission. At the time of a examination previous to the violation, he came and attended as a spectator, but as he said nothing about his former conduct no notice was taken of him as a schollar. A few weeks since he came to meeting on the sabbath & tarried through the night. He appeared friendly and serious, & said he wanted to come to school again. The necessity of order, the evil of his former conduct in then leaving the school &c were set before him. He appeared to feel the force of the remarks,—said he had done wrong and was sorry for it. He was told that we still loved him, & should always be glad to do him good, but if he was again received to the school it must be in a way to shew all the schollars that such conduct was bad, & that he never intended to be guilty of the like again. He has now given full satisfaction to the teachers, & to the school; & we expect he will be obedient and faithful, as this has formerly been his general character.

Br. Thompson left us this morning with his family to remove to Hightower. He goes to establish a blacksmith shop there at this own expense, according to arrangements made when Mr. Evarts was here, expecting we shall have a local school there in a few months. He considers himself and family devoted [to] the cause of missions, & was willing to go as an assistant missionary under the direction of the Board, or at his own expense, as should be thought most conducive to the general good. His steady habits, faithful christian conduct, & devotedness to the cause, which have been daily manifested since he has been employed in the mission, are worthy of our imitation: and although he & his family will now conduct their secular concerns independent of the mission, we consider them in _effect_ attached to it.[34] As Br. Thompson failed in getting horses for a light wagon to accomodate the family, it was not thought advisable for his aged mother to go at this time, she will continue with us untill an easy mode of conveyance can be provided for her. Sister Nancy Thompson, being needed here more than in her brothers family, will continue with us.

[June] 22. Br. Butrick left us expecting to preach at Mr. Hicks' tomorrow—then proceed to Taloney & spend some time there & in other places in that part of the nation. God in his providence shall appear to direct. A great door appears to be opened among this people, both for preaching & schools: may the Lord thrust in laborers, and bless the means of his own appointment.

This evening the father of the boy who went away last week came to enquire respecting it.[35] The boy it appears made only some trifling excuses for going home, & said he wanted to go and live with Mr. Hall. {The father who lives near Mr. Hicks', says Mr. Hall sent word by the daughter of Mr. Hicks who has been for some time at that school, that he wanted Horace to come and live with him: & that this was told to the boy before he went home.} We told him we did not board many children at Taloney, & that the boy could not go there. He appeared satisfied with this, & with our former treatment of his son, & wished us to take him back. We concluded to receive him on the acknowledgment of his fault; & a promise not to repeat it. He says he will send him back as soon as he has ploughed out his corn. He would do it immediately but being captain of the Light horse, & called away on this business, he requested that we would permit the boy to stay, as he now is at home, long enough to do this ploughing, which he knows not how to get done in season without him.[36] To this we consented; & he promised that the boy would return within two weeks.

Sab. [June] 23. Br. Samuel J. Mills & some of his little company came in this morning. Br. Reece interpreted the afternoon discourse; then made a short address of his own: after which Br. Mills, by request, spoke to the congregation, prayed and sung a hymn. He had no lack of words, appeared very devout in prayer and sung with animation; but br. Reece could not recollect after meeting so as to give us the substance of his remarks except that he was greatly rejoiced in meeting the dear brothers, & sisters here once more in the house of God.

[June] 24. Received three new schollars, one boy and two girls. One of the girls was brought by Br. Mills' company; they also brought three boys and one girl that have been absent since vacation. There are some of the schollars in that neighborhood that would have returned at this time but they have the measles there. Br. Mills left his son, called Jeremiah Evarts, at home sick with them.[37] This disease prevented several adults from coming to receive religious instruction. Br. Reece came and spent some time interpreting for us. It appears that two of Br. Mills company think they have found the Saviour. One a woman between 40 and 50, the wife of a Cherokee man called Fields—We therefore call her Mrs. Fields. She has been here with her husband several times to be instructed, & has attended regularly to Br. Mills' meetings on the sabbath. She mentions a certain time when

she was here with her husband, that the words of truth sunk into her heart, have been there ever since. She speaks of her old sins as bad things flung away which she shall never wish take up again.—The other is the young man mentioned on the 6th inst. as having been at school, & left us under serious impressions. His name is John Wanuh. He says after he went away he thought much more of what we had told him than he ever did here—that he continued always to pray— and thinks the Lord has had mercy on him & given him a new heart. Always since that he feels as if he had found a great prize.

[June] 25. Mr. Hoyt, & br. Mills went out to visit some of the members of the church—Mrs. Fields and one other woman went with them.

Gave the name of Samuel Worcester to a full Blooded Cherokee boy agreeably to a request from two Societies, viz. Juv. Brainerd Soc. of Beverly Ms. & the female members of the Tabernacle Church Salem, Ms [Massachusetts].[38]

[June] 26. Not able to say anything of consequence on religious subjects to our visitors for want of an interpreter: Some of them say they must return home to attend to their corn. As they were about to depart one of them requested one of the sisters to write to her, & tell her everything that she must do, & she would take it to one who could read & interpret it for her. This was suggested in consequence of our having no interpreter at the time to talk with them.

[June] 27.—Br. Mills, the two hopeful converts, and one woman are with us. Mr. Hoyt went with them to brother Reece's. They had a very interesting meeting there. At the close of it Br. Mills said this had been the day of all days to him—he had received more knowledge, light & joy than ever in any one day before. Mrs. Fields & John Wanuh appear well. From Br. Reeces they went to visit the sick woman in that neighborhood. A number of Cherokees there. Br. Mills talked and prayed with them.

[June] 28. Mr. Hoyt went this morning with our visitors to Br. Milo Hoyts' to get his wife to interpret. They had not been long there before they were interrupted by the sickness of Mrs. Fields. She was taken with pain in her stomach, & could not be dissuaded from setting out to return to the Mission house, & on her way was taken with a fit. Dr. Butler was sent for, he bled her &c—in little more than an hour she revived. We sent a waggon over in the afternoon and brought her in. Learn that she has been subject to such fits.

[June] 29. Mrs. Fields is still feeble—Dr. Butler went early this morning to visit the sick woman near Br. Reece's. Some months ago she was given over by the Cherokees, her disease being considered incurable. Dr. Butler was called. Medicine had the desired effect, & being administered under his direction for some time she had so far recovered as to ride abroad. The doctor, being pressed with other business thought it duty to discontinue his visits.

Dr. Butler returned about 11 o'clock. He found the woman as low if not lower than he had ever seen her. She appears to have taken cold—the neighbors say she bathed in the river.[39] Her husband, who talks some English, says she did not. He is probably afraid the Dr. will be offended if he knows she has been so imprudent.—Just as Dr. Butler returned he was called on to visit sister Coody. She was nearly two weeks ago violently seized with cramping through the whole system—Br. Butler was then called and administered to her speedy relief. She was left in a feeble state, & he visited her two or three times; but discontinued his visits sooner than he would have done but for his pressing calls in the secular concerns of this mission. Mr. Hoyt, & other members of the mission have visited her since, and we have heard from her almost every day as getting better. The messenger says she now has another turn like the first.

Sab. [June] 30.—Dr. Butler went early to visit the woman near Br. Reece's: just as he returned he was called in haste to sister Coody's, & thus obliged to abstain from public worship. Br. Reece is also necessarily absent to day.

Br. Samuel J. Mills was admitted to full communion: he might have been received sooner, but could not be here at a proper time. As some members of the church and most of the congregation understand Cherokee it was proposed that Br. Mills should make profession of his Faith, & purpose to serve the Lord in his own language, and according to his own mind & feelings. Opportunity was given him to speak before the vote was taken to admit him to the communion. He spoke about fifteen minutes, & with much feeling, particularly towards the close. A number of Cherokee men were present, who heard with solemn attention, and one of them covered his face to hide his tears. After communion, and the close of public worship, the church was detained, & Mrs. Fields & John Wanuh were examined & admitted as candidates for baptism.

After meeting, a number of Cherokee men came into the house, & among them an old man much respected by his people, who has been a constant attendant on the sabbath for some time. Br. Mills talked to them a long time with much engagedness; & they listened with solemn attention: but there was no one to hear who could tell what was said. Many among this people appear to be prepared to received instruction; & in some instances there is a shaking among the dry bones.[40] Some of the oldest schollars have been anxiously inquiring, & apparently under deep impressions, for a little time past, & some begin to express a hope: but whether there be life, or whether these dry bones can live, the Lord knoweth. We are loudly called to unremitted exertion—to fervent prayer—to a feeling sense of our entire dependence, & to humble submission to the divine will.—

Ard Hoyt, J.C. Elsworth, Elizur Butler

Brainerd July 6th 1822

Dear Mr. Evarts Sir,
You will learn from the journal that my time is much occupied in attending on the sick. For a week or fortnight medicine has occupied most of my time. If the measles should prevail this summer my time must probably be entirely devoted to medicine. This day I have sold clothing to the amount of $20 for money and supplies.
I mention these things as the reason why our accounts are not forwarded. I am in hopes I shall be enabled to forward them soon. The committee business which has lately devolved on me adds to my labors.
The Committee you appointed feel it their duty to forward soon, an estimate of the probable expense of the mission for the ensuing year.
We have likewise to forward a short list of medicine & some other articles forgotten when you were here.

Yours affectionately
Elizur Butler

J. Evarts Esq.

Brainerd Mission Journal July 1822

July 1st 1822. Dr. Butler was taken up the whole day visiting the sick, and did not get home to attend the Monthly concert.—Br. Mills would have left us to day but Mrs. Fields is still unwell, and his son who he brought with him to the school is taken sick, probably with the measles. We therefore expect this disease will spread among the schollars. John Wanuh and one woman (the last of br. Mills' company except Mrs. Fields) left us this morning.

Business meeting. Br. Dean rendered the acct of the smith shop, Joiner shop, & Mills.

Smiths shop C^r

By work done for Brainerd	$24,68
" dto pay recd in money	10,00
" dto in produce	2,89
" dto charged customers	9,84
" Anvil & vise sold	23,00
By Iron & steel sold	44,79
	115,20

D^r

" Iron bought of Mr. Cobb	361,74
Balance against the shop	246,54

Joiner shop C^r

By sundry articles for mission house	$9,12
" dto dto house by the creek	1,62
" Repairing waggons [?]	15,00
" Articles sold	3,50
Total amt for June	29,24

No account has yet been taken of stock used in joiners shop

Value toll corn recd for June	$14,75
dto Boards sawed	6,47
	21,22
Tending mills & [?]	7,50
Balance in favor of mills	13,72

[July] 2. Showers of rain prevented our getting the last of our wheat and timothy hay. Wheat is very light this season, being much injured by the rust. The timothy turns out well, but is thought not to be quite so large as it was last season. It is thought the Mission may greatly derive more profit from grass than was at first expected. The piece included last spring for pasture has hitherto been found sufficient for the missions horses—working oxen—calves—sheep, & some other cattle. But it is not [*word unreadable*] pasture—working horses &c need some corn on account of the quality of the [*word unreadable*].

[July] 3. Br. Mills, and Mrs. Fields are still with us on account of the boy who has the measles. He appears likely to go through well, but they do not want to leave him untill they can see him better. After the wednesday lecture br. Mills (by request) addressed the schollars and prayed. Dr. Butler, after visiting sis. Coodey went to br. Reece's neighborhood, & found the woman who had been raised almost to health by his instrumentality, had fallen a victim to her imprudence; or perhaps to the mistaken notions of her relatives. She died yesterday. It appears that she had been heated in a Hot house, and while in a high state of perspiration plunged into a river.[41] This is one of the Indian methods of curing the sick: but, in a case like hers, nothing could have been more injudicious.[42] Ignorance & superstition mutually foster each other, as it respects both soul and body. There are numbers in that neighborhood, lately from the upper towns, who still adhere to the old custom of a sacrifice and dance, before they eat green corn or beans. A number of them were at work for br. Reece in the field, & he brought them green beans before they had had their dance.[43] Several immediately remonstrated, accusing him of great wickedness. He labored in vain to convince them of their error—As he and one of his old neighbors sat down to eat, the others all refused to partake, and left the field. We believe this antient custom is nearly done away in all the lower part of the nation: but those in the mountains have had, comparatively, very little opportunity for instruction. It was there the family mentioned in our Journal of 28th May, was destroyed for the supposed crime of witchcraft, about ten years ago. But br. Reece says there has been a very great and astonishing improvement in every part of the nation since that time, & particularly within the last 5 years.

Mr. Butrick returned this evening. He brings pleasing intelligence from Taloney. Numbers there are awakened to a serious concern for their salvation, & 3 or 4 express a hope.—Sis. Hall is again in a very feeble state of health, & had kept her room for several days. The remainder of the family in good health & actively engaged.

[July] 4. Mr. Hoyt and three of the sisters went out to visit one of the neighbors.

Mr. Butrick finds his scripture translations very useful. He spent much of the day in reading to br. Mills & Mrs. Fields. They sit & hear with great attention—say they can understand the words, & think they know something of the meaning.[44]

[July] 5. Brs. Blunt & Darius Hoyt with three of the sisters went into br. Reece's neighborhood & had an interesting visit at br. Reece's and one other family where they speak English.

The Rev. Thomas Roberts, and Mr. Evan Jones from the Baptist station in the Valley towns, called on us.[45] They left the mission family in health, & their school has been well attended—They have at this time a vacation of the school. N⁰ of schollars 65. The loss of their Mills by highwater has retarded the building at the station—They are rebuilding their Mills—The grist mill is already in operation, & the saw-mill expected to be soon.

Three of the boys were absent from school this afternoon. They were seen on the path which leads to where it is said there is a ball play three or four miles from us.[46] From the character of these plays, and the intemperance which generally attends them, they must have a demoralizing effect. We therefore do not allow the children under our direction to attend them. This was known to at least one of these boys, who has been with us several years. About 2 weeks since, he asked permission to attend one of these plays, and was told that no one of our schollars could ever be permitted to attend them.

[July] 6. At the opening of the school this morning Mr. Hoyt, & Dr. Butler attended with br. Elsworth, and examined the boys who were absent from school yesterday. They had been at the ball play—It appears that the youth, who has been longest in school, enticed the other two. One of the two has been in school but a few weeks, & does not understand English. He appeared to be in a great degree ignorant of the evil of going from school without permission—& totally so of the evil of ball plays—was much grieved that he had done wrong, and ready to promise strict obedience for the future. We thought best to grant him a free pardon. The other, though the youngest of the three, has been longer at the school, and understands English, he was therefore fined. But the leader, having been long in school, and taught to speak English from his childhood being able to read the word of God, and thoroughly acquainted with the rules of the school, and being told by his teachers, but a few days ago that no schollar could ever be permitted to go from the school to the ball play, was thought to merit expulsion—and the welfare of the school appeared to require it. We endeavored to make all the schollars understand the reasons of our proceeding, and required him to leave the school.[47]

Sab. [July] 7. Mr. Roberts preached. Afternoon discourse interpreted as delivered. The boy mentioned on the 14th ult as having left the school, whose father came on the 22nd to enquire respecting it returned and in the presence of the school frankly made the acknowledgments that were required of him.

[July] 8. The husband of the woman, who died near br. Reece's last week came to request Mr. Hoyt to go tomorrow and preach at his house on account of her death.

Br. Dean went out after a Millwright, we having heard nothing from the one expected.

[July] 9. Our brethren from the Baptist mission left us this morning—they would have gone yesterday but for the rain—We have reason to be thankful, for this very agreeable interview, which we trust has been for mutual edification. As we have felt our hearts united while together, so we believe the bonds, which by divine grace unite the two missions, will be strengthened and conformed by all the intercourse we may have with each other. They go to br. Hicks' and thence return circuitously through the eastern part of the nation. As they were on the way down the Agent informed them that the stipend from Government for this station was continued, with the addition of Fifty dollars a quarter for this year, & that he expected to have for us within a few weeks, $600, the first semiannual payment for 1822.

Mr. Butrick also left us this morning, in company with br. Mills and Mrs. Fields. He expects to go home with br. Mills, & spend a little time in that neighborhood to instruct the candidates for baptism, & assist in fanning the breeze which appears to be passing over that place. May the Holy Spirit work by him confirming the truth by his gracious influences.

Mr. Hoyt went agreeably to the request of yesterday. From 70 to 80 persons (including a number of children) assembled at the place where the woman died, & gave serious attention to conversation, & a sermon interpreted by br. Reece. The old man, who has attended so constantly at Brainerd on the sabbath for some time was present, & at the close feelingly expressed his approbation of all that had been said. Hired a man to tend the mills. We know not how he will suceeded, as he has but little experience in a grist mill, & none in a saw mill, but we thought best to try him, as the saw mill has been still the greatest part of the time since the last of May, for want of a sawyer.

[July] 11. In meeting for business Resolved, That the vote respecting three measures on the role both be rescinded.

Major Lowrey & Mr. Andrew Ross from Wills town & Mr. John Ross visited the school this afternoon.[48] They appeared well satisfied with the progress of the schollars.—Mr. Lowrey addressed them in Cherokee. Mr. A. Ross saw Mr. Chamberlin;—says he preached at Chattooga last friday & expected to spend the sabbath in br. Mills neighborhood, & then to go on to Hightower, & Taloney—Br. John Arch was with him as interpreter.

Br. Dean returned this evening—He has engaged Mr. Alexander of Rhea County to do the Millwright work of the shop; & expects he will be here next week.

[July] 12. {Mr. Hoyt went out this morning expecting to visit two or three families. Sis. Chamberlin went with him for the benefit of her health, which she is gaining slowly. Riding in fair weather is very beneficial to her. Several showers near the middle of the day so interrupted them that they visited but one family. They passed a new building about 3 miles from Brainerd, called by some a school house & by others a meeting house—It is probably intended for both purposes, & is nearly finished.}

A number of the children are complaining—we expect they are coming down with the measles.

[July] 13. The man lately engaged to tend the mills has been complaining several days, thinks he has the fever & ague—and on that account left us today to return to his family. We have sent for another to take his place.

[July] 15. The man who was sent for on saturday to tend the mills came this morning & commenced his work.

Business meeting—Question. How shall work done at the joiner shop be [?ainated]. The stock shall be charged to the shop, & when [*hole in ms*] ordered for the mission they shall be estimated as when sold. Question: Shall the tools that are made for the blacksmiths shop be charged to the shop? Answered in the affirmative—Resolved that sis. Sarah Hoyt be released from the charge of the girls out of school; and that sis. E. Elsworth have that charge & the charge of the clothing given to the teacher of the girls school.—The reasons for this change are it is not thought best for sis. Dean in her present circumstances,[49] & particularly in prospect of the measles coming into the school to continue in the school—and sis. Sarah does not think her health, and strength sufficient for the care & labor that has devolved upon her.

[July] 16. The Millwright came, & several hands with him. We hope now to proceed with the triphammer shop without further interruption. In consequence of word left by br. Dean when out a man came to hire who is acquainted with the blacksmith business; as he offers to work low; in the smiths shop or out as he may be needed, & as br. Dean must be considerably out of the shop with the workmen it was thought best to employ him.

[July] 17. One man who had been employed by us a few days, not long since, came again & wished to be hired. He was rejected on account of having used profane language, & expressed Infidel sentiments in the presence of another hired man when here before. He gave further evidence of his unfitness to be employed here by threatening to fight the young man who had informed against him.

We fear that a part of the very small crop of wheat will be nearly or quite destroyed by the frequent rains. It is now more than two weeks since the last of it was cut, & we have had rain nearly every day since. It was thought it might do to come in this afternoon, but as br. Vail was harnessing the horses to commence hauling another shower prevented. So much of it already sprouted as to render what is now in the field unfit for bread—The oats are still out.

Such was the prospect of fair weather this morning that two men were employed to commence mowing the wild grass in the savannah. If these showers continue we shall be obliged to stop them. The two men came in from the savannah after dinner & say the meadow is covered with water, we shall therefore be obliged to leave it for the present.

[July] 18. The boy mentioned the 7th inst. was absent from school without leave yesterday afternoon—On being called to an account at the opening of the school this morning, he had no cause to offer, but said he knew it was wrong when he went away into the woods, and [*hole in ms*] giving any reason for his conduct—Various questions were put in order to [*hole in ms*] out the reason of this strange conduct. He answered them all very frankly except the one directly to the point—on this he remained silent; but without any appearance of obstinacy or moroseness—At length this question was put to him Did you do this because you thought we should dismiss you from the school for this disobedience? He answered that he did. On being

asked why he wished to leave the school, he remained silent as on the first question, but answered other questions as before—By which it appeared that he was not dissatisfied with any treatment he had received here—was not offended with anyone of the missionaries or schollars—that he wished to get more learning, but did not expect he should have left the school at this time. As the boy treated us with proper respect & appeared to pay strict regard to truth, the subject was laid over for further consideration, & he permitted to take his seat, & proceed with his studies as heretofore. During the intermission after dinner, Mr. Hoyt conversed with the lad alone—and he said that the only reason why he wished to leave the school was that (to use his own words) "He felt uneasy." He was advised not to think of obtaining relief by changing his place, but to apply to the Saviour who alone could give him rest and peace: but, if he was determined to go, we would send for his father, & if he thought best he should go in a more honorable way. He desired time to think of it untill tomorrow.

[July] 19. The lad mentioned yesterday not appearing contented, we sent for his father.

One of the chiefs of Wills Valley, a very respectable man, of mixed blood who speaks both languages, and has considerable school education, called on us and visited the schools. By request he made a short address to the boys in Cherokee. The substance of his remarks as we are told, was, that he himself had obtained his education with great difficulty—a little in one place and a little in another—There was then no such opportunity for Cherokees as they now had. The good white people had sent them schools at a great expense, asking no pay from the Cherokees, & much better schools than he had—They should be very thankful for these privileges—attend to every thing their teachers told them—always be obedient in every thing, and learn as fast as they could every day—that they could be a great advantage to them and to their people.

He says the people of the Valley think much of the preaching they have lately heard, and desire to hear more—they would be glad if we could have regular appointments there—once in two weeks—a month—or as often as we can. We were also glad to hear him say that the people do not think hard of the missionaries for not giving them a school—they believe we are doing all we can—& hope they shall not have to wait longer than till next fall. He assures us that a desire for instruction, and confidence in the supporters of mission, is continually increasing in all parts of the nation.

[July] 20. Finished bringing in and threshing what wheat could be saved from the small piece on the bottom land—found it to measure only about 8 bushels. This is all that we get from about 3 acres.

[July] 21. Br. Reece attended the forenoon service—at the close of the sermon a short summary of what had been said was given to br. Reece and by him interpreted & this was all the public interpretation we had this day as br. Reece was unable to attend in the afternoon by reason of ill health.

[July] 22. There being again a prospect of fair weather two men were set to mowing wild grass—but not in the savannah we have formerly mowed, as that is very wet and grass light this season. It is found that a savannah on the east side of the creek, about the same distance of the other is much dryer and better this season. We can there cut as much wild grass as we please.
Meeting for business. Resolved that br. Vail have charge of getting Hay and the Timothy seed.
Mr. Hoyt went to br. Reeces neighborhood—he had so far recovered his health as to ride abroad, and there being no other competent interpreter, the day was spent in visiting such families as can speak english. At one place however a number came together, and a little plain talk was interpreted by a woman. In this neighborhood they are enlarging their cornfields, and beginning to make a considerable show of industry. It is said none of them work on the sabbath.

[July] 24. A man hired for the purpose set out this morning with a light waggon to take our aged sister Thompson to Hightower. Sisters Nancy Thompson & Anna Hoyt went with her, as it was thought unsafe for a person of her age & infirmities to attempt such a journey without female assistance. The three brethren, Butrick, Chamberlin & Parker all came in, from different ways, nearly at the same time this evening. Br. John Arch is with Mr. Chamberlin, & some boys for the school with Mr. Butrick. Mr. Chamberlin has been through Wills Valley to Creek path—there engaged br. John to go with him as interpreter, thence through a part of Wills Valley to Chattooga, Turnip mountain, the Ridges settlement, Hightower and Taloney, a distance (including his return to Brainerd) of between three & four hundred miles.[50] He was well received in every place, found the people ready to converse, & hear attentively, & many of them exceedingly anxious for schools.[51]—There appears to be a necessity laid upon us to have at least three new schools commence before

winter—Viz. At Wills Valley, Hightower, & Turnip town.[52] The people had put up a house for br. Thompson—While they were raising the house an old chief came—required them all to stop their work—sent for those that were out cutting logs—collected them all under a tree & gave them a long talk; after which sometime was spent in conversation—& then all returned again to their work with great animation. The young man who was educated here, (called Calvin Jones) and who is now there with br. Thompson, was present and communicated the substance of the talk, & conversation.[53] He says the Chief reminded the people of the great number of Blacksmiths in the nation who were bad men—& told them if they had not full evidence that this was a good man, they must not strike another stroke for him. Witnesses then came forward (Calvin was one of them) and testified to the character of br. Thompson. The old chief then said "Go on—build him a good house and let this house be between you and him, for a perpetual witness of your mutual friendship." The chief then turned to br. Thompson & said, "This must now be your home—you must live & die & be buried here". Calvin says one man enquired very seriously of him if br. Thompson could be a good man, & a blacksmith. He thought all blacksmiths were bad men. At Taloney he found the seriousness spreading. None have expressed a christian hope except those who have been before mentioned—These still appear well—

Mr. Butrick has been to Turnip town, Hightower, and Beaver Dam. This latter place lies on the south side of Coosa river, opposite to Turnip town. Its situation agreeable, its land fertile, its inhabitants apparently industrious, and anxious for a school—He found the people as usual anxious for instruction both Divine & literary.—Br. Parker has come with a waggon for some mechanical work, & other articles for Taloney.

[July] 25. As Mr. Chamberlin agreed with br. John only for the time he should be out untill his return to Brainerd we had conversation with him on the subject of continuing this service; & particularly on the compensation he should receive. As he must now provide for himself, or depend on the mission, it was thought best that he should be paid a definite price for the time he should be employed as interpreter, and clothe himself from his wages at his own discretion. We proposed ten dollars a month, which is the usual pay of a common laborer. With this he is well satisfied—If there are any intervals when he is not

wanted to go out as interpreter, he will attend to study and assist here as formerly without pay.

[July] 26. Miss Mary K. Rawlings who has been here since about the first of June, returned to her Uncles—A young man (son of Mrs. Fields who stands a candidate for baptism) who came with Mr. Butrick, appears very seriously enquiring after the way of salvation. He proposes to stay a few days for further instruction.

[July] 27.—The schools were not kept today on account of the great number of children with the measles. Only about 10 of each school were able to attend. Br. Blunt is also down with the measles, and br. Ellis unable to work—not yet certain what his complaint is. Raised the lower part of the trip hammer shop.

Mr. Butrick took br. John Arch with him, & went out to meet an appointment to preach tomorrow about 12 miles south—Mr. Chamberlin goes north about 15 miles where most can understand without an interpreter.

[July] 29. Br. Ellis' complaint proves to be the measles—Find it very difficult for those who are well to get along with the necessary business of the family and to take care of the sick. We have reason to be very thankful that so many of the mission family have had this complaint before; & that a merciful God has so constructed our mortal frame that this disease seldom returns a second time: also that we have a physician in the family, & all who have taken the disease appear to be going safely through—Both schools continue with but few schollars able to attend.

Meeting for business. Resolved that sister Butler have charge of teaching the girls who are able to attend school, for the present. Resolved that br. Vail have charge of the fence, feeding the fattening ox, repairing the bridge on the road to Mr. Coody's, attend to br. Ellis' charge untill he recovers, & have liberty to hire two men to assist, who shall be under his direction so long as shall be necessary.

[July] 30. Br. Parker left us to return to Taloney. While waiting here for the mechanics to make some necessary articles for that branch of the mission, he has been assisting in the labors here; so that we have enjoyed the pleasures of a social visit, and frequent seasons of religious worship and conference with little or no loss of labor to the mission. "How good, and pleasant it is for brethren to dwell together in unity."[54]

[July] 31. About 3 ock this afternoon the hired man with the two sisters returned from Hightower. Mother Thompson endured the fatigues of the journey with very little inconvenience. They arrived to breakfast with br. Thompson and family on saturday morning, and found all well, with satisfactory prospects—the women are very attentive and kind to sister Thompson.—The natives (whether by design or mistake is not known) had appointed sabbath as the day to put up the shop. Br. Thompson being told that they were coming after so many days to build the shop, observed that would be the sabbath, and therefore the work must not be done on that day. This being told to one of the chiefs, he said one man must not think to come in and rule the nation at once. On hearing this br. T returned answer, that they were in their own country, and must not think that he would desire to direct them in their business in any respect—they must do as they pleased; but as he knew the command of God forbidding work to be done on that day, if they came he could not assist them, or even go out to look at the work. Thus the matter rested untill sabbath morning when only five or six men came. These said they did not know it was the sabbath—laid their axes away in the bushes, & with pleasant countenances departed. About the midle of the day a number of men, women & children collected—said they thought the man who came yesterday was a missionary, & they had come to hear preaching. Their mistake was corrected—one of the Cherokee women being able to interpret. She told br. Thompson if there was no Missionary then he must preach, as the people had come to hear preaching, and were very unwilling to go away without it. He told them, as well as he could, the difference between himself and a preacher of the gospel— that they must never think he could preach—but if they desired it, he would read from the good book for the woman to interpret, and also sing and pray with them. Accordingly as many as could crowded into the house, & the remainder stood about the door and window—were attentive while these exercises were performed, & then withdrew apparently well satisfied. As the sisters set out on their return early on monday morning they met large companies of men with their axes going to put up the shop. The woman who interpreted on the sabbath was herself affected to tears. Among others things she has manifested her regard to br. & sis. Thompson, by giving them the loan of four cows, with young calves.—All the boys of the school except about 10 have had the measles at this time, & we expect 7 or 8 of these have yet to pass through this disease, as we cannot learn that more than 2 or 3

have before had it. All, except three, were able to take supper this evening at the common table.—The girls are behind; as none of them took it from the first boy. About half of them are now under the complaint, and none have so far recovered as to return at their common table; but all appear to be doing well. As this disease generally leaves the eyes weak it will probably be some time before the schools can resume their former standing—yet we hope to keep them in such continued operation as to prevent the children from scattering. Six whose parents live near have been taken home, by permission, to be nursed untill they shall be able to attend school. The remainder are still with us.

The boy whose father was sent for on the 19 inst. is yet with us, and has had the disease. His mother came at the time we sent for his father, and said he was from home on business, but she thought he would come and see us when he returned. We have not since heard from him—nor does the boy say anything more about his uneasyness.

Ard Hoyt, Elizur Butler, Wm Chamberlin, J.C. Elsworth

Brainerd Journal

August 1, 1822. Mr. Butrick left us to return to Taloney.

[Aug.] 3. The father of the discontented boy came last evening, & this morning brought in an interpreter to talk with us—He speaks no english. The substance of his remarks was, That he should have come sooner but his business would not permit—he had given his son a long talk, & thought he would no more be so foolish, but would hereafter be obedient & stay out his time contentedly—that he had always been glad of the coming of the missionaries since he became acquainted with them, & understood their business—& that the people all over the nation are seeing more & more clearly the great good of having such teachers among them. Perhaps he did not know we had been informed that he was at first a violent opposer, & had talked so high to Mr. Hicks on the subject that he had ordered him out of his presence—but we were pleased with the strictness of his varacity in the qualification—since he became acquainted & understood the business—& his conduct has manifested that this was not long after the commencement of the mission.

We believe it is not only in our presence, but also among their own people, that many consider it an honor to have been among the first to discuss the national advantage of these institutions, & that it is, by many at least, considered a mark of a weak mind not now to see it.

Sab. [Aug.] 4. Mr. Chamberlin spent this sabbath with us & preached in the forenoon. Such is the opening for preaching at those places which he has lately visited, & also in the other places, that, although this is our communion season, it was his intention to have left us last week on a second tour; & he would have done so, but for the sickness of the family, the prospect of his children taking the measles, & sister Chamberlin's feeble health. Under these circumstances it was thought best that his interpreter should go to Taloney & thence round to meet him at Chattoga next Friday.

[Aug.] 5. Br. Butler having some business at Mr. Ross', & br. Blunt being in convalescent, they both went with the light waggon, took two of the sisters, & visited several families.

[Aug.] 6. Mr. Chamberlin went to br. Reeces,—several of the neighbours came in, with whom he read conversed prayed & sang. Br. Reece interpreted.

[Aug.] 7. Several of the boys having injured themselves by eating green peaches before they had recovered from the measles, it was thought best to forbid anyone pulling peaches from the trees, & to annex a penalty for disobedience. Several of the boys violated this order & were yesterday punished. It appears that two of them took offense, & went off last night.

[Aug.] 8. Mr. Chamberlin left us this morning.

[Aug.] 9. Mr. Hoyt spent part of the day in pastoral visits. We find it difficult without taking up too much of our journal, so to mention the various visits of Mr. Hoyt, as to give the Prud. Com. a correct idea of them; & on this account it has not been our practice untill of late, to mention them, nor even now to notice them all. A little part of this small congregation is so located, that by riding circuitously 12 or 14 miles four or five families may be visited in a day, but in general it is most convenient not to visit more than one or two families at a time, & part of a day is commonly sufficient for that. These short seasons spent in pastoral visits except there be some occurrence worthy of particular notice, we think may well be left to pass as we leave other small circumstances unnoticed in the journal.

Animals & fowls from the woods are constantly seeking to feed upon our growing corn—the one by day & the other by night. We are therefore obliged to keep an almost constant watch. At little before day this morning one oppossum, & three Raccoons were found in the corn & killed.

[*Aug.*] 10. A gentleman from Blount Co. (Mr. Canada) called on us yesterday partly on business. He spent the afternoon in the schools, & looking over the farm, Mills &c. He left us this morning after assuring us that though his business failed, he did not regret his journey. He appeared to take a lively interest in the children, & thought his neighbours would cheerfully contribute for the support of the Mission.

Sab. [*Aug.*] 11. Br. Reece was with us again. He was unable to interpret one Sabbath, & has been absent two sabbaths since. We have had no interpreter the three last Sabbaths, & did not know we could have one today soon enough to give notice—none of those who usually attend on account of his interpreting were present, yet, for the sake of the children & two or three who were with us from a distance, & also to keep up the course of having the afternoon sermon interpreted when we can, the discourse was interpreted.

[*Aug.*] 12. This morning another Raccoon was driven from the corn & killed. We hope by hunting them continually as they come in to prevent their destroying any great quantity of the corn. They have however already pulled down much more than we could have expected from such short depredations. They are far worse upon the corn of this country than so many hogs. The ears being all too high for them to reach, they are obliged to climb the stalk. As they ascend the stalk breaks, & falls, leaving all upon it to perish the kernel being not yet sufficiently formed to be any use. Thus in a very short time a single Raccoon or oppossum will destroy more corn than would be sufficient for his support for months; most of the corn thus broken down being left untouched.

A Gentleman from N. Carolina (Mr. McCrea) politely called & visited the schools. He expressed satisfaction in the appearance & progress of the children—their safe & cleanly keeping of their books &c. & gave it as his opinion that the public would not suffer the institution to languish for want of support.

Aug. 14. Sister Elsworth took her bed early last evening with symptoms which indicated an approaching fever. This morning with symptoms more alarming she was put under the operation of medicine. The measles are still prevailing. New cases occur frequently.

[Aug.] 16. Mr. Chamberlin returned. He expected to have been out till after the next sabbath, but his horse becoming lame by the loss of a shoe, he found it necessary to shorten his rout. By going out so as to preach next sabbath 12 miles from Brainerd, he will have fulfilled all his appointments. Br. John Arch met him according to arrangement at Chattuga on the 9th inst, & has returned with him.
He found br. Mills & some others in his neighbourhood apparently as much engaged as ever. There he saw the two boys who left us on the night of the 6th. Their parents say they shall bring them back.
Sister Elsworth appears some better today, but is not able to sit up. Br. Elsworth took his bed this afternoon.

[Aug.] 17. Br. Parker, his wife & daughter arrived from Taloney. They have employed a hired man at Taloney & br. Hall writes, that he thinks that br. Parker & family might be more profitably employed at Brainerd than there, & if the brethren here think with him, he shall be satisfied to have them remain here. Br. Parker concurs in this opinion. Br. Vails daughter, Caroline, about 3 years old, is thought to be in a critical situation. The measles have turned, but she does not recover as the other children have done. Sister Elsworth's fever continues, & she is to day not so well.

Sab. [Aug.] 18. Br. Elsworth appears somewhat relieved by the medicine he has taken, but is unable to go out of his room. We were again with out an interpreter. Br. Reece is probably unwell. We greatly need a steady interpreter at this place.
Mr. Butrick & Mr. Chamberlin both came in this evening. At br. Hicks' where Mr. Butrick preached, the congregation was small. Mr. Chamberlin preached 12 miles from Brainerd, found almost all the people of that vicinity assembled, and attentive to what was said through the interpreter. In the Congregation Mr. C. observed many children. He thinks a good school might be collected there if we would furnish a teacher: And also at another place about 15 miles south of that, where the people have manifested a readiness to attend preaching whenever they have been invited.

[Aug.] 19. Br. & sister Vail & the remainder of the mission family with them are all called to mourning. This morning about 9 O'Clock the Spirit of their dear Caroline was called away by Him, who doth not afflict willingly, nor grieve the children of men. This is the first death except infants that has taken place in the Mission family at Brainerd.

Sister Elsworth has had a very sick day. She is so affected by noise that we have stoped the ringing of the bell, entirely, & use our utmost endeavours to keep all still around the mission house. Br. Elsworth has a high fever, & is nearly in a state of mental derangement.

Last evening br. G. Halsey had a fit of the ague followed by a high fever. He is today beginning a course of medicine.

The man who is employed to attend to the mills recvd intelligence that his wife was very low with a fever, & left us.

Meeting for business. As br. Parker has come with his family bringing a letter from br. Hall, from which, & from the statements & brs. Butrick & Parker, it appears that the brethren Hall & Parker thought it would be more for the interest of the mission, for br. Parker & family to reside at Brainerd, & that they have come expecting a decision of the brethren on the subject therefore Resolved that we think it expedient under existing circumstances for br. Parker & family to continue here untill the pleasure of the Prud. com can be known. Also Resolved, that br. Butler prepare a joint letter to be sent to the Cor. Sec. on the above subject.

[Aug.] 20. The schools were suspended this forenoon to attend the funeral of br. Vail's child. Its remains were deposited near the feet of Dr. Worcester.

[Aug.] 21. One of the boys ~~Lewis~~ was absent from school this morning. When enquiry was made for him, some of the boys said they saw him a little time before going out on the road. As his mother, who has been making Conuhanuh for us some days left us to return home a short time after the boy went away,[55] &, followed him on the same road, we suspect he has gone with her.

Mr. Butrick left us this morning to return to Taloney. He led a horse for the boy to ride back, who has gone to take the horses and waggon brought by br. Parker.

The hired carpenter, D. Clark, was taken sick yesterday,—keeps his bed today; & has considerable fever.

Sab. [Aug.] 25. Mr. Chamberlin is out without his interpreter, as the people where he went, about 15 miles up the Tennessee river, mostly understand English: but we had little use for the interpreter here, as few attended meeting who do not understand our language. Hearers of this description came principally from two neighbourhoods, and we learn that a man belonging to one of these was bitten by a snake in the other, & for a time thought to be dying. Possibly this prevented the people from coming to meeting today. Or the information that we should have an interpreter might not have been sufficiently circulated.—But we fear the anxiety to hear the gospel which was manifested by some when we had a interpreter every sabbath is somewhat abated.

[*Aug.*] 26. Darius Hoyt has kept the boys school since br. Elsworth was obliged to leave it. He was taken down yesterday, & today Mr. Chamberlin has taken the school.

In business meeting, Read the joint letter prepared by br. Butler to be sent to the Cor. Sec., which was unanimously accepted.

Read a letter from Mr. Charles Stodard of Boston, to Mr. Chamberlin requesting him to select a boy to be placed in his family, to bear the name of Benjamin Blydenburg Wisner, stating that the first semi-annual payment for his support had been paid into the Treasury at Boston.[56] Agreed that Mr. Chamberlin be allowed to select a boy agreeable to the above request.

Br. Dean rendered the acct of the blacksmith shop & mills from July 1st to Aug. 12 inclusive which are as follows:

Smiths Shop	$ ¢	Gristmill	$
Recd in Cash	11,68½	Cr By toll corn	18,25
" " produce	3,72	Dr to tending	6.50
" " labour	30,98	Balance in favour	11,75
Work done for M.S.	28,61	Sawmill	
do do for Taloney	4.50	Cr by plank & boards	58,55
	$80,12 [57]	Dr to tending, repairing	
		& getting logs	21.08
		Balance in favour	37.47

Shop Dr		
To laying tongs 1,00 iron		8,95
$0,45 hire of smith	$7,50	___
Balance in favour of shop		71.17

Aug. 27. We have now five sick who require constant attendance & so situated that four persons must be up every night & in addition to this br. Vail youngest child is sick with the measles, so as to prevent his rendering any assistance at this time in watching. Our neighbors are very kind on rendering assistance when called on as far as they are able, but few of them understand taking care of the sick in our way.[58] Br. McPhaerson came to our assistance last week, & brought one of his daughters with him. They proposed to stay with us and assist by night or day as long as we should need their help; but on the fourth day he was called home by notice of sickness in his own family. His daughter still continues with us. Dr. Butler visited br. McPhaerson's family. They are getting better.

[Aug.] 28. Br. McPhaerson sent for his daughter being himself sick.

[Aug.] 30. An elderly man & two youths came from br. Mills neighbourhood. They inform that the other part of the precious company expected from that place at this time are all detained by sickness either in their persons or their families.
We hear of fever prevailing in different parts of the [nation?] at this time more than at any other since the commencement of the Mission.
Dr. Butler has been unwell for two or three days, & for [2 *words unreadable*] days at least should have kept his room but for the sick in the family, yet on their account he did not give up to take his bed untill this evening.

[Aug.] 31. There is a man here from br. Mills' neighbourhood, known among the Cherokees by a name which signifies wicked, the English call him Jack,—the common appellation which has been [?n] when speaking of him is Old wicked, or wicked Jack.[59] It is said that in externals he is entirely reformed. He expresses a great desire to stay some time, for the purpose of farther instruction in religion but says it is not right to spend his time in idleness; if we [want?] him to work he shall be very glad to stay. This he said at [*hole in ms*] of the day, a considerable portion of which had been spent [?] him, & others, endeavouring to impart that instruction which he came to seek. He was very readily told that he should have [*hole in ms*] immediately after the sabbath.
Dr. Butler has had a very sick day, & it was [*hole in ms*] to send early in the morning to Blount Co. for a physician.

Sept. 1. Br. John Arch left us early this morning to go find a physician. We hope he will be able to obtain Dr. McGhee of Maryville, who we are informed has relinquished the practice of physic, for the study of Theology.[60]

A very considerable number of Cherokees attended public worship today, & listened with solemn attention while br. Reece interpreted. They also listened with the same attention while he spoke to them sometime from his own knowledge after sermon. Almost the whole mission family were detained from public worship by sickness. Sister Vail, though not visited with the fever, is brought exceedingly low by some debility of the stomach, which for two days past, occassioned frequent & excessive vomiting.

Dr. Butler continues quite sick, yet for most of the time ~~he is favoured with a clear mind, so that~~ he is able not only to prescribe for himself, but to give advice respecting others, & information concerning our business.

As many of the family as were able, & could be spared from the sick, attended the monthly concert at the usual time.

Although we had great reason to humble ourselves under the hand of God upon us, yet it was very comforting to reflect that whatever might become of us, the cause for which so many fervent prayers are offered in faith, & which has the promise of Jehovah for its support, must prevail. Br. Ellis attended this meeting, & it is the first time he has been able to attend public worship for more than nine weeks.

[Sept.] 4. Mr. Butrick returned from Taloney.

[Sept.] 8. Br. John Arch returned. He waited some time in Maryville, in hopes of having a physician return with him, & at last came back without any. Dr. McGhee could not come in consequence of sickness in his own family. We do not so much regret the disappointment as we have had no new cases of fever since Dr. Butler's; and from the change of the weather—hope we shall not: & the sick are all or nearly all getting better.[61]

Dr. Butler except at intervals, which have not been long, has been able to prescribe for the sick, so far as their cases could be represented to him in his room.

[Sept.] 9. Meeting for business. Resolved that br. Vail tend the grist mill—that br. Blunt take charge of the boys out of school, & that br. Parker take his place in the kitchen.

[Sept.] 13. Br. John Arch left us to meet certain appointments of Mr. Chamberlin, as neither he, nor Mr. Butrick could go with him at this time.

[Sept.] 15. Sister Elsworth came down stairs for the first time since her sickness. She is still very feeble & was obliged to take a bed as soon as she got down.

[Sept.] 16. Meeting for business. Resolved that br. Dean obtain hands and finish the [*hole in ms*] floom immediately.
Nearly all business has been suspended since the commencement of the sickness [*hole in ms*] the necessary business [*hole in ms, 4-5 words missing*] that [w?d] some white men to cut & secure the tops of the corn, which they have done with the assistance of the boys. It is necessary that the mill race should be cleared before the sawmill can run, there being now scarcely water enough for the gristmill and it is thought necessary for the waste floom to be prepared to draw off the water before the race is cleared; and if this is not done soon we fear the weather [will] be so cold that labourours will not be willing to work in the mud and water as they must do to clear the race. We therefore deem it of great importance that the waste floom should be finished as soon as possible.

[Sept.] 17. Br. Dean went after a carpenter to finish the waste ~~gate~~ floom. Br. Butler & Sister Elsworth were taken out a short distance in a carriage, & returned again to their rooms, not greatly fatigued, & apparently refreshed by the exercise & the pure air.
Purchased six fat steers for beef, valued at ninety dollars, paid for them in blankets, bed quilts & comfortables. It was thought we had put up a sufficient quantity of pork last winter to last the year round, & some thought more than we should need; but in this we are disappointed, having now only all a few pieces of salt pork left; this would all have been eaten weeks ago, if we had not supplied the table with fresh to save it. We have already consumed this season about 2300 of beef & about 2000 of fresh pork besides some venison, two sheep and a number of fowls. Since the first of this month we have killed two beeves, twelve hogs from the pen, all of which have been consumed in the family. Our family during this time has not been unusually large,—we have but few hirelings, & the schools are not full, several of the schollars went home when sick with the measles, and have not yet returned; neither are our children great [*word missing-hole in ms*]. It may then be asked how we can account for the

consumption of so much flesh in so short a time? We can only say we have had little else, except for the sick, but corn bread & meat. Could we so manage to have plenty of vegetables—increase the quantity of milk & furnish our table with a greater variety, it would not only greatly lessen the quantity of meat, but make our diet more comfortable, more [hea?y] & we believe less expensive.

> Ard Hoyt, Wm Chamberlin, John Vail, Henry Parker, E. Dean, A. Blunt, E. Butler

> Brainerd 20th Sept. 1822

Dear Sir,

To save postage I occupy this corner to inform you that I have this day drawn on you in favor of Thomas McDowall, $100— payable thirty days after [?ight]. This draft Dr. Butler will send to Augusta. Yours of August 14th [*hole in ms*] the departed of the family [*hole—3 to 4 words missing*] course of mail.

From this journal you will learn something of the dealings of God with his family nearly to this time—I can now add that, thro, the great mercy of our Redeemer, the sick, or rather convalescent, are all recovering very fast, except Br. Elsworth, & he is gaining slowly— Two nights have now passed since it was necessary to have a watcher continually up—& all, except Br. Elsworth, expect to get into the waggon to day— I think we might set out on the Agency next week, but Mr. Anderson advises that we make our first effort in Blount,[62] & that the way be prepared by attending a sacramental occassion on the 2nd Sabbath in Oct—on this account we think it best not to go out untill about the 1st of October.

> Yours in the labors & hands of the gospel,
> Ard Hoyt

J. Evarts, Esqr

Brainerd Mission Journal 1822

Sept. 20. Br. Ellis went out to meet br. John Arch at Turnip mountain.[63] He is still feeble but we hope riding will be for his health—if it is, he will probably ride with br. John & visit the several places where Mr. Chamberlin has appointments—read, pray, & converse both in public and private, and thus endeavor to keep up the attention of the people untill Mr. Chamberlin can again enter into these labors.

[*Sept.*] 21. Mr. Butrick went out with one of the school boys, of whom we have hopes, as lately brought into the kingdom, expecting to spend sabbath at the preaching place 12 miles south.

The sick are all convalescent—have been able to do without constant watching two nights, & all except br. Ellsworth and sis. Vail are able to ride out. May God in mercy sanctify unto us this season of affliction, and prepare us for the blessing of restored health.

[*Sept.*] 22. Br. Elsworth was carried to the waggon and rode a short distance. Mr. Butrick returned this evening—found the people as usual ready to hear. He thinks the youth he took with him will soon make a good interpreter.

[*Sept.*] 23. As it was thought it would be necessary for Mr. Chamberlin to go into Tennessee to assist in soliciting donations and in that corse there would be no one to teach the school untill the sick should be restored, we determined about 2 weeks ago to vacate the schools before the set time, and appointed this day for the parents to come for their children. Accordingly the schools were examined this day and vacated for five weeks. We hope and trust the summer has not been spent in vain, but the schools have necessarily been much retarded by the measles among the children, and the fever in the Mission family. Yet our God has not forgotten to be gracious—we hope for some who came last spring in natures darkness that they now go out enlightened by renewing grace. If their lives are spared, time will probably strengthen or destroy this hope.

Meeting for business.

Resolved that no person have a right to purchase articles for the Mission but the steward, unless particular direction be given by the brethren, or he be requested by the steward, excepting articles rec^d for Smith work or other labor, and that in such cases the articles be delivered immediately into the hands of the Steward, or placed in such deposits as are, or may hereafter be provided.

Resolved, That br. Blunt have charge of the mills, and mechanical work, except blacksmithing, and that the resolutions respecting br. Vails tending the mill and br. Dean's obtaining hands and finishing the waste floom be rescinded. It is thought necessary to make this change in order that br. Dean may attend to the Blacksmiths shop, and br. Vail be more at liberty to attend to other things. Some of the neighbors think hard that they must come repeatedly with small jobs of work and cannot get them done, even when the blacksmith is but a few rods from the shop, and br. Dean thinks he cannot attend to blacksmithing, and at the same time have charge of the floom &c—and br. Blunt will now be relieved in his charge of the boys by their absence during vacation.

Sept. 24. Dr. Butler walked to sis. Congers, after having walked a little in the Mission yard. Sis. Ellsworth walked into the garden, and Darius to the carriage and back, Br. Ellsworth begins to feel his best a little in his room.

Received a letter from the Cor. Sec. The Pru. Com. think our estimate of supplies for the coming year of flour, and pork are high. If the price of flour is so much above corn as to make it more expensive, when we take into consideration the saving of meat when wheat bread is eaten, we suppose it may [be] best to purchase less flour—and if other articles of food can be obtained as a substitute, or in part a substitute for meat, we can doubtless live more comfortable, and certainly more agreeable to our inclination, with much less meat: but so far as flesh must be eaten, we are confident that it is much cheaper, and more for the health of the family, to purchase pork in the proper season so as to have always plenty of salt pork. This we have always intended to do but have never yet done, because the quantity consumed has always exceeded our calculation; and this is owing in a great measure to our having never succeeded according to our expectations in raising vegetables for our table. How we may succeed in time to come we cannot tell, but of this we are confident, that we shall now have stronger resolutions to lay our plans for this object, or greater confidence of success in time to come than we have had in time past. The mission is at this time suffering a daily loss from the want of salt pork. Yesterday morning we killed a hog which weighted upwards of 100 lb.—the whole of it except the head, and feet, was brought onto the table at dinner, and eaten by a less number than our ordinary family, exclusive of those who board at the creek. The average quantity of fresh meat (and we have eaten considerable salt) since the 1st of this month, is 150 lb per day.

Mr. J.G. Ross and wife, from Creek Path, made us a visit.[64] Mr. Ross left a donation of $5.00 observing that he was much indebted to the mission, and hoped to be able to pay more hereafter.

[Sept.] 25. Brs. Ellis, and John Arch returned. The people had kept the time and assembled without further notice at Turnip mountain, but at the other places on this side, they were only expecting Mr. Chamberlin soon, and said six weeks was too long for them to keep time, if they could be told three or four days before the time they could know it, and would all attend. It is not surprising that they should find it difficult to number accurately for forty-two days, where they have no sabbaths, no weeks, nor any other way of reckoning but to count the days as they passed one by one. At Turnip mountain they keep the sabbath, and could therefore the more readily keep time.

One of the children in packing clothes last night to be in readiness to go with her parents this morning, put up a number of garments, of different sizes, which were not her own, and among these a tablecloth belonging to the mission—Her parents were both here, but said they had no knowledge of the child's putting up any thing which did not belong to her. We had a long talk with them in the presence of the child, and endeavored to impress on their minds the importance of parental government, as enjoined in the word of God, and told them if they had not been present we should have felt it our duty to correct the child; but as they were here, and the evil had been committed while they were here, we thought more proper that the correction should be by their hands, and should leave the child with them.

[Sept.] 26. Mr. Butrick left us again for Taloney. Br. Parker went with him to pack up some things which they have left at Taloney, and to bring some clothing which is at this time needed for himself, and family.

[Sept.] 27. Mr. Hoyt went out on pastoral visits for the first time since Dr. Butler was confined. Purchased 60 bu. potatoes at the ware house and brought one waggon load home.

Finished two small bridges, one over the mill race, just above the new floom, and the other over the small drain which runs between the race and the bottom land above it—The object in building these bridges is to get the timber, and wood from the bottom as we clear it.—We have now about 100 cords of coal and fire wood cut there, which should come off soon lest a rise in the creek take it away.

Meeting for business.

After seeking divine direction, and deliberately considering the question, Will it be expedient at this time to take measures for commencing a school in Willsvalley? Resolved, That br. Ellis go to

Willsvalley, take with him br. John Arch to interpret and propose to the chiefs to commence a school there as soon as they wish, if they will provide a suitable house, and board the teacher at their own expense.

Sept. 28. Dr. Butler after being about same this morning, and attending to considerable business, took his bed, affected with a pain in the head, followed with fever. We think he has gone beyond his strength and taken some cold.

Sab. [Sept.] 29. Dr. Butler still affected with the headache—some better than yesterday afternoon.
Mr. Chamberlin, and his interpreter, spent the sabbath at the preaching place 12 miles south. They returned this evening—had an agreeable meeting.

[Sept.] 30. Dr. Butler has had a chill, followed with fever, and we fear his relapse will prove a serious one.
An aged white man with a Cherokee family who resided about 20 miles from us died a few days ago. His son called to day requesting one of the brethren to preach a funeral sermon at his house. As br. Butrick is absent & Father Hoyt, & br. Chamberlin expect to leave us tomorrow, he was told no one could go. He replied he would wait till they returned.

Oct. 1. Father Hoyt, & br. Chamberlin left us for the purpose of performing an agency in Tennessee to solicit donations to the Board, and make arrangements for our obtaining supplies from that quarter. With painful emotions they gave us the parting hand on account of the continued feeble health of the family.
Br. Butler continues quite feeble had another chill, and considerable fever to day. Br. Parker arrived from Taloney in good health.
A Cherokee woman from Creekpath brought us a letter with pleasing information from our br. & sis. there. The woman is a subject of serious impressions.

[Oct.] 2. Br's. Ellis, & John Arch left us for Willsvalley to make arrangements for commencing a local school. But four of the brethren are now left who are able to attend to any of the business here. Br. Parker is constantly employed in the kitchen. Br. Vail is employed in his family, as his wife continues quite unwell—gathering corn, and attending to various business about the house, and barn. Br. Blunt is attending to the sick, seeing to the business at the mills, and repairing

the boys tools. Br. Dean, and a hired blacksmith are constantly employed at the shop. It seems impossible for either of these brethren to leave their charges, and yet we have the following business which it seems extremely necessary should be done this fall.—That the Triphammer shop which is not half completed should be finished— That a large quantity of stone should be drawn the distance of two miles, and laid in a wall around our flooms to secure them from high water; that our race be cleaned, and enlarged so that we may obtain sufficient water for our mills, and shop; that 40 or 50 dollars be laid out on our mill-dam to prevent as some of the brethren suppose several hundred dollars cost next season (The earth the south east side of the mill dam is composed of loam. It is found lately that the water is soaking through this from the mill dam so as to form a little stream which is constantly enlarging.) Could a brother be employed with Cherokees, or with white men this might probable be secured with less expense than the sum already mentioned. Tho' hands might be obtained to do this work we fear it would not be done to purpose. That a small convenient washhouse be built across or near the race, which would probably before spring pay the expense in the health of our sisters. That our girls school house be plastered, and painted which would save to the mission $330,00. That considerable repairs be made to the boys cabins. That there be an additional covering to our lumber-house, dining room & kitchen. That, according to the direction of the Cor. Sec. a brick kiln be burned, and that our Ware-house have a floor, and rough ceiling, that our corn if any should be brought down the river might be safe from all intruders. According to the directions of the Cor. Sec. respecting money, and our estimate which we wish not to exceed, we see no way how this, or even a small part of this business can be accomplished.

Oct. 3. Two of the natives called on us for seed wheat. We engaged to the first one three bushels all that we could spare untill we ascertain what we want for our own use. Our miller again rec^d word that his family was sick. Tho' he had been here but a short time he has left us again. Unless we have some person who is well acquainted with the saw mill, and grist mill that can be depended on they will evidently soon be so damaged that we must send for a Millwright to repair them. If our resources would permit we should consider it our immediate duty to hire a good Sawyer, and Miller whom we should have to pay something like $300, a year. We are now paying common laborers $25 in money per month, more than we should be justified in doing were it not for sickness. These hands are assisting br. Vail, and br. Blunt in their charges.

Br. Ellsworth is in a very nervous state but able to walk with two assistants. He is recovering slowly. Sis. E. is able to sew a little, and attend some to the concerns in her room. Darius who did not have a run of the fever tho' he was brought quite low is recovering so fast that we hope he will be able to attend the boys school on their return. Those who were unwell at the creek walk from there to the mission house daily. One of the sisters is engaged in writing the journal as a brother dictates who is unable to write. Two of the sisters attend mostly to the sale of clothing, and accounts.

We learn from a traveller this evening that Messrs. Hoyt, and Chamberlin are detained about 25 miles from us on account of Mr. Hoyt's ill health.

[Oct.] 4. Br. Chamberlin returned late last evening to get a waggon. Finding it very fatiguing for Father Hoyt to ride on horseback he thought perhaps he could go in a waggon. He left us early this morning.

Sab. [Oct.] 6. Being destitute of a preacher our meeting was conducted by one of the laymen—had a sermon read in the forenoon & afternoon.—Towards evening a traveling man called wishing br. Butler to visit his Father at Mr. Coody's who had been travelling three days in a state of mental derangement, with his family. Br. Butler gave him some medicine but was unable to visit him.

[Oct.] 7. The travelling man who called yesterday for medicine came over this morning wishing some assistance in burying his Father who died last evening at 10 Ock. About 3 Ock the corpse was brought. All the exercises we could have, for want of preaching was prayer, & singing. He left a widow, and 13 children to mourn his loss. They were moving from near Darien Geo. to the upper part of Alabama or lower part of Tennessee to exchange a sickly neighborhood for one more healthy.

Oct. 9. Br's. Ellis, & J. Arch returned—were prospered according to expectation. Br. C. expects the house to be in readiness next week. His boarding place is about 2 miles from the school house.

Sister Nancy Thompson hearing that her sister was very sick in the vicinity of Maryville was anxious to visit her. No way could be provided for safe conveyance unless some one of the mission family accompanied her. Br. Blunt (being almost worn out by attending on the sick) not being able to labor much, it was supposed it would be much for his health to take a short journey. It was also supposed by his accompanying a person to Blount County who was well acquainted with many of the inhabitants might, particularly at this time, be instrumental in preparing the way for donations in provisions &c. He accordingly left us this morning accompanied with sis. Nancy expecting to be gone about two weeks.

150 fish were caught in the trap this morning.

[Oct.] 11. Br. & sis. Potter arrived from Creekpath.

[Oct.] 12. This morning about 10 ock br. & sis. Proctor arrived.[65] Most of their journey was uncommonly pleasant when compared with that of former missionaries. They manifest much gratitude on account of the constant kindness they recd. on the way from the well wishes of the dear Redeemers cause. Towards the last of the journey br. P. experienced much inconvenience from the intermitting fever. A few hours after his arrival he had a turn of the fever & ague.

Recd a small bundle of clothing from the female Newel Academy Tennessee.

[Oct.] 13. Exercises as usual. Br. Potter preached.—
Sister Dean was confined—has a fine son.[66]

[Oct.] 15. We have to day 22 Cherokees at work for us clearing the race and chopping. They are all from br. Reece's neighborhood, and are at work for the purpose of getting money to pay their annual tax.[67]

[Oct.] 17. Br. & sis. Potter left us for the purpose of visiting br. Hicks, and from thence to go to Taloney. Br. Butler is recovering health and is able to attend to a little business having had no ague & fever for a week past. Br. Proctor is also gaining health.
Br. Conger returned. His health is somewhat improved, but he has still a pain in his breast attended with a slight cough.

[Oct.] 19. The large field was cleared of corn and fodder. The amount of corn was 315 bu. The labor done in the field was estimated at $101. The corn gathered from the field near the barn was 11 bushels, and from that near the school house 10. We can make no calculation on the green corn used. It was principally gathered from the two last mentioned fields.

Rec^d a letter from Br. Kingsbury containing the painful intelligence of the death of sis. Kingsbury.[68] On the 15th Sept. she sweetly fell asleep in Jesus.

[Oct.] 20. Sabbath—Exercises forenoon and afternoon. Two sermons were read.

[Oct.] 21. Account of smith's shop from August 13 to Sept. 30.

Rec^d in cash ———————————————	$14,00
" Do-produce ———————————	4,06
Do-labor———————————————	6,81½
Work done for the mission———————	25,02¼
Do for Creek Path ———————	,75
Charged to customers———————	8,31¼
Work done for the triphammer shop ———	17.05
	76,01
Expenses of the shop	7.12½
	68,88½

To day we expected the mail carrier from Knoxville would bring us some Per. Bark, but we are disappointed.[69] Owing to the sickness this season we have used considerable bark. It was supposed we had a good supply but for three weeks past we have had but little. To day brs. Proctor, Butler, & Darius have a turn of the ague & fever. A hired man, and one of br. Congers children have also the intermitting fever. Various substitutes for the Bark have been used with good effects but proved not sufficient to break the fever. We see more & more the importance of having a good supply of medicine constantly on hand as no general supply can be obtained short of Knoxville.

Meeting for business. Resolved that measures be taken as far as possible to furnish br. Proctor with the articles mentioned by him in a list presented this evening.—

Resolved that brs. Potter, Proctor, & Butler be a Com. to make proposals to the brethren concerning the buildings to be erected at Hightower.

[Oct.] 23. This forenoon br. Blunt and sis. Nancy Thompson returned from Tennessee. We had great occasion to be thankful when we found they had brought us a little Bark.

Special meeting for business, Resolved that we hire Mr. Cary to burn 2000 bushels of coal.[70]

Br. & sis. Potter returned from Taloney—found the family there well.

[Oct.] 25. Br. & sis. Potter left us for Creekpath.

[Oct.] 26. Brs. Proctor and Butler rode half a mile to the mill dam. Br. Butler has not been so far from the mission building before for eight weeks, having had in this time the bilious cholic, remitting, and intermitting fevers.[71]

[Oct.] 27. *Sabbath.* Rainy the fore part of the day. Two sermons read as on previous sabbaths.

A Cherokee man and his wife with a small girl came, as they say, twenty miles this morning (in season to attend the first meeting) for the sole purpose of receiving religious instruction. Neither of them speak English. They appear quite serious particularly the woman & wished some way might be devised so that they might keep the day of the week, for they wished to observe the sabbath. After some conversation respecting the best way one of the Cherokee laborers mentioned his manner of keeping the day of the week correctly. This was by setting the first letter of each day of the week beginning with monday in a horizontal line on a strip of paper. The new Cherokee said that if he forgot to notice his paper one day he would lose his reckoning. He then suggested this addition: to paste his paper upon a flat, and thin piece of wood, and underneath each letter burn a hole, and on monday put a stick in the hole under the letter M and each succeeding day move the stick.

[Oct.] 28. After some further conversation with the Cherokee and his wife upon the way of salvation they left us promising to come again soon and leave a little daughter of theirs to attend school.

Meeting for business, Resolved, That br. Ellis have charge of the boys school for the present. Resolved that br. Blunt be released from the mills, and mechanical business. Resolved, that br. Vail have charge of the mills.

Our schollars are returning.—In contrasting the present situation of the mission family with what it was at the time the children left us, we have great occasion to speak of the goodness and mercy of our God. At that time br. and sis. Elsworth, Br. Butler, br. Darius, sis. Vail, and two hired men were unable to wait on themselves. When br. J. Arch was absent for a Physician neither of the seven persons mentioned were able to rise from their beds without assistance. A part of the time br's. Chamberlin and Butrick had symptoms of the fever, and were hardly able to be about to see to any business. Br. Elsworth was for several days considered in a dangerous condition. Sister E. was brought into a weak, and helpless state but not considered dangerous. One of the hired men was also for a while dangerously ill. O that the Lord would sanctify to us this season of affliction. All are now convalescing, also able to labor some excepting br. Elsworth (whose sickness is followed by an afflicting nervous complaint,) and sis. Vail. Br. Elsworth walks about but little. We trust the Pru. Com. see and feel the importance of either sending a physician to this place who can be wholly devoted to his profession, or relieving br. Butler in his charges.[72]

We understand by private letters, that an opinion is prevailing at the North, that we are burdened with clothing, that we have it at such an amount it is impossible to dispose of it. This is confirmed by those who have lately arrived from N. England. The idea was red [read]; by at least some, from what was said in the Herald in perhaps a note by the Editor; about a year ago. Some partial articles of clothing we may have to such an amount that they cannot be used at present or disposed of for the benefit of the mission. Of the Blankets, Bed quilts, Comfortables, and Coverlids, we had last spring we have not left more than twelve excepting those in use. We now refuse selling. We have no more shirts, pantaloons, hats, shoes, large vests, no frocks large enough for girls fourteen years old, and no factory of any kind. If it is asked how the articles have been disposed of? We answer, some have been sold for ready money, one hundred and fifty dollars worth exchanged for beef, considerable for other provisions, several hundred dollars worth went to Local schools, and considerable given Cherokees & white people for labor. Blankets, quilts, Coverlids and comfortables have been sold for from two to ten dollars, each. Wool hats at two dollars, mens shoes at $2,00 and mens shirts at $1.50. White factory at 37½cts. per yd, striped at 56 cts. All of these articles are very saleable.

Many of the Natives esteem it a great privilege to bring various sorts of provisions here & exchange for blankets &c. Others deem it as great a privilege to labor for clothing. We have in some instances had eight and ten at work at a time for clothing. This is the season of the year when they need this article most; yet it seems now we must deny them. When we can profitably employ the Cherokees we esteem it our duty and privilege, as it may be of great benefit to them in a spiritual as well as for temporal point of view.

J.C. Elsworth, Henry Parker, Sylvester Ellis, A.E. Blunt, Elizur Butler

Mr. Frederick Elsworth arrived on the 29th all in good health.

E. Butler

Brainerd Mission Journal

Oct. 29 1822. Rev. Mr. Wilson and lady called on us on their way to join Mr. Stewart in the Chickasaw nation.

[Oct.] 30. Br. & Sr. Wilson left us this morning—Though their visit was short it was highly gratifying to us. O that the Lord would send forth laborers to these western wiles untill they shall bud and blossom as the rose, and resound with the praises of redeeming love.

This afternoon we had the gratification to welcome as assistant laborers at this establishment Mr. Frederick Elsworth and wife from Vermont.[73] His brother [Oliver] a minor accompanied him, also Miss Burnham from Lenox, Massachusetts on her way to join the mission at Elliot.

[Oct.] 31. The sweet potatoes which had not been previously used in the family were dug and brought in—they measured 70 bushels.

Nov. 4. Meeting for business. Agreed to hire Thomas James for one year at $10 a month to be paid half money and half in clothing.—Resolved that Br. F. Elsworth have charge of the farm; and of cutting and drawing logs for the saw-mill; also that he have under his charge (if needed) the span of horses he brought on and 3 yoke of oxen.—Agreed to build a wash house by the mill race opposite the mission house 16 by 22 feet.—Resolved, that in addition to the mills br. Vail have charge of the horses and oxen not otherwise engaged—of the hogs, cows & other cattle when up, & of the drawing not otherwise assigned.

Agreed that the steward provide br. Vail with a hired man.

The Com. on Hightower buildings report, that in their opinion the following plan of buildings should be adopted Viz. One double cabin one part 18 by 22, the other 18 x 20, leaving a covered space between of 10 feet. The school house 24 by 30 and such out buildings as br. Proctor may think proper. Report approved & accepted.

Nov. 5. Dr. Butler & br. Proctor set out for Hightower, to look out a site for the buildings, and make preparations for br. Proctors family— They took br. John Arch for interpreter. We fear their health is still too feeble to endure the fatigues and exposures of the journey, but are anxious to have the business there progressing as fast as possible. This afternoon Mr. Hoyt, and Mr. Chamberlin returned.—They have been unable to prosecute their business to the extent they might have done had it not been for Mr. Hoyts feeble health, yet we hope some good has been done—They were very kindly received by professors of religion wherever they went, & considerable donations of corn have been obtained for the mission.

[*Nov.*] 9. Mr. Butrick went out for the purpose of preaching tomorrow (15 miles up the river) a funeral sermon, which had been promised after Messrs. Hoyt, & Chamberlin should have returned—He will probably go thence to the Highwassee, & be out several days. Mr. Chamberlin went out expecting to preach at Mr. Hicks' tomorrow, go thence to the Hightower, and there take br. John Arch with him on a tour of several weeks.

Sab. [*Nov.*] 10. Both sermons in English—Br. Reece though present in the morning, not being able to attend and interpret in the afternoon.

[*Nov.*] 12. Great rains yesterday and to day. Chickamauga rising very fast.

[*Nov.*] 13. Br. F. Elsworth, & others employed in floating logs from the new clearing—The water being higher than usual at this season of the year. Mr. Chamberlin returned—& with him the dear Choctaw youth McKee, & Israel Folsom. These young men spent a few days here when lads going on to the school. McKee four years ago last May, and Israel about 5 months after. It was truly gratifying to see them now returning to their people with the advantages of their admirable improvement in manners, in school education, and in the knowledge of the doctrines of Christ, and above all to find in one of them such evidence of a renewal after the divine image—Mr. Chamberlin, being unable to proceed on account of the rains and highwater, will continue here untill his interpreter returns.

[Nov.] 14. Dr. Butler returned. We were surprised to see him at this time—supposing the creeks to have been impassable—and he had been equally surprised to see the water in this part of the country so high, there having been very little rain at Hightower and Taloney— Appearances at Hightower are pleasing, but the principal chiefs being absent attending council it was thought not best to commence the building untill they should return.

Mr. Butrick returned.—Meeting for business, Resolved that sister Burnham, with McKee & Israel Folsom be permitted to take a waggon and horses for their conveyance to Mayhew—they leaving the same there for the use of the Choctaw mission.

Nov. 16. Mr. Butrick went out to spend the sabbath in Br. Reeces neighborhood. Mr. Chamberlin being unwell and having no interpreter will spend sabbath here.

Sab. [Nov.] 17. Br. & sister Dean presented their infant son for baptism—He is named Chester Wright. After the baptism br. Blunt, & sister Harriet Elsworth were married in the presence of the congregation.

[Nov.] 18. Meeting for business, Resolved that Mr. Hoyt, & br. Vail assist the steward in taking an Inventory of the articles that br. Conger is to take from the mission. Resolved, that Deacon Elsworth have charge of plaistering the chamber of the girls school house.—The brethren appointed to take an Inventory of articles to be taken by br. Conger, asked for definite instructions.—Resolved that they take an account of all articles except wearing apparel, and affix a valuation to each article, except those which br. Conger brought into the mission without a valuation.

[Nov.] 20. The old king (Pathkiller) called to make us a visit. He attended the wednes. Lecture, made a short speech to the congregation (a number of Cherokees being present) after which he visited both schools. Mr. E.[Elijah] Hicks coming in early in the evening we were providentially furnished with a good interpreter. The king appeared much pleased with this opportunity of conversing with us—expressed great satisfaction in what he was again permitted to see here, and in what was doing for the general instruction of his people. He spake with approbation of the laws which the young chiefs are introducing, so different from their former customs, and

manifested a pleasing hope concerning the future prospects of the nation, mixed with some foreboding fears.[74]

[Nov.] 21. Br. John Arch has returned from Hightower. When he left there the chiefs had got home from the council, and had appointed wednesday the 19th for the people to meet and make arrangements for putting up the buildings, and to do any other business which should be necessary for the school: but as it was expected Mr. Chamberlin would be here waiting for his interpreter it was thought best for John to be on his way before the meeting. Br. John was told that some of the lower class of people, influenced by certain white men who occassionally trade among them, were making some objections against having a school—But he says the chiefs pay no attention to them.

[Nov.] 22. The king being detained yesterday by rain, spent a second night with us. He left us to day with warm expressions of gratitude and good will.

Sab. [Nov.] 24. Two young men members of the school were examined today as to their hope in Christ, and admitted candidates for baptism. They are supposed about 20. One of them is a full Cherokee could speak no English when he came, and now speaks but poorly—The other is a half white, and was taught to speak English when young. They are both in the most forward class in the school, possessing natural abilities of some promise.[75]

[Nov.] 25. Br. Conger, and family removed from the mission expecting to go to a place which he has purchased in Blount Co. Tenn. Sister Burnham, and the young Choctaws who are returning to their people left us to pursue their journey. Mr. Chamberlin, and his interpreter go with them as far as Creek path; and from thence they will have but 200 miles to Mayhew. May the God of Jacob guide them through.
Meeting for business, Concluded that br. Frederick Elsworth move into the house left by Br. Conger, and that the hired men board there. Resolved that a dividend of groceries be made for the creek, and that the proportion be according to the number of adult persons in the mission family, allowing for Mr. Hoyt [*hole in ms*] portions.[76] The questions was asked shall we recommend to the Pru. Com. to purchase br. Milo Hoyt's improvement? Answed in the affirmative.

[Nov.] 26. Mr. Butrick being about to go [to] Taloney and Hightower, sister Nancy Thompson went with him in order to visit her brothers family, and perhaps remain with them, as she has heard they are sick.

[Nov.] 28. Br. Milo Hoyt cannot consistently wait for an answer respecting his improvement untill we can hear from the Pru. Com. He has now an opportunity, (if he takes it immediately) of getting a place in Wills valley that will suit him, and a person is now here wishing to take his improvement if we do not. He offered his place to the mission sometime ago, and told us a few weeks since that he thought it his duty to dispose of it, and take that place in Wills Valley. The question was then brought before the brethren, and it was thought not best for the mission to take his place. Under this impression he has made his arrangements, but still has it in his power to give us the refusal. Considering the difficulties that may arise from having a stranger, possessing large property, settled so near us, and the advantages of having more opened land for immediate improvement it was thought best to agree at once to take the place.

[Nov.] 29. Several boys of the school (Jeremiah Evarts for one) have manifested a desire to be sent to the F. M. School. We think these desires have been excited by seeing the improvement of the young Choctaws, and hearing from them concerning the good people of the north. We hear also that some of the elder Cherokees have (by the same means) been excited greatly to desire, that their sons may be favored with the same privileges. One man said, he loved his children as well as any body, but he should be willing to have them all go, even if he should never see them again—and that he was determined to send at least one, if he did it at his own expense.—

Ard Hoyt, Henry Parker, E Dean, E. Butler

My Dear Sir—

As you may perhaps be surprised to see the first notice, in our Journal of the Purchase of Br. Milo Hoyts improvements.
We had not forgotten what you said to us on that subject, but circumstances seemed to call for an immediate decision—Some weeks since Br. Milo offered us the improvements, (as he was wishing to move to Wills Valley) but we declined taking them from what had already been said by you on the subject. Mr. Fox Taylor a wealthy half breed having about a dozen negroes made proposals to Br. Milo to

purchase his place[77]—It was the opinion of the Br. generally that it would be duty for us to purchase the place under existing circumstances—

Mr. Taylor was anxious to know immediately.

There are about 23 acres cleared & fenced well & nearly the whole will do for corn & Potatoes the ensuing year—He has a good well which some of the sisters say is preferable to creek water for washing, a double Cabin all which he offers for $300,00, $30, in cash & the rest in trade such as cattle, clothes &c.

Yours with respect
J.C. Elsworth
Elizur Butler

I have now about 14 pair of trace chains promised & shall probably want as many more during the year. They can probably be got in Boston for $1,00 a pair & here they sell for $2,50 & $3,00. There is no profit in making them here for $3,00. Could you send me 25 pair I should be very glad.

yours affectionately,
E. Dean

Brainerd Mission Journal

Dec. 2. The water again high. Br. F. Elsworth, Oliver Elsworth, and five Cherokees are engaged, with canoes, floating logs (and trees for fire wood) from the new clearing above the mills.

Meeting for business. Agreed that Br. Blunt repair the cabin by the tool house for his family, and that the cabin behind the kitchen be removed for the boys—also that some of the young cattle be killed for beef—if needed—Agreed also that Messrs. Timberlake, Brown, and Tailor[78] and Mr. McPhearson (if to be obtained) be hired with their teams to haul corn from the ware-house, when it arrives—& that Deacon Elsworth be furnished with a horse to go and try to hire a girl for sister Vail. Our reason for proposing to hire these teams to haul the corn as it arrives is, that the corn cannot be considered safe to remain in the ware-house, as the streams are all now full & heavy rains might raise the Tennessee so as to bring its water into the ware-house, as was the case two years ago. When this house was built it was supposed to be above the highest water, but as an uncommon rise of the river has reached it, we choose to be on the safe side.

[Dec.] 3. The ground is covered with a light snow, and the day quite cold. Began to kill pork to lay down for the coming year. At 12 ock ice formed upon the north side of a killed hog, hanging in a fair sun: the boys in the school were obliged to suspend writing on account of the freezing of their ink. We sometimes regret that we have not a Thermometer that we might at least ascertain the degree of cold and heat in our very great and sudden changes. Not a week since a brother who lately came from the north found the nights so warm that he could not sleep.

[Dec.] 5. On this and the two preceding days we killed 65 hogs, of our own raising—18 had been killed before since the first of September—83 in the whole—W^t of those killed at this time 7031.—Killed before 2298—total 9329—average a fraction over 112 for each hog.—

[Dec.] 6. Col^n A. B. Campbell brought notice this morning that he had brought the boat with corn, and landed it a little above the ware house—He has brought only 610 bushels of donated corn—As he was obliged to come off with the boat sooner than was at first expected, some of the donors from high waters and other circumstances, did not get their corn on in season.

Donors from whom corn is received are,

John Montgomery	50	Andrew Early	10	Saml Houston & others	40
James Berry	30	Robert Scott	12	George Ewing	12
Wm Keith	15	A.B. Campbell	15	James Ewing	12
Doct A. McGhee	55	Benj^m Alexander	15	Robert Hook	12
James McNutt	20	Wm Wallace	15	Thomas Caldwell	12
J Houston	26	J Gillespie	15	Wm Ewing	12
John M. Rankin	10	John Rankin	15	John Ewing	12
Thomas Hunter	20	John Carson	5	John M. Colack	8
Ja^s W. Stephenson	12	Charles McLure	12	Thos Dearmin	5
Ja^s Henderson	10	James Breant	12	Nathaniel Wood	4
George Henderson	10	John Wood	5	John Eagleton	8-3/4
Robert Woods	6	Wm Gillespie	12	Asa Anderson Junr	10
Elias Deburk	6	Joseph Tilford	40	Joseph Alexander	10

These donations were all from the upper part of Blount county.

[Dec.] 9. Meeting for business. Resolved, that the vote respecting a brother travelling over ten miles without permission be rescinded.— Question. Have the brethren any objections to paying Mr. R. Taylor 2,50 & br. McPhearson 2,00 a day for the use of their team.
Answ^d None.
Resolved, that one of our own teams or one that is hired, be employed constantly at drawing coal wood untill it is all drawn.
Two hired teams brought corn to day from the ware-house—and two other teams came in for the purpose of hauling tomorrow.

[Dec.] 10. Deacon Elsworth went out to engage pork and try to hire a girl for sister Vail in Tennessee.

[Dec.] 11. The boy called Horace Loomis who was discontented last summer, and by his fathers pursuasion or command induced to continue in the school, left us to day without giving us any notice of his intention to leave the school or in any way manifesting dissatisfaction to any of the mission family.—The boys say (since his departure) that he has been often talking about leaving the school.[79]
Br. Proctor returned this evening and brought with him Brs. Bascom & Gibbs and a principle chief from Hightower, Sis Nancy Thompson also returned with them.[80] We learn by Br. Bascom that the young men from the F. M. School have all arrived safe in the nation, and some of them are expected to be here in two or three days—The health of Elias Boudinot and John Ridge has improved on the journey.[81]—
It appears that some of the people of Hightower have had their zeal dampened by reports and sayings of certain white men who occasionally trade among them, and therefore do not proceed with the buildings as fast as might otherwise have been expected. They have put up the body of a dwelling house 18 x 20 & put on the roof. The buildings were going on so slow that Brs. Proctor & Butrick thought best for br. Proctor to return and bring the chief with him, that he might learn what was doing here and in other places, and that Br. Proctor might advise with the brethren here as to the expediency of hiring some help to forward the buildings.
It appears that many from Alabama and Georgia are so sanguine in their expectations that the Cherokee will give up that part of the country that they are exploring it to look the best places for settlement, and some have actually come on with their families

supposing the land had been ceded.—While so many white people are grasping for their land it is no wonder if the poor misinformed Cherokees sometimes suspect that missionaries (under cover) have the same object in view.

[Dec.] 12. Meeting for business. Br. Proctor present—After hearing Br. Proctor report respecting the state of business at Hightower—Concluded it would be best to hire a man to assist in making preparations there: & that the Cherokee called Wicked Jack (if to be obtained) he hired for that purpose.
Resolved that Br. Vail go with the 4 horse team to take Br. Proctors goods to Hightower—& that Br. Proctor take from this place three cows for the use of his family & the old one for beef. Resolved that measures be taken to hire four of the expected youths from the F.M. School, one for this place and one for each local school.

[Dec.] 13. Dean Elsworth returned this morning, having accomplished the business on which he went.
Mr. Chamberlin, and br. J. Arch returned—Sis. Burnham and her company left Creek Path on wednesday the 4th inst. Mr. Chamberlin accompanied them 10 miles ~~from Creek Path~~. As they travelled comfortably and with good speed we hope they are by this time near to Mayhew.
Meeting for business—Mr. Chamberlin found the people in Wills Valley still anxious to have a family attached to their school—They live so scattering that there is no place to which their children can generally be collected at a school and board at home[82]—They propose to put up all necessary buildings for the family and school and to provide food for such children as cannot go home for their board, and thus have them boarded at the school. Therefore Resolved that Mr. Chamberlin remove with his family to Wills Valley as soon as suitable buildings are erected, provided we can obtain a teacher for that place.
We have this night 39 horses to feed, besides those usually kept at Brainerd, last night we had 35, and have not had less than 25 any night this week; 20 of those now here belong to teams in our employ, bringing up corn.

[Dec.] 14.—The girls of the school, with a little assistance from one or two of the sisters, have quilted a bed quilt on each of the four evenings past. These quilts are made from old cloth and fetch from six to seven dollars each.—They were made particularly to sell to the Cherokees & please them very much.

The teams brought in the last of the corn from the warehouse—
This day the trip hammer was put in operation.
David Tawcheeche & Kapooly with the baggage waggon arrived this evening.[83] Coln Campbell and Mr. Alexander having taken the corn boat to Huntsville arrived this evening on their return home.

Sab. [Dec.] 15. Br. Hall arrived early this morning with Thomas Basil[84]—Mr. Bascom preached in the forenoon, but thought it unsafe for him to do more than deliver the sermon and offer the concluding prayer on account of a cold which has affected his lungs. In other respects his health is improved by the journey—At the close of the afternoon exercises Br. Gibbs addressed the congregation and offered the last prayer. Such witnesses of the power of the gospel, by the grace of God, to civilize & christianize Indians, we think may well encourage those who are engaged in this work, and at least suspend the opposition of those who would discourage it as a hopeless undertaking.

[Dec.] 16. Mr. Bascom & br. Gibbs set out this morning on their way to Mayhew by Creek Path. They left their waggon with us, and one horse; took one horse from us that was supposed better able to perform the journey & proceeded on horse back.
We requested Br. John Arch to endeavor to learn from Mr. Beamer (the principal chief from Hightower) the present feelings of his people, and also his own feelings, respecting the projected school there.[85] He says Mr. Beamer favors it, but says many people from Georgia have been talking against the school, and that some of the chiefs and many others retain their word. He does not think so many children as was expected will at first attend the school: but thinks the disaffected will after a while see the benefit of the school and send their children.
Meeting for business. Brs. Hall & Proctor present. Br. Hall was permitted to make arrangements with Thomas Basil as interpreter for Taloney—& also to hire a man to labor at that place. As the Cherokee man proposed at the last meeting to be hired for Hightower, chooses to stay here, therefore Resolved that Thomas James go and labor at Hightower.—Question. Can any arrangements be made to assist the steward so that he can have time to purchase our supply of pork, & prepare the accounts to forward to the Treasurer—Ans. Br. J.C. Elsworth take charge of the trading to releive [relieve] the steward. Resolved that Br. Ellis have charge of the school. As it appears we

have no horse that can be spared for Mr. Chamberlin that is suitable for him to ride, Therefore, Resolved that he be permitted to buy a horse for his particular use—Our pork might have been engaged early without going after it, but the steward then mailed for instructions from Boston. The season is now so far advanced that he can wait no longer.

[Dec.] 17. Colⁿ Campbell & Mr. Alexander, having spent sabbath and monday with us, visited both schools, and joined with us in several precious devotional seasons, left us this morning to return to their families. Mr. Alexander had never visited the station before—We feel that this visit has added to our particular acquaintance & friends one more, who will exert in Blount Co. an influence favorable to the mission.—Br. Hall left us in company with the above visiting brethren, expecting to go to the Agency, attend to some business in Tennessee near that place, and thence return to Taloney.

[Dec.] 18. Mr. McCoy, (a chief from Wills Valley,) called to know our decission respecting a family's going there.[86] He is greatly pleased with their prospects—says the people will come in from a distance of 25 miles to put up the buildings—they have plenty of pork and corn—and there will be no want of provisions for the children, that cannot go home to board. ~~They are now opening~~ A waggon road ~~in no place less than 18 feet wide~~ is now opened from the Tennessee river, through the Valley to the southwestern boundary of the nation, a distance of one hundred miles ~~90 miles of it are already completed~~. The contemplated cite for the school is on or near this road, and about equally distant from each end of it, so that a preacher settled there will have an opening of 50 miles each way for his labors up and down the Valley—crossing the mountain 10 miles east is one of our present preaching places, and 27 miles is Turnip mountain. The south-western end of this road is 35 miles from Creek Path—Mr. Chamberlin & his interpreter left us on a short preaching tour—They expect to be at Turnip Mountain next sabbath, and return this way so as to be at Wills town the sabbath following.

[Dec.] 19. Br. Proctor left us to return to Hightower. Br. Vail went with the large waggon loaded with such articles as it was thought best to take from this place, and a hired man to assist by the way in driving three cows and a fat ox, and to labor a short time when there. The old chief returns with them, we think with favorable impressions. On

account of sister Proctors feeble health and particular circumstances, she will remain at Brainerd untill spring.

[Dec.] 20. We have recvd the following boxes of clothing Viz., One from Salisbury V^t valued at $63,42 left for the use of the school at Taloney—One from first Society of Ashford Con. containing articles from Westford second Society in Ashford valued at $40 with $3 in money: articles from the first Soc. were not valued, with these there was also $1,00 in money—and one box from the centre Meeting house Mite Society Oglethorpe Co. Geo. valued at $37,75—Letters were written to each of these places to day, giving notice of the safe arrival of their respective donations.
Thomas Basil having visited his relations in this vicinity returned to us yesterday, and to day left us on his return to Taloney.

[Dec.] 21. The school boys with Br. Ellis, have cut and split fit for the fire, and laid up in piles 16-1/2 cords of wood in one week and one morning over: Br. Blunt being too much engaged in coopering to go out with them at this time. Br. Mills, not knowing that any one from us was to be in his neighborhood at this time, came in. Mr. Chamberlin's rout being circuitous, Br. Mills did not meet him or hear of him by the way.

[Dec.] 23. Mr. Chamberlin with Br. John Arch, his interpreter, returned. Hearing on their way out that Br. Mills had gone to Brainerd, they made their tour a little shorter than was at first intended; being anxious to get to Wills town as soon as practicable.
About a dozen Cherokee men and women from different parts were providentially with us this evening; and brother Reece. After early supper and family prayers they were seated in the common room, a Cherokee hymn sung, prayer offered by Br. Mills & another hymn. Religious conversation being proposed the visitors listened with solemn attention, but had nothing to say. The three Cherokee brethren spake in turn, a discourse of some length was interpreted, the three brethren again took the subject, and the long evening was concluded by a Cherokee hymn. The visitors appeared attentive and serious through the whole, but no one made enquiry or reply. Such opportunities of communicating instruction would much more frequently occur, if we had always a good interpreter at hand.
In meeting for business Mr. Chamberlin brought in a list of articles which it was supposed would be needed in the family at Willstown,

consisting of kitchen and table furniture, agricultural tools, meat casks, cows &c which was approved and accepted.

As we are informed that Calvin Jones has returned from Br. Thompsons to his fathers and is wishing to come and finish learning the miller trade here, it was determined that he be permitted to return to the shop here, provided he will come on such terms as we shall think proper—& that Mr. Hoyt write to Mr. Hicks requesting him to converse with Calvin on the subject.

Dec. 24. One of the large boys who left the school last summer without leave, and was received again in the fall on his acknowledgment & promise to continue steady in the school & behave well left us sometime last night without any known cause except his own changable feelings. He has taken with him a blanket and some clothing which we had furnished him. Perhaps he thought he had a right to take them: but we consider all clothing, blankets &c which we furnish the children of the school only as given for their use while here, unless we see fit to give them when, by our consent, they leave the school.[87] We therefore require this youth to send back all that he has taken from us, and br. Mills says he will see that he does it.

[Dec.] 26. Mr. Chamberlin and his interpreter left us for Wills town, and Br. Mills to return to his family—

Late this evening Mr. Butrick returned, bringing with him John Vann, Elias Boudinot, & Stand, a brother of Elias.[88]

[Dec.] 28. Mr. Butrick with br. John Vann went into Br. Reece's neighborhood, and expects to spend sabbath there. John Vann's brother Joseph, who has large property and a large family, wishes him to make his house his home, and is unwilling to have him make any permanent engagement with us as interpreter. He has however consented that he should spend a few months in this way—

Elias Boudinot thinks it his duty to spend the winter with his mother. He and the four other pious young men who returned with him appear to be devoted to the cause, and much engaged to do all in their power for the instruction of their people: we trust this will be found a great acquisition to the strength of the mission: and that their appearance and conversation will do away many prejudices.

Sab. [Dec.] 29. Mr. Butrick and his interpreter returned this evening.

The wing partition between the girls school and working rooms was raised, and all the children with the mission family, and several visitors, were convened this evening, in our large room, for religious worship, & to give our young Cherokee brothers an opportunity to speak to the children. Brs. Boudinot & Vann both prayed, one in English and one in Cherokee, and Br. Vann addressed the children in his own tongue at considerable length.

[Dec.] 30. Br. Boudinot & Vann, with some others, spent the day with us, and visited both schools.—

[Dec.] 31. Acct. of Blacksmith shop from Oct. 1 to Dec. 31 is derived viz.   C^r

By recvd in cash $31,25, in product 56,81 in labor 36,29 $124,35
"dto Iron 7,68 Work done for mission, including local
    schools ,   116,55   <u>124.23</u>
                                          248.58

    charged to customers $77
            D^r

To repair of tools 10,07, Iron 7,68   17,75
To hire & board of man to work in shop   <u>56.00</u>
Balance in favor of shop, inclusive of what is charged
to customer which will come into the acct when paid   <u>73.75</u>
                                          <u>$174,83</u>

Ard Hoyt, Elizur Butler, J.C. Elsworth

Brainerd Jan. 6th 1823

Dear Sir,

    Soon after you left here there arose something of a question concerning the duty of the committee you appointed. We found a difference of opinion on the subject, and felt a delicacy, on our part, (as we recd no particular instructions from you) towards performing what we supposed was required of us. It seems that perhaps a majority of the brethren supposed that you had substituted this committee for the superintendent and that their only business was to superintend under the directions of the brethren the temporal concerns of the mission; or in other words relieve Mr. Hoyt so that his time might be occupied wholly in the concerns of the church. Your committee could not reconcile this with your direction for them to meet every monday to plan business for the following ten days, or your idea that there would be but little business for the brethren to attend to in the general meeting—We concluded to write you immediately on the subject, but on a little reflection, and particularly considering that your arrangements when here were made only for the summer and fall, we thought we could receive instructions from you until nearly the time other arrangements would be made.

We would not convey the idea that hardness has existed between the brethren and committee: it has been far otherwise, we have avoided as much as possible giving any occassion for it; in fact we have thought it best to remain almost inactive as a committee.

We have waited until the commencement of the new year and have heard of no different arrangements—as heretofore we consider ourselves [entirely?] under the direction of the Prude. Com. and if they still wish us to attend to the temporal concerns of the mission we wait for advice and instructions—If providence should relieve us from this responsible situation we would rejoice in it.

Yours with due affection and obedience
J.C. Elsworth , Elizur Butler, E. Dean

Jany 1st Br. Vail returned with the waggon from Hightower. He had a prosperous journey, came by way of Taloney for the purpose of bringing Br. Parkers beds and other articles he had left there. On their way out Brs. Vail & Proctor with Mr. Beamer, the chief stoped at Br. Hicks', & learned by him that the chief from Hightower (Mr. Beamer) was highly pleased with all he saw here—and said the children were well dealt by. He returns to his district much engaged to forward the school.

[Jan.] 3d Mr. Butrick having been detained here by ill health thru the sabbath went out this morning by request to preach a funeral sermon in Br. Reece's neighborhood. Brs. Boudinot & Vann went with him.

[Jan.] 4. Mr. Butrick & the two brothers who went with him returned in season to attend preparatory lecture—
Mr. Potter came in from Creek Path—

Sab. [Jan.] 5. Previous to the administration of the Lord's supper, James H. Williams and David Carter were baptized, and David Taucheeche, John Vann, and James Fields presented a letter of recommendation from the chh in Cornwall, and were received as members of this chh. Thomas Basil was also recommended in the same letter; but he, having gone to Taloney before the letter was received has not yet been formally admitted.
It is yesterday five years, since those of the mission family who have been here longest, came on to this consecrated ground. In a retrospect of these years, while we see much to lament and be ashamed of, we are constrained to exclaim "What hath God wrought?"[1] In this time there have been added to the chh here (exclusive of missionaries and assistants) 26 adults, (including Thomas Basil) we believe nearly the same number to the chh of the United Brethren—and at Creek Path 10 adults & 16 children of believers have been baptized at Creek Path, and 49 at this place—Near the frontier of Tennessee and Georgia numbers of this people within these five years have made a profession of faith in Christ and connected themselves with other denomina-

tions. In our several congregations we count some who are hopefully pious that have not yet made a public profession of religion. Although in comparison to the mass of this people, this is a day of small things, yet is in not to be despised. To God be all the praise.

[Jan.] 6. Mr. Butrick left us in company with Br. Vann. They go circuitously to Taloney, expecting to visit Br. Vann's mother and other relations by the way.

Meeting for business. Br. Potter present. Considering the importance of having a faithful man permanently to tend the mills, and that James Shelton (the man who has been employed by the mission from the first untill last spring, and always found faithful) is willing to return and take the mills if we can agree on the terms, but wishes to make a little trial before proposing the terms on which he will return, Therefore resolved that James Shelton be hired to tend the mills one month at $26.—Question by Br. Potter. Will the brethren send a boat load of boards and plank to Creek Path by the 1st of March? Ans. It is not certain, but we will if we can.   Question. Shall a joint letter be prepared to the Pru. Com. respecting a family to be sent to Creek Path as assistants? Ans^d-in affirmative. Question. Will the Com. recommend that a supply of salt be kept to be exchanged for corn, beans &c. Ans^d in affirmative.

[Jan.] 7. Mr. Potter left us in company with Br. Boudinot. Br. Boudinot has agreed to go with Mr. Potter to Creek Path, but must go first to Youkalooga [Oothcaloga] to his mothers to get cloathes &c. Mr. Potter will go with him and return to Creek Path that way.

[Jan.] 10. The Captain of the Light horse came, with four of his men, having in custody a man who has been suspected of stealing and killing hogs belonging to the mission. The officer says Mr. Hicks directed him to bring the suspected person here, and if their appeared sufficient evidence to justify a trial, to bring the case before the Judge. The circumstances are as follows.—From a company of hogs running in the woods the largest have from time to time been missing—the neighbors on both sides of us have been naming this man as one who was killing them, and intimating that he ought to be prosecuted— saying there was evidence enough against him. In this way we were almost compelled to do something, and get braced to enter a formal complaint lest we should fail in proof. It was thought best to write to Mr. Hicks, stating facts just so far as we knew them, and asking his advice. The first we have heard from our letter is the officer with the

accused under his guard—They will all wait here untill the witnesses have time to come in.

About two thirds of the schollars of both schools, consisting of the best spellers, were collected this evening in the girls school house, for an exercise in spelling—They took first a long lesson of about 300 words which had been given them in a difficult part of Websters spelling book—and afterwards spelled about as many more among which were nearly all the longest words in that book ~~which had not been given them as a lesson at this time~~ each schollar spelling in his turn—In the whole exercise but 6 words were missed, and each of these was in every case spelled correctly by the second scholar they were put to—not more than one missed in a hundred.

[Jan.] 11. Several witnesses came in the morning and testified respecting the accused man as having killed hogs in the woods &c to which he replied—We understand the captain of the Light horse considers the evidence sufficient to justify a trial. The company left us after dinner. This captain is the father of the boy we call Horace Loomis, who left the school on the 11 ult. He appears still anxious that this boy should continue at school and requests the privilege of bringing him back once more. As the father has always been steadfast, and the boy behaves well when here, we consented to try him again.

[Jan.] 13. In meeting for business—Decided that we have a new gate in the place of the old one at the Northeast end of the mission yard similar to the one across the lane in front of the yard—and that Br. Blunt have charge of building a poultry house and yard.

[Jan.] 16. The fish trap which had been broken down in time of highwater probably by some log or tree drifting over it was repaired this afternoon at the expense of many cold and wet feet, several of the brethren wading for some time in deep and cold water—We had expected to loose the benefit of taking fish through the best part of the season; and probably we have improved the only time we shall soon have when it could have been repaired, as rain this evening indicated a return of highwater.

[Jan.] 17. Rev. Messrs. Vancourt and Williamson, missionaries under the direction of the General assembly, on their way to Mississippi called on us.

[Jan.]18. Br. Thompson came in with a waggon from Hightower. He left all in good health. Br. Proctors goods had not been brought on as

was expected, & he had suffered some inconvenience and hindrance in completing the buildings from the want of tools which are thus left behind; but he had nevertheless been able to keep on with the work.

Sab. [Jan.] 19. Mr. Vancourt preached in the forenoon from Isa. 63:9, first clause, and Mr. Williamson in the afternoon from 1st John 5:4. In the evening the mission family and children being assembled, were addressed by each of our visiting brethren in turn. By all their discourses we have been instructed and edified, and have reason to be thankful to God and these his servants for this precious season.

[Jan.] 20. Messrs. Vancourt and Williamson continued with us and visited both the schools. They expressed satisfaction in the progress of the children, and encouraged them to go forward—In meeting for business the pecuniary accounts of the two Local schools for the last 6 months, as rendered by Mr. Potter and Br. Hall were read. Also a letter from Br. Proctor and one from Mr. Chamberlin. Resolved that we furnish boards for the buildings at Willstown as mentioned in Mr. Chamberlins letter—Also that we furnish Br. Thompson with iron and steel from the smiths shop at the discretion of Br. Dean.

[Jan.] 22. Our visiting brethren Messrs. Vancourt & Williamson having tarried with us a day longer than they expected, on account of high waters, left us to pursue their journey.—They expect to go by Willstown, Creek Path & Mayhew. Our prayers & best wishes accompany them.

[Jan.] 27. Br. Thompson left us to return to Hightower. He has been detained to the present time by highwater. The Chickamauga is still so high that the mills cannot run. Considerable damage has been done by the water pressing around and under the safe gate which was placed across the race, and also under the saw mill floom.[2] We this day commenced repairing. Had the stone wall been finished which was from the first contemplated to save the banks, there is reason to believe this damage would not have occurred. It is however, but small.

In meeting for business resolved that Br. Dean have charge of the business pertaining to the Smiths shop including all persons employed to labor in and for said shop—making all necessary preparations for it, and that the hired help and apprentice (if we should have any) board at his family. Resolved that our stated meeting for business be only on the evening of the first monday in each month—and that special meetings be called at the request of two or more brethren. As br. J.C. Ellsworth has now no special charge of the children, Resolved that he be released from the charge of the clothing and that so much of the clothing as it is thought best to lay by for the children be under the direction of those who have charge of the children out of school, and that the remainder be kept in the middle store room under the charge of the steward.

[Jan.] 30. For a number of weeks past the boys (except those employed about the house and barn) have been cutting firewood in five companies, each company being tasked 3 cords a week—the present week have been formed in 6 companies, four to five in each company. Notwithstanding the weather has been cold and uncomfortable. They have performed their tasks with their usual alacrity, each company having cut and piled its three cords before thursday night. Br. Blunt works with them, but cuts and piles his wood by itself.

[Jan.] 31. Some addition has been made to the saw mill floom and the breach so far stoped that the grist mill was put in operation this evening, and will be kept running most of the night, as our own family, and many of the neighbors, have for several days been out of meal.[3]

Meeting for business called in consequence of communication this day received from the Cor. Sec.—Read the two letters from the Cor. Sec. one of Oct. 18, and one of Dec. 23, and Jan. 3—After conversing on the subject of farming &c for the coming season, Resolved that Brs. Vail, J.C. Elsworth & F. Elsworth be a Com. to lay our plans for cultivating the various fields, & for our farming business generally for the next season, agreeably to the suggestions of the Cor. Sec, and present said plan to the brethren at our next meeting.

It appears from the mill books the value of boards and timber sawed from July 15, to Jan. 31 inclusive is—————— $161,24
Toll corn received during same time—————— 85,00
* Expense of getting logs, tending and repairs during s^d time <u>108,83</u>
Profit of mills for 6½ months <u>$137,41</u>
Account of Smith Shop for Jany 1823
Recd in cash $5,00, produce 37,54, labor 14,48½ $57,02½
Work done for Mission including 2,12½ for Creek Path <u>44,91</u>
101,93½

Shop D^r
To making and repairing tools 3,50
To files 18,00, hire of Smith 14,75   36.25
Balance in favor of shop   65.68½

Amount of work charged to customers which is left to be
brought into account when paid is $59,46.

*The late repairs, & addition to the floom, not being finished, are not
included. We learn that the venerable Col^n Meigs, U.S. Agent, departed this life after a short illness, on Tuesday 28th of this month. He has
ever been a firm friend of the mission, & ready to further its
opperations by all means in his power.
The U. States Commissioners to treat with the Cherokees for land,
have been at the Agency since the 15th—The Cherokees gave early
notice that they should not meet them on this business, as they had no
more land to spare.[4] The Com^s after waiting a few days, sent
messengers thro. the nation to the chiefs to induce them to come in,
but, we are informed, they all still refuse to attend.—
The Prud. Com. may wish to know the state of health in the mission
family, through the blessing of our covenant God, the brothers all
enjoy a comfortable state of health, yet those who had the fever do not
appear to have fully recovered their former strength & ability to
sustain fatigue & exposure. Sister Vail is entirely confined to her
room, & mostly her bed. Sis Butler is recovering from an ill turn
which has kept her from business for a short time—the remainder of
the sisters in usual health—Children healthy, & schools progressing
satisfactorily—but have not been filled since last spring vacation—
present number 42 boys & 23 girls, besides children of missionaries.

A. Hoyt, H. Parker, A.E. Blunt, E. Butler

Brainerd Mission Journal Feby 1823

Feb. 3^d Meeting for business. Comt. [committee] appointed to report a
plan for farming, not having completed their plan asked a longer time
which was granted. Agreed that Br. J.C. Elsworth have charge of the
cattle and hogs, and that he be allowed to purchase a poney to be
under his direction for the purpose of bringing them in—Resolved
that all our Irish potatoes now on hand be saved for seed—The
question was asked will the brethren think it expedient that Br. F.

Elsworth move up to the mission house? Ans, if he chooses, and a place can be found for him.—The Pru. Com. may wish to know the reasons for Br. Elsworth's removing. There appears not to be sufficient room for both families at the creek—most who labor on the farm, (especially including the boys) must be at the mission house, and he will be as much or more in the midst of his business here, & Sis Elsworth is too feeble to perform the hard labor of the family there.

[*Feb.*] 5. A Cherokee brought in 11 hogs killed, weighing upwards of 2000 lbs—also a company of 11 natives brought in a drove of 21 hogs to be killed here. The men thus brought in by business tarried for the night—Being providentially furnished with a good interpreter the evening was spent endeavouring to lead their minds to a knowledge of Christ & to persuade them to seek salvation through him accompanied with some remarks on the missionary operations of the day & their effects. All listened with unwearied attention, but said little—An elderly man who appeared as a father in the company told a friend after the evenings discourse that the missionary was very good to spend so much time in teaching Cherokees whenever they came here.

[*Feb.*] 6. The men who brought in the drove of hogs, waiting to kill and weigh them, remained with us another night. At the request of the oldest man (who we find is the father of four of the young men) this evening was spent as the last. An attempt was made to draw the father into conversation, or in some way to get his ideas on religious subjects; but he frankly confessed his entire ignorance & desired to be taught. The attention of this evening was the same as the last.
These people have no objections to raise, nothing to oppose to what we say—The great difficulty lies in awakening their attention, and then coming down to their uninformed minds, so as to make them understand. On one subject however they readily understand, & quickly reply, (viz.) the evil of drinking whiskey. They acknowledge it is bad; but white people make it, and bring it to them.

[*Feb.*] 7. Very cold—Br. Ellis not being able to warm the boys school-house so as to keep them in any degree comfortable, dismissed the school—A snow of 2 or 3 inches which fell yesterday, lies unsoftened, which gives the appearance of a northern winter. Twenty-eight boys, in companies of four each, had cut and split their 21 cords of fire wood this week before the snow fell. Br. F. Elsworth removed from the creek, & for the present will take part of the cabin with Br. J.C. Elsworth, back of the girls school-house. Br. Dean only remains at the creek. He proposes to entertain such travellers as it is found necessary to take in—and the hired men (except such as are employed in or about the smiths shop) will board at the mission house in the common family.

[Feb.] 8. Cold continues—Clear day, yet the snow remains as it was.— The Cherokee, called Wicked Jack, (whose real name we now learn is Jack Wicket) who came to us some months ago saying he wished to be here in order to learn about the Saviour, and on that account, proposed himself as a laborer in the family has lately expressed a desire to receive baptism.—His story is that untill within about a year he spent all he could get in whiskey and was often drunk. Being discarded by a near relative, on whom he had partly depended, he came to Br. Mills' neighborhood friendless and disconsolate. When he heard br. Mills talk about the Saviour—the evil of drinking whiskey &c & since that time he had left drinking & been seeking the knowledge of Christ. For a time, he resided in the family of Br. Mills, and then came here—His conduct since he came to us, has been unexceptionable—and he expresses a hope that he has experienced a saving change.—
Br. Parker having been indisposed for a short time, was this morning obliged to leave business and take his room.

[Feb.] 10. Special meeting for the purpose of hearing and deciding on the report of the Com. appointed to form a plan of farming for the coming season.—The Com. presented their report, which was accepted and is as follows. Viz. That we plant with corn & Irish potatoes the large field bought of br. M. Hoyt, containing about 23 acres—and sow with oats and timothy the small field bot of s^d Br. which contains 3 or 4 acres—that the field West of the boys school-house of 4 acres, & about 10 acres above the Smith shop (including the former little field of about 3 or 4 acres the remainder new clearing) be planted with corn—part of the field adjoining the garden to be planted with sweet potatoes, the remainder sowed with oats.—The two small fields lying on each side by the road leading to the creek, to be planted and sown (if seed can be procured) with garden vegetables—and that the large field south of the house be sowed with oats, or summer fallowed for wheat.

[Feb.] 11. Mr. Chamberlin and Br. John Arch returned. Br. E. Boudinot & sisters Susannah & Catharine Brown from Creek Path came in company with them. It is with great pleasure we receive visits from these young converts—Br. Arch went from Wills town to Creek Path,

and thence returned to Brainerd by Chattooga, and arrived here at the same time as Mr. Chamberlin, though he had not seen him from the time he left him at Willstown.

{Br. Arch says he finds most of the people entirely ignorant of the gospel, except in the vicinity of the missions—that he begins to discover the light when he gets within 40 miles of Brainerd. The people every where are willing to hear, and he desires nothing more for this life but to spend his days in training his people—He is willing to spend his whole time travelling with a preacher, and would gladly do any thing in his power if it were possible that he could himself be prepared to preach the gospel to them. If we had another evangelist to travel among this people we think he might be employed with great prospects of usefulness.}

They have put up a double cabin at Willstown, for a dwelling house— each room 20 ft. square—story & a half, calculating the chambers for the childrens lodging. The school house is not yet up; nor is the dwelling house finished—It has been too cold for Cherokees, & indeed for anyone to work at such business—

False tales, of almost every description are circulated among this people against missionary operations. The following is a specimen. A traveller, who in the language of the world, would be called a gentleman, put up at the house of a chief for the night. Finding that a son of the chief could speak English, he entered into conversation with him, pretending to be a great friend of the Cherokees—Among other things, he told the young man, the missionaries were a very dangerous people—that with all their pretensions to friendship, they were endeavoring to ruin the nation, that they might get the country—Many people had long known this, and now they had full proof of it—The missionaries had been in secret correspondence with Governor Clark [of Georgia], in laying the plan for the commissioners to come and treat for their country—That the safety of the nation required that they [missionaries] should be driven out of the country immediately[5]—He observed further, that the Choctaws had got their eyes opened, & were determined at all hazards to drive the missionaries out of their country—The young man enquired if all this was certainly true.—Receiving for answer that there was full proof of it, the youth replied, that he was himself well acquainted with the missionaries, & all their operations—that he had been to the north among the people whence the missionaries came—and that he had just been reading a letter from a Choctaw chief, entreating for more missionaries, he must therefore see that he knew the whole to be false—It is perhaps unnecessary for us to say, it is too late in the day for such idle reports to have their intended effect upon the Cherokees[6]—

Meeting for business relative to the contemplated school at Wills town. Resolved that Br. Darius Hoyt, go with Mr. Chamberlin, as teacher of that school—and that sister Anna Hoyt go for a time to assist in the family—also resolved that the light two horse waggon be assigned to that school.

[Feb.] 13. The hired man returned from Hightower—They had finished the dwelling house or rather cabin—Br. Proctors sister had come out from Georgia to assist him, and they expected immediately to commence house-keeping. They had not commenced the school-house. The Cherokees being barefoot, and almost destitute of cloathing could not work in such cold weather. They would build the school-house as soon as the warm weather commenced—& there was prospect of a very large school, at least at the commencement. Br. P. writes that the natives there are greatly addicted to drinking, gambling & dancing.—but they express a desire to be instructed, and he has no doubt would very generally attend on preaching, if they had a preacher and interpreter.

Br. Parker is still confined to his room, and mostly to his bed—but we hope he is on the recovery. His complaint appears to be a very heavy cold—which threatened a pleurisy but by timely application of medicine is now likely to pass off.[7]

[Feb.] 15. Last evening a waggon arrived from Augusta, loaded with various articles for the mission—among which are 10 packages containing donations of clothing and other articles from societies & individuals as follows—One box put up at Cazenovia [N.Y.] May 25, 1822, valued at $161. [8]—One box from female Alms Society, Benson V^t valued at $55,85—One from Mrs. Paine, Athens, Penn. containing sundry articles from Ithaca N.Y. which articles from Ithica were valued at $22,08,—those from Mrs. Paine not valued—One box from New marlborough, Mass. valued at $131,73—One from Harperfield Geo., without bill, or letter, containing the following articles (viz.) 2 blankets, 2 sheets, 1 skirt, 1 pillow, 1 bed tick, 4 pr stockings, 1 pr mittens, 1 pr shoes, 3 pillow slips, 1 towel, 1 pr pantaloons, 1 small shirt, 1 coat, 1 cap, 2 small remnants torn cloth & one of factory—One chestnut barrel; first directed on it to care of Henry Hudson Esqr Hartford Con. without bill or letter containing the following articles—

2 yds cotton & wool, striped, 2 bed quilts, 3 vests, 12 shirts, 6 aprons, 5 pr mittens, 1 skirt, 1 frock, 1 towel, 1 pr pantaloons, 4 pr stockings, 2 handkerchiefs, 1 blanket, 4 remnants of linen, and a few other small articles.—One small box place unknown, containing 1 coverlet, 1 blanket, 1 sheet, 3 pr stockings, 1 skirt, 2 collars, 1 [spe?], 1 pr pantaloons, 2 small frocks, thread & yarn—One dto from Mrs. Ann [H?] Shippen Livingston Phila., put up by Mr. Ralston Esqr containing sugar, tea, pamphlets, & other articles not estimated—One box from Dorcas Soc. Unionville, Orange Co. N.Y. valued at $44,35.—One box from Females of Bridgewater Susquehanah Co, Penn. containing 1 bed quilts, 1 coverlet, 3 sheets, 4 shirts, 10 towels, 1 table cloth, 5 pr pillow cases, 15 pr stockings, 1 apron, 8 pocket Hkfs, 2 shawls, 1 pr pantaloons, 4 pr shoes, 1 hat, 1 doz. spoons, 8-1/4 yds towel cloth, 1 [surcoat?], 1 pr scissors, sundry small articles, as thread, stocking yarn, tracks, paper, quils &c. It appears from a letter found in this box, that it was put up Nov. 14, 1821 & designed for Eliot. The above articles were all in good order, those which had been longest packed having recd no damage. We are under renewed obligations to God & his people for this timely assistance.

After one or two warm days, just enough to dissolve the snow, the cold has returned upon us with increased strength—Br. Parkers symptoms of speedy recovery are checked. He suffers very considerably from the piercing cold which presses in from every side of his open cabin. It is impossible to keep his room warm. The labor of our barefooted [boys?] has been suspended for more than a week—they have been much interrupted in their labor heretofore for want of shoes. It has been said that many poor children among the white people are obliged to go without shoes, and we have [?] whether it was our duty to ask the christian public (while so many objects were pressing upon their charity) to furnish shoes for their children but we believe, aside from the object of making them more comfortable that the additional labor which they might perform, particularly the largest of them, would be a full compensation for shoes. Some have been furnished, but in general the shoes are too small—many of our children requiring shoes of a full size for men, & women—If they could also have hats it would be a great convenience, & would do away their practice of wearing handkerchiefs like turbans round their heads.[9]

[Feb.] 17. Br. Boudinot left us to return to his parents. His health still improving.

[Feb.] 18. The cold having moderated, br. Parker is again on the mend—Sister Susannah Brown left us on her return to Creek Path—Catharine will continue with us a few weeks.[10]

[Feb.] 20. Meeting for business.—Resolved that br. Ellis have charge of the boys in school & out—that br. Blount [Blunt] assist him in laboring with the boys, & Cornelius A. Hoyt assist him in the school house and out of school when necessary[11]—Resolved that there be only an annual vacation in the schools in this place, & that this commence on tuesday next after the first sabbath in August & continue four weeks.

[Feb.] 21. Mr. Aaron Crosby from Cambridge N.Y. called to spend a few days with us.

[Feb.] 22. The weather has become mild & br. Parker has so far recovered as to walk out of his cabin into the house.

[Feb.] 24. Mr. Crosby visited the schools. He expressed satisfaction in the progress the children are making. Mr. Chamberlin, who has been unwell since his return from Willtown, is so far recovered as to be able to attend to business. It appears we did not fully understand the people of Willstown when they said they would put up the buildings for the family & school. Mr. C. when last there, learned that when the Cherokees say they will build a man a house, mean only that they will put up the logs, & make the roof. When this is done they consider the house built. The person who is to occupy can then make his chimney, doors &c at his leisure. Finding they were not fully understood they proposed to build our chimney—which is so much more than they expected. It is thought best not to insist any further. We have therefore to finish the house at the expense of the mission. Doors, windows sash, boards for the floors &c are to be prepared here.

[Feb.] 25. Began to plow the small field by the joiner shop which is to be improved as a garden. Two sisters of Br. Elias Boudinot were this day brot to the school. The oldest about 15, the youngest about 8.[12]

[Feb.] 27. Mr. Crosby left us on his journey homeward. This short acquaintance has endeared him to us as a christian brother & friend of missions.—Recd a letter from Br. Mills, which he says was written in the presence of all his congregation, most earnestly intreating us to send him a teacher. He thinks they have been promised a school: & expects the teacher of the school will also instruct them in religion.

[Feb.] 28. Dr. Butler was called this morning to visit a sick man within about ten miles of the Agency.

Notices to accompany the Journal for Feb.

[Feb.] 28. We have now in school 43 boys and 28 girls, among them are the following names, given by Societies, or individuals, who are supposed to contribute to the Treasury at Boston for their support, except the benefactors of Eli Smith, who send their donations directly here, where they are entered in our acct with the Treas of the Board, viz: John Emerson—Boston Recorder[13]—Thomas Witherspoon—Elizabeth Kean—Nicholas Patterson—Caroline Smelt—Benjamin Tappan—Samuel Spring—Ralph Wells Gridley—Moses Hoge—Manasseh Cutler—John Knox Witherspoon—Samuel Worcester—Eli Smith—John E. Latta—Wheeler Gilbert—Louisa Battelle—Edward HopFull—Josiah Meigs—There are also the following beneficiaries absent on account of ill health, but expected to return soon: John D. Paxton, David Parker, Vinson Gould—To visit a sick mother—Bethuel Dodd. Mindwell Woodridge Gould is a relative of Vinson, and will probably return when he does. We have long lamented the absence of three promising girls, who were beneficiaries, viz. Ann Porter—Mary Mason—& Betsey Mayhew—Just as we are preparing this part of our journal to forward to the Com. Mr. Butrick has returned and brought some pleasing intelligence respecting the three last mentioned girls—particulars will be forwarded in their place, in the journal of next month.[14]

> Ard Hoyt, D.S. Butrick, E. Dean
> J.C. Elsworth, H. Parker, Elizur Butler

Brainerd mission journal

1823

March 1st Dr. Butler returned having visited the sick man, been to the agency, and transacted business there, and again visited the sick man on his return.[15]

March 2nd Mr. Chamberlin though not sufficiently recovered from his indisposition to ride abroad to preach, was able to take the afternoon exercises.

Two persons were by the church examined and recvd—one as candidate for baptism—the other for communion—The former is the Cherokee, mentioned in the journal August 30, as known by the appellation of wicked Jack he chooses to bear the name of Jack or John Crawfish.[16] He has been a faithful laborer in the mission family since that time, and is now about to return to Br. Mills's to labour with him during the season of raising corn.

From Jack's relation it appears he not only received his first impression with Mr. Mills but thinks he there experienced a radical change in the temper and desires of his heart, yet knowing at that time but little about the Savior, the change appears much greater and more apparent since he came to us. He knows of no particular time of conversion, or special change, since he came here; but thinks his love to God hatred of sin, and sense of his own unworthiness, have been gradually increased, as he has learned more and more of revealed truth. His progress in the knowledge of divine things has been very considerable for his advantages; but must necessarily have been greatly retarded by his ignorance of our language—we having always to communicate by means of an interpreter. If we mistake not he clearly understands the fundamental principals of our most Holy religion, and we hope will prove a comfortable assistant to Br. Mills.

The candidate for communion, is a young woman who was baptised about two years since as a member of the household of believing parents, and has recently obtained a hope.

[*March*] *3.* Business meeting. The sisters presented the following declaration and request viz. As sisters Chamberlin and Anna Hoyt are expected soon to leave us for Wills town and several of the sisters who remain are in feeble health, it seems necessary that sister J.C. Elsworth have many cares besides that of the girls out of school which is particularly assigned her by the brethren, and it is thought Sister Sarah Hoyt's health will now admit of her taking more cares than she has been able to the winter past, the sisters request that the charge of the girls out of school as well as in—be given to her—she being willing to take it as long as her health will permit, it being understood that sister Elsworth will still assist in some parts of the charge—Resolved that the sisters request be granted.

Resolved that Mr. Chamberlin be permitted to hire a man to labor at Willstown for one month and that the horse left here by Mr. Bascom in exchange be assigned to Mr. Chamberlin—Directed that a letter be written to the general post office, requesting that the mail may be opened at Wills town.

Question: shall the time spent by Br. Dean in the concerns of the Mission not connected with the shop be mentioned in connection with the accounts events of the shop.—Ans. in the affirmative.

Account of smiths shop for February—

Recvd in money———————————————	$12,12½
dtto in produce———————————	15,27
dtto in labour———————————	16,59
dtto Iron———————————	4,84
work done for mission———————————	_73,22_
	122,04

charged to customers which will be brought into acct when collected 31,00.

D^r

To 950 bushels coal at $5 ———————————	47,50
" hire and board of Journeyman———————————	14,50
Repairing tools ———————————	3,00
—Brass———————————	_1,75_
	66,75
Balance in favor of shop ———————	55,29

Br. Dean spent four days out of the shop.
The board of the hired smith in the above acct and in former acp^t is estimated at one dollar a week. We think this is too low, and in future it will be called 1,25—

[*March*] 4th The youth who was dismissed from the school last summer for going to a ball play contrary to orders, having made satisfactory acknowledgment and manifested a disposition to conduct well in future was again admitted to the school.

One of the evangelists, with Br. Thomas Basill interpreter returned this afternoon.[17] They left Taloney Feb. 4th. The first day travelled about 15 or 20 miles—spent the evening with the chief of the town, and some of his neighbors who came in.[18] Early the next morning the people assembled. Among the first was John the father of Ann Porter and Mary Mason and Betsey Mayhew, with his family. The evangelist in his journal writes, "I knew neither of the girls, but Mary and Betsey took their seats near me, and surprised me by uniting in singing Cherokee hymns. I immediately made enquiry, and found that the dear girls, who have been the hope and expectation of many Christians, were before me. Mary can still read. She and Betsey wish to attend school at Taloney as it is nearer their parents than Brainerd.

Ann Porter was more hopeful, and as she is now a young woman I did not make may enquiries about her; though perhaps she also desires further instruction. The whole family appeared peculiarly neat and descent. Their father appears serious, and anxious to hear the gospel." We now learn that he is the person who has been at Taloney and is mentioned by Mr. Hall as the serious enquirer. Since the above mentioned time—the evangelist with his interpreter, has been traveling from place to place chiefly among the mountains, where they found the cherokees more thickly settled than in any other part of the nation. They were cordially received and found the people ready to assemble and hear what they had to say. They rarely found a person who could speak any english.

[March] 6th The situation of the people at Turnip mountain and the importance of soon commencing a school there has for a long time lain with great weight upon our minds; and more especially so since we received the last letter from Br. Mills—He has claimed a promise since the Cor. Sec. was here and we fear longer delays will be attended with very serious evils; especially if they continue willing to do as they have encouraged. Having for several days past taken the subject under serious and we trust prayerful consideration; the brethren came together this evening according to previous appointment, and resolved that Br. John C. Elsworth go to Turnip mountain and, if such assistance will be given by the people as we expect, make preparations for commencing a school there.

[March] 7th A messenger having been sent for Dr. Butler again to visit the sick man he was called to on the 28 ult, he set out very early this morning intending to go and return before he sleeps although the distance is estimated at 28 or 30 miles.

Br. Proctor came in from High Tower. The importance of having a school there increases in his view, the more he becomes acquainted with the people and the wretched situation, which exceeds every thing he could have imagined without being an eye witness—The buildings have progressed very slow. For a time he feared their luke warmness to labor arose from disaffection, but was soon satisfied it was nothing but indolence and cold weather. He has done most of the work on the buildings with his own hands, and the hired man that was with him a few weeks. The dwelling house is finished and comfortable. The logs were put up for a large school house; and the people promise to work on it during his absence—They appear very friendly—Dr. Butler returned this evening about 11 Oclock. He found his patient in a most distressed state—spent about four hours with him, and had the satisfaction of seeing him greatly relieved—

[March] 10. Br. Parker has so far recovered his health as to resume his former charges and labors.

[March] 11. Br. John Arch returned from Creek Path found all well there staid but one night—

[March] 12. Br. and Sis. Proctor were this morning blessed with the gift of a first born son. Both mother and child are in comfortable circumstances.
Dr Butler left us about 10 Oclock to visit again the sick cherokee.—He would have gone yesterday or the day before, but heavy rains and highwater rendered it impracticable for him to go and return in a day. As he can now be spared for a longer time he will try to get round the high waters—
Br. J.C. Elsworth expected to have set out for Turnip mountain on monday, but was detained by high water. He sat out this morning but had not proceeded far before he was convinced that the creeks in that direction seem yet too high, and turned back—
Dr Butler returned about 10 Oclock this evening. When within 6 or 7 miles of the place he learned that the man was dead, and turned immediately back. It appears the sick man was greatly relieved by the Drs prescriptions when he last visited him, but soon after he came away he eat a large quantity of food, and died the night following—

[March] 13. Long and copious showers of rain are continued and the streams, alternately falling and rising, each sucessive rise being higher than the last—

[March] 14. Br. Parker is again obliged to leave his work on account of ill health—He appears to have taken a new cold—

[March] 16. Recvd a letter from Br. Hall.—The hopeful converts who have been for some time on trial continue to give increasing evidence of a genuine change—one or two more have recently obtained a hope—Arrangements having been previously made that Br. Hall should appoint the time when the first converts should receive baptism, he informs us that, he (agreeably to the desire of all the candidates) has appointed next sabbath and expects Mr. Hoyt with some of the cherokee brethren from the church will go out soon

enough to spend Saturday with them, which day they have appointed for a feast—

[*March*] 17. Meeting for business—
As Br. Proctor while at hightower was obliged to labor on the buildings and therefore could not clear and fence for a garden, &c,— concluded that it will be best to hire a man to labor there for 1 or 2 months if a suitable man can be obtained.
Question, Shall Br. Vail hire a girl to take care of his wife, and give two dollars a week, if one cannot be hired for less. Answered in the affirmative.

[*March*] 19. The water still keeping up too high for a waggon to pass to Taloney, we find it necessary to put off the business there untill sabbath after next.
Br. J.C. Elsworth set out this morning to make a second trial to get over the creeks to Turnip mountain.
Br. Proctor also left us to return to hightower. It is expected sis. Proctor will follow him by the aid of some one from this place, as soon as her health and strength will permit.

[*March*] 21. Mr. Chamberlin set out to go to the agency on business for the mission.—

[*March*] 22. Mr. Alen Gleason, assistant missionary for the Choctaw mission, arrived in good health.[19] He has been 9 weeks on his journey, being obliged to ly by one week on account of the lameness of his horse. He received in donations $30 and expended $16,81-1/4.—

[*March*] 24. Mr. Harper, a gentleman from Adams County, Penn. journeying for his health, called to make us a visit. James Harvey Williams, by his request and the advise of his mother and brothers, was this day placed as apprentice in the blacksmith shop for the term of four years.
Br. McPherson set out with his team loaded with boards and other articles for Will town.
Mr. Chamberlin returned late this evening—not being able to leave the Agency untill 3 Ock afternoon.

[*March*] 25. Mr. Chamberlin and family (including Anna and Darius Hoyt) being commended to the grace of God, left us, for Wills town. The children (especially those who have been here longest at school) were much affected at parting with their former teachers. Br. Vail goes with them with the four horse waggon.

[March] 26. D. Campbell Esq and Mr. G.W. Campbell Licentiate from the State of Maine, called to visit the schools—

[March] 27. Messrs. Campbells and Harper visited the schools.

[March] 28. Mr. Harper left us this morning, after testifying his good will by a donation of $4,00 observing it was not in his power at this time to do more.

Br. Vail returned this evening after 9 oclock—on the first day an axeltre [axletree] of the waggon broke. While he waited to exchange this for another, Mr. Chamberlin went on with the light waggon and family. The next day the wind was so high that Br. Vail could not cross the Tennessee—(The lookout mountain being at this time impassable for waggons, they are obliged to go around it by crossing the river twice). On the third day Br. Vail crossed the river once, and again the waggon broke down, he obtained another waggon, which also crushed under his load before he got to the second crossing place. He then took a horse from the team and came up with Mr. Chamberlin and Br. McPherson at evening, within 18 miles of the station: and on the next day returned with his broken waggon, as mentioned above—If practicable Mr. Chamberlin will get a team at Wills town to come after the left goods, should he fail in this we must try to send them on in some way after Br. McPherson returns.

[March] 30. Mr. Campbell preached, both forenoon and afternoon, to our instruction and edification.

> Ard Hoyt, John Vail, Henry Parker, J. C. Elsworth,
> Frederick Elsworth, E. Butler, E. Dean

Brainerd mission journal

1823

April 1st Mr. Alexander McCoy of Willstown & Miss Sarah Hicks, daughter of Mr. Charles R. Hicks were this day married in the presence of the scholars, the mission family and some of their relatives—who came with them to witness the ceremony.[20]

Br. Elsworth returned—The people at Turnipmountain recvd with joy the proposals he had to make—Br. Mills readily offered an improvement containing such buildings as, with very little repairs, would answer the present purpose—At first it was thought best to commence the school at that place, but it being suggested that there was a much better spring at another place, which would be equally convenient for the people, & probably more healthy; and that they could soon put up the necessary buildings there; it was thought best not to decide positively on the place untill Br. and Sis. E. should have moved down—And then, if it is thought best to have new buildings, they will put them up—

[April] 2nd Mr. Campbell preached the Wednesday lecture, & afterwards both he & his brother attended during the school hours to hear the children read &c &c.

[April] 3rd An invitation having been previously given to all the mission family to attend a wedding at Mr. D[aniel] Ross'; as many as conveniently could went over—found a respectable number of guests assembled & witnessed the marriage of Mr. Elijah Hicks to Miss Margaret Ross, daughter of Mr. D. Ross,—after which about 50 persons partook of an excellent wedding feast.[21] We never demand a marriage fee, but Mr. Hicks politely presented to Mr. Hoyt nine silver dollars, which were accepted as a donation to the mission.

[April] 4th A number of our cherokee friends have come in from a distance to attend the solemnities of a communion season—

[April] 5th The schools were suspended & religious exercises attended both forenoon & afternoon.—At the close of the second service three candidates for communion, & two for baptism, were examined, & permission granted them to come forward tomorrow.—Mr. Brigham, agent of the board came in this evening—

Sab. [April] 6. Mr. Campbell preached in the morning—After sermon, James Harvey Williams, David Carter, and Polly McPhearson, renewed their confessions of faith, entered into covenant with the church, and were admitted to full communion—after which the members of this church, one member from the church at Springplace, and our visiting brethren united in the solemn ordinance of supper. Mr. Brigham preached in the afternoon, & after sermon, John Crawfish & Elizabeth Fields were baptized—and a woman called Acha was examined and recvd a candidate for baptism.—

[April] 7th The two schools passed a satisfactory examination.

Meeting for business

Br. Dean rendered smith shop acpt for the month of March as follows:

Cr

By recvd in money ——————————————	$ 7,00
" " " produce 29,57, in labor 20,35 ———————	49,92
" " " Iron 4,50 pd J. Ross 15,25 ——————	19,75
" pd Milo Hoyt———————————	6,75
" work done for mission———————	<u>44.56</u>
	127,98

Charged to customer (including Iron)
& steel sold to Br. Thompson $96,95

Dr

To Iron 5,67 hire and board of smith 19,75 —	25,42
repairing tools ———————	<u>3.50</u>
	<u>28.92</u>
Balance in favor of shop	99,06

Br. Dean has spent in the course of the month 8 days in burning lime and plastering girls school house & 4 days in various other concerns of the mission.—Read the resolutions of the Pru. Com: as contained in the letter last recvd from the Cor. Sec. and his instructions to us relative to the superintendence of the secular concerns: & Resolved that Br. Dean have charge of carrying to effect the resolution of the Pru. Com. relating to the carpenters shop.—

Resolved that the Pru. Com. be requested to send on a person to act as superintendent of secular concerns.—

[April] 8th Br. Gleason left us to pursue his journey to Mayhew. He continued here longer than he would have done in expectation that the sore back of the horse he rode would heal so that he could take the same beast on with him but (the sore still remaining) he has taken the horse brought by Br. Proctor.

[April] 9th The Mr. Campbells having been detained with us longer than they expected, have by their affectionate & christian deportment greatly endeared themselves to the mission family—They took their leave of us this morning—making a donation to the mission of thirty dollars.—

Br. Vail went with the waggon & one span of horses to take part of the left load to Willstown: he will not again attempt so large a load upon the old waggon.—

[April] 12. The parents of several of the children have been in, expecting a vacation this spring, & to take the children home with them. We feared they would not all hear that the vacation was not to be untill August & that some might be anxious to have their children go home as heretofore; but all who have yet come have appeared to be well satisfied, after hearing our reasons; & after staying a while, have returned cheerfully without the children—
The chief called Shoe boots, from Hightower came to make us a visit.[22] He says they were finishing the school house when he came away— Br. Vail returned, he found the family at Willstown in usual health— without floor, door, or window in their house,—Mr. Chamberlin and Darius hard at work clearing their garden place &c. Mr. C. had permission to hire a man to assist in bringing forward this business, but it appears he has not found one—

Sab. [April] 13. Mr. Brigham preached forenoon and afternoon; his discourses were very acceptable both for instruction and edification—

[April] 14. Shoe boots, after thanking us for what we were doing for the children here, & assuring us that it gave him great pleasure, took an affectionate leave of us to return home—saying he hoped they should soon have a school at Hightower, & that their children would some day appear like these. Three chiefs of the Arkansas Cherokees returning from Washington City [the federal capital] called and spent a short time with us; one of them is half brother to David & Catharine Brown.[23] He says the missionaries on the Arkansas are much beloved, and greatly respected by the people—

[April] 5. Mr. Brigham left us this morning on his return.—
A few weeks ago two children that had not been returned since vacation last fall were brought and left here without our permission, or knowledge; untill those who brought them were gone—As they had forfeited their standing in the school by absence it became a question whether they should be permitted to go into the school—but as they were left on our hands, & could not be turned off without some trouble, they were suffered to remain—Last evening two women, connexion of that family, came and took supper with us— afterwards, while we were engaged in family prayer—they went off with the children. We can think of nothing which would induce them to such conduct except the expectation of obtaining clothes which might be put onto the children.—A few articles had been given them which were taken away.

We shall advise with Mr. Ross what is to be done in this case.—
Two small boys have also left us without leave—They probably remembered the last spring vacation, and were unwilling to be deprived of a like season this spring—We are sure their parents will disapprove their conduct, & have no doubt they will soon send them back—

[April] 16. Mr. Ross advises that we send to the parents of the children taken by the two women—& if they do not return them with a promise of keeping them steady at school, that we exact of them the expense which have been incurred here by their children. Agreeably to this advice we sent Br. J. Arch to give notice to the parents. He returned this evening—says the parents disapprove the conduct of the women in taking the children, & of the children in going with them. They say when the children first came they thought they would drive them immediately back—but afterwards consented to let them stay a few days untill their father could have time to come with them—He promises to bring them as soon as he can go to Mr. Hicks' on some business, and return.—

[April] 19th Sisters began to wash at the new washhouse.—It is placed over the mill race, opposite the mission house—and the water raised by a pump—It is intended to set the kettles in the house over arches, but at present they are hung upon crotches out of the house.

[April] 20th The father of the children to whom John Arch went on the 16th came with the children.—He says he thought there was vacation, and told the young women if it was so they might bring the children—but if not they must not bring them—

[April] 21st Two of the oldest schollars John D. Paxton & Tilman Rose both in the highest class, having for some time conducted in many little things not agreeable to our wishes we have thought it might be as well for the school if they were away, they now manifesting a desire to leave the school were told we were willing they should go— & they left us this morning. We are sorry that any should leave the school in a surly mood, as these have done, but as we have given them no cause of complaint, we had reason to believe they would only grow worse if detained.—Tilman Rose is the boy that was dismissed last summer for disobedience in going to a ball play, & recvd again the winter past.[24]

[April] 22nd We were again called to the painful joyous scene of dismissing a family from Brainerd to commence another local school— Such parting seasons remind us of those we experienced before we came onto mission ground.—As we then rejoiced that a door was opened for carrying the gospel into the wilderness; so now we rejoice that our God is opening the way for us to penetrate still deeper into these barren wilds, bearing that precious seed which will soon cause the "wilderness to become a fruitful field, & the fruitful field as the garden of the Lord"[25]—Br. Vail went with the larger waggon to carry the goods—Br. John Arch to assist in driving the cows, & bring back the light waggon in which Br. & Sis Elsworth rode.—

[April] 26. Brs. Vail & John Arch returned, they has a prosperous journey out—arrived at Turnip mountain on the third day & came back in two days—They were all cordially recvd—& entertained the night after their arrival by Mr. Lasley a white man with a cherokee family— In the morning Br. Vail took the goods to the house Br. Mills offers, but did not wait for him & other neighbors to come in—Br. & Sis. Elsworth are to go into that house for the present, but is expected they will put up new buildings a short distance from that place.—Br. Vail thinks it is 70 miles to Turnipmountain by the present waggon road.

[April] 29th Mr. Butrick came in from Taloney. Sabbath before last he spent at Hightower and on monday witnessed the first opening of a school there. Last sabbath they had an interesting day at Taloney. Six adults (four males and two females) and twenty one children were baptised—a church was formed, & as the persons baptized had been candidates for that ordinance over the usual time, they were admitted also to full communion—& the sacrament of the Lords supper administered. Although we have been for several months looking with joyful anticipation to this day, yet the fact that another vine is planted in this wilderness, under circumstances of so much promise, gives a new spring to our hopes & joys, such we cannot attempt to describe.—Let God have all the praises, & our hope be alone in him.

[April] 30. One of the brethren expected to have gone with Sis. Proctor to Hightower this week. Heavy rains have raised the creek so that they are now impassable in that direction. Though the goodness & mercy of God the general health of the Mission family has been as good during the month which is now closing as has been usual in months past. At present all except sister Vail are able to be about and attend to business and she is so much better as to need little attention except to prepare her food. When we reflect on our spiritual state we have great reason to be humbled before God & his people. The religious excitement which has been very considerable in many of our children appears in most of them to have subsided, & left no visible token of repentance, we have however hope for the Sandwich Islander, & perhaps for one or two others.

As we have said nothing about our gardening or farming business in our daily journal it may perhaps be proper to mention here at the close of the month, that our prospects for culinary vegetables, in tolerable plenty, are favorable. A very good hired gardener, with several of the school boys have been constantly employed in that line when the weather would permit. We have found a considerable lack of seeds which will be a great loss unless we receive a supply from Augusta, where we have sent for them. Should these fail our prospects in this line will be less favorable. In farming, we have sowed the small field, west of the boys school house, containing about 4 acres with oats. The greatest part of the large field in front of the Mission is plowed: also a considerable part of the 22 acres over the Creek is plowed, & we expect soon to plant it with corn.

Ard Hoyt, Elizur Butler, Henry Parker, A.E. Blunt, E. Dean

Brainerd mission journal

May 1st 1823 Br. Vail set out for Willstown with such a load as he thinks the waggon will bear, consisting of bedding & other articles which were expected to go when the family moved, some meat &c— We are this afternoon called to rejoice in another addition to the mission family, a son born to Br. & sis. Butler.—

[May] 2nd Mr. Butrick left us to return to Taloney—Since the refreshing season there last summer it has been thought best that he should make Taloney his home, & spend as much time there as could be consistent with his urgent calls as an evangelist—We greatly need one or two more to labor in that office, & regret that Mr. Chamberlin has been detained so long in putting up buildings & making other preparations at Willstown—

[May] 5th Meeting for business, Br. Dean rendered acpt of smith shop for April as follows—

Shop C^r
By recvd in money ——————————— $ 8,00
  " Labor 24, produce 9,75 ——————— 33,75
  " Iron ,75———————————————— ,75
  " work done for Turnip mountain school 25,86½
  " " for Creekpath school ——————— 28,61½
  " " for Mission Brainerd ——————— 45.86
                                         142,84
Charged to customers to be brought in when paid 31,95
  D^r
To Iron bought from boat 107,00
  " repairing tools 2,50   109.50
  Balance in favor of shop   33,34

Br. Blunt requested permission to remove the cabin now standing below the kitchen, and repair it for his family—which was granted—

[May] 6th Br. Vail returned from Willstown. Sis. Chamberlin having measurably recovered from her late illness, & learning the state of the sisters at this place, thought sis. Anna might be more needed here than there, at least for the present, she therefore returned with Br. Vail—

The attention to preaching at Willstown is encouraging—They have commenced a sabbath school—A number of blacks & some cherokees attend & appear very anxious to learn—They are promised Testaments as soon as they have learned to read.—They have not opened the school on account of the school house not being in readiness—

Mr. Chamberlin has thought it not best for him to do any thing to that house, or to begin the school untill the people will themselves prepare the house—It is thought they will now have it ready in a few days—Special meeting called this evening to determine what cows shall be sent to Willstown &c   Resolved that Mr. Hoyt & Br. Parker be a Com. to select three cows for Willstown, & provide a hand to drive them. Resolved that the white mare be exchanged for the bay horse left by Br. Gleason with Br. Milo Hoyt—Resolved that Brs. Butler & Dean be a Com. to furnish a man to plow while Br. Vail goes to Hightower with Sis. Proctor—

Resolved, that Brs. Parker and Dean be a Com. to see that the roofs of the dining room kitchen & lumber house are repaired—

[May] 7th Br. Vail set out with Sis. Proctor for Hightower—

This afternoon the old king (Path killer) came to make us another visit. He soon enquired for John Arch to interpret—He was out on business but came in at evening—After supper the king related with apparent reserve, some of the decisions of the late council against disposing of their land—but in a little time he became quite open, and told us plainly that he was afraid of the white people; and distressed for his children (meaning the people of his nation) He desired to live here while he lived, but as he had but little time to stay, it was not much matter on his own account, but he was night and day grieved for his children that he should leave behind, lest the white people would give them no place to live, and they would be driven from the earth—We endeavored to soothe the poor old man by mentioning some things which we thought calculated to inspire a confidence in the government of the U.S. particularly in their father the president [Monroe]; and to show that he felt towards them as his children, and desired their best good and also that almost all the white people considered them as brothers, and wished to do them good—He replied, If we have a little brother who is poor & does not know well how to take care of himself, I do not think it is right to try to get away from him the little all that he possesses has: I think we should be willing to have him keep his little, and try to teach him how to use it that he may be better able to take care of himself—He acknowledged their father the President had always given them good talks, but he did not think they had been well kept—& proceeded to give us what he called a history of this business since his own time—for substance as follows—President Washington agreed where the line should be— had it run and marked—and told them this should always be the line between the Cherokees and white people—soon after there must be another treaty and another line—again another treaty and another line—and so on—always telling them this shall be the last line and always using the same reasons when they wished for more land viz. you have more land than you want,—you can live much better if you leave hunting, raise cattle, hogs, corn and cotton—make your own clothes, and have your bread and meat always at hand—if you do this then you dont want so much land—This he said was all good, but many did not at first like it, and they had great disputings about it: now they had done with their disputes, almost all were following this advice of their father, & could live very well on the little land they had—only they wanted their children instructed and trained to work—Soon these would be men and women: and the nation would then be rich and happy on their little land—and would not repine for what they had given to the U.S.—But now (said he) the Georgians seem determined to take this last little: & are willing to leave my children to go back and be lost—This grieves me so that I can think of nothing else, only that white people kill my people, and no notice is taken of it. He then gave in detail a long list of murders which had been committed in the nation by the whites, and the murderers not brought to justice. He said four of his own family had been murdered by white men in time of peace, and he never could get any satisfaction for it[26]—That just in that part of the nation where he lived, twelve persons had been murdered by the whites since the Creek war, and no murderers killed for it—It was not so among red people—if a person of one nation killed one of another, they always gave up the murderer—and if a cherokee killed a white man they always gave him up—He had after sent word to the president about these things. He knew there were good people among the whites, but knowing all these things as he did, he could not but be afraid of white people.—

[May] 8. The greatest part of the forenoon was spent with our good friend the king, & chiefly in conversation on religious subjects. He says when he was young they told him we went to another country when we died—that there were many people there, & great towns & villages—but they never talked much about this—He does not know whether they got the idea of a future state from their own minds, or in some way from the book of God—He did not choose to visit the schools this time saying he was tired and lame—& wanted to be on his way home. He would try & come again soon when he could stay & see the schools—for he always felt that he was at home among his children when here.

[May] 12. In meeting for business, Resolved to hire Robert Waters (a Cherokee) to labor on the farm, or otherwise as needed, for 7-1/2 months—or untill the close of the present year—
Resolved that Brs. Elsworth, Vail & Parker, be a committee to devise a plan for building stables or sheds, for visitors horses, mission cows &c—& report the same to the brethren, that (if approved) it may be sent to the Pru. Com. for their approbation—

[May] 15. Br. Vail returned and with him sis. Nancy Thompson—
Although the journey out was fatiguing for sis. Proctor & her young child, yet a kind providence carried them through without any material injury to health—Br. Proctor writes "The school here

continues to prosper—the number is increasing, and some little circumstances have greatly strengthened us in the belief that the school is much thought of by the people here especially by some Chiefs and head men. We have had about 25 scholars who have attended very regularly—they are very promising & very obedient"—Sis. Nancy says the children come decently clothed, & clean.—

Br. Vail returned by way of Turnip mountain—Br. & sis. Elsworth were in good health. Br. John Crawfish is at work with them at $10 a month, pay half clothing & half money—They are now in the house offered by Br. Mills, & are putting in a piece of corn in his old field—They all think it best to put up new buildings at the large spring as was before talked of—but as they are all now so much engaged in their cornfields, it is thought not best to commence buildings, untill they get a little over their business—Br. E. gives a very pleasing account of Br. Mills little congregation—he thinks he has never seen more serious attention in any part of the nation—On the sabbath previous to the first monday, Br. E. informed the congregation (consisting of about 30) of the monthly concert, & proposed a meeting for that purpose the next day, at about 4 O clock, The people began to assemble an hour or two before the time, & about all who were present on the sabbath came in.—

The cherokee who interpreted on the sabbath came a distance of 5 or 6 miles to be present at this meeting.—

[*May*] 16. Meeting for business—Recd letters from Brs. Proctor & Elsworth. They both ask for interpreters—Brethren can at present do no more than they have done—having before recommended to employ the young brothers who came from Cornwall if we could—the Pru. Com. having also recommended the same—If interpreters can be obtained we can then consult where it will be best to send them. Br. Elsworth needs a horse to plough.—

Resolved that Brs. Vail & Dean select a horse for Turnip mountain—As the particular charge of our cattle has been assigned to no one since it was given to Br. J.C. Elsworth Resolved that Br. Butler have charge of the cattle—

[*May*] 22nd Mr. Bascom arrived with three Choctaw youths on their way to Cornwall.

[*May*] 23rd Meeting for business, Br. Bascom present—

Resolved that Br. Vail, Dean & Elsworth, make arrangements with Mr. Bascom respecting a horse to carry him to N. England—As the youth expected to go on with Mr. Bascom from Creek path has failed on account of ill health, & as it is yet uncertain whether any will be sent from Taloney, several of the boys now in school were talked of under the question who can be obtained, to fill their places—Resolved that Mr. Hoyt, Mr. Bascom, and Br. Ellis, decide according to their discression whether John Brewer—John E. Latta, or David Carter, or either of them be selected to fill the two places—

Sab. [*May*] 25th We were favored with the ministrations of Mr. Bascom, whose health is so far restored that he was able to preach both forenoon & afternoon. Cornelius A. Hoyt after relating his religious experience & being examined by the chh, was admitted a candidate for communion—

[*May*] 26th Waggon arrived with Iron & other articles from Augusta—

[*May*] 27th We sent Br. John Arch out to look for Vinson Gould & Mindwell W. Gould—two beneficiaries who have not been brought in since they went out last fall—their parents having removed from their former [residence?]. Mr. Chamberlin came in from Willstown— They are not prepared to take scholars to board with them, but have commenced a school for the small number whose parents live sufficiently near to board them at home—The school was commenced on the 12th inst.—Last sabbath many more people assembled than could be accomodated in their little house. Sis. Chamberlins health is not so good since sis. Anna left her. Mr. Butrick also came in this evening with a youth from Taloney to go on with Mr. Bascom to Cornwall. They are in usual health & prosperity at Taloney and Springplace—
Recvd a letter from Mr. Hicks, enclosing one sent through him from the people of Turnipminetown (a place lying north or north east from Taloney) requesting a school & blacksmith.—Mr. Hicks desires that their request may be granted if possible—

[*May*] 28. Mr. Butrick preached the Wednesday lecture—

[*May*] 29. Mr. Butrick left us, to return to Taloney & the region round about, taking with him Br. James Fields interpreter—Mr. Chamberlin also left us to return home, taking sis. Anna with him—

[May] 30. Br. Arch returned & brought Vinson with him—Mindwell is lame by a swelling—They think she will be able to come in two weeks, & promise to bring her—

We think it best in general (if we can) to send after children that are not returned, as they appear often to be kept by their parents through mere sloth, or inattention—or some trifling thing—which is no hindrance to our regaining the children when they are applied for—These children are glad of the opportunity to return.—

In behalf of the brethren
Ard Hoyt

Brainerd mission journal

1823

June 1st Mr. Bascom again preached to our little congregation. We had expected the boy we call Benjamin Tappan to go on with Mr. Bascom; his mother and other relatives had consented—but his mother came to day and gave counter orders—it being her choice that he should stay here—Many of our largest scholars are anxious for an enlarged education—& would be very willing to go to Cornwall or almost any other place to obtain it—most of their parents also appear willing that they should stay at school as long as there is any thing for them to learn, but they are not willing they should go so far away. We do not know a single full Cherokee who is willing to permit his son to go out & be educated among white people.

[June] 2nd Mr. Bascom with five lads for the F.M.S. took leave of us this morning.[27]—Br. David S. Tarcheehe, is now here. He thinks it duty to assist his father on his farm through this summer; and then he is willing to be employed in the mission any way that shall be thought best; but (other things being equal) it is his choice to teach a school—He thinks he shall be glad to commence about October.

In meeting for business Resolved That Br. Blunt have charge of cleaning the cellars, drains and door yards, & of shearing the sheep—

[June] 4th 2600 lb bacon, which had been previously bargained for, arrived from Tennessee, for which we pay 13 cents pr pound—The $338 which we pay for this bacon would have purchased last fall about 10,000 lb pork—It would be much better if we could have milk, and other articles of light food, in plenty and eat less meat—But so far as meat must be used it is undoubtedly the best economy to put up a sufficient quantity of pork in the cold season—

[June] 9th Meeting for business—Resolved that Br. F. Elsworth have charge of the mills—From January to March we were expecting Mr. Shelton to come and make arrangements for taking the mills. He was expected to tend them on hire untill we could hear from the Pru. Com.—& then if the Com. approved, & we could agree, to take them on [shares?]. He waited in this state of suspense untill the 21st of March when Mr. Chamberlin, being at the agency on business, called on Mr. Shelton—He had not heard that we wished him to come, and therefore, supposing we did not want him he had made arrangements for his summer business, & did not know how he could dispose of it, but said he would think of it and in about one month come down and see us—This is the last we have heard of him: It is now thought best that Oliver Elsworth should steadily tend the mills & as Br. F. Elsworth thinks it will add but little to his present charge, to include the mills, under these circumstances, they were assigned to his care as above—

We have had rain every day of the present month, untill this day.

[June] 10th Dr. Butler set out to go again to the agency for the purpose of adjusting with the present agent all accounts & business transactions which have occurred with the former agent.[28]

Finished new roofing [on] the dining room and kitchen—The shingles, (or boards) of these roofs had most of them considerably decayed, & also the poles by which they were supported—These have all been taken off & the place of the rotten shingles & poles supplied with new, & a third course of shingles added: we think these roofs are now better & tighter than when the buildings were first erected. Since the kitchen roof was thus repaired, we have had two or three violent storms & find it as dry as any room on the premises—We have also, within a few weeks past, removed the cabin that stood back of the kitchen to the northwest end of the second range (back of the girls school house) & put to it a new floor, roof & chimney, with a rough piazza in front, wide enough for a bedroom in one end making it a very comfortable residence for Br. & sis. Blunt. We have also put new roofs after the manner of the above, on the cabin where Br. Elsworth resides, & on the meal house.

The new ground above the mills requiring yet much labor to prepare it for seed, it is thought impracticable to raise corn on it this season;

Br. Elsworth therefore thinks of preparing it for turnips, & perhaps to sow it with timothy, with the view of preparing it for a meadow.

[June] 11th After the Wednesday lecture, our schools pass a short examination; at which time the teachers give a written certificate of the conduct of the scholars for the week past.

The girls certificate to day, after mentioning their good behavior both in school and out contains the following summary of their labor between schools since monday of last week, viz. They have made fifty hunting frocks, besides hemming a number of handkerchiefs & some other sewing, in addition to their usual work in other branches of labor which is assisting in the dining room, in the milking, in all the washings, doing the whole of their own washings & ironing, most of the ironing for the mission family & boys, & mending the boys clothes. During the above time in working hours three of the girls have been employed with sis. Elsworth, two with sis. Dean, one with sis. Vail, one with sis. Butler, and one with sis. Blunt. The whole number of girls is thirty one, leaving only 23 for the above mentioned labor. The Com. will not receive this as a specimen of what is done every eight days, but only as a sample of dexterity in certain hours of work—

Having mentioned the number of the girls, we will just say the number of boys is 45—making the whole number now with us 76. In numbering scholars we never include children of missionaries.

Dr. Butler returned this evening. The agent treated him with polite attention, was well satisfied respecting the account & paid him $375. For the remainder we must wait untill an estimate of money wanted at the agency for the next quarter can go to the war department, & returns be made—

[June] 12th Mr. Shelton came in this evening proposing to make trial of the mills as was talked of last winter. When Mr. Chamberlin saw him in march he thought he could have made arrangements to come within a month from that time; but his business had been such that he could not leave untill the present time.—

[June] 13. Meeting for business, Resolved that Brs. Butler, Elsworth & Dean, be a Com to make arrangements with Mr. Shelton respecting our mills, including the dam race &c—Finished the coal house near the blacksmiths shop—

[June] 14ᵗʰ Br. Elsworth with the hired men are cutting and drawing timber for flooms &c—about the mills—Mr. Shelton being hired to complete what of the original plan has been left undone as taking the rock out of the race &c & to do what is now thought necessary to put the mills in complete opperation.

[June] 17ᵗʰ The boys finished hoeing the corn over the crick for the first time. It is supposed there are about 21 or 22 acres in the field, about 5 not cultivated, & about 1-1/2 of potatoes, leaving about 15 acres of corn, this is all the corn we have this season, except a little planted in the small piece on which are cultivated only culinary vegetables. Under this culture we have from 3 to 4 acres, about 1/3 in corn and potatoes, & the remainder in common garden vegetables— In these pieces & in the gardens, we have a hired gardener constantly employed with some of the boys whenever the weather will permit— We have also in a piece by themselves, about 3-1/2 acres of sweet potatoes. We suppose the Com. have expected to find in the journal notice of the time of beginning & ending of certain parts of the agricultural business during the past important part of the year—but these have been so interrupted by other business that the journalist has not been able to distinguish them—The farmer is now employed with the ox team, drawing timber for an extension floom, to be placed in the mill race in front of the mills & shops—

[June] 18ᵗʰ The Rev. Mr. [Hugh] Dickson & [Rev.] Mr.[D.B.] Johnson called on us on their return from Monroe, & Mayhew to South Carolina.²⁹ Mr. Johnson only had been to Mayhew. The missionaries at Mayhew were in health, & the mission prosperous. Mr. Johnson was highly pleased with the appearances & prospects there—Mr. Dickson has been out as a delegate from the society under whose patronage the mission to the Chicasaws is conducted—He expresses high satisfaction in the state of their mission there, & the interviews he has had with the chiefs—Their prospects are much more flattering than he expected—
They visited our schools, & appeared pleased with the appearance of the children—

[June] 19. Messrs Dickson & Johnson, being in haste to pursue their journey, left us this morning about 9 oclock. They came by Creek path & Willstown, & have turned considerably out of their way in order to visit the different stations in this region—They go by Spring place &

Taloney—The mother of the girl to whom we had given the name of Mindwell Woodbridge Gould came in, & told us she had brought Mindwell to a place which is about 12 miles from us, & the girl then complaining on account of her lameness (which the mother says has been the cause of keeping her) she had left her—She wished to send and bring her in—Accordingly Br. John Arch went out & brought her in—she appears to have nearly recovered of her lameness, & we hope will soon be quite well—(The clothes sent for Mindwell & also those sent for Vinson, by their beneficiaries; fit them very well though they might have been a very little larger, as they are for growing children.)

[June] 21st A fish was found in our trap this morning four feet in length & 2-1/2 in circumference, weighing 47 lb. This we believe is the largest we have taken in the trap, though it is said larger have been taken from these waters. Messrs Spencer, Whitlesey, & Goodand, the two former from Conn. the latter from V^t, having at this time a vacation in schools they are teaching in Georgia, came out to see Brainerd—

[June] 23. Our visiting friends, having a journey of about 250 miles to return home to their schools, cannot spare longer time to stay with us.—With their good wishes, they left a donation of $10 for the use of the mission, & set out on their return this morning—
Br. J.C. Elsworth came in late this evening, having rode from Turnip mountain since 6 oclock A.M.—His chief business is to get a horse to plough their corn. Br. John Crawfish lives with him & is very faithful in his work, & lively in religion—The native professors there appear well, & some others serious—
Br. E. & his hired man have been chiefly employed in the corn field— He expects soon to commence clearing on the site for the new buildings, & for a field near it—

[June] 24th Mr. Butrick came in from Taloney, & with him a youth of the Sanders family of that place[30]—The school at Taloney & Hightower prospers, & the attention to preaching in that region is not diminished. Mr. McChord from Lawrence Co, Alabama, on his way to Tennessee, spent the afternoon with us—visited both schools, looked over the premises, mills, shops, &c[31]—

[June] 25th Mr. McChord left us this morning assuring us that he was exceedingly well pleased with the schools, & general order of the mission—He thought we should find it profitable to pay more attention to [?ing]—Mr. Butrick and his young companion left us this afternoon to return to Taloney by way of Mr. Hicks'—Br. Elsworth set out on his return home by moon light this evening—

[June] 27th Rev. I. Walke, of the baptist denomination called on us.

[June] 28th Mr. Walke visited the schools &c—

[June] 29th Mr. Walke preached morning and evening—
He expressed great satisfaction in the appearance of the schools, the children on the sabbath, & the congregation—

[June] 30th Our visiting brother left us this morning to pursue his preaching tour in Tennessee—We feel much obliged to him for his friendly visit—In a review of the past month we have great reason to admire the forbearing goodness & mercy of our God—While we have by our slothfulness & stupidity in spiritual things, provoked him to cut us off by some sudden stroke, or at least to remove us from this his holy service, he has only chastised us as a kind father, by withdrawing the cheering & enlivening influences of his spirit, and in gentle powers saying, "return unto me, & I will return unto you."[32] O that we might now be wise, & harken to his voice, that our backslidings may be healed! To our shame we must say, it is an awfully stupid time at Brainerd—Will the Pru. Com. pray for us?
But notwithstanding we know these things exist within us as a mission family, & that there is very little seriousness among our unconverted children, yet, through the goodness of God, the external concerns of the chh & the schools continue much as they were. We were apprehensive that the putting over the vacation to August would create some uneasiness in the children, & also in some of their parents—but in regard to the latter (so far as we know) they have been all well satisfied—Some of the children have left without cause, but these with one or two exceptions, have all been stopped by us in the outset, or sent back by their parents—A good degree of contentment is now manifested in the school, and some ambition to prepare for the examination—
We have with us 47 boys & 33 girls—which is more than we have had at any one time for 18 months past—
This addition to the numbers of schollars now with us, above that mentioned on the 11th is occasioned by the admission of two girls, &

the return of some boys who were then absent without leave—The health of the family has been usually good for the month past—

Ard Hoyt, E. Dean, H. Parker
Elizur Butler, Frederick Elsworth, A.E. Blunt

The Cor. Sec. will please notice a P.S. on the next page—

P.S. We have omited to mention that but a very limited supply of clothing for the children has been sent to us this year—We are already obliged to make for them, & fear it will be difficult for us to keep them decent untill their benefactors can be informed, & forward us a supply—The readiness of our Sisters to furnish clothing in the infancy of the mission, as the first intimation that they would be useful—& the super abundance sent to this place untill notice was given that we had more than was then immediately necessary, induces a belief that there is now the same readiness to grant a supply if our wants could be definitely known. We think it would be well to make a note in the Herald stating our need—if it can be done so as not again to turn this branch of benevolence too much this way—

Brainerd mission journal

1823
July 1ˢᵗ A fish was taken from the trap this morning which weighed 48-1/2 lbs.
Br. Vail rode out on business relating to corn which was to have been brought to us last fall—& if this cannot be obtained to purchase—we having only about 20 bushels on hand—

[July] 3ᵈ Br. Vail returned—No prospect of getting the corn that was promised so as to meet our present necessities—but corn can be bought about 40 miles up the river for 50 cents a bushel—A few hours after Br. Vail returned we were offered corn from a boat that will be at our ware house tomorrow at the same price we must give if we go up the river after it. If the corn is good we shall purchase a supply for the remainder of this season—
Br. Thomas Basil entered into agreement to work in the smiths shop four years on the same terms of Harvey Williams—

[July] 4ᵗʰ Br. & sis. Vail were this day called to rejoice in the birth of a Son—Sis. Vail, though she has for many months been confined

entirely to her bed, appears as comfortable as women generally in child bed—the babe appears healthy & strong—
Purchased the corn which was offered yesterday; & have now enough for the present season—

[July] 7th Meeting for business—
Br. Dean rendered acct of smiths shop for May & June.

Recvd in money	$ 33,00
do " produce———————————	15,15
do " labor———————————	25,00
Work done for Mission viz. Brainerd ——	172,98
Willstown ———————————	19,73
Turnip mountain ———————————	_22.00_
Charges to customers $78,31	_$287.86_
Shop Dr To 1000 bu coal ———————	50,00
Tools & stock from Boston ———————	596,53
Tools repaired & made ———————	_3.80_
	650,33
Balance against shop	_$362.47_

The expense for hired smiths to be brought into the account next month—
Br. Elsworth rendered acct of mills from June 9 to July 5th.

Gristmill Cr by 40 bu corn		$20,00
Dr to labor & board of hand	11,69	
[Peeking?] stones & repairing	2,00	_13.69_
Balance in favor of mill		6,31

Saw mill from 9 June to July 5th

Dr to 25 logs @ [?]	10,42	
labor & board of hand	4,25	14,67
Cr by 3551 ft. mostly at 3¢		_59.70_
Balance in favor of mill		_45.03_

[July] 11. The girl hired to nurse sister Vail having been unwell several days went home—We do not expect her to return—

[July] 12. Sis. Elsworth being unwell, & expecting soon to be confined, it is thought she may be more comfortable with sister Dean—on this account they removed their lodging to Br. Deans—

For eight successive days we have had thunder & rain every day—In the midst of these thunder showers, which are very comon in this country, we observed a notice in the Boston Recorder of the providential escape of a Mr. Spooners family in Long Island, while the house was rent by the lightning in a most extraordinary manner—their escape being attributed to the repellent property of feathers—which is further confirmed by the escape of a bird while his cage was demolished by the electrical fluid—This reminds us of a fact which took place before our eyes last season. During a heavy thunder storm some persons were looking out from the back door of the mission house, when the lightening was seen to descend upon or near a small tree about 10 or 12 rods from the door, from which a smoke instantly assumed as from the singing (singeing) of feathers, & as soon disappeared—From the circumstance of the smoke asscending immediately after the descent of the lightening, some persons ran out to examine the place, & found a small bird lifeless near the tree; his feathers burnt & his body torn—No other effect of the lightening was to be observed.

[July] 14. Shut the water out of the mill race, for the purpose of deepening it &c.

[July] 19. meeting for business—Question. Will the Brn. advise the steward to contract with Mr. J. Ross for two thousand bushels of corn to be delivered at the barn & mill in the course of next fall at 45¢ per bushel? Answered: What is purchased should be delivered here; the quantity left with the steward—
Resolved, that Brs. Vail, Elsworth, & Dean, be a Com. to say whether the old two horse waggon be sold, & if so, at what price—
The 26,00 of bacon which was brought in on the 4th of June has all been consumed with the addition of one beef & br. Parker thinks at best 200 lb of side pork which was put down last winter, has been eaten during this time—

[July] 25. Showers of rain for a few days past have somewhat interupted the workmen in the race, & this afternoon the water rising in the creek burst over the temporary dam which had been flung across the head of the race to keep it dry while we were working in it; it is therefore thought best to dismiss the hands, & wait a more favorable time to finish this work. The new floom by the mills is completed, & much of the rock taken out, so that if no more is done we shall have more water at the mills than before—

We have had a wet season so far—The Tennessee river is very high, & we are told much damage has been done to the cornfield on its margin by the overflowing of the waters—

[July] 28. Br. & sis. Elsworth were this day made the joyful parents of a fine son. Mother & child under comfortable circumstances—

[July] 29. In meeting for business, Resolved that a division be now made of our labors agreeably to the resolution of the Pru. Com. contained in letter of Feb. 19.—Resolved that Brs. Vail, Blunt & Ellis be a Com. to report to the next meeting what parts of agricultural business will be necessary to employ the boys—Resolved that we send for Mr. Alexander to come & repair the mills, & for Mr. Harris to tend them.

[July] 30. Br. Vail set out to go to Rhea Co—for a mill wright & miller, & some other business—Br. & Sis. Elsworth came in from Turnip mountain this evening, & Br. Milo Hoyt, & Sis. Chamberlin with them—Br. Elias Boudinot & some other cherokee friends, also came in to day.—

The neighbors at Turnip mountain have assisted in puting up the body of a house—some boards are in readiness for the roof & plank for the floor. Br. E. hopes to be able to remove into it in a few days after his return; as the waters of the Coosa have lately overflowed its banks, & the place where they have lived being near the river will probably be unhealthy. Br. E. says the rain has kept the people back in puting up buildings.

[July] 31—The health of the mission family for this month has been much as usual. Sis. Vail (though apparently on the mend) is still unable to rise from her bed, or to be placed in a chair.

Six or eight of the children have had the fever & ague, which in most cases has been removed in a few days. ~~This is a complaint which we [?] has [?] before visited this place~~ Whether it be occasioned by the mill pond, or the state of the atmosphere this wet season is not certain but it is supposed to proceed from the pond & race.—From the 4th to the end of the month the thermometer ranged at sunrise from 72 to 80—noon 74 to 88—Sunset 76 to 90—15 days of this time have been showery.[33]

Ard Hoyt, Henry Parker, Elizur Butler, E. Dean

Mission Journal Brainerd

1823
August 1st Mr. Potter came in, accompanied by Mr. Hadden, a Licenciate from South Carolina, who has been [missionating?] in Alabama—one of the schollars called Joseph, nephew of John Arch, came with Mr. Potter—no others are expected from Creek Path— Shortly after these Mr. Chamberlin arrived with his family, & others from Willstown—Then Mr. Butrick, & others—Br. & sis. Hall & some others at Taloney are detained in consequence of the children having the hooping-cough. Br. Mills, & his company from Turnip-mountain also came in this evening—Brainerd is now favored with a dear & precious company, who have come up to participate in the holy feast.—Br. Proctor & his company are yet behind—

[Aug.] 2nd Br. Proctor, Sis. Thompson, & others from Hightower, came in this morning—
This day was devoted to religious exercises preparatory to the communion—Prayer meeting at 8 ock—public worship at 10—Mr. Hadden preached.—
Public worship in the afternoon at 2—services in cherokee, except the prayers—Brs. Reese, Arch & Boudinot, each in turn, addressed the people.
The chh then reexamined John Crawfish & Cornelius A. Hoyt, candidates for communion, & voted to admit them tomorrow—Acha, candidate for baptism, was also reexamined—she is to be baptised tomorrow. Three persons from Turnip mountain, & Kapooley (the Sandwich islander) offered themselves to be examined as candidates for baptism—Some of them gave a short relation, & answered a few questions—but it being too late to go through, adjourned till after public worship tomorrow—

Sab. [Aug.] 3. A large congregation for this place assembled in & around our little house of worship. After sermon by Mr. Butrick, Acha, & her six children, were baptized. She takes the name of Mary in addition to her former name. Three of her children are members of the school, two of which are beneficiaries, & bear the names of Elizabeth Kean and Wheeler Gilbert—John Crawfish & C.A. Hoyt renewed covenant, & were admitted to the communion—Among the communicants were seven Cherokee youths between the age of 20 &

27, all able to read the scriptures, & communicate to their people in their own tongue.

At the close of worship in the afternoon the chh resumed the examination of candidates for baptism—& admited Kapooley—& the three persons from Turnip mountain viz. Polly, a woman whose hair is nearly white by age—A-muh-noi (english Noisy Water) aged about 30—& Charles Fields, about 22.[34] The mother of Charles is baptized, & would probably have been now admited to communion, but she was not able to be present.

The Com. will understand that we admit none as candidates for baptism who do not give hopeful evidence of piety: this evidence is however expected to increase, as to be more fully confirmed, before they are admited to the ordinance.

This sabbath, we trust, has been a refreshing & encouraging season to many souls—& we indulge the hope that good impressions have been made, which will not soon, or easily, be effaced. The work is the Lords—to Him we joyfully commit it—& to his name be ascribed all the praise—

[Aug.] 4*th* The schools passed the usual course of examinations, it is thought to as great satisfaction as on any former occasion.

After a short intermission, the children formed at the mission house, & returned to the school house in procession, where (with many others) they witnessed the union of their teachers in the bans of matrimony.[35]

At 3 Ock, more than 200 persons (including the children) dined on the best fare our humble circumstances could afford. After which the children, with most of our Cherokee friends who came to spend this solemn & joyful season with us, took leave in a cheerful & affectionate manner—The vacation is to continue four weeks.

We have reason to praise the Lord that we are permited to enjoy such privileges, & to witness such scenes in this wilderness.

August 5*th* General meeting for business, all the brethren from the local schools, except Br. Hall, present.

A season spent in prayer & singing—

Communications relative to the general concerns of the mission from the Cor. Sec. & Treasurer, read—Also Records of business meetings at Brainerd since the last general meeting.

Mr. Chamberlin had permission to hire a man for 2 or 3 months—& to use his own discretion whether to bring the water from the spring to his house in logs, it being 40 or 50 rods.

Resolved that Mr. Hoyt attend the next council at New town, & present to them a writen statement of the present situation of the schools in the nation under the patronage of the A.B.C.F.M.[36]—seek to know whether the plans of the missionaries meet the approbation of the Council & also tender the Council our thanks for the kindness with which we have been recvd by them & their people—and in case of Mr. Hoyts failure that he appoint a person to carry the statement, & perform the business above mentioned.

Resolved, that at all our general, monthly & special meetings, at the request of any brother, it shall be the duty of the moderator to call for a prayer before we proceed to any further business.

Agreed to let Br. Proctor have a horse from Brainerd for Hightower school; & if the horse Br. Proctor brought on was charged to that school—that the school be credited the same as before charged, said horse having been kept at Brainerd—Adjourned untill after breakfast tomorrow.

[Aug.] 6th Met according to adjournment—

Reports from Creek Path school & Hightower, read—

No report being recd from the Taloney school—

Resolved that Br. Hall be requested to forward one to Mr. Hoyt—

Resolved that Br. Proctor be permited now to erect the remaining buildings for which permission was granted last fall—

The Com. appointed on the 29th ult. to Report to the next meeting what parts of agricultural business will be necessary to employ the boys, presented the following Report, which was read & accepted, viz—

"Brethren, your Com. respecting the share of the work necessary for the employment of the boys, submit the following, viz. That the boys can improve the fields belonging to the mission on this side of the creek, excepting the new field above the blacksmiths shop—provided that two healthy brothers labor with them out of school, and one of them have the direction of the business—& have liberty on pressing or urgent occasions, to hire assistance as he shall think necessary, to enable him to prepare the labor so as not to hinder the boys in so great a degree as to be an essential injury to the crops: also that he shall have charge of as much teams as shall be sufficient to do all the labor, & if rightly managed, all the various kinds of labor without hurry or confusion—Also that the boys be furnished with a sufficient supply of utensils, & a sufficiency of carts, Waggons, harness &c—["]

Resolved, That Brs. Vail & Blunt be appointed to labor with the boys, & that Br. Vail have direction of the business, in pursuance of, & agreeably to the above report—

Resolved that the two yoke of oxen that have been much used this summer be assigned to the mills; & the lined & whitefaced steers occasionally if wanted—

Resolved that the one horse waggon & harness be sent to Turnip mountain.

As the young men from Cornwall decline entering the service of the mission as proposed in the Cor. Sec.'s letter, Therefore Resolved, that we deem it expedient to employ them occasionally as we do other Cherokee converts.

[Aug.] 7*th* Mr. Butrick—Br. Proctor, Sis. Thompson, & Mr. Beamer (chief from Hightower) took leave of us—Also Br. Milo Hoyt & wife—Darius Hoyt, & Cornelius—the latter to spend a part or all the vacation at Wills Town. We begin to feel almost alone at Brainerd.

[Aug.] 8*th* Special meeting for the purpose of rightly understanding, & fixing definitely some particulars under the late arrangment of business—

Question, Who shall direct as to cuting & hauling wood; & taking care of visitors horses—   Answd Br. Vail—

Who shall take care of the stock   "   dto

Who shall take charge of killing & taking care of meat   dto

Shall Br. Butler have charge of fencing & cultivating as a garden, the small field between the barn & the farm house, & also of the present garden?   Answd yes—

Who shall have charge of rebuilding the fish trap, & repairing the dam—   Ansd The brethren at the Creek—

Resolved that Brs. Vail, Butler & Dean be a Com. to examine & report whether we build a new ware house, or repair the old one—if they think best to build—the size & place where—

[Aug.] 11*th* Brs. Potter, Chamberlin & Elsworth (the two latter with their wives) having been detained to the present time on business of their respective stations, all left us today—Also Oliver Elsworth, who goes to reside with his brother at Turnip-mountain.

Br. & Sis. Ellis went out, expecting to visit Taloney—Hightower, & perhaps some other of the stations, before they return. This journey is undertaken with a particular view to his health, which has not been good for some time.—Only two of the schollars (except Kapooley) remain with us; yet on counting we find we can still number a very considerable family at Brainerd—the gardener—two hired men who work at the creek but board at the mission house—the interpreter— the above mentioned schollars, & the mission families (including infants) number twenty seven at the old place.—Brs. Elsworth & Dean, with their wives & babes, two apprentices & one journeyman in the smiths shop make nine boarding at the Creek—in all thirty six— Br. Vail's little girl has the ague & fever.—

[Aug.] 12. Br. Blunt is striving to bring forward the coopering business in the absence of the boys. He has brought from the woods a fine bunch of staves & heading which he got out last winter. He finds it will not do in this region to leave this timber long exposed to the weather as is often practiced at the north—& the sawmill not affording boards or slabs to make a shed over it, his next business (Br. Elsworth being unwell) is to get logs & saw boards for this shed.

The lathe, to run by water, which was brought on by Mr. Conger, is now in opperation, when needed in the small room attached to the blacksmiths shop.

Mr. Henning from S. Carolinia made us a visit—

[Aug.] 13. Brs. Vail, Butler & Dean, with Br. McPhearson for a guide, went to look out a road & place for a ware house, on this side of the creek.

[Aug.] 16. Meeting for business. The Com. on the subject of warehouse reported that they are undecided. Whereupon it was determined not to build. Concluded to offer the two yearling colts for sale—

[Aug.] 17. Br. Blount unwell, symtems of a fever.—We think more of it as it was about this time last year that the fever commenced—

[Aug.] 20. Br. Blount keeps his bed & requires constant attendance. Kapooly came in from work this evening unwell—

[Aug.] 21. Br. Blount still runing down—Kapooly keeps his bed—high fever—

[Aug.] 22. Br. Blunt rested last night but his fever returns again to day. Kapooly still keeps his bed—This mail brought us six numbers of the

Evangelical & litterary Magazine, commencing with the present year published at Richmond Va. We have also lately recd three numbers of the Family Visitor a weekly paper—published at the same place. Our thanks are due to some unknown friends, probably the proprietors of these useful publications, for the valuable donation.

We have also recvd in the same way for several years—The Religious Remembrancer published at Philadelphia—The Religious Intelligencer from Newhaven, & the Boston Recorder. All these form a rich variety & excellent religious & litterary treat, to our numerous family, & to many of our occasional visitants.[37]

[Aug.] 23. Noah Vail taken with fever & ague—Anna Hoyt sick; uncertain to what it will turn.—

[Aug.] 25. Br. Blunt, Kapooly & Sis. Anna, all confined to their beds—Noah Vail & Almira Parker have ague & fever, Electa Vail the little girl who has been under the latter complaint for sometime now begins to escape her regular fits, & we hope is on the recovery—Sis. Vail still unable to sit up—

[Aug.] 26. Br. & Sis. Ellis returned—They have visited Taloney, Hightower, Turnipmountain, & Willstown—found all in usual health, except, Br. Hall. He was able to keep about & attend to the school, but is troubled much with pain in the breast & debility—

On their journey they found a number of their scholars, & were much gratified by the warm affection manifested by all they saw—

It is hoped the journey will prove beneficial to the health of Br. Ellis; but the stages have been too long for his strength—he returns much fatigued—

[Aug.] 27. One of the girls, who remains with us through the vacation, attacked with ague & fever.

[Aug.] 29. The old fish trap having decayed, was taken out & a new one put in—

[Aug.] 30. Most, or all our sick, are now convalescent—Except Br. Blunt & Kapooly, the complaints have all been light—& these have been far less malignant than the fever of last year—Mr. Butrick came in with Br. Cornel. Hoyt from Willstown—Mr. Butrick has been traveling with Br. Boudinot for interpreter, parted with him this morning about half way between this & Willstown, to which place Br.

Boudinot was to return to spend sabbath with Mr. Chamberlin, & then to come on & over take Mr. Butrick here.

[Aug.] 31. Sab. Six of the scholars returned—Mr. Butrick preached to our little congregation—
In concluding the journal for this month during most of which the schools have been vacated, we desire to record the goodness of God, in that the necessary chastisement by sickness in the mission family has been laid upon us in the absence of the children that the well could have more leisure to attend upon the sick—that the health of so great a proportion of the family has been preserved, & that He has so speedily sent healing mercy that on the first return of the children we can say there is no fever among us—Br. F. Elsworth continues unable to attend to much business—he has had neither fever nor cough—has complained chiefly of want of appetite & sleep, & for some time untill of late his strength has been running down—it appears now to be stationary, or, as he hopes, gaining—Sis. Vail has found herself able to walk two or three steps, & for a short time to sit in a chair.

Ard Hoyt, John Vail, H. Parker, E. Butler

Brainerd Mission Journal

1823
Sept. 1. The gristmill has for some time been out of repair, & we have been expecting a workman to put it right—It has now entirely failed so that we can grind no more—Br. Dean set out for Rhea Co. to hasten the millwright.

[Sept.] 2nd The time set for vacation having closed, the schools commenced this day, with 13 boys & 10 girls—We learn that some of the absent children have ague & fever, the seeds of which were probably taken here. We think it likely that some of the parents will for a time delay bringing their children from an apprehension that Brainerd is at this time a sickly place—but our apprehensions on this subject arise simply from the state of facts, & not from any thing we have heard—

[Sept.] 3rd Br. Elias Boudinot came in for the purpose of joining Mr. Butrick again, with the expectation of proceeding to the Valley towns—Mr. Chamberlin came with him on business—Br. Dean also

returned & brought a millwright with him—We being out of meal, the first job of the millwright was to put the mill in opperation so as to grind for present use—In about two hours he had it runing so that it grinds very well for the present, it will however require considerable labor to put it in good repair—We greatly need a miller with sufficient skill to keep the mill in order—

[Sept.] 4th Br. Boudinot's horse failing, Mr. Butrick went on without him—He expects to go by Taloney & take an interpreter from that place—

[Sept.] 5. Dr Butler set out for Taloney—Br. Hall desiring his advise respecting a complaint with which his little daughter has for a long time been afflicted—

[Sept.] 8. Br. Reece, & 19 of his neighbors, are employed cleaning the mill-race—For the first day we are to pay over to the collector of the national tax fifty cents for each man—this being the amt of their annual pole tax—For the remainder of the time they are to have 62 1/2 cents per day, payable in clothing or smiths work.—

[Sept.] 9. Br. Frederick Elsworth set out to travel for his health—He goes into Tennessee—undecided how far he may travel or when returns—
Dr Butler returned late this evening—He left Taloney after breakfast, not expecting to come through in a day—He thinks if he had set out early he might have reached home about dark—
They had an interesting time at Taloney on the Sabbath—The sacrament of the supper was administered—Br. Mills with his son Jerh Evarts was there—After the close of the usual exercises Br. Mills addressed the people with his wanted animation & solemnity, & it was supposed he detained them more than hour, all siting quietly & hearing with solemn attention to the last—

[Sept.] 11. Harvey Williams, who went a few days ago to visit his friends, we hear is sick with Ague & fever—

[Sept.] 12. A waggon arrived this evening from Augusta, with Iron & other articles for the mission. There are 8 boxes & 1 bbl, containing donated articles, as follows, viz. Box fr. J.M. Soc., of Rodman Jefferson Co, N.Y., containing cloth, clothing & 5 dollars in money,

Estimated value (including money)	$56,27
Barrel from Orwell Vt—Cloth & clothing—estimated	77,78

Box from Ogden Monroe Co, N.Y.—dto— $48,67
dto from Ten. Char. Soc. Carleton V^t dto—   45,92
dto, containing articles from Berkshire Tioga Co—N.Y.
Valued at $42,25, also from Benevolent Ladies
In Ovid, Seneca Co, N.Y.—$14,11—total valuation   56,36
Box fr. Great bend Pa— estimated value   28,54
dto—Utica N.Y.—without bill or valuation, containing the following
articles—19-1/2 yds linen cloth—1 pr sheets—2 blankets—1 Quilt—2
shirts—2 pr pillow cases—1 pr pillow ticks—1 boulster tick—3
towels—3 small remnants homemade—5 pr socks—1 pr boots, thread
& yarn—
One large box, put up by Deacon A. Thomas Utica & containing
articles from Madrid, Lawrence Co, N.Y. without bill or estimate—&
one Box of Bibles & Testaments from Philadelphia Bible Soc,
containing 25 Octavo bibles, 50 dto N. Testaments—50 bibles duo
decimo, 50 dto N. Testaments.
We are under great obligations to this Soc. for having furnished Bibles
& Testaments for charitable distribution as we have needed, from an
early day of the mission—& also for the encouragement of a
continued supply. As this people are learning to read, the call for this
charity is fast increasing. A number have been sometime anxiously
waiting the arrival of this box—The cloths—clothing & beding, will
also all be useful—Our thanks are due to the Father of mercies, & to
each individual of his dear children who have thus contributed to the
supply of our wants—

[Sept.] 17. Sis. J. Elsworth taken down—Ague & fever—

[Sept.] 18. Mr. Hoyt was called to attend a weding in the neighborhood. The Bridegroom was educated in Mr. Gambolds school at
Springplace—the Bride at Brainerd—The industrious habits & very
respectable behavior of this couple afford a pleasing prospect of
future usefulness to themselves & others—Meeting for business—
Resolved that Mr. John McTier be hired (if he can be obtained on
reasonable terms) to tend the mills for one year—He was married last
spring to a sister of Br. Thompson—& will expect to have one of the
cabbins, & board himself. He & his wife are both professors, in
communion with us—Resolved—That a black woman be hired to
labor in the family at the Creek, & that the hands employed there
board in that family—

[Sept.] 19. Sis. Dean obliged to take her bed—cold chills with fever. The mill-wright having done what he supposed was immediately necessary to the mills put them in opperation last evening, & left early this morning—Soon after the mill-wright left us we attempted to grind, after considerable time of trial, a logg broke, & the family must be again out of bread for want of meal—

[Sept.] 20. A millwright on his journey, providentially called on us last evening—He consented to tarry to day, & put the mill in opperation— a few bushels were ground soon enough to make bread for the sabbath—We have suffered much loss in the mills for want of a good miller who could keep them in repair—

Sab. [Sept.] 21. But a small part of the family able to attend meeting— Sis. Deans fever runs high—

[Sept.] 22. Br. Vail confined to his house—Sis. Deans fever quite high—The D^r was called from his bed in the night to visit her—

[Sept.] 25. Br. Dean has the fever & ague—The whole family at the creek are now down, except the two apprentices—& they are too feeble to do much—all are down at Br. Vails, except Noah, & the little girl, & they have not fully recovered. Br. J.C. Elsworth, hearing of the feeble state of Frederick, & not knowing that he was from home, came in for the purpose of taking him to Turnip mountain, if it was thought best—He left the family there in health—

[Sept.] 26. Br. Dean is able to walk about & see a little to business— The sick all appear to be geting better—

[Sept.] 26. Br. Frederick Elsworth returned—He has had the ague & fever slightly for several days, on which account it is not easy to determine whether the journey has been beneficial.

[Sept.] 30. Darius Hoyt came in from Willstown after the D^r for Mr. Chamberlins little son, who is dangerously ill—The sick here being all on the mend Dr Butler set out immediately for Willstown—As he is unacquainted with the road, & would be liable to miss the path in the night, Cornelius Hoyt went with him—
We have had in the family about 30 cases of ague & fever & billious fever—chiefly of the former—&, through the goodness of God, they have all very soon been brought under the power of medicine—We

have great reason to be thankful that we have a physician on the spot—

Children bearing the following names as beneficiaries now belong to the schools at Brainerd—viz, John Emmerson—Boston Recorder—Thomas Witherspoon—Elizabeth Kean—Nicholas Patterson—Benjim Tappan—Samuel Spring—Ralph Wells Gridley—Morris Hoge—Manassah Cutler—John Knox Witherspoon—Vinson Gould—Mindwell Woodbridge Gould—Samuel Worcester—Eli Smith—John E. Latta—Bethuel Dodd—David Parker—Wheeler Gilbert—Louisa Battelle—Edward Hop Full—Josiah Meigs—Saml B. Wilson & William Kerr—

Caroline Smelt, was supported here as a beneficiary untill the last vacation, when, being adopted into the family of Milo Hoyt by consent of her mother; she was taken to reside in his family, & to finish her education at his expense—Ann Porter (a former beneficiary) was taken from the school by her father, & is now married.[38] Mary Mason & Betsey Mayhew, are now in the school at Taloney—John D. Paxton has finished his school education, & is now in the family of Mr. Charles R. Hicks—Boston Recorder is now able to read the paper, if his benefactor please to send it to him—

> Ard Hoyt, Henry Parker, E. Butler
> E. Dean, A.E. Blunt

Brainerd Journal

1823

Oct. 1. This day was observed by the church (agreeable to previous appointment) as a day of fasting, humiliation & prayer. Bread, & a piece of cold meat, was given to such of the children as did not choose to abstain from food; but all were required to abstain from play, & to attend worship, in the family, & in public; which was so arranged as to occupy a considerable part of the day. The duty of keeping a fast—the occasions which called for it—& the manner in which it should be kept were stated & illustrated from many passages of scripture—and we think there is reason to believe the ordinance was made profitable to all who attended upon it.

Br. J.C. Elsworth having made arrangements to take his brother Frederick with him to Turnip mountain, did not think it best to stay & keep the fast with us—They accordingly set out for Turnip mountain in the morning—Dr Butler was also under the necessity of traveling on his return from Willstown.

He arrived at home a little after midnight having been absent only 35-1/2 hours. The distance he has traveled twice over is supposed to be 60 miles—He left the sick child somewhat better, & it was hoped the means would be blessed for his recovery.

Cornelius Hoyt (who went to point out the path) waits to assist at Willstown untill Darius Hoyt returns—We are very glad of the Doctors speedy return, as there are several new cases of the ague & fever among the schollars since he went out.

[Oct.] 2nd A cherokee woman came with two female servants, desiring us to hire them—alledging that she suspected some white men designed to steal them, & she was therefore afraid to keep them at home. We agreed to let them stay four weeks on trial.

[Oct.] 3rd Meeting for business—all the brethren able to attend—The following questions were put, & all answered in the affirmative—viz. Shall it be left to Mr. Hoyt & the teachers of the schools to take such measures to keep the schollars steady at school as they shall think proper?
Shall we ask the Council to grant us a permit to hire John McTier as a miller for one year?
Is it thought necessary to ask permission to hire single men, or those who do not bring a family with them?

[Oct.] 4. Br. Vail was able to come to the common table for breakfast, & all the children except one—All the family are now able to walk abroad, with the exception of this one schollar, Sis. Dean & Sis. Vail. The divine blessing has, in a remarkable manner, attended the use of means for the recovery of the sick.
Cornelius Hoyt returned this evening. Mr. Chamberlins child became worse soon after the Doctor left, & is considered in a very dangerous state: Sis. Chamberlin was also quite sick—

Sab. [Oct.] 5. Considering the state of the family at Willstown it was thought duty to send a female to their assistance immediately. Therefore Sis. Ellis, accompanied by Cornelius, set out early to go to them—Another of the schollars taken with the ague & fever to day—

[Oct.] 7th Meeting for business—As Br. F. Elsworth is absent, & not likely soon to be able to attend to business if he should return, Therefore Resolved That the business about the mills which was under his charge be given for the present to Dr Butler, & that part of the farm which was assigned to him to Br. Vail—& that Br. Parker have charge of the ox team & hauling logs to the mill—

Br. Dean rendered acc^t of smiths shop for July & August as follows: Shop C^r

By recvd in cash $24,00, labor 9,53, produce 2,42½	$ 35,95½
" cloth 2,62½ pd John Ross 27,51	30,13½
" Work for Willstown school	11,05
" dto Turnipmountain 20,25, Creek Path 87,50	107,75
" " Brainerd	135.56
	$320,65

D^r

To 1150 lb Iron 82,00. [Freight on Dto] 1,25	83,25
" Hire & board of smith in shop	101,50
Repair of tools &c.	8.00
	192.75
Balance in favor of shop	127,90

Br. Dean has spent about half of the time tending mills, building fish trap, work in race, farming &c or rather in overseeing this business.

[Oct.] 9. Meeting for business. Resolved that travelers be entertained at the Creek as in time past—& that the vote respecting hired man boarding there be rescinded, except as respects those employed in or about the Smiths Shop—

Resolved that Brs. Parker & Butler be a Com. to provide a house or cabbin for the miller.

Advised to purchase, if practicable, seed wheat sufficient to sow 12 or 15 acres of the corn field across the Creek—

Cornelius Hoyt returned from Willstown—He left Sis. Ch^n [Chamberlin] & the child somewhat better, but it was thought necessary for Sis. Ellis to continue there a few days longer—

Dr Butler taken with the ague & fever—Several who had escaped the fits for some time have it return again upon them—This is thought, (at least in some cases) to be occasioned by discontinuing the bark too soon; which would not have been done but for the present scarcity of that medicine.

Br. Ellis, though not afflicted with the prevailing complaint, is frequently too unwell to attend to the school.

[Oct.] 11. Br. Vail again down with the fever.

[Oct.] 12. Br. & Sis. Blunt were called to rejoice in the birth of a daughter—both mother & child likely to do well—

[Oct.] 15. Br. John Arch returned from a circuitous tour in which he has been to the eastern extremity of the nation, & visited his relations & many of his former acquaintance. He finds a very pleasing change since he traveled in those dark regions a year ago. Then he found multitudes who had never heard of a Savior, & almost all quietly pursuing the old way—Now in every cabbin where he visited, they were inquiring with a becoming seriousness. He says all the cherokees in these parts are now prepared to receive missionaries, & he wants to go & spend one year on the Arkansaw in hope that they also may in like manner be prepared. He returned by way of Newtown, & spent the last sabbath with the Council. They have passed a law that no business shall be done in Council on the sabbath, or in the vicinity of Council during its sessions—On the sabbath every one was cleanly dressed, & the outward observance was strict, & solemn. They desire to have preaching every sabbath—

[Oct.] 16. Sis. Ellis returned, accompanied by Darius Hoyt—The child still continued feeble, but was hopefully on the mend. Mr. Chamberlin & Darius have found it necessary to spend most of their time in labor on the buildings, & in clearing around them. Mr. C. is now ingaged building a stone chimney for the kitchen, in which he makes an oven & place for ashes. He has expected to hire some person to do this work, but not being able to hire it done, he thinks it duty to do it himself rather than wait any longer. We should be very sorry to have him kept so much from his ministerial labors if it could be avoided, but they can have but a small school untill the buildings are finished.
Meeting for business to consider what shall be done to relieve Br. Ellis in his charge during his present feeble state of health. Resolved, That Brs. Vail, Butler & Blunt, have charge of the boys out of school, including the sabbath school, & other catechitrial instruction & government on the sabbath—& that one of them go into the school when Br. Ellis is not able.
Resolved, That for the present Br. Parker & his wife be relieved from the charge of the kitchen, & that we hire a cooper for one or two months.

[Oct.] 17. Gen. Calvin Jones, from North Carolina, made us a very friendly visit.[39] He appears cordially to approve of the missionary opperations, & thinks there should be a printing press employed in

the nation—says, if it should meet the approbation of the Board, he will contribute to the expense of its establishment according to his ability—

[Oct.] 18. The boys have spent some time diging sweet potatoes, but they are found to be scarcely worth digging—From the seed of thirty bushels they have got only twelve bushels, & these very poor—The loss is supposed to be occasioned partly by the ground not being well prepared, & chiefly by their having been overrun with grass—
Mr. Butrick came in from Taloney—He has had an interesting tour in the Valley towns since he was here—Last Sabbath he organized a church at Hightower, consisting of Br. Proctor, his wife & Sister, Br. Thompson, his wife & mother, six in all. Three of the natives were admited candidates for baptism—

[Oct.] 19. Mr. Butrick preached from Matt. 18:20[40]—

Oct. 21. Br. J.C. Elsworth came in with Br. Frederick. The improvement in his health during these three weeks of his absence is truly surprising—Almost immediately after his arrival at Turnip mountain, he went to work, & labored all the time he was there. His appetite & digestion is extremely good, & he has nearly or quite gained all the flesh he had lost.

[Oct.] 23. Mr. Butrick left us, having detained here a day or two longer than he intended in consequence of being somewhat unwell—He expects to spend next sabbath with the Council, as it is their desire to have preaching every Lords day—
Br. Vail walked out of his room for the first time after his relapse—

[Oct.] 24. Br. J.C. Elsworth left us to return to his family—

[Oct.] 28. As the two black women hired 4 weeks ago are about to leave us, it becomes necessary to make some new arrangements for the kitchen, or for Br. Parker to return to it—& his help is greatly needed in the business abroad, particularly on account of the ill health of Br. Vail & others—Meeting for business to determine what shall be done in this case—Concluded to endeavor to furnish Mrs. Parker such help as will enable her to perform the business of the kitchen without him.
Resolved that Br. Butler be released from the charge of the mills, & Br. Parker from hauling logs, as soon as Br. Elsworth thinks he is able to resume the charge of S^d business—

[Oct.] 31. Cases of fever & ague, in various forms & degree, have been too frequent in the month that now closes to admit a particular mention of them as they have occured. But few of the mission family have entirely escaped—new cases are still frequently occurring—& some who had nearly recovered are down again as bad as ever.—Br. Ellis after being obliged to leave the school for a few days, as mentioned on the 9th, resumed it again, but was soon obliged to leave it, & is now confined to his bed—Cause of his complaint not fully understood—The schools have been continued, but the number of schollars able to attend has been small (the boys school has averaged of those able to attend about 30 or 32—the girls perhaps 18). Many of the children have not returned at all since vacation, & some who returned have gone home sick. Five schollars, who have been absent since vacation, were yesterday brot in from one place, four of them have had the ague & fever—This complaint is this year more common than usual in the country around us, but we think the mill pond is one great cause of its prevailing more at this place—But though we speak of natural causes, we would acknowledge the hand of our offended God; knowing "that afflictions do not spring from the dust."[41]—We desire the prayers of the Prud. Com. that this affliction may be sanctified to us—& that our merciful Father will in his own best time prepare us for the blessing of health—

Ard Hoyt, John Vail, Elizur Butler, A.E. Blunt, H. Parker

Brainerd, mission journal for Nov—1823

Nov. 3. In meeting for business Dr Butler rendered a/c of the mills from Oct 7 to the present time, as follows.

Saw mill Dr to labor by McTier	$12,33
Smiths bill, & carpenters work on log wheels	4,50
Hauling logs 2,62½—one file ,62½	3,25
	20,08
Cr By plank scantling &c	73,87
Balance in favor of sawmill	53,79
Grist mill Dr to pd McTier for grinding	$5,45
Cr By 32-3/4 bu toll corn	16,37½
Balance in favor of Gristmill	10,92½

Resolved that the expense of building floom, clearing Race, repairing dam &c should be charged to a/c of mills & shop, & that 1/4 be put to the shop. Also that deer skins be purchased to make mockisons for the boys—and that Corn blades be purchased to feed travelers horses—Adjourned to thursday evening for the purpose of reviewing a/c of mills & shop proir [prior] to Oct 7th—

[Nov.] 4th Mr. E. Smith, on his way from Georgia to the Seminary at Andover, came round this way for the purpose of visiting the mission—

[Nov.] 5. Mr. S. spent the day with us visiting the schools &c—

[Nov.] 6. Mr. Smith took an affectionate leave, after manifesting his friendship by a donation of Two dollars; observing he should be glad to do more, but was not able, having to defray the expense of his intended course at Andover from avails of his late school in Georgia—Meeting for business this evening according to adjournment.
Br. Elsworth sent in a/c of mills up to Oct. 6th as follows—

Grist & Sawmill Dr

To 120 ft of floom	$130,00
labor of Cherokees in race	37,00
Hire of men to work in race with Mr. Shelton	50,00
Building wall above Coal house	12,00
1½ month spent by Br. Dean	30,00
" Repairs of mill, by Mr. Alexander	33,50
new saw mill saw $10. file ,50	10,50
Hire & board of hands	6,00
dito of McTier	7,50
—work in the dam	6,75
	323,25
Deduct for charged to Smith Shop	56,31
	266,94

Cr

By 24 bu. toll corn	12,00
" 3000 1¼ inch boards	37,12
" 600 rough edge do	3,75
	52,87
Balance against the mills	214,07

A/C of Smiths shop for Sept & October

Cr By recvd in cash	$28,80
" do in produce	94,39
" " labor	6,17

Work done for mission, including

$21 for Turnip mountain & $6, for Willstown	<u>97,91</u>
	<u>227,27</u>

D^r

To hire & board of hands	30,00
Repairs	5,00
" Work done in race & on dam	<u>56,31</u>
	91,31
Balance in favor of shop	$135,96

Br. Dean thinks he spent five weeks of this time out of the shop—
Mr. Chamberlin came in this evening from Willstown on business—
His wife & child are in somewhat better health than they were, but are
both still feeble. He cannot be prepared to board schollars untill a
team can go from this place with boards—Salt—Meat—casks &c.

[Nov.] 7. Mr. Chamberlin left us early this morning to return home—
Mr. Ross has returned from the Council. We learn that the Chiefs
would not consent to cede any land, although great efforts were made
on the part of the Commissioners[42]—Our letter to the council was well
recvd—& they have directed Mr. Hicks to appoint a Com. to meet the
deputation from the Prud. Com. whenever they arrive—The proposal
for a national school was thought well of by the Council, but they did
not think best to act definitely upon it untill they could get more
information.[43] It was therefore laid over—The Council appointed a
delegation of four to go to Washington, & lay before the President
[Monroe] some things which they call grievances; but they appear
determined not to part with their land on any conditions—[44]

[Nov.] 11. Mr. Alex^r McCoy with his wife made us a visit. He confirms
what we had before heard respecting an attempt to bribe some of the
most influential chiefs to cede their land—A head man of the Creek
nation, half-blood, attended with the Commissioners—He pretended
great friendship for the Cherokees—& in his private interviews with
some of the principal Chiefs, insinuated that the whites would have
their country at all events, & this would be a good time to put money
in their own pockets, & no one but confidants should know it—that
he himself had done so in a late sale of Creek lands &c—They
concealed their feelings & suffered him to go on—holding conferences
with him & he with the Com. untill he made them a writen promise of
sums to individuals amounting to $19,000—& afterwards verbals of

$10,000 more—making in the whole Twenty nine thousand dollars—which he assured them the Com. would pay in hand, & keep the whole a secret if they would continue their influence with the Com. & persuade the Council to sell the country—After proceeding thus far, the Cherokee chiefs who were in the secret, made a full disclosure of the whole in open council (the Creek being present) reading the letter in which the $19,000 was promised—The Creek, (greatly agitated) attempted an apology; but soon, in the utmost confusion, left the council, mounted his horse, & fled away. The Council have ordered the whole to be reported to the chiefs of the Creek nation—& to the President, if he desires it—[45]

[Nov.] 12. Gave the name "Lydia Huntley" to a full cherokee girl, supposed to be nine years old, not large of her age—We have taken the first child which we thought of sufficient promise to meet the wishes of the benefactors, which has offered since we knew that a child could be supported here bearing the name—It appears the name was sometime ago mentioned in the Herald, & it was expected we would notice it, & give out the name accordingly—But it being in the list of donations, which we do not always get time to look over, it was not noticed—We have, not long since, recvd information that a schollar may be supported here bearing the name of Samuel B. Wilson—We intend giving this name as soon as we can be satisfied to which schollar it will be best to give it—
Meeting for business—Resolved that Br. Parker have charge of hauling wood for the fires—

[Nov.] 14. Br. Gage & wife—Br. Bliss & Sisters Hutchinson & Thatcher arrived[46]—Their journey from N. England has been pleasant & prosperous—

Sab. [Nov.] 16. About 7 Ock this evening it pleased God to receive by death one of the schollars—a girl about 12 years of age, who has been in the school about 7 months. This is the second death that has taken place among the schollars at this place since the commencement of the school. May this afflicting dispensation serve to quicken us to greater diligence & faithfulness in leading these dear children to a knowledge of the truth, while they are spared to us, & we to them.

[Nov.] 19. Br. Wright & wife, arrived, & informed us that Mr. Moseley & other fellow laborers, may be expected soon—[47]

[Nov.] 20*th* Meeting for business—As it appears Br. Gage is instructed to remain at this place, or at some local school in this nation, untill Mr. Evarts arrives, & for ought that appears, this is left to his own discretion,[48] The following question was put, Will the brethren advise Br. Gage to assist Br. Blunt so long as he thinks it his duty to remain at Brainerd? Also, shall Sis. Gage take charge of the girls school, so long as Br. Gage thinks it his duty to stay at Brainerd? Brothers answered in the affirmative—Resolved, that Cornelius A. Hoyt have charge of ringing the bell, & that a man be hired to drive the horse team, & be under the direction of Br. Vail—

We hope the fever & ague has nearly left us, but most of the brothers & sisters who have been afflicted with it are still too feeble to perform much labor. Br. Ellis is still quite low, & requires constant attendance—the whooping-cough was brot into the family on the return of schollars after vacation. Dr Butlers children both have it, the youngest very bad, so that they require the attendance of both father & mother much of the time—& Br. Vails babe is dangerously ill with it, & himself too feeble to labor if his family were in health—We mention these things here that the Com. may see our reasons for the above arrangement of business—

Br. Holland & wife—Br. Hemingway, & sisters May & Sawyer, arrived this evening[49]—Soon after their arrival the mail brot us three letters from the Cor. Sec. dated Oct 27-& 28 and Novr 1st—These letters give us the first information we have had (except from the persons themselves) of the sisters who are sent out this fall, & of their destination. Only Messrs. Moseley & Crane, with their wives are now behind—The last of these letters has found a quicker passage from Boston than any one before sent to this mission—

[Nov.] 21. Gave the name of Samuel B. Wilson to a promising youth supposed about 18 years old who has been in school only since Oct 9th—He is a full Cherokee, & when he came knew nothing of the English language, or a letter of the alphabet—He has for some days been spelling in words of two syllables—and has neither friends nor property to assist him—We also this day selected a boy to bear the name of Samuel Lincoln—He is a poor orphan, about 9 years old, who has been in the school but one week, but of promising appearance—In these two cases we have departed from our general practice of selecting beneficiaries from schollars that have been some time proved, because we have none of that class who have not already

received english names, & we are unwilling to keep these benefactors in suspense any longer, as we learn that money has been sometime since contributed for the support of children to bear these names, the knowledge of which has but lately reached us—in the latter case but yesterday—and because we think if the benefactors had the same knowledge of these lads, & their circumstances that we have, they would heartily concur in thus giving their names.—

Meeting for business in consequence of instructions from the Cor. Sec. recvd yesterday.

Resolved that Sis. Gage have charge of the girls out of school, & that Sis. Hutchinson assist her, & that Sis. Ellis be released—The charge of the girls school being given to Sis. Gage yesterday; she now has charge of the girls in school & out—

Resolved That the charge of the boys school be given to Br. Gage—

Resolved that Dr Butler be released from the charge of the boys which was given him in connection with Brs. Vail & Blunt & that Br. Hemmingway assist Br. J. Elsworth [in] his charge—that Br. & Sis. Holland proceed to Creek Path—Br. Parker resume his charge in the kitchen, & that hauling of wood return to Br. Vail—Br. J. Elsworth resumes only the charge of the mill. We have sowed 13-1/2 bu wheat & 3 bu of rye, in the field over the Creek, under the care of Br. Vail—& it is expected he will see to gathering some potatoes which are still in that field—bringing over the corn that was raised on it, repairing the fence &c—as the whole farming business is now under his care—

[Nov.] 25. Br. Holland, his wife, Br. Bliss, Sis. May & Sis. Thatcher, after a season of social prayer & praise, took leave of us for their respective stations—The two former for Creek Path, untill the deputation arrives, the latter for the Choctaw mission—

They go in company by way of Willstown, as far as Creek Path—Br. & Sis. Wright wait a little longer in hope that Mr. Moseley may come up—whose arrival has been expected for several days—

Mr. Moseley & wife, arrived this evening—He has been detained a little by the breaking of his waggon, & also has been obliged to travel more slowly on account of his baggage having been increased by donations of light articles from time to time, which, though small in themselves, & collectively not amounting to very much, had made his load too heavy for the horse—In other respects their journey has been pleasant & prosperous—He left the broken waggon at Mr. Ross' ferry—7 miles back; and walked in, Mrs. Moseley riding the horse—

At the ferry he met the brethren on their way to Creek Path, where they concluded to wait untill he & Br. Wright can come up—

[*Nov.*] 26. Oliver Elsworth came in from Turnip mountain. The school was commenced there on monday 17th inst. with 9 schollars—one has been added since.

[*Nov.*] 27. As Mr. Ross is called to go on a delegation to Washington, & cannot see to the delivery of the Corn which he has engaged to the mission, he wishes us to receive it at the warehouse, at 37-1/2 cents per bushel.[50] A meeting for business was called, & a resolution passed to receive the corn at the warehouse, according to Mr. Ross' proposal—

[*Nov.*] 27. Mr. Butrick (with Br. Andrew Sanders interpreter) came in this evening.[51] On this tour he has visited all the local schools, & found the several families in comfortable health. He is particularly anxious that help may be speedily granted to Willstown that Mr. Chamberlin may be at liberty to ride & preach—

Sab. [*Nov.*] 30. Mr. Moseley preached in the morning from 1 Cor. 5:11. Mr. Butrick in the evening from Col. 3:2—We have reason to be thankful for their instructive & edifying discourses—
Thus, in much mercy, we are brot to the close of another month—The lives of the mission families & their children, & the lives of the schollars (except one) are yet spared—Nearly all the Cherokee children now with us, are able to attend school, but numbers of the mission family are yet quite feeble, & some very sick—Br. Vail—one of his children, Br. Elsworth & wife & Br. Dean & wife still have the ague. Dr Butlers two children have been dangerously sick & the oldest is still so, & Br. Ellis is yet confined to his bed.

In these seasons of affliction, & interruption of our labor, it is an unspeakable consolation to know & feel, that both we, & the people for whose sake we gladly spend & are spent are in the hand of the Lord; who can & will raise up support instruments for the accomplishment of his own purposes of mercy & grace—In his hand we would submissively lie—to be raised up or cast down, as seemeth good in his sight—We have only 50 schollars with us, 39 males & 11 females—There are about 100 on the list as belonging to the school—

Previous to the sickness there was a prospect that we should very soon be again obliged to reject applicants for want of room.

Ard Hoyt, Elizur Butler, Henry Parker, A.E. Blunt

As this was closing for the mail Dec^b 5
Mr. Evarts letter of Novr 12th was recvd—

Brainerd Mission Journal for the
Month of Dec. 1823

Dec. 1st Messrs. Moseley & Wright, with their wives left us early this morning to pursue their journey. They would have left us last week but were detained to get Mr. Moseleys wagon repaired and their horse shod. In order to save expense in crossing the river they will attempt to go over the mountains. Brs. Butrick, Saunders and Dean went to assist them.

In meeting for business Br. Elsworth rendered act. of mills as follows;

Sawmill C^r By 12593 feet lumber	129,43
D^r	
To pd for sawing $21, —51 logs $25,50———	46,50
" two days packing boards 1,50———	1.50
Balance in favor of mill	$81,43
Gristmill C^r By 32 bushels toll corn	$16,00
D^r To 1/3 for attendance———	5.33
Balance in favor of G. Mill———	10,67

Br. Blunt expressing some doubt as to his having charge of coopering since his having care of the boys—It was voted that Br. Blunt have charge of the coopering and such hands as might be employed in it.

[Dec.] 2nd Br. Butrick left us for Taloney—

[Dec.] 3rd Oliver Elsworth left us to return to T. Mountain.

[Dec.] 6th Brought in the last of the corn from the field over the creek; 230 bushes have been gathered from that field and about 50 bushels of Irish potatoes—

[Dec.] 8th Br. John Arch left us for Wills Town expecting to travel as interpreter with Mr. Chamberlain—

[Dec.] 10ᵗʰ Being unable to hire a cooper that will answer our purpose, Br. Blunt concludes that he must in a degree, omit his labor with, and for the boys, and Make our meet casks himself—The following appears to be the state of the family at present—
5 hired females (including Sis. Nancy & the aggregate of whose wages including board at ,75¢ per week is   37,00
5 males $10. per month board per week 1,25   77,00
2 smiths wages and board   51,75
1 sawyer who boards himself [say?]   26.00
                                                                                      191,75
34 of the mission family including Thomas Bassil (apprentice) Total 47 besides the children of the schools— 47 children including Kapooly and Sis Deans girl—If these children were boarded at the $1. per week, it would cost only about as much as we are now paying for hire, and board of laborers, who are chiefly engaged for the sake of earning support for the children.

[Dec.] 11ᵗʰ Br. McTier cut his knee badly—will probably be some time kept from his work.

[Dec.] 13ᵗʰ Darius Hoyt came from Wills Town for the purpose of going to Maryville.[52]

[Dec.] 15ᵗʰ Mr. Hoyt having been confined, with the rheumatism, and in a measure helpless, for a number of days, the journal has been neglected. Though he has had a most afflicting attack, from appearances this evening, we hope he will soon recover; and that the mission will not be long deprived of his valuable services.

Since the last date our four horse team has been to Wills Town, and carried meet casks, and other necessary supplies for that school— By the return of the wagon and several other sources, we learn many at W. Town anxiously enquire the way of Salvation; that they will travil from fifteen to twenty miles to attend an evening meeting, and though they are very scattered will attend to the amount of 60 or 70. May the Son effect a work there which shall be for the Glory of his great name—

[Dec.] 17ᵗʰ Heard of the death of Louisa Battell.[53] She left the school about two months since with symptoms of consumption, her mother supposing she would give medicine that would soon remove the disease.

Louisa was a very promising girl though we have to say she gave little or no evidence of piety—We regret that none of the mission family had the privilege to visit her in her last sickness—

[Dec.] 28th Sabbath. This is the third Sabbath we have been deprived of Mr. Hoyts ministry. Met as before and a sermon read. We hope and pray that our dear Pastor may be speedily restored to us and that we may submit to the chastisement without a murmur.

[Dec.] 31st Within a few days past 4 boys and one girl have been brought to school. All except one boy are old scholars who have been home awhile with their friends.

At a meeting for business on the 27th it was thought best not to hire 2 black girls who have been in our employ for some time. It was thought best not to hire a black man who was offered.

A. E. Blunt, E. Butler

Epilogue

As the last "t" was crossed and the last "i" dotted, the missionaries completed the final *Brainerd Journal* entry in December 1823. After the ceasing of the official *Brainerd Journal*, missionaries kept readers, supporters, and benefactors informed of Brainerd events and daily life through letters or articles published in the *Missionary Herald*. For instance, the June 1824 *Missionary Herald* printed the following article concerning the missionaries' health:

> The members of the mission family are as well at present as they have been for several months. Still there is much sickness among them. Mr. Hoyt has not been able to leave his room since December, and a great part of the time has not been able to turn himself in bed. Mr. Ellis has been quite deranged, a part of the time, for months, and is quite feeble. Mr. Blunt is confined by sickness, and has been since December. Several of the women are also in a very poor state of health.[1]

In addition to receiving letters and articles meant for publication, personal visitation to the missions provided another means for the American Board to keep in touch with its missionaries. From December 1823 to May 1824, Jeremiah Evarts made a five month trip to assess the Cherokee and Choctaw missions' operations. To begin his journey, he visited the Cornwall Foreign Mission School where he joined former Brainerd student David Brown, who had been attending the Cornwall school. Together, Evarts and Brown journeyed southward; along the way Brown gave speeches at such places as Yale College, Newark, New Brunswick, Princeton, and Philadelphia. In January 1824, Evarts journeyed to Washington where he met John Ridge. John, another former Brainerd student, had accompanied his father, Major Ridge, a member of a Cherokee delegation sent to Washington at that time. This delegation brought to President Monroe their tribal grievances concerning injustices perpetrated against the Cherokees by other Indians tribes, by the U.S. Indian

Agent, and by the U.S. government. Evarts spent time with the Cherokee delegation and various congressmen.

Evarts continued his journey southward, finally reaching Brainerd in March 1824. There he conducted another investigation and composed lengthy letters concerning the mission's organization and administration.[2] Evarts remained at Brainerd and the other mission stations through April 1824, after which he proceeded to the Choctaws at Mayhew. Back in New England by early summer 1824, he recommended to the Prudential Committee that the missions reorganize. Subsequently, the following news article appeared August 1824 in the *Missionary Herald*:

> It had been the opinion of the Prudential Committee, for a considerable time that the objective of the Board would be promoted by diminishing the number of persons residing at Brainerd, and expending more missionary labor at the smaller stations. To accomplish this end, it was necessary, that there should be new assignment of duties to a large part of the missionaries, and assistant missionaries, now attached to the Cherokee mission.[3]

To "diminish" the number of people at Brainerd and "expand missionary labor," the Prudential Committee recommended that Ard and Esther Hoyt and Sylvester and Sarah Ellis move to Willstown and that the Chamberlins remain at Willstown, where Chamberlin was to continue as an evangelist touring the Cherokee Nation. Meanwhile Potter and Butrick were to continue as touring evangelists, while John Elsworth was to return to Brainerd. John's brother, Frederick filled the vacancy created by John's departure from Haweis-Turnip Mountain. At Brainerd, John Elsworth was assigned to teach the boys' school and to superintend the secular concerns at Brainerd while the new missionary, Sophia Sawyer, was assigned to teach the girls' school. Dean, Parker, Blunt, and Hemmingway were also to remain at Brainerd, but Dr. Butler was relocated to Creekpath, where he was to teach the school. There was no change in the assignments for Hall at Carmel or Proctor at Hightower. Vail and Holland were provided a new station, called Candy's Creek, about twenty-five miles northeast of Brainerd. They opened this station by the end of 1824.[4]

Although never mentioned in the journal, Sequoyah's invention, the Cherokee syllabary, rapidly expanded the Cherokees' quest for education. It took little time for any Cherokee to learn to read and write in the new syllabary. After 1828 the Cherokee people could read their own newspaper, read the new constitution, and read tracts and documents printed in their own language.[5]

A friend and teacher of the Cherokees, Samuel Austin Worcester, arrived in the Cherokee Nation in 1825. This Samuel was the nephew of Samuel Worcester, the deceased American Board Corresponding Secretary. The younger Worcester first worked at Brainerd, but the American Board continued the mission expansion in 1827 with a station at the New Echota capital. Worcester subsequently moved to New Echota in December 1827. The former Foreign Mission School graduate Elias Boudinot also moved to this location to begin his new job as editor of the nation's newspaper.[6] On behalf of the Cherokee Nation, Worcester secured a printing press, with the unique capability to print documents in the new Cherokee syllabary as well as print in English. Because of his abilities in languages and his learning the new syllabary, Worcester worked along side Elias Boudinot in publishing the bilingual *Cherokee Phoenix*. Worcester was instrumental in the Cherokees' latest advance in "civilization" and, therefore, earned the Cherokee name A-tse-nu-sti, or "the messenger." After the Removal he continued to work among the Cherokees, securing another press and establishing another newspaper, called the *Cherokee Advocate*.[7]

Regarding the Cherokees who played a part in events reported in *Brainerd Journal*, some died at a young age, while others went on to be leading figures in Cherokee history serving their Nation well during the Removal, the Trail of Tears, and afterwards. Catharine Brown died on July 18, 1823 at age twenty-three succumbing to the same disease, tuberculosis, which took her brother John's life and later took her brother David's life on September 15, 1829. Before his death, David translated, with his father-in-law George Lowrey, the New Testament into the Cherokee syllabary.[8]

John Arch worked tirelessly for the American Board missions as an interpreter. He not only interpreted and taught at the Creek Path Mission, but also worked with the Brainerd evangelists as they toured the Cherokee Nation covering hundreds of miles in the Nation. His evangelizing efforts were described in William Chamberlin's and Daniel Butrick's "Private Journals" found in the American Board Papers.[9] Arch also worked as an interpreter at the Willstown mission. When Jeremiah Evarts returned to Brainerd in early 1824, John Arch accompanied Evarts on his trip through the Cherokee and Choctaw Nations. Soon after this trip, disease took its toll on John Arch; he curtailed his endeavors somewhat but continued to work on translating portions of the New Testament. Sadly for the missionaries and the Cherokees, at the young age of twenty-eight, John Arch died on June 18, 1825.[10]

Samuel J. Mills, who was known only by the name "Enquirer" in the early *Brainerd Journal*, later became an important lay-preacher and was often referred to as an "Exhorter." In 1828 a movement called "White Path's Rebellion" took place among a group of traditionalist Cherokees protesting the Christian influence and the new Cherokee Constitution. A rebel council drew up a resolution, which Samuel J. Mills signed, against the new Cherokee Constitution. Even though he participated in this rebellion, he still befriended the missionaries and continued to work as lay-preacher at the Haweis Mission formerly known as Turnip Mountain.[11]

In their offices as Principal Chief and Assistant Principal Chief, Pathkiller and Charles Hicks served only a little more than three years after the close of *Brainerd Journal*. Both died in early 1827 when the Cherokees were rising to their full potential as a sovereign nation. Though both Pathkiller and Hicks ardently supported a unified Cherokee Nation, they never saw the new constitution put into action because the Cherokee Nation adopted their new constitution on July 26, 1827, six months after their deaths.

Immediately after the enactment of the Cherokee Constitution, the federal government increased pressure for cession of more Cherokees land. The U.S. Commissioners swooped down on them thinking the time was ripe because the old chiefs, who supposedly opposed the sale of land, had died. The surrounding states hoped that the new Cherokee leadership would sell or cede the remaining land. But the Cherokees, united through their new constitution, withstood the pressure. Under the new constitution, during elections held at the fall 1828 Council, John Ross became Principal Chief while George Lowrey assumed the office of Assistant Principal Chief.

The *Brainerd Journal* foreshadowed many future events. For instance the subject of removal filtered continuously through the journal. After the close of the journal, the United States and the Southern states escalated pressure for all Indian tribes in that region to cede their remaining land and to emigrate west. In the period 1826 to 1827, the Creeks capitulated to government pressure by ceding their land in Georgia.[12] While the Creeks abandoned their land to Georgia, the Cherokee Nation grew in strength as a sovereign nation.

Just as the Cherokee Nation centralized its tribal government, Andrew Jackson was elected President. He supported the Southern states by saying that no sovereign nation, such as the Cherokee Nation, should be allowed to exist within the boundaries of a state or territory of the United States.[13] Simultaneously with Andrew Jackson becoming President, Georgia seized control of all Cherokee land by passing a series of laws aimed directly at the Indians, effectively nullifying all Cherokee laws. In other words, Georgia said the Cherokee Constitution had no validity in that state.

Several other major events took place which greatly affected the Cherokees' lives while paving the road for eventual removal from their native lands. After Georgia passed these laws against the Cherokees, faithful Cherokee supporter, Jeremiah Evarts, under the pseudonym, William Penn, counteracted this pressure for removal by writing a series of essays now known as the "William Penn" essays.[14] During the Jackson administration, these essays became a rallying point for the opposers of Indian Removal when Congress debated the Indian Removal Bill. Despite well-meant efforts to defeat the bill, the Removal Act passed Congress May 28, 1830.[15] Georgia now set in motion the next series of laws aimed at the Cherokee Nation. Among other stipulations, the Cherokee government could no longer hold any councils within Georgia boundaries, and the law now required all whites living within state boundaries to declare an oath of allegiance to Georgia.[16] The Georgia law also provided for a Georgia Guard to enforce the new laws within the Cherokee Nation. These last laws also affected the American Board missionaries residing within the area now claimed by Georgia. Samuel Worcester and Elizur Butler refused to take the loyalty oath, so they went to prison, where they not only engaged in evangelizing activities, but Dr. Butler made shoes, and Rev. Worcester worked in a prison cabinet shop.[17] The United States Supreme Court tried Samuel Worcester's case; in their decision rendered in *Worcester v. Georgia*, the highest court ruled in favor of the sovereignty of the Cherokee Nation.[18] However, no governing power supported the Supreme Court's ruling, so Georgia ignored the decision. In the end, Worcester and Butler spent eighteen months in jail, but they appealed, and finally Governor Wilson Lumpkin of Georgia released them.

In 1835, when the situation became intolerable for missionaries in Georgia, they established two new missions in Tennessee: one at Red Clay, just north of the Georgia state boundary, and one called

Running Waters near Nickajack on the Tennessee River. Prior to this move to Red Clay and Running Water, the American Board attempted to open another new mission, Amohee, near the Candy's Creek Mission, but this mission closed only two years later in 1833.[19] As a result of Georgia's pressure and legislation, the missionaries now in 1835 concentrated their religious activities in Tennessee, Alabama, and other parts of the Cherokee Nation which lay beyond the borders of Georgia.

Even with the Cherokee advance in "civilization" and the Cherokees taking on white man's ways, Georgia and the United States government did not alter their policy concerning the Cherokee Nation; complete removal was still the goal of the white leaders. The Cherokees became "civilized;" they formed a central government, passed new laws to be more like their white neighbors, learned English, learned the white man's way of farming, learned to read and write in the new Cherokee syllabary, and even established and printed their own newspaper. "Many white Americans considered them to be the most 'civilized' of all native peoples," but the United States yielded to the whites' pressure for new land; land needed and demanded in large amounts.[20]

Life became more harsh for Cherokees as Georgia surveyed all Cherokee land and then held a land lottery for white settlers.[21] The whites soon seized control of the former Cherokee homes and plantations turning the rightful Cherokee owners out of their own homes. Finally, to secure removal of all Cherokees, the United States and a small faction of Cherokees signed the 1835 Treaty of New Echota. This small Cherokee faction agreed to remove all Cherokee inhabitants from Georgia, Tennessee, North Carolina, and Alabama, and they agreed for all Cherokees to emigrate to Indian Territory.[22] When the Removal finally took place two years later, it was one of the lowest points in Cherokee history. The United States Army herded thousands of people into stockades to await removal and to prepare for what today Cherokees and non-Cherokees refer to as "Trail Where We Cried" or "The Trail of Tears." Starting with early "roundups" in 1838, many Cherokees perished of depravation, disease, and starvation. By 1840, a year after the last detachment arrived in the West, over 4,000 Cherokees had died as a direct result of the Removal and its aftermath.[23]

Many of the American Board missions remained in operation up to the Removal. The first small mission station called Taloney (later

Carmel Mission), located sixty miles southeast of Brainerd, opened in 1819 and continued as a mission until 1839. The mission station at Creek Path remained in operation until 1837. The Creek Path site is today mostly underwater in the Guntersville Reservoir in Alabama. A magnolia tree growing on a small island in the reservoir marks the only visible remains of the Creekpath Mission where Catharine Brown taught.[24] The Willstown Mission continued until 1839; today Fort Payne, Alabama is near the former mission site. The Hightower Mission, which opened in 1823, closed eight years later in 1831. The mission near Samuel J. Mill's home at Turnip Mountain became the Haweis Mission. Dr. Butler and his wife were reassigned to the Haweis Mission in 1826. Mrs. Butler died there in 1829; a grave and historical marker on Georgia Highway 20 reminds the traveler of the existence of the Haweis Mission and events in the Butlers' lives as missionaries to the Cherokee Indians.[25] Haweis closed in 1834; its site was near present day Rome, Georgia. The Candy's Creek Mission which opened in 1824, continued to operate until 1839. Today the location of the former mission is in Bradley County, Tennessee, fourteen miles from Red Clay, Georgia.[26]

The Brainerd Mission remained a center for Christianizing and "civilizing" the Cherokees, but eventually closed in August 1838 when the Cherokees removed to the West. All the missionaries vacated their stations in the East, but some did move west with the Cherokees. Today a cemetery is the only remains left of the Brainerd Mission; the monuments and grave markers are surrounded by a chain link fence. The land which formerly was the mission grounds is now a shopping center located in the area which became Chattanooga, Tennessee.[27]

Shortly after the completion of the emigration west, three signers of the Treaty of New Echota—The Ridge and former Brainerd and Cornwall students John Ridge and Elias Boudinot—were executed by a small secret group who were invoking the Blood Law. A majority of Cherokees opposed the treaty; a small faction of individuals, fraught with grief and "long-smoldering resentment," took action against the signers because this small faction viewed the signing of the treaty, without the entire nation's approval, as the action which precipitated much suffering of the Cherokee people and the deaths of loved ones during the Removal.[28]

The American Board missionaries were prolific writers, documenting important events in the Cherokee history. Just as they wrote the *Brainerd Journal* telling of the early days of their missionary endeavors, they also wrote many letters documenting the years up to the removal and missionary involvement in the "Trail of Tears." Elizur Butler, the Brainerd Mission physician, described in letters the suffering in the holding stockades before the long trip to the West.[29]

Some missionaries migrated west with the Cherokees and established new missions in Indian Territory. Even though the Cherokee Nation went through more turbulent years following the removal, good sprang forth, as the Cherokee Nation finally united the newly arrived Cherokees from the Eastern Nation with the "Old Settlers" in the West and ultimately established their own Cherokee operated schools. The *Brainerd Journal* had earlier recorded the Cherokee desire for their own schools, but it was not until the 1840's that the Nation passed various acts which established eleven lower education schools and two schools of higher learning. These last two became the Cherokee Male and the Cherokee Female Seminaries which opened in 1850.[30] By this time the Nation was in control of the education process leaving the missionaries to focus on their evangelizing efforts. Letters and documents exist telling of the American Board's involvement in the Cherokee Nation subsequent to the Removal including events in the Cherokee Nation before the Civil War when the American Board finally discontinued their missions among the Cherokees.

The American Board missionaries recorded a vast amount of letters and documents dealing with one of the most turbulent times in Cherokee history. For today's historians, scholars, and readers, those documents in archival form or microfilm, or in transcriptions such as this one, constitute a rich source of information about the history of the Cherokee Nation, as well as the history of the missionary movement and life on the ever-changing and moving frontier.

Table #1

List of Places in the Cherokee Nation

---

1. Wills valley 40 or 50 miles long. Two or three preaching stations. Mr. Mckoy, one of the best interpreters, can read & write, and is a man of general information. Maj. Lowrey also talks both languages. All in darkness. Beautiful land, springs of water, mill seats &c, lying between the Lookout, & Raccoon mountains, on Wills Creek.
2. Squirrel Town lies between Raccoon Mountains & Tennessee river.
3. Crow Town & Sauta on the Ten. river perhaps 20 miles above Creek Path.
4. Turkey Town perhaps 30 or 40 miles long, is I believe bounded by Lookout mountain, Alabama, the Creek line, and Chatoogy, lying on the Coosi river. The king, his first counselor, & many other old chiefs live in this Town, all in darkness. A beautiful country. Between two & three hundred in-habitants.
5. Chattoogi bounded by Turkey Town, Lookout, Raccoon Town, Turnip Town, & the Creek line. Watered by the Coosi, & Little river, Chattogi creek, & other small streams & Springs. Good land.
6. Turnip Town, lies on the Coosi river, bounded by Chattoogi, Dirt Town, Ysu ki lo gi or Hightower & the Creek line. Br. Mills, Mr. Fields, & sister Lestley live in this Town.
7. Hightower lies on the Hightower river, & two roads leading from Georgia to Alabama. It is watered by a number of beautiful creeks. Good land. Large population, perhaps 50 or 60 miles in length. Upwards of 200 families.
8. Hickery Log, lies 20 miles above Hightower, on the same river, & the same roads. The Cherokees live compact on the river. Two white men with Cherokee families a few miles from them have a school for their children. The teacher is hired from Georgia. Twenty miles above this is the settlement of Mr. Blackburn on the Federal road from Georgia to E. Tennessee.
9. On the way from Taloney to Hightower is Sa li ga i & Pine log lying on Creeks by those names. The people generally in the most entire darkness. No road passes near them. Pine log is a most beautiful place. The town is compact, one or two common fields, on the creek. Perhaps between two & three hundred inhabitants.

Table #1

List of Places in the Cherokee Nation

10. Fifteen miles from Pine log is Y pu ki lo gi on the Coosiwatee, perhaps 30 miles below the town of that Name. Here is a church of the United brethren. Father Gambold Pastor.
11. Shoemake Town lies 12 miles from Spring place, near the direct road to Knoxville. I believe about 40 families.
12. Thomas Foreman's town, about 8 miles this side of the Agency.
13. Sleeping Rabits town lies on the road leading to the Agency, perhaps 15 miles from Brainerd.
14. Going Snakes Town 5 or 6 miles I believe from Mr. Wolfs.
15. Three killers Town perhaps 12 or 13 miles from Brainerd up the principle branch of Chickamaugah.
16. Tesy's Town 27 miles up the same Creek.
17. Broom Town 20 miles from Three killers, on the head waters of Chattoogi Creek. A beautiful country. Perhaps 200 inhabitants.
18. Raccoon Town between Broom Town & Chattoogi.
19. Dirt Town East of Raccoon Town.

Source: Papers of the American Board, ABC 18.3.1 v.2: 168

Table #2

A List of Persons, who belong to the Mission at Brainerd, May 17, 1822

Rev. Ard Hoyt, born at Danbury, Con.	Oct 20, 1770
Ordained at Wilksbarre, Penn.	Aug 26,1806
Arrived on Mission ground	Jan 4, 1818
Mrs. Esther Hoyt, born at Southbury, Con.	Jan 18, 1774
Sarah Hoyt, born at Danbury, Con.	Oct 11, 1794
Anna Hoyt, born at Danbury, Con.	May 1, 1802
Darius Hoyt, born at Danbury, Con.	Nov 11, 1804
Cornelius Adams Hoyt, born at Wilksbarre, Pen.	July 23, 1807
Rev. Daniel S. Butrick, born at Windsor, Mass.	Aug 25, 1789
Ordained at Boston, Mass.	Sept 3, 1817
Arrived on Mission ground	Jan 4, 1818
Rev. William Chamberlin, born at Newbury, Vt.	Feb 20, 1791
Ordained at Hartford, Pen.	Nov 12, 1817
Arrived on Mission ground	March 10, 1818
Mrs. Flora Chamberlin, daughter of Rev. A. Hoyt,	
born at Danbury, Con.	July 7, 1798
Catharine B. Chamberlin born at Brainerd	July 4, 1819
Amory N. Chamberlin, born at Brainerd	Nov 29, 1821
Mr. Abijah Conger, born at Rockaway, New Jersey	May 4, 1782
Arrived on Mission ground	Nov 10, 1819
Mrs. Phebe Conger, born at Bridgehampton, New York	March 27, 1781
Anna J. Conger, born at Rockaway, New Jersey	Aug 30, 1804
David Conger, born at Rockaway, New Jersey	March 6, 1808
Hedges T. Conger, born at Rockaway, New Jersey	Aug 2, 1811
Sophia P. Conger, born at Rockaway, New Jersey	Aug 31, 1815
Elisabeth A. Conger, born at Rockaway, New Jersey	Sept 17, 1817
Cynthia Conger, born at Brainerd	Feb 5, 1822

Table #2

A List of Persons, who belong to the Mission at Brainerd, May 17, 1822

Mr. John Vail, born at Hanover Township, New Jersey	Oct 9, 1788
Arrived on Mission ground	Nov 10, 1819
Mrs. Julia Vail, born at Warrack Township, New York	April 1, 1789
Noah Vail, born at Hanover Township, New Jersey	Nov 21, 1809
Mary Ann Vail, born at Hanover Township, New Jersey	Oct 30, 1814
Caroline Vail, born at Hanover Township, New Jersey	July 11, 1819
Electa J. Vail, born at Brainerd	July 28, 1821
Dr. Elizur Butler, born at Norfolk, Con.	June 11, 1794
Arrived on Mission ground	Jan 10, 1821
Mrs. Esther Butler, born at Canaan, Con.	Sept 15, 1798
William Smith Butler, born at Brainerd	Aug 25, 1821
Mr. John C. Ellsworth, born at Chatham, Con.	Feb 22, 1793
Arrived on Mission ground	Nov 25, 1821
Mrs. Eliza Ellsworth, born at Greensborough, Vt.	Dec 25, 1797
Miss Harriet Ellsworth, born at Chatham, Con.	Sept 25, 1790
Mr. Erastus Dean, born at Bristol, Vt.	May 13, 1798
Arrived on Mission ground	Jan 12, 1822
Mrs. Sally Dean, born at Byfield, Mass.	Sept 23, 1796
Mr. Sylvester Ellis, born at Randolf, Vt.	July 29, 1798
Arrived on Mission ground	April 10, 1822
Mr. Ainsworth E. Blunt, born at Amherst N.H.	Feb 22, 1800
Arrived on Mission ground	April 12, 1822

Source: Papers of the American Board, ABC 18.3.1 v.2: 162

Table #3

Names of those who have been admitted to the church at Brainerd–
the time when admitted–
supposed age at the time of admission–
remarks.

Names	Dates	Age	Remarks
Charles Reece	Feb 1, 1818	30	is a half breed–has a family
Jane Coodey	Feb 1, 1818	35	is a half breed–is wife of a white man
Sally McDonald	Mar 29, 1818	35	is a half breed–is a widow
Susannah Nave	Mar 29, 1818	33	is a half breed–is wife of a white man
Catharine Brown	Mar 29, 1818	19	is a half breed
Lydia Lowry	Mar 28, 1819	16	is a half breed–is wife of Milo Hoyt
Anna McDonald	June 13, 1819	73	is a Cherokee–is wife of a white man
John Arch	Feb. 20, 1820	23	is a Cherokee
David Brown	April 30, 1820	19	is a half breed
Samuel J. Mills	Oct 14, 1821	35	is a Cherokee–has a family of 6 children
Anna McPhearson	Oct 14, 1821	53	is a Cherokee–is wife of a white man
Greenbury Pardue	Mar 29, 1818	24	is a white man–now a Methodist
Anna Hoyt	May 3, 1818	15	is a daughter of Father Hoyt
Milo Hoyt	April 30, 1820	20	is a son of Father Hoyt
Daniel McPhearson	Sept 3, 1820	55	is a white man–the husband of Anna
Darius Hoyt	Oct 14, 1821	16	is a son of Father Hoyt
Juno	May 17, 1818	55	is a black woman of Mr. Ross'
Robin Martin	July 7, 1818	35	is a free black
Ned	July 7, 1818	30	is a black man of Sally McDonald's
Sally	Aug 16, 1818	25	is a black woman of Fox Taylor's

Source: Papers of the American Board, ABC 18.3.1, v.2: 176.

Table #4

A Catalogue of the Cherokee Scholars that belonged to the School at Brainerd

Name	Time of entry	AD	Supposed age	Time of leaving	Cherokee name	Explanation	Place of Residence	Improvement	Character
Edward Brown	Sep 2	1817	15	Jul 9 1818	Nã tý	Edward	Arkansas	Could read & write	Respectable
Catharine Brown	Jul 9	1817	18	Apr 9 1820	Kã tý	Caty	Creek Path	Read & write	A very promising young woman. Attends school with Br. Potter
Elias Boudinot	Aug 18	1817	14	May 20 1818	Te kuh nah sté sky	Pick him up & put him down	Arkansas	Could spell & write on the slate	Unknown
Thomas Basil	Jun 19	1817	14	May 23 1818	Tau tsoo wãh	Redbird	Cornwall, Con.	Good	Pious
Jonas Coe	Jun 14	1817	7		Ah wih tuh yãy	A Deer is coming	Brainerd		
Jeremiah Evarts	Sep 12	1817	9		Woy kuh ke ské	Take a pigeon out of the water	Brainerd		
John Gambold	Dec 26	1817	9		E low í		Brainerd		
George	Mar 20	1817	12	Dec 3 1819	Skah quaĥ	Swan	Chickamauga Court house	Could read & write	Mediocrity
Jack	Jun 14	1817	11		Tsãh kih	Jack	Brainerd		
David Brainerd	Dec 16	1817	9		Tsu hluh	Fox	Brainerd		
Horace Loomis	Jun 14	1817	9		Wow sutta skih	Bush shaker	Brainerd		
James H. Williams	Jun 14	1817	12		Kaw killuh nuh he tuh	long hair	Brainerd		
James Fields	Jul 31	1817	14	Oct 23 1818			Cornwall, Con.	Good	Pious
Levi Timberlake	Jul 31	1817	8	Sep 17 1819	Oo kuh lõu guka	a leaf	Near the mouth of the Chick-amauga	Read & write	Mediocrity
Susannah Hanley	May 20	1817	9				Brainerd		
Peggy	May 20	1817	9	Feb 13 1818			Arkansas	Good	Unknown

Table #4

Name	Time of entry	AD	Supposed age	Time of leaving	Cherokee name	Explanation	Place of Residence	Improvement	Character
Elsey Wilson	Jan 5	1818	12	Sep 16 1818			Fortville	Read & write	Was married to a white man a few days. Parted from her husband by her Cherokee friends. Maintains good character
Peggy Wilson	Jan 5	1818	10	Sep 16 1818			Alabama	Read & write	Unknown
Collins McDonald	Apr 8	1817	10	Aug 6 1819	Ke nuh te tuh	Rising Fawn	Springplace at school	Read & write	Good as a scholar
Ruth Falling	Jan 24	1818	14	Aug 27 1818			Coosa watee	Read & write	Married to a half breed by the name of Shepard, Respectable
Betsey Burns	Mar 30	1817	10	Oct 28 1819			Agency	Read & write	Respectable young woman
Jane Woodward	Feb 12	1818	6	Feb 23 1819			Blue Springs	Read in easy lessons	Unknown
Eliza Holt	Feb 17	1818	7	Aug 6 1819			Clarks Ferry	Read & write	Respectable
John Walker	Jan 8	1818	11	Jan 16 1818			Chickamauga Town		Unknown
Rachel	Nov 21	1817	9	Jan 30 1818			Broomstown		Unknown
Tooker	Nov 21	1817	9	Bef Jan 1818					Unknown
Elishah Yale	Nov 21	1817	10	Jan 30 1818					Unknown
William Coodey	Jun 10	1817	9	May 6 1819	Kuh whe sit tah	parch corn	Rossville	Read & write	A Respectable Clerk in a store
Thomas Woodward	Jun 13	1817	13	Bef Jan 1818			Blue Springs	Spell in 2 syllables	Doubtful
Allen Radcliff	Jun 13	1817	12	Bef Jan 1818	A lun nih	Allin	Ool ta woh	Spell in 2 syllables	Industrious
Sun nè koo yàh	May 25	1817	9	Bef Jan 1818	Sun ne koo yah		Broomstown		Unknown

Table #4

Name	Time of entry	AD	Supposed age	Time of leaving	Cherokee name	Explanation	Place of Residence	Improvement	Character
Jack	Mar 20	1817		Bef Jan 1818	Oo ne skoo koo	Oak ball			Unknown
James McPharson	Feb —	1817	11	Feb 24 1822	Too wa yuh luh	Boald [bold] hunter	Chickamauga	Read & write	Industrious
Rachel Lowrie	Apr 4	1817	10	Jun 21 1819			Willstown	Read & write	Respectable young lady
John Ridge	May 14	1817	10	Bef Jan 1818			Cornwall, Con.	Read & write	Thoughtful
Nancy Ridge	May 14	1817	14	Bef Jan 1818				Could read & write	Married a white man & died in 1819.
Madison Riley	May 19	1817	9	Bef Jan 1818	Es kau la en nâh	Bug head	Creek path	Good	Respectable
Luney Riley	May 23	1817	16	Bef Jan 1818			Creek path	Good	Respectable
Nelson Riley	May 23	1817	15	Bef Jan 1818			Creek path	Good	Respectable
Mariah Ross	Jul 1	1817	12	Bef Jan 1818			Lookout	Good	Respectable young lady
Polly Coody	Jul 7	1817	10	Jun 5 1818			At her fathers in the neighborhood	Read & write	Respectable young lady
Eliza Sevier	Jul 24	1817	18	Bef Jan 1818			Near the Agency	Read & write	Married to a white man from Richmond, Virginia by the name of Ross, Respectable
Jack Walker	Aug 9	1817	20	Jan 16 1818	Tsu lik tsee	Entrails	Calhoon	Read & write	Respectable young man
Cău nõ wēē lēē	Aug 29	1817	8	Bef Jan 1818	Cău nõ wēē lēē	Walking through the weeds	In the Cherokee Nation		A Creek girl (Character unknown)
Ebenezer Kingsbury	Feb 23	1818	9	Apr 10 1818	Tsū nuh lon skuh	an improbability you cannot do	Broomstown		
Henry Buckingham	Feb 23	1818	8		Cun ne yaw stah	Sharp arrow	Brainerd	Read & write	Rather dull
Robin Burns	Mar 9	1818	11	Oct 15 1819	Clo gă sy	a field	Chickamauga	Read in easy lesson & write	Was not at school steady, Rather wild

Table #4

Name	Time of entry	AD	Supposed age	Time of leaving	Cherokee name	Explanation	Place of Residence	Improvement	Character
Lucy Fields	Sep 5	1817	11	Apr 4 1820				Read & write	A respectable young lady
Delilah Fields	Mar 24	1818	9				Brainerd		
Robin Vann	Mar 24	1818	15	Dec 7 1819			Near Clarks ferry	Read & write	Respectable person
William Holt	Mar 24	1818	12	Aug 6 1819			Near Clarks ferry	Read & write	Respectable
Lydia Lowrey	Apr 10	1818	15	Oct 29 1819			Near Brainerd	Read & write	Married to Milo Hoyt. She makes a good wife & a respectable woman
Polly Hair	Apr 11	1818	13	Aug 15 1818			Chickamauga	Spell in words of two syllables	Mediocrity
Aries Williams	Apr 16	1818	15	Sep 5 1818	Teel tuh ta gih	jumper	Arkansas		Unknown
Lyman Beecher	Apr 16	1818	6	Aug 22 1818	Nai u ta gih	stone thrower	Arkansas		Unknown
Robin Fields	Apr 27	1818	10		Tsick uh lĕ lĕ	a small bird*	Brainerd		
John Brewer	Apr 27	1818	9				Brainerd		
Jane Reece	Apr 27	1818	6				Brainerd		
John Vann	May 5	1818	16	Sep 12 1818			Cornwall, Con.	Read & write	Pious
Thomas Tailor	May 11	1818	7	Nov 14 1821	Tse quh loo ih yuh	Bird pecking	Springplace	Read in easy lessons & write indifferently	A very good scholar in Br. Smiths school
Charles	May 12	1818	14	Aug 18 1818			Arkansas		Unknown
Walter Holt	May 14	1818	9	Aug 6 1819			Near Clarks ferry	Read & write	Respectable
David Harlin	May 16	1818	10	Sep 30 1818			Near Agency	Read & write	Unknown
Peggy Wolf	May 19	1818	13	Oct 28 1819			Big Spring	Read & write	Respectable young lady
Denis Wolf	May 19	1818	8	Oct 15 1821	Ook too klah wuh	Eyebrows	Big Spring	Read & write	Respectable
Anna Claunuh	May 21	1818	10	Dec 31 1818			Creek Path	Read in easy lesson	A good scholar in Br. Potters school
Polly Blackwood	Jun 8	1818	8	Oct 15 1821			Coo sy waw tee	Read & write	Respectable
Susan Reece	Jun 8	1818	8				Brainerd		
Archy Willson	Jun 11	1818	18	Jan 11 1819			Alabama	Read & write	Unknown

Table #4

Name	Time of entry	AD	Supposed age	Time of leaving	Cherokee name	Explanation	Place of Residence	Improvement	Character
Cyrus Kingsbury	Jun 15	1818	12	May 1 1819	Tse squh nē tuh	young bird	Chickamauga		Unknown
Timothy Dwight	Jun 15	1818	15	Aug 15 1818	To wos kēē	swimmer	Chickamauga		Not good, forfeited his name
Sally Katchum	Jun 17	1818	11				Brainerd		Doubtful
Walter McDonald	Jul 3	1818	6	Aug 26 1818			Pea vine		Doubtful
Nancy Ākè	Jul 3	1818	15	Aug 26 1818			Pea vine		Doubtful
Jedediah Morse	Jul 3	1818	10	Aug 26 1818	Te kun nu wa té sky	making holes deeper	Pea vine		Doubtful
Cynthia Pack	Jul 8	1818	9	Jun 18 1819			Nickojack	Read & write	Respectable young lady
Jane Tailor	Jul 13	1818	7				Brainerd		Unknown
Mary Duning	Jul 16	1818	7				Broomstown	Read	
Calvin Jones	Jul 17	1818	18	Mar 24 1821	Tsu yaw nuh	Horns	Brainerd		Learning the blacksmith trade, hopefully pious
Polly Burns	Sep 24	1818	15	Jun 30 1819			Nickojack	Read & write	Respectable young lady
Lydia Carter	Sep 29	1818	4	22 Aug 1820	Te tah te yow sky	one who runs too fast to be taken	Dead	Spell in words of four syllables	Was taken to the Arkansas by order of the government with the view of sending her to her own nation. The journey was too great.
Nancy Melton	Nov 30	1818	14	Jul 2 1819			Alabama	Read & write	Married to a white man
Anne Wolf	Nov 30	1818	9	Oct 15 1819			Big Spring	Read & write	Promising
Jesse Hicks	Dec 7	1818	16	May 15 1819			Fortville	Read & write	Promising
Edward Hicks	Dec 7	1818	14	Dec 14 1821			Fortville	Grammar, common arithmetic, Burrels Astronomy	Promising

Table #4

Name	Time of entry	AD	Supposed age	Time of leaving	Cherokee name	Explanation	Place of Residence	Improvement	Character
Polly Hicks	Dec 7	1818	12	Aug 1821			Taloney	Read & write	Promising
Darcas Fields	Dec 7	1818	12	Aug 1821			Fortville	Read & write	Promising
John Newton	Dec 7	1818	14				Brainerd		
William Brewer	Dec 9	1818	6		Ta kah huh tuh	Scaly	Brainerd		
Sally Brewer	Dec 25	1818	15	Apr 16 1821			At Maj Browns	Read & write	Hopefully pious
George Murphy	Dec 28	1818	12		Tsu hloh gwoh		Brainerd		
George Lowrey	Dec 29	1818	14	Jul 13 1819	Kun ne guh	Black hairs	Wills Town	Read & write	Hopeful, Industrious
Jackson	Jan 7	1819	11	Nov 3 1819	Kul tuh suh yoh whah	Snipes	Big Springs	Spell in words of two syllables	Doubtful
Torrey	Jan 7	1819	7	Nov 3 1819			Big Springs	Spell in words of two syllables	Doubtful
Selz Timberlake	Jan 18	1819	13	Sep 17 1819			Near the Agency	Read in Testament	Unknown
Ebz Fields	Jan 18	1819	7				Brainerd		
Jefferson Pack	Jan 22	1819	10	Jan 18 1819**	Oo naw leh	Wind	Nickojack	Read & write	Promising
Jane Lowrey	Jan 22	1819	4	Feb 19 1819			Chickamauga		Unknown
John Arch	Jan 27	1819	25	Oct 15 1821			Creek Path	Read & write	Pious
Harriet Newel	Feb 3	1819	10		Ka hu guh		Brainerd		
Henry Axtel	Feb 15	1819	6		Tih guh skih	Drowner	Brainerd		
Tilman Rose	Feb 22	1819	13		Tille oo kum muh	Ches[t]nut soup	Brainerd		
Fanny Woodbury	Mar 15	1819	5	May 25 1819	Wot tĕ yo hy		Coosewattee		Unknown
Susan Watts	Mar 25	1819	9	May 29 1819	Yock sih		Chatoogy		Doubtful
Julian Watts	Mar 25	1819	7	May 29 1819	Tse kä eh	Taking away			
Charles Stowful	Mar 29	1819	12	May 1 1819	Sah ge uh		Willstown	Read in easy lessons	Unknown
Susan Still	Apr 12	1819	15	May 16 1820			Chickamauga		Married in the Cherokee Nation
Akĕ	Apr 24	1819	8	Oct 29 1819			Willstown		Unknown
Tsu ke tsuh nä hý	Apr 24	1819	11	Aug 8 1820	Tsu ke tsuh nä hý	Daily	Willstown		Unknown
Oo tsĕ tsuh tuh	Apr 24	1819	13	Aug 8 1820	Oo tsĕ tsuh tuh	Corn Tassels	Willstown		Unknown
George Killion	May 6	1819	8	Feb 16 1820			Tennessee State	Read in easy lessons	Unknown

Table #4

Name	Time of entry	AD	Supposed age	Time of leaving	Cherokee name	Explanation	Place of Residence	Improvement	Character
John	May 6	1819	14	Apr 16 1821	Yuh wih guh nih hih	Man strikes	Coosewattee	Read & write	Mediocrity
Jack Griffin	May 17	1819	13	Apr 16 1821	Ah heüh ta gih	Jumping in the water	Chattooga	Read & write	Lead away by bad company
Nicholas Patterson	May 22	1819	11		Oo tun tah stee	Listener	Brainerd		
Samuel Spring	May 31	1819	13	Apr 15 1821	Ta kuh tō kuh	Standing	Going Snakes town	Read & write	Has forfeited his name by staying away, & it has been given to another
Caty	Jun 4	1819	5	Oct 29 1819			Turnpike		
Manasseh Cutler	Jun 8	1819	8		Sul lō lüh né tüh	Young squirrel	Brainerd		
Tulskooaiĥ	Jun 8	1819	6	Nov 18 1820	Tulskooaiĥ	Bowing	Coosewattee	Spell in words of three syllables	Doubtful
Jane Shell	Jun 8	1819	12	Apr 15 1821			Going Snakes town	Spell in words of three syllables	Unknown
Diany Dryhead	Jun 8	1819	9	Oct 15 1821			Coosewattee	Read in easy lessons	Promising
Ullē tsuh	Jun 14	1819	13	Jan 20 1820	Ul lē tsuh		Little Cai u guh	Read & white	Unknown
Tun noo wih	Jun 14	1819	8	Jan 20 1820	Tun noo wih		Little Cai u huh now dead	Read & write	Was killed by being thrown from a horse
Teel tuh ta gih	Jun 21	1819	16	Jul 24 1820	Teel tuh ta gih	jumper	Wills town	Spell in words of 2 syllables	Doubtful
Tse tse kuh noo we a huh	Jun 21	1819	13	Aug 10 1820	Tse tse kun noo we a huh	a Ren [wren] going under	Wills town	Spell in three syllables	Doubtful
Bethuel Dodd	Jul 5	1819	5				Brainerd		
Alexander Otter lifter	Jul 10	1819	11	Nov 17 1819	Kun nos kē skē	Thief	Shoe make town	Spell in 2 syllables	Doubtful
Daniel	Jul 19	1819	9				Brainerd		
Tsah noo wa nuh	Jul 19	1819	16	Jan 9 1822	Tsah noo wa nuh	John is gone	Fort Armstrong	Read & write	Hopefully pious, attends family prayers with his people
David Parker	Jul 19	1819	6		Oo ta le tuh	Hid	Brainerd		

Table #4

Name	Time of entry	AD	Supposed age	Time of leaving	Cherokee name	Explanation	Place of Residence	Improvement	Character
Oo tse tsuh tuh	Jul 19	1819	11	Dec 20 1819	Oo tse tsuh tuh	Corn Tassels	Unknown	Made but little improvement	Turned away from school for bad conduct
Ann Porter	Jul 19	1819	13	Apr 15 1819	Anna John		expected at B. soon	Read in Testament	Promising. She has been absent on account of misunderstanding.
Mary Mason	Jul 19	1819	10	Apr 15 1819	Polly John		Do	Do	They were at home a short time on account of sickness. Their father sat out to bring them, but hearing on the way that we would not take them again, he turned back.
Dick	Jul 21	1819	25	Sep 10 1819			Turnpike		Unpromising
Alexander Sanders	Jul 29	1819	10	Nov 20 1819			Taloney		In Br. Halls School
James Sanders	Jul 29	1819	14	Nov 20 1819			Taloney		In Br. Halls School
Ool stoo John D. Paxton	Aug 3	1819	18	Mar 19 1822	Ool stoo	A leaf	Fortville	Read & write	Left the school in a fit of obstinacy, though his general character is good.
Woi kuh ke skē	Aug 5	1819	9	Jul 27 1820	Woi kuh ke skee	Pigeon out of the water	Chickamauga	Spell in 3 syllables	Not promising
Riley Thornton	Aug 15	1819	12		Oo tso nuh tih	Rattle snake	Brainerd		
John Osage Ross	Oct 11	1819	4	Aug 22 1820	Sah suh	A goose	City of Washington	Spell in two syllables	Osage captive
Samuel Candy	Oct 13	1819	16	Nov 16 1821	Tu a loŏ ky	Jealous	Chatunooga	Read & write	Doubtful
Jack Candy	Oct 13	1819	12		Quh law sih oo tlah wuh	Frog skin	Brainerd		
Oo ke tu tly	Aug 30	1819	16	Sep 10 1819	Oo ke tuh tly	Feather	Unknown		Unknown

Table #4

Name	Time of entry	AD	Supposed age	Time of leaving	Cherokee name	Explanation	Place of Residence	Improvement	Character
Ut tai uh tsuh ky	Sep 30	1819	6	Aug 10 1820	Ut tai uh tsuh ky	Lost	Willstown	Spell in two syllables	Unknown
David Brown	Oct 11	1819	18	Apr 22 1820			Cornwall, Con.	Read & write	Pious
Uh ne a lih	Nov 4	1819	10	Jul 27 1820	Un ne a lih	Howling	Chickamauga	Spell in easy lessons	Unknown
Stuesty	Dec 17	1819	12		Stuesty	Key	Brainerd		
Vinson Gould	Dec 30	1819	6		Sequh ne yaw	Hog shooter	Brainerd	Read in easy lessons	
Jackson	Dec 30	1819	20	Mar 10 1820			Chickamauga	Read in easy lessons	Very unpromising (a thief)
Thomas L	Jan 25	1820	12	Mar 13 1820	Tsu tuh yun luh tuh	Shadow	Brainerd		
Joseph Meigs	Jan 31	1820	12		Ut tuh suh	War club	Creek Nation		Run away from the school because the boys called him a Creek
Tsu he suh tuh	Feb 7	1820	10	Feb 21 1820	Stu he suh tuh**	Dew	Sumach town	Spell in three syllables	Unknown
Thomas Griffin	Mar 20	1820	8	Apr 16 1821	Oo y hun ttuh	Cold	Chattooga		Doubtful
Walter	Mar 20	1820	12	Apr 16 1821			Te squh la skuh	Do	Doubtful
Moses	Mar 20	1820	11	Apr 16 1821			Te squh la skuh	Do	Doubtful
David Carter	Apr 10	1820	14				Brainerd		
Tsu ttuh	Apr 10	1820	12	May 20 1821	Tsu ttuh	Fox	Duck Creek	In words of three letters	Unpromising
Watte keh	May 6	1820	8	Jul 10 1820	Watte keh	Bey	Te squh la skuh		Unknown
Tsah lih	May 6	1820	6	Jul 10 1820			Te squh la skuh		Unknown
Jesse	Jun 18	1820	15	Aug 25 1820	Oo ne na ke te ye	White killer	Eu kul loo ga	Spell in 4 letters	Ran away from the school
Tse stu ke hle huh	Jul 13	1820	18	Aug 28 1820	Tse stu kuh hle huh**	Sleeping Rabbit	Creek path	Read & write	Unpromising
Glover Thornton	Aug 10	1820	10		Tau osuh	Musketoe [mosquito]	Brainerd		
Smith Thornton	Aug 10	1820	8		Tul lah too	Cricket	Brainerd		

Table #4

Name	Time of entry	AD	Supposed age	Time of leaving	Cherokee name	Explanation	Place of Residence	Improvement	Character
Benjamin Tappan	Sep 4	1820	12		At tle taw heh	Runner	Brainerd		
Thomas Brewer	Sep 6	1820	6		Hoo suh taw hnih	Key	Brainerd		
Wheeler Gilbert	Sep 12	1820	6		Tene saw keh	Let us go across	Brainerd		
George Candy	Sep 25	1820	13		Tăy a wuh	a hollow weed	Brainerd		
Louisa Botell [Battelle]	Sep 20	1819	10				Brainerd		
Elsey Tsu ih	Oct 18	1819	6				Brainerd		
Jane	Nov 20	1819	11				Brainerd		
Nancy	Nov 20	1819	11				Brainerd		
Patience	Dec 16	1819	8		Hah na loo gà hih	Run after	Brainerd		
Lucy	Dec 16	1819	12				Brainerd		
Sally	Jan 16	1820	7				Brainerd		
Lydia	Jan 16	1820	7	Apr 12 1820			Chickamauga		
Tuker	Feb 8	1820	15	Aug 29 1820			Creek path	Read in easy lessons	Unknown
Mindwell W. Gould	Mar 23	1820	4				Brainerd		
Nancy Fields	Mar 8	1820	8	Jun 27 1820			Creek path		Fine scholar in Br. Potters school
Ruth Fields	Mar 8	1820	6	Jun 27 1820			Creek path		Fine scholar in Br. Potters school
Jane Thompson	Apr 30	1820	6	Apr 15 1821			Springplace	Read in the Testament	A good scholar in Br. Smiths school
Polly	May 27	1820	5	Mar 27 1821			Broomstown	Spell in three syllables	Unknown, taken from the school by her grandmother after the death of her mother.
Sally Harris	Aug 28	1820	13	Nov 23 1820			Taloney	Spell in two syllables	Unknown
Nancy Tailor	Sep 4	1820	5				Brainerd		
Dinah Murphey	Sep 22	1820	8				Brainerd		
Rachel Murphey	Sep 22	1820	6				Brainerd		

Table #4

Name	Time of entry	AD	Supposed age	Time of leaving	Cherokee name	Explanation	Place of Residence	Improvement	Character
Kuh nuh Se nih	Dec 6	1820	15		Kun nuh se nih	Drag[j]ing	Brainerd		
Dick Benge	Dec 4	1820	9		Tse stuh nuh	Craw fish	Brainerd		
Edward Hopful	Nov 6	1820	8		Oo koo goo	Owl	Brainerd		
Ta kuh nuh nuh	Dec 4	1820	14	Jul 14 1821	Ta kuh nuh nuh	Two roads	Creek Nation	Spell in two syllables	Ran away from the school
Kuh luh nuh hih	Feb 7	1821	8		Kuh lun nuh hih**	Fritter	Brainerd		
Kos suh he lih	Feb 7	1821	6		Kos suh hee lih**	Stoopin	Brainerd		
George McPherson	Feb 6	1821	7				Brainerd		
Oo ta lih tuh	May 7	1821	12		Oo ta lih tuh	Hid	Brainerd		
John Wilkison	May 8	1821	11	Sep 11 1821			Nickojack	Spell in two syllables	Doubtful
Wm. Wilkison	May 8	1821	9	Sep 11 1821			Nickojack	Spell in two syllables	Doubtful
Charles Downing	May 14	1821	13				Brainerd		
William Downing	May 14	1821	11				Brainerd		
Johnston Reece	May 15	1821	7				Brainerd		
Samuel Spring	May 9	1821	11		Sa lu gih	Flute	Brainerd		
Kun noo we a huh	Jan 12	1821	10		Kun noo e a huh**	Going under	Brainerd		
Lacy Willson	May 7	1821	6				Brainerd		
Moses	Aug 9	1821	11				Brainerd		
Tot tsu la nuh	Aug 9	1821	9		Tot tsu la nuh	Arise	Brainerd		
John Rackley	Feb 11	1819	8				Dead	Could read & write	
Wm. Reece	Nov 10	1821	5				Brainerd		
Tuh ne suh nih	Nov 6	1821	13		Tuh ne suh nih	Eat it all	Brainerd		Grandson to the King (Pathkiller) a bright boy
Cah too luh skuh	Nov 3	1821	11		Kah too luh skuh***	Dirt track	Brainerd		
Skah tah	Feb 8	1822	11				Brainerd		
Woh yih kil luh	May 8	1822	11		Woh yih kil luh	Pigeon off of the ground	Brainerd		

Table #4

Name	Time of entry	AD	Supposed age	Time of leaving	Cherokee name	Explanation	Place of Residence	Improvement	Character
Kul luh gē nuh	Feb 7	1822	13		Kulluh gē nuh	Buck	Brainerd		
Kun na hē yuh	Dec 1	1820	9		Kun na hē yuh	Leave a part	Brainerd		
Patsey Benge	Dec 20	1820	7				Brainerd		
Diana Fields	Dec 20	1820	9				Brainerd		
Jane McPherson	Feb 6	1821	8				Brainerd		
Nancy Booth	Sep 20	1819	8	Apr 15 1821			Chickamauga		
Caroline Smelt	Sep 8	1820	7				Brainerd		
Betsey Fields	August	1821	7				Brainerd		
Mariah Mackentosh	May 3	1822	10				Brainerd		
Jack Foster	Nov 29	1819	8				Brainerd		

* Chickadee

** Date of leaving probably miscopied by Cataloguer

***Two different spellings of Cherokee name

Source: Papers of the American Board of Commissioners for Foreign Mission, ABC 18.3.1 v.2: 159-161.

Table #5

Additional list of students who attended Brainerd School, with comments.

Name	Comments
Mahala Wells	Entered April 6, 1817; White girl whose father resides in the nation.
Samuel Worcester	Entered May 25, 1817; Sun e ky yah, Indian name.
Grace S. Meigs	Entered June 9, 1817; White girl, granddaughter of the Agent.
Emily S. Meigs	Entered June 9, 1817; White girl, granddaughter of the Agent.
James Hervey	Entered June 14, 1817; Hakh lu nah hee tah. Long Hair.
Barbara McClellan	White children belonging to the family we hired.
William McClellan	Dto
Adaline McClellan	Dto
Samuel Newell	
Nehemiah Porter	
Adam Empie	
James Wilson Tilman	
Christian Streik	
William George Patterson	
Ezra Ripley	
Nicholas Patterson	Run away
Benjamin Tappan	Run away
Manasseh Cutler	Run away
John Knox Witherspoon	Run away
John E. Latta	Run away
Kapooly	Sandwich Islander, probably 21 years of age, Websters spelling book, a poor scholar.
William Brewer	a half breed, 12 years. English grammar passing. Reads & spelt very well as did the three immediately following. Talents about middling, rather a quarrelsome boy.
Wiley Glover Thornton	a half breed, 11 years. English grammar passing. Rather insolent & negligent.
Bethuel Dodd	a full Cherokee, 10 years. Sounds of the letters as they occurred in reading. Industrious & well behaved. Moderate Talents.
Smith Thornton	a half breed, 9 years. English grammar passing. A good boy with good talents. Very promising.
Thomas L. McKenney	full Cherokee, 14 years. English Reader. Well disposed. Not so attentive as he should be.

Table #5

Name	Comments
George McPherson	3/4 white, 10 years. English Reader. Does pretty well.
James Coe	full Cherokee, 12 years. Definitions in spelling book. Talents of a mediocrity, Very indolent.
David Parker	full Cherokee, 10 years (Did not recite as he was unwell). Indolent, a poor scholar. Now at school, but will be dismissed.
Eliphalet Wheeler Gilbert	a full Cherokee, 12 years. A brother of T. L. McKenney. Common Talent, sounds of letters. Well disposed. Married Ann Porter.
Thomas Witherspoon	full Cherokee, 13 years. Sounds of letters. Talent above mediocrity. Not very industrious.
John Emerson	full cherokee, 13 years. Sounds of letters. Good talents. Pretty industrious.
Samuel Worcester	full Cherokee, 12 years. Definitions in spelling book. Very good boy & very promising.
Moses Harris	half breed, 13 years. Spelling book. Small talents & little industry.
Edward Hopful	full Cherokee, 9 years. Spelling book. A promising boy as to talents; but rather roguish & mischievous.
James Taylor	7/8 white, 8 years. Spelling book. Sounds of the letters. Respectable talents, learns well. Needs correction occasionally.
Jack Spears	half breed, 13 years. Spelling book, sounds of letters. Very steady, sedate, industrious boy. Talents not above mediocrity.
Samuel Spring	full Cherokee, 14 years. Arithmetic. Well behaved, industrious boy. Talents good.
Wiley Thornton	half breed, 16 years. Arithmetic. Talents good, apt to learn, hates work, addicted to levity & slothfulness.
Jack Candy	3/4 white, 14 years. Arithmetic. Good talents & good behavior.
John Murphy	full Cherokee, 12 years. Syllables of three letters. Good boy to work, here but a little while.
Samuel Lincoln	half breed, 8 years. Words of two syllables. A good little boy, well behaved, makes good proficiency in his studies.
Lacy Wilson	3/4 white, 8 years. Words of two syllables. His character promising as far as known.

Table #5

Name	Comments
Ralph Wells Gridley	half breed, 7 years. Words of three syllables. Talent above mediocrity. Himself well behaved.
William Kerr	full Cherokee, 14 years. Words of three syllables. A poor scholar, very good to work.
Kaskalo (chair or stool)	full Cherokee, 13 years. Words of three syllables. A slothful & ill behaved boy with poor talents.
William Reese	half breed, 8 years. Words of three syllables. A very good little boy & very promising.
Moses Hoge	full Cherokee, 7 years. Words of three syllables. Talents fully equal to mediocrity. Behavior not so good.
Thomas Brewer	(brother of William Brewer), half breed, 10 years. Words of three syllables. Learns well, behavior bad.
Henderson Harris	(brother of Moses Harris), half breed. Words of three syllables. 9 years. Talents respectable, behavior not so good.
David Spears	(brother of Jack Spears), half breed, 10 years. Words of three syllables. A dull boy, behavior tolerably good.
Walter McDonald	half breed, 10 years. Words of three syllables. Talents not promising, behavior about as good as common.
Charles Downing	1/4 white, 15 years. Went home a week since, to be absent 4 weeks, for the purpose of helping his mother plant some corn. He is a boy as worthy of patronage as any in the school, good talents, good behavior, pleasant disposition.
James Carey	3/4 white. 12 years. Went home 3 weeks ago by permission, to stay a week, but has not returned. Common talents, bad disposition.
Eli Smith	full Cherokee, 18 years. Went home a week since by permission, to be about two weeks, a good talent & well behaved.
Johnson Foreman	7/8 white, 15 years. May be ranked among the best boys in every respect. Went home on a visit 3 days ago, to be absent a week.
Samuel B. Wilson	full Cherokee, 18 years. Has been absent a week to assist his mother. Talents very good, behavior rather boyish, sometimes saucy.

Table #5

Name	Comments
Johnson Reece	(brother of William Reece), half breed, 10 years. Is now sick here with the ague & fever & will soon be removed home. A very promising boy, both in talents & behavior.
George Candy	(a brother of Jack Candy), 3/4 white, 18 years. Absent today to attend the mail carrier, & show him where to pass the high water. Very good as to conduct, his talents not above mediocrity.
Boston Recorder	full Cherokee, 18 years. A well behaved youth. Very rarely requires even a reproof. Absent now by permission.
Betsey Mayhew	at home
Lydia Huntley	
Jane Wilson	half breed, 13 years. Was at school here two years ago, then absent till within a few weeks since. She did not retain all her letters when she returned, but now reads in words of two syllables. Talents small. Disposition unsteady, of as little promise as any children in the school.
Anna Spears	half breed, 9 years. Reads & spells in words of two syllables. An active child, learns to work better than to read, sullen temper.
Mindwell Woodbridge Gould	full Cherokee, 11 years old. Returned to school lately, after a long absence. In the same class as the preceding. A promising child, pleasant temper, pretty apt to learn.
Polly Hwa kwa	full Cherokee, 9 years. In the same class as the preceding. Has been in school only since last fall. Of a quick temper, easily governed, a promising & very affectionate child. (She is sister to Elizabeth Kean, and her mother is a member of the church.)
Margaret McDonald	half breed, 12 years. Just begins to read in the Testament. Is quick to learn, has a pleasant disposition.
Catherine Spears	half breed, 10 years. In the same class with the preceding. Slow to learn, good disposition.
Polly Wati	3/4 Cherokee, 10 years, (a sister of Elias Boudinot) in the same class as the preceding, has been in school a year. A very promising child.

Table #5

Name	Comments
Nancy Wati	(a sister of E. Boudinot) has been in school a year or nearly. Reads in the Testament, is 17 or 18 years old. A very amiable girl, & apt to learn.
Sally Bob	full Cherokee, 13 years old. Testament. Sullen temper, quick to learn.
Betsey Hare	full Cherokee, 12 years old. Testament. Appears pretty well.
Nancy Reece	half breed, 9 years old. Testament, (a child of Charles Reece). An active child, apt to learn & apt to work.
Patsy Benge	12 years, half breed. Testament. Has a pleasant disposition, but does not love books.
Elizabeth Kean	full Cherokee, 16 years. American Reader. Spells words in reading lessons. Pretty good disposition. Talents for work good, for learning about as good as common.
Nancy Taylor	7/8 white, 12 years. American Reader. Spells words in the reading lessons. These two last are the only pupils in the first class. They, & several others, were examined in the abbreviations, sounds of letters, numerals, &c. There is no pupil so apt to learn as this child, of uneasy temper, very active.
Nelly	a half breed, 13 years. Reads in syllables of two letters. Has read but just commenced as learner. Not much opinion formed of her character.
Katawtlanuh	(a sister of Nelly) 9 years. Learning her letters. Appears well as to temper, not apt to learn.
Ya tsoo	(a daughter of Six killer) 10 years. Learning her letters. Full Cherokee. A wild creature just from the woods.

Compiled and arranged from various lists of students in the American Board Papers, ABC 18.3.1, v. 2: 189, 205-207; ABC 18.3.1, v. 3: 9-10.

Table #6

List of Persons at Taloney Mission.

Moody Hall, born at Cornish	Dec 1, 1789
Joined the mission	Mar 1817
Isabella Hall (Miss Murray) born at Lansingburgh	Apr 25, 1792
Louisa Jennet Hall born	Dec 27, 1818
Henry Parker, born at Litchfield, Con.	Mar 22, 1791
Removed to Ohio when ten years old	
Joined the Mission	Jan 1822
Philena Parker (Miss Griffin) born at Simsbury, Con.	Feb 10, 1792
Removed to Ohio in 1814	
Philena Almira, born in Con.	Dec 2, 1813

Source: Papers of the American Board, ABC 18.3.1, v. 2: 166.

Table #7

Names of those who belong to the church at Creek Path, year baptized &c.

Name	Baptized	Age	Remarks
John Brown Jr.	1820	25	is a brother to Catharine—is a half breed now dead
Susannah Brown	1820	30	is a half breed—widow of the above John
Mary Davis	1820	35	is a half breed—the wife of a white man
Sally Fields	1820	35	is a half breed—wife of a half breed has a lovely family
Susan Brown	1820	18	is a half breed—is sister to Catharine
Lydia Lovett	1820	30	is a half breed—is a widow
James Spencer	1821	30	is a half breed—has a family
John Brown Sr.	1822	60	is a half breed—father of Catharine
Sarah Brown	1822	60	is a half breed—mother of Catharine

Polly Gilbreth is a half breed–is hopefully pious–is the wife of a wicked white man, who probably keeps her from the church.

Millie Gunter is a half breed–the wife of a half breed–is the sister of Lydia Lovett–is hopefully pious but probably kept back by her husband.

Source: Papers of the American Board, ABC 18.3.1, v. 2: 176.

Notes

In citing works in the notes, short titles have been used and are identified with the following abbreviations:

ABC   Archival Papers of the American Board of Commissioners for Foreign Missions, Houghton Library, Harvard University.

ASP   *American State Papers*, Class 2: Indian Affairs. vol. 2., edited by Walter Lowrie, Walter S. Franklin, and Matthew St. Clair Clarke (Washington, D.C.: Gales and Seaton, 1832, 1834).

BJ   "Brainerd Journal," ABC 18.3.1, v.2: 1–94.

"Catalogue"   "A Catalogue of the Cherokee Scholars that belonged to the school at Brainerd," ABC 18.3.1, v. 2: 159–161. (See Table #4.)

M–208   National Archives. U.S. Government. Bureau of Indian Affairs. Records of the Cherokee Indian Agency in Tennessee, 1801–1825. Reference Group 75, Reels 7–9. Microfilm 208.

"List"   "A List of Persons who belong to the Mission at Brainerd, May 17, 1822," ABC: 18.3.1, v.2: 162. (See Table # 2.)

MH   *Missionary Herald*.

"Members"   "Names of those, who have been admitted to the church at Brainerd,"ABC: 18.3.1, v.2: 176. (See Table # 3.)

OED   *Oxford English Dictionary*, J.A. Simpson and E.S.C. Weiner, eds. (Oxford: Clarenden Press, 1989).

Tracy, "History"   "History of the American Board of Foreign Missions," in *History of American Missions to the Heathen*, Joseph J. Kwiat, ed., 1840; reprint (New York: Johnson Reprint Corp., 1970).

All scripture references are from the Kings James Version.

1. Kingsbury, Hall, Williams to Worcester, November 25, 1817, ABC 18.3.1, v.2: 99–101.

2. Mark 16:15.

3. For further information on the religious revival and the missionary motivation to evangelize, see: John A. Andrew III, *Rebuilding the Christian Commonwealth: New England Congregationalists and Foreign Missions, 1800–1830* (Lexington: University of Kentucky Press, 1976); John A. Andrew III, *From Revivals to Removal: Jeremiah Evarts, the Cherokee Nation and the Search for the Soul of America* (Athens: University of Georgia, 1992); Robert F. Berkhofer, Jr., *Salvation and the Savage: An Analysis of Protestant Missions and American Indian Response, 1787–1862* (Lexington: University of Kentucky Press, 1965); William G. McLoughlin, *The Cherokees and Christianity, 1794–1840: Essays on Acculturation and Cultural Persistence,* ed. by Walter H. Conser, Jr. (Athens: University of Georgia Press, 1994); and William G. McLoughlin, *Cherokees and Missionaries, 1789–1839* (Norman: University of Oklahoma Press, 1995).

4. For further information on Gideon Blackburn, see William G. McLoughlin, "Parson Blackburn's Whiskey, 1809–1810" in *The Cherokee Ghost Dance: Essays on the Southeastern Indians, 1789–1861* (Macon, Ga.: Mercer University Press, 1984), 365–384; V.M. Queener, "Gideon Blackburn," *East Tennessee Historical Society Publication* 6 (1934): 12–28; Edwin J. Best, "New Providence Presbyterian Church," *The Blount Journal* 2 no. 2 (Nov. 1986): 2–8.

5. For the Moravian's work in the Cherokee Nation, see Rowena McClinton, "The Moravian Mission Among the Cherokees at Springplace, Georgia" (Ph.D. diss., University of Kentucky, 1996); McLoughlin, *Cherokees and Missionaries;* and Muriel Wright, *Springplace: Moravian Mission and the Ward Family of the Cherokee Nation* (Guthrie, Okla.: Co–operative Publishing Co., 1940).

6. For an in–depth study of Evan Jones' work among the Cherokees, see William G. McLoughlin, *Champion of the Cherokees: Evan and John B. Jones* (Princeton: Princeton University Press, 1990).

7. Samuel Worcester, educated at Dartmouth College, became the pastor of the church in Salem, Massachusetts in 1802. Starting in 1810, as corresponding secretary for the American Board, he devoted the remainder of his life, until his death in 1821, to this mission outreach. See *BJ* entries for May 25–June 7, 1821, for Worcester's visit to the

Brainerd Mission. *National Cyclopaedia of American Biography* (New York: James T. White & Co., 1909), 1: 178–179.

8. The young New Englander Samuel J. Mills was one of the promoters of a world–wide missions outreach program which resulted in the American Board in 1810. Mills grew up hearing from his mother about missions to the "heathen," hearing stories about David Brainerd, and hearing about other missionaries. His mother said of him, "I have consecrated this child to the service of God, as a missionary." Mills was then educated with such a goal in mind by attending Andover Theological Seminary. Tracy, "History," 28.

9. *First Ten Annual Reports of the American Board of Commissioners for Foreign Missions* (Boston: Crocker and Brewster, 1834), 12.

10. William E. Strong, *The Story of the American Board: An Account of the First Hundred Years of the American Board of Commissioners for Foreign Missions* (Boston: The Pilgrim Press, 1910), 36.

11. *First Ten Annual Reports*, 135.

12. McLoughlin, *Cherokees and Missionaries*, 108.

13. Kingsbury to Worcester, December 16, 1816, ABC 18.3.1, v.3: 7.

14. A goal of the American Board was for Butrick to learn the Cherokee language. Samuel Worcester wrote the brethren: "That some of you should as soon as possible acquire a knowledge of the language of the Natives, we deem of very great importance. At each station there should be at least one well acquainted with the language of the Tribe, & one who is a preacher." The letter then instructed the brethren to designate a person to learn the language. Worcester to Hoyt, Kingsbury, Butrick, Hall, Williams, March 14, 1818, ABC 1.01, v.3: 36–38; McLoughlin, *Cherokees and Christianity*, 28–29; McLoughlin, *Cherokees and Missionaries*, 134–135.

15. Berkhofer, *Salvation and the Savage*, 112–113.

16. Robert Sparks Walker, *Torchlights to the Cherokees: The Brainerd Mission* (New York: The Macmillan Co., 1931), 329.

17. These original letters, reports, and journals are found in the American Board Archives at the Houghton Library, Harvard University, or copies of the originals are on microfilm produced by Primary Source Media, previously known as Research Publications.

18. For best sources see Bernard W. Sheehan, *Seeds of Extinction: Jeffersonian Philanthropy and the American Indian* (Chapel Hill: University of North Carolina Press, 1973); Theda Perdue and Michael D. Green, eds., *The Cherokee Removal: A Brief History with Documents* (Boston: St. Martin's Press, 1995); William G. McLoughlin, *Cherokee*

Renascence (Princeton: Princeton University Press, 1986); McLoughlin, *Cherokee Ghost Dance, Cherokees and Missionaries, The Cherokees and Christianity*; William L. Anderson, ed., *The Cherokee Removal, Before and After* (Athens: University of Georgia Press, 1991); Andrew, *From Revivals to Removal*; Francis Paul Prucha, *American Indian Policy in the Formative Years: The Indian Trade and Intercourse Acts, 1790–1834* (Cambridge: Harvard University Press, 1962); Ronald N. Satz, *American Indian Policy in the Jacksonian Era* (Lincoln: University of Nebraska Press, 1975); and Thurman Wilkins, *Cherokee Tragedy: the Ridge Family and the Decimation of a People* (Norman: University of Oklahoma Press, 1988).

19. Berkhofer, *Salvation and the Savage*, x–xi.

20. Berkhofer, *Salvation and the Savage*, 1–15; Sheehan, *Seeds of Extinction*, 119–147.

21. In *Cherokee Renascence*, William McLoughlin discusses in-depth the Indian policies of various presidential administrations. Francis Paul Prucha looks at how the state and national governments set policy for all Indian tribes in *American Indian Policy in the Formative Years*. Another book by McLoughlin, *Cherokee Ghost Dance: Essays on the Southeastern Indians*, includes an essay entitled "Thomas Jefferson and the Beginning of Cherokee Nationalism," 73–110. Ronald Satz looks at the effects of Andrew Jackson's policy in *American Indian Policy in the Jacksonian Era*.

22. See Reginald Horsman, *Race and Manifest Destiny: the Origins of American Racial Anglo–Saxonism* (Cambridge: Harvard University Press, 1981); and Robert F. Berkhofer, Jr., *The White Man's Indian: Images of the American Indian from Columbus to the Present* (New York: Alfred A. Knopf, 1978).

23. For a look at pre–Revolutionary War traditional Cherokee society, see John Philip Reid, *A Law of Blood: The Primitive Law of the Cherokee Nation* (New York: New York University Press, 1970); Tom Hatley, *The Dividing Paths: Cherokees and South Carolinians Through the Era of Revolution* (New York: Oxford University Press, 1993); and Charles Hudson, *The Southeastern Indians* (Knoxville: University of Tennessee Press, 1976). Also see McLoughlin, *Cherokees and Missionaries*, 18–23; McLoughlin, *Cherokees and Christianity*, 157–158; McLoughlin, *Cherokee Renascence*, 3–16.

24. McLoughlin, *Cherokee Renascence*, 36.

25. Ibid., 36.

26. Ibid., 36.

27. Ibid., 106–107.

28. For more information on the development of roads in the Cherokee Nation, see McLoughlin, *Cherokee Renascence,* 77–104. For a detailed description of the area which the Federal Road traversed, see "Retracing the Old Federal Road" in *Placenames of Georgia: Essays of John H. Goff,* Francis Lee Utley and Marion R. Hemperley, eds. (Athens: University of Georgia Press, 1975), 349–360.

29. McLoughlin, *Cherokee Renascence,* 88–89.

30. Clemens de Baillou, "The Chief Vann House at Spring Place, Georgia, the Vanns, Tavern and Ferry," *Early Georgia* 2 (1957): 3–11; E. Raymond Evans, "Highways to Progress: Nineteenth Century Roads in the Cherokee Nation," *Journal of Cherokee Studies* 2 (Fall, 1977): 394–400.

31. For a complete story of the sale of the hunting grounds, see McLoughlin, *Cherokee Renascence,* 92–108.

32. The split between the Upper and Lower Town Chiefs and also Doublehead's killing are discussed in *Cherokee Renascence,* 109–127.

33. Ibid., 146–160.

34. Cherokees ceded this land through treaties signed in 1805 and 1806. Charles C. Royce, *The Cherokee Nation of Indians* (Chicago: Aldine Publishing Co., 1975), 256.

35. *BJ,* November 25, 1818.

36. Royce, *The Cherokee Nation of Indians,* 256.

37. The Civilization Fund Act, passed in 1819, provided funds for the mission schools among the tribes so the missionaries could have the necessary facilities and implements to accomplish their goals. McLoughlin, *Cherokees and Christianity,* 60.

38. The missionaries stated that a "hunting frock came a little below the knee, is open before and fastened around the middle with a girdle, of their own making." Kingsbury to Worcester, June 30, 1817, ABC 18.3.1, v.3: 9–10.

39. For the traditional Cherokee myths of Selu, see James Mooney, *Myths of the Cherokee and Sacred Formulas of the Cherokees, from the 19th and 7th Annual Reports B.A.E.* (Nashville: Charles and Randy Elder Publishers, 1982); for a more contemporary view, see Marilou Awiakta, *Selu: Seeking the Corn–Mother's Wisdom* (Golden, Colo.: Fulcrum Publishing, 1993).

40. For the Cherokee traditional views of kinship, marriage, clans, and revenge laws, see Hudson, *The Southeastern Indians,* 184–257;

Reid, *A Law of Blood*; and V. Richard Persico, Jr., "Early Nineteenth–Century Cherokee Political Organization," in *The Cherokee Indian Nation: A Troubled History*, Duane H. King, ed. (Knoxville: University of Tennessee Press, 1979), 92–109.

41. For an in–depth look at the role of Cherokee women in society and the Cherokee reaction to the government's "civilization" effort see Theda Perdue, *Cherokee Women: Gender and Culture Change, 1700–1835* (Lincoln: University of Nebraska Press, 1998) and several articles by Theda Perdue: "Women, Men, and American Indian Policy: The Cherokee Response to 'Civilization'" in *Negotiators of Change: Historical Perspectives on Native American Women*, Nancy Shoemaker, ed. (New York: Routledge, 1995), 90–113; "Southern Indians and the Cult of True Womanhood," in *The Web of Southern Social Relations, Women, Family and Education*, Walter J. Fraser, Jr.; R. Frank Saunders, Jr.; and Jon L. Wakelyn, eds. (Athens: University of Georgia Press, 1985), 35–51; "Nancy Ward," in *Portraits of American Women: From Settlement to Present*, G.J. Barker–Benfield and Catherine Clinton, eds. (New York: St. Martin's Press, 1991), 83–100; "Cherokee Women and the Trail of Tears," in *Journal of Women's History* 1, no. 1 (Spring 1989): 14–30.

42. See Table #1: "List of Towns" which described the size of a few Cherokee "towns."

43. McLoughlin, *Cherokee Renascence*, 139–140, 161–162, 284. Also see Charles Hicks' description of clans found in the April 16, 1818 *BJ* entry.

44. See Reid, *Law of Blood*, 143–152 for information on Cherokee traditional views of inheritance.

45. McLoughlin, *Cherokee Renascence*, 71.

46. Hamilton, trans. and ed., "Minutes of the Mission Conference Held in Springplace," *The Atlanta Historical Bulletin* 16 (Spring 1971): 35.

47. For other information about Cherokee rituals and myths, see Mooney, *Myths of the Cherokee and Sacred Formulas of the Cherokee*; Hudson, *The Southeastern Indians*; and James Adair, *History of the American Indians*, ed. Samuel C. Williams, (1775; reprint, Johnson City, Tenn.: The Watauga Press, 1930).

48. See *Panoplist* 14 (September 1818): 415–416.

49. Worcester to B. King, April 28, 1819, ABC 1.01, v.3: 144–145.

50. Berkhofer, *Salvation and the Savage*, 25–27.

51. *BJ*, July 2, 1821.

52. "Catalogue."

53. Evarts, "Memoranda," May 8, 1822, ABC 18.3.1, v. 2: 155.

54. Worcester to Hoyt and Other Brethren at Brainerd, May 6, 1819, ABC 1.01, v.3: 148–152.

55. Hoyt to Evarts, July 24, 1820, ABC 18.3.1, v.3: 62.

56. Ray Nash, *American Penmanship, 1800–1850* (Worcester: American Antiquarian Society, 1969), 59.

Notes for 1817

1. Cyrus Kingsbury, born November 22, 1786, was educated at Brown University and Andover Seminary. Under the American Board he received permission from the Cherokee Council in 1816 to open a mission. He arrived at Chickamauga Mission on January 13, 1817 though the first *BJ* entry is dated January 18, 1817. The missionaries called the mission Chickamauga[h] for the first year, but when Jeremiah Evarts, visited the mission in 1818, he wrote regarding the mission's name:

As Chickamaugah comprehends a considerable district, extending up and down the creek of that name, and including an Indian village near the Tennessee, it has been thought best by the missionaries, Mr. [Elias] Cornelius, and myself, that the missionary station should receive a new name . . . . BRAINERD, in affectionate remembrance of that able, devoted, and successful missionary.

Evarts referred to David Brainerd, a missionary to Indians in New England and Delaware from 1742–1747 and fiancé to Jerusha Edwards (Jonathan Edward's daughter) at the time David died. Kingsbury left Brainerd in 1818 to open Eliot Mission in the Choctaw Nation.

The mission was located in present Tennessee, six miles from the Tennessee River on the Chickamauga, which was usually navigable up to the mission. The site was 140 miles southwest of Knoxville, Tennessee; 7 miles east of Lookout Mountain; 155 miles northwest of Athens, Georgia; and 2 miles north of the Georgia–Tennessee state line. *Panoplist* 14 (July 1818): 339; Walker, *Torchlights*, 41–42; Henry Warner Bowden, *Dictionary of American Religious Biography* (Westport, Conn.: Greenwood Press, 1977), 61–62; E. Raymond Evans, ed., "Jedidiah Morse's Report to the Secretary of War on Cherokee Indian Affairs in 1822," *Journal of Cherokee Studies* 6 (Fall, 1981): 64; ABC 18.3.1, v.3: 7. For the life of David Brainerd, see Jonathan Edwards, *The Life of David Brainerd*, ed. Norman Pettit, vol. 7 of *The Works of Jonathan Edward* (New Haven: Yale University Press, 1985).

2. John McDonald, Cherokee Chief John Ross' grandfather, was born about 1747 at Inverness, Scotland. McDonald at age nineteen came to Charleston, South Carolina. While engaged in trading in the Fort Louden area, he met and married a Cherokee woman, Anna [Anne] Shorey, daughter of the interpreter William Shorey. McDonald held the Cherokee people in great regard, for he not only married a Cherokee woman, but he also took the Indian's side on many issues especially since the Cherokees had supported his side, the British side, during the Revolutionary War. Later the McDonald family moved to the Lookout Mountain area on the Chickamauga Creek near present day Chattanooga. Mollie, the McDonald's daughter, also married a trader, Daniel Ross. The McDonald home site, purchased as the location for the Brainerd Mission, included twenty–five acres, the buildings, and improvements. Gary E. Moulton, *John Ross, Cherokee Chief* (Athens: University of Georgia Press, 1978), 3; Grace Steele Woodward, *The Cherokees* (Norman: University of Oklahoma Press, 1963), 84–85, 140; Emmet Starr, *History of the Cherokee Indians* (1921; reprint, Muskogee, Okla.: Hoffman Printing Co. Inc., 1979), 474, 582; Henry Thompson Malone, *Cherokees of the Old South: A People in Transition* (Athens: University of Georgia Press, 1956), 54–56.

3. The missionaries were concerned about morality and sinning. They probably had questioned Mr. McDonald on his view of sin, and his answer to them probably was that he did not think he sinned and did not think he did "anything wrong."

4. The Cherokees began acquiring African–American slaves in the eighteenth century. The planter elite, who increasingly came to control the economy and government of the Cherokee Nation in the nineteenth century, depended on slave labor to expand their land holdings. The American Board hired African–American slaves from their Cherokee masters through the period of this journal, but later, in 1826, missionary Daniel Butrick protested slave–hiring, and the Dwight Mission prohibited the practice. See Theda Perdue, *Slavery and the Evolution of Cherokee Society, 1540–1866* (Knoxville: University of Tennessee Press, 1979); Theda Perdue "Cherokee Planters: The Development of Plantation Slavery Before Removal," in *The Cherokee Nation: A Troubled History*, 110–128; Robert T. Lewit, "Indian Missions and Anti–Slavery Sentiment: A Conflict of Evangelical and Humanitarian Ideas," in *Mississippi Valley Historical Review* 50 (1963): 39–55.

5. Missionaries, like other Americans in the early nineteenth

century, often described Indians (and other people of color) in terms of their ancestry. They tended to link race and personal qualities, such as industriousness. Although missionaries occasionally affirmed the ability of "full-blood" children, they clearly believed that European ancestry enhanced a child's likelihood of success. See William Ragan Stanton, *The Leopard's Spots: Scientific Attitudes Toward Race in American, 1815–1859* (Chicago: University of Chicago Press, 1960); Berkhofer, *The White Man's Indian* ; and Horsman, *Race and Manifest Destiny* .

6. Charles Reece (Reese), born about 1788, fought in the Creek War. A missionary letter stated about his war service: "He was one of the three intrepid Cherokees, who at the battle of Horse Shoe, swam the river in the face of the enemy & brought off their Canoes in triumph. (The President has lately presented him with an elegant Rifle as a reward for his bravery.)" In reference to Cherokee marriage customs as practiced by Charles Reece, leaving one wife and taking up with another wife was not so much a "trait in Indian character" as following the Cherokee custom that a man and wife were free to separate at any time, and that in a marriage, no binding contract existed between a man and wife. Even though the New England Congregationalists opposed this Cherokee custom of polygamy, Reece joined the Brainerd Church on February 1, 1818. Reece was baptized and gained church membership because by the time Reece joined the church, one wife had died, he left the other two sisters, and now only lived with the new wife; but to avoid any future situation such as this one, the Brainerd missionaries wrote the Board in Boston for advice concerning converts who practiced polygamy. Worcester replied by saying that "A convert who has more than one wife should be required to separate himself from all but his first wife." But the Board went on to say that a man who "puts away" a wife must treat her "prudently and with kindness."

Charles Reece later became a member of the Cherokee National Council and also tutored a subsequent American Board missionary, Samuel A. Worcester, in learning the Cherokee syllabary. Reece often interpreted for the preachers at Brainerd. He died in 1845 while in Texas looking for Sequoyah who had gone there earlier. For a discussion of traditional Cherokee customs relating to marriage and "divorce" see Chapter 12 of Reid's *A Law of Blood.* Kingsbury, Hall, Williams to Worcester, November 25, 1817, ABC 18.3.1, v. 2: 99; Hoyt, Hall, Chamberlin, Butrick to Worcester, September 25, 1818, ABC

18.3.1, v. 2: 116; Worcester to Hoyt and the brethren, November 11, 1818, ABC 1.01, v.3: 99–101; Gary E. Moulton, *Papers of Chief John Ross* (Norman: University of Oklahoma Press, 1985), 2: 730; "Members"; McLoughlin, *Cherokees and Missionaries*, 205.

7. Psalm 84:10.

8. Kingsbury probably preached at the home of Henry and Susannah Ross Nave. The next year, on March 29, 1818, Susannah Nave, John Ross' younger sister, joined the Brainerd church. In a letter dated April 11, 1817 from John Ross to Indian Agent R.J. Meigs, Ross stated that Henry Nave "lives on the road 6 miles from the river . . ." The Naves must have been neighbors to the Brainerd Mission since the mission stood about eight miles from the mouth of the Chickamauga where it joined the Tennessee. The *BJ* stated March 12, 1817, "the creek on which we live is navigable for large boats about 2 miles from its mouth. From this place to the Mission house is about 6 miles by land . . ." "Members"; Starr, *History of the Cherokee Indians*, 410, 582; Moulton, *Papers of Chief John Ross*, 1: 30.

9. Southerners, from whom Cherokees learned how to keep livestock, let the livestock forage in the woods and rounded them up for sale or slaughter. However, the Brainerd missionaries expressed their New England opinion about this Southern herding method when they wrote:

cattle & horses will live well in this country the year round if suffered to run at large; but those of the above dispositions, if suffered thus to run, will get out of our reach, give us much trouble in looking after them, & occasion great loss in their labor, or in their milk. Some pasture fields & a little meadow, would save all this trouble & loss.

In another letter they went on to say: "Cows running in the woods here yield but very little milk, & cannot be got up even with this except while the sucking calf has his share of it." These passages point out the difference in the southern herding method of letting livestock run in the woods whereas the New England method of farming restricted the dairy cows to a pasture providing easier access for milking. Forrest McDonald and Grady McWhiney, "The Antebellum Southern Herdsmen, A Reinterpretation," *Journal of Southern History* (1975): 147–66; Frank L. Owsley, *Plain People of the Old South* (Baton Rogue: Louisiana State University Press, 1949), 24–50; Hoyt, Kingsbury, Butrick, Chamberlin, Hall, Williams to Worcester, March 18, 1818, ABC 18.3.1, v.2: 104; Hoyt, Butrick, Hall, Chamberlin to

Worcester, April 10, 1819, ABC 18.3.1, v. 2: 124.

10. The Cherokees maintained a tradition of generosity and hospitality, and they expected missionaries to reciprocate. Cherokees often visited the mission, as two did on January 24, and sometimes strained meager supplies. In a letter the missionaries commented on this Cherokee trait of hospitality:

> The general character of the natives here is very different from that of the indians who have for generations been surrounded by & living among the whites .... If a friend or stranger calls on him he makes him welcome to the best his house affords; & if he is not treated in the same manner where ever he calls, he thinks he is not received as a friend.

Cherokee attitudes about generosity may also explain why they often kept clothing that the missionaries provided to children—they needed the clothing and the missionaries presumably had given it to them. See *BJ* entry for December 24, 1822. Hoyt, Butrick, Chamberlin to Worcester, December 21, 1818, ABC 18.3.1, v. 2: 120; J.P. Evans, "Sketches of Cherokee Characteristics," *Journal of Cherokee Studies* 4 (Winter, 1979): 10–20; Hudson, *The Southeastern Indians*, 311–312.

11. This meeting place was probably the home of Joseph Coody (Coodey) and Jane (Jennie) Ross Coody. Jane Coody, sister of John Ross, joined the Brainerd Church on February 1, 1818. Joseph and Jane lived near Lookout Mountain with Jane's father, Daniel Ross. In the 1820's the Coodys moved near Jane's brother John at Rossville, where the Coodys operated a tanyard. "Members"; Starr, *History of the Cherokee Indians*, 410; Emmet Starr, *Old Cherokee Families* (Oklahoma City: Baker Publishing Co., 1988), 1: 143; Moulton, *Papers of Chief John Ross*, 2: 719.

12. Mechanical work refers to specialized skills such as carpentry, blacksmithing, tanning, shoemakers, or wheelwrights.

13. Born about 1767 and probably the son of white trader Nathan Hicks and a Cherokee woman, Charles Hicks served as Assistant Principal Chief under Pathkiller from 1817 until January 6, 1827 when Pathkiller died. Hicks then became Principal Chief for two weeks until he died January 20, 1827. While Hicks was Assistant Principal Chief and since Pathkiller spoke no English, Hicks interacted with the whites and served as an interpreter. Hicks supported the educational process set up by the various missionary groups. In 1812 at the Springplace Moravian Mission, Hicks converted to Christianity. Upon baptism, he took the name "Renatus" meaning "renewed." Hicks lived

at Fortville in the vicinity of the Red Clay Council grounds that Ard Hoyt visited in November 1818. Jedidiah Morse wrote in 1822 that Hicks lived just seven miles from the Brainerd Mission. The Cherokees held seven councils at Fortville between December 1817 and April 1823. The convening of councils near Hicks' residence demonstrates the influence which Charles Hicks held in the Cherokee Nation, because as Assistant Principal Chief, the Councils convened in Hicks' vicinity rather than being held near the residence of Principal Chief Pathkiller and the old Cherokee chiefs who lived at Turkey Town. Hicks, Major Ridge, George Lowrey, and John Ross all rose to power during the time period of 1816 to 1819, the years when the Council convened in Fortville. Despite his bout with scrofula (tuberculosis), Hicks proved an effective chief. See *BJ* June 3, 1821 note. Moulton, *Papers of Chief John Ross*, 2: 724; Rowena McClinton Ruff, "Notable Persons in Cherokee History: Charles Hicks," *Journal of Cherokee Studies* 17 (1996): 16–27; Brian Butler, "The Red Clay Council Ground," *Journal of Cherokee Studies* 2 (Winter, 1977): 142–144; Evans, eds., "Jedidiah Morse's Report," 76; Wright, *Springplace*, 46 n.

14. The "Moravian Mission Diary" for February 10, 1817, elaborated on this incident:

> an Indian murdered his wife and three children. He had put the bodies in a potato cellar, shut the doors carefully, and went away. Subsequently, the snow fell and there were no footprints seen from his dwelling. Since the doors were not opened, this roused the attention of several neighbors, who then proceeded into the house. They looked throughout and finally found the murdered bodies. Immediately, the murderer was tracked down and discovered a few miles away at a relative's sitting by a fire. At first glance, he was shot without further ado.

McClinton, "The Moravian Mission," 454.

15. The United States government promoted a plan to set aside a tract of land in Arkansas for Cherokees to emigrate to and live upon. In return the Cherokees would give to the United States a proportional amount of surplus hunting grounds. In 1816 Andrew Jackson and Gov. Joseph McMinn of Tennessee urged the Cherokees to cede unneeded land. In addition, the United States Commissioners offered an enrollee for emigration either a blanket, a rifle, and aid in their removal; or, if the Cherokee chose to stay, the Cherokee received 640 acres of land and citizenship. But the government's push for

removal not only caused division between the leadership of the Cherokees, but caused division in individual families as seen in this entry. See McLoughlin, *Cherokee Renascence*, 220–246.

16. The Cherokees wrote several memorials as they desperately tried to prevent an entire removal of the Cherokee Nation to lands west of them. Traditionally in Cherokee politics the women were silent, but the situation had become so critical that the women spoke out through this memorial and two other memorials on the same topic: opposition to removal. At the time of this journal entry, the stage was being set for a "talk" between the U.S. government and the Cherokee leaders; again the federal government intended to pressure the Indians for land and for removal. The "talk" resulted in the Treaty of 1817 by which the Cherokees ceded land to the government as well as agreed to a plan for reserves and removal, but only those Cherokees who favored removal left for the West, with the majority who opposed removal staying in their Eastern homelands.

The Memorial of the Cherokee women addressed the "council at Ostanalee"; in part it stated:

We have heard with painful feelings that the bounds of the land we now possess are to be drawn into very narrow limits. The land was given to us by the Great Spirit above as our common right, to raise our children upon, & to make support for our rising generation. We therefore humbly petition our beloved children, the headmen and warriors, to hold out to the last in support of our common right, as the Cherokee nation have been the first settlers of this land; we therefore claim the right of the soil. We well remember that our country was formerly very extensive, but by repeated sales it has become circumscribed to the very narrow limits we have at present. Our Father the President advised us to become farmers—to manufacture our own clothes, & to have our children instructed. To this advice we have attended in every thing as far as we were able. Now the thought of being compelled to remove [to] the other side of the Mississippi is dreadful to us because it appears to us that we, by this removal, shall be brought to a savage state again; for we have, by the endeavors of our Father the President, become too much enlightened to throw aside the privileges of a civilized life. We therefore unanimously join in our meeting to hold our country in common as hitherto.

Hoyt, Hall, Butrick, Chamberlin to Worcester, July 25, 1818, ABC
18.3.1, v. 2: 113. For a discussion of Cherokee women and the removal
question, and two other petitions drawn up by the Cherokee women
protesting removal, see Perdue and Green, eds. *The Cherokee Removal*,
122–126.

17. Principal Chief John Ross served during the turbulent years
preceding the Cherokee Removal, the years of reunification, and
during the Civil War. John Ross, one of nine children, was born on
October 3, 1790 to Daniel and Mollie Ross. John lived in both the
Cherokee world of his mother and the "white man's" world of his
father who wanted his son to be educated. John had a private tutor
and also attended an academy in Kingston, Tennessee. Growing up,
he lived at Turkey Town, Willstown, and until 1827 at Rossville in the
Chickamauga area (near present day Chattanooga) where he had a
landing for river boats, a store, and a warehouse. As a land owner
with slaves and an agricultural enterprise, he also participated in
Cherokee politics during the years of the *BJ* going as a delegate to
Washington first in 1816 and then also in 1819. A well-respected
Cherokee leader, he served as President of the National Committee.
By 1827 he and his wife Quatie and their family moved to a new home
at the head of the Coosa River near New Echota. After the enactment
of a new constitution in 1827, Ross was elected Principal Chief in
October 1828; he thereafter made many trips to Washington on behalf
of the Cherokees to plead their case to retain their native homelands
in the Southeast. Gary E. Moulton wrote an extensive biography
about John Ross entitled *John Ross, Cherokee Chief*; Moulton also
compiled Ross' letters which are published in two volumes entitled,
The Papers of Chief John Ross. Gary E. Moulton, ed., *Papers of Chief John
Ross* 2 vols. (Norman: University of Oklahoma Press, 1985), 1: 3–11.

18. The Agency refers to the Indian Agent's location at the
Hiwassee Garrison. After Return J. Meigs took over as Indian Agent,
the U.S. military garrison moved in 1807 from Southwest Point
(Kingston, Tennessee) to the new location on the west bank of the
Tennessee River opposite Jolley's Island and the mouth of the
Hiwassee River at the southern limit of territory ceded in 1805 by the
Cherokees to the United States. At this site the Agency consisted of
the agent's house and office, the sub-agent's house, a small magazine
to store ammunition, and small buildings to store provisions. All
these buildings were constructed as log cabins. The Agency moved
again to a peninsula of land in the Hiwassee River near Calhoun,

Tennessee, where Meigs occupied the new Agency in late 1820. Quite often the missionaries traveled to the Agency to discuss financial and other business matters with the Indian Agent. Meigs to John C. Calhoun, February 22, 1819, M-208, reel 8; James S. McKeown, "Return J. Meigs: United States Agent in the Cherokee Nation, 1801–1823," (Ph.D. diss, Pennsylvania State University, 1984), 422–423; Theodore C. Mercer, "A Note on Rhea County." *Tennessee Historical Quarterly* 35 no. 1 (Spring 1976): 92–94

19. Published sources claim John and Anna McDonald had only one child, Mollie McDonald, the mother of Chief John Ross. However, this February 16 entry indicated John and Anna possibly had another child by stating that George McDonald was the son of John McDonald, the former occupant of the mission house. This entry also gave another clue that the journal writer was correct in the identification of George McDonald as the son of John McDonald: the entry stated that the deceased person had many relatives who attended the Brainerd Church. Passages of the *BJ* (see January 26 and February 2, 1817) already identified church attendees as Joseph and Jane Coody and Henry and Susannah Nave. Both Jane Ross Coody and Susannah Ross Nave would then be nieces of George McDonald, since they were the daughters of Mollie McDonald and Daniel Ross. They were most likely the relatives who would not be attending the church services that day. A catalogue of students who attended the school at Springplace also provides evidence that George McDonald existed. Descendants of George McDonald trace their lineage to George McDonald through Collins McDonald, a student at Brainerd and later at Springplace. The Springplace catalogue indicated that Collins' parents were George McDonald and Sarah (Sally) Scott McDonald, and that Collins' sisters Polly and Maria also attended the Springplace school. Sally Scott McDonald presumably was the daughter of Sarah Hicks and Walter Scott. Other evidence exists which points to Collins McDonald being a descendant of John McDonald: the 1835 Cherokee census shows that Collins McDonald (Collins' name was misspelled as McDaniel) of Oothcaloga Creek was the descendant of a reservee. In this case, the reservee who Collins descended from was his grandfather, John McDonald, who signed up for reserve #14 in "the right of" his Cherokee wife, Anna McDonald. Starr, *History of Cherokee Indians* 410; George M. Bell, *Genealogy of "Old & New Cherokee Indian Families"* (Bartlesville, Okla.: G.M. Bell, 1972), 278; Penelope Johnson Allen, *Leaves from the Family Tree*, (Easley, S.C:

Southern Historical Press, 1982), 220; Adelaide L. Fries, trans. and ed., *Records of the Moravians in North Carolina*, (Raleigh: The North Carolina Historical Commission, 1968), 8: 3791; James W. Tyner, ed., *Those Who Cried, the 16,000*, (Pryor, Ok.: Pryor Printing, 1974), 80; McLoughlin, "Experiment in Cherokee Citizenship, 1817–1829" in *Cherokee Ghost Dance*, 181; Gary Moulton letter to transcribers, September 10, 1997; Tom Mooney, telephone conversation with transcribers, September 5, 1997; Jerry L. Clark, Rose Guthrie, Virginia Vann Perry, and Rowena McClinton, correspondence and telephone conversations with transcribers, January 1998.

20. Settlements refer to the area outside of the Cherokee Nation where white settlers developed towns. Quite often the missionaries wrote of going on business to Washington, Rhea County, Tennessee, a town north of the Brainerd Mission up the Tennessee River. For instance, in the June 27, 1818 *BJ* entry, Moody Hall went to the settlements; the same entry then specifically defined the settlement as Washington, Rhea County, Tennessee. The missionaries traveled to these places on dirt paths, but travelers also used the Federal Road that crossed through the nation leading to Nashville with the Brainerd Mission located along that road. *Panoplist*, December 1817, 563–564.

21. Kingsbury hired Mr. McClelland (McClellan) and family who Kingsbury described as:

> a decent and pious family to live with, & to assist us. They have 3 children, the youngest about 3 years old. I engaged to give them 10 dollars per month & board them. They have two good horses, & four milch cows, of which we can have the use. The man is handy with tools, & we shall have much work to do the first year, & as I have not at present means of purchasing horses & cows, I think if the Society have no objections, I should still like to retain them for a season.

A June 1817 list of Brainerd students showed Barbara, William, and Adaline McClellan, as "white children belonging to the family we hired." Kingsbury to Worcester, June 30, 1817, ABC 18.3.1, v. 2: 7–8.

22. Cyrus Kingsbury anticipated the arrival of assistant missionaries sent by the American Board.

23. Brethren Hall and Williams referred to Moody Hall and Loring S. Williams. Hall, born in Cornish, New Hampshire, on December 1, 1789, married Isabella Murray, born in Lansingburgh, New York, April 25, 1792. Williams, born in Pownal, Vermont on June 28, 1796, married Matilda Loomis, born in Winchester, Connecticut,

October 20, 1793. Hall previously studied the Lancastrian teaching method which the mission school used. In 1818, while the Halls remained at Brainerd, the Williams and Kingsbury moved to Eliot Mission in the Choctaw Nation. Tracy, "History," 336, 338.

24. In 1801, the Moravians established Springplace located three miles east of the Connesaga River near the Georgia to Tennessee public road. On October 19, 1805, Rev. John Gambold and his wife, Anna Rosina Kliest Gambold, came to Springplace to evangelize and supervise the mission and school. Under the Gambolds, the second Cherokee to be converted to Christianity was Chief Charles Hicks. At the Springplace Mission Church such people as Margaret Scott Vann, widow of James Vann; Clement Vann and his wife Mary Christina Vann; William Hicks and his wife Sarah Hicks; and the wife of Major Ridge, Susanna Catherine Ridge, all became Christian. Future Cherokee leaders Elias Boudinot, John Ridge, and John Vann received their education at the Springplace Mission School. For additional study of the Springplace Mission, the Gambolds, and the original journal written by the Gambolds, see McClinton, "The Moravian Mission Among the Cherokees at Springplace, Georgia." Evans ed., "Jedidiah Morse's Report," 61–62; McLoughlin, *Cherokees and Missionaries*, 35–53, 60–68; Wright, *Springplace*, 33–48; Hamilton, "Minutes of the Mission Conference" 15 (Winter 1970): 38.

25. Here the journal writer shifted to letter abbreviations for the missionaries' last names: Br. W. referred to Loring Williams, Br. K. to Cyrus Kingsbury, Br. H. to Moody Hall.

26. This statement is a good example of how missionaries linked race and culture.

27. In Alabama, Fort Armstrong was a few miles above Turkey Town on the Coosa River. Andrew Ross and John Ross ran a "merchandising operation" at Fort Armstrong for a few years. During the Creek War, Andrew Jackson's troops were involved in skirmishes at Emuckfau and Enotachopo in order to protect Fort Armstrong where the Cherokee regiment was stationed during the war. Moulton, *John Ross, Cherokee Chief*, 9; Moulton, *Papers of Chief John Ross*, 1: 19; Benjamin W. Griffith, *McIntosh and Weatherford, Creek Indian Leaders* (Tuscaloosa: University of Alabama Press, 1988), 143.

28. The journal writer referred to Gideon Blackburn who, until 1810, operated several schools for Cherokees working under the Union Presbytery. In 1804 he established his first school at the Hiwassee River near what is today Charleston, Tennessee. Blackburn

did not actually teach the school himself, but acted in a supervisory position. He also founded and became the first pastor of the New Providence church in Maryville, Tennessee. Reverend Isaac Anderson, on the Visiting Committee for the Brainerd Mission, became pastor of this church after Gideon Blackburn stepped down. McLoughlin in *Cherokee Ghost Dance* showed a different side of Blackburn's involvement in the Cherokee Nation when he pointed out that Blackburn ran a whiskey distillery and shipped the goods down the Coosa River into Creek territory where the Creeks seized the whiskey. McLoughlin contented that this incident may be the real reason Blackburn's schools closed in 1810. Blackburn left New Providence Church about the same time as he closed down his schools for the Cherokees. After the closing, he organized a school in Franklin, Tennessee, served at several other churches in Tennessee and Kentucky, served as president of Centre College, and helped found Blackburn College in Illinois. McLoughlin, *Cherokee Ghost Dance*, 365–384; McLoughlin, *Cherokees and Missionaries*, 51–81; Queener, "Gideon Blackburn," 17–18; Inez E. Burns, *History of Blount County, Tennessee: From War Trail to Landing Strip, 1795–1955* (Nashville: Benson Printing Co., for The Tennessee Historical Commission, 1957): 138–139; Best, "New Providence Presbyterian Church," 4.

29. One person hired to work at Brainerd was Robert Gamble, of Rhea County, Tennessee. Through a contract signed on February 12, 1817, Indian Agent R.J. Meigs hired Gamble to build a school house. A second contract was signed by Gamble to build for the mission a 52 by 20 foot two-story residence house, with double piazza, eight doors, five windows, and plank floors. Gamble was paid $425.00 to build this house. Meigs to Gamble, February 12 and 21, 1817, M-208, reel 7.

30. The Cherokees experienced a scanty harvest in the fall of 1816; by spring of 1817 their corn was depleted, so they turned to the missionaries and the United States government for help. Numerous letters exist in the Cherokee Agency Papers where the headmen of Cherokee towns wrote to Meigs asking for help in procuring corn for their families. For instance Samuel Riley wrote:

> they are in a state of starvation it appears that all the Nabering [neighboring] town is Starving to wit Wilstown turkey town crowtown Creek path & Sauoty—I am told that some of turkey town peopel [people] was hear sometime ago & stated that they had not eate any Bred for three weeks only thin Gruell—if

you should think proper to furnish the above mentioned town with small quantity of Corne each.
Riley to Meigs, March 5, 1817, M-208, reel 7.

31. The missionaries spoke metaphorically where they likened the Cherokees' physical need for corn to the spiritual need for the "Bread of life:" Jesus Christ.

32. In May 1822, Evarts compiled a list of the students who attended the Brainerd Mission School between 1817 and 1822. This list identified the two students who came to Brainerd May 14, 1817, as John Ridge and Nancy Ridge. They stayed at the Brainerd School for less than seven months since they left the school before January 1818. The "Moravian Mission Diary" sheds some light on one possible reason Nancy Ridge left school: "Nancy Ridge was here [Springplace], and she left in a hurry. We think she did not want to seek us out because we had heard from our Chickamauga brothers that she had behaved indecently at their school." Another reason the two Ridge students may not have stayed very long at Brainerd is that their parents, especially their mother, had a habit of quickly taking her children out of a school. Major Ridge lamented this type of decision as seen in the December 11, 1816 entry in the "Moravian Mission Diary:" "The Ridge admitted now that he knew that if he had let his children stay at Springplace, they would have learned much more and he understood how much they lost by leaving." John and Nancy Ridge attended the Springplace school in 1810. For more information on John Ridge, see *BJ* entry for July 4, 1817, and note. See also Wilkins, *Cherokee Tragedy*. "Catalogue"; McClinton, "The Moravian Mission," 440, 503; Fries, *Records of the Moravians in North Carolina*, 8: 3791.

33. The "Moravian Mission Diary" recorded on May 4, 1817, that "Mr. Williams [the Brainerd missionary] again held the morning service and proceeded home after breakfast. Our Brother and Sister Crutchfield had presented him with a cow and calf for the mission at Chickamauga, and another was loaned for use this summer." McClinton, "The Moravian Mission," 471.

34. The "Catalogue" indicated three Riley boys and two girls entered Brainerd around May 21. Susannah Hanley and Peggy (no last name) both age 9, entered May 20; Madison Riley, age 9, entered May 19 while Luney Riley, age 16, and Nelson Riley, age 15, entered May 23 (rather than May 21 as the *BJ* notes.) Only Susannah Hanley still attended Brainerd when the "Catalogue" was drafted in 1822. Peggy departed September 16, 1818, and the three Riley boys left

"Before Jan 1818." Little is known of Susannah or Peggy. However, the Rileys lived near Creek Path. Madison, Luney (Loony), and Nelson Riley's father, Samuel Riley, married two Cherokee sisters, *Gu lu sti yu* and *Ni go di ge yu*; because the two mothers belonged to the Long Hair clan, the sons belonged to the Long Hair clan. Samuel and his wives had a total of sixteen children. The oldest Riley sibling, Richard Riley, became a "leading figure of the Cherokee bourgeoisie," acquiring wealth through his saltpeter business and the sale of powder to the United States Army. "Catalogue"; Starr, *History of the Cherokee Indians,* 432, 475; McLoughlin, *Cherokee and Missionaries,* 127.

35. This new student, identified by his Cherokee name—*Sun nek oo yah*—resided in Broomstown in 1822. "Catalogue."

36. The date of this letter is non-chronological. As Ard Hoyt explained, Br. Kingsbury and Hall requested after Hoyt arrived in 1818, that Hoyt prepare the journal and include the previous six months, January to June 1817, based on notes provided by Kingsbury. Hoyt assumed the task of writing the official journal and for the next few years (January 1817 to April 1820) wrote the journal and forwarded it to Massachusetts. After 1820 Hoyt shared the responsibility of writing the journal with Butrick, Chamberlin, Darius Hoyt, an unidentified female, and others who helped compile the journal.

37. Often preachers read printed sermons which they received from the mission board or which the missionaries read from the religious periodicals received. This sermon was by Rev. George Burder, Secretary of the London Missionary Society, a society which maintained close contact with the American Board. Burder also wrote many sermons which were later published in a volume entitled *Village Sermons* used at the missions. *First Ten Annual Reports,* 16; Tracy, "History," 108.

38. Although the missionaries occasionally managed to hire Cherokees, particularly just before they had to pay the national poll tax, the missionaries usually had difficulty finding wage laborers. The reason for the difficulty was that the Cherokees held land in common, and any Cherokee was free to cultivate unused land if it did not infringe on the rights of another. This meant that Cherokees who wanted to farm could work for themselves without investing capital in land. McLoughlin, *Cherokee Renascence,* 292; Perdue and Green, eds., *The Cherokee Removal,* 25.

39. Born in 1803, John Ridge, the son of Major Ridge and Susanna Wickett Ridge, became a respected Cherokee leader. John received an

education first at Springplace and later at Brainerd; he then received a higher education at the Foreign Mission School in Cornwall, Connecticut. Ill part of the time while at Cornwall, he suffered from scrofula, the same disease from which Charles Hicks suffered. While in New England, John fell in love and ultimately married Sarah Northrup on January 27, 1824; their marriage caused heated controversy because an Indian, John Ridge, was marrying a white woman. In 1835 Major Ridge, John Ridge, Elias Boudinot, and a few others who believed in the inevitability of Cherokee removal, signed the Treaty of New Echota which provided for the removal of the entire nation to Indian Territory. After the end of the removal, a group of Cherokees, who opposed the signing of the New Echota Treaty, killed Major Ridge, John Ridge, and Elias Boudinot on June 22 1839. See Thurman Wilkins, *Cherokee Tragedy: The Ridge Family and the Decimation of a People,* an excellent book on the Ridge family, John Ridge's Cornwall years, the controversial signing of the Treaty of New Echota, and the Cherokee Trail of Tears. Chapter One gives the background information and family history of *Kah nung da tla geh,* Major Ridge. Moulton, *Papers of Chief John Ross,* 2: 730; Wilkins, *Cherokee Tragedy,* 119–153.

40. The "Catalogue" does not indicate which two students were dismissed. It lists all students who left in 1817 as leaving "before Jan 1818" and suggests no reason for students leaving, such as being dismissed. However, a letter in the American Board files refers to this dismissal, but does not identify the students. The letter stated:

Two lads who were half breeds, & who had been at school considerably in the settlements, we were obliged to dismiss for obstinate and persevering disobedience to orders. A smaller br. of theirs has continued with us ever since, & the father has lately solicited us with great importunity to take his two older sons again and had declared himself more than willing to pay for them.

Kingsbury, Hall, Williams to Worcester, November 25, 1817, ABC 18.3.1, v. 2: 99–100.

41. American Board Agent Elias Cornelius toured the Southeastern United States and visited various mission locations. He talked with government officials in Washington about the state of the Indians as well as collected donations as he passed through towns on his tour. *The Panoplist* 13 (December 1817): 563; *First Ten Annual Reports,* 128.

42. Mark 8:36.

43. I Corinthians 11:28.

44. Luke 22:19; I Corinthians 11:24–28.

45. "Articles of Faith & Covenant adopted by the Chh. of Christ at Chickamaugah" is part of the American Board Papers, September 28, 1817, ABC 18.3.1, v. 2: 98 .

46. II Corinthians 6:2.

47. From Acts 2:37.

48. "Saul" refers to Saul of Tarsus (Paul) on the road to Damascus where, blinded by light, he heard Jesus speaking to him. See Acts 9:4.

49. Rev. Matthew Donald, a member of the Visiting Committee, acted as one of the local overseers of the Brainerd Mission for the ABCFM. *First Ten Annual Reports*, 195.

50. Referred to often as Father Hoyt, Rev. Ard Hoyt, born in Danbury, Connecticut, on either October 20 or October 23, 1770, was a self-educated pastor. On September 12, 1792, Hoyt married Esther Booth, born in Southbury, Connecticut January 18, 1774. They later moved to Wilkes-Barre, Pennsylvania, where he was ordained August 26, 1806. They came to the Brainerd Mission with six of their seven children: Sarah, Flora, Milo, Anna, Darius, and Cornelius whose ages ranged from the oldest, Sarah, age 21, to the youngest, Cornelius, age 10. The five oldest all worked in positions similar to missionary assistants at Brainerd or one of the outlying mission stations. In 1824 Hoyt and most of his family moved to the Willstown Mission where he died in 1828. Tracy, "History," 335; David W. Hoyt; *A Genealogical History of the Hoyt, Haight, and Hight Families* (1871; reprint, Camden, Maine: Picton Press, 1993), 255–270, 374, 417–418; Walker, *Torchlights to the Cherokees*, 43; "List."

51. Rev. Daniel Sabin Butrick, born at Windsor, Massachusetts, on August 25, 1789, was ordained at age twenty-eight in Boston on September 3, 1817. Working as an evangelist after his arrival, he spent much of his time on tours around the Cherokee Nation. Butrick desired to learn as much as he could about the Cherokees and their language. The *BJ* often referred to him as Br. B. During the time he was at Brainerd he was unmarried; in 1827 he married Elizabeth Proctor. During his life as a missionary, Butrick wrote two journals which are part of the American Board collection. The first journal described his tours through the Cherokee neighborhoods as he evangelized during the years 1819–1845. The second journal examined the language and culture and included such topics as clan vengeance,

priesthood, and public ceremonies among many other topics. Another collection of Daniel Butrick's writings is found in the Payne-Butrick Manuscripts at the Newberry Library. Cherokee documents expert Paul Kutsche described this collection of Butrick's writings as "probably the most important single manuscript describing aboriginal Cherokee culture." "List"; Tracy, "History," 335; Walker, *Torchlights*, 43; Marion L. Starkey, *The Cherokee Nation* (New York: Alfred A. Knopf, 1946), 133–134; Paul Kutsche, *A Guide to Cherokee Documents in the Northeastern United States*, (Metuchen, N.J.: Scarecrow Press, 1986), 177–178, 332–342, 409. See Lee Irwin "Different Voices Together: Preservation and Acculturation in Early 19th Century Cherokee Religion," and "Antiquities of the Cherokee Indians from the Collection of Reverend Daniel Sabin Buttrick," *Journal of Cherokee Studies*, 18 (1997).

52. Born at Newbury, Vermont, on February 20, 1791, Rev. William Chamberlin was ordained at Hartford, Pennsylvania, November 12, 1817. Chamberlin became the school teacher as well as itinerant preacher at Brainerd when Cyrus Kingsbury left Brainerd to establish Eliot Mission in the Choctaw Nation. The *BJ* referred to Chamberlin as Br. C or spelled his name *Chamberlain* at times. The other missionary, Elisha P. Swift, was ordained in Boston on September 3, 1818, along with Daniel S. Butrick. At this time Swift had no mission assignment, so he was touring and evangelizing. In early December 1817, Chamberlin left Wilkes-Barre, Pennsylvania, and met Swift at Pittsburgh where together they acted as agents for the Board and collected donations in Ohio, Kentucky, and Tennessee for the missions. *First Ten Annual Reports*, 158, 189; "List"; Tracy, "History," 335; Walker, *Torchlights*, 44.

Notes for 1818

1. On their way to the Brainerd Mission on December 31, 1817, the large Hoyt family stayed near Springplace with Johnston McDonald, a relative of the John McDonald family, as recorded in the "Moravian Mission Diary":

> There were nine pilgrims in the total count, who came together, namely the Reverend Mr. Ard and Mrs. Esther Hoyt with three sons and daughters from Wilkesbarre, Pennsylvania, and the Reverend Sabin Butrick from Boston .... Among those present was our Johnston McDonald who lodged the dear company in his house free of charge, since

they were our friends and missionaries.
Also see *BJ* entry for March 19, 1818, and note. McClinton, "The Moravian Mission," 525–526.

2. I Samuel 3:18.

3. Job 30:23.

4. Job 12:10.

5. Proverbs 29:18.

6. John 7:37: "In the last day, that great day of the feast, Jesus stood and cried, saying, If any man thirst, let him come unto me, and drink."

7. The Cherokees' first recorded law, enacted September 11, 1808, established "regulating parties . . . . to suppress horse stealing and robbery of other property . . . and to give their protection to children as heirs to their fathers' property, and to the widow's share." Often called the Lighthorse, these "regulating parties" heard witnesses, reached decisions, and inflicted punishment on the spot. Furthermore, the United States government had previously outlawed the Cherokee traditional custom of clan revenge and instead the Lighthorse, a police force, would be the internal policing agency concerning bodily crimes, horse thievery, and policing of the roads within the nation. *Laws of the Cherokee Nation: Adopted by the Council at Various Periods. Printed for the Benefit of the Nation* (Tahlequah: Cherokee Advocate Office, 1852; reprinted Wilmington, Del.: Scholarly Resources, Inc., 1973), 3–4; McLoughlin, *Cherokee Renascence*, 44–46, 89.

8. Catharine Brown came to the Brainerd School on July 9, 1817, at age eighteen. The missionaries described her as "genteel in her appearance & amiable in her manner; knows the English language well when she came to live with us, & could read indifferently in words of three letters." After ninety days of school she "reads well in the Bible & writes tolerable good hand." Her father, John Brown Sr., whose Cherokee name was *Yau nu gung yah ski*, and her mother, Sarah, whose Cherokee name was *Tsa luh*, both had Cherokee mothers, but each of John and Sarah's fathers were white or partly Indian. Neither of Catharine's parents spoke English. Two of Catharine's brothers attended the school: David, and half-brother Edward. Edward Brown arrived at Brainerd September 12, 1817, at age 15 and left the school July 9, 1818. By 1822 Edward moved with his father to Arkansas while Catharine lived at Creek Path. The "Catalogue" stated he could read and write and possessed a "respectable" character. Edward, John, David, and Catharine all had

the same father; however, while Catharine, John, and David's mother was Sarah, Edward's mother was John Brown Sr.'s third wife, Betsy or Wattee. Betsy and John Brown had four children: Polly, Alexander, Susan, and Edward. The *Memoir of Catharine Brown* referred to Edward as Edmund. "Catalogue"; Kingsbury, Hall, Williams to Worcester, November 25, 1817, ABC 18.3.1, v. 2: 99-100; Rufus Anderson, *Memoir of Catharine Brown, a Christian Indian, of the Cherokee Nation* (Philadelphia: American Sunday School Union, 1832), 10–11.

9. "Federal City" was Washington, the capital of the United States.

10. This young girl nicknamed "Little" Peggy was listed in the "Catalogue" as Peggy with no other last name and no Cherokee name. She started school on May 20, 1817, and left the school February 13, 1818. The missionaries indicated her improvement at the school as "good" and her character as "unknown." In 1822, she was listed as living in Arkansas.

11. The missionaries spoke of ignorance in regards to the God of the Bible and His precepts of religion, that is, ignorance of Jesus Christ as Savior and Lord.

12. Women and men lived largely separate lives in traditional Cherokee society. Women worked in the fields together, raised their children jointly in extended households, and shared rituals and experiences associated with childbirth and menstruation. The fact that these women lived and traveled together reflects the strong bonds that women shared. For a full discussion of the social life of Cherokee women see Perdue, *Cherokee Women: Gender and Culture Change, 1700–1835*.

13. Evarts wrote of Jane Coody: "She remains uniform & stable, considering circumstances. Her husband is a Methodist." Evarts, "Memoranda," May 14, 1822, ABC 18.3.1, v.2: 155.

14. No other students were listed in the "Catalogue" as having come to the school in November other than Eliza Holt and Jane Woodward, and they are already accounted for in other entries.

15. The "Catalogue" identified this girl as Jane Woodward, age 6, living at Blue Springs in 1822. She left the school February 23, 1819; she could "read in easy lessons."

16. The Cherokees were matrilineal, that is, they traced kinship through women alone rather than bilaterally, through both mothers and fathers, as Europeans did. This meant that the Cherokees did not consider fathers to be blood relatives of their children who belonged solely to their mothers' clan. Reid, *A Law of Blood*, 35–48.

17. Robin Martin. See *BJ*, May 3, 1818.

18. The girl was Eliza Holt, age 7, who lived at Clarks Ferry in 1822. She could read and write when she left the school August 6, 1819. "Catalogue."

19. This John Brown was son of Colonel Richard Brown, who was son of John Brown Sr. by his first wife. This John Brown was Catharine's nephew. Several sources referred to Richard Brown having a son named John: a missionary letter referred to Chief John Brown, son of Col. Dick Brown. On the "Register of Persons Who Wish Reservations" in 1817, John Brown Jr. signed for Reservation #57 and listed his place of residence as "the late residence of his father, Col. Richard Brown. In this *BJ* entry the journalist referenced the death of Richard Brown and mentioned the facts that Catharine accompanied her relative, John Brown. Alexander was Catharine's half-brother who had a different mother (Wattee or Betsy), but the same father as Catharine. Washburn to Green, August 12, 1839, ABC 18.3.1, v. 10; McLoughlin, *Cherokee Renascence*, 54–55, 266; McLoughlin, *Cherokee Ghost Dance*, 182; Anderson, *Memoir*, 11.

20. Although William Chamberlin left Pennsylvania at the same time the Hoyt family left Pennsylvania to come to Brainerd, Mr. Chamberlin went by a different route through Pennsylvania, Ohio, Indiana, Kentucky, and Tennessee preaching on behalf of the missionary effort and raising donations for the missionary cause. *MH* 14 (August 1818): 387 note. See also *BJ*, December 15, 1817.

21. There is a possibility that two women named Sally McDonald existed. The Sally McDonald identified in the strike-out was most likely the widow of George McDonald since the Brainerd church member list shows Sally McDonald, as "a widow." Born Sarah (Sally) Scott, she was the daughter of Walter Scott and Sarah Hicks. See *BJ* for February 16, 1817 and June 7, 1818. However, the "Moravian Mission Diary" written by missionaries John and Anna Gambold stated in 1815 that a Sally McDonald was the sister of Johnston McDonald and lived with her brother at Coosawattee. Other Moravian documents identified Johnston as the son of Charles McDonald; therefore, this Sally McDonald of "The Moravian Mission Diary" was probably the daughter of Charles McDonald of Selikoi. The "Moravian Mission Diary" stated that this Sally McDonald had a daughter named Polly Blackwood. A Polly Blackwood, age 8, was a student at Brainerd from June 8, 1818 to October 15, 1821. But by 1822, Polly lived at Coosawattee—the same location which the Sally McDonald of the

"Moravian Mission Diary" had earlier lived with her brother Johnston. In short, possibly two Sally McDonalds may have lived in the area around Brainerd and Springplace. Presumably one was the wife of George McDonald and was referred to in the *BJ*, while the other was the sister of Johnston and referred to in the "Moravian Mission Diary." McClinton, "The Moravian Mission," 304n, 351, 358 387n, 408; Hamilton, "Minutes of the Mission Conference," 15 (Winter 1970): 60, 74; "Catalogue"; Jerry L. Clark, telephone conversations with transcribers, January 1998.

22. Chamberlin and Flora Hoyt, Ard Hoyt's daughter, knew each other before coming to the mission since Chamberlin had studied for the ministry under the care of Ard Hoyt in Pennsylvania. *MH* 14 (August 1818): 387n.

23. The Brainerd Church received four new members on March 29, 1818: Greenbury Pardue, age 24, a white man; Sally McDonald, a widow of age 35; Susannah Nave, age 33 and the wife of a white man; and Catharine Brown, age 19. "Members."

24. Springplace, the Moravian Mission under John Gambold, was located on the east side of the Connesauga River and near the Old Federal Highway in Georgia, in what is now Murray County. The Moravians were not pleased with the fact that the members of the Moravian Church were attending the Brainerd Church: "We are grieved . . . because they [the missionaries at Brainerd] endeavor to draw some of our tried members to them, both by ingratiating ideas and by verbal and written invitations to communicate with them." Goff, *Placenames of Georgia*, 357; Hamilton, "Minutes of the Mission Conference," 16 (Spring 1971): 48.

25. Isaiah 25:6.

26. The missionaries explained part of the creation story: "And God said, Let there be lights in the firmament of the heaven to divide the day from the night; and let them be for signs, and for seasons, and for days, and years."

27. The mission was organized and run according to a set of rules established by the Prudential Committee in 1812 which instructed missionaries that they must devise a plan of parliamentary procedure, with a presiding officer, a treasurer, and secretary, so the missionaries could pass resolutions concerning operation of the mission. They were to communicate such resolutions to the Prudential Committee as well as to communicate through a journal whatever activities or thoughts were of interest to the missionaries or the Prudential

Committee. *First Ten Annual Reports*, 40.

28. See *BJ* entry for July 26, 1818, and note for an explanation of the difference in the spiritual belief system of each culture.

29. Hosea 3:4.

30. The original manuscript of the entries for April 10–18, 1818, are not in the archival documents at the Houghton Library, but the journal entries for those dates did appear in the *Missionary Herald* in 1818. Even though the journal entries are not archived or on microfilm, the entries for April 12, 13, 15, 16 and 18 are of extreme importance, so the entries for those dates are included in this transcription, quoting from the *Missionary Herald* (September, 1818): 414–416.

31. Paraphrase of Matthew 23:13.

32. Colonel Return Jonathan Meigs accepted the post of Indian Agent at age sixty-two after retiring from the army. Cyrus Kingsbury wrote that Meigs was:

> a worthy old gentleman upwards of 80 years of age, but retains to a wonderful degree, the use of his bodily & mental functions. He has for many years resided among the Cherokees, as the government agent & will probably continue in that office so long as he shall be able to discharge its duties. He may be relied upon as a firm & substantial friend to the object of the mission.

Meigs held the agent position for twenty-two years, from 1801 to 1823. As part of George Washington's Indian civilization program, agents, such as Meigs, were sent to Indian tribes to administer the government's program which included promoting farming and distributing useful instruments of civilization such as plows, spinning wheels, and looms. The agent was also responsible for distribution of annuities due to the Cherokees, but in return for the aid which the government gave the Indian, the agent was to work on the government's behalf and secure more land cessions from the Indians. Meigs took this part of the job seriously, participating in all the negotiations for land cessions. Meigs, like other Indian Agents, was an administrator who encouraged the missionaries to work among the Indians and to bring education to them. Kingsbury to Worcester, May 8, 1816, ABC 18.3.1, v.3: 3. See McKeown, "Return Jonathan Meigs: United States Agent in the Cherokee Nation, 1801–1823." See also Malone's chapter about Return J. Meigs in *Cherokees of the Old South* and Francis Paul Prucha's *American Indian Policy in the Formative Years*.

33. The Glass, one of the Lower Town Chiefs, moved south after 1777 to the Chickamauga area with other "Chickamaugans" led by Cherokee Dragging Canoe. The Glass lived in the Lookout Mountain area. As early as 1808 The Glass favored removal. He was one of eight who signed the Treaty of 1816 which sold away 2.2 million acres of Cherokee land to the United States. He and other Lower Town Cherokees later moved west to Arkansas. For more on Dragging Canoe and the Chickamaugans, see E. Raymond Evans "Notable Persons in Cherokee History: Dragging Canoe," *Journal of Cherokee Studies* 2 (Winter 1977): 176–189; James Pate, "The Chickamauga: A Forgotten Segment of Indian Resistance on the Southern Frontier" (Ph. D. diss. Mississippi State University, 1969); and Pat Alderman, *Nancy Ward: Cherokee Chieftainess and Dragging Canoe: Cherokee-Chickamauga War Chief* (Johnson City: Tenn.: The Overmountain Press, 1990). The Glass to Meigs, August 16, 1819, M-208, reel 8; McLoughlin, *Cherokee Renascence*, 20, 133–134, 209–211.

34. Agent Meigs promised schools to the Arkansas Cherokees; he also said that he would encourage agriculture and "manufacturing" among them when they got to the Arkansas. Meigs to Pathkiller, August 9, 1817, M-208, reel 7.

35. See *BJ* for July 3, 1822, and note for more information on the Green Corn Ceremony.

36. Mooney elaborates on this Cherokee custom by relating the different accounts of the new fire ceremony. Mooney referred to John Howard Payne who in 1835 also described this ceremony saying that it was part of the annual spring festival where the fire in the town center was replaced and rekindled for the new year. Prior to this rekindling of the fire for the new year, people engaged in the ceremonies of purification and sacrifice. Mooney, *Myths of the Cherokees*, 502–503.

37. See *BJ* for July 3, 1822, and note for more on the Cherokee ritual of "going to water." Also see James Mooney, "The Cherokee River Cult," *Journal of Cherokee Studies* 7 (Spring, 1982): 30–36.

38. Hudson, *The Southeastern Indians*; Adair, *History of the American Indians*; Mooney, *Myths of the Cherokee and Sacred Formulas of the Cherokees*; and Frank Gouldsmith Speck and Leonard Broom, *Cherokee Dance and Drama* (Norman: University of Oklahoma Press, 1983) all contain additional information about Cherokee ritual and ceremony.

39. Missionary movement advocates in the early 1800's used the term "monthly concert" for meetings to promote their cause. Evangel-

ists sometimes relied upon collections of addresses or sermons such as those found in Enoch Pond's "Short Missionary Discourses or Monthly Concert Lectures." R. Pierce Beaver, *Pioneers in Mission* (Grand Rapids: William B. Eerdmans Publishing Co., 1966), 3–4.

40. The journalist referred to the impending arrival of Jeremiah Evarts, American Board Treasurer. See *BJ* entry for May 8, 1818.

41. Evarts visited the Brainerd Mission to travel, relax, and collect information from the brethren concerning the affairs of the mission. While there, Evarts attended a Cherokee Council where removal was the topic of concern. He reassured the Cherokees that should there be a general removal, the American Board would provide a mission and school for them in the new area. From Brainerd, Evarts wrote to the Boston headquarters an informative letter describing the area surrounding the mission, the mission's buildings and house, the fish caught in the stream, the mill, classroom and prayer time, the mission family, the schedule for each day, the teaching system in the schoolroom, the dining situation, the out-of-classroom work performed by the girls and boys, the evangelizing done by the Brainerd church, the Visiting Committee, and a short review of the establishment of the mission. Evart's letter is another view of the Brainerd Mission which enhances the material in the *BJ*. For the letter see *The Panoplist and Missionary Herald* 14 (June 1818): 275–278 and 14 (July 1818): 338–347. *First Ten Annual Reports*, 190–197; Tracy, "History," 71.

42. Quite often Christians referred to a person's relationship with God as their "walk" with God; therefore, the missionaries had not had enough time to observe the black man's and woman's commitment to Christ through their actions or "walk" (for "walk," see II Corinthians 5:7; Galatians 5:16, 25). The black man could be Ned who joined the church July 7, 1818. He was listed on the church membership roll as age 30 and belonging to Sally McDonald who had joined the church previously on March 29, 1818. The woman mentioned could be another woman named Sally who joined the church August 16, 1818. Sally, age 25, belonged to Fox Taylor. "List."

43. The Choctaw student, McKee Folsom, came from a large and influential Choctaw family descended from a Scotch-Irish trader to the Choctaws. McKee's father, Nathaniel Folsom, had two wives and twenty-four children. Walker, *Torchlights*, 152–153; Clara Sue Kidwell, *Choctaws and Missionaries in Mississippi, 1818–1918* (Norman: University of Oklahoma Press, 1995), 60.

44. Joseph McMinn (1758–1824), born in West Marlborough, Chester County, Pennsylvania, came to Hawkins County, Tennessee, early in his life. He served many years in public office starting in 1794 when he served as a member of the territorial legislature of Tennessee. He was speaker of the state senate three times and in 1815 became governor of Tennessee, an office he held until 1821. McMinn felt that Indians within the borders of Tennessee presented a "problem for the whites," so he pushed for Indian removal. He felt it "was an injustice to withhold lands from the white settlers with no object than to serve the Cherokee and Chickasaw Indians for a hunting ground." While governor, McMinn succeeded in securing from the Chickasaws the western portion of Tennessee. He also served as a U.S. Commissioner to secure Cherokee land and served from 1823–1824 as U.S. Indian Agent after Meigs' death. McMinn died November 17, 1824; later McMinn County, and McMinnville in the county of Warren, both in Tennessee, were named in his honor. McLoughlin, *Cherokee Renascence*, 206–215; Dumas Malone, ed., *Dictionary of American Biography*, vol. 6, pt. 2 (New York: Charles Scribner's Sons, 1961), 145–146.

45. Gov. McMinn, along with Andrew Jackson and David Meriwether of Georgia were the commissioners who negotiated and pressured the Cherokees to give up eastern land in exchange for land in the Arkansas. In Tennessee and Alabama, many white intruders settled on Cherokee land, land that the government allowed the whites to stay upon while it persuaded the Cherokees to cede. McLoughlin, *Cherokee Renascence*, 221–222.

46. Hebrews 2:9.

47. Kingsbury left Brainerd to set up a new mission in the Choctaw Nation. In a letter to American Board headquarters, the Brainerd brethren said, "it was given unanimously as our opinion that Brother Kingsbury & brother & sister Williams will be the most suitable persons to select for this service, & that it will not be expedient to send any more from this establishment at present." Kingsbury established the first Choctaw mission near the Yalobusha River in the Western District, naming the mission, Eliot Mission (also spelled Elliot), in honor of John Eliot, a missionary to the Algonquin Indians in early colonial New England. In 1646 John Eliot was one of the first missionaries who endeavored to learn an Indian language. Tracy, "History," 13; Hoyt, Kingsbury, Butrick, Chamberlin, Hall, Williams to Worcester, March 18, 1818, ABC 18.3.1, v.2: 104; Kidwell,

Choctaws and Missionaries, 29–30.

48. Elias Cornelius and Jeremiah Evarts took three Cherokee young people and one Choctaw student to the Cornwall, Connecticut Foreign Mission School (F.M.S.). The American Board ran the school from 1817 to 1826 in the secluded town of Cornwall, Connecticut. The school's director, Rev. Herman Daggett, had once been Elias Cornelius' teacher. The American Board sent to the Foreign Mission School promising young students from around the world to obtain an evangelical higher education in the hope that the students would return to their native land as leaders in converting their fellow people to the Christian way of life. The school trained the youths to serve as missionaries, schoolmasters, interpreters, and doctors. Students from China, Malay, Bengal, India, and the Sandwich Islands attended the Foreign Mission School.

The first of the Cherokee students mentioned was Buck Oo Watie, who adopted the name Elias Boudinot (also spelled Boudinott) after he met Elias Boudinot, the American Bible Society president. While at Cornwall the young Boudinot met Harriet Gold, a white woman; their subsequent romance and marriage caused much discontent among New Englanders. Historian Thurman Wilkins stated the situation succinctly: "A storm then broke in Cornwall." The Boudinot-Gold romance and marriage came on the heels of another Cherokee, John Ridge's, marriage to a white New England woman. This controversy over the two marriages caused much racial conflict in Cornwall including Elias Budinot's image being burned in effigy and threats to his life. When Elias came from the Cherokee Nation back to Cornwall for his wedding, he arrived disguised, fearing a lynching party. He married Harriet Gold on March 28, 1826. In the autumn of 1826, the Cornwall school closed with the announcement that "the great objects, which it was designed to accomplish, can now be more easily and effectually attained by other means." The story of Cornwall and the marriages is well told in Thurman Wilkins' *Cherokee Tragedy*.

The second Cherokee student who went north was Charles Hicks' son, Leonard Hicks, who had previously attended Springplace school in 1813; and the third Cherokee student was Redbird, who was renamed Thomas Basil at Cornwall. The Choctaw student going to the school with them was McKee Folsom. Wilkins, *Cherokee Tragedy*, 112–153; Theda Perdue, ed., *Cherokee Editor: the Writings of Elias Boudinot* (Knoxville: University of Tennessee Press, 1983), 6, 9; Walker, *Torchlights*, 152–163; Fries, *Records of the Moravians in North Carolina*, 8:

3791.

49. An usher was an assistant to a schoolmaster or head teacher, an under master, or assistant master. *OED*, 19: 358.

50. A Visiting Committee was organized for the mission school consisting of reputable people who lived in the vicinity of Brainerd. The members were to "make an annual visitation of the school for the purpose of examining its general state and management, its expenditures & improvements; and making a report to be exhibited to the Board, to the U.S. government and to the public." Each member was also to collect donations for the American Board. The Visiting Committee for 1818 consisted of Cherokee Agent R.J. Meigs and Rev. Isaac Anderson, pastor of First Lebanon Presbyterian Church in Knoxville and later New Providence Church of Maryville, Tennessee. He founded the Southern and Western Theological Seminary which later became Maryville College. Ard Hoyt would have had much contact with him since Anderson also served as superintendent of the Synod of Tennessee, clerk of the Union Presbytery, and secretary of the East Tennessee Missionary Society—organizations with which the mission maintained relations. Others on the committee were Col. David Campbell of Knox County and Col. Francis A. Ramsey of Knox County, a founder of Lebanon Presbyterian Church in Knoxville. His father helped found the former State of Franklin and Knoxville. Francis Ramsey's son was the famous historian, J.G.M. Ramsey who wrote *The Annals of Tennessee to the End of the Eighteenth Century*. The last two members of the committee were Rev. Matthew Donald and Daniel Rawlings, president of Tennessee Academy in Washington, Tennessee. Worcester to Rev. Isaac Anderson, February 14, 1818, ABC 1.01, v. 3: 26; *First Ten Annual Reports*, 195–197; Allen, *Leaves from the Family Tree*, 344, 347; *History of Tennessee: From the Earliest Time to the Present, Together with an Historical and a Biographical Sketch of the County of Knox and the City of Knoxville* (1887; reprint, Easley, S.C.: Southern Historical Press, 1982), 810, 890–891, 1031; Best, "New Providence Presbyterian Church," 5–7; Mary U. Rothrock, ed., *The French Broad-Holston Country: A History of Knox County, Tennessee* (Knoxville: East Tennessee Historical Society, 1946), 367–368, 467–468.

51. See *BJ* for May 28, 1818, and note about Visiting Committee and Isaac Anderson.

52. The report was a summary of the Visiting Committee's observations of the mission, the students, the missionaries involved, with an account of Kingsbury's farewell as he left for the new

Choctaw mission. Anderson, Donald, Campbell to the Prudential Committee, May 29 and June 2, 1818, ABC 18.3.1, v.2: 109–110.

53. There is no way to positively identify this older potential student. The entry states he went to the Agency and would come back to enter the school, but no student of this age came back to enter the school in the next several weeks or months.

54. The missionaries could be referring to Ned, the African-American of Sally McDonald. Sally was a convert and a member of the Brainerd Church by this time. See *BJ* entries for February 16, 1817, and March 19, 1818, and notes for those dates. The student they referred to in this passage could be Collins McDonald, the son of George McDonald and Sarah (Sally) Scott McDonald. A student with a Cherokee name of Rising Fawn, Collins McDonald, came to the school April 8, 1817, at age 10, and left Brainerd August 6, 1819; by 1822 he lived at Springplace to where Sally McDonald had also moved. Collins McDonald was born December 23, 1807, and married Narcena Adair on March 20, 1832. He led an eventful life: in 1839 he assisted George Hicks in leading a detachment of Cherokees on the removal, but then went back to Georgia to live. In 1836 Collins had been a rather affluent Cherokee planter in the Oothcaloga Valley along Oothcaloga Creek, but by 1842 he was reduced to a financial state that he had no means to move to Indian Territory even though he and many other Cherokees still residing in Georgia desired to join the rest of the Cherokee Nation. Collins McDonald finally was able to move west in 1867. "Catalogue"; Moulton, *Papers of John Ross* 1: 344, 701, and Letter, Thomas Fox Taylor to John Ross, July 12, 1843, 2: 140–141; Don. L. Shadburn, *Cherokee Planters In Georgia, 1832–1838* (Rosewell, Ga.: W.H. Wolfe, 1990), 36, 49; Jerry L. Clark, descendant of Collins McDonald, telephone conversations with transcribers, January 1998; Starr, *History of the Cherokee Indians*, 103, 641; Bell, *Genealogy of Old and New Cherokee Families*, 278.

55. Wade A. Horton takes an in-depth look at the role of the missionary women at the Brainerd Mission in his dissertation entitled "Protestant Missionary Women as Agents of Cultural Transition Among Cherokee Women, 1801–1839" (Ph.D. diss., Southern Baptist Theological Seminary, 1991). He focuses on passages such as this *BJ* entry in his study of the female's role at the mission—a woman's role which is often overlooked in other history books.

56. See *BJ* for May 28, 1818, for information on Daniel Rawlings. For resolution of the Wilson lawsuit see *BJ* for October 16, 1818.

57. "Catalogue" identified the children as Walter McDonald, age 6; Nancy Ake, age 15; and Jedediah Morse, age 10; all three children left the school August 26, 1818, and in 1822 were living in Peavine.

58. The Cherokee language was quite difficult for an English speaking person to learn. American Board missionary Daniel Butrick was commended by the Moravians for trying to learn the language, when the Moravians had never even attempted to do so. Very few white people in the early 1800's fluently spoke Cherokee as a second language except John McDonald, John Ross' grandfather. Hamilton, "Minutes of the Mission Conference," 16 (Spring 1971): 52–53.

59. In their endeavor for moral purity, the missionaries were concerned about keeping boys and girls separate because, traditionally, Cherokee boys and girls experimented sexually. They swam together nude and joked in what missionaries considered to be a very lewd fashion. For the traditional Cherokee, the only real restriction was against having sex with members of a person's own clan. Not surprisingly, horrified missionaries tried to keep boys and girls apart or under constant supervision. Jeremiah Evarts commented upon this Cherokee custom: "The intercourse between the young of both sexes was shamefully loose. Boys & girls in their teen would strip & go in to bathe, or play ball together naked. They would also use the most disgustingly indecent language, without the least sense of shame." Evarts, "Memoranda," May 1, 1822, ABC 18.3.1, v.2: 154; 197–201; Reid, *A Law of Blood*, 42–46.

60. Isaiah 62:1.

61. See *BJ* entry for October 15, 1818, for possible identification of Rev. Brown.

62. "Catalogue" stated that Edward Brown left the school on July 9, 1818. He started school September 2, 1817, at age fifteen, so there is some discrepancy concerning his age. His place of residence in 1822 was listed as Arkansas. The "Catalogue" also stated "he could read & write" and was "respectable."

63. Psalms 68:18: "Thou hast ascended on high, thou hast led captivity captive: thou hast received gifts for men; yea, for the rebellious also, that the Lord God might dwell among them."

64. History has shown that the missionaries were correct in their assumption that cotton did not grow well where they lived. The growing range of cotton started south of them at 31° latitude and west of them in middle Tennessee. Cotton grew east of the Appalachians "starting at the northeastern boundary of North Carolina and curved

gradually southward due to the influence of the Appalachians." Maps of the growing regions show that cotton never was produced in areas close to Brainerd. Lewis Gray, *History of Agriculture in the Southern United States to 1860* (Washington: The Carnegie Institute of Washington, 1933), 888–891

65. The Cherokee were not nomadic. They lived in permanent villages and cultivated large fields of corn, beans, and squash. War and disease caused population decline; the relative peace that began in 1794 permitted the population to grow. For a description of their permanent towns and their system of agriculture see Hudson, *The Southeastern Indians*, 211–222, 272–309.

66. The treaty of July 8, 1817, encouraged a change in the Cherokee ownership of land by one of two methods: either by complete removal of the Cherokees as supported by General Andrew Jackson or by accepting a reserve of 640 acres and citizenship. Most Cherokees wanted neither option; they did not want to remove, and they did not desire individual ownership of land because Cherokee land had always been held in common. In mid-1817 the U.S. government began negotiating to enroll Cherokees to emigrate to the Arkansas with an offer of a rifle, a blanket, and transportation to Arkansas. In February 1818 Chief John Jolly, brother of Tahlonteskee, with 331 Cherokees left on 16 boats to emigrate to Arkansas. Another group left shortly after; the emigration was funded by the United States government for $21,255.00. After this emigration, bitterness and animosity existed between the Eastern and Western Cherokees over the signing of this treaty. Meigs to Calhoun, February 19, 1818, M-208, reel 7; McLoughlin, *Cherokee Renascence*, 228–239; Royce, *The Cherokee Nation of Indians*, 84–91.

67. "Catalogue" identified the girl as Mary Duning, age 7; she left the school March 4, 1821, and could read and write. In 1822 she lived in Broomstown.

68. Cherokees usually did not strike their children. Parents treated their children with a more indulgent attitude as in the case described in an entry for September 5, 1818. In fact, for the May 29, 1819 entry, the grandparents of two of the students complained that their girls had been whipped by the missionaries, and so the girls were withdrawn from the school because of the whipping. John Philip Reid explains the lack of chastisement:

> White men marveled that Cherokee children were never
> chastised 'with blows' .... they simply were treating children as

they treated everyone and disciplined them by methods at least as effective as the rod of an English schoolmaster. When a Cherokee uncle poured water over a child, or headmen dry scratched unruly youths in the town's council house, they were holding them up to ridicule, the same satirical sanction used to check antisocial aggressiveness in adults.
Reid, *A Law of Blood*, 242–243.

69. Romans 1:15–16: "I am ready to preach the gospel to you . . . . For I am not ashamed of the gospel of Christ: for it is the power of God unto salvation . . . ."

70. The five Cherokees were Charles Reece, Jane Coody, Sally McDonald, Susannah Nave, and Catharine Brown. The three African-Americans were Juno (owned by Mr. Ross), Robin Martin (free man), and Ned (owned by Sally McDonald). The one white man was Greenbury Pardue, who by 1822 had become a Methodist. "Members."

71. See Romans 2:15.

72. Here the missionaries' statement that the Cherokees were "stupid, ignorant & unconcerned" demonstrated that they did not understand the Cherokee spiritual belief system. The missionaries' opinions grew from cultural expectations; that is, the missionaries expected that every rational thinking, "civilized" man would contemplate his relationship with God, sin, and life after death. According to the missionaries and Christian society, such preoccupation with God, sin, and after-life was the "natural state" for man. The *BJ* April 9, 1819 entry stated this belief when the missionaries report that "there is nothing among this people to oppose the Gospel . . . . They have not . . . . a system of false religion, handed down from their fathers, which must be overturned." McLoughlin in *Cherokee Renascence* explained that the missionaries not only felt that the Cherokees had no belief system, but also found that the Cherokee language lacked words for "heaven, hell, devil, grace, soul, guilt . . . or sin." Thus missionaries found that their beliefs and the beliefs of the Cherokees differed on basic issues. Differences in beliefs also involved the missionaries' concept of after-life versus the Cherokee concept of life after death. In II Corinthians 5:8 Paul talked of heaven as the place where the believer resides with God and where after-life is, for the Christian, living in the presence of God forever—to be absent from the body (that is dead) is to be present with the Lord. The Cherokee concept of the after-life projected a life similar to this life where souls of dead slipped back and forth at will, often through the portals of

dreams, visions, and spiritual omens. The Cherokees had no one "Great Spirit," who created all, but rather had many spirits with which the Great Spirit blended. The missionaries also found their beliefs in contrast to the Cherokees' beliefs in reference to "sin." The Cherokees believed that all life existed in balance, a harmony of man, nature, and spirits. For example, a man was balanced by a woman, hunting was balanced by farming, Cherokee was balanced by non-Cherokee. For the Cherokees, then, murder may or may not be a "sin" depending on whether the murder corrected an imbalance—in which case it would not be a "sin"—or if that murder created an imbalance disrupting, the harmony of man and nature—in which case evil would befall the man or woman, the family, and/or the tribe that created the imbalance through the act of murder. The concept of "sin" as disobeying God was foreign to the Cherokees for the evil came, many times, from a man violating the balance of nature. If a man killed a deer without the proper ceremony, imbalance occurred, and evil came upon him and his family. Therefore, when Cherokees told the missionaries they rarely thought of the after-life or of sin, nor had they considered themselves wrong doers or sinners, they were telling the truth from their perspective because concepts of sin did not exist. Therefore, the work of the missionary became more complicated in that he not only had to make the "unsaved" Cherokees aware of their personal sin— "For all have sinned and fall short of the glory of God" (Romans 3:23)—but he had to make the Cherokees aware that sin existed at all. See McLoughlin, *Cherokee Renascence*, 358–359; McLoughlin, "Fractured Myths: The Cherokee's Use of Christianity," in *The Cherokees and Christianity*, 152–187; and Berkhofer, *Salvation and the Savage*, 51–55.

73. Isaiah 60:2.

74. The *MH* added the following footnote to the July 29 excerpt of the *BJ*: "On account of the advanced age of Mr. and Mrs. Hoyt, compared with the other missionaries, they are called 'father and mother.' Their age is somewhat under 50." *MH* 14 (December 1818): 567. As in previous trips away from the mission, Father and Mother Hoyt probably headed north into Tennessee to such a place as Washington, Rhea County, Tennessee where the missionaries regularly went to conduct business affairs. Previously Hoyt and Kingsbury left for the settlement to transact business in Tennessee riding almost fifty miles to their destination—this location could easily be Washington. See *BJ* February 2 and 7, 1818.

75. Brainerd church member's list identified her as Sally, age 25, "a

black woman of Fox Taylor's." "Members."

76. The "Catalogue" contains no listing for a youth entering on this exact date; however, the name Calvin Jones appeared for July 17. Because Evarts compiled the "Catalogue" ex-post facto in May 1822, for the students who entered the school in July, Evarts wrote the same word, one after another for four entries. During the writing of the list, he could have continued with "July" for the fifth entry—Calvin Jones—even though the entry should have been August.

77. Zechariah 3:2.

78. This girl might be Ruth Falling, who, according to the "Catalogue," left the Brainerd School on August 27, 1818. This date could be in error since the "Catalogue" was compiled four years after she left. She was the correct age of fifteen, and she previously attended the school at Springplace starting in March 1812. The "Moravian Mission Diary" does not necessarily state that she was "dismissed" but does state that she had "heart to heart talks" with the Moravian missionaries. Ruth was the daughter of Nancy Vann Falling and John Falling who was killed by his brother-in-law, James Vann, in a duel. Nancy Falling then remarried a man named Samuel Tally. The "Moravian Mission Diary" contains an entry for August 1, 1817, which does point to discord in the Falling-Tally family which might also indicate that Ruth had less than a contrite spirit:

> the Negroe Reene came to us in great distress and difficulty. Her mistress [Nancy Falling Tally] and her husband Tally had thrown her daughter Ruth Falling out of the house. She finally fled to her grandmother, the elderly Vann. Now Reene would like to encourage her mistress to think better of her daughter, and she went to her place.

"Catalogue"; McClinton, "The Moravian Mission," 457, 489–490, 492; Fries, *Records of the Moravians in North Carolina*, 8: 3791; McLoughlin, "James Vann," *Cherokee Ghost Dance*, 56–57.

79. Cause for dismissal from Springplace included "persistent unruliness, gross offenses, seduction, and the like." Hamilton, "Minutes of the Mission Conference," 16 (Spring 1971): 40.

80. In Cherokee society, uncles often behaved in ways that Europeans associated with fathers. Because the Cherokees were matrilineal, a child's closest male relatives were maternal uncles. Hudson, *The Southeastern Indians*, 187; Reid, *A Law of Blood*, 38–40.

81. II Corinthians 7:5.

82. Just cause existed for the gentlemen's confusion concerning

the denominational affiliation of the Brainerd missionaries. The mission was mainly associated with the New England Congregational churches. But there were no established Congregational churches in the South, so the Brainerd Church associated with and received support from the Union Presbytery of Eastern Tennessee. The Congregationalists and Presbyterians even though not the same denomination, joined together in their missionary efforts on the frontier. The two denominations did not always agree on politics or doctrines; for instance, the Presbyterians supported the frontier views of Indian removal as lead by Andrew Jackson, while the Congregationalists did not. McLoughlin, *Cherokees and Missionaries*, 110–111.

83. Thurman Wilkins identified this daughter of Major Ridge as Nancy, who died in childbirth. Her husband was Ricky, an Indian. "Catalogue" listed Nancy as a student entering on May 14, 1817, at age 14, but she left school before January, 1818; Nancy "married a white man and died in 1819." However, this journal entry stating that "Br. Butrick will go to preach a funeral sermon" was dated September 1818. *Cherokee Tragedy*, 116.

84. When the journalist wrote "the field appears white for harvest," he was referring to John 4:35 where Jesus Christ talked to his disciples about evangelizing among the unbelievers.

85. The journal writer referred to John Ridge, a former Brainerd student. Prior to his short stay at Brainerd, John received an education at Springplace. Then, John Ridge stayed at the Brainerd school for only a few months in 1817 and was withdrawn from school before January 1818. Next, Major Ridge sent John to a school in Knoxville where he remained for only a short while. John needed a more advanced education than that available at Knoxville, so Major Ridge approached the American Board missionaries with the idea of John Ridge going to the Foreign Mission School in Connecticut. *Cherokee Tragedy* gives a full account of John Ridge's journey to Cornwall, education, and experiences while there. Wilkins, *Cherokee Tragedy*, 97–153; Hoyt, Hall, Chamberlin, Butrick to Worcester, September 25, 1818, ABC 18.3.1, v.2: 116.

86. Dempsey accompanied John Ridge to New England. In a letter to Worcester, the missionaries reported that Dempsey was "in the nation from New York who expected soon to return, & would probably be willing to take charge of the youth. Fortunately the s^d Dr. D. soon arrived, on his way to Yookillogee . . . The Dr. having shewn

a satisfactory recommendation from the Mayor of sᵈ city . . . [we]trusted him under his care & protection." Hoyt, Hall, Chamberlin, Butrick to Worcester, September 25, 1818, ABC 18.3.1, v. 2: 116.

87. "Catalogue" listed that Elizabeth Wilson and Peggy Wilson left the school on September 16, 1818. They both entered January 5, 1818, when Elizabeth was 12 and Peggy was 10. The "Catalogue" stated Elizabeth "was married to a white man and in a few days parted from her husband by her Cherokee friends. Maintains a good character." Evarts wrote this statement about her in 1822 when she was just 16 years old. Her place of residence was listed in 1822 as Fortville, and she could read and write. In 1822 Peggy, who could also read and write, lived in Alabama.

88. Proverbs 13:15.

89. No laws traditionally bound Cherokees in marriage, and they separated with ease. The husband simply moved out leaving his wife and children in the house that belonged to them and their lineage. He returned to his own relatives and a house occupied by his mother and/or sisters until he took a new wife and moved in with her. When Cherokees, like Charles Reece (see *BJ* January 25, 1817), entered polygamous marriages, they often married sisters who continued to live together with their shared husband. Unrelated wives caused great hardship because they had separate houses, and the husband constantly moved from one wife and family to another. See John Philip Reid, *A Law of Blood*, 113–122 for a full discussion on marriage, "divorce," property rights, and polygamous marriages among the Cherokees.

90. The missionaries were grieved and shocked due to the ill feelings which existed within the Hoyt family and between the Hall and Hoyt family. In February 1819 Daniel Butrick wrote a lengthy letter to Samuel Worcester explaining the prior year's disturbances between the two families. These disputes stemmed partly from Sarah Hoyt siding with the Halls against her own family, and such petty actions as who ate with whom. Sarah preferred to eat with the Halls instead of her own family; Mrs. Hoyt expressed that Mrs. Hall used more sheeting than she ought to use for her own bedding, and the Hoyts expressed that the Halls should have their washing done with the other families' washing "to save the time of the black woman." Much talk occurred amongst the two families finding fault with each other until a proposal was made for all concerned to turn to the Bible: they were to write out Matthew 18:15–18, commit it to memory, and

recite these verses every morning for one month. Butrick explained:

Each one also promised not to talk of the faults or failings or improprieties of a brother or sister in his or her absence either to husband or wife or parent or child, or brother or sister . . . . But even this measure was ineffectual. In a few days br. & S. Hall talked as before & they said the other family had before violated the promise . . . . The time for the Sacrament of the Lords supper drew nigh. The preparatory lecture was appointed the Saturday previous. When the day came the situation of the family was such that some of the members thought the sacrament should be postponed. Br. & S. Hall & S. Sarah said there were some things in the way to their communion. It was agreed to postpone the ordinance. A sermon was preached to answer the appointment for the lecture. After sermon F. Hoyt & br. Hall had conversation, & br. Hall concluded that if the difficulties could be removed from S. Sarah's mind, he would be willing to commune. Accordingly S. Sarah, br. & S. Chamberlain & S. Anne, were desired to meet, when S. Sarah stated distinctly wherein she thought she had been injured, & after hearing their, & some other remarks, she was willing to commune with them. The next day we went to the table of our blessed Lord and had truly a refreshing season. But Mother Hoyt, & S. Hall were unable to meet with us, their thoughts continued still on their difficulties, & soon the families were again involved . . . . About this time our joint letter of Sept. was written, & our difficulties abroad & discouragements stated, without explanation in order to awaken our feelings, & call the attention of the Board. S. Hall thought the other family did not pay that attention to her they ought, considering her very ill health. At length, Br. & S. Hall & S. Sarah agreeable to the advice of the family, left for Knoxville.

Butrick to Worcester, February 24, 1819, ABC 18.3.1, v.3: 115–118.

91. Exodus 15:26.

92. American Board agent Elias Cornelius met this "little Osage captive" in November 1817 when he camped near some Cherokee warriors who had been in a battle with Osage Indians. The Cherokees took her captive after they scalped her mother and father. When warriors showed Cornelius their "prize of war," Cornelius' heart went out to the little captive as he tried to befriend her. He decided to

pursue ransoming her from the Cherokee warriors. While in Natchez, Mississippi, he told the story to Mrs. Lydia Carter, who paid $150.00 ransom for the girl. The Indian who had the girl lived only sixty miles from Brainerd. The missionaries at Brainerd were completely informed of the situation and the ransom money left with them. Word was sent to the United States government for help in rescuing her from a "half-breed" named A. Price "who gave a horse in exchange" for the little girl. The story picks up with this journal entry. See *BJ* for December 1, 1818, and note for more on the Osage War and Osage captives. Walker, *Torchlights*, 71–77; Cornelius to Meigs, July 17, 1818, M-208, reel 7; Cornelius to Calhoun, July 7, 1818, M-208, reel 7; Hoyt to Meigs, October 23, 1818, M-208, reel 7.

93. The Chamberlins adopted the Osage girl giving her the name Lydia Carter after her benefactor. Walker, *Torchlights*, 77.

94. In 1818 Rev. Glenn became pastor of a Presbyterian church in Jonesboro where previously Dr. Charles Coffin had served as pastor from 1808 to 1818. Coffin also preached at the Harmony Church in Greenville. In 1818 Glenn took over as pastor of the Jonesboro church, while in 1820 Christopher Bradshaw became the minister at the Harmony Church. *East Tennessee History: Reprinted from Goodspeed's History of Tennessee*, reorganized and indexed by Sam McDowell, (Hartford, Ky.: McDowell Publications, 1978.), D26, D38.

95. Eschol was the valley where Moses sent out spies to gather grapes signifying the fruitfulness of the land. See Numbers 13:23–24 and 32:9, and Deuteronomy 1:24. J.D. Douglas, ed., *New Bible Dictionary* (Wheaton, Ill.: Tyndale House Publishers, 1982), 348.

96. Missionaries Kingsbury and Williams arrived in June at the Choctaw Mission, but did not build their house until August. Living through their first hot southern summer and suffering greatly from the weather, Kingsbury and Williams both had dysentery and fever. Mrs. Williams almost died from "bilious fever." When Peter Kanouse arrived, he was ill from "consumption" or tuberculosis, so he left the mission in early October. The missionaries' health situation greatly affected their ability to establish their mission; Kingsbury finally opened the school on April 19, 1819, even though the buildings were not completed. Kidwell, *Choctaws and Missionaries*, 30, 33.

97. The woman could possibly be the wife of Dr. John Brown, an Irish, Presbyterian minister, who was president of the University of Georgia from 1811 until 1816. Prior to Dr. Brown's presidency of the University, Josiah Meigs, brother of Cherokee Indian Agent, Return

Jonathan Meigs, was president of the University from 1801 to 1811. The Georgia 1820 Census listed a Josiah Newton who was also mentioned briefly in Hull's *Annals of Athens* as a supporter of missionary societies in Athens. Ernest C. Hynds, *Antebellum Athens and Clark County Georgia* (University of Georgia Press, Athens, 1974), 72; *Index to United States Census of Georgia for 1820 Compiled Under Auspices of the Georgia Historical Society*, 1963 (reprint, Baltimore: Clearfield Co., 1989), 109; Augustus Longstreet Hull, *Annals of Athens, Georgia, 1801–1901* (Athens: Banner Job Office, 1906), 26, 88–93.

98. See *BJ* entry for June 27, 1818, for beginning of the lawsuit filed by James Wilson.

99. The objectionable articles may involve a statement in the church's covenant that members of the church must:

> renounce forever, as objects of chief pursuit, the World, its pleasure, its riches, its honors, and our own private interest as infinitely inferior, in worth, in excellence, and in glory, to the worth, the excellence and the glory of the ever-blessed God . . . . to appoint us to the sacred work of building up the Kingdom among the poor and benighted heathen, and to suffer us, as we do this day, to associate ourselves into a Christian church, we do cheerfully give ourselves to each other as brethren . . .

In other words the Cherokees would be required to give up all their old beliefs and old way of living, and the Indian should become a "carbon copy of a good white man." However, the missionaries were calling the Indians their equal by calling them their brethren. Historian Reginald Horsman states that "Between 1815 and 1850 the American Indians were rejected by the white society. Before 1830 there was a bitter struggle as those who believed in the Enlightenment view of the Indian as an innately equal . . ." The whites in the surrounding areas opposed the missionaries' effort to "civilize" the Cherokees with the goal of integrating them into white society. "Covenant of the Church at Chickamauga." September 28–30, 1817, ABC 18.3.1, v.2: 98; Berkhofer, *Salvation and the Savage*, 10; Horsman, *Race and Manifest Destiny*, 190.

100. Peter Kanouse was on his way back to New England from the Eliot Mission where he had been an assistant missionary. Worcester wrote of Kanouse that he was a church elder about 34 years of age, a blacksmith who owned a small farm, and was previously employed as a school master. From Rockaway, New Jersey, and born in 1784, he served a short time at the Eliot Mission

from August 29, 1818 to October 5, 1818, and left the mission due to illness. He suffered from consumption as soon as he arrived, became worse, so returned home. Israel Folsom received an education at the Foreign Mission School from 1820 to 1821; he then went back to the Choctaw Nation where he worked with missionary Alfred Wright on a translation into Choctaw of the *Book of Luke*. Folsom also worked as an interpreter. Worcester to Hoyt, Kingsbury, Butrick, Hall and Williams, March 14, 1818, ABC 1.01, v.3: 36–38; Tracy, "History," 339; Kidwell, *Choctaws and Missionaries*, 30; Grant Foreman, *The Five Civilized Tribes* (Norman: University of Oklahoma Press, 1989), 37.

101. The Cherokees, R.J. Meigs, and Gov. McMinn of Tennessee met for a second time in 1818 to discuss removal of the Cherokees as well as an exchange of land for the Arkansas Cherokees. Removal had previously been discussed in June 1817 at a meeting with U.S. Commissioners Andrew Jackson, David Meriwether, and Gov. Joseph McMinn. In 1817 a treaty was signed by some, but not all of the Cherokee chiefs. Those signing the treaty thought they were executing a compromise treaty allowing them to remain on their "lands and follow the pursuits of agriculture and civilization." Yet, in reality, they gave up 651,000 acres of land in Georgia and Tennessee in exchange for the land in Arkansas. The treaty also provided for enrollment of Cherokees to emigrate to the Arkansas lands. This provision created a dilemma for the Cherokees because by Cherokee law, enrollment to go to Arkansas would deprive a Cherokee of his status as a Cherokee citizen. So the individual Cherokee sat wedged between the two governments: The United States encouraged enrollment and the move to Arkansas while the Cherokee Council stated that if a Cherokee enrolled, he was breaking the Cherokee law of 1817 concerning disenfranchisement.

In 1818, the Cherokees protested the Treaty of 1817 by writing several memorials and by going to Washington D.C. As governor of Tennessee, McMinn supported opening all Indian lands to settlement by whites; he also acted as a commissioner whose main job was to encourage emigration and removal of the Indians. The Cherokees held a council in June and July 1818 to protest McMinn's actions. The Council also passed a law on July 7 saying that any Cherokee, who agreed to sell land held in common by the Cherokee Nation without the approval of the entire council, would be subject to death. Another council was set for November 1818 where McMinn would be present. The Cherokees worried that McMinn and the commissioners would push for a total exchange of land and a total removal especially since McMinn felt that the Cherokees were hostile to the government's position. A missionary letter affirmed the tension:

> The Cherokee Nation is in great commotion. The U.S. commissioner appointed a talk on the 20 ult. at Agency. Pathkiller & the upper town chiefs appointed a talk at Mr. Hicks' on the 28th. A large number from the lower towns, disposed to emigrate have collected at the Agency. The U.S. Commissioner is with them—we do not hear that they are doing anything at the Agency, but it is said they are waiting to hear from the council at Mr. Hicks', where the Pathkiller, & chiefs from 40 or 50 towns are deliberating. We hear of no quarreling, & hope there will be none. All appear friendly to your missionaries, & say they shall want schools whether they go or stay.

McLoughlin, *Cherokee Renascence*, 228–246; Hoyt, Chamberlin, Butrick to Worcester, October 28, 1818, ABC 18.3.1, v. 2: 119.

102. James Fields, who also attended the Springplace School in 1817 and attended the Brainerd School from July 1817 to October 1818, attended the Cornwall School from 1820–1823. When the prospect of Fields attending the school was mentioned, the missionaries wrote to the Board:

> One of our eldest boys, called James Fields .... who is about 17 years old & has been a member of our family & school about a year, manifested a great desire to go on to that school ... . The lad continued to manifest a great anxiety—told us though he was a poor boy who had no father to help him yet he had a horse, saddle & bridle, & thought his uncle would help him to money sufficient to bear his expenses on the road, if we would only consent to let him go .... He went to his uncle & other friends—they were willing he should go, but could furnish only 40 dollars in money; this he said being all his uncle had.

Hoyt, Chamberlin, Butrick to Worcester, October 28, 1818, ABC 18.3.1, v.2: 119; Walker, *Torchlights*, 155; Fries, *Records of the Moravians in North Carolina*, 8: 3792.

103. See *BJ* for October 27, 1818, and note for explanation of purpose of the convened council.

104. Pathkiller was the Principal Chief of the Cherokees from 1808 until his death in 1827. He spoke no English, so Assistant Principal Chief Charles Hicks interacted more with English speaking people

and acted as interpreter for Pathkiller, while Major Ridge did much of
the oratory and wielded his own political influence. Pathkiller's
Cherokee name was *Nanohetahee* or *Nunnahidihi* which means "he kills
in the path." Moulton, *The Papers of Chief John Ross*, 2: 729.

105. The daughter of Major George Lowrey and Lucy Benge,
Lydia Lowrey, age 15, arrived at the school on April 10, 1818, and
attended until October 28, 1819. The "Catalogue" written in 1822,
listed her then as living near Brainerd, that she could read and write
and "she makes a good wife and a respectable woman." In 1820 Lydia
married Milo Hoyt, Ard Hoyt's son. Later, Lydia, wrote one of the
first hymns in the new Cherokee syllabary. On January 19, 1834, Milo
and Lydia enrolled for emigration. They left Wills Valley with a
family of ten people, arriving at Fort Smith, Arkansas on May 16,
1834. Eventually Lydia and Milo separated, with Milo living in Ohio
and Lydia living with her father near Tahlequah, Indian Territory.
Lydia died July 10, 1862; she was "lifting a calf from a well and never
recovered." Milo died near Bowling Green, Indiana, during or
immediately after the Civil War; he had been a member of an Indian
Union Regiment with his son, Hinman B. Hoyt; they both served as
doctors. "Catalogue"; Jack D. Baker, trans., *Cherokee Emigration Rolls
1817–1834* (Oklahoma City: Baker Publishing Co., 1977), 49; Mrs.
Philip Viles, "McSpadden," in *History of Rogers County* (Tulsa: Heritage
Publishing Co., 1979), 299–300.

106. The missionaries had much trouble with an appropriate
spelling of this Cherokee location. Various spellings of this location
appear throughout the *BJ*. Current Cherokee history books show the
location spelled as one of two ways: *Oothcaloga* or *Oochgelogy* with
most maps deferring to *Oothcaloga*. Located sixty miles southeast of
Brainerd near the location of where the Cherokees would establish
their capital at New Echota, Oothcaloga was also the site of Major
Ridge's home and plantation. The missionaries described this place as
"about 35 miles from Father Gambold's near the center of the nation.
The people in this neighborhood we believe are most of them steady,
industrious farmers . . . they have a good grist mill, excellent spinning
and steams of water, and a good tract of land." The Brainerd
missionaries did nothing about establishing a school here because
when Butrick inquired on the subject, he learned "that their former
teacher was still there, unwilling to leave till the expiration of his
term, and hearing their earnest request to have a school established
when this man's time had expired, he returned." Hoyt, Butrick, Hall,

Chamberlin to Worcester, April 17, 1819, ABC 18.3.1, v.2: 123.

107. The journalist referred to John 5:24: "Verily, verily, I say unto you, He that heareth my word, and believeth on him that sent me, hath everlasting life, and shall not come into condemnation; but is passed from death unto life."

108. Luke 17:5.

109. As an alternative to removal west, the Treaty of July 8, 1817 contained a provision to grant United States citizenship to heads of families who wished to reserve 640 acres of land near the Cherokee homelands. To protect the Cherokees from being pressured to sell their land to whites in the future, the treaty placed a "temporary entail." This entail prevented the sale of the reserve during the lifetime of the grantee. Cherokee families who signed up for a reserve included Pathkiller, Daniel Ross, John McDonald for his wife Anna, John Ross and John Ross' brothers, Lewis and Andrew Ross, and several in the Brown family including Catharine Brown's father and half-brother, John Sr. and Alexander, and John Brown, Jr., son of Colonel Richard Brown. These reserves were discriminatory because although the United States government had it within their power to grant the Cherokees federal citizenship, the Cherokees would be living under the jurisdiction of a state where the white people were still racially biased and were not willing to accept the Cherokees as equals, but only as "men of color." The Southern whites viewed Indians in this category; therefore, under state laws the Indians had no rights other than owning land and paying taxes. They were discriminated against because on the state level, they were barred from voting, holding any type of office, serving in a state militia, or testifying in a court against a white man, marrying a white person, or sending a child to a public school. McLoughlin, "Experiment in Cherokee Citizenship, 1817–1819," in *Cherokee Ghost Dance*, 153–191; *Cherokee Renascence*, 212–213; *Cherokees and Missionaries*, 111–112; David Keith Hampton, compiler, *Cherokee Reserves* (Oklahoma City: Baker Publishing Co., 1979), 13.

110. The "great talk" referred to a meeting starting November 13, 1818, between the emigration superintendent, Gov. McMinn of Tennessee, and the Cherokee Indians. McMinn tried to persuade the Cherokees that ceding land was for their benefit; by giving up their land and moving, they would be happier and more prosperous. McMinn sharply pointed out to the "King, Chiefs, Headmen, and Warriors of the Cherokee Nation," if 5,000 Cherokees remained on 5

million acres in the eastern homelands, they would not advance as a society; that they must become industrious, but if they inhabited so much land, then they would lead a life of idleness. McMinn proposed that all Cherokees should remove west of the Mississippi, and the United States should pay them $100,000 and pay all expenses of removal. He also encouraged the taking of reserves. When the Cherokees refused, he offered to double the amount, but the Council still refused wholesale emigration. ASP, 481–489.

111. The missionaries elaborated more in a letter written several weeks after the "great talk" was over. They wrote:

All the chiefs, head-men & warriors, were unanimous in the determination to hold their country as long as possible: being willing however to cede a due proportion for the emigrants, according to the late treaty, as soon as the census is taken. Since the council they have determined to send a delegation to Washington to lay their case before the President, & if possible, to get some renewed assurance that they shall not be driven out of their country; & that the white people, who are intruding upon them by thousands, shall be driven back.

The delegates are to meet at Knoxville on their way the first of January. Our dear brother Hicks is one of them, & will doubtless be glad to correspond with you [Samuel Worcester] while at Washington. They do not expect to return untill spring. Our neighbor, Mr. John Ross, who is well known to Esqr Evarts, is another of the delegates, & a good pen man.

Hoyt, Butrick, Chamberlin to Worcester, December 21, 1818, ABC 18.3.1, v. 2: 120.

112. For the Cherokees who had already moved west to Arkansas, life was not peaceful. They moved into an area used by the Osages, but the Cherokees needed access to the hunting grounds through Osage land. Great hostility raged between the Arkansas Cherokees and the Osages over this access and also over the Osages stealing Cherokee horses. In October 1817 the Cherokees attacked the Osages, destroyed a village on the Verdigris, killed thirty-eight Osages, and captured over one hundred people. Diplomacy and the United States government ended the hostilities with the Osages ceding land and giving Cherokee access to the plains and hunting grounds through the Osage land. In October 1818, William Clark, of the Lewis and Clark expedition, now Superintendent of Indian Affairs at St. Louis, secured a treaty between the Osages and Western Cherokees. John

Ross eventually went after this Osage boy. See *BJ* entry for October 10, 1819. Willard H. Rollings, *The Osage, An Ethnohistorical Study of Hegemony on the Prairie-Plains* (Columbia, University of Missouri Press, 1992), 236–241; Royce, *The Cherokee Nation of Indians*, 93–94.

113. Hoyt stated in a letter that the sister belonged to a "half-breed by the name of Fields—Would it not be well if we could obtain her to be educated with her Sister?" "Osage girl now with us" referred to Lydia Carter. Hoyt to Meigs, October 23, 1818, M-208, reel 7.

114. During October 1818, three U.S. Commissioners, Choctaw Agent John McKee, Senator Daniel Burnet of Mississippi, and General William Carroll met with the Choctaw chiefs to discuss plans for a Choctaw removal as proposed by Secretary of War John C. Calhoun. During the meeting the Choctaws unanimously rejected the idea of a land cession and removal. Plans for further talks on the subject were put off for one year. Arthur H. DeRosier, Jr. *The Removal of the Choctaw Indians* (Knoxville: University of Tennessee Press, 1970), 46–47.

115. The Moravians also complained about the difficulty of gathering a congregation for worship; however, they laid the blame for the scattering of the Cherokee families squarely on the United States government: "congregating in communities is not suitable for the Cherokees under their conditions and that even the [U.S.] government would not welcome it, since it is endeavoring to make agriculture the main occupation of the Indians and therefore goes to pains to have them live in dispersed localities. Therefore it follows that no effort can be made to gather our converts at one spot." As seen in the *BJ* entry, the Brainerd brethren were quite aware of this difficulty, so they turned to itinerant preaching where one of the missionaries traveled out on Saturday to meet a gathering in a location some distance away, preached on Sunday, and then returned to the mission on Monday. Later Chamberlin and Butrick left Brainerd for tours lasting weeks or even several months. Hamilton, "Minutes of Mission Conference," 16 (Spring 1971): 36; William Chamberlin and Daniel Butrick, "Private Journals," ABC 18.3.1, v.3.

Notes for 1819

1. The chiefs in this entry are identified in other passages within the *BJ*. The king was Principal Chief Pathkiller, who lived at Turkey Town. (See *BJ* for November 2, 1818). A *BJ* entry for June 26, 1820, identified the other chief as The Boot. Further identification is found in a letter in the Cherokee Agency Papers which specifically identifies

"a Cherokee chief named Chulio, alias The Boot." Also, Cherokee historian William McLoughlin clearly identified Chulio as The Boot who was also called Shoe Boots. However, the Brainerd missionaries seemed to make a distinction between The Boot and Shoe Boots. Butrick while on a preaching tour of the southern part of the Cherokee Nation wrote that he:

> Rode to the Boots in Turkey Town 25 miles. This man I believe is some like a prince regent. He attends to business when the king is absent or in ill health, and is his Creek interpreter. Though a Cherokee, he was brought up among the Creeks, and though he now lives with the Cherokees & is one of the principal chiefs, yet he is also a chief, and attends the councils of the Creek Nation.

While there Butrick smoked a peace pipe with The Boot, and The Boot requested that Butrick call his wife and him "mother" and "father" because the Boot and his wife considered Butrick as their own son. Just three weeks after this visit with The Boot at Turkey Town, Butrick wrote that he visited Hightower at The Feather's, and The Feather sent for the other nearby chiefs. Butrick went on to say that, "Br. John [Arch] spent some time in conversing on the evil of drinking. They appeared sensible of it & one[,] the great Warrior Shoe Boots, said he was determined to drink no more." In a period of just three weeks, Butrick identified that The Boot was from Turkey Town, and that Shoe Boots lived near the Feather's at Hightower. The *BJ* itself later stated that Shoe Boots lived at Hightower. See *BJ* entry for April 12, 1823 which says, "The chief called Shoe boots, from Hightower came to make us a visit." Also, Adriane M. Strenk has written an analysis of Shoe Boots and the Cherokees in her Master's Thesis: "Tradition and Transformation: Shoe Boots and the Creation of a Cherokee Culture," (Lexington: University of Kentucky, 1993). Butrick, "Private Journal," ABC 18.3.1, v.3: 143–144; McLoughlin, *Cherokee Renascence*, 343–345; "Cherokee Indian Talk," June 11, 1818, M-208, reel 7; Meigs to John C. Calhoun, August 10, 1819, M-208, reel 8; McLoughlin, *Cherokees and Missionaries*, 42.

2. Daughter's name was Louisa Jennet Hall.

3. Upon hearing of this, Worcester responded: "Milo is the young hero of the Mission; may he ever acquit himself in the Divine warfare, with equal heroism & success, as in the affair with the robber. . . ." Worcester to Hoyt, August 27, 1819, ABC 1.01, v.3: 210–211.

4. The missionaries previously requested that the New England

mission board look into the possibility of sending ready-made clothes from donors in the North. Clothing donations would ease the missionary wives' burden of sewing by hand enough clothes to clothe approximately fifty to sixty students. The mission board agreed to this request. See *BJ* June 19, 1818, where this request was made.

5. Luke 6:35.

6. John Arch was born about 1797 in the Smoky Mountains of North Carolina where many traditionally cultured Cherokees lived. John Arch's Indian name was *Atsi* or *Atsee*. John's *Memoir* stated that his Cherokee name must have sounded similar to the English name of "Arch" which would explain his assumption of the name Arch. John went on to be educated at Brainerd; he was an interpreter for the missionaries, toured mission stations, and died from a condition referred to as "dropsy" in 1825. "Memoir of John Arch, A Young Cherokee Man," Boston: Massachusetts Sabbath School Society, 1844), 1, 13; Walker, *Torchlights*, 201–213.

7. The journalist was paraphrasing a well-known Bible verse, Proverbs 22:6: "Train up a child in the way he should go: and when he is old, he will not depart from it."

8. The missionaries here referred to Anna [Anne] McDonald, wife of John McDonald and grandmother to John Ross. She eventually was admitted to church membership on June 13, 1819. The missionaries supposed her age to be about seventy-three and said that "she is perhaps as universally respected & beloved as any woman of the nation. She has been a constant attendant in the means of grace since the commencement of this mission." Hoyt, Hall, Chamberlin, Butrick to Worcester, July 25, 1818, ABC 18.3.1, v.2: 114; "Members."

9. Paraphrase of Isaiah 35:1.

10. Isaiah 25:6.

11. Psalms 126:3.

12. The "dance" was almost certainly a religious ritual. Cherokees commemorated important events such as harvest or victory, redistributed goods, and responded to disease, famine, and other disasters by holding public ceremonies. These involved singing, dancing, and consuming "medicine," a spiritually purifying decoction. Missionaries quickly realized that these dances were not social events and forbade students and converts to attend them. Occasionally they cited the drinking that they believed took place as the cause for the prohibition, but the underlying reason was that dances were the public expression of traditional Cherokee religion. See Speck and

Broom, *Cherokee Dance and Drama*.

13. Battle Creek was located in what is now Marion County, Tennessee, the area where George Lowrey and his brother John Lowrey lived. John Lowrey was a cattle and stock trader and owned a ferry on the Tennessee River at the mouth of Battle Creek on the Georgia Road. The actual "town" spread out about fifteen miles long. Battle Creek received this name because of a battle which occurred near the mouth of the creek during Colonel James Ore's expedition to the Nickajack towns in 1794. The Lowreys lived at Battle Creek until just after the Treaty of 1819. John Lowrey died prior to the allotment of reserves, so his widow, Elizabeth, and George Lowrey, each took reserves on their respective land in this area which was ceded to the United States. However the Agency recorded problems with white settlers who moved into the adjacent ceded area:

the Cherokees have suffered much in their neighborhood of Battle Creek, by the depredations of unprincipled white men. There appears to have been a remarkable degree of hostile feeling between the frontier settlers and the Indians in that quarter, in course of which, the settlers murdered two Indians.

The losses included horses and other livestock; for instance, George Lowrey lost twenty-three horses valued at a total of $920.00. The two Lowrey families along with other families, later moved from their reserve to the northern end of the Wills Valley in what is now Fort Payne, Alabama. Allen, *Leaves From the Family Tree*, 151; Meigs, "Claims List," July 13, 1819, M-208, reel 8; Marybelle W. Chase, trans., *Records Of The Cherokee Agency In Tennessee, 1801–1835* (Tulsa: M.W. Chase, 1990), 13.

14. The delegation of Cherokee leaders went to Washington to speak with President Monroe and Secretary of War Calhoun. In a December 18, 1818 letter, Pathkiller instructed Hicks and the delegation to address "the outstanding provision of the Treaty of 1817, especially as it regards their relationship with the Arkansas Cherokees and the distribution of annuities between the two groups." In addition to Hicks, the delegates included John Ross, John Walker, John Martin, Gideon Morgan, Lewis Ross, Teeyonoo, George Lowrey, Cabbin Smith, James Brown, Chestoo Culleaugh, and Currohee Dick. The result of the negotiations included a land cession of an equitable amount of land in the Eastern Nation in proportion to the number of Cherokees who had emigrated to Arkansas under the Treaty of 1817, but there was great debate concerning the exact number of Cherokees

who had already removed under the provision of this treaty. "Names of the Cherokee Delegation now in the City," February 9, 1819, M-208, reel 8; Moulton, *The Papers of Chief John Ross*, 1: 31–32; Royce, *Cherokee Nation of Indians*, 98.

15. Acts 28:15.

16. For the delegates trip, see *BJ* of February 12, 1819 and note. A letter from the missionaries to American Board headquarters further explained the results of the delegates' trip to the federal capital:

> In our last [letter] we informed you that the chiefs at the late council had refused to exchange their land, & also that a delegation was to be sent to Washington to lay their case before the President, and, if possible, to get some renewed assurances that they shall not be driven out of their county . . . . we are told, in confidence, that the delegates have full power to negotiate an entire exchange of country if they think best, after a conference with the President.

As it turned out, the delegates to Washington were successful in preventing removal, but it was more the economic situation of the United States as well as Congress' reaction to the availability of money to remove Indians that worked in the Cherokees' favor. However, the Cherokees did agree to another land cession. Hoyt, Butrick, Chamberlin to Worcester, January 11, 1819, ABC 18.3.1, v.2: 121; McLoughlin, *Cherokee Renascence*, 247.

17. Paraphrase of Romans 11:33: "how unsearchable are his judgments, and his ways past finding out."

18. Spunk was a slender slip of wood tipped with brimstone and used for conveying or producing fire. *OED*, 16: 370–371.

19. Paraphrase of James 1:17.

20. When the missionaries wrote about agriculture, they did not mean traditional farming performed by women. The Cherokee division of labor, however, was difficult to change. See Perdue, "Women, Men, and Civilization."

21. In 1821 the Moravians did establish another mission and church at this location under missionary John Gambold's guidance.

22. The Moravians were much in favor of separate schools for boys and girls. They said, "experience has taught that it is not advisable to have both sexes together and that it could lead to unpleasant consequences in the future." By October 1819, the Moravians were only accepting boys. Hamilton, "Minutes of the Mission Conference," 16 (Spring 1971): 39.

23. As Corresponding Secretary, Samuel Worcester oversaw all missionary activity. The missionaries sent all journals and letters to him, and he faithfully replied and conveyed to the missionaries all Prudential Committee decisions. The journal often referred to this committee by the abbreviation: Pru. Com. Because the Cherokees feared that the federal government would remove them from their homelands, a Cherokee delegation went to Washington in 1819 to discuss this serious matter. The Prudential Committee in their minutes of February 6, 1819 resolved that, along with the Cherokee delegation, the American Board would send Worcester to Washington to "promote the general design of the Board for civilizing and evangelizing the Indian nations." Worcester was to:

confer with the delegates of the Cherokees as to the best means of securing to them the benefits of Christian instruction, and to the Board the full and permanent value of its establishment in the Cherokee country; and to do all in his power to promote the objects of the Board in regard to the improvement of the Indians generally.

After Worcester went to Washington on their behalf, the Cherokees expressed appreciation as seen in a letter they wrote to Worcester:

Mr. John Ross in a letter to us . . . . says, 'I had the pleasure & satisfaction of becoming acquainted with the Rev. Dr. Worcester, who has been here several days, & been very active in promoting much good towards our welfare & future happiness. I cannot express my feeling oatitude in behalf of the Cherokee Nation to those religious societies who have so much softened the hearts, & influenced the minds of the Gentlemen of congress, as well as heads of departments, towards the interest of the poor red children of nature.' Your [Worcester's] interview with the Delegates at Washington has done much good to the cause—they speak of it with great satisfaction.

Tracy, "History," 76–77; "Worcester's Parting Address," *MH* 15 (August 1819): 374–375; Hoyt, Butrick, Hall, Chamberlin to Worcester, April 10, 1819, ABC 18.3.1, v.2: 124.

24. David A. Sherman served as principal of an academy in Knoxville which operated in a building earlier vacated by the East Tennessee College in 1809. The college opened again in 1820 with the academy and college in the same location where Sherman served as both principal and president. *History of Tennessee*, 875–876.

25. On March 3, 1819, Congress passed the Civilization Fund Bill which appropriated $10,000 each year to further the "civilizing" of Indian tribes including education for Indian children. The money could be appropriated as the President and Secretary of War saw fit and could be used for construction of schools. The United States employed suitable individuals or groups (such as the ABCFM missionaries) to carry out this "civilizing" and education effort. Fortunately, the Brainerd Mission was a beneficiary of this fund. Prucha, *American Indian Policy*, 219–222.

26. General Edmund Pendleton Gaines, an army officer, surveyed the road from Nashville to Natchez; he also served as a treaty commissioner, worked on running the boundary line between the Creeks and Cherokees, and later in his life worked among the Creeks investigating the controversy over the signing of the Treaty of Indian Springs. He also is known as the military officer who placed Aaron Burr under arrest in February 1807. For the life of Gaines see James W. Silver, "Edmund Pendleton Gaines and Frontier Problems, 1801–1849" *Journal of Southern History* 1 (August, 1935), 320–344. Griffith, *McIntosh and Weatherford*, 166, 187, 261; Walker, *Torchlights*, 99.

27. Worcester wrote the missionaries that President Monroe had been invited to stop by Brainerd on his tour from Augusta through the Cherokee Country to Tennessee. Worcester stated: "He may reach Brainerd about the first of June." Worcester to Hoyt & the Brethren at Brainerd, April 23, 1819, ABC 1.01, v.3: 137–138.

28. Monroe reminded Meigs that a balance of $200 to $300 was due to the mission; he wrote, "Let it be paid." Monroe also suggested that the expense of the new building not exceed $400 to $500 and that the new school "on the Eastern side, will be considered on my return to Washington." Here he referred to the prospect of a school in the Taloney district. Monroe to Meigs, May 27, 1819, M-208, reel 8.

29. "Catalogue" listed the two girls as Susan Watts, age 9, and Julian Watts, age 7, who had entered the school just two months earlier on March 25, 1819. In 1822 they lived at Chatoogy.

30. In 1816, Presbyterian, Reformed, and Associate Reformed churches organized the United Foreign Missionary Society. The society desired to establish mission stations in the Missouri Territory, specifically among the Western Cherokees, the Osages, and the Caddos. Their purpose was to make "husbandmen" of the Western Cherokees, to provide education, and to provide teachings in "moral sentiments" which would be derived from teaching them religion. Job

Vinal and Epaphras Chapman had the full support of the government in setting up a new mission among the Western Cherokees. However, the American Board also proposed setting up a mission among the Western Cherokees and felt that "it seems not desirable that different societies should be engaged with the same tribe. The field is sufficiently wide, & each Society may take its allotment." Vinal and Chapman finally went on to the Osages and negotiated to set up a mission among them. Vinal died at Fort Smith from a fever, but Chapman proceeded with the plans for the mission named Union among the Osage on the west bank of the Grand River. Ultimately the United Foreign Mission Society gave up the Western Cherokee country to the American Board missionaries. Subsequently, in 1826, the United Foreign Mission Society merged with the American Board. Meigs to Western Cherokee Chiefs, Meigs to Reuben Lewis (Agent to the Arkansas Cherokees), and Meigs to Gov. Clark of the Arkansas Territory, June 14, 1819, M-208, reel 8; Grant Foreman, *Indian and Pioneers: the Story of the American Southwest Before 1830* (New Haven: Yale University Press, 1930), 94; Tracy, "History," 139; R. Pierce Beaver, *Church, State, and the American Indians* (St. Louis: Concordia Publishing House, 1966), 61, 72; Worcester to Thomas L. McKenney, April 24, 1819, ABC 1.01, v.3: 138–141; *MH* 19 no. 7 (July 1823): 213.

31. Born in 1790, Isaac Fisk, from Holden, Massachusetts, served as blacksmith and farmer at Eliot until he died September 19, 1820. The American Board's 1819 Annual Report stated that Fisk was "in the prime of life." Dr. William W. Pride, a physician and teacher from Cambridge, New York, on his way to the mission to be the missionary physician at the Choctaw Mission, worked in this capacity at Eliot from August 1, 1819, to October 20, 1820, and then moved to the Mayhew Mission. Worcester to Hoyt and other Brethren at Brainerd, April 23, 1819, ABC 1.01, v.3: 137–138; Tracy, "History," 339; Kidwell, *Choctaws and Missionaries*, 39; *First Ten Annual Reports*, 244.

32. Known first as Taloney, later Carmel, the mission and school was located in what is now Pickens County, Georgia, near present day Talking Rock, one half mile from the Old Federal Road. In this same area was Sanderstown, the home of Cherokee George Sanders. Goff, *Placenames of Georgia*, 353.

33. Concerning Gillespie's supplying the mission with provisions, the missionaries wrote to Samuel Worcester:

A responsible & wealthy farmer, who resides about 60 miles above [us] on the bank of the Tennessee, offers to engage to supply the institution, at a fair price, for a number of years, if we will provide a place of deposit at the mouth of the creek, & engage to take our supplies of him. In that case he will procure a keel boat, & keep it for the purpose, but cannot be at the expense of such a boat unless he can be sure of our market. This man will be able to furnish from his own farm (which lies on the bank of the river) wheat, rye, corn, pork & rice sufficient for all our wants . . . . This man can afford to deliver these articles much cheaper than we can by looking them up ourselves, as he will have them all for market within himself, & as convenient to be brought to us as they can be obtained anywhere.

From a prominent Tennessee family, Colonel George Gillespie purchased in Rhea County a 1000 acre plantation, called "Euchee Old Fields." Gillespie served as trustee of Tennessee Academy at Old Washington and in 1818 began his term as "commissioner for valuing Cherokee improvements in the ceded territory under the treaty of 1817." Hoyt, Butrick, Hall, Chamberlin to Worcester, April 10, 1819, ABC 18.3.1, v.2: 124; Allen, *Leaves From the Family Tree*, 90.

34. See *BJ* entry for January 31, 1819 and note.

35. In the "Catalogue" Mary Burns was not listed, but a Betsey Burns and Polly Burns were listed. Nancy Melton arrived at Brainerd November 30, 1818, at age 14 and left shortly after her baptism, on July 2, 1819. In 1822 her place of residence was Alabama; she could read and write, and she had married a white man. "Catalogue."

36. The Chamberlins named their daughter Catharine Brown Chamberlin after Cherokee student, Catharine Brown. See *BJ* entry for August 8, 1819.

37. *Woy kuh ke ske*, age 9, arrived at the school on September 12, 1817. The missionaries renamed him Jeremiah Evarts in honor of the American Board Treasurer who had visited the mission and school. In 1822 the Cherokee student Jeremiah was still attending the school. On July 19, 1819, one of the four who entered the school was Daniel, age 9. Jeremiah's brother was most likely this Daniel since the *BJ* for October 14, 1821, said that Jeremiah's father, Samuel J. Mills and four of his children including a son, Daniel, were baptized. "Catalogue."

38. The upset student was John Arch; see *BJ* September 5, 1819.

39. Alfred Wright, born on March 1, 1788, at Columbia, Connecticut, was educated at Williams College in Massachusetts and Andover Theological Seminary; after his graduation in 1814, he

decided to devote himself to missionary work but was delayed several years due to ill health. He served at the Choctaw missions at Mayhew, Goshen, and Wheelock. He married Harriet Bunce of Charleston, South Carolina; Harriet worked with Alfred at the Goshen Mission starting in June 1825. In Wright's eventful life he learned the Choctaw language, published sixty books and tracts in the Choctaw language, translated and printed in Choctaw all of the New Testament and parts of the Old Testament, provided medical services as the only doctor around the Wheelock mission, and pastored a church with over 570 members. *First Ten Annual Reports*, 245; Tracy "History," 338; Foreman, *Five Civilized Tribes*, 80–81.

40. Concerning the Osage boy, the Cherokees stated that Turtle Fields bought the boy and gave a horse worth $100.00. Fields wanted to raise the boy in his own family, but instead left the boy with an old friend and after that the man died. The man's widow then sold the boy to a white man. Pathkiller, the Boot, the Speaker, Wososey to the Missionaries, Friends & brothers, copy to Meigs, December 16, 1819, M-208, reel 8.

41. Although the referenced letter to the Brainerd brethren from Moody Hall is not found in the American Board papers, other letters dated at the same time were written concerning an ongoing conflict of authority over who made the final decisions relating to the establishment of the Taloney mission. The Brainerd brethren previously passed resolutions regarding the establishment and operation of Taloney with the understanding that Moody Hall would abide by such resolutions. See *BJ* entry for July 29, 1819. Hoyt wrote in a letter to Worcester:

He [Hall] considers himself now entirely detached from this establishment as much as the brethren who were sent to the Choctaws . . . . that it belongs to him alone to direct everything which concerns the new school. We should not be so much allarmed at this . . . . and our present belief that he does not intend to proceed in our original plan. He conceives the new school will be as distinct from & as independent of this as the one with the Choctaws.

The letter continued by describing Hall's enlarged plans for the local school and a farm and concluded by saying: "In short his whole plan, so far as has come to our knowledge, appears to be, not for a local school, as proposed by us, but for an establishment, as he calls it, very different from what we expected." The letter also complained of his attitude while at Brainerd previous to the set up of the Taloney mission. Hoyt to Worcester, July 3, 1819, ABC 18.3.1, v.3: 42.

42. John G. Kanouse and his wife, originally from Rockaway, New Jersey, arrived at the Eliot Mission on August 29, 1818, but were released from duty on August 30, 1819, after serving only one year. Kanouse "did not consider himself engaged, like the rest, for life . . . ." Tracy, "History," 339; *First Ten Annual Reports*, 199, 241, 293.

43. The letters referred to in this entry concerned the dispute at Brainerd involving Moody Hall and the Brainerd missionaries who had previously written to the Corresponding Secretary on February 24, 1819, regarding whether Hall should abide by the decisions and resolutions of the brethren at Brainerd or whether he should function independently from the Brainerd establishment such as Kingsbury acted independent of the Brainerd Mission. Worcester responded in May 1819 by exhorting them to a vigilant spirit to work in harmony among themselves and not to impeach the motives or character of each other. Worcester wrote two letters on August 26, 1819; one to Hoyt and the brethren at Brainerd and the other letter to Hall. In these letters Worcester plainly stated:

> The Local Schools are not to be independent establishments, but branches of the Primary Institution. The mission is one; & the whole, including the Primary Institution & its several Branches, is to be under the same general superintendence, & subject to the same general rules & regulations.

To Moody Hall he also wrote:

> general rules must be observed: to the general interests of the cause every private & subordinate consideration must yield . . . Dear brother, we hope better things of you . . . . You will make it your care to have all matters relative to your station, determined with mutual good understanding, & brotherly harmony as soon as possible . . . .

Unfortunately, the Brainerd brethren were not able to keep this dispute quiet among themselves as even the Moravians were well aware of it when they wrote in 1819: "At present the missionaries at Brainerd are somewhat at odds among themselves; yet this does not prevent us from cherishing Christian love for them . . . ."
Worcester to Hoyt and Brethren at Brainerd, May 6, 1819, ABC 1.01, v.3: 148–152; Worcester to Hoyt and Brethren at Brainerd, August 26, 1819, ABC 1.01, v. 3: 206–207; Worcester to Hall, August 26, 1819, ABC 1.01, v.3: 209; Hoyt to Worcester, July 3, 1819; ABC 18.3.1, v.3: 42;

Hamilton, "Minutes of the Mission Conference," 16 (Spring 1971): 48.

44. The missionaries named the boy John Osage Ross. In a letter the missionaries stated that:

the Osage boy whom we sought to obtain last winter is now brought to us. The Cherokee who claimed him as prisoner did not go to the Arkansas. News reached us in August that the boy had been sold for a small sum to a white man, an intruder in the nation. Soon after we heard that this man had sold him for $150. Application was made to the chiefs, & by them to the Agent. He immediately issued a precept to rescue the boy & place him under our care to await the orders of the President. Mr. J. Ross pursued after, & found the boy within 15 miles of the mouth of the Catawba, a distance of 250 miles from Brainerd.

Hoyt, Butrick Chamberlin to S. Worcester, October 20, 1819, ABC 18.3.1, v.2: 131.

45. In this entry the journalist referred to Romans 9:15: "I will have mercy on whom I will have mercy, and I will have compassion on whom I will have compassion." He also referred to Mark 16:15: "Go ye into all the world, and preach the gospel to every creature."

46. See *BJ* September 30, 1819 and note. The brethren were still trying to resolve the dispute regarding establishing Taloney based on Brainerd's resolution for no farm at the new local school versus Moody Hall's determination to buy a farm.

47. Born in Randolph, Vermont, on July 25, 1793, Cephas Washburn married Abigail Woodward, born in Randolph, Vermont, on August 22, 1797. Washburn's sister was Mrs. Alfred Finney, Susanna Washburn Finney. (See *BJ* for November 12, 1819, and note.) The Washburn family stopped at Brainerd on their way to the American Board's Eliot Mission in the Choctaw Nation. In 1821 the Finneys moved west to establish the Dwight Mission among the Western Cherokees, and the Washburns moved also. The mission, established with permission from the Western Cherokee Chief, John Jolly, was named in honor of Timothy Dwight, former president of Yale College. Cephas Washburn was the minister at the Arkansas mission; he died there March 17, 1860. Tracy, "History," 335; Walker, *Torchlights*, 44–45; Foreman, *Indians and Pioneers*, 93–94.

48. Ephesians 1:11.

49. Rewording of Psalm 77:19.

50. Rewording of Ecclesiastics 9:10.

51. Steiner, born in Pennsylvania in 1758, taught at a boy's school and later went on a missionary trip into the Indian tribes of Ohio in 1789. He was responsible for establishing the first Moravian mission among the Cherokees. Later he was principal at the Moravian's Salem Academy. A full report of Abraham Steiner's trip into the Cherokee Nation is found in Samuel Cole Williams, ed., *Early Travels in the Tennessee Country, 1540–1800* (Johnson City, Tenn.: The Watauga Press, 1928), 445–525. Hamilton, "Minutes of the Mission Conference," 15 (Winter 1970): 86–87.

52. The missionaries referred to James Vann, a wealthy and influential mixed-ancestry Cherokee, who assisted the Moravian Church in obtaining Cherokee land being vacated by Robert Brown near his own home. The Federal Road to Knoxville was near the Vann home and the Springplace Mission. McLoughlin, *Cherokees and Missionaries*, 47; de Baillou, "The Chief Vann House," 3–11.

53. Several years passed before the Moravians opened their school, and then they opened the school only because the Cherokee chiefs threatened them with expulsion from the Nation. The Moravians' theory was that first they would convert the Cherokee parents to the Christian way of life; after enough parents were converted, then the missionaries would open a school. The Moravians hesitated opening a boarding school because they could not afford the expense of boarding, feeding, and clothing students, and these missionaries had not settled near an area where large numbers of students could attend a day school and return home at night; therefore, the Moravians took several years to accomplish the task of opening a school—much to the disappointment of the Cherokees. McLoughlin, *Cherokees and Missionaries*, 43–47.

54. From 1799 to 1803 the United States continually pressured the Cherokee leadership for the right to run a federal highway through the center of the Cherokee Nation. The Cherokees opposed this road because they knew that the whites would increasingly use this road and increasing conflicts would erupt between the whites and Indians in the form of theft, violence, and murder. A road would also increase the opportunity for white settlement and encroachment on Indian land. The government, especially after Thomas Jefferson took office, argued for the road, saying that it was of absolute necessity for settlement, trade, and military strategy. The United States negotiated for several years to compel the Cherokees to grant this right of way and until 1803 the Cherokee answer had been "no." In October 1803,

the so called "progressive" Cherokee chiefs, fourteen in all, signed an agreement with the United States thinking they would reap an economic advantage by running such enterprises as ferries within their nation. James Vann was one leader who signed this agreement knowing that he personally would benefit from the building of the road. He seized the opportunity to run a tavern and lodge, rent horses, and run a ferry along the Federal Road. Even though fourteen Cherokee leaders signed this agreement, more than one hundred leaders were present at the negotiations, but not all present signed, showing that many Cherokee leaders, especially the Upper Town chiefs, opposed this road. For a look at James Vann's personal and political life see William McLoughlin, "James Vann: Intemperate Patriot, 1768–1809," in *Cherokee Ghost Dance* and McLoughlin, *Cherokee Renascence*, 77–91. For further information on the Vanns, see de Baillou "The Chief Vann House." Also see chapter entitled "The Old Federal Road" in Goff, *Placenames of Georgia*, 349–360.

55. The group of assistant missionaries on their way to Brainerd consisted of Abijah Conger, John Vail, John Talmage, and their families—all from Rockaway, New Jersey. Conger, born in New Jersey on May 4, 1782, married Phebe, born March 27, 1781, at Bridgehampton, New York. The Conger's family consisted of five children: Anna, David, Hedges, Sophia, and Elizabeth ranging in age from eighteen to two years old. The "Tenth Annual Report" gave details of Conger's offer of missionary service saying that he was a carpenter, a cabinet maker, a cooper, a blacksmith, and also skilled at farming. It further stated that "for six years in his youth, he was a schoolmaster, and for the two last years has been a principal teacher in a Sabbath school."

John Vail, a farmer, born at Hanover Township, New Jersey on October 9, 1788, married Julia, born April 1, 1789 at Warrack Township, New York. In the few weeks just prior to leaving Rockaway, New Jersey, the Vails lost two sons to an epidemic. The Vails, nevertheless, left for Brainerd with their three remaining children: Noah, Mary Ann, and Caroline ranging in age from four months old to ten years.

John Talmage (also spelled Tallmage) was a blacksmith who married Abijah Conger's sister just before the departure. A minor, George W. Halsey, not related to anyone in this group, came with them to serve a short time. "List"; Evarts, "Memoranda," April 27, 1822, ABC 18.3.1, v.2: 154; *First Ten Annual Reports*, 235–236, 281;

Tracy, "History," 336.

56. In the first decade of the nineteenth century, Agent Meigs displayed opposition to sharecropping because it was a way for wealthy Cherokees to relieve their wives of farming without having to do the work themselves. The Cherokees themselves came to oppose sharecropping because their employees tended to become squatters after their contracts were terminated, and as a result, wealthy Cherokees turned increasingly to African-American slaves for agricultural labor. The law passed by the Council on October 26, 1819, actually applied to "schoolmasters, blacksmiths, millers, salt petre and gun powder manufacturers, ferrymen and turnpike keepers, and mechanics," and it did not prohibit them. The law simply required that their employers obtain a permit from the Council and accept responsibility for their good behavior, and it allowed them to clear and cultivate twelve acres "for the support of themselves and their families." *Laws*, 6.

57. Albert Finney, born at Harvard, Massachusetts in 1790, left from Randolph, Vermont, bound for the Eliot Mission. He married Susanna Washburn also born at Randolph, Vermont. Finney and Cephas Washburn arranged to meet at the Brainerd Mission to complete their journey to Eliot together. Finney worked at the Eliot Mission only a short time and then moved on to establish a new mission, the Dwight Mission for the Western Cherokee, near Little Rock, Arkansas; he served there until he died June 13, 1829. Tracy, "History," 79, 335; Walker, *Torchlights*, 44.

58. Moody Hall stated the following regarding Mr. Gahagan and his employment status at Taloney:

> A Mr. Gahagan, who is we trust a pious man, has offered to labor for me at Talloney, till the buildings are erected gratis, if I will then take him into my family & instruct him, he at the same time assisting in the labors enough to pay for his board. He is of the Methodist order . . . .

Hall to J. Evarts, October 6, 1819, ABC 18.3.1, v.3: 176.

59. Abijah Conger brought with him from New Jersey all the tools necessary to perform the farming and mechanical work. He brought machinery for the sawmill, a turning lathe, carpenter's tools, blacksmith's tools, bellows, anvils, cabinet maker's tools, cooper's and mason's tools: all worth a total value of $700.00 for which the Brainerd missionaries later asked the U.S. government to pay. Their request for reimbursement was turned down. A. Conger to Meigs, April 1, 1820,

Calhoun to Meigs, May 8, 1820, M-208, reel 8.

60. David Brown, brother of Catharine Brown, entered the Brainerd school on October 11, 1819, where he remained until April 22, 1820; the "Catalogue" listed him as eighteen years old and "pious." David attended the Foreign Mission School at Cornwall where, from 1820 to 1823, he received a well-rounded education. He went on to Andover Theological Seminary and studied Hebrew and Greek. Brown then came back to the Cherokee Nation where he worked on translations and promoted Sequoyah's new syllabary. In September 1825, Brown was the first person to bring the Cherokee syllabary to the attention of government officials in Washington. He and father-in-law, George Lowrey (Brown married Lowrey's daughter, Rachel), used Sequoyah's syllabary for translating the New Testament into Cherokee from the Greek language. Like his sister Catharine, David succumbed to consumption; he died in September 1829. "Catalogue"; Mary Alves Higginbotham, "Creek Path Mission," *Journal of Cherokee Studies* 1 (Fall, 1976): 77, 82; Anderson, *Memoir*, 125–126.

61. In this passage the journalist was not referring to Sequoyah's written Cherokee language. The journalist was most likely referring to writing the Cherokee language according to a system devised by John Pickering, a philologist, who worked in association with the American Board. The Board was tying to develop its own system for writing native languages. See Theda Perdue, "The Sequoyah Syllabary and Cultural Revitalization," in *Perspectives on the Southeast: Linguistics, Archaeology, and Ethnohistory*, Patricia B. Kwachka, ed., (Athens: University of Georgia Press, 1994), 116–125.

62. "Dear company" referred to missionaries Washburn and Finney and their wives who eventually established the Dwight Mission to the Cherokees.

63. Andrew , brother of Principal Chief John Ross, married Susannah Lowrey, daughter of George Lowrey. Andrew and Susannah lived in the Wills Valley of Alabama. He was active in Cherokee politics and served in 1828 as a judge of the Cherokee Supreme Court. On December 29, 1835, Andrew Ross, along with Major Ridge, Elias Boudinot, John Gunter and a few other Cherokees signed the Treaty of New Echota, the treaty which lead to the removal of the Cherokees to Indian Territory. Starr, *History of the Cherokee Indians*, 367, 410; Moulton, *The Papers of Chief John Ross*, 2: 732; Moulton, *John Ross, Cherokee Chief*, 72–73.

64. Rev. William Eagleton, born in Blount County, Tennessee,

held a position as professor of language and science at the Southern and Western Theological Seminary. He pastored the Cumberland Presbyterian Church and for thirty-six years pastored the Presbyterian Church in Murfreesboro, Tennessee. Samuel T. Wilson, *A Century of Maryville College: A Story of Altruism, 1819–1919* (New York: J.J. Little and Ives Co., 1916), 73–75; *East Tennessee History*, A36, B21; "Eagleton Family Bible Records," *The Blount Journal* 3, no. 1 (May 1987): 39–41.

65. Hebrews 2:9.

66. Eagleton served as principal of the Rittenhouse Academy in Kingston, Tennessee.

67. Visiting Committee's Report, December 13, 1819, ABC 18.3.1, v.2: 133–34.

68. The government's "civilization" program was indeed working quite well for the Cherokees who farmed and produced more than they used themselves; thus, they had turned to "civilized" methods of economy—producing enough to sell for profit (or in the case of Reece to donate some of his surplus to the mission). A Cherokee elite evolved consisting of several Cherokee families who had now developed plantations and grew quantities of corn for sale. See William L. McLoughlin and Walter H. Conser, Jr., "The Cherokee Census of 1809, 1825, and 1835," in *Cherokee Ghost Dance*, 215–250.

69. The joint letter written on December 25, 1819, reviewed the circumstances of Moody Hall moving to the Taloney station and taking with him from Brainerd a large number of articles which he did not account for as directed by the brethren; also Hall requested large sums of money for the building of his log cabin at Taloney. The Brainerd brethren felt expenditures of this kind should have gained approbation in regular meetings according to resolutions passed at Brainerd. The missionaries refer to the third item of contention in the following quote from the joint letter:

> that he [Hall] has had a number of boxes brot to him from Athens & from Knoxville—that he is selling articles of merchandise to the natives, some of which were sent him by Mrs. J. [N?] of Athens to sell to the Indians—He writes to us that he has an acct. at Knoxville which he wishes us to pay, but does not mention the sum for what the debt was contracted— he writes also that he has a bushel of Timothy seed, a part of which he can spare to us, if we want—We cannot tell what he can want any for, unless he improves a farm—& he knows our

opinion is decidedly against that, unless the Com. send on a farmer for that place—He said he shall want at least $2000 before he can get started & as he never makes his calculations high enough to meet his plans, we know not at what point he will stop if suffered to go on.

Hoyt, Vail, Chamberlin to Worcester, December 25, 1819, ABC 18.3, v. 2: 135–136.

Notes for 1820

1. George M. Erskine started his life in slavery, but the Union Presbytery purchased his freedom. After studying under Isaac Anderson of Maryville, Erskine received his license to preach in 1818. He went to Africa in 1828, becoming the first foreign missionary from that presbytery. Wilson, *A Century of Maryville College,* 29–30

2. The student's Cherokee name was *Tsu tuh yun luh tuh,* meaning "shadow," with a "white" name of Thomas L., age 12. "Catalogue."

3. Twelve year old *Ut tuh suh* (War club) was renamed Joseph Meigs. On March 13, 1820, he "ran away from the school because the boys called him a Creek." The agent referred to was R.J. Meigs. See *BJ* February 16, 1820. "Catalogue."

4. Butrick wrote in his journal for February 1820 that he performed the marriage ceremony for Richard Taylor and Susan Fields at Major Brown's. Taylor lived just ten miles from Brainerd as noted by Chamberlin, who had several times spent the night at Taylor's and wrote that he rode ten miles back the next day to Brainerd. Richard Taylor was a well-known Cherokee leader who had first distinguished himself in the Creek War and received a bounty land warrant after the war. He signed many treaties, served in various Cherokee political offices, as well as led a removal detachment. Taylor served as Assistant Principal Chief from 1851 to his death in 1853. "Journal of Daniel Sabin Butrick," ABC 18.3.3, v. 4, February 1820; Chamberlin, "Private Journal," ABC 18.3.1, v.3: 25. Moulton, *The Papers of Chief John Ross,* 2: 736; Starr, *Old Cherokee Families,* 1:139; James Manford Carselowey, *Cherokee Notes* (Tulsa: Oklahoma Yesterday Publications, 1980), 15–16, 45.

5. Hoyt wrote of the wedding: "My son Milo is married to our sister Lydia Lowrey—We were all well pleased that it should be so, & hope the union will be productive of good to the mission." Butrick added in his journal for February 1820 that the wedding ceremony was performed by Father Hoyt. Several years after this marriage

between a white man and a Cherokee woman, Butrick commented on marriages between Cherokees and whites by comparing Boudinot's marriage situation with that of Milo Hoyt and Lydia Lowrey:

> All of our Christian friends at the North will be much affected by the late transactions at Cornwall. . . . It is known that Milo Hoyt married a Cherokee without censure from the Board or Christian public . . . It is known also that there is nothing between the two lids of the bible to forbid such marriages.

Hoyt to Worcester, March 4, 1820, ABC 18.3.1, v.3: 52; Butrick to ABCFM, September 17, 1825, ABC 18.3.1, v.4: 18; "Journal of Daniel Sabin Butrick," ABC 18.3.3, v. 4, February 1820.

6. Dr. Joseph Churchill Strong was a supporter of missionaries among the Cherokees and a corresponding member of the American Board. When Mrs. Hall became ill in 1818, the Halls left the mission and traveled to Knoxville, Tennessee, where she was under the care of Dr. Strong. Moody Hall in a letter stated: "He [Strong] has kindly offered us a room & all the assistance in his power." At a later date when Hall met with a Cherokee delegation to Congress, Strong was also in attendance, spending "an evening with them, in conversation about the school, & about the Nation making a reserve . . . ." Dr. Strong also urged the Brainerd missionaries to have one person stationed there acquainted with medicine and offered to assist in this training, possibly even training Hall. Strong later provided smallpox vaccinations for the Brainerd students. In 1828 Strong was mayor of Knoxville, and in 1830 he became president of the East Tennessee College. His active support of education is seen when he donated a lot for the site of the Knoxville Female Academy and also served on its board of trustees. See *BJ* November 18, 1820. ABC 18.3.1, v. 3: 164, 167; *First Ten Annual Reports*, 208; *History of Tennessee*, 870, 874–877; Rothrock, ed., *The French Broad-Holston Country*, 492–493.

7. The first plan was for David Brown and John Arch to go to the Foreign Mission School in Connecticut. John Arch turned down the opportunity to go saying he preferred to remain in the Nation interpreting for the missionaries. The possibility was then raised that John Brown might go to the F.M.S. with David. In the end John Brown did not go. Hoyt, Conger, Vail, Butrick, Chamberlin, Talmage to Worcester, December 6, 1819; Letter Hoyt, Butrick, Chamberlin to Worcester, March 9, 1820, ABC 18.3.1, v. 2: 132, 138.

8. Located approximately one hundred miles southwest of the Brainerd Mission, The Creek Path Mission and school were

established and located in Alabama near what is now Guntersville. See Higginbotham, "Creek Path Mission," 72– 86.

9. See *BJ* for December 24, 1819, and note for the background on this communication to Moody Hall.

10. One of three people with the last name of Leuty lived in Rhea County around 1820 and possibly worked at Taloney. William A. Leuty was one of the first merchants in Washington, Rhea County, Tennessee. He owned land and slaves leaving an estate worth $29,922.69 when he died. He had two half-brothers, David and John, who also lived in Rhea County. David, also a merchant, ran a tavern. Letter from Citizens of Washington, Rhea Co. to Meigs, March 21, 1817 M-208, reel 7; Allen, *Leaves from the Family Tree*, 146–148; *East Tennessee History*, A41.

11. Darius Hoyt attended college at Southern and Western Theological Seminary (Maryville College); subsequently he became an ordained pastor, and in 1828 became professor of languages at the college. He also was editor of the *Maryville Intelligencer*, a weekly religious newspaper. After his death in 1837, he was praised for being "a good linguist, a shrewd critic; of a very mild, quiet, inoffensive spirit, and of a remarkably amiable disposition. He loved the students and they loved him." Wilson, *A Century of Maryville College*, 75–76; Hoyt, *A Genealogical History of the Hoyt Family*, 418.

12. Chattooga was southwest of Brainerd along what is today the Georgia-Alabama border in Chattooga County, Georgia. The Cherokee town took its name from an earlier abandoned Cherokee village by the same name near South Carolina. The name was spelled throughout the *BJ* in numerous ways, just as the name had been spelled different ways throughout history: Chattooga, Chatooga, Chatuga, Chattugie, Chattoogee, Chatugee, and Chatugy. Goff, *Placenames of Georgia*, 58–61.

13. The blacksmith hired was Mr. Espy; see *BJ* for April 8, 1820 and note.

14. This was Isabella Hall's third child born in the three years she had been at this mission. See *BJ* for January 10, 1818, for the birth of the first child—a son who died at childbirth. See *BJ* for January 2, 1819, for news of a girl born to the Halls on December 27, 1818, while in Knoxville.

15. Taking misspellings into account, only one person with a last name of Espy (Espey) was listed on the Georgia 1820 Census: James Espey. In his 1822 "Memoranda," Jeremiah Evarts referred to the

former millwright as Mr. Espey. *Index to United States Census of Georgia for 1820*, 47; Evarts, "Memoranda," May 7, 1822, ABC 18.3.1, v.2: 155.

16. The millwright was responsible for designing and setting up the mill and all of its parts. Grist means corn, so a gristmill ground corn. The mill race was the stream which started as far away as half a mile and ran to the mill from the dam, but in the case of the Brainerd Mission's setup, the race was three-quarters of a mile long. Sometimes the race was as wide as six feet, approximately three feet deep, and usually braced with some sort of planking or crossbars of wood which kept the sides of the race from caving in. Marion Nicholl Rawson, *Little Old Mills* (New York: E.P. Dutton, 1935), 20, 101, 148–149.

17. Shoemake was a town which "lies 12 miles from Springplace, near the direct road to Knoxville." The population of Shoemake was about forty families. "List of Places in the Cherokee Nation," ABC 18.3.1, v.2: 168.

18. The Gunter family lived at Creek Path and Guntersville, Chattooga district. Old man Gunter was probably John Gunter, a Welshman, who married Catherine, a relative of George and John Lowrey. Gunter operated a powder mill in the Cherokee Nation. He died in 1835. Starr, *History of the Cherokees*, 367, 472; Starr, *Old Cherokee Families* 2: 114.

19. Conger's oldest daughter, Anna Jackson Conger born at Rockaway, New Jersey, on August 30, 1804, at this time was age 15. "List"; Fries, *Records of the Moravians in North Carolina*, 8: 3792.

20. Tombigbee in the Choctaw Nation became the American Board mission known as Mayhew founded by Cyrus Kingsbury on the *Oak tib be ha* Creek. The mission was named Mayhew in honor of Thomas Mayhew, who in the mid-seventeenth century, worked among the Indians in the Martha's Vineyard area. He died in 1646, and his father, also named Thomas Mayhew, continued the work among the Indians. Tracy, "History," 13; Kidwell, *Choctaws and Missionaries*, 43–44.

21. Proverbs 14:4.

22. Hoyt wrote of her: "Mary K. Rawlings, a niece of D[aniel] Rawlings, Esq. of Washington, is now with us, & wishes to be permanently attached to the mission—She appears to possess a true missionary spirit—but is somewhat delicate in her habits of living, & rather a feeble constitution." Hoyt to Evarts, July 24, 1820 and October 12, 1821, ABC 18.3.1, v.3: 62.

23. In 1819 the Baptist Board of Foreign Missions (BBFM) received permission from the federal government to open missions in the Valley Towns of the Smoky Mountains, an area inhabited mostly by traditionalist Cherokees. Thomas Dawson, a teacher trained in the Lancastrian teaching method, was from Georgetown, South Carolina. Rev. Humphrey Posey from Haywood County, North Carolina, was an itinerant preacher; he became a missionary under the BBFM on December 1, 1817. Dawson and Posey set up a mission and a school on the Hiwassee River in what is now southwest North Carolina; the establishment consisted of eighty acres, three houses, a farm and a school. The Valley Towns Mission was set up in an organizational manner where the missionaries were able to live a life with some privacy. This Valley Towns style of living differed from Brainerd which was communal where all the Brainerd missionaries' property and possessions such as books and household goods were contributed to the common stock. Furthermore, Brainerd's missionaries ate with the children and drew no salary from the establishment. Jeremiah Evarts wrote a lengthy description of the Valley Towns Mission in his 1822 "Memoranda." Note the differences which Evarts must have observed as Mr. Posey talked while the two men rode horseback to John Ross':

> In going & returning I conversed with Mr. Posey, in reference to the Baptist Mission, in the Valley Towns, of which he is the Superintendent. It is situated about 100 miles east of this, in the State of N. Carolina, 6 miles north of the line of Georgia. The school now consists of 60 children, supported in the mission family .... The establishment consists of a preacher, schoolmaster, blacksmith, two farmers & a hired man. This spring 80 acres of corn have been planted; last year 800 bushels were raised. The plan of the station is this: The pupils eat & lodge by themselves, forming own family, & eating at own table; the family being under the care of the teacher, with the aid of two or three young women. The other families live by themselves, entirely independent of each other, and draw substantial provisions from the common stock. Beside this they have an allowance from the Treasury of $70 for each man, $50 for each woman, & $20 for each child; from which they supplied themselves with clothes, & sugar, tea, coffee, &c. Mr. Posey's family consisted of himself, his wife, & six children: of course his allowance was $240, annually. Each family had

cows from the common stock; and when the pork was killed, it was divided among the different families.
Evarts, "Memoranda," May 6, 1822, ABC 18.3.1, v. 2: 154; McLoughlin, *Cherokees and Christianity*, 152–153; James W. Moffitt, "Early Baptist Missionary Work Among the Cherokees," *East Tennessee Historical Society Publication* 12 (1940), 16–17.

24. The journal reflects a change in handwriting which appears to be William Chamberlin's writing starting with the April, 30, 1820 entry and continuing until November 18, 1820.

25. Talmage and family had arrived at the mission five months earlier. See *BJ* for November 10–11, 1810.

26. Because of the lack of a blacksmith for the Cherokees, the missionaries' concern over Talmage leaving can be seen in a letter:

the expectations of the natives had been highly raised in regard to the blacksmith business—we had engaged to take one or two apprentices—had told them we were ready ... how could we hold up our lives to the natives—what would they think of missionaries, if we trifled in this manner. If one had a right to go at any time, simply because he pleased, another had—all might go & what would become of the mission?

Hoyt went on to say concerning the Cherokee point of view:

the Prud. Com. will see the importance of sending another blacksmith as soon as possible, when they consider the pledges we have given the Nation in regard to this business; but they can never fully realize the deep interest the natives take in this branch of the mission, unless they were on the grounds; to witness the great inconvenience they [the Cherokees] often experience from the want of implements of husbandry, the imposition they suffer in having bad tools put upon them, & the great eagerness with which they flock to the shop for work & the annuity of the chiefs to have some of their sons taught this business, by serving as apprentices in a shop where their moral principles will not be contaminated. We have no doubt the Com. will do all in their power to furnish one truly devoted, & a good workman. In our opinion much depends on this branch of the business. In a pecuniary point of view, a good workman would make the business very serviceable—as a great accommodation to the natives it would conciliate their favor—& a faithful servant of Jesus who *loved their souls*, might be preaching Christ to some of them every day.

The underlining is original writer's. Worcester's reaction to Talmage's decision was also one of shock: "We are not a little astonished & grieved at the resolution of Mr. Talmage to leave the mission . . . . It is a dereliction of duty, a breach of faith, which cannot be too deeply deplored." Hoyt to S. Worcester, May 5, 1820, ABC 18.3.1, v.2: 140; Worcester to Hoyt, June 8, 1820, ABC 1.01, v. 4: 152–153.

27. This new house became known to the missionaries as the "house by the creek." See *BJ* for April 12, 1820. The construction of the house only took them three weeks to complete; this description is a good example of a frontier log cabin with a dog trot.

28. Paraphrase of Matt. 9:38.

29. The essence of the thought is from I Corinthians 11:23–29.

30. The entry referred to the "Tenth Annual Report of the ABCFM" dated September 17, 1819, listing the charge to the new missionaries (including Talmage) going to Brainerd:

These . . . . men, have given themselves to the service, on the same principle with the missionaries and assistants now at the stations,—as an engagement for life; consecrating themselves, their faculties, and their earnings, to the sacred and benevolent object of christianizing and civilizing the Aborigines; and expecting no earthly compensation but a comfortable maintenance.

The brethren were perplexed because to them, Talmage had dedicated himself for the rest of his life to the mission cause, but Talmage was now breaking that commitment, let alone leaving the mission without the necessary blacksmith. *First Ten Annual Reports*, 236.

31. Elijah Hicks (1796–1856) was the son Charles Hicks and Clerk of the Cherokee Nation. In 1827 he was President of the National Committee. From 1832 to 1834 he was editor of the Cherokee newspaper *Phoenix*; Hicks opposed Cherokee removal in his newspaper writings. In 1834 under the harsh laws the state had set against the Cherokees, Georgia confiscated the press of the *Phoenix*. During the removal Hicks was captain of a Cherokee detachment. After the removal he continued to be active in Cherokee politics. See *BJ* for May 25, 1818 and note. Walker, *Torchlights*, 198; Starr, *History of the Cherokees*, 410, 599; Moulton, *Papers of John Ross*, 2: 724–725.

32. Numbers 10:29.

33. II Samuel 1:20.

34. I Corinthians 10:12.

35. See *BJ* for May 6, 1820, and note about the Annual Report.

36. The entry referred to Dr. Moses Waddel, president of the University of Georgia from 1819 to 1829. Hynds, *Antebellum Athens and Clarke County*, 29, 73.

37. Matthew 6:32 and Luke 12:30.

38. The entire story of Adam Hodgson's early 19th century tour of the United States is found in *Remarks During a Journey Through North America in the Years 1819, 1820, and 1821*, New York: 1823. (Ann Arbor, Mich.: University Microfilms, [n.d.]). Hodgson's remarks about Brainerd are found in Letter 6 from New York, pp. 48–65. See Walker, *Torchlights*, 138–140 for a short account of Mr. Hodgson's journey.

39. Under former Brainerd missionaries Loring Williams and his wife, a third school for the Choctaws was put in operation at Bethel near Upper French Camp on December 11, 1821. Kidwell, *Choctaws and Missionaries*, 57–58.

40. This resolution was particularly aimed at Abijah Conger. Concerning this situation, Evarts stated later:

An instance of Mr. Conger's anti-missionary conduct is the following. Soon after he came hither, he commenced selling goods on his private account. When inquired of respecting it, he said he had a few remains of a store, in which he was interested; & that the Prudential Committee told him he might sell them. He agreed, however, to let Mr. Ross sell the articles. Soon afterwards he was selling again, till, after repeated remonstrance, he took them away to Tennessee. Mr. Vail has said that Mr. Conger bought these articles in New York, on purpose to sell.

"Memoranda," May 7, 1822, ABC 18.3.1, v.2: 155 .

41. See *BJ* January 1, 1819, and note for information on The Boot.

42. Vinson Gould came to Brainerd on December 30, 1819, at age six. His Cherokee name was *Sequh ne yaw* meaning "Hog shooter." Mindwell Gould came to Brainerd on March 23, 1820, at age four. They were both still attending the school when the list of students was compiled in May 1822. "Catalogue."

43. Medway was also known as Midway, and sometimes referred to as Midway Church, the site of a large church first built in 1754 by Puritans who left their Massachusetts colony. The first name resulted from colonists who named the site Medway after the River Medway in England. Rev. Murdoch Murphey was the pastor of Midway Congregational Church from 1811 to 1823. He also had been a

missionary in South Carolina. Kenneth K. Krakow, *Georgia Place Names*, (Macon: Winship Press, 1975), 146; James Stacey, *History of the Midway Congregational Church of Liberty County, Georgia*, (Newnan, Ga.: S.W. Murray, Printer, 1903), 35, 71–74, microfiche.

44. In 1820 Catharine's parents, John and Sarah Brown; her brother and sister-in-law, Capt. John Brown and Susannah; and her sister Susan all had joined the church at Creek Path. "Members."

45. Under Thomas C. Stuart (Stewart) and David Humphries, an extensive educational system was set up for the Chickasaws by the South Carolina-Georgia Synod. Stuart and Humphries arrived in June 1820, setting up a mission near McIntoshville, the Chickasaw Agency, and naming their school "Monroe" after President James Monroe. They went on to establish several more schools among the Chickasaws. Since the Chickasaw language is similar to the Choctaw language, these missionaries taught the Chickasaw students using the Choctaw written language that Cyrus Kingsbury had adapted by using English letters to represent the Choctaw language's sounds. In 1827 the South Carolina-Georgia synod missionaries and the schools were placed under the ABCFM. Arrell M. Gibson, *The Chickasaws* (Norman: University of Oklahoma Press, 1971), 110, 112, 113.

46. Meigs to Hoyt, August 10, 1820, M-208, reel 8.

47. A New Englander, General James Miller (1776–1851) fought in the War of 1812. From 1819 to 1825, he was the first territorial governor of the Arkansas Territory. His location at the "Post of Arkansas" consisted of a village of log cabins and an Indian trading post. By late 1820, the seat of government moved to Little Rock which at the time was also a village of log houses. Miller resigned the governorship in 1825 to return to Massachusetts as collector for the port of Salem. *The National Cyclopaedia of American Biography*. vol. 10 (New York: James T. White & Co. 1909), 183.

48. This John Rogers was probably John Rogers Jr., son of John and Elizabeth Emory Due Rogers. He married Elizabeth Coody. He and his family had emigrated to Arkansas by this date. In a letter Hicks refers to John Rogers taking the little boy back to his people by request of the Arkansas Cherokees. Rogers in 1839 became Chief of the Cherokee Nation West. Moulton; *Papers of John Ross*, 2: 731–732; Starr, *Old Cherokee Families* 1: 268; Hicks to Meigs, October 27, 1820, M-208, reel 8.

49. This little sister was Chamberlin's infant daughter, Catharine. *MH* 18 (January 1821): 22.

50. I Samuel 3:18.

51. See chapter entitled "A Young Osage Prisoner" for the story of these two Osage children in Walker, *Torchlights*, 71–84.

52. The "Catalogue" identified the girls as Dinah Murphey, age 8, and Rachel Murphey, age 6.

53. The Creek Path chiefs were George Fields, Turtle Fields, The Speaker, Wausausey (or Wasosey), Bear Meat, John Brown, The Mink, Parched Corn Flour, George Guess (Sequoyah), Young Wolf, Two Killer, Clubfoot, Arch Campbell, Night Killer, James Spencer and John Thompson. McLoughlin, *Cherokee Renascence*, 266.

54. Wausausey rose to leadership in the Cherokee Nation at the time of the 1808–1809 disagreement between the Upper and Lower Towns regarding selling of the old hunting grounds. After this division among the Cherokee leadership, a National Committee was appointed to conduct the affairs of the nation. Two years later Wausausey was included among this committee. Wilkins, *Cherokee Tragedy*, 51.

55. See *BJ* for April 24, 1820, and note for information on Miss Rawlings' arrival at Brainerd.

56. Sister Crutchfield was Margaret Ann Crutchfield, Charles Hicks' niece. The funeral took place October 22, 1820, at Springplace. "Biography of Our Late Brother Charles Renatus Hicks, Second Principal Chief of the Cherokee Nation." *United Brethren Missionary Intelligencer* 2, no. 1 (1827): 402.

57. Title added interline and in a different handwriting.

58. The Council passed the law concerning the missions on October 26, 1820. *Laws*, 13–14.

59. The Council instituted a poll tax of fifty cents on each head of household and each single man under the age of sixty "paid into the National Treasury [and] to be applied for such purposes as the National Committee and Council shall deem proper." The council also derived income from licenses, contracts, and bond forfeitures as well as interest on money loaned from the National Treasury. Most of the Nation's income, however, came from annuities, annual payments from the United States for land cessions under the terms of treaties. In 1825 the Council suspended the poll tax for two years, and finally instituted an indefinite suspension in 1829. *Laws*, 48, 87, 93–94, 139.

The Council established district Councils on October 20, 1820. These Councils usurped the judicial functions of clans and the legislative role of town councils. The Council also apportioned representation in the National Council among the districts, an act which further reduced the power of town councils and limited participation in government. In 1822 the Council established a National Superior Court to hear appeals. *Laws*, 11–15, 28.

60. According to Robert Hooper in *Lexicon–Medicum; or Medical Dictionary; Containing an Explanation of the Terms*, the medical dictionary which the missionaries used at Brainerd, they counteracted the poison by using antimonial wine as an emetic medicine made of "one scruple tartarized antimony" (the chemical element Sb) four ounces distilled water, and six ounces wine. Sweet oil was an edible mild oil available from Georgia. Catharine Brown Chamberlin was born July 4, 1819, so she was one year, four months old at the time of ingesting the poison. "List of books belonging to the Cherokee Mission Library," ABC 18.3.1, v. 2: 163–164; Robert Hooper, *Lexicon-Medicum; or Medical Dictionary* (London: Longman, Hurst, Rees, Orme, and Co., 1820), 62; William A. Craigie and James R. Hulbert ed., *A Dictionary of American English on Historical Principles.* (Chicago: University of Chicago Press, 1940), 4: 2279.

61. The students were often renamed in honor of a New Englander or other supporter, who either was associated with a group providing support for the child, or in honor of people associated with the American Board. As can be seen from this list, boys were named in honor of American Board founder, Rev. Samuel Spring, and missionary, Samuel Newel. A girl was named in honor of Mrs. Samuel Newel, Harriet Newel. Rev. Samuel Spring, a minister at Newburyport, was also a member of the Prudential Committee, and Vice President of the Board. Samuel Newel and his wife Harriet, were the first missionaries to be sent out by the American Board. They went to India where they had a poor reception by the British government because of the War of 1812 between England and the United States. The Newels were forced to leave on a ship which was battered about in a storm lasting one month. A few weeks later, the Newel's new born girl died, and shortly thereafter Harriet Newel died of consumption. Samuel Newel continued on as a missionary and helped found a mission in Ceylon. Strong, *Story of the American Board*, 3; *First Ten Annual Reports*, 62.

62. Smallpox inoculation was first used in England in 1721 and was in widespread use there in the 1740's. The inoculation was also in widespread use in the colonies in the early eighteenth century due to the disease's spread in the Americas among the colonists as well as

among the Indians where the disease was so deadly. William H. McNeill, *Plagues and Peoples* (Garden City: Anchor Press/Doubleday, 1976), 249–251.

63. Butrick wrote the journal November 21, 1820 to June 9, 1821. The Western Theological Seminary, founded in 1819 by the Presbyterian church, was actually known as the Southern and Western Theological Seminary. The college was founded by Rev. Isaac Anderson who was a friend to the missionaries and a member of the Visiting Committee. In 1842 the Seminary was renamed Maryville College. The early history of the seminary and college can be found in Samuel T. Wilson's *A Century of Maryville College*. Burns, *History of Blount County*, 138–140.

64. There were three Richard Fieldses in the Cherokee Nation, but at least one person can be eliminated from the possible identification. The first Richard Fields (1762–1827) was a leader of the Cherokees during Doublehead's leadership. This Richard Fields, who was married to Jennie Buffington, Elizabeth Hicks, and Nancy Timberlake, emigrated to Texas after the Treaty of 1819, so he can be eliminated because he had most likely emigrated West by the date of this journal entry. The second Richard Fields (1803–1879) married *Ghi yo gu* and is the brother of Charles and James Fields and the son of John Fields and Elizabeth Wickett. This Richard Fields is a possibility because his brother Charles attended Brainerd. The third Richard Fields is the son of George Fields and Sarah Coody. He lived at Creek Path, living in the Chatooga District and was in the Seminole War in 1818. He owned a ferry, a grist, and a saw mill. Later in life he was associate justice of the Cherokee Supreme Court, and he was Chief Justice from 1855 to 1857. He is the most logical possibility for identification of the Fields mentioned since he was from Creek Path. McLoughlin, *Cherokee Ghost Dance*, 87; McLoughlin, *Cherokee Renascence*, 158; Starr, *History of the Cherokee Indians*, 306; Moulton, *The Papers of Chief John Ross* 2: 722.

65. The "Catalogue" listed a student with a Cherokee name of *Tse stu ke hle huh* and the explanation of his name as Sleeping Rabbit. He came to the school July 13, 1820, at age eighteen and left the school August 28, 1820. He could read and write, but was "unpromising." In 1822 he lived at Creek Path.

66. The child was Dollie (Dolly) Eunice Hoyt. When grown, Dolly married, on December 3, 1846, Amory Nelson Chamberlin, who was born November 29, 1821 at Brainerd Mission. Amory was the son of William Chamberlin and Flora Hoyt Chamberlin, who was Dolly's

paternal aunt. Starr, *Old Cherokee Families*, 2: 114; Starr, *History of the Cherokees*, 369; Wright, *Springplace*, 81.

67. Having known the Hoyts and Chamberlin in Pennsylvania, Anne Paine volunteered her services to help at Brainerd. On October 4, 1818, she wrote of her very delicate circumstances: "Mr. Paine's health for several years has not been good. He believes a release from the cares of a family to be the only remedy." Mrs. Pain stated that Mr. Hoyt's work at Brainerd had inspired her, and she was now volunteering to come with her four sons age twelve and younger. Letters were written back and forth for months while negotiations went on between Mr. and Mrs. Paine and the American Board. A legal separation finally was drawn up between the Paines where Mr. Paine agreed to pay his wife $400.00 per year, and she received in support $200.00 per year for the children. At the mission she supported herself instead of being maintained as a missionary through American Board donations. She wrote an insightful notebook describing her journey to Brainerd from Pennsylvania, her three month stay at the mission, and Cherokee customs. See excerpts of Anne Paine's journal in Walker, *Torchlights*, 193–200. Ann Paine, "Notebook," ABC 18.3.1, v.3: 328–329; "Candidate Department," ABC 6, v.1: 102–112; Worcester to Mr. & Mrs. Paine ABC 1.01, v.4, 3–6, 104–107, 174–175; Worcester to E. Strong, ABC 1.01, v.4: 109–110, 177–178.

Notes for 1821

1. William Potter, born in Lisbon, Connecticut, February 1, 1796, married Laura Weld born October 12, 1800, at Braintree, Vermont. Dr. Elizur Butler, born at Norfolk, Connecticut, June 11, 1794, married Esther Post, born at South Cannan, Connecticut, September 15, 1798. Neither Potter or Butler had a formal college education. Previous to offering his service as a missionary, Butler had worked on a farm, in a tanyard, and as a shoemaker. In preparation for his service at Brainerd, Butler studied grammar, geography, arithmetic, and composition. He then studied medicine, anatomy, diseases, and surgery under Dr. Milo North where Butler received more concentrated training than in a school. In 1831 Butler, along with Samuel Austin Worcester (one of the most famous of the Brainerd missionaries), was imprisoned by the Georgia Guard for refusing to obtain a permit to work as a missionary in the state of Georgia. Butler was in prison until 1833. Subsequently, Butler became an ordained minister in 1838. In 1850 he was chosen as steward of the Cherokee Female Seminary in

Indian Territory. Walker, *Torchlights,* 45–46; Worcester to Butler, March 14, 1820, ABC 1.01, v. 4; Candidate Department; ABC 6, v.1: 96–101.

2. Worcester's letter discussed Mr. & Mrs. Potter and Mr. & Mrs. Butler coming to Brainerd. Also Anne Paine and her four sons were to join these two couples in Pennsylvania for the journey to Brainerd. The letter also discussed the plans for work assignments: Butler to work at Brainerd, Potter to go to Creek Path, and Mrs. Paine to help with instructing at Brainerd. By the time of this resolution, the missionaries had arrived at Brainerd and the plan of work assignments begun. Worcester to Hoyt and other missionaries, November 13, 1820, ABC 1.01, v.4: 205–206.

3. The *Missionary Herald* reported that this day was also the coldest day of 1820 in New England. *MH* 17 (September 1821): 285.

4. Rev. Eli Smith, originally from Hollis, New Hampshire, moved to the frontier and pastored a church in Frankfort, Kentucky. Smith was acquainted with Isaac Anderson of Maryville; Smith helped Anderson recruit young New England ministers to come to East Tennessee and minister on the frontier. Quite often the Brainerd students were named after a pastor who had organized a "cent" society which collected donations for missions. One Brainerd student was supported through donations from the Frankfort, Kentucky Cent Society which in 1822 paid $12.00 to support a child named Eli Smith. Wilson, *A Century of Maryville College,* 36; *MH,* 18 no. 4 (April, 1822): 114.

5. Only one of the three children born on February 5, 1821, to the Congers was still alive in May 1822 when the "List" was prepared. The surviving daughter's name was Cynthia, although the "List" shows her birth date as February 5, 1822, not 1821. See *BJ* February 28, 1821, when the second baby died.

6. For details on Catharine Brown's work at the Creek Path Mission see Higginbotham, "Creek Path Mission," 72–86; and Rufus Anderson, *Memoir of Catharine Brown.*

7. A tierce was a forty to forty-two gallon container; usually a tierce was used for liquids such as wine or sometimes was used to hold provisions such as beef, pork, coffee, sugar, or tobacco. The Brainerd Mission received dry goods in this tierce which was transported over dirt roads in a wagon. *OED* 8: 75.

8. The Conger's oldest child was Ann Conger who went to Springplace for further education. See *BJ* April 15, 1820.

9. After Miss Rawlings left her missionary service Hoyt wrote: "The education of Miss Rawlings was not sufficient for a teacher, and her constitutional strength was not sufficient for hard labor. By advice of her friends she has been attending school in Washington, and still manifests a great desire to be attached to this or some other mission." Hoyt to Evarts, October 12, 1821, ABC 18.3.1, v.3: 84.

10. Most likely this sermon was about proper prayer life. The topic for the sermon, "closet duties," was from Matthew 6:6 which says, "but thou, when thou prayest, enter thy closet, and when thou has shut thy door, pray to thy Father which is in secret; and thy Father which seeth in secret shall reward thee openly." Prayer life was an important part of the day for the missionaries as well as the students, who had an organized time of prayer each evening.

11. Milo and Lydia Hoyt had been living under the mission's support; at this time they were moving onto their own improvements and supporting themselves. Ard Hoyt had requested permission from the Prudential Committee to let Milo Hoyt take articles from the mission's supplies equal in value to some items which the Hoyt family had brought with them from Pennsylvania. Hoyt to Evarts, March 9, 1821, ABC 18.3.1, v.3: 72.

12. Representing the American Board, Samuel Worcester was on a tour of the Indian missions.

13. A list, "Blount County, Tennessee, 1820 Census of Manufacturers," shows that Alexander Hannah was in the blacksmith business and that he had three people working at his establishment. *East Tennessee Roots*, 6, no. 3 (Fall 1989): 116.

14. See BJ for December 20, 1820, and note for entry about Mrs. Paine's arrival at Brainerd.

15. Only one student was listed as entering the school on this date: Lacy Willson, age 6. "Catalogue."

16. The only two students arriving on this date were John Wilkison, age 11, and Sym Wilkison, age 9; both lived near Nickajack in 1822. "Catalogue."

17. Intermittent fever was another term for "fever and ague" or what is now called malaria where a person suffers from "cold, hot, and sweating stages, in succession, attending each paroxysm, and followed by an intermission or remission." At the time of the Brainerd Mission, doctors thought that ague and fever was caused "from stagnant water, or marshy ground . . . . acted upon by heat . . . ." Hooper, *Lexicon-Medicum*, 351.

18. A stricture was a "diminution, or contracted state of some tube, or duct, of the body; as the esophagus, intestines, urethra . . .&c." Hooper, *Lexicon-Medicum*, 844.

19. Strangury was "difficulty of making water, attended with pain and dripping." From the Latin for *a drop* and *urine*. Hooper, *Lexicon-Medicum*, 844.

20. Worcester used a bark known as Peruvian Bark to treat his ailments. Accidentally discovered prior to 1638, this bark of the cinchona tree was one of three varieties found in Peru which yields medicinal quinine, an 1820 treatment for intermittent fever. This bark also treated typhus, acute rheumatism, gangrene, venereal ulcerations, scrofula, and dropsy. The dried bark was named after Francisca Henriquez de Ribera (1576–1639), Countess of Chinchon who was treated and cured of a disease through its use. Hooper, *Lexicon-Medicum*, 111, 218–220.

21. *Excarius* or *exarius*, an extremely hard to decipher word on the handwritten manuscript, appears to be a misspelling of a medical term which was probably known in the era; two possibilities exist. The word could be a misspelling of a form of the word *scrofulous*, a common ailment among the Cherokees, a disease which affected Charles Hicks. Or the handwritten word could be a misspelling of the medical term *exarma* which means a tumor or swelling. Either 1820's medical term certainly described Hick's medical problem. The *BJ* on August 2, 1821, described Hick's condition as a "white swelling of the thigh," although the journal writer crossed out this description. In 1820 the medical definition of a scrofulous condition was "hard indolent tumours of the conglobate glands in various parts of the body, which after a time suppurate and degenerate into ulcers, from which, instead of pus, a white curdled matter, somewhat resembling the coagulum of milk, is discharged." Hicks' condition continued to worsen, for a year later Chamberlin wrote: "Sabbath, Br. Hicks was about to have the bone taken out of his leg, but he had the operation suspended that he might attend meeting." Hicks, when young, was so bothered by this condition that he traveled all the way to South Carolina seeking medical attention for his disease. Hectic Fever (*Febris Hectica*) was a fever which broke out at noon and then was "greater in the evening, with slight remissions in the morning, after nocturnal sweat . . . . symptomatic of scrophula"; or the daily rise of temperature in active tuberculosis. Hooper, *Lexicon-Medicum*, 350, 797; Thomas L. Stedman, *Stedman's Medical Dictionary*, Norman Burke Taylor, ed.

(Baltimore: Williams & Wilkins Co., 1957), 1270; Wilkins, *Cherokee Tragedy*, 99; Ruff, "Notable Persons in Cherokee History: Charles Hicks," 23; Chamberlin, "Private Journal," November 9, 1822, ABC 18.3.1, v.3: 30. See *BJ*, August 2, 1821.

22. An unidentifiable journalist wrote the entries from June 11, 1821 to August 2, 1821.

23. Powelton, in Hancock County, Georgia, was named after an early resident by the name of Powell. The Methodists, Baptists, and Presbyterians established churches here. Powelton Academy, a coeducational school with female teachers, was established in 1811. Many of this academy's headmasters and teachers were from New England, especially Middlebury College. Forrest Shivers, *The Land Between: A History of Hancock County, Georgia to 1940*, (Spartanburg, SC: The Reprint Company, Publishers, 1990), 107–108; Robert G. Gardner, *Cherokees and Baptists in Georgia* (Atlanta: Georgia Baptist Historical Society, 1989), 34–35; Krakow, *Georgia Place Names*, 183.

24. Isaiah 45:22: Look unto me, and be ye saved, all the ends of the earth: for I am God, and there is none else.

25. Evarts' 1822 "Memoranda" identified the various locations where the Brainerd missionaries preached. He wrote of a meeting place at "Threekillers 14 S. of Brainerd, at the court house, 50 hearers—Preaching always by an interpreter; but one person there, who understands English." Other places where the Brainerd missionaries preached were at Tessey's town 27 miles south; Fortville at Mr. Hicks' house, 17 miles southeast where Mr. Hicks acted as interpreter; Richard Taylor's 9 miles southeast; and Fox Taylor's 10 miles northeast. At this same time the Cherokees also were requesting that Brainerd missionaries preach at Foreman's town, the Lowreys, the Agency, Mr. Reeces, as well as other places. "Memoranda," May 14, 1822, ABC 18.3.1, v. 2: 155.

26. In 1821 the Moravians established a second mission and school in the heart of the nation where many influential Cherokee leaders lived. Consisting of a house and twelve acres, it was purchased from Mr. Joseph Crutchfield, and was close to the new Cherokee capital of New Echota. John Gambold, previously at the Springplace Mission, remarried after the death of Mother Gambold and came with his new wife, Anna Maria Schulz Gambold, to open this second mission. Gambold to Meigs, May 18, 1822, M-208, reel 9; McLoughlin, *Cherokee and Missionaries*, 146–148; McClinton, "The Moravian Mission," 537.

27. The generous donation probably came from Martin D. Hardin (1780–1823), a lawyer, soldier, and United States Senator. Living in Frankfort, Hardin became a leading lawyer and politician. He served in the Kentucky State House of Representatives and in 1812 became Kentucky's Secretary of State. In 1816 he served as a United States Senator for a short time to fill a vacancy. Dumas Malone, ed., *Dictionary of American Biography* vol. 4, pt. 2, (New York: Charles Scribners' Sons, 1960), 246–247.

28. Part of the wheel hoop, the husk was an encasement around a millstone or a circular wooden box made to fit the millstone's shape. A husk was also known as a "vat, "hoop," or "curb." The husk could be made of white pine or poplar. The wood was cut into boards eight feet longer than the circumference of the mill stone and soaked in water several days. The pieces were then bent to form a circle and nailed to secure the circular shape. Rawson, *Little Old Mills*, 142.

29. Mr. Alberty (or Alberti) lived in the Taloney area. In July 1819 Moody Hall tried to buy Mr. Alberty's Taloney area farm for the mission station, but by August 1819, Alberty declined to sell saying to Hall that he "was unwilling to have a school house near his spring." Later the missionaries heard a report "that Br. Hicks wished Mr. A. not to sell at present . . . ." Hoyt, Butrick, Chamberlin to Worcester, August 30, 1819, ABC 18.3.1, v. 2: 130; Hall to Worcester July 22, 1819, August 1, 1819, ABC 18.3.1, v.3: 173, 174.

30. Cherokees who opposed drinking felt that the introduction of alcohol into their nation was a consequence of the "civilization" program and the government promoting the idea that Cherokees become like white men. In this case the "civilization" program backfired. As the Cherokees took on white man's education, agriculture, and social values, intoxication from liquor increased and the image of the "drunken Indian" emerged. Consequently, some whites felt this image was an "unlikely candidate for civilization." To counteract this image, missionaries preached against the vice of drinking (see *BJ* for July 10, 1818 for an example of the missionaries' horror of drinking), while the government tried to combat drinking through various Federal Trade Intercourse Acts. From the early colonial days, white traders were restricted in the trading of ardent spirits to the Indians. In addition, early federal laws forbade such trade by placing a fine on the trader and excluding foreign traders. Such laws proved fairly ineffective. As Indians ceded more land to the U.S., more white people moved into the newly acquired territory.

However, liquor restrictions did not apply to these citizens because the Federal law restricted the sale of liquor only on Indian titled land. In 1802, the Federal government implemented more rules which forbade trading ardent spirits among the Indians. If traders engaged in such activities, then their license would be taken away. But, the exact area of jurisdiction for this law was in question, and the Indians managed to find areas to buy the liquor and to bring back into the Nation the spirits for their use. Furthermore, the traders came into the Nation selling illegally, and they penetrated so deeply into Cherokee country that officials were unable to stop them. That liquor was readily available to the Indians can be seen in the number of distilleries in operation in Rhea County, Tennessee. The "Rhea County, Tennessee, 1820 Census of Manufacturers" identified fourteen legal whiskey distilleries in the county, but no census exists for the illegal distilleries that could have also contributed to illegal whiskey trade among the Indians. In nearby Blount County there were forty-seven legal distilleries in operation, so whiskey was amply produced and available. Laws aimed at stemming the flow of liquor into the Indians areas were directed at both the licensed and unlicensed traders. See *BJ* entry of September 24, 1821, for another of the missionaries' discourses on the problem of liquor. McLoughlin, *Cherokees and Missionaries*, 93; Prucha, *American Indian Policy*, 102–138; Sheehan, *Seeds of Extinction*, 232–240; Burns, *History of Blount County*, 243. For an in depth look at Indians and the alcohol problem, see Peter Mancall, *Deadly Medicine: Indians and Alcohol in Early America*, (Ithaca: Cornell University Press, 1995); and Izumi Ishii's Masters Thesis, "The Cherokee Temperance Movement: An Internal Struggle for a Sober Nation Before the Trail of Tears." University of Kentucky, 1996.

31. Electa J. Vail was born at Brainerd July 28, 1821, per "List." With this entry for July 28, Ard Hoyt took over as journalist.

32. The man was Mr. Fields; his son was the student named David Brainerd. See *BJ* for August 20, October 13, and December 15, 1821.

33. Mr. Fields was the Enquirer's (Samuel J. Mills) uncle and also David Brainerd's (the Cherokee student) father. This Mr. Fields is not the Richard Fields mentioned on November 24, 1820, because the Richard Fieldses mentioned in the earlier entry were probably born in 1803; thus at the time of this entry in 1821, they both were only eighteen years old. Starr, *History of the Cherokee Indians*, 306, 308–310.

34. Mrs. Persis Lovely was the widow of Colonel Meigs' Sub Agent, Major William Lovely, who had died in February 1817. Grant

Foreman, *Pioneer Days in the Early Southwest* (1926; reprint, with an introduction by Donald E. Worcester, Lincoln: University of Nebraska Press, 1994), 36.

35. The *BJ* recorded the start of hostilities, and the "Journal of the Dwight Mission" recorded the end of hostilities in 1822:

> August 12, 1822: Heard the result of the Peace Talk, between the Cherokees and Osages. The long and bloody war between them has at length terminated. The chain of peace is made bright and riveted upon them; and the friendly pipe is smoked by them in harmony. They agree to bury the hatchet and live together as brothers, on conditions of a restoration of prisoners by the Cherokees, and the payment of $300 as damages by the Osages.

MH 19, no. 3 (March 1823): 81.

36. The Butlers named their baby William Smith Butler. "List."

37. The journalist referred to land ceded through the Treaty of 1817 where the Cherokees gave up several tracts of homeland for land in Arkansas upon which the emigrating Cherokees of 1817 settled. The chiefs at Wills Valley may refer to people such as George Lowrey. He had previously resided at Battle Creek, where he took a reserve on his land under the treaty of 1817, but later moved from the reserved land to Willstown where he felt he could live in an environment free from the encroachment of white settlers. In 1822 the chiefs of Wills Valley were still asking for a school as seen in William Chamberlin's "Private Journal" where he recorded: "Went with Mr. McCoy, & Mr. Lowry to the Spirits. Turtle Fields and some others being there, I conversed with them respecting a school, found they were still anxious to have one, but they were peculiarly anxious to have a family come . . . ." Chamberlin had been holding preaching services at George Lowrey's home, with Alexander McCoy interpreting. The Spirit was also known as Captain Spirit; later he became a Christian under the teachings of the missionaries at Brainerd and took the name John Huss. He became an ordained native preacher in 1834. Royce, *The Cherokee Nation of Indians*, 91–100; Chamberlin, "Private Journal," December 1, 1822, ABC 18.3.1, v.3: 30; McLoughlin, *Cherokees and Missionaries*, 131, 133. See also *BJ* February 11, 1819 and note.

38. The brackets show the missionary journalist's indication of paragraphs not to be published in the *MH* as the writers had done many times before. In this case, though, the second paragraph starting with the words, "It is perhaps generally believed," was published

anyway. *MH* 18 (January 1822): 14.

39. Butrick was the journalist for the next section of the journal from October 1, 1821 to November 15, 1821.

40. The *MH* contained the following footnote concerning this student: "David Brainerd is a very promising Cherokee boy, to whom the missionaries gave the name, which he now bears. The parents of this boy are mentioned, in the place here referred to, as a gray headed man and his wife." David Brainerd was named after the eighteenth century missionary who was a missionary to the New England Indians—the same David Brainerd for whom the Brainerd Mission is named. *MH* 18 (January 1822): 15.

41. The missionaries gave "The Enquirer" this new name in honor of New Englander, Samuel J. Mills. See Introduction and note.

42. Dr. Charles Coffin was president of Greenville College from 1810 to 1827; he thereafter became president of East Tennessee College. Earlier in Coffin's life he belonged to a church in Newburyport, Massachusetts, where Dr. Samuel Spring was the pastor. This Samuel Spring was a founding member of the ABCFM in 1810. Coffin also studied theology under Dr. Spring. In 1804 when Coffin was ordained as vice-president of Greenville College, Dr. Spring delivered a "Discourse" at the ceremony. Coffin was also a member of the East Tennessee Missionary Society. *East Tennessee History*, D25; Rothrock, ed., *The French Broad–Holston*, 399–400.

43. Miss Conger went to a school known today as Salem College. This educational institution has been in existence since April 1772 when it was opened by the Moravian Church as the Salem Female Academy. See Frances Griffin's *Less Time for Meddling: A History of Salem Academy & College, 1772–1866* (Winston-Salem: John F. Blair Publisher, 1979).

44. The "Catalogue" stated Samuel Candy left the school on November 16, 1821. On October 13, 1819, Samuel, at age 16, entered the school with Jack Candy, age 12. Samuel's Cherokee name was *Tu a loo ky*, meaning "jealous." Samuel's residence in 1822 was listed as Chatunooga; he could read and write; his character was "doubtful."

45. Among Cherokees, this young man reflected a broader redefinition of masculinity that created anguish, confusion, and lawlessness among many youths. Masculinity traditionally had been measured by a man's daring exploits in war and hunting. Now, those ways of proving one's manhood were being taken away by the American government's plan for "civilizing" the Indians. McLoughlin,

"Cherokee Anomie, 1794–1810: New Roles for Red Men, Red Women, and Black Slaves," *The Cherokee Ghost Dance*, 9–11.

46. In 1822 the "Catalogue" listed John Rackley, age 8, as having entered the school on February 11, 1819.

47. Hall's report of the Taloney school was contained in a letter written to the Brethren at Brainerd October 10, 1821. He touched on such topics as the delay of locating a suitable site, the building of the school and dwelling house, a report on the livestock, the progress of the students, and meetings on Sunday for Cherokees and blacks. He then launched into a lengthy narrative of the "afflictions and trials" of his personal family as regards their health reminding the Board of the death and burial of his two babies and the constant burden of illness. He wrote: "sickness has been our most constant lot. Twice has my dear wife been brought to the gates of death . . . ." He then complained that the "unfaithfulness of labourers has not only been a trial but an expensive evil." It could be that the brethren first voted not to send this report to the Prudential Committee because of the many complaining comments in the letter, but later in the *BJ* entry for November 26, 1821, the brethren at Brainerd voted to forward this same report to the Prudential Committee. Hall to Brethren at Brainerd, October 10, 1821, ABC 18.3.1, v.3: 198–199.

48. John C. Elsworth (Ellsworth), born in Chatham, Connecticut, February 22, 1793, married Eliza Tolmar, born in Greensborough, Vermont, December 25, 1795 or 1797. The Elsworths worked at the Haweis-Turnip Mountain Mission in 1823–24. Harriet Elsworth, John's sister, born at Chatham, Connecticut, September 25, 1790, married Brainerd missionary Ainsworth Blunt. See *BJ* November 17, 1822. Tracy, "History," 336; "List."

49. The *MH* edited this passage to read "pulmonary complaint." The journalist used the more precise medical terminology for the day, peripneumonia, which was defined in 1820 as a condition with a weak pulse, a pain in the chest or side, difficulty in breathing, a livid color, a cough. "If relief is not afforded in time, and the inflammation proceeds with such violence as to endanger suffocation, the vessels of the neck will become turgid and swelled . . . so as to impede the circulation . . . and the patient will soon be deprived of life." *MH* 18 (April 1822): 105; Hooper, *Lexicon-Medicum*, 703–704.

50. Amory Nelson Chamberlin, born at Brainerd, November 29, 1821, later married Dolly Eunice Hoyt on December 3, 1846. Dolly, also born at Brainerd, was the daughter of Milo and Lydia Hoyt.

Amory served as a Cherokee interpreter for the Council and was a superintendent of the Cherokee Male and Female Seminary in Indian Territory. "List"; Starr, *Old Cherokee Families*, 2: 114; Starr, *History of the Cherokee Indians*, 555.

51. Shortly thereafter, Dr. Butler reported to the Prudential Committee that "this morning Mr. Hoyt is very much recovered having had a comfortable night. From appearances we may suppose in a few days he will be able to resume his labors." Butler to Evarts, November 30, 1821, ABC 18.3.1, v.3: 87.

52. Consumption, the disease which took the lives of Catharine Brown, her brothers John and David, and convert John Arch, was a common disease among people living at that time. Consumption was the general word used, but tuberculosis was the underlying cause for this disease which was contagious and known today to be a streptococcal infection. According to the 1820 *Lexicon-Medicum Dictionary* used at the Brainered Mission, early nineteenth century doctors believed that those people prone to come down with the disease were in:

> particular employments exposing artificers to dust, such as needle-pointers, stone-cutters, millers &c . . . . violent passions, exertions, ... frequent and excessive debaucheries, ... drinking freely of strong liquors, . . . continuing to suckle too long under a debilitated state, . . . the application of cold, either by too sudden a change of apparel, keeping on wet clothes, lying in damp beds, or exposing the body to suddenly cool air, when heated by exercise . . . .

Hooper, *Lexicon-Medicum*, 687–688; Harold W. Jones, Normand L. Hoerr, and Arthur Osol, ed., *Gould's Medical Dictionary*. (Philadelphia: The Blackiston Co., 1941), 349; Stedman, *Steadman's Medical Dictionary*, 1482.

53. Evarts recorded Moody Hall's account of Jeremiah Hill joining the mission:

> He [Hill] left the state of Maine, with an intention of setting up a school in the Creek Nation, by his own perseverance & skill. He went thither, but found it impracticable. He then came to Taloney, & hired himself out to our mission, till he could learn whether he was received as a missionary. He did not wait, however, for an answer; but went to Brainerd, where he labored about 3 weeks. He then went to the northern part of the nation, near the Hiwassee, with a view of setting up a

private school. He could not get the people to do any thing for his support. He has planted six acres to corn, in order to support himself; & has taught Sabbath school.
"Memoranda," May 8, 1822, ABC 18.3.1, v.2: 155.

54. Philo P. Stewart, born in 1799 and from Pawlet, Vermont, was an assistant missionary bound for Mayhew. Tracy, "History," 339.

55. Identification of the books and periodicals the missionaries referred to is as follows:

Christian Observer, a Presbyterian family newspaper published religious articles, biographical sketches, and essays.

The *Panoplist*, a religious magazine started in 1805 by Congregationalist Jedidiah Morse, attacked the new doctrines of Unitarianism espoused by Harvard Divinity School. The *Panoplist* was the "leading spokesman for foreign missions." Backed by the American Board, the *Panoplist* published sermons and articles on doctrine. In 1808 it merged with the *Massachusetts Missionary Magazine* and reported missionary news. Jeremiah Evarts succeeded Morse as editor of the *Panoplist* in 1810. By 1821 the *Panoplist* became the *Missionary Herald*. News of the Brainerd Mission was often published in the *Panoplist* and *Missionary Herald*; many times the periodical published verbatim excerpts from the mission's journal.

The "Henry on prayer book" could be one of two books written by Matthew Henry (1662–1714); one possibility was *A Method for Prayer, with Scripture-expression, Proper to be Used Under Each Head*. The other possible book was *Prayers in Scripture Expressions, for the Use of Families*. Matthew Henry was an English Presbyterian minister whose most famous work was his *Commentary on the Whole Bible* which he started work on in 1704.

The Rise and Progress of Religion in the Soul by Philip Doddridge (1702–1751), spoke about Christian life. Jean Hoornstra and Trudy Heath, eds., *American Periodicals, 1741–1900: An Index to the Microfilm Collections*, (Ann Arbor: University Microfilm, 1979), 57–58, 131, 142; Bowden, *Dictionary of Religious Biography*, "Jedidiah Morse," 317–318; Andrew, *Rebuilding the Christian Commonwealth*, 20; Leslie F. Church, "Forward," *Commentary on the Whole Bible* (Grand Rapids: Zondervan Published House, 1961), vii–xi.

56. Henry Parker, born at Litchfield, Connecticut, March 22, 1791, married Philena Griffin, born at Simsbury, Connecticut, February 10, 1792. Tracy, "History," 336.

57. Daniel Butrick wrote the journal to November 15, 1821. A

change of handwriting appears for the section of journal from November 15, 1821 to July 1822. See *BJ* entry for January 3, 1822, where writing was assigned to William Chamberlin.

Notes for 1822

1. The *MH* printed this *BJ* entry and edited the minister's name to read *Rev. Marshall*, but did not print his first name. *MH* 18 (September 1822): 284.

2. Erastus Dean, born in Bristol, Vermont, May 13, 1798, married Sarah Coleman from Montpelier, Vermont; she was born at Byfield, Massachusetts, September 23, 1796. Tracy, "History," 336.

3. The missionaries sent a letter to the Prudential Committee concerning plans for a 55 by 30 foot, two story mission house with a cellar under the entire building. The main floor was to have a dining room 30 feet square and a kitchen 30 by 25 feet. They planned bedrooms on the second floor. The cost of the building they estimated at $3,000.00. In addition, to ease the burden of the women cooking for such a large group, they requested a "Slaters London patent steam kitchen & hot air roaster advertised in a Philadelphia paper" which would also save on the expense of wood with which to cook. Hoyt, Conger, Butler, Chamberlin, Dean, Elsworth to Evarts, February 1, 1822, ABC 18.3.1, v.2: 147.

4. No corresponding missionary letter specifically identified this head man of Willstown, but the Brainerd brethren were friendly with several Cherokees whom Chamberlin and Butrick associated with on their tours into that area. This head man could have been George Lowrey, Alexander McCoy, The Spirit, Turtle Fields, or John Benge. Chamberlin, "Private Journal," ABC 18.3.1, v. 3: 30; Butrick, "Private Journal," ABC 18.3.1, v. 3: 151–152.

5. The missionaries told the Willstown headman that the American Board would take the Willstown school under consideration. The brethren wrote "If provision should be made for Hightower we hope Wills Valley will at least be furnished with a single teacher otherwise they may feel neglected." Hoyt, Butrick, Chamberlin, Vail, Conger, Dean to Evarts, March 8, 1822, ABC 18.3.1, v.2: 148.

6. The entry referred to the widow of Samuel Worcester; he died at Brainerd in June 1821, and obviously the mission had kept his horse.

7. Lydia Lowrey Hoyt, being their closest neighbor, now lived on

a farm approximately one-half mile away. See *BJ* February 16, 1821.

8. Missionary writer was actually referring to Turnip Mountain. See *BJ* for July 24, 1822 and note, which explains the difference between Turnip Mountain and Turnip Town.

9. Jesus' Sermon on the Mount, found in Matthew 5–7 with parallel passages in Luke 6:20–49, has been viewed as a discourse on a Christian's "road to salvation" and also Christ's expression of God's relation to man and His involvement and sovereignty in the individual's daily life. The Sermon is also a "character sketch" of the believer and a "description of the quality of ethical life" expected of the believer. Hoyt may have spent much of the afternoon explaining how a Christian was expected to live—touching on such topics as murder, forgiveness, adultery, impurity, offenses one against another, marriage and divorce, Christian love, prayer, fasting, and dress. All these ways of living had become part of the Euro-white values which the missionaries were trying to impart (or impose) upon the Cherokees. See also *BJ* for February 5, 1822. *The Revell Bible Dictionary*, (Old Tappan, N.J.: Fleming H. Revell Company, 1990), 908; Douglas, ed., *New Bible Dictionary*, 1088–1091.

10. Catharine Brown was with her brother John Brown in his last days. She kept a journal in 1821 and 1822. In September 1821, Catharine, her brother John, and his wife, Susannah, traveled to Blount County, Alabama to a "sulphur springs" to seek a cure for John. The three slept in a tent on the ground. She recorded, "Brother John drinks the water, and bathes in it, but has yet received no benefit. I do not feel so well as I did before I came here, and almost wish to return immediately. Perhaps it is lying on the ground, that makes me feel sick." She was with him again in January and February of 1822. On January 14, 1822, Catharine wrote, "have not attended school since last vacation, having been at home taking care of my sick brother. He has failed very fast the past week. I fear he will not live many days." By January 30, she wrote, "Brother John is senseless most of the time. I fear he is to remain but a little while in this world . . . . Our great consolation is, that our dear brother will soon be freed from pain, and rest in the bosom of his dear Jesus." On February 2, Catharine wrote, "Evening, Brother John is no more." After recording the death of her brother her diary ends. Anderson, *Memoir*, 71–76.

11. In a list of donors, the *MH* identified the medicine's donor as Dr. John H. Kain. Rogersville is in Hawkins County, Tennessee. *MH* 18 vol. 2 (February 1822): 56.

12. The journal writer referred to Thomas Dawson, the teacher from the Baptist mission and school in the Valley Towns, Cherokee Nation. See *BJ* April 27, 1820 and note.

13. Butrick's journal covering this itinerant tour of the Cherokee Nation is found in the American Board Papers: ABC 18.3.1, v. 3: 143–147, January 3–February 28, 1822. While on this tour Butrick and Arch visited Hicks, the Coodys, the Rosses, Benges, the Barks, Gunter's Landing, Sister Fields, Wa-sa-si, The Boot in Turkey Town, Pathkiller, S.J. Mills, Major Ridge, Pettit, Alberty, The Feather, and other chiefs. It was while on this visit in Turkey Town that Butrick smoked the peace pipe with The Boot.

14. In a letter the missionaries elaborated on the subject of the school in the Hightower district:

> Br. Hicks speaks of this Town as being the most important place in the nation for a local school. It is the largest town, containing two hundred or more families & is perhaps 30 miles long. It lies on the Hightower river, & the road leading from Georgia to Alabama, about 40 miles from the Georgia line,—about the same distance from some of the creeks, and also the same from the school at Taloney. The chiefs numbered the children of a suitable age to attend school, and within a reasonable distance & found them to be 67, besides others who would probably board with their friends there who now live at a distance. They propose building houses both for the smiths shop [which the Cherokees had requested the missionaries to set up for them] and school.

Hoyt, Butrick, Chamberlin, Vail, Conger, Dean to Evarts, March 8, 1822, ABC 18.3.1, v.2: 148.

15. In this letter to Evarts, Butler expressed his conflict with trying to be physician and steward-treasurer of the mission at the same time. Butler to Evarts, March 16, 1822, ABC 18.3.1, v.3: 288.

16. The journalist referred to the New Testament parable of the prodigal son found in Luke 15:11–32.

17. Sylvester Ellis, born July 29, 1798, arrived at Brainerd from Randolph, Vermont. This teacher and farmer at the school and mission later married Sarah Hoyt. They left the mission on May 22, 1824, when they moved to the Willstown Mission, but in 1832 they came back to Brainerd. "List"; Walker, *Torchlights*, 52.

18. Ainsworth Blunt, born February 22, 1800, in Amherst, New Hampshire, functioned as a farmer and mechanic at the mission. After

arriving at Brainerd, he married Harriet Elsworth. They had two children who died at the mission and were buried in the Brainerd Cemetery. The journalists occasionally spelled his name Blount. After the removal of the Cherokees, Blunt stayed in the area which later became Chattanooga and helped organize the Presbyterian Church of Chattanooga. When the mission closed in 1838, Blunt came into possession of the mission's pewter tankard, cup, and platter which the Presbyterian Church used at its first communion held June 28, 1840. Walker, *Torchlights*, 49–50; "List"; Zella Armstrong, *The History of Hamilton County and Chattanooga, Tennessee*, Vol. 1 (Chattanooga: The Lookout Publishing Co., 1931), 72–73, illustration facing p. 78.

19. The missionaries often gave the Brainerd students a "white man's" name taken from the benefactor who sponsored their education at the mission. Other times a student might be named after a minister who headed a missionary society in his locale. The donor then received a letter at least once a year from the mission or student relating the student's progress at the school. The sponsor or benefactor relationship provided income for the mission as well as a "pronounceable" name for the missionaries to call the student. Sums donated for the support of students ranged from a low of $10.00 to a high of $120.00 with the normal donation approximately $30.00 for a year's education. Berkhofer, *Salvation and the Savage*, 37; Henry Hill to Hoyt, February 11, 1824, ABC 18.3.1, v.2: 189.

20. William Goodell acted as an agent of the American Board. Before Brainerd was established, he helped explore locations for the purpose of setting up missions to the Southeastern Indians. However, after the trip to Brainerd in 1822, Goodell embarked on his own missionary endeavors, first working at a mission in Beirut where there was much opposition to Christian missionaries. He then moved on to open a mission in Constantinople where two months after his arrival his home burned down. He was successful in translating the Old and New Testament into Armeno-Turkish, but died during the world wide cholera epidemic of 1832. Strong, *Story of the American Board*, 35–36, 83, 88, 90, 103; Charles E. Rosenberg, *The Cholera Years* (Chicago, University of Chicago Press, 1962), 14–98.

21. Evarts was now the Corresponding Secretary. Even though in poor health, he undertook this trip through the Southeastern Indian missions to view the threat of Indian removal as well as the state of the missions. During his stay at Brainerd, he conducted an investigation of the mission's organization, operation, and secular

concerns such as the mills and farm. Evarts' findings resulted in the 1822 document entitled "Memoranda Relative to the Cherokee Mission" which criticized the operation and running of the mission and farm. Evarts undertook another tour of the Indian missions starting in December 1823 and thereafter became an avid supporter of the Indian's rights to remain in their homeland. He later toured New England and elsewhere raising donations to support Indian missions. Subsequently he wrote the *William Penn Essays* which strongly opposed Indian removal. See Andrew, *From Revivals to Removal* for an in-depth look at Evarts' life; also see Prucha, ed., *Cherokee Removal: The "William Penn" Essays and other Writings of Jeremiah Evarts.* "Memoranda," ABC 18.3.1, v.2: 154–157.

22. Evarts' detailed report said that Hoyt was negative about planting the field, claiming Hoyt felt that because the field was worn out, it should be left unplowed except for planting wheat. Evarts reported the other missionaries expressed a "qualified affirmative" that the "field would pay for cultivation." Evarts opinion was that corn should be planted quickly on 10 acres, and 15 acres should be seeded with wheat and rye. Evarts, "Memoranda," May 7, 1822, ABC 18.3.1, v.2: 154.

23. The question of letting one of the females leave Brainerd was answered in the negative because the women at the mission had engaged in very hard labor the previous year and many of them were worn out. It was a burden for the women to engage in academic teaching, teaching out-of-school "civilizing" tasks, cooking, cleaning, and doing laundry for over one hundred people. Consequently, the missionaries were reluctant to let one of the female workers leave at this time. The labor of the female department was one of the issues discussed while Jeremiah Evarts was at the mission. As he listened to the men give reports of the domestic tasks performed by the women, he heard two sides of the issue, one that the women were not doing their work well, as reported by Dr. Butler, and the opposing side as reported by Daniel Butrick that the women were overburdened. For instance on May 11, 1822, Evarts wrote that:

> In regard to Mrs. Chamberlain's hard labors, Dr. B. said that she took charge of the kitchen, & washing; that her plan was to have the Cherokee girls do all the labor, & herself superintend; that the girls did not like to work with her, because she never took hold herself; they said they had rather work with sister Sarah; that complaint was made by

the children, that the kitchen work was done wretchedly. . . .
that Mrs. C. would go out to wash in the night, & in the rain,
& finish before 9 o'clock, & the clothes would look as though
they had only been dipped into water.

On May 10, 1822, Daniel Butrick wrote a formal letter to Evarts and in
it addressed the issue of the hard labors performed by the women,
especially Flora Chamberlin:

> Permit me to say a word respecting our dear sister
> Chamberlin. She has ever been a dear sister to me. The last
> year as you probably know was a trying time with the sisters
> here. Sister Chamberlin for a considerable time was obliged,
> with the help of a few school girls to perform all the washing
> for upwards of a hundred persons, besides teaching the girls
> school. In order to do this she was often obliged to arise at
> midnight or a little after, & go to the creek, frequently in the
> rain & commence her labours. I told her then & told father
> Hoyt, that it was entirely too much, but no other seemed
> practicable, as we could not obtain help & sister Sarah was
> obliged to be at br. Halls, or labouring in the kitchen . . . . or
> attending to her mother & Darius who were sick. By such
> labours, & by fatigues, which women are seldom called to
> pass through, her constitution is doubtless affected, & of any
> one here I think she deserves commiseration.

Evarts, "Memoranda," May 11, 1822, ABC 18.3.1, v. 2: 155;
Butrick to Evarts, May 10, 1822, ABC 18.3.1, v.2: 172.

24. When Evarts visited Hicks, the chief expressed his views
against a large boarding school such as Brainerd and was much in
favor of smaller schools. See quote from Hicks in the Introduction to
this book. "Memoranda," May 8, 1822, ABC 18.3.1, v.2: 155.

25. A triphammer, used in a blacksmith shop, was a pressure-
loaded, foot operated, heavy hammer that rose on an idler pulley.
When the blacksmith tripped the foot treadle, the hammer came
down with rapidity and force. The operator used this machine for
making medium or small size forgings. Robert H. Harcourt,
Elementary Forge Practice (Peoria: The Manual Arts Press, 1917): 86

26. Even though the missionaries compiled later lists of students
attending the Brainerd school, they never compiled another list such
as the "Catalogue" which listed dates for students entering the school
before May 1822.

27. If Cherokees could prove a person to be a witch, that person

was executed. A witch was amoral, so could steal a person's years of life away and add those years to the witch's own life. They also believed that witches could read a person's mind and cause evil to happen to the other person. Witches could transform themselves into other shapes, animals, or birds. Witchcraft was a capital offense, but in 1824 the Arkansas Cherokees passed a law against killing people who were suspected of witchcraft. Hudson, *The Southeastern Indians*, 173–183, 362–365. See also Raymond D. Fogelson, "The Conjurer in Eastern Cherokee Society," *Journal of Cherokee Studies* 5 (Fall, 1980): 60–87 where he discusses the difference between conjuring (the practice of traditional Cherokee medicine) and witchcraft.

28. Scrofula was a glandular swelling, an obsolescent term referring to tuberculosis with symptoms of eczematous eruptions, ulcerations, glandular swellings or tuberculosis of the glands, bones, or joint. This was the disease which also afflicted Charles Hicks and John Ridge. *Steadman's*, 1270.

29. C^r and D^r stand for Credit and Debit, accounting term which the missionaries used to indicate income and expenses.

30. This Turnip Town was actually the location which the missionaries later referred to as Turnip Mountain, ultimately becoming the Turnip Mountain-Haweis Mission.

31. See *BJ* for June 24, 1822 which identified him as John Wanuh.

32. "List of Places in the Cherokee Nation" described Turkey Town as "perhaps 30 or 40 miles long, is . . . . bounded by Lookout mountain, Alabama, the Creek line, and Chatoogy, lying on the Coosa river. The king [Pathkiller], his first counselor, & many other old chiefs live in this Town, all in darkness. A beautiful country. Between two & three hundred inhabitants." The list's compiler used the term "darkness" to refer to the state of the Cherokees' souls in reference to knowledge of the white man's God. ABC 18.3.1, v. 2: 168.

33. See *BJ* for March 19 and 20, 1822.

34. The *MH* stated, "Mr. Thompson had been employed several months as a blacksmith, at Brainerd. He is from Blount County, Tennessee." *MH* 18 (October, 1822): 306.

35. The boy was Horace Loomis. See *BJ* for June 14, 1822.

36. See *BJ* for January 18, 1818, and note for explanation about the Cherokee Lighthorse Guard.

37. Chamberlin described Jeremiah Evarts' and his family's extreme illness:

We called at Br. Mills & I was much affected to see the

situation of his family. He was at Brainerd taking care of a sick son; his wife & seven children were all taken down at once with the measles. She said for one or two days she had nearly lost her senses. It appeared to her like a dream. She barely remembered that her children were crying around her in great distress, crying for water & she had neither strength nor inclination to give it to them. She said for two or three days they did not eat a mouthful of food, or take a drop of medicine. They were now considerably better.

Chamberlin, "Private Journal," July 7, 1822, ABC 18.3.1, v.3: 25.

38. Worcester, who had died at Brainerd, had been the preacher at the Tabernacle Church.

39. Cherokees engaged in regular bathing in creeks and rivers for ceremonial purposes as well as cleanliness, believing that if they bathed every day, they would live a long life. They plunged into the cold water every morning before eating any food. Hudson, *The Southeastern Indians*, 324–325.

40. The journalist's statement "there is shaking among the dry bones" refers to the Bible passage found in Ezekiel 37:1–14 which explains how those who are without God can be transformed to ones with spiritual lives. In the passage God is speaking of the spiritually dead among the Israelites who would then be spiritually reborn upon hearing the word of God. Likewise the Cherokees when hearing the spiritual truths from the missionaries would have a new spiritual life.

41. Many tribes besides Cherokees used the sweat bath (hot house) as a cure-all for illness. In the eighteenth century James Adair wrote about the Cherokees' practice of plunging in the river in extremely cold weather. But he also stated that the Southeastern Indians practiced bathing "as a religious duty, unless in very hot weather, which they find by experience to be prejudiced to their health." Mooney, *Sacred Formulas of the Cherokees*, 333–335; Adair, *History of the American Indians*, 126; Hudson, *The Southeastern Indians*, 324–325.

42. For more information on traditional Cherokee medicine and bathing in rivers, see Mooney, *Sacred Formulas of the Cherokees*; and two articles by Mooney, "Cherokee Theory and Practice of Medicine," and "The Cherokee River Cult," *Journal of Cherokee Studies* 7 (Spring, 1982) 25–36.

43. Held in late summer, the Green Corn Ceremony was one of the Cherokees most important ceremonies, a ceremony of thankful-

ness and gratitude for a successful corn crop since corn was a main food sources. The ceremony which lasted several days contained rituals of eating great quantities of food, of fasting, of cleaning public buildings and individuals' homes; a time of renewal, a time of abstinence from many social contacts, of purging and purifying themselves, a time for ceremony involving the medicine bundle, a time for making a new fire for the coming year, a time of ceremonial dancing and then of igniting new fires in their homes for a new season. After these rituals and ceremonies were concluded, the women cooked food for another feast and another ceremonial dance. The last ceremony involved going to water to purify themselves, then another dance. The Cherokees (and other Southeastern Indians) were then ready for a new year after cleansing themselves of the impurities and sins of the former year. See April 16, 1818 *BJ* entry for Hicks' explanation of the ceremony. Hudson, *The Southeastern Indians*, 365–375; Adair, *The History of American Indians*, 105–117; Speck and Broom, *Cherokee Dance and Drama*, 45–54.

44. In the crossed-out words, the journalist referred to Butrick learning the Cherokee language and translating the Bible passages for attendees who only knew Cherokee.

45. Baptists Rev. Thomas Roberts and Rev. Evan Jones went into Western North Carolina to evangelize among the Valley Towns populated by many Cherokee traditionalists. For over fifty years Jones and his son John B. Jones ministered to and worked on behalf of the Cherokees, first in the Eastern Nation and later in Indian Territory. Jones opposed removal and Andrew Jackson's policies, but when the time came for Cherokee removal, he walked the "Trail of Tears" with his Cherokee friends. He continued to work among the Cherokees, even serving as a chaplain in an Indian regiment during the Civil War. Because the Cherokees accepted Evan and John Jones as true friends, historian William McLoughlin pointed out that Evan Jones "had the unique honor of being officially admitted as a full member of the tribe with a pension from the Cherokee treasury for his long and faithful service to the Cherokee Nation." For a complete study of Evan Jones' and his son, John B. Jones' life work among the Cherokees, see William McLoughlin's *Champions of the Cherokees: Evan and John B. Jones*. McLoughlin, *Cherokees and Christianity*, 30–33, 51–108, 146.

46. The Cherokee ball play, similar to the North American game of lacrosse, was played with two ball sticks made of hickory or pine wood bent to look like a long spoon and then laced with leather to

form the "bowl of the spoon." Using a small leather ball and the two ball sticks to catch and throw the ball, they played on a large field with a goal post. Testing players' swiftness, accuracy, and cunning, they scored a point by striking the pole with the ball; twelve points won the game. Ball play, often an alternative to war, was rough, so participants were often injured. The players went through special training, abstinence, and a fast for the two to three weeks before the game. They held a ball play dance which began the evening before the game and continued until dawn the day of the game. The dance involved ceremony and a special incantation pertaining to the athlete's abilities to play the game the next day. The ritual of "going to water" just before the game involved sacred formulas where the priests told the players the myth of the birds who would examine the fate of the ballplayers. See James Mooney, "The Cherokee Ball Play," *Journal of Cherokee Studies* 7 (Spring, 1982): 10–24 ; Hudson, *The Southeast Indians*, 408–421; Mooney, *Myths of the Cherokee*, 230; Mooney, *Sacred Formulas*, 395–397.

47. See *BJ* for April 21, 1823, where the expelled boy was identified as Tilman Rose.

48. George Lowrey, Assistant Principal Chief under John Ross in the years 1828–1829 and 1843–1851, also acted as Principal Chief while John Ross went to Washington for parts of 1845, 1846 and 1848. Lowrey, one of the first Cherokee leaders to see Sequoyah's Cherokee syllabary in use, later wrote "The Life of George Gist" which tells the story of Sequoyah's invention of the Cherokee alphabet. During the removal, Lowrey and John Benge led one of the first detachments of Cherokees out of their eastern homelands and into Indian Territory during the fall and winter of 1838. Cherokee historian Grace Steele Woodward called him the "Cherokee's George Washington." His tombstone monument inscription aptly sums up his life:

George Lowrey, Born at Tahskeegee on Tennessee River about 1770. Died October 20, 1852, Age 82 years. Erected by order of the National Council. Many years a Member of the Church of Christ. Ruling Elder of the Church at Willstown. Deacon of the Church at Park Hill. He fulfilled the duties of every Office well. An Honest Man. A Spotless Patriot. A Devoted Christian. Visited President Washington as Delegate from the Cherokee Nation 1791 or 92. Captain of the Lighthorse 1810. Member of First National Committee of 1814. One of the Delegation who negotiated the Treaty of 1819. Member of the Convention who formed the Constitution in 1827. Also that of 1839. Elected Assistant Principal Chief 1828 and often afterwards. At his Death a Member of Executive Council. Filled various other public Offices.

For a sketch of Andrew Ross, see *BJ* for December 9, 1819 and note. T.L. Ballenger, "Major George Lowrey" (talk delivered at the Lowrey Family Reunion, Tahlequah, Oklahoma, 1964), 6; Major George Lowrey, "Notable Persons in Cherokee History: Sequoyah or George Gist," *Journal of Cherokee Studies* (Fall, 1977): 385–392; Grant Foreman, *Indian Removal* (Norman: University of Oklahoma Press, 1972), 308–309; Woodward, *The Cherokees*, 215; Tombstone inscription transcribed by J.B. and P.G. Phillips.

49. Sister Dean was approximately six to seven months pregnant at this time. See *BJ* entry for October 15, 1822.

50. For a time in the journal, the missionaries seemed to use the name Turniptown and Turnip Mountain interchangeably to refer to the area where Br. Mills lived. In actuality, Turnip Town (or Turnipminetown) and Turnip Mountain were two different locations. The *BJ* entry for June 6, 1822, stated that Turnip "Town" was near Chatooga, along with other places such as Creek Path and Hightower which all lie in a line south of Brainerd about 50 miles. This July 24, 1822 entry identified Beaver Dam on the south side of the Coosa River, opposite to Turnip "Town," but this same location was identified here as Turnip Mountain. The missionaries established the Haweis-Turnip Mountain mission on what is now Georgia Route #20, seven miles west of Rome and about one mile north of the Coosa River. On the other hand, a May 27, 1823 entry identified Turnipminetown: a place lying north or northeast of the Taloney mission. This town was a place located southeast of Brainerd in what is now Gilmer County, Georgia, four miles northeast of Ellijay. About this time Ard Hoyt wrote a letter concerning Turnipminetown desiring a local school, which confirms that this second location was a different name and location. However, later in the journal the missionaries seem to differentiate between the two Turnip "town" locations by referring to Br. Mills' location south of Brainerd as Turnip Mountain, and the location east of them as Turniptown. Gardner, *Baptists and Cherokees*, 57–58; Krakow, *Georgia Place Names*, 238; Hoyt to Evarts, August 14, 1823, ABC 18.3.1, v.3: 104; Charles O. Walker, *Cherokee Footprints* (Jasper, Ga.: C.O. Walker, 1988), 30.

51. An account of Chamberlin's tour of May to July 1822 is found

in the American Board Papers. See William Chamberlin's "Private Journal," ABC 18.3.1, v.3: 25–28.

52. Mission stations were eventually established at all three places. This Turnip Town was actually Turnip Mountain, where Samuel J. Mills, "The Enquirer," lived and witnessed about religion among his people. The name of the station at Turnip Mountain was later changed to Haweis, "in memory of a venerable friend of missions in England, lately deceased, whose widow had given £50 to the Board for Indian mission, on condition that one of the stations should bear his name." Mr. John C. Elsworth set up this station at Turnip Mountain. The mission at Hightower (Etowah) was set up by Mr. Isaac Proctor who arrived October 12, 1822. See *BJ* and note for that day. After the establishment of the mission station at Hightower, a period of anti-mission sentiment erupted over the chief's complaints concerning Proctor's teaching methods and corporal punishment, over complaints concerning the missionaries preventing the new converts from attending the Cherokee town house, over conflicts between traditionalist Cherokee and the missionaries use of hymns and communion, and over problems between slave and Indian masters once the master became Christian. The third new mission at Willstown was set up by William Chamberlin. Tracy, "History," 118; McLoughlin, "Cherokee Antimission Sentiment, 1823–1824," in *Cherokee Ghost Dance*, 385–396.

53. This former Brainerd student was probably given the name Calvin Jones in honor of General Calvin Jones of North Carolina who had visited the mission in 1819, but this 1819 visit was not recorded in the journal. See *BJ* October 17, 1823 note. "Catalogue" says of Calvin Jones the student, that he came to school at age eighteen and in May 1822 was learning the blacksmith trade.

54. Psalm 133:1.

55. Conuhanuh or Con-nau-ha-nah was a dish made of corn or "hominy prepared with lye leached from green hardwood ash." Milo and Lydia Hoyt's daughter, Lucy Lowrey Hoyt Keyes or Wahnenauhi (meaning: Over there they just arrived with it), wrote a manuscript in 1889 containing her knowledge of Cherokee customs and history. She wrote that Conuhanuh was a principal dish of food for the Cherokees. Jack Frederick Kilpatrick, ed., "The Wahnenauhi Manuscript: Historical Sketches of the Cherokees, Together with Some of Their Customs, Traditions, and Superstitions." *Bureau of American Ethnology Bulletin* 196, no. 77. (Washington: United States Government Printing

Office, 1966), 179, 192.

56. This student was named after a New England preacher, Rev. Benjamin Blydenburg Wisner (1794–1835), who was ordained pastor at the Old South Church in Boston on February 21, 1821. Rev. Wisner, was the American Board's Corresponding Secretary during the 1830's. Wisner wrote important letters concerning the American Board's position on Cherokee Removal, as well as, their views on Elizur Butler and Samuel Worcester being imprisoned by Georgia. ABC 1.3.1, v. 1; Leonard Woods, "The Grand Theme of the Christian Preacher: A sermon delivered at the Old South church in Boston, at the Ordination of the Rev. Benjamin B. Wisner, Feb. 21, 1821," (Andover: Flagg and Gould, 1821).

57. Error in journalist's addition.

58. Likewise the missionaries probably did not understand the traditional Cherokee practice of medicine. For a look at Cherokee medicine see Mooney, *Sacred Formulas of the Cherokees*, 319–368; and Mooney, "Cherokee Practice of Medicine" *Journal of Cherokee Studies* 7 (Spring, 1982): 25–29

59. See *BJ* for February 8, 1823, for more information on Jack who later took the name Jack Crawfish.

60. Dr. Alexander McGhee was an early settler and physician of Maryville, Tennessee, after the town's founding in 1795. *East Tennessee History*, B28.

61. In a letter sent two weeks prior to this date, Hoyt described in full detail the extent of those suffering from various illnesses:

Respecting the family Br. Ellis has been quite feeble since he had the measles, or what we supposed was the measles. He is now just able to take care of himself, but not to assist in the family. Four of the mission family & two hired men are down with a fever, each requiring one or more watchers every night. Sis. Elsworth was taken on the 13th of August, has been apparently on the borders of the grave, & is now unable to rise from her bed without assistance. Br. Elsworth was taken down three days after, leaving the school to my son Darius, who has been in as assistant thro the summer. Soon after Mr. Clark (the carpenter) & George W. Halsey were taken down in the same manner—on the 25th Darius was taken, & Mr. Chamberlin who had just returned from a tour took the school. Last friday Dr. Butler was brot to his bed, & on saturday his fever run very high—under these distressing & alarming circumstances it was thought best to send to Maryville for Dr. McGhee, who has relinquished the practice of physic & is studying theology with Mr. Anderson. John Arch left us early sabbath morning to go for him & has not yet returned. I should also mention Sis Vail among the sick, tho, with another complaint, yet perhaps not less distressed than any of the others. Their three youngest children were among the last who has the measles, & were all very bad & the youngest but one, after enduring the complaint many days, was taken from them by death on the 19th ult. This bereavement, together with the long anxiety during the sickness bore hard upon her feeble frame & while thus reduced her stanch from same cause became too debilitated to digest her food—repeated & excessive vomiting ensued & continued for several days untill her life was nearly spent. Br. Vail has been, & still is, obliged to spend nearly all his time with her. Under these circumstances you will readily see we have had as much as we could all well do to take care of the sick, keep the family together, & continue the schools. A merciful providence has sent us a very cool salubrious air for a few days, which gave us reason to hope that the spreading of the fever is checked. Most of the sick appear to be mending, perhaps I may say all except my Son Darius—his case is still doubtful. Dr. Butler is so much better today that we hope his fever will not run on as in all the other cases—but there is by no means certain. Such a season you will readily see we never before had at Brainerd.

Hoyt to Evarts, September 6, 1822, ABC 18.3.1, v.3: 89.

62. The "effort" referred to the missionaries' tour of the surrounding white communities to raise donations for the missionary cause.

63. An unknown female penned the journal for September 20, 1822 to February 28, 1823, with one of the other missionaries dictating the journal to her. See *BJ* for October 3, 1822.

64. This entry probably referred to John Golden Ross who married Elizabeth Ross, daughter of Daniel and Mollie Ross. John and Elizabeth's son, William P. Ross, was Principal Chief of the Cherokees after John Ross. Starr, *History of the Cherokees Indians*, 410, 582; Moulton, *Papers of Chief John Ross*, 2: 734.

65. Isaac Proctor, born May 6, 1784, at Ipswich, Massachusetts, functioned at the new mission at Hightower as a teacher and farmer, but also worked at the American Board mission at Carmel (Taloney),

and Amohee. His wife, Fanny, was from West Bloomfield, New York. Walker, *Torchlights*, 52; Tracy, "History," 336.

66. The son born was named Chester Wright Dean. See *BJ* for November 17, 1822.

67. The poll tax had been enacted in 1820, but the impetus to comply may have stemmed from impending legislation passed on November 13, 1822, which empowered tax collectors to seize and sell the property of those who did not pay. *Laws*, 29.

68. The wife of Cyrus Kingsbury, Sarah B. Varnum from Dracut, Massachusetts, traveled to New Orleans to marry Kingsbury on December 24, 1818, and then joined him at the American Board mission at Eliot. She then moved on with her husband to the Mayhew Mission where she lived until her death. Tracy, "History," 338.

69. Per. Bark was Peruvian Bark or Cinchona. See *BJ* for May 28, 1821 and note.

70. Mr. Cary (or possibly Pary) was presumably making charcoal for the blacksmith. Charcoal, which burns at a hotter temperature than wood, is made by burning wood while restricting the air supply. Charcoal production requires an enormous supply of wood, and industrial production largely turned from charcoal to coke (coal burned with restricted air) in the eighteenth century. *OED*, 3: 34

71. In the nineteenth century, doctors believed bilious fever was a disease which arose from over production of bile, which could result in digestive disturbances, furred tongue, constipation, headache, vertigo, or jaundice. The term was also used to describe disorders of the liver. Hooper, *Lexicon-Medicum*, 126; *Stedman's*, 182.

72. Butler asked relief from his job as the mission's steward.

73. Born in 1795, Frederick Elsworth, from Greensborough, Vermont, married Miss Coleman, born in Montpelier, Vermont. In 1824 they accepted reassignment to the mission station at Haweis. The young brother was Oliver Elsworth. Tracy, "History," 336.

74. In its annual meeting in November 1822, the Council voted to refuse "any cession of land, being resolved not to dispose of even one foot of ground." The most radical step the council took was the establishment of a superior court at New Town (New Echota). The Council also passed laws regulating slaves, authorizing turnpikes, requiring written records of district courts and providing payment to court clerks, prohibiting drinking and card-playing within three miles of council houses, prohibiting embezzlement of letters, empowering district judges to appoint light horse companies, authorizing property

seizure for non-payment of taxes, and reducing taxes on merchants and peddlers. *Laws*, 23–30.

75. From a list of the Brainerd students compiled in 1824, several possible identifications exist for these two baptized students. Eli Smith, Samuel B. Wilson, and the student named Boston Recorder were all listed as "full Cherokee" and were all 18 years of age. No one on the list was 20 years old in 1824. George Candy was also 18 years old, and listed as "3/4 white," so he could be the second student mentioned as "half white." ABC 18.3.1, v.2: 205.

76. "A dividend of groceries be made for the creek" referred to the missionary assistants and laborers who lived in another house nearer the creek. Br. Conger and his family earlier vacated this house; Frederick Ellsworth now occupied it. The missionaries divided the food supplies proportionally between the families at the main house and those residing in the house near the creek.

77. Fox Taylor and brother Richard Taylor were the sons of Jennie Walker and Charles Fox-Taylor. Charles and his mother emigrated to America from Scotland and settled near the Cherokee Nation where Charles later married Jennie Walker, a granddaughter of the beloved woman, Nancy Ward. Therefore, Fox Taylor and Richard Taylor were Nancy Ward's great-grandsons. Starr, *The History of the Cherokee Indians*, 350.

78. The man named Tailor can be identified as Richard Taylor by cross-referencing the *BJ* entry of December 9, 1822 where the brethren referred to the men's help and providing the use of their wagons: this time the missionary wrote of Mr. R. Taylor who could be Richard Taylor. Mr. Timberlake could possibly be Richard Timberlake who was granted under the treaty of February 27, 1819, a reserve of land where he resided within the chartered limits of Tennessee Territory. Timberlake received a fee-simple reserve because as head of a Cherokee family he was "believed to be a person of industry and capable of managing their property with discretion." Other Cherokee heads of households who received this type of fee-simple reserve were Edward Gunter, Fox Taylor, Elizabeth Lowrey widow of John Lowrey, George Lowrey, John Benge, and Richard Taylor mentioned above. Hampton, *Cherokee Reserves*, 13; McLoughlin, "Experiment in Cherokee Citizenship, 1817–1829," in *Cherokee Ghost Dance*, 158.

79. See *BJ* for June 14 and June 22, 1822.

80. This chief could be either John Beamer or Thomas Pettit with whom the missionaries were quite friendly, or the chief could

possibly be Shoe Boots, who in early 1823 was also inquiring about a school at Hightower. See *BJ* for April 12, 1823. Chamberlin visited Beamer and Pettit in May 1822 on an evangelizing tour in that neighborhood. He discussed with both chiefs the possibility of putting up a blacksmith shop and a school at Hightower. Chamberlin, "Private Journal," ABC 18.3.1, v.3: 25.

81. Boudinot and Ridge, former Brainerd students, returned from the Foreign Mission School in Cornwall, Connecticut after having received a higher education at that school. Rev. Reynolds Bascom was on his way to serve as a missionary to Indians; Adin D. Gibbs was on his way to the Choctaw Nation. Gibbs had also attended the Foreign Mission School. The "Ninth Annual Report" said of Gibbs that he was:

> one of our Aborigines, was born in Pennsylvania, is a descendant of the Delaware tribe, speaks the English language fluently, and impressively, makes laudable progress in study, is a professor of religion, and highly adorns the character of a Christian. He is exemplary in all his conduct; and his character procures him influence among his fellow students. He was religious before he joined the school, which was in April last.

These two men accompanied John Ridge, David Steiner, John Vann, James Fields, and Thomas Basil home from Cornwall, Connecticut. The group sailed south to Charleston; Elias Boudinot also sailed south having left Cornwall approximately at the same time as the previously mentioned students, but Elias traveled on a different ship. The two groups met at Charleston; Bascom and Gibbs accompanied all the former students the remainder of the way to Cherokee country. When James Fields returned to the Cherokee Nation, he was described as being "dressed in fine calf boots, blue pantaloons, silk velvet vest, fine beaver hat, with silver band. His gown was made of red flowered calico, reaching nearly to the ground, with a cape over the shoulders trimmed with a blue fringe." Wilkins, *Cherokee Tragedy*, 123, 134; *First Ten Annual Reports*, 203.

82. "List of Places in the Cherokee Nation" described Wills Valley as 40 or 50 miles long. ABC 18.3.1, v.2: 168.

83. *Tawcheeche* (also spelled *Tawcheechy* and *Darcheechee*) and Kapooly were two students who had been educated at the Foreign Mission School and now returned to work in the Cherokee Nation. *Tawcheeche*, given the white man's name David Steiner, had first been educated at Springplace under John Gambold and subsequently was educated at Cornwall. Numerous references to this Cherokee student

are found in the "Moravian Mission Diary" where his name was spelled Dazizi. Tawcheeche's (Dazizi's) religious nature and also his relationship with his father, Tiger, and mother are shown in Moravian entries such as: "In the evening, his [Tiger's] son Dazizi usually entertained him with translations of a few historical pieces from the bible; the father showed great pleasure at this." An entry for December 1, 1816 stated that "Dazizi talked with them the entire evening about the story of the dear Savior who gave His life for all men, what He did, what stance He took." Other entries show how he spoke out against Indians drinking alcohol. Even though he was educated at Springplace, he never joined the church there because they refused to admit him (the Moravians depended on the "lot" in order to make decisions such as church membership, and the answer repeatedly came up "no" in reference to his admission), so he joined the Brainerd church.

Kapooly (also spelled Kapooley) came from the Sandwich Islands (Hawaii). McClinton, "Moravian Mission," 318, 326, 330, 353, 381, 411, 428, 438, 491, 535; Tracy, "History," 108; Walker, *Torchlights*, 157; Wilkins, *Cherokee Tragedy*, 119–121; Hoyt, Butrick, Hall, Chamberlin to Worcester, October 6, 1818, ABC 18.3.1, v.2: 118.

84. Thomas Basil, another former Brainerd student, left the Cherokee Nation to be further educated at the Foreign Mission School. His Cherokee name was *Tautsoowah*, but the F.M.S. named him Thomas Basil in honor of Deacon Thomas Basil of Lansingburg, New York. After returning to the Cherokee country, the newly educated Basil often acted as an interpreter. After his education at Cornwall, the missionaries had hoped Basil would go among his people and spread the gospel, but in later life he forsook religion. Instead, he became a blacksmith. Walker, *Torchlights*, 157.

85. John Beamer, a wealthy Cherokee Chief, at first supported the missionary effort and asked for a school in his area; he joined the mission church established at Hightower, but by 1827 he left the church because of discontent over the church preaching against Cherokee customs such as conjuring, ballplay, and dancing. McLoughlin, *Cherokees and Missionaries*, 227–228.

86. Paul Kutsche identifies this chief as Daniel McCoy, although Daniel's brother, Alexander McCoy, the clerk of the Cherokee Council, had been a visitor at Brainerd on other occasions. Furthermore, William Chamberlin had been to Willstown from December 7 to 11, and talked with Mr. McCoy, as well as with Mr.

[George] Lowrey, the Spirit, Turtle Fields, and others about the idea of a school at Willstown where the parents would furnish provisions for their own children. It is quite possible that this Mr. McCoy to whom Chamberlin spoke was Alexander McCoy who lived one mile from Lowrey. Chamberlin had spent time with Alexander McCoy in June 1822 when Chamberlin performed a marriage ceremony for Mr. Jones and widow Peggy Stevens at Alexander McCoy's home. Alexander McCoy also acted as interpreter for Chamberlin on occasion. See *BJ* November 11, 1823. Kutsche, *A Guide to Cherokee Documents*, 161, 507; Chamberlin, "Private Journal," June 19, 1822 and December 10, 1822, ABC 18.3.1, v. 3: 26, 30.

87. The Cherokees, who culturally were brought up with the quality of hospitality and generosity, felt that once the missionaries had given the clothes to them, the clothes were theirs to keep.

88. John (George) Vann, the son of James Vann, attended the Moravian school. The "Moravian Mission Diary" of November 5, 1816 recorded that "Around evening Joseph Vann came and asked would we take his brother John, around eleven years old, into the school. Since he was our former pupil and future neighbor, we could not refuse." John attended the F.M.S. at Cornwall from 1820 to 1822. As the half-brother of Joseph Vann (known as "Rich Joe"), John was less well-known than Joseph. When Joseph Vann found that John was desirous of attending Cornwall, Joseph "furnished him with a horse & $100 to bear his expenses .... John is a sober studious youth, of good moral character...." Stand Watie, the brother of Elias Boudinot, signed the 1835 Treaty of New Echota and in 1839 was a target for murder along with the Ridges and Boudinot, but Stand Watie escaped the attempt. After the removal of the Cherokees, Watie served as leader of the Treaty Party which stood in opposition to John Ross' faction. As a Confederate General during the Civil War, Watie carries the fame of being the last Confederate general to surrender. For the Vann family story see de Baillou, "The Chief Vann House," *Early Georgia* 3–11. For the life story of General Stand Watie see Kenny A. Franks' book, *Stand Watie and the Agony of the Cherokee Nation* (Memphis: Memphis State University, 1979). Also "The Moravian Mission Diary," contains many entries concerning the time when Stand Watie was a student at Springplace. Hoyt, Butrick, Hall, Chamberlin to Worcester, October 6, 1818, ABC 18.3.1, v.2: 118; McClinton, "The Moravian Mission," 436; Wilkins, *Cherokee Tragedy*, 119; Fries, *Records of the Moravians in North Carolina*, 8: 3792.

1. Numbers 23:23.

2. Possibly the journalist used the term "safe gate," to refer to the mill's safeguard, a strong stone wall at the side of a brook which guarded and protected the mill if flood water surged. The "floom" was the flume, or sluice, a passage for water which had a gate to control the flow of water. Rawson, *Little Old Mills*, 101, 106.

3. The dependence of the mission's neighbors on the grist mill gives some indication of how acculturated the Cherokees had become. Traditionally Cherokees pounded corn with a wooden mortar and pestle. For a detailed account of the Cherokee's traditional way of preparing corn see Hudson, *The Southeastern Indians*, 302–307 and Adair, *History of the American Indians*, 437. Also see Joan Greene and H.F. Robinson, "Maize Was Our Life: A History of Cherokee Corn," *Journal of Cherokee Studies* 11 (Spring, 1986): 40–49.

4. The Cherokee leaders had resolved in October 1822 not to sell land or even treat on the subject. Before Meigs died, the leaders wrote to him saying they were "determinedly opposed to disposing of one foot of land and therefore have determined not to meet any commissioners on the subject of Treaty for land." Commissioners James Meriwether and Duncan G. Campbell came to the Cherokee Nation for a meeting set for January 15, 1823, even though Meigs had warned them of the determined "no" to any meeting to treat. "Resolution" signed by more than 50 Cherokee leaders, New Town, October 23, 1822, M-208, reel 9; John Ross, Pathkiller, Going Snake, [Chickaulchse?], and Major Ridge to Meigs, October 26, 1822, M-208, reel 9; Meriwether and Campbell to Meigs, November 22, 1822, M-208, reel 9.

5. Words in brackets per *MH* 18 (June 1823): 171. Gov. Clark was John Clark.

6. There was some anti-mission sentiment among the Choctaws; after 1821 Robert Cole, the speaker and leader of the Choctaws, gave harsh criticism of the mission schools. He criticized the curriculum, the manual labor expected of the children, and the child-rearing at the school. He also complained that the Eliot school was in session only a few hours a day. Cyrus Kingsbury, organized more day schools in the Choctaw Nation instead of depending on the large, permanent boarding schools such as Brainerd. Other Choctaw leaders, though, were supportive of the missionaries' presence in the Choctaw Nation

and requested additional schools in their districts. Besides the isolated incident of anti-mission sentiment among the Choctaws, the Creeks were also prejudiced against white man's institutions, so missionaries were not as welcomed in the Creek Nation as in the Cherokee Nation. In 1822, the Baptists received permission from a Creek chief to establish a mission among the Creeks, but permission was for a school, not for preaching, because the Creeks were prejudiced "against white man's institutions" still clinging to their traditions and customs. Kidwell, *Choctaws and Missionaries*, 54–55, 65; Angie Debo, *The Road to Disappearance* (Norman: University of Oklahoma Press, 1941), 84–85.

7. In the early nineteenth century pleurisy was defined as a condition resulting from exposure to cold causing inflammatory problems of the lungs. The symptoms were acute pain in the side and a cough. Hooper, *Lexicon-Medicum*, 700–701.

8. Identification of state per *MH* 18 (June 1823): 172n.

9. This passage illustrates an example of the missionaries' ethnocentric attitude because they felt their New England style hat was preferable over the Cherokee traditional turban.

10. Susannah Brown was the widow of Catharine's brother, John Brown who had died February 2, 1822.

11. Cornelius Hoyt was the youngest child of Ard and Esther Hoyt. He moved with his family to Willstown and then attended Yale College and became a pastor of churches in Ohio. He also was a professor of mathematics at Reform College of Iberia where he served as the preacher. In 1866 Cornelius wrote a lengthy biographical sketch of Ard Hoyt which outlined his father's early life, Ard's missionary years, and a touching account of his father's death at the Willstown mission. See Hoyt, *A Genealogical History of the Hoyt Family*, 255–269 for Cornelius' sketch.

12. Elias Boudinot's two sisters who attended the school were Nancy and Polly, although Dale and Litton listed Boudinot as having four sisters: Nancy, Mary Ann, Elizabeth, and Susan. The Brainerd School records indicated that Nancy had attended school one year, read in the Testament, was 17 to 18 years old, amiable, and willing to learn. The records indicated that Polly was 10 years old, could read somewhat, had attended school one year, and was "promising." "School for Girls, March 31, 1824," ABC 18.3.1, v.2: 207–208; Edward Everett Dale and Gaston Litton, eds., *Cherokee Cavaliers: Forty Years of Cherokee History As Told in the Correspondence of the Ridge-Watie-*

Boudinot Family (Norman: University of Oklahoma Press, 1939), Genealogy Chart.

13. This student's benefactor was the periodical by the name of *Boston Recorder*, and the student was so named after his benefactor.

14. See *BJ* entry for March 4, 1823.

15. Several people wrote the journal for the remainder of 1823; Ard Hoyt wrote the portion for July 30 to August 12 and September 1 to November 30. The other journalists cannot be identified.

16. See also *BJ* entry for February 8, 1823, for more information on John Crawfish, who apparently went by several names: Wicked Jack, Jack Wicket, and Jack or John Crawfish.

17. The journalist was referring to Daniel Butrick who left on February 4, 1823, and toured the Valley Towns and the Baptist Mission Station. He also visited John Arch's mother. Butrick, "Missionary Tour to the Valley Towns," ABC 18.3.1, v.3: 148–150.

18. In his journal, Butrick identified the head chief as The Rabbit and brother to *Tsu li o wu*. ABC 18.3.1, v.3: 148.

19. According to other published sources, this missionary's first name was Anson. From Hartford, Connecticut, he went to the Choctaw Mission at Emmaus (Mississippi) working there from May 1823 to June 1824. He then moved on and worked at Hachah (Mississippi) from June 1824 to May of 1826, later working at the Mayhew Mission from April 1827 to May 1831. Gleason married Bethiah W. Tracy, born 1803 in Lebanon, Connecticut. Tracy, "History," 339: Kidwell, *Choctaw and Missionaries*, 125 map.

20. A friend of the missionaries, Alexander McCoy was Clerk of the Cherokee Council. See *BJ*, April 1, 1823. The marriage to Sarah Hicks was his second; he previously was married to Aky Gunter. Residing near Chickamauga, he also owned a ferry boat. McCoy was active in the Cherokee government before and after the removal. Moulton, *Papers of John Ross*, 2: 727.

21. Margaret Ross was John Ross' sister, the second youngest child of Daniel and Mollie Ross. Elijah Hicks was Charles Hicks' son. Traditional marriages were far more informal and normally involved an exchange of corn from the bride and meat from the groom. Starr, *The History of the Cherokee Indians*, 410, 599; Walker, *Torchlights*, 198; Hudson, *The Southeastern Indians*, 198.

22. See *BJ* entry for January 1, 1819 and note.

23. The "half brother to David and Catharine Brown" was Walter Webber, a merchant with a store near the Dwight Mission among the

Western Cherokees. Webber was a trader and chief who read, wrote, and spoke English. In all four chiefs went to Washington City: Black Fox, Walter Webber, John Rogers, and John McLamore. Webber died April 11, 1834, of consumption, the same disease which took siblings Catharine, David, and John. Webber Falls in the Arkansas River derived its name from Walter Webber. Foreman, *Indians and Pioneers*, 255, 264 note; Carselowey, *Cherokee Pioneers* (Adair, OK: J.M. Carselowey, 1961), 10.

24. See *BJ* for July 6, 1822 and March 4, 1823.

25. A slight rewording of Isaiah 32:15.

26. Pathkiller could be referring to his nephew Charles, who was murdered by a man named Gabriel Morris "in the Big Ca near the Chocktaw Nation" supposedly because Charles sat on Morris' horse. Morris said he acted in "self defense," that he "had no other alternative, but to kill or be killed" because Charles had struck out at him with a Tomahawk, so Morris repeatedly struck at Charles' with a piece of wood; Charles died eight days later. Pathkiller to Hicks, June 24, 1821, M-208, reel 9; Letter by Ezekiel Nash and John Halbart, June 21, 1821, M-208, reel 9.

27. The two students who left for the Foreign Mission School were David Carter and John Sanders. Carter or *Tawah* attended the Cornwall School for one year and then was dismissed for unknown reasons. In later life he became an influential leader holding such positions as editor of the *Cherokee Advocate*, Judge of the Cherokee Supreme Court, and superintendent of schools. John Sanders attended the Cornwall School until 1824, lived in the Cherokee Nation until 1837, and moved west before the Trail of Tears. Walker, *Torchlights*, 157–158; Carselowey, *Cherokee Pioneers*, 56.

28. The present agent was Joseph McMinn. (See note about McMinn in *BJ* entry for May 15, 1818.) The "former agent" referred to Return Jonathan Meigs who died in January 1823.

29. Moody Hall in his journal from the Taloney Mission also wrote of these two missionaries when they stopped at the Taloney Mission. Monroe, near McIntoshville, the Chickasaw Agency, and the Natchez Trace, was the American Board mission station in the Chickasaw Nation established in 1821. Mayhew was one of the Choctaw missions; for more information see *BJ* entry for April 15, 1820. Hall, "Journal," June 20, 1823, ABC 18.3.1, v.3: 243; Gibson, *The Chickasaws*, 110.

30. Although the particular youth mentioned in this *BJ* passage

cannot be identified, the Sanders family (consisting of brothers George, Alexander, John, Andrew, and David) was a large family who lived in the vicinity of Taloney. Several brothers became converts at Taloney and sent many children to the school there. While at the Taloney mission Jeremiah Evarts wrote of one Sanders brother:

> Toward evening Mr. George Sanders came in. He is one of several brothers, half-breeds, who have become rich. He early began to make money; & is now said to have bushels of silver. He has been known to lend $1000 or $2000 at a time, to persons in whom he can place confidence. Yet his own James did not know the alphabet, when Mr. Hall came here (a youth of 17 years.) Mr. John Sanders is said to keep a very good house of entertainment. All the brothers are neighbors, & are very friendly to Mr. Hall.

Evarts continued: "Mr. Andrew Sanders, his wife, & her sister, called to see me at the school house. . . . His father was a soldier from New Hampshire, in the Revolutionary army, who deserted, settled here, & married an Indian woman. He died several years ago, & left many descendants." Historian Emmet Starr recorded that George's father's name was either Michael or Mitchell, that he was an Englishman who married Susannah, a Cherokee of the Bird clan. George Sanders was one of the signers of the treaty of July 8, 1817, and helped to "lay off" the Cherokee capital at New Echota.

The following excerpt from a Moody Hall letter shows how the Sanders family changed from opposing the missionary effort to supporting the school and religious efforts at Taloney. Hall wrote that "Mr. Alex Sanders [is] asking questions & [is] an altered man, moving to within two miles of the school expressly for the purpose of sending all his children to school." Chamberlin wrote of Alexander Sanders:

> he is the man who killed [James] Vann, & assisted in killing Doublehead. He has always spread terror where ever he went. He is the Africaner of the Cherokee Nation. But the Spirit of God is now evidently working with him . . . he appears very anxious to receive instruction. He says he has been a great enemy to the mission, but is now sorry for it he did not then know any better.

Mr. John Sanders also expressed an interest in what the missionaries taught. Hall wrote of John Sanders that Sanders:

> had of late thought much on religious things. This man keeps a noted publick house, half a mile [distant?] and in consequence

of his frequent intercourse with wicked white men, had contracted strong prejudices against religion & had spoken much against the work when it first began here. But now his heart is touched & his ears open to instruction. Last evening I appointed a meeting when a great number met. Five brothers (the Sanders) were present. Having opened the meeting, I gave liberty for any one to speak on the subject of our meeting who wished. Br. Andrew first spoke with much animation & after him all the rest spoke in their turn, in their own language. One said. 'Our friend Mr. H. has been here a long time telling us of the good things, & trying to do us good, but instead of believing him we believed the wicked white men—but we now know that he is our friend & tells us the truth, and it is time for us all to leave our bad ways, walk in that good way which he tells and try to prepare for a better world.' O what has God wrought. A few months ago all these men would occasionally attend meetings with as little apparent concern as the beast that perish. Now they are all attentive.
Evarts, "Memoranda," May 2, 1822, ABC 18.3.1, v.2: 154; Chamberlin, "Private Journal," ABC 18.3.1, v.3: 25; Hall to Evarts, July 22, 1822, ABC 18.3.1, v.3: 208; Starr, *History of the Cherokee Indians*, 374, 473; Starr, *Old Cherokee Families*, 1: 119.

31. Mr. McChord might have been either Joseph or James McCord who lived in Moulton in the northeast part of Lawrence County, Alabama. Joseph McCord was a member of the Alabama State Legislature in 1824; his brother James served in the same capacity in 1835. They were inn keepers in Alabama. James Edmonds Saunders, *Early Settlers of Alabama* (1899; reprint, Greenville, S.C.: Southern Historical Press, 1977), 116.

32. Malachi 3:7.

33. Catharine Brown, Brainerd Mission's "first fruits of their labor" and the promising young woman who went to Creek Path to teach at that mission station, died on July 18, 1823, just past 6 A.M. of "consumption." It is odd that the journalist did not record this event in the journal since it was quite common for the writer to record events of either joy or sorrow such as when the *BJ* recorded the death of Catharine's brother, John Brown. A complete story of Catharine Brown's life is found in the *Memoir of Catharine Brown, a Christian Indian, of the Cherokee Nation* by Rev. Rufus Anderson. Also see Walker, *Torchlights to the Cherokees* for an entire chapter devoted to

this Cherokee woman. Anderson, *Memoir*, 111.

34. Charles Fields could be the son of John Fields and Elizabeth Wickett Fields. Noisy Waters, from Turnip Mountain, later acted as an interpreter for John Elsworth at the Haweis-Turnip Mountain Mission. Starr, *History of the Cherokee Indians*, 309; Elsworth to Evarts, August 25, 1823, ABC 18.3.1, v. 3: 312.

35. This was the wedding of Sylvester Ellis and Sarah Hoyt. On May 26, 1823, Ard Hoyt wrote to Jeremiah Evarts asking permission for Sarah and Sylvester to marry. They were the teachers at the school at this time. *MH* 20 (January, 1824): 2; Walker, *Torchlights*, 52; Tracy, "History," 336; Hoyt, *Genealogical History of the Hoyt Family*, 417; Hoyt to Evarts, May 22, 1823, ABC 18.3.1, v.3: 99; "List."

36. New Town was New Echota, the Cherokee capital. The Council House, Supreme Court, the printing office of the *Cherokee Phoenix*, the post office, and the residences of Elias Boudinot and Alexander McCoy were located here.

37. Nathan Pollard's *Evangelical and Literary Magazine,* a missionary and religious magazine out of Richmond, Virginia, published literary and philosophical items, book reviews, poetry, and historical articles. The *Family Visitor*, also a magazine published in Richmond, Virginia by Nathan Pollard, usually was thought of in later years as a temperance weekly. The *Religious Remembrancer* was a Presbyterian family newspaper which later became the *Christian Observer*. The *Religious Intelligencer*, published between 1816 and 1837 in New Haven by Nathan Whiting, contained "the principal transactions of various Bible and missionary societies" and "progress reports of missions to the American Indians." The *Boston Recorder*, published in Boston by Nathaniel Willis from 1817 to 1824, was a Congregationalist magazine printing religious news of Bible societies, missionary societies, tract societies, and missionary work. Hoornstra and Heath, eds., *American Periodicals, 1741–1800: An Index to the Microfilm Collections*, 57–58, 60, 67–68, 119–120, 218.

38. Ann Porter married Eliphalet Wheeler Gilbert, a former Brainerd student. ABC 18.3.1, v. 2: 189.

39. General Calvin Jones had visited the Brainerd Mission prior to 1823, for John Ross wrote a letter to Calvin Jones stating:

> The Cherokee Nation owes much to your visit and description
> of the mission school at Brainerd .... I trust the period is not far
> distant when the Cherokees will evince to the world, that
> American Indians, are capable of civilization and improve-

ment of the highest degree—time and good management will realize this fact.

During his lifetime Calvin Jones was a physician who lived in Johnston County, North Carolina; a major general of the North Carolina Militia, 7th Division during the War of 1812; a trustee of the University of North Carolina; a chief of police in Raleigh; and a trustee of Raleigh Academy; as well as founding a newspaper in Raleigh. By 1832 he retired to a 30,000 acre estate in Tennessee. Moulton, *Papers of Chief John Ross*, Ross to Jones, July 3, 1819, 1: 36–37, 2: 743; Malone, ed. *Dictionary of American Biography*, vol. 5, pt. 2: 163.

40. Matthew 18:20: For where two or three are gathered together in my name, there am I in the midst of them.

41. Paraphrase of Job 5:6.

42. At the October 1823 Cherokee Council, the United States government represented by Commissioners Duncan G. Campbell and James Meriwether, tried to persuade the Cherokees to cede more land. Indian Agent Joseph McMinn also appeared before the Cherokee Council. Georgia pressured the United States to make good on the Compact of 1802, under which Georgia claimed all the land in Western Georgia now held by the Cherokees. Those representing Georgia and the United States tried various forms of manipulating, threatening, and bribery upon the Cherokees. The Cherokee Council did not give in to the pressure. Major Ridge articulated the sentiments: "Not one more foot of land to the whites." Letters and "Journal of Proceeding of the Commissioners," October 1823, M-208, reel 9; Wilkins, *Cherokee Tragedy*, 143–146; Moulton, *John Ross*, 24–25.

43. Concerning the Cherokees' proposed national free school which the October 1, 1823 council would consider, Hoyt wrote that the Council wishes

to know if we will engage to furnish a suitable person to superintend sd school (should one be established) who would be ready to enter on the charge a year from next fall—also whether we would be willing to employ one or two of the young men from Cornwall, now members of this church, as teacher in sd school at our expense. The principal teacher to be paid by the nation .... The idea of proposing a school of this kind to be established at Newtown I think originated in conversation which was held with some of the chiefs on the subject of a Classical ~~& Theological~~ school to be established at Brainerd, as mentioned in my letter of June 4th. I believe the proposers of the new school have not yet determined whether it shall be of higher order, or to admit those who have recvd no education, as we have hitherto done at this place. I understand Mr. Ross is for the former & Mr. Hicks the latter, and most members favored the idea of this kind of school.

Actually the national school had been in the plans since the treaty of 1819, but the government failed to follow through on setting aside a tract of land in the proper manner. For several years the council discussed the matter and opinion was divided as to secondary or elementary level teaching. The Cherokees waited a long time to have their own school; finally in the 1850's the Cherokee Male and Female Seminaries were established in Tahlequah, Indian Territory. Hoyt to Evarts, August 7, 1823, ABC 18.3.1, v.3: 103; Hoyt to Evarts, August 19, 1823, ABC 18.3.1, v. 3: 104; McLoughlin, *Cherokee Renascence*, 314–315; Malone, *Cherokees of the Old South*, 157;

44. The delegation consisted of Major Ridge, John Ross, George Lowrey, and Elijah Hicks. The delegation's mission was to ask the United States government to do away with the Compact of 1802, to ask for the removal of McMinn as Indian Agent, to demand payment promised to the Cherokees since 1804 for land known as "The Wafford Settlement," to seek relocation of the Cherokee Agency, and to seek help in collecting taxes on white traders.

It was while this delegation was in Washington that a humorous incident occurred at Tennison's Hotel regarding George Lowrey. The Cherokee delegation was eating dinner one night. John Ross' nephew recalled the incident:

Major Lowrey possessed an eminent degree of wit and quick retort so common among the Cherokees of the older stamp, which gave so much zest to their social life, and he could be sarcastic when the occasion required. It is related of him that on one occasion, when at the city of Washington as a delegate, he listened to a speech by a member in one of the halls of Congress which was unsparing in denunciation and invictive against the Indians, charging them, among other things, with living on roots, wild herbage and disgusting reptiles. Lowrey boarded at the same hotel with the speaker and many other members of congress, and at dinner called repeatedly in a loud voice to the waiter to bring him some of those 'roots' (a dish of sweet potatoes), each time taking a small one to be able to protract the calling, and remarked to his fellow boarders, 'We

Indians are very fond of roots; these are the kind of roots we live on.' This, as intended, directed the general laugh against the orator of the morning.

Quoted in Mrs. William P. Ross, *Life and Times of Honorable William P. Ross* (Fort Smith, Arkansas: Weldon & Williams Printers, 1893) from an article by William P. Ross, "Major George Lowrey, Formerly Assistant Principal Chief of the Cherokee Nation," *Indian Journal*, (August 17, 1876): 9.

45. The journal writer's account of the bribery is a good rendition, but the names of those involved must be added to complete the story. The head man of the Creek Nation was General William McIntosh who along with six or seven Creek chiefs attended the meeting of the Cherokee leaders and Commissioners Duncan Campbell and James Meriwether. McIntosh's position in the Creek Nation was roughly on the same stature as the Cherokee Chief Major Ridge. The bribes were extended to John Ross, Alexander McCoy, and Charles Hicks. In a letter to John Ross dated October 21, 1823, at Newtown (New Echota) William McIntosh wrote:

> I am going to inform you a few lines as a friend. I want you to give me your opinion about the treaty whether the chiefs will be willing or not. If the chiefs feel disposed to let the United States have the land part of it, I want you to let me know. I will make the United States commissioners give you two thousand dollars. A. McCoy the same and Charles Hick $3000 for present, and nobody shall know it . . .

He included a footnote to the letter saying: "the whole amount is $12000. You can divide among your friends. exclusive $7000." John Ross read this letter to the Council on October 24 in the presence of McIntosh. Pathkiller and twenty-eight members of the Cherokee General Council then wrote a letter to the head men of the Creek Nation saying that McIntosh was no longer welcome in the Cherokee Councils, and they "suggest a careful watch over him." After an address by Major Ridge denouncing McIntosh, the Creek chief rode away as fast as he could, and the U.S. Commissioners left the Council in a hurry. McIntosh had been offered $7,000.00 by the commissioners from Georgia for his part in the secret negotiations. After the incident, the Cherokee Council decided to send a delegation to Washington. (See *BJ* for November 7, 1823 and note.) Later in the Creek Nation negotiations took place between the United States and the Creek Nation. Under pressure from the State of Georgia, William McIntosh signed a treaty on behalf of the Creek Nation agreeing to complete removal of the Creek Nation. As a consequence, the Creek National Council declared that McIntosh was a traitor and ordered his execution for signing the treaty; the execution was a foreshadow of what would happen thirteen years later when the Ridge family signed the treaty for Cherokee removal. U.S. Commissioners to Cherokee Chiefs, Cherokee Chiefs to McMinn and Commissioners, October 1823, M-208, reel 9; Moulton, *The Papers of Chief John Ross*, 1: 53–55; Griffith, *McIntosh and Weatherford*, 213–217, 232–254; Michael D. Green, *The Politics of Indian Removal* (Lincoln: University of Nebraska Press, 1982), 75–97; Wilkins, *Cherokee Tragedy*, 144–146; Moulton, *John Ross*, 25; Janet and David G. Campbell, "The McIntosh Family Among the Cherokees," *Journal of Cherokee Studies* 5 (Spring, 1980): 7–9.

46. The five travelers went to various American Board missions in the Choctaw Nation. Br. Gage and wife were David Gage and Betsy Putnam Gage from Lyndeborough, New Hampshire, on their way to the Emmaus Mission in Southeast Mississippi where they served from June 1824 to January 1833 as assistant missionaries. Br. Bliss was Ebenezer Bliss from Clarkson, New York, born in Springfield, Massachusetts. He served at the Goshen Mission to the Choctaws from May 1824 to May 1831. Lucy Hutchinson from Lyndeborough, New Hampshire, served first at Brainerd for a short time before moving onto the Mayhew Mission; in 1825 she married Zechariah Howes who was serving at the Eliot Mission. The Gages and the Howes were assistant missionaries. Philena Thatcher, born in 1804 in Hartford, Pennsylvania, worked at the Eliot Mission starting in December 1823. In 1831 she married Ebenezer Hotchkin from Richmond, Massachusetts, who was a missionary at Goshen, Clear Creek, and Good Water. Tracy, "History," 338–339.

47. Born in 1795, David Wright from Newport, New Hampshire, and wife, Lucinda Washburn Wright from Montpelier, Vermont, born 1802, served as assistant missionaries at a mission named Aiikhunnuh established in 1824. Mr. Moseley was Samuel Moseley from Montpelier, Vermont, born on September 27, 1790, at Mansfield, Connecticut. As a graduate of Andover, he went into the Choctaw Nation as a full missionary. He served at Mayhew just a short time, from December 12, 1823, until his death on September 11, 1824. Mrs. Moseley (Sarah Curtis born June 1, 1793, at Hanover, New Hampshire) was released from her missionary activities in March 1828. Tracy, "History," 338–339.

48. Jeremiah Evarts made another trip to the Brainerd Mission in April 1824; see Epilogue.

49. These new missionaries had assignments at various Cherokee missions. William Holland, born in Belchertown, Massachusetts, February 7, 1798, married Electa Hopkins, born in Hanover, New Hampshire, May 9, 1797. They worked at Brainerd from November 1823 to November 1824. Then they moved to the new mission at Candy's Creek where Holland functioned as teacher and farmer. See William R. Snell, "Candy's Creek Mission Station 1824–1837," *Journal of Cherokee Studies* 4 (Summer, 1979). Born in 1793, Josiah Hemmingway from Windsor, Massachusetts, worked at Brainerd as a farmer until 1826 and then moved to the Carmel Mission (Taloney). Born May 4, 1792, Sophia Sawyer, from Rindge, New Hampshire, taught the girls' school at Brainerd from 1823 to 1829, then moved to New Echota, and later to a school at Running Water. In 1837 she moved west before the removal. There she resided with John Ridge's family and taught school independently. For more information on Sophia Sawyer's work among the Cherokees, see Kimberly C. Macenczak, "Sophia Sawyer, Native American Advocate: A Case Study in Nineteenth Century Cherokee Education," *Journal of Cherokee Studies* 16 (1991): 26–37. Tracy, "History," 336–337; Walker, *Torchlights*, 52–53.

50. Ross was part of the delegation of four influential Cherokees who journeyed to Washington to lay their grievances before President Monroe. See *BJ* for November 11, 1823, and note.

51. See *BJ* for June 25, 1823, and note about Andrew Sanders.

52. Darius Hoyt was preparing to leave for Maryville to attend school at the Southen and Western Theological Seminary which later became Maryville College. Earlier Ard Hoyt had written the American Board about the idea of Darius attending college:

> My son Darius . . . mentioned his earnest desire to study with a view to the ministry—or some other employment in the missions for which a more enlarged education would be necessary—but to be prepared to preach the gospel to this people under the direction of the mission is the great object of his desire. Considering his industrious & studious turn, & readiness to retain & communicate what he has learned, his acquaintance (so far as I know) all recommend this course— thinking it probable that you would approve of it, & having no pecuniary resources at my command to assist him at this time, I wrote Mr. Anderson a few lines of enquiry respecting the

seminary .... it appears by his answer that he supposed my son was ready to go at any time .... that he was to bring books, Latin grammar, Dictionary &c boarding—is at $1.50 per week, tuition nothing.

Darius was licensed to preach in March 1827 and ordained soon after. He died in August 1837 at age 32. Hoyt to J. Evarts, July 10, 1823, ABC 18.3.1, v.3: 102; Hoyt, *A Genealogical History of the Hoyt Family*, 418.

53. Louisa Battelle (Botell) came to Brainerd on September 20, 1819, at the age of 10, so she was fourteen years old at the time of her death. "Catalogue."

Notes for Epilogue

1. *MH* 20 (May, 1824): 168.

2. For documents describing this trip, see Jeremiah Evart's letters to Rufus Anderson and Henry Hill dated December 15, 1823 to May 3, 1824, ABC: 11, v.1: 243–314.

3. *MH* 20 (August 1824): 248–249.

4. Ibid.

5. For further information on Sequoyah see Grant Foreman, *Sequoyah*, (Norman: University of Oklahoma Press, 1938); Perdue, "The Sequoyah Syllabary and Cultural Revitalization"; and Major George Lowrey, "Notable Persons in Cherokee History: Sequoyah, or George Gist," *Journal of Cherokee Studies* 1 (Fall, 1977): 385–393.

6. For Boudinot's writings as editor of the *Cherokee Phoenix* see Theda Perdue, ed., *Cherokee Editor: The Writings of Elias Boudinot*.

7. For the life of Samuel Austin Worcester see Althea Bass, *Cherokee Messenger*, with Introduction by William L. Anderson (Norman: University of Oklahoma Press, 1996).

8. For information about David Brown's work as translator see Althea Bass, *Cherokee Messenger* and Higginbotham, "The Creek Path Mission," 72–86.

9. Chamberlin's and Butrick's journals are found in the American Board Papers, ABC 18.3.1, v.3.

10. John Arch's work as interpreter and teacher in the Cherokee Nation is found in detail in the "Memoir of John Arch, A Young Cherokee Man."

11. McLoughlin, *Cherokees and Missionaries*, 224.

12. For the story of the Creeks' land cessions and removal see, Michael D. Green, *The Politics of Indian Removal: Creek Government and*

Society in Crisis, and Angie Debo, *The Road to Disappearance.*

13. Robert V. Remini, *The Legacy of Andrew Jackson: Essays on Democracy Indian Removal, and Slavery* (Baton Rogue: Louisiana State University Press, 1988), 48–49.

14. See Prucha, ed., *Cherokee Removal: The "William Penn" Essays and other Writings* .

15. See Perdue and Green, eds., *The Cherokee Removal;* and Remini, *Legacy* for information on the Indian Removal Bill.

16. Remini, *Legacy*, 69.

17. Walker, *Torchlights*, 275.

18. Remini, *Legacy*, 69.

19. Malone, *Cherokees of the Old South*, 101; Walker, *Torchlights*, 70.

20. Anderson, "Introduction," *Cherokee Removal*, vii.

21. Douglas C. Wilms, "Cherokee Land Use in Georgia Before Removal," in *Cherokee Removal Before and After*, 9–13.

22. Remini, *Legacy*, 74–77; see also Perdue and Green, eds., *The Cherokee Removal*; and Wilkins, *Cherokee Tragedy.*

23. Russell Thornton, "The Demography of the Trail of Tears Period: A New Estimate of Cherokee Population Losses," in *Cherokee Removal: Before and After*, 75–95. For a look at the fluctuations in the Cherokee population as a result of war, disease, the "civilization" pro–gram, and removal, see Russell Thornton, *The Cherokees: A Population History* (Lincoln: University of Nebraska Press, 1990).

24. Higginbotham, "The Creek Path Mission," 72.

25. Roger D. Aycock, *All Roads to Rome* (Roswell, Ga.: W.H. Wolfe Associates, 1981), 23.

26. Walker, *Torchlights*, 69–70.

27. Theda Perdue, "Letters from Brainerd," *Journal of Cherokee Studies* 4 (Winter, 1979): 4; Duane H. King, conversation with transcribers, April 19, 1996.

28. Wilkins, *Cherokee Tragedy*, 329–339.

29. See Butler's letters to David Green, ABC 18.3.1, v. 10: 66–77.

30. "An Illustrated Souvenir Catalog of the Cherokee National Female Seminary, Tahlequah, Indian Territory 1850–1906," *Journal of Cherokee Studies* 10 (Spring, 1985), 119. For an in-depth history and analysis of educating young women at the Cherokee Female Seminary, see Devon A. Mihesuah, *Cultivating the Rosebuds: The Education of Women at the Cherokee Female Seminary, 1851–1909* (Urbana: University of Illinois Press, 1993).

Bibliography

I. Primary Sources
A. Manuscripts:

Papers of the American Board of Commissioners for Foreign Missions, 1811–1919. Archives, Houghton Library, Harvard University.
ABC 1.01   Letters to Domestic Correspondents.
ABC 6   Candidate Department.
ABC 18.3.1, v. 2   Cherokee Mission, previous to September, 1824.
ABC 18.3.1, v. 3   Cherokee Mission, from individual missionaries.
ABC 18.3.1,
  v. 4 & 5   Cherokee Mission, September 1824–1831.
ABC 18.3.3, v. 4   Journal of Daniel Sabin Butrick, 1831.

B. Published Primary Sources:

Adair, James. *The History of the American Indians.* Edited by Samuel Cole Williams. 1775. Reprint. Johnson City, Tenn.: The Watuaga Press, 1930.

Dale, Edward Everett and Gaston L. Litton, eds. *Cherokee Cavaliers: Forty Years of Cherokee History as Told in the Correspondence of the Ridge-Watie-Boudinot Family.* Norman: University of Oklahoma Press, 1995.

First Ten Annual Reports of the American Board of Commissioners for Foreign Missions. Boston: Crocker and Brewster, 1834.

Fries, Adelaide L., trans. and ed. *Records of the Moravians in North Carolina.* Vol. 8. Raleigh, N.C.: The North Carolina Historical Commission, 1968.

Hamilton, Kenneth G., trans. and ed. "Minutes of the Mission Conference Held in Springplace." *The Atlanta Historical Bulletin.* 15 (Winter 1970): 9–87 and (Spring 1971): 31–59.

Hodgson, Adam. *Remarks During a Journey Through North America in the Years 1819, 1820, and 1821.* New York, 1823. Ann Arbor, Mich.: University Microfilms, [n.d.].

Laws of the Cherokee Nation: Adopted by the Council at Various Periods. Printed for the Benefit of the Nation. Tahlequah: Cherokee Advocate Office, 1852; reprinted Wilmington, Del.: Scholarly Resources, Inc., 1973.

Moulton, Gary E., ed. *The Papers of Chief John Ross.* 2 vols. Norman: University of Oklahoma Press, 1985.

Mooney, James. *Myths of the Cherokee and Sacred Formulas of the Cherokees from the 19th and 7th Annual Reports B.A.E.* Reprint. Nashville: Charles and Randy Elder Booksellers, 1982.

Perdue, Theda, ed. *Cherokee Editor: The Writings of Elias Boudinot.* Knoxville: University of Tennessee Press, 1983.

Prucha, Francis P., ed. *Cherokee Removal: The "William Penn" Essays and other Writings of Jeremiah Evarts.* Knoxville: University of Tennessee Press, 1981.

Ross, Mrs. William P. *The Life and Time of the Honorable William P. Ross.* Fort Smith, 1893. New Haven: Research Publications, 1975. Microfilm.

Williams, Samuel Cole, ed. *Early Travels in the Tennessee Country, 1540–1800.* Johnson City, Tenn.: The Watuaga Press, 1928.

Woods, Leonard. "The Grand Theme of the Christian Preacher. A sermon delivered at the Old South Church in Boston, at the Ordination of the Rev. Benjamin B. Wisner, February 21, 1821." Andover: Flagg and Gould, 1821.

C. Newspapers and Periodicals:

"Biography of Our Late Brother Charles Renatus Hicks, Second Principal Chief of the Cherokee Nation." *United Brethren Missionary Intelligencer* 2, no. 1 (1827): 400–402.

Missionary Herald and *The Panoplist*, 1817–1824.

D. United States Government Documents:

American State Papers, Class 2: Indian Affairs. Ed. Walter Lowrie, Walter S. Franklin, and Matthew St. Clair Clarke. 2 vols. Washington, D.C.: Gales and Seaton, 1832, 1834.

National Archives. United States Government. Bureau of Indian Affairs. Records of the Cherokee Indian Agency in Tennessee, 1801–1835. Reference Group 75. Reels 7–9: Correspondence and Miscellaneous Records. Microfilm M-208.

II. Secondary Works
A. Books:

Alderman, Pat. *Nancy Ward, Cherokee Chieftainess and Dragging Canoe, Cherokee-Chickamauga War Chief.* Johnson City, Tenn.: The Overmountain Press, 1990.

Allen, Penelope Johnson. *Leaves from the Family Tree*. Easley, S.C.: Southern Historical Press, 1982.

Anderson, Rufus. *Memoir of Catharine Brown, a Christian Indian of the Cherokee Nation*. Philadelphia: American Sunday School Union, 1832.

Anderson, William L., ed. *Cherokee Removal: Before and After*. Athens: University of Georgia Press, 1991.

Andrew, John A. III. *From Revivals to Removal: Jeremiah Evarts, the Cherokee Nation, and the Search for the Soul of America*. Athens: University of Georgia Press, 1992.

— *Rebuilding the Christian Commonwealth: New England Congregationalists and Foreign Missions, 1800–1830*. Lexington: University of Kentucky Press, 1976.

Armstrong, Zella. *The History of Hamilton County and Chattanooga, Tennessee*. Vol. 1. Chattanooga: The Lookout Publishing Co., 1931.

Awiakta, Marilou. *Selu: Seeking the Corn-Mother's Wisdom*. Golden, Colo.: Fulcrum Publishing, 1993.

Aycock, Roger D. *All Roads to Rome*. Roswell, Ga.: W.H. Wolfe Associates, 1981.

Baker, Jack D., trans. *Cherokee Emigration Rolls, 1817–1835*. Oklahoma City: Baker Publishing Co., 1977.

Barker-Benfield, G.J. and Catherine Clinton, eds. *Portraits of American Women: from Settlement to Present*. New York: St. Martin's Press, 1991.

Bass, Althea. *Cherokee Messenger: A Life of Samuel Austin Worcester*. With Introduction by William L. Anderson. Norman: University of Oklahoma Press, 1996.

Beaver, R. Pierce. *Church, State, and the American Indians*. St. Louis: Concordia Publishing House, 1966.

Beaver, R. Pierce, ed. *Pioneers in Mission*. Grand Rapids: William B. Eerdmans Publishing Co., 1966.

Bell, George Morrison, Sr. *Genealogy of "Old and New Cherokee Indian Families."* Bartlesville, Okla.: G. M. Bell, 1972.

Berkhofer, Robert F., Jr. *Salvation and the Savage: An Analysis of Protestant Missions and American Indian Response, 1787–1862*. Lexington: University of Kentucky Press, 1965.

— *The White Man's Indian: Images of the American Indian from Columbus to the Present*. New York: Alfred A. Knopf, 1978.

Bowden, Henry Warner. *Dictionary of American Religious Biography*. Westport, Conn.: Greenwood Press, 1977.

Brown, John P. *Old Frontiers, the Story of the Cherokee Indians From Earliest Times to the Date of their Removal to the West, 1838.* 1938. Reprint. Salem, N.H.: Ayer Co. Publishers, 1986.

Burns, Inez E. *History of Blount County, Tennessee: From War Trail to Landing Strip, 1795–1955.* Nashville: Benson Printing Co. for The Tennessee Historical Commission, 1957.

Carselowey, James Manford. *Cherokee Notes.* 1960. Reprint. Tulsa: Yesterday Publications, 1980.

— *Cherokee Pioneers.* Adair, Okla.: J.M. Carselowey, 1961.

— *My Journal.* Adair, Okla.: J.M. Carselowey, 1962.

Carter, Samuel III. *Cherokee Sunset: A Nation Betrayed, A Narrative of Travail and Triumph, Persecution and Exile.* Garden City, New York: Doubleday and Co., 1976.

Chase, Marybelle W. trans., *Records of the Cherokee Agency in Tennessee, 1801–1835.* Tulsa: M.W. Chase, 1990.

Church, Leslie F. "Foreword." *The Matthew Henry Commentary.* Grand Rapids: Zondervan Publishing House, 1960.

Craigie, William A. and James R. Hulbert, eds. *A Dictionary of American English on Historical Principles.* Chicago: University of Chicago Press, 1940.

DeRosier, Arthur H., Jr. *The Removal of the Choctaw Indians.* Knoxville: University of Tennessee Press, 1970.

Debo, Angie. *The Road to Disappearance.* Norman: University of Oklahoma Press, 1941.

Douglas, J.D., ed. *New Bible Dictionary.* Wheaton: Tyndale House Publishers, 1982.

East Tennessee History: Reprinted from Goodspeed's History of Tennessee. Reorganized and Indexed by Sam McDowell. Hartfort, Ky.: McDowell Publications, 1978.

Eaton, Rachel Caroline. *John Ross and the Cherokee Indians.* Menasha, Wis.: George Banta Publishing Co., 1914. New Haven: Research Publications, 1975. Microfilm.

Edwards, Jonathan. *The Life of David Brainerd.* Edited by Norman Pettit. Vol. 7 of *The Works of Jonathan Edwards.* New Haven: Yale University Press, 1985.

Fairbank, Alfred J. *The Story of Handwriting: Origins and Development.* New York: Watson-Guptill Publications, 1970.

Fogelson, Raymond D. and Richard N. Adams, eds. *The Anthropology of Power.* New York: Academic Press, 1977.

Foreman, Grant. *The Five Civilized Tribes.* Norman: University of Oklahoma Press, 1934.

— *Indians and Pioneers.* New Haven: Yale University Press, 1930.

— *Indian Removal: The Emigration of the Five Civilized Tribes of Indians.* Norman: University of Oklahoma Press, 1932.

— *Pioneer Days in the Early Southwest.* 1926. Reprint, with an Introduction by Donald E. Worcester, Lincoln: University of Nebraska Press, 1994

— *Sequoyah.* Norman: University of Oklahoma Press, 1938.

Franks, Kenny A. *Stand Watie and the Agony of the Cherokee Nation.* Memphis: Memphis State University, 1979.

Fraser, Walter J., Jr.; R. Frank Saunders, Jr.; and Jon L. Wakelyn, eds. *The Web of Southern Social Relations: Women, Family, and Education.* Athens: University of Georgia Press, 1985.

Gardner, Robert G. *Cherokees and Baptists in Georgia.* Atlanta: Georgia Baptist Historical Society, 1989.

Gearing, Fred O. *Priests and Warriors: Social Structure for Cherokee Politics in the 18th Century.* American Anthropological Association, Memoir 93. Menasha, Wis.: American Anthropological Association, 1962.

Gibson, Arrell. *The Chickasaws.* Norman: University of Oklahoma Press, 1971.

Goff, John H. *Placenames of Georgia: Essays of John H. Goff.* Edited by Francis Lee Utley and Marion R. Hemperly. Athens: University of Georgia Press, 1975.

Govan, Gilbert E. and James W. Livingood. *The Chattanooga Country, 1540–1976.* Knoxville: University of Tennessee Press, 1977.

Gray, Lewis C. *History of Agriculture in the Southern United States to 1860.* Washington: Carnegie Institute, 1933.

Green, Michael D. *The Politics of Indian Removal: Creek Government and Society in Crisis.* Lincoln: University of Nebraska Press, 1982.

Griffin, Frances. *Less Time for Meddling: A History of Salem Academy and College, 1772–1866.* Winston-Salem: John F. Blair Publisher, 1979.

Griffith, Benjamin W. *McIntosh and Weatherford, Creek Indian Leaders.* Tuscaloosa: University of Alabama Press, 1988.

Hampton, David Keith, comp. *Cherokee Reserves.* Oklahoma City: Baker Publishing Co., 1979.

Harcourt, Robert H. *Elementary Forge Practice, a Textbook for Technical and Vocational Schools.* Peoria: The Manual Arts Press, 1917.

Hatley, Tom. *The Dividing Paths: Cherokees and South Carolinians Through the Era of Revolution.* New York: Oxford University Press, 1993.

History of Athens and Clarke County. Athens: The McGregor Co., printed for H.J. Rowe Publisher, 1923. Microfiche.

History of Tennessee: From the Earliest Time to the Present; Together with an Historical and a Biographical Sketch of the County of Knox and the City of Knoxville. 1887. Reprint. Easley, S.C.: Southern Historical Press, 1982.

Hooper, Robert. *Lexicon-Medicum; or Medical Dictionary: Containing an Explanation of the Terms.* London: Longman, Hurst, Rees, Orme, and Co., 1820.

Hoornstra, Jean and Trudy Heath. *American Periodicals, 1741–1900: An Index to the Microfilm Collections.* Ann Arbor: University Microfilms, 1979.

Horsman, Reginald. *Race and Manifest Destiny.* Cambridge: Harvard University Press, 1981.

Hoyt, David W. *A Genealogical History of the Hoyt, Haight, and Hight Families.* 1871. Reprint. Camden, Maine: Picton Press, 1993.

Hudson, Charles. *The Southeastern Indians.* Knoxville: University of Tennessee Press, 1976.

Hull, Augustus Longstreet. *Annals of Athens, Georgia, 1801–1901.* Athens: Banner Job Office, 1906. Microfiche.

Hynds, Ernest C. *Antebellum Athens and Clarke County Georgia.* Athens: University of Georgia Press, 1974.

Index to the United States Census of Georgia for 1820. Compiled Under Auspices of the Georgia Historical Society, 1963. Reprint. Baltimore: Clearfields Co., 1989.

Jones, Harold Wellington, Normand L. Hoerr, and Arthur Osol, eds. *Gould's Medical Dictionary.* Philadelphia: The Blackiston Co., 1941.

Kidwell, Clara Sue. *Choctaws and Missionaries in Mississippi, 1818–1918.* Norman: University of Oklahoma Press, 1995.

Kilpatrick, Jack Frederick, ed. "The Wahnenauhi Manuscript: Historical Sketches of the Cherokees, together with Some of Their Customs, Traditions, and Superstitions." *Bureau of American Ethnology Bulletin 196,* No. 77. Washington: United States Government Printing Office, 1966.

King, Duane H., ed. *The Cherokee Indian Nation: A Troubled History.* Knoxville: University of Tennessee Press, 1979.

Krakow, Kenneth K. *Georgia Place-Names*. Macon, Ga.: Winship Press, 1975.

Kutsche, Paul. *A Guide to Cherokee Documents in the Northeastern United States*. Metuchen, N.J.: The Scarecrow Press, 1986.

Kwachka, Patricia B., ed. *Perspectives on the Southeast: Linguistics, Archaeology, and Ethnohistory*. Athens: University of Georgia Press, 1994.

McLoughlin, William G. *The Cherokees and Christianity, 1794–1870: Essays on Acculturation and Cultural Persistence*. Edited by Walter H. Conser, Jr. Athens: University of Georgia Press, 1994.

McLoughlin, William G. with Walter H. Conser, Jr. and Virginia Duffy McLoughlin. *The Cherokee Ghost Dance: Essays on the Southeastern Indians 1789–1861*. Macon, Ga.: Mercer University Press, 1984.

McLoughlin, William G. *Champion of the Cherokees: Evan and John B. Jones*. Princeton: Princeton University Press, 1980.

—*Cherokees and Missionaries, 1789–1839*. Norman: University of Oklahoma Press, 1995.

—*Cherokee Renascence in the New Republic*. Princeton: Princeton University Press, 1986.

McNeill, William H. *Plagues and People*. Garden City: Anchor Press, 1976.

Malone, Dumas. *Dictionary of American Biography*. New York: Charles Scribner's Sons, 1961.

Malone, Henry Thompson. *Cherokees of the Old South: A People in Transition*. Athens: University of Georgia Press, 1956.

Mancall, Peter C. *Deadly Medicine: Indians and Alcohol in Early America*. Ithaca: Cornell University Press, 1995.

Marriott, Alice. *Sequoyah: Leader of the Cherokees*. New York: Random House, 1956.

Mihesuah, Devon A. *Cultivating the Rosebuds: The Education of Women at the Cherokee Female Seminary, 1851–1909*. Urbana: University of Illinois Press, 1993.

Moulton, Gary E. *John Ross, Cherokee Chief*. Athens: University of Georgia Press, 1978.

Nash, Ray. *American Penmanship, 1800–1850: A History of Writing*. Worcester: American Antiquarian Society, 1969.

National Cyclopaedia of American Biography, New York: James T. White and Co., 1909.

Owsley, Frank L. *Plain People of the Old South*. Baton Rogue: Louisiana State University Press, 1949.

Perdue, Theda. *The Cherokee*. New York: Chelsea House Publishers, 1989.

— *Cherokee Women: Gender and Culture Change, 1700–1835*. Lincoln: University of Nebraska Press, 1998.

— *Slavery and the Evolution of Cherokee Society, 1540–1866*. Knoxville: University of Tennessee Press, 1979.

Perdue, Theda and Michael D. Green, eds. *The Cherokee Removal: A Brief History with Documents*. New York: St. Martin's Press, 1995.

Prucha, Francis Paul. *American Indian Policy in the Formative Years*. Cambridge: Harvard University Press, 1962.

Rawson, Marion Nicholl. *Little Old Mills*. [New York]: E.P. Dutton and Co., 1935.

Reid, John Philip. *A Law of Blood: The Primitive Law of the Cherokee Nation*. New York: New York University Press, 1970.

Remini, Robert V. *The Legacy of Andrew Jackson: Essays on Democracy, Indian Removal and Slavery*. Baton Rogue: Louisiana State University Press, 1988.

The Revell Bible Dictionary. Old Tappan, N.J.: Fleming H. Revell Company, 1990.

Rogers County Historical Society. *The History of Rogers County, Oklahoma*. Claremore: Heritage Publishing Co. for the Claremore College Foundation, 1979.

Rollings, Willard H. *The Osages: An Ethnohistorical Study of Hegemony on the Prairie-Plains*. Columbia: University of Missouri Press, 1992.

Rosenberg, Charles E. *The Cholera Years: the United States in 1832, 1849, and 1866*. Chicago: University of Chicago Press, 1962.

Rothrock, Mary U., ed. *The French Broad-Holston Country: A History of Knox County, Tennessee*. Knoxville: East Tennessee Historical Society, 1946.

Royce, Charles C. *The Cherokee Nation of Indians*. Chicago: Aldine Publishing Co., 1975.

Satz, Ronald N. *American Indian Policy in the Jacksonian Era*. Lincoln: University of Nebraska Press, 1975.

Saunders, James Edmonds. *Early Settlers of Alabama*. 1899. Reprint. Greenville, S.C.: Southern Historical Press, 1977.

Shadburn, Don L. *Cherokee Planters in Georgia, 1832–1838*. Roswell, Ga.: W.H. Wolfe Associates, 1990.

Sheehan, Bernard. *Seeds of Extinction: Jeffersonian Philanthropy and the American Indian*. Chapel Hill: University of North Carolina Press, 1973.

Shivers, Forrest. *The Land Between: A History of Hancock County, Georgia to 1940*. Spartanburg, S.C.: The Reprint Company Publishers, 1990.

Shoemaker, Nancy, ed. *Negotiators of Change: Historical Perspectives on Native American Women*. New York: Routledge, 1995.

Simpson, J.A. and E.S.C. Weiner ed. *Oxford English Dictionary*. 2nd Edition. New York: Oxford University Press, 1989.

Speck, Frank Gouldsmith and Leonard Broom. *Cherokee Dance and Drama*. Norman: University of Oklahoma Press, 1983.

Stacey, James. *History of the Midway Congregational Church of Liberty County, Georgia*. Newnan, Ga.: S.W. Murray, Printer, 1903. Microfiche.

Stanton, William Ragan. *The Leopard's Spots: Scientific Attitudes Toward Race in America, 1815–1859*. Chicago: University of Chicago Press, 1960.

Starkey, Marion L. *The Cherokee Nation*. New York: Alfred A. Knopf, 1946.

Starr, Emmet. *History of the Cherokee Indians and Their Legends and Folk Lore*. 1921. Reprint. Muskogee, Okla.: Hoffman Printing Co., 1984.

— *Old Cherokee Families: Notes of Dr. Emmet Starr*. Edited by Jack D. Baker and David Keith Hampton. 3 vols. Oklahoma City: Baker Publishing Co., 1988.

Stedman, Thomas L. *Stedman's Medical Dictionary*. Edited by Norman Burke Taylor. Baltimore: Williams and Wilkins Co., 1957.

Strong, James. *The Exhaustive Concordance of the Bible*. McLean, Va.: MacDonald Publishing Co., [n.d.].

Strong, William E. *The Story of the American Board: An Account of the First Hundred Years of the American Board of Commissioners for Foreign Missions*. Boston: The Pilgrim Press, 1910.

Thornton, Russell. *The Cherokees: A Population History*. Lincoln: University of Nebraska Press, 1990.

Tracy, Joseph. "History of the American Board For Foreign Missions," Joseph J. Kwiat, ed. *History of American Missions to the Heathen, from Their Commencement to the Present Time*. 1840. Reprint. New York: Johnson Reprint Corporation, 1970.

Tyner, James W., ed. *Those Who Cried: The 16,000: A Record of the Individual Cherokees Listed in the United States Official Census of the*

Cherokee Nation Conducted in 1835. Pryor, Okla.: Pryor Printing Co., 1974.

Walker, Charles O. *Cherokee Footprints.* Jasper, Ga.: C.O. Walker, 1988.

Walker, Robert Sparks. *Torchlights to the Cherokees: The Brainerd Mission.* New York: The Macmillan Co., 1931.

Wallace, Anthony F.C. *The Long Bitter Trail: Andrew Jackson and the Indians.* New York: Hill and Wang, 1993.

Wilkins, Thurman. *Cherokee Tragedy: The Ridge Family and the Decimation of a People.* Norman: University of Oklahoma Press, 1988.

Wilson, Samuel Tyndale, *A Century of Maryville College: A Story of Altruism, 1819–1919.* New York: J.J. Little and Ives Co., 1916.

Woodward, Grace Steele. *The Cherokees.* Norman: University of Oklahoma Press, 1963.

Wright, Muriel H. *Springplace: Moravian Mission and the Ward Family of the Cherokee Nation.* Guthrie, Okla.: Co-operative Publishing Co., 1940.

B. Articles:

"An Illustrated Souvenir Catalog of the Cherokee National Female Seminary, Tahlequah, Indian Territory, 1850–1906." *Journal of Cherokee Studies* 10 (Spring, 1985): 115–183.

"Antiquities of the Cherokee Indians from the Collection of Reverend Daniel Sabin Buttrick. *Journal of Cherokee Studies* 18 (1997): 27–51.

Best, Edwin J. "New Providence Presbyterian Church." *The Blount Journal* 2, no. 2 (November 1986): 2–8.

"Blount County, Tennessee, 1820 Census of Manufacturers." *East Tennessee Roots* 6, no. 3 (Fall 1989): 116.

Butler, Brian M. "The Red Clay Council Ground." *Journal of Cherokee Studies* 2 (Winter, 1977): 140–153.

Campbell, Janet and David G. "The MacIntosh Family Among the Cherokees." *Journal of Cherokee Studies* 5 (Spring, 1980): 4–16.

de Baillou, Clemens. "The Chief Vann House at Spring Place, Georgia, the Vanns, Tavern and Ferry." *Early Georgia* 2 (1957): 3–11.

"Eagleton Family Bible Records." *The Blount Journal* 3, no. 1 (May 1987): 39–41.

Evans, E. Raymond. "Highways to Progress: Nineteenth Century Roads in the Cherokee Nation." *Journal of Cherokee Studies* 2 (Fall, 1977): 394–400.

— "Jedidiah Morse's Report to the Secretary of War on Cherokee Indian Affairs in 1822." *Journal of Cherokee Studies* 6 (Fall, 1981): 60–77.

— "Notable Persons in Cherokee History: Dragging Canoe." *Journal of Cherokee Studies* 2 (Winter, 1977): 176–189.

Evans, J.P. "Sketches of Cherokee Characteristics." *Journal of Cherokee Studies* 4 (Winter, 1979): 10–20.

Fogelson, Raymond D. "The Conjuror in Eastern Cherokee Society." *Journal of Cherokee Studies* 5 (Fall, 1980): 60–87.

Greene, Joan and H.F. Robinson. "Maize Was Our Life: A History of Cherokee Corn." *Journal of Cherokee Studies* 11 (Spring, 1986): 40–52.

Higginbotham, Mary Alves. "Creek Path Mission." *Journal of Cherokee Studies* 1 (Fall, 1976): 72–86.

Irwin, Lee. "Different Voices Together: Preservation and Acculturation in Early 19th Century Cherokee Religion." *Journal of Cherokee Studies* 18 (1997): 3–26.

Lewit, Robert T. "Indians Missions and Anti-slavery Sentiment: A Conflict of Evangelical and Humanitarian Ideals." *Mississippi Valley Historical Review* 50 (1963): 39–55.

Lowrey, Major George. "Notable Persons in Cherokee History: Sequoyah, or George Gist." (Introduction and transcription by John Howard Payne, 1835.) *Journal of Cherokee Studies* 1 (Fall, 1977): 385–393.

McDonald, Forrest and Grady McWhiney. "Antebellum Southern Herdsman: A Reinterpretation." *Journal of Southern History* (1975): 147–166.

McLoughlin, William G. "Who Civilized the Cherokees?" *Journal of Cherokee Studies* 13 (1988): 55–81.

Macenczak, Kimberly C. "Sophia Sawyer, Native American Advocate: A Case Study in Nineteenth Century Cherokee Education." *Journal of Cherokee Studies* 16 (1991): 26–37.

"Memoir of John Arch, A Young Cherokee Man." Compiled from Communication of Missionaries in the Cherokee Nation. Boston: Massachusetts Sabbath School Society, 1844.

Mercer, Theodore C. "A Note on Rhea County." *Tennessee Historical Quarterly* 35 (Spring 1976): 92–94.

Moffitt, James W. "Early Baptist Missionary Work Among the Cherokees." *East Tennessee Historical Society Publication* 12 (1940): 16–27.

Mooney, James. "The Cherokee Ball Play," "Cherokee Theory and Practice of Medicine," and "Cherokee River Cult." *Journal of Cherokee Studies* 7 (Spring, 1982): 10–36.

Perdue, Theda. "Cherokee Women and the Trail of Tears." *Journal of Women's History* 1, no. 1 (Spring 1989): 14–30.

— "Letters From Brainerd." *Journal of Cherokee Studies* 4 (Winter, 1979): 4–9.

Queener, V. M. "Gideon Blackburn." *East Tennessee Historical Society Publication* no. 6 (1934) 12–28.

Ruff, Rowena McClinton. "Notable Persons in Cherokee History: Charles Hicks." *Journal of Cherokee Studies* 17 (1996): 16–27.

Silver, James W. "Edmund Pendleton Gaines and Frontier Problems, 1801–1849" *Journal of Southern History* 1 (August, 1935), 320–344

Snell, William R. "Candy's Creek Mission Station, 1824–1837." *Journal of Cherokee Studies* 4 (Summer, 1979): 163–185.

D. Unpublished Works:

Ballenger, Thomas L. "Major George Lowrey." Talk delivered at the Lowrey Family Reunion, Tahlequah, Okla., 1964.

Horton, Wade Alston. "Protestant Missionary Women as Agents of Cultural Transition Among Cherokee Women, 1801–1839." Ph.D. diss., The Southern Baptist Theological Seminary, 1991.

Ishii, Izumi. "The Cherokee Temperance Movement: An Internal Struggle for a Sober Nation before the 'Trail of Tears.'" Master's thesis, University of Kentucky, 1996.

McClinton, Rowena. "The Moravian Mission Among the Cherokees at Springplace, Georgia." Ph.D. diss., University of Kentucky, 1996.

McKeown, James. "Return J. Meigs: United States Agent in the Cherokee Nation, 1801–1823." Ph.D. diss., Pennsylvania State University, 1981.

Pate, James. "The Chickamauga: A Forgotten Segment of Indian Resistance on the Southern Frontier." Ph.D. diss., Mississippi State University, 1969.

Strenk, Adriane M. "Tradition and Transformation: Shoe Boots and the Creation of a Cherokee Culture." Master's thesis, University of Kentucky, 1993.

Index

In the Indians of the Southeast series

William Bartram on the Southeastern Indians
Edited and annotated by Gregory A. Waselkov
and Kathryn E. Holland Braund

Deerskins and Duffels
The Creek Indian Trade with Anglo-America, 1685–1815
By Kathryn E. Holland Braund

Cherokee Americans
The Eastern Band of Cherokees in the Twentieth Century
By John R. Finger

Choctaw Genesis 1500-1700
By Patricia Galloway

The Southeastern Ceremonial Complex
Artifacts and Analysis
The Cottonlandia Conference
Edited by Patricia Galloway
Exhibition Catalog by David H. Dye and Camille Wharey

An Assumption of Sovereignty
Social and Political Transformation
among the Florida Seminoles, 1953–1979
By Harry A. Kersey Jr.

The Caddo Chiefdoms
Caddo Economics and Politics, 700-1835
By David La Vere

Cherokee Women
Gender and Culture Change, 1700-1835
By Theda Perdue

The Brainerd Journal
A Mission to the Cherokees, 1817-1823
Edited and introduced by Joyce B. Phillips
and Paul Gary Phillips

The Cherokees
A Population History
By Russell Thornton